# AN EPOCH AND A MAN

# AN EPOCH AND A MAN
## MARTIN VAN BUREN
## AND HIS TIMES

DENIS

TILDEN

LYNCH

MCMXXIX

HORACE LIVERIGHT
NEW YORK

*To*

MY WIFE

2 l
2 7

# CONTENTS

CHAPTER                                           PAGE

   I. MEN WHO FEARED NOT . . . . . . . . .   15
       The contract—Prayer and baptism.

  II. TWO WHO WERE NEVER PARTED . . . . .   20
       Buys Greenwich Village—Van Buren's boast—
       His birth.

 III. SOME THINGS THAT HAPPENED IN THE VAN BUREN
       TAVERN . . . . . . . . . . .   26
       The unsought honor—The great at the tavern.

  IV. WHEN WE DANCED THE CARMAGNOLE . . . .   30
       A republican ode.

   V. THE HARDSHIPS OF HIS BOYHOOD . . . . .   33
       His first case—Justice for the judge—The boy
       keeps the faith.

  VI. PERSECUTED FOR HIS BELIEFS . . . . . .   39
       His first convention—Hamilton's son—The assas-
       sination—Christmas suffering.

 VII. THE SPOILS SYSTEM AND ANOTHER DUEL . . .   48
       A Scot who became Dutch—The second duel ends
       —Burr as an actor—Edward the Great—Aristides
       quotes Horace—Van Buren no longer fears hun-
       ger.

VIII. HE RESOLVES TO SUBORDINATE POLITICS . . .   59
       He rejects Burr—On freedom of opinion—Coun-
       sels Burr's second.

  IX. THE CLINTONS WAR ON THE LIVINGSTONS . . .   67
       The importance of tavern keepers—The jest on
       the gallows — Improving on Periander — Van
       Buren's marriage.

   X. SURROGATE . . . . . . . . . . . . .   75
       New York rebels.

  XI. HIS ENCOUNTER WITH A VAN RENSSELAER . .   79
       Noblesse oblige—Van Buren challenged.

v

CHAPTER    PAGE

XII. HE ACQUIRES NEWSPAPER NOTORIETY . . . . 85
Two dogs who snarled—Silenus laughs at Solon—
Elected State Senator.

XIII. THE WAR OF 1812 DIVIDES US . . . . . . 91
The friends of peace—The mob—The cannon in
the void—The dealer in flesh—Revolutionary
heroes—The last stand—Maryland, My Maryland
—The worm turns.

XIV. THE BREAKFAST AT ROSA KEESE'S BOARDING HOUSE 109
Scavengers—The new leader at work—Waiving
the classics—Clinton wronged—A master to the
people—Opponents are traitors—Van Buren earns
a kiss.

XV. HIS HUMANE DECISION . . . . . . . . 124
The "Cow Case"—Fighting the banks—An old
strain—Scott predicts—A great blackguard—Just
another rebuff—The right to secede—Cæsar's
extra.

XVI. ATTORNEY GENERAL . . . . . . . . 140
His runaway slave—The sheriff who stole.

XVII. HIS FAVORITE ARTIFICE . . . . . . . 145
Allen's price—"Kick or be kicked."

XVIII. HE WARS WITH CLINTON . . . . . . . 151
The snuffbox eloquent—Weak sisters—Meets a reverse—Clinton's star rises.

XIX. HE SPURNS CLINTON'S PEACE OFFER . . . . 161
How they used the Bible—His mother's faith—
The secret plot—A widower—Jackson's "toast
accurst"—Epistolary spouting—A punitive expedition.

XX. HE IS REMOVED AS ATTORNEY GENERAL . . . 177
The Livingstons condole—Twenty gallons of wine
—The sheep and the goats—An ancient device—
The hand of tragedy.

XXI. THE STARVATION LAWS . . . . . . . . 188
"A man or a pig"—Peterloo.

XXII. RUFUS KING'S DEBT TO VAN BUREN . . . . 193
The spoils letter—The high minded—Prayer to a
rhymester.

# Contents

CHAPTER                                                             PAGE

XXIII. SHORN OF ALL HIS HONORS . . . . . . .   200
The old order protests—Reform and revenge—
The fox scents the bait—Rufus King reciprocates
—The schools in politics.

XXIV. WHEN THE DUTCH REJECTED HIM . . . . .   211
The Convention—Palaver for The Patroon—The
"Mad-caps"—"The poor ye have always"—The
record remains—A speech, not an epigram—Re-
stricted suffrage—"Thus gods are made."

XXV. UNITED STATES SENATOR . . . . . . .   229
Rufus King's odd rôle—A sordid scramble.

XXVI. JEFFERSON'S GRANDDAUGHTER AMUSES . . . .   235
"Unprompt gallantry"—Sayings of Hibernicus—
Clinton's scorpions.

XXVII. THE IRON HAND . . . . . . . . . . .   242
His Majesty, Noah I—An élite boarding house—
Monks who may marry—A fly spins a web.

XXVIII. LEADER OF THE RADICALS . . . . . . .   251
His "art and business"—Nativism—On Mr. Astor's manners—"Shallow knaves"—"Envenomed
malignity" — Jefferson astonishes — Unclouded
glories.

XXIX. HIS FOLLOWERS HANGED AND BURNED IN EFFIGY   266
Indians and wild Irish—La Fayette remembers—
Killing a man too dead.

XXX. INTRIGUING CLAY OUT OF THE PRESIDENCY . .   273
King's man mystified—Clay fears militarism—
The Patroon doubts—He prays.

XXXI. ADAMS TURNS AGAINST VAN BUREN . . . .   283
A father to his son—"Delicate and ensnaring"—
Demosthenes drunk—Puritan and Blackleg—
Punctilio—Pistols at ten paces—Clay asks a sec-
ond shot—A new word—An audacious speech—
Judges are human—An unkept promise.

XXXII. HE MAKES USE OF ADAMS . . . . . . .   307
A woman's way—What Buchanan did—A false
bar sinister—The germ of bigotry.

XXXIII. HOW HE BECAME GOVERNOR . . . . . .   317
Father to son—Perfume and gossip—A lovely act.

*Contents*

CHAPTER                                                        PAGE
XXXIV. SECRETARY OF STATE . . . . . . . . .   324
    Why Jackson wept—Two tragedies—Friday finds
    a valet—"My Dutch brother"—Peggy O'Neale
    snubbed—The ladies conspire—Springing the
    mine—The prologue—A statesman's reward—"An
    old man, broken . . ."—Livingston muses.

XXXV. MINISTER TO ENGLAND . . . . . . . . .   346
    Wassail—The indictment—Marcy revises Livy—
    "You will be made V. P."—"The monster."

XXXVI. VICE PRESIDENT . . . . . . . . . . .   357
    A Tory's farewell—Society's new lion—A cellar
    and a closet—Harpies of the Republic—Orestes
    to Pylades—A petty Louis XVI—Jackson's prop
    —A pinch of snuff—Feast and forget—A State
    indorses a mob—A duel or a beating—Presiding
    with pistols—The dynasty dies hard—Burn books
    and hang men—An oration in Dutch—Jackson's
    guide—Adams makes comparisons—A just stand
    —Victory—Hungry men—After the riot.

XXXVII. PRESIDENT . . . . . . . . . . . . .   400
    A distant ray of light—A tribute and a prayer—
    Progress makes a panic—Hone's dire prophecy
    —A man attacks a citadel—A world revulsion—
    The Panic Session ends—An epic battle—The
    midnight massacre—A trying hour—"Our Prince
    John"—The first fifty years—A veteran is hu-
    mored—striking a balance.

XXXVIII. A PRESIDENTAL TOUR . . . . . . . .   428
    Honors—Snubs—The heart has a tongue—The
    champagne dinner—Roses and hyacinths—The
    old man eloquent—The Bank collapses—A sneer
    may be immortal—The gold spoons—Prince
    John's toast—An appeal to the senses—A lion and
    a lioness—"Van is a used-up man"—A nation
    sings—An advertisement—Strange pipe-layers—
    Van Buren's blow—"Nothing to regret."

XXXIX. HOW HE ENDURES THE REVERSE . . . . .   465
    Triumph in defeat—Fair-weather friends—Pity
    for the victor—A gala performance—"Thrice wel-
    come home"—In retirement—Impeaching a Presi-
    dent—The second conspiracy—Bryant pens an

# *Contents*

epitaph—Rare courage—Spurning the Presidency
—The two-thirds rule—Slavery ascendant—The
first dark horse—The white oak.

XL. THE IDEALIST . . . . . . . . . . . 496
His father's footsteps—Prince John in jail—A
poet's humor—Polk's treachery—Idealism em-
bryonic—". . . and fellow-traitors"—Colonel
Van Buren—The root of the evil—A call to arms
—The Buffalo convention—The banner of Free
Soil—A wag of Virginia.

XLI. THE FREE SOIL MOVEMENT GAINS . . . . . 520
One woman's "No"—The lethal cup—Literary labors—Seward fans the flames—Van Buren goes
to church—The other John Brown—Van Buren's
slogan—Reënters Peggy O'Neale—His "happiest
years"—Lincoln's policy—The farewell letter
—The last salute.

# LIST OF ILLUSTRATIONS

MARTIN VAN BUREN . . . . . . . . . . *Frontispiece*
    From a Photograph from Life

FACING PAGE

MARTIN VAN BUREN'S BIRTHPLACE . . . . . . . . . 24
    Etched by Edith Nankivell after a Contemporary Woodcut

HENRY CLAY . . . . . . . . . . . . . . 48
    After a Mezzotint by H. S. Sadd

MARTIN VAN BUREN . . . . . . . . . . . 96
    After an Engraving by H. W. Smith. (The earliest likeness)

ALBERT GALLATIN . . . . . . . . . . . . 148
    From the Painting by Chappel

MRS. MARTIN VAN BUREN . . . . . . . . . . 164
    After an Engraving by J. C. Buttre

WILLIAM L. MARCY . . . . . . . . . . . . 192
    After an Engraving by J. C. Buttre

JOHN VAN BUREN . . . . . . . . . . . 256
    After an Engraving by J. C. Buttre

MARTHA JEFFERSON RANDOLPH . . . . . . . . 288
    After an Engraving by J. Serz

ANDREW JACKSON . . . . . . . . . . . 336
    After an Engraving by H. B. Hall

EDWARD LIVINGSTON . . . . . . . . . . . 352
    After a Drawing by J. B. Longacre

MARTIN VAN BUREN . . . . . . . . . . . 384
    From a Painting by Inman

SMITH THOMPSON VAN BUREN . . . . . . . . 416
    From a Tintype Owned by Ellen Van Buren Pell

ANGELINA SINGLETON VAN BUREN . . . . . . . 448
    After an Engraving by J. C. Buttre

MARTIN VAN BUREN . . . . . . . . . . . 480
    After an Engraving by H. B. Hall, Jr.

MARTIN VAN BUREN . . . . . . . . . . . 544
    The Last Photograph, Taken in 1862

# AN EPOCH AND A MAN

# AN EPOCH AND A MAN
## Martin Van Buren and His Times

### CHAPTER I

JASPAER FERLIN could read and write, so he sat himself down
in the dimly lighted notary's office in Amsterdam, and laboriously
perused the parchment which bound him to sow, grow, and cultivate tobacco in the New World for a term of three years, as the
*bouwknecht* of Marinus Adriaensz van der Veere. After signing
the contract, he handed the quill to Marijin, as Marinus was
called in the vernacular. Then Marijin read aloud the document
to which Jaspaer had scrawled his name while three other young
Dutch farmers listened. Eyes bulged as they heard the provision in the agreement stipulating that in the event of discovery of
"any mines, minerals, pearl fisheries or the like, they shall dis-
close the same to no one but the Patroon or his agents, who shall
make them a handsome present therefor according to the importance of the matter." There were gold and silver and pearl fisheries over there! The contract further bound them to "submit
themselves to the sovereignty of the High and Mighty Lords the
States General of these United Netherlands, to the supreme power
and direction of the Chartered West India Company in general,
and of the aforesaid Rensselaer in particular." And Marijin
wrote the names of the three dreaming farmers, and they in turn
scratched their marks: whereupon Marijin heaved a sigh of relief.
He had labored three or four months without rest to find farm
servants who would meet with the favor of Kiliaen van Rensselaer,
wealthy diamond merchant of the city, whose grant of land running twenty-four miles north and south, and forty-eight miles east
and west, with the North, or Hudson's, River dividing the manor
in equal halves, would not be valid until he had colonized it.

One of the farmers who bound himself to toil in the New
Netherlands near Fort Orange, destined to be the site of New

York's State capital, was described in the contract as "Cornelis maesen van Buyrmarsen." This was the notary's misspelling of Buyrmalsen, or Buurmalsen, a hamlet near Buren, in the province of Gelderland. And all that is known of the ancestry of Cornelis is told in this brief line which translated reads: "Cornelis son of Maes of Buurmalsen."

This contract was signed and dated the 27th of May, 1631. On the first Monday of the following July, the Jonker, Kiliaen van Rensselaer, appeared before the Amsterdam Chamber of the West India Company, of which he was a director, and obtained permission to ship on the *d'Eendracht*, Marinus van der Veere and the three farmers, together with the wife and child of his agent, eight heifer calves, material for a saw and grist mill, millstones, hoes and other implements of husbandry. We know from the Van Rensselaer Bowier Manuscripts that all arrived safely at Rensselaerswyck, save one of the heifers, which did not survive the rigors of the voyage.

Before the year 1633 Van Rensselaer—we shall henceforward use a capital V after the manner of later days—had complied with the terms of the grant. He had settled fifty males above the age of fifteen years on his manor on the upper Hudson. But to the Patroon the settlement of the Rensselaerswyck was only part of a broader scheme, the colonization of all the New Netherlands, that the sturdy ships of the Company might have a station in the New World where they could obtain grain, cattle and other supplies on their voyages between the homeland and their destinations in the fabled West Indies and the still more fabled Brazil. He induced many farmers to settle in Manhattan; and his only act of folly, or rather bad judgment, was his advocacy of the appointment of the vacillating Wouter Van Twiller, husband of his niece, as Governor of the New Netherlands. Equally important with the cultivation of the soil and the protection of its tillers from hostile Indians was the collection of funds to support a minister and a schoolmaster; for this, too, was a condition under which he held the land as a perpetual fief from the Company. Van Rensselaer and his agents had complete jurisdiction in civil and criminal cases, including the power of capital punishment. When the extreme penalty was imposed the condemned was returned to Holland where his appeal was heard and his fate determined. The

Patroon appointed the magistrates, and exercised other manorial rights, including "hunting, fowling, fishing, and the rights of the wind." And he maintained an armed force for the common weal.

The record is silent respecting Cornelis Maesen until the summer of 1634, when we find that on August 2 he was charged twelve guilders and eighteen stivers for clothes and brandy. As nothing stronger than wine could be retailed in the colony under the Dutch régime, we know that Cornelis bought a wholesale quantity of this most potent of firewaters. The amount charged against him represented $5.16, a sizable sum for those days, when it is recalled that eight years before the Indians sold the entire Island of Manhattan to Peter Minuit, Van Twiller's predecessor, for sixty guilders, or twenty-four dollars. The terms of Cornelis Maesen's contract stipulated that he "shall receive the first year f60, the second year f70, the third year f80"; and he was advanced twelve florins or guilders upon signing the contract with his mark.

Shortly after the $5.16 was deducted from the $92 he earned in his three years' service to Marinus Adriaensz van der Veere, agent of the Patroon, Cornelis returned to the Fatherland where his brother Hendrick lived, and likewise a little maiden named Catelijntje Martense, daughter of a man named Martin. Catelijntje lived in the ancient town of Houten, a brisk morning's walk from Cornelis's own village of Buurmalsen. Nothing save love or high adventure would induce a man to cross and recross the Atlantic three hundred years ago in a small wooden ship that took months to make the stormy passage. And that Catelijntje looked upon Cornelis with more than passing affection is evidenced by her accompanying him to the New Netherlands to brave the perils of the most primitive frontier life. The date of their marriage is not known, but it was probably in the latter part of 1635 or in the early months of 1636.

No record exists of the contract under which Cornelis came to this country the second time; but letters of the Patroon reveal that Cornelis had a lease direct from him and was not beholden to any other man. He now had his own farm—as a tenant of Van Rensselaer. This agreement was executed in the summer of 1636, and, with this in his pocket, he persuaded a young farmer, named Cornelis Teunisz, from Westbroeck, in his wife's Province of Utrecht, to go along as his farm laborer, as he had gone with Marinus Adriaensz van der Veere five years before. And on September 25, Cornelis, his wife, and his *bouwknecht,* sailed for the wilds of the New Netherlands in the ship *Rensselaerswyck.*

The commander of the vessel, Captain Jan Tjebkews Schellinger, being prudent, sailed for England, and made inquiries at Plymouth, Falmouth, and other ports for ships bound for the New World. Schellinger was not concerned over the personal valor of his crew; for these seemingly peaceful Dutchmen were ready to fight at the drop of the hat; or even on less provocation when liquored up. There was more safety in numbers from marauders at sea.

One of the crew who had signed a contract to work as a smith on the Patroon's manor, after filling himself and his assistant with many and varied drinks in an English tavern, picked a quarrel with his apprentice, who felled him with a stout blow. The smith was taken aboard and nursed by his wife while the prow of the *Rensselaerswyck* was pointing toward the final goal of most on board. And when her nursing was over the widow of the smith turned her attention to the wife of Cornelis Maesen, who was in need of the solace and attention of one of her own sex. We find in the ship's log under date of Friday, January 3, 1637, this entry: "About two o'clock in the night a boy was born. His mother is Caetelin." The Captain had his own way of spelling the name of the wife of Cornelis. Three months and one day later, on Wednesday, March 4, 1637, the *Rensselaerswyck* dropped anchor in the harbor of New Amsterdam, hard by the cluster of huts nestling under the walls of the fort above which floated the orange, white, and blue tricolor; and against the eastern sky were silhouetted the vanes of Van Twiller's windmill. "God be praised for our safe voyage thus far," the pious sailor wrote in the log that day.

In the first boatload ashore were Cornelis Maesen, and his wife, and their infant son, accompanied by their faithful friend and servant, Cornelis Teunisz. Catelijntje pressed her child a little closer as they passed groups of Indians who were trading rich peltries of beaver for knives and beads and other trinkets. The place was swarming with soldiers. Presently the little party arrived at the wooden church, a few steps from the fort, situate on what is now Pearl street, between Broad and Whitehall streets. And as they prayed in the dimly lighted, barn-like structure, even the mother, had she been vouchsafed the vision of the destiny of the new land, would have doubted that one of her descendants, two hundred years from that very day, would be made the ruler of a mighty nation; for it was on March 4, 1837, that Martin Van Buren was inaugurated the eighth President of the United States. The next Sunday, all four paid a second visit to the church, and Dominie Everardus Bogardus baptized Catelijntje's first-born Hendrick.

For twenty-two days the *Rensselaerswyck* lay at anchor off the fort; and on March 26, being assured by Indians and traders who came from the north, that the ice in the river had broken up, Captain Schellinger hoisted sail and began the last lap of his voyage. In the evening of that day, he cast out anchor at Sapokanican, in later years the village of Greenwich, and now part of New York City. A dozen more days the *Rensselaerswyck* battled the icy river and the head winds from the north; and on Tuesday, April 7, the ship anchored off Fort Orange, "the end of our voyage upward," as the log of Captain Schellinger has it.

## CHAPTER II

FORT ORANGE proper was "a miserable little fort built of logs," with eight or ten guns—"four or five pieces of Breutil cannon and as many swivels." The settlement, as Father Jogues found it some seven years after Cornelis Maesen and his family became part of it, consisted of "about one hundred persons who reside in some twenty-five or thirty houses built along the river." The soil on the margins of the stream and on the islands near the post alone was tilled. Wild berries grew in abundance, and native grapes, white and blue. The waters teemed with the majestic sturgeon and lesser fish. Turkeys, teal, swans, geese and pigeons flocked by the thousands. Deer were so plentiful at times that the Indians sold them for a loaf of bread, a knife, or a tobacco pipe. De Vries noted on December 30, 1639, that the usual price of a deer was "cloth worth six or seven guilders."

Cornelis worked hard. And with him slaved, and willingly, his *bouwknecht*, Cornelis Teunisz from Westbroeck, who, at the end of six years fared forth as his own master; and in time was appointed magistrate of the colony. From the Patroon himself we learn, that in the year of the visit of De Vries to Fort Orange, Cornelis was building a dwelling house for himself and his growing family. Again, when the Patroon found that his agent was having trouble with some of the farmers over the terms of their leases, he wrote him to consult with the farmer from Buurmalsen. In another letter from Amsterdam the Patroon directed his representative to let Cornelis Maesen have a fair choice of the farm workers who were about to arrive in the settlement, because, as Van Rensselaer put it, he had been very helpful to him. Cornelis was prospering.

We gather from the Patroon's correspondence that his gratitude toward this unlettered farmer arose from his capacity to smooth out the difficulties between the Patroon's agent and the dissatisfied tenant farmers, persuading them to live up to the spirit of their contracts, which usually called for one-tenth of the produce of the farm. The Patroon would not yield in these disputes. He was charitable at home, where he was one of the founders of the orphan asylum at Nieukirk, and generous to his tenantry here. We find him ordering his officer not to look for rent from this one for a year, or another for two or three years, because things had not gone well with them. But he could not bear the very thought of being imposed upon. "I do not want to be defied by those I have made men," he once wrote.

In 1644, when Cornelis was a tenant farmer for seven years, he paid in tithes one hundred bushels of wheat, oats, and rye, "and some peas." His annual yield must have averaged at least a thousand bushels of grain, for two years after this sole remaining record of his earnings, he bought "a house and plantation" from Volckert Evertsen on the Island of Manhattan. The property adjoined that of Wouter Van Twiller and Thomas Hall. The latter was a leader on the unsuccessful expedition of the English against Fort Nassau. The plantation was in the heart of the place called Sapokanican, and extended north from Christopher street to Fourteenth street, and westward from a line near Greenwich avenue to the North River,—the boundaries, roughly, of New York's present-day Greenwich Village. The date of the purchase was October 24, 1646.

It is not difficult to imagine the thoughts of Cornelis Maesen when he obtained the deed to this plantation on the Island of Manhattan itself, close to a ready market in New Amsterdam, where one met men from all parts of Europe, and what was even more pleasing to call to mind—there would be no more tithes to the Patroon. All that he raised would be his own. It is fair to assume that in the beginning of the year 1648, after he had held title to the farm on Manhattan Island some fifteen months, he thought of removing to his own place.

Cornelis and Catelijntje now had five children; Marten, who was next to Hendrick; Maes, barely a head taller than his sister Styntje, and little Tobias, a babe in arms. There would be many heartbreaks in Rensselaerswyck when those children set sail for New Amsterdam, some 145 miles south, for every one in the settlement loved them. None would miss them more than Cornelis Teunisz from Westbroeck, who came over with their parents, and was uncle to all of them.

Hendrick, just turned eleven, could almost do the work of a man. And so could Marten. As for babbling Styntje, she was breaking hearts even now. We can hear the fair Catelijntje, her mother heart beating faster with every word of praise, forcing from smiling lips a gentle reproof to Uncle Cornelis, and the steadfast friend vigorously protesting that no one could spoil such children.

In the midst of all this happiness the tragedy which stalked the family fell upon them, staggering the little settlement; and for years no one talked of it save in whispers. Such was the lasting impression it made that early translations of the records of Rensselaerswyck retain the line in the original: *Beyde op eenen dagh zyn begraaven*—Both were buried on the same day. The date is given as "about April 8, 1648." On the following Shrove Tuesday, the farm implements, stock, and household effects were auctioned off, and Uncle Cornelis became father and mother to the five little children. The plantation and house on the Island of Manhattan was sold to Rutger Jacobsen for 1,500 guilders. He paid part in wampum, or seawant, and was slow in paying the remainder; for nine years later, on January 13, 1657, he was haled before Deputy La Montagne and acknowledged a debt of 660 guilders on the "parcel of land in Manhattan," promising to pay within a year "in good strong seawant," with interest in beavers.

Uncle Cornelis always kept a watchful eye on the children of his friend and one-time master, and there exists an affidavit, dated August 19, 1662, wherein he described himself as formerly a magistrate; and that he came to this country in 1636 in the ship *Rensselaerswyck*, in the service of the said Cornelis Maesen; that he served him for six years and that the said Hendrick Cornelis Maesen was born on the ship, and that all the other children were born here.

This affidavit was made to identify the children of Cornelis and Catelijntje Maesen as the niece and nephews of their father's brother, Hendrick, who had died in Cuijlenborch, leaving them his heirs. This is all that we have regarding the relatives in the Netherlands of Cornelis Maesen. The affidavit, which is supported by Jan Verbeeck, "formerly Councillor of the Colony of Rensselaerswyck," is likewise of value in definitely establishing this country as the birthplace of Marten, the second son, and not

Houten, as asserted by some genealogists. Marten, Maes, Styntje,
and Tobias were born on the farm leased from the Patroon in
Greene Bosche, or as it was spelled when many of the old Dutch
place names were Anglicized, Greenbush. The leasehold is placed
both on the eastern bank of the Hudson, and on Papcanee, or
Papsknee Island; and although there is nothing determinative
in the documents, their study inclines to the conclusion that Cornelis Maesen's farm was on the island.

Where or how the children lived after their bereavement is
not known; but the records they made show that they inherited
in full measure the qualities of leadership of their father. This
was especially true of Marten, the American primogenitor of the
President whose proud boast was that he was the first head of the
Republic to be born after the Colonies had declared their independence. Marten, in 1700, was a Captain in the command of
Colonel Pieter Schuyler, and in the same outfit we find as Major,
Dirck Wessels Ten Broeck, free merchant, one of the first alder-
men of Albany, recorder of the Colony and, more important to
us, husband of the charming Styntje. Hendrick, too, was a
soldier, and served in the Patroon's forces which manned Fort
Cralo, on the Van Rensselaer farm at Greenbush, when word
reached the settlement in the summer of 1663 that the Indians
had massacred the Dutch at Esopus, some sixty miles down the
river. Maes, for some baffling reason, when the Dutch began to
use surnames, following the English occupation in 1664, called
himself Bloemingdael. Tobias alone died without issue.

The descendants of Hendrick and Marten called themselves
Van Buren, because of an error of their father, whose boyish
recollection of the pronunciation of Buurmalsen, their father's
village, was Buren Malsen, as they spelled it in the power of
attorney executed for their sister and two brothers in applying
for the inheritance left by their uncle Hendrick.

About this time Marten married Maritje Quackenbosh, who
bore him nine children on the farm on Constapel's Island, near
Albany. A year before the birth of the third, who was called
Pieter, Marten acquired title to part of a large tract of land
at Kinderhook, which had been purchased from the Indians in
1666 by Styntje's husband, for himself and Pieter, and two of
their neighbors.

At the age of twenty-three, on January 15, 1693, Pieter married Ariaantje Barentse and settled on his father's farm, sixteen miles south of Albany. Nine children were also born to them. Their second child was baptized Marten. When Marten Van Buren arrived at the age of twenty-eight he married Dirckie Van Aelstyne, and like his father and grandfather before him, he was the parent of nine children. His fifth child was baptized Abraham on February 27, 1737. This fixes his birth as about the 17th of the month, as it was the custom in the Dutch Reformed Church to christen a child when he was ten days old.

The farm house in which Abraham was born was a long, low, clapboarded structure, one and one-half stories high. The roof was steep, the better to shed the heavy snows. Two brick chimneys at either end of the house, with their comfortable fire-places, were familiar to stagecoach passengers on the old New York and Albany Post Road in Abraham's youth, if not before his birth. Prior to the late fall of 1759, when Abraham was twenty-two, there is no record extant of the farm house being used as a tavern; but tradition has it the stopping place of soldiers of George II throughout the whole of the six years' campaign against the French in their marches between New York City and the Canadian frontier. Immediately adjoining was a smaller structure, somewhat similar in design. This was the kitchen for the patrons of the inn.

Nearly three months after the surrender of Quebec, Colonel James Montresor, Chief Engineer in the Provinces of the forces of George II, set out from Albany for New York in four sleighs. On Saturday, December 15, a cold northeast wind brought a heavy fall of snow, delaying his departure until noon of the following Tuesday, and in the late afternoon, Montresor drew up at the swinging sign in front of Van Buren's tavern. Snow and the growing darkness partly concealed a pawing horse of black and red and gray, the proud work of the forgotten village artist.

We can see the upper half of the door open gently; then the remainder of the door swung back by a black slave, while Mine Host Van Buren rushes out and bows the Colonel in, bidding him welcome in broken English; later we hear him shouting in Dutch to the negro to heap more logs on the fires; now he is personally waiting on Montresor in the private room, pouring the wine and serving the spirits, while voices are muted in the tap room, as is the custom in respectable inns when one's betters are supping. Van Buren's was not a tippling house for teamsters.

In the morning this quiet soldier and maddeningly laconic diarist resumed his journey, taking a full week to reach the city.

And Abraham continued to preside over the tavern which he inherited from his father along with the land and the slaves; and cultivated the farm, selling the surplus to neighbors. Sometimes he sold to those who never paid, and ofttimes gave of his store to the needy. He was the most popular man in the village. but his lack of thrift caused the good wives to warn their daughters against accepting the attentions of Abraham Van Buren. Little did this worry Abraham, who never knew the lack of boon companions to while away the heel of a dull evening.

Then came the Revolution, and the peaceful Abraham found his fixed ideas of thirty-nine years turned topsy-turvy. He who a few days ago was without an enemy, now found himself hated by the Tories of the neighborhood. Next he astonished his Whig cronies as much as if he had joined the supporters of the Crown by marrying the Widow Van Alen, ten years his junior. There was more of the love of pity than love of the senses in the heart of the bachelor turned benedict, although the Widow Van Alen was good to look upon. The only dowry she brought him was three little children: two sons and a daughter. And she bore him five children, the first two being girls, Dirckie and Jannetje, who were born while the guns of the revolting Colonists were thundering their pæans to the Rights of Man; and then came Martin, and two other sons, Lawrence and Abraham.

# CHAPTER III

Martin Van Buren was born December 5, 1782, and was baptized by Dominie Johannes Ritzema ten days later in the Dutch Reformed Church at Kinderhook, where his uncle Pieter Van Beuren, a deacon of the church, and Catarina Quackenbosh promised to see that he would be brought up in the faith of his fathers. That Christmas Eve! The infant made it seem as no other Christmas before to Mine Host Abraham. Two daughters had come first and he was beginning to doubt that he would have a son. Not that he did not love those two lovely little girls and the three children his wife brought as her dot; but this baby was his own son. And he sang with the children the Christmas song that he had sung as a child, as his fathers before him:

Sint Nikolaas, goed heilig man!
Doe je beste tabbard an;
Rydt er mee naar Amsterdam,
Van Amsterdam naar Spanje,
Van Spanje naar Oranje;
En brengt de kinders wat:
Noten van Muskaat,
Appeltjes van Oranje,
Pruimpjes van Spanje,
Peertjes van die hogenboom—
Sint Nikolaas zal koom!

And all the grown-ups took up this invocation to Santa Claus, none doubting that the good holy man would put on his best cloak and ride to distant climes and return with nuts from Muscat, apples from Orange, plums from Spain and pears from the high trees. And how fervently the children sang the last line: St. Nicholas shall come!

Then slender white clay pipes, a yard and a half long, were taken from their deep box-like repository on the wall, filled with home-grown tobacco; and Schiedam was poured and a toast drunk to the holy friend of the children. There was much twitting

26

of the older ones. Any wrongful act done during the year, no matter how well concealed, would be revealed on the morrow, for *goed Sint Nikolaas* would put a twig of the silver birch in the culprit's stocking. The very little tots firmly believed this, and some had trouble in finding sleep on the night before Christmas; but their seniors who could remember distinctly four or five Christmases, smiled knowingly. They knew that this was teasing invention of the grown-ups; for never yet had Santa Claus put a piece of birch in their stockings; although all, in their innocence, thought they richly deserved it.

In the midst of the merry-making sleigh-bells were heard outside. The sleigh stopped at the door. Some of the juvenile hearts beat faster. Could it be *goed Sint Nikolaas?* Hopes were dashed when it was discovered that it was only a late traveler, and one who spoke only English at that! The Yankees—all who were not Dutch were Yankees—called *Sint Nikolaas* by a most amusing name: Father Christmas.

It was a real merry Christmas. The war was over and the signing of the articles of peace was daily expected. Meanwhile New York continued to be governed by George Clinton who, in the following year, made the father of little Martin a Captain of militia, an unsought honor that sat irritatingly on him. He was flattered, but he knew nothing about troops. True, he could handle a musket or fowling piece as well as the next. But drilling troops was beyond him. So in time he resigned his commission, which had been given to him because of his influence among the Whigs. His tavern was used as the polling place during the three days of election, a circumstance which made it the rendezvous of partisans throughout the year.

Only those possessed of freeholds could vote under the State constitution adopted in 1777. The wealthier, who owned land worth £100—a pound in New York currency had a value of $2.50—over and above all debts charged thereon, were privileged to vote for all elective officials; but the less fortunate, freeholders with an equity of £20, might only vote for members of the Assembly; and the same privilege was extended to those who paid forty shillings a year rental. All the Van Burens in Kinderhook of voting age—and there were a few—could qualify under the first provision: seven of them were listed as owners of slaves in the first United States census, Martin's father owning six negroes in the year 1790.

This wealth of the tavern-keeper was more fancied than real. He was noted for his improvidence, and had borrowed on all he possessed. Quackenbosh's tavern was taking much of the custom that had originally been his; and his wife, noted for her sagacity, grew daily more concerned over the fate of the family. It was plain that the education she had hoped for her children could not be theirs, save by dint of the hardest of personal struggles and self-sacrifice. And a little property—a freehold of the value of $250—and education were alone required to enable a youth to become like those who sometimes stopped at the tavern. Even little Mat had to work most of the year. He made occasional visits in the winter months to the village school, half buried in a knoll, where the light was so miserable that it was difficult to read. After school, on many a winter afternoon, little Mat trudged through the snow, dragging a sled weighted with vegetables to the home of some more fortunate family.

It was a pity, thought the mother, that he should have to labor so hard when he should be studying. The schoolmaster said Mat could write better English than any one else in his class. The boy was a great talker and was never at a loss for a word, and this natural talent was whetted by the badinage of the patrons of the tavern. It did seem wrong that this yellow-haired stripling with his merry laughing blue eyes should be kept at work more fitted for a man, or at least a husky boy of twelve; he would not be that old for another two years. In these times of depression she would fall back on her faith in a crucified Jesus, and recall the words of the Twenty-third Psalm. The words she knew were in Dutch: she had never heard their English equivalents.

As the children grew up they learned the language of the Yankees, although at the family table Dutch was spoken. Much of the talk in the tavern was political, and little Mat, as he listened, observed that no matter how warm the argument waxed, his father kept silent, or maintained a strict neutrality, as behooved those who presided over these places that have long since been only memories. And as election time drew nigh, most of the lawyers of the county, and some from Albany and New York, stopped at the inn, and after a drink or two, were ready to harangue all who would listen. They never lacked an audience. They bought drinks for all.

It was a feast for eye and ear to visit the tavern on these occasions. These canvassers wore richly colored coats and breeches of velvet, silken hose, silver buckles, and cocked hats set on their powdered wigs; and talked as only the richly dressed could talk. Kinderhook then was the center of everything on the west bank of the Hudson between Albany and Poughkeepsie: the City of Hudson, which was later to supplant it in importance, was but a small settlement of Rhode Island Quakers. And to feel the pulse of this vast territory with its thousands of votes, one had to visit the taverns. Alexander Hamilton, Aaron Burr, and John Jay were patrons of the Van Buren inn. All these were frequent visitors at the home of the wealthy Peter Van Schaack —whom Jay welcomed back in 1785 after he returned from his banishment to England for his Toryism—and at the home of another rich Kinderhook family, the Van Nesses, whose place lay some two miles south of the Village.

## CHAPTER IV

WHEN Martin had passd his tenth birthday he heard strange talk in the tavern: men were publicly rejoicing over the beheading of Louis XVI; strange stories of stranger scenes in the large cities were told; and there was much said of heroic France fighting the rest of Europe to save the republic she had established. This was dividing the people: some favored active support of the French cause, while others were for following the course mapped out in Washington's proclamation of neutrality. None of the tales recounted in the tavern could exaggerate the actual happenings in New York and Philadelphia after the arrival of Citizen Edmond Charles Genêt, minister from France, in the spring of 1793.

After Genêt landed from the French frigate *L'Ambuscade* at Charleston, the ship preceded him to Philadelphia seizing English vessels along the way. A series of banquets were given the impetuous young Frenchman at the Nation's Capital. Through the quiet streets of the staid old Quaker town the French sympathizers paraded, singing the Marseillaise, and performing that mad dance of the French Revolution, the carmagnole: the burden of the sanguinary song that accompanied it was borne by students, creoles from the West Indies, and other French refugees who had sought sanctuary in the city.

In Girard Square stood a pole topped with the red cap of liberty. School boys and girls, dressed in red, white, and blue, made a demonstration in front of the residence of the British minister. On the night of May 23, at the dinner given in honor of Genêt, attended by Governor Mifflin and other Pennsylvanians of note, a roasted pig which graced the table was accorded the name of the executed French King, and the head of the porker was severed from the body to symbolize the fate of the luckless monarch. The head was presently carried on a salver to each guest, who, as he donned the red cap, mangled the pig's head with a table knife, and exclaimed: "Tyrant!"

Jefferson, then Secretary of State, indorsed Genêt's mission, saying: "He offers everything and asks nothing." Quasi-secret organizations were formed, patterned after the Jacobin Clubs of Paris. They were called Democratic Clubs or Societies; their members addressed each other as citizen and announcements of marriages of these French sympathizers told of the wedding of Citizen John Doe to Citizeness Mary Roe.

Toasts were drunk everywhere to the success of the armies of France. In Philadelphia, in violation of Washington's proclamation of neutrality, Genêt was fitting out a privateer when stopped by Governor Mifflin. Undaunted, the Frenchman left for New York, where salvos of cannon and the pealing of bells announced his landing; dinners were given in his honor, and the carmagnole was performed in the streets of Manhattan Island; and tri-colored cockades were worn by many citizens. At all these assemblies the Marseillaise was sung; but the extreme was reached at a meeting of the local Democratic Society where this parody of "God Save the King," written by Thelwall, an English republican, was chorused:

> God save the guillotine!
> Till England's King and Queen
>     His power shall prove;
> Till each anointed knob
> Affords a clipping job,
> Let no rude halter rob
>     The guillotine.

> France, let thy trumpet sound—
> Tell all the world around
>     How Capet fell;
> And when Great George's poll
> Shall in the basket roll,
> Let mercy then control
>     The guillotine.

> When all the sceptred crew
> Have paid their homage due
>     The Guillotine
> Let Freedom's flag advance
> Till all the world, like France,
> O'er tyrants' graves shall dance
>     And peace begin.

Associations of merchants throughout the North held counter demonstrations, and condemned the fitting out of French privateers. Jefferson had now repudiated Genêt, and joined with Washington in demanding his recall. John Jay and Rufus King in a letter to a New York newspaper accused the minister of having threatened to appeal to the people from the Government's refusal to lend aid to the French in accordance with the Treaty of Alliance of 1778. But Genêt did not leave the country: the guillotine awaited him in France. To the ægis of Governor Clinton he owed his safety, whose daughter he married; and he spent the remainder of his life as a gentleman farmer.

The political activities of Genêt widened the gulf between the Federalists and the Anti-Federalists; and the latter began to be known as Republicans. The Federalists, under the leadership of Hamilton, derisively dubbed the Republicans democrats, by way of perpetuating the memory of *L'Ambuscade*, which Genêt had renamed *Little Democrat*. Jefferson, whose ardor for the French revolutionists never waned, accepted the tag as a badge of honor, and the Republicans referred to themselves as democrats, spelling the word, however, with only a small *d*. It was to be many years before the name was to denominate a party. Of course the Republicans did not turn the other cheek. The Federalists were pro-British and their leaders had been bribed with British gold. The proof? The charge was repeated. This is supporting testimony on the hustings.

Abraham Van Buren was an ardent Republican. His son Martin also professed the faith of Jefferson.

## CHAPTER V

Young Martin's brief schooling ended before he reached his
fourteenth year, but by that time he had put in some periods of
study at the Kinderhook Academy—no one knows how much
scraping his mother did to manage this—where he learned the
rudiments of Latin, and not much else besides. Until he was well
on in years he wrote a most atrocious scrawl. In the summer or
very early fall of 1796 Martin was articled to a lawyer. Washington had declined to be a candidate for a third term, smarting
under attacks couched, as he phrased it, "in such exaggerated and
indecent terms as could scarcely be applied to a Nero, to a notorious defaulter, or even a common pickpocket." They derisively
called him the Stepfather of His Country. He said that he would
rather be in his grave than in the Presidency. But the hatchers of
campaign canards had not drawn upon the argot of the brothels;
this was to await a later day, when Van Buren's opponents
fashioned a bar sinister in their forge of falsehoods, and held it
up to public gaze with an elaborately embroidered tale purporting
to account for it.

Young Martin's employer was Francis Silvester, a just and
honorable man, son of Judge Peter Silvester, "the first lawyer of
Kinderhook," statesman and jurist, who married a sister of Peter
Van Schaack. He was related to nearly every one of importance
throughout the countryside. There was high honor in serving as
Francis Silvester's law clerk.

It should be noted here that the Silvesters were ardent Federalists; and it should also be observed that while Peter Van
Schaack had been a Tory in the war, his brother-in-law had served
as a member of the First State Provincial Congress. On his father's
side Van Buren's preceptor was descended from Nathaniel Syl-
vester (*sic!*) the first resident proprietor of the Manor of Shelter
Island, obtained under a grant in 1666 from Charles II. All the
Silvesters were dandies. Francis wore silver buckles on his square-
toed shoes. His clerk, as became a disciple of Jefferson, wore laces

in his. The year Van Buren began his seven years' clerkship, the
father of his employer was elected to the aristocratic State Senate,
for none save landowners of considerable size were nominated
for this body by either party—the State Constitution provided
that they should be freeholders with a holding worth not less than
£100, a sum sufficient in those days to purchase at least two lots
on Broadway, near Wall street. The Senate was a highly important body, as its members, sitting with the Chancellor and the
judges of the Supreme Court, constituted the Court for the Correction of Errors. This was in keeping with tradition; it was only
proper that the landed interests should be preferred: the Van
Rensselaers were but one of a few families who owned most of the
land on either bank of the Hudson by virtue of manorial grants.
Here slavery existed, the only region outside of the South and
the shores of Narragansett Bay where human beings were bought
and sold. Elsewhere in the North it meant social ostracism to
own a slave.

When Martin first appeared in the law office he wore coarse
linen and rough woolens his mother had spun and woven. Part of
his duties was to sweep out the office and dust the furniture and
books, and to keep the logs blazing in the fireplace on cold days.
This work has never yet failed to afford a small boy an opportunity to soil his clothes. A spot on a garment was an offense in
the eyes of a Silvester. The greater part of the boy's time was
spent in copying the pleadings in chancery and the less interesting technical forms of common law, in serving papers, and in
carrying his preceptor's green bag to court. Another task was
to sleep in the store of Cornelius Silvester when his clerk was
absent for the night. Cornelius was a brother of Francis, kind and
generous, and young Van Buren did not lose by slumbering behind
stacks of merchandise in the rear of the establishment.

Toward the end of Van Buren's first year as a law student,
Francis Silvester talked at length on the imperative need of
always wearing the very finest apparel. The next day Silvester
looked in vain for his law clerk; and the day following he was
also absent. On the third day young Van Buren reappeared. The
lawyer looked at the boy and quickly turned away to hide a grin;
and Martin merely bade him good morning. Not a word was said
about his absence, for the boy, from his cocked hat to his silken

hose, was a sartorial counterpart of his preceptor. The name of
the waggish benefactor of Martin who took him to Albany and
made him over in point of dress, is not recorded by his kinsmen
or others who have told this story. We are inclined to believe
that he was Cornelius Silvester, who took more than passing
interest in the lad's progress.

Minor actions were tried before justices of the peace, who
generally held court in a tavern; and here the blindfolded goddess functioned in most primitive fashion. In some counties of the
State—the Dutch counties, as they were called—the justice invariably spoke broken English. A bottle of whiskey was usually
on the table of counsel "to be used as the trial progressed, whenever it should be necessary to solve an intricate question." Levi
Beardsley, a distinguished counsel of the day, and one-time President of the New York State Senate, has described these village
courts in his amusing *Reminiscences*. Here is one:

> The defendant was a noted fighter, a hard drinker and . . .
> amused himself, while the jury was being summoned, with drinking,
> and playing with an old dirty pack of cards on one end of the bar-
> room table. The jury being in attendance, the justice called the par-
> ties, and had the warrant returned, and then directed the plaintiff
> to state the nature of his demand; which, being done, he with great
> humility, and in broken English, asked the defendant, whom we will
> call Mr. C.: "Well, Mr. C., what do you say to dat?" "What do I
> say to that?" says the defendant; "I say that you are a d——d old
> fool." "Oh! tut, tut," says the justice, "dat may very well be, Mr. C.,
> but what has dat to do with this case?" At this stage of the proceed-
> ing the defendant knocked down the constable, threw the cards in the
> justice's face, kicked over the table, and cleared out . . .

The spectators did not hesitate to show their displeasure
when a verdict was not to their liking, sometimes mauling the
luckless jurist. Important cases involving property rights were
tried before juries, and sessions were invariably held at night
that witnesses might not be taken from their work.

Beardsley recalls a sitting where "a crowd assembled, and
as usual, took sides with the parties; but in this instance, were
nearly unanimous for one of the parties, and in opposition to the
justice, who, they thought, favored the wrong party." During the

trial, some of the spectators, who were drinking "freely at the bar of the country tavern," resolved that they would show their contempt for judicial authority in a manner to make the judge the laughing stock of the county if he rendered a verdict in keeping with his unjust rulings. He did.

After court adjourned, those who had drunk long and copiously formed a circle around his honor, and "commenced urinating on him from every direction." When this unpopular judge realized what was happening to him "he set up an outcry and escaped from the crowd, but brought actions of assault and battery against the perpetrators, which in due time the defendants settled, by paying costs and making suitable amends to the distinguished jurist."

Although the administration of justice in these courts was of the crudest sort, and decisions ofttimes dictated by political passions, the lawyers who practiced before them, with rare exceptions, were veritable Chesterfields. In their relations with one another sharp practice was almost unknown. Causes tried before justices of the peace were frequently entrusted to the law clerk, and not a few of our great jurists of a century ago argued their first case in a country tavern.

In a tavern at Valatie, a village near Kinderhook, Van Buren made his professional début. He was there on business for his office, and had to wait until a jury case was finished. Aaron Gardinier, a scion of an old Kinderhook family, was of counsel in the action. It was not an important cause; and when the evidence was presented, Gardinier turned to the little law clerk who sat beside him and said: "Here, Mat, sum up. You may as well begin early." Van Buren, whose head did not reach the lawyer's shoulder, was lifted up on a chair, and began summing up the case for Gardinier's client. At first his voice was low and halting, but presently he was speaking in the hurried, racing fashion that was later to be the despair of the shorthand reporters. For his labor Van Buren received a silver half-dollar. He was not much more than fifteen years of age.

In this same year, following the State election of 1798, Van Buren had his first serious conflict over politics. News of the victory of the Federalists was brought to the village by Colonel Elisha Williams, the leading Federal lawyer of Columbia County, who was destined soon to be Van Buren's chief legal adversary. Williams, a noted orator and famed throughout the State for his splendid qualities of heart and mind, called on the Silvesters with the intelligence. The head of the family, Peter Silvester, was re-elected State Senator; John Jay was elected Governor for a second term, and the Patroon—in New York, although there were many patroons, the prints of the day always referred to *the* Van Rensselaer as the Patroon—was again chosen Lieutenant Governor. The tidings was the signal for firing the cannon in the village square; and how much powder was consumed, or how much wine, no record tells, but the drinking and firing of the cannon continued through the night. In an upper room of the Silvester home all the male Silvesters gathered, attended by Williams, and other Federalists, including Van Buren's older half-brother, James I. Van Alen. All were drinking and singing patriotic songs and voicing their praise of Federalists and Federalism, and their contempt for Republicans and Jacobinism. At the height of the jubilations Van Buren had occasion to visit the room, but declined to celebrate the victory of the Hamiltonians. In relating the incident he said:

Cornelius Silvester . . . having observed the state of my feelings came out and pressed me earnestly to join them. Having declined his invitation, which was given with delicacy and kindness, I retired to his store, where I slept in the absence of his clerk. Some time after midnight I heard a knocking at the door, and on opening it, admitted Mr. Silvester himself. At his instance I returned to my bed, and he placed himself by its side, and for more than an hour occupied himself in presenting the reasons which ought to induce me to adopt the politics of the Federal party, and solicited me to do so with a degree of earnestness and obvious concern for my welfare which I could not but respect. After hearing him out, I replied calmly that I appreciated thoroughly the kindness of his feelings, and was well satisfied of the purity of his motives, but that my course had been settled after much reflection, and could not be changed. He paused a moment, and then took my hand and said he would never trouble me again on the subject, and would always remain my friend.

The attempt to convert a lad who had six years to go before he could vote was doubly inspired. Cornelius Silvester was an ardent Federalist and felt that, in all probability, young Van Buren, because of his local fame as a boy-lawyer, would make a picturesque figure on the hustings, and that one or the other of the two parties would soon enlist him as a campaigner. The second and dominating motive was the concern of the merchant for the lad's future; he suspected that his brother would not suffer in his office one who held political views at variance with his own.

That is the only incident Van Buren has left us of his youth, a youth filled with the hardships of poverty, which the poor have learned to endure; and the hardships wantonly inflicted by the fortunate, which lead to reprisals. Van Buren was well acquainted with the first: he was soon to know the second.

# CHAPTER VI

VAN BUREN as a boy answered his own definition of an old-school Dutchman—"immovable, obstinate, and imperturbably good-natured." He was frankly that. He had not yet learned to wear a mask.

In time the village heard of the fruitless midnight mission of Cornelius Silvester to the bedside of the boy of fifteen. Mine Host Abraham beamed broadly at his tavern bar. What joy it gave the Van Nesses! They had a new story to retail to Aaron Burr on his next visit. Old Peter Van Ness, who commanded his own company in the British invasion of Canada, and led a regiment at the capture of Burgoyne at Saratoga twenty-one years later, could hardly bear the sight of a Federalist. A kinsman, Captain Abraham Van Ness, who was to have taken part in the Battle of Saratoga, was captured by sympathizers of the Crown while he was home on furlough, taken from the house, and assassinated. Old Peter was now living quietly on a farm a good two miles south of the village on the Post Road. One of his sons was distinguished as a lawyer; a second, William P. Van Ness, was studying law in the office of Edward Livingston, then noted chiefly because he was the brother of Chancellor Livingston, who was defeated for Governor by Jay. Burr was fond of Livingston's law clerk; and Billy Van Ness worshiped Burr.

A year or so passed before young Van Buren first encountered the petty persecution of the Federalists. He made cautious inquiries as to when Billy Van Ness was expected to make his next trip from New York to Kinderhook, as he wanted his advice. And when they met Mat told his troubles to Billy, four years his senior, but ever so much wiser in the eyes of Van Buren, because, like Francis Silvester, and the Van Schaacks, he had a sheepskin from Columbia College. Mat related some of the petulant scenes with his instructor. Billy could see no reason for being distressed by anything a Federalist might say from Hamilton down. If he were a year or two older he would have his own law

39

office and Mat could study with him; but, after all, there was
no need to worry; he could go to New York anyway, which teemed
with lawyers. Young Van Buren was cheered by the reassuring
words of the worshiper of Burr, who was to blast the youth's
career as well as his own. Thereafter, the occasional bickerings
were received with a less heavy heart. His reading, apart from law
books, was of the most trivial character. He preferred a rod
and one of Kinderhook's quiet trout streams, or one of the many
neighborhood ponds, where lurked the wary bass and the wily
pickerel, to the volumes of Shakespeare on Silvester's shelves.
But he read every Republican journal, periodical, and pamphlet
that fell into his hands.

Van Buren's appearances in court became more frequent, and
the presence of the yellow-haired boy before a jury no longer
excited comment. He earned the merited plaudits of the Republicans of Columbia County when he won a case tried by a justice
and jury in Nathan Deyo's tavern. The opposing counsel was
Elisha Williams. Oliver Wendell Holmes, in *The Poet at the
Breakfast Table*, tells us that when he asked a New Yorker—"a
scholar and a writer of note"—one who had known every one
worth knowing in his long career: "Who, on the whole, seemed
to you the most considerable person you ever met?" Holmes expected him to name Henry Clay, or Daniel Webster, or "one of
the great ex-Presidents whose names were known to all the world."
His unnamed scholar and writer of note answered, very deliberately: "Take it altogether, I should say Colonel Elisha Williams
was the most notable personage I have met with." Elisha Williams
was the first to congratulate Van Buren when the verdict was
rendered.

Van Buren had passed his seventeenth birthday when he encountered Williams in the legal arena. Earlier in the year, Jefferson had made a profession of his political faith in a letter to
Elbridge Gerry—each one of the articles of the creed Van Buren
knew by heart—and in 1800 the essentials of the credo of republicanism were incorporated in the platform on which he defeated
John Adams. Against two great dangers Jefferson warned the
people: the gradual monarchizing of the young Republic; and the
building up of a powerful partisan machine through the creation
of needless offices, lest this, too, destroy the freedom so dearly

bought. "I am for a government rigorously frugal and simple," wrote Jefferson, "applying all the possible savings of the public revenue to the discharge of the national debt; and not for a multiplication of officers and salaries merely to make partisans, and for increasing, by every device, the public debt, on the principle of its becoming a public blessing."

Van Buren campaigned for Jefferson, and the Republicans of Columbia County rewarded the eighteen-year-old youth by electing him a delegate to the Republican Congressional caucus in Troy. It was known in advance that John P. Van Ness, older brother of young Van Buren's friend Billy, would be the choice of the Trojan meeting. Van Buren was broke. He could not go to Troy without money. Timidly he confided in Van Ness, expecting the aspirant for Congressional honors to offer to lend him the needed sum. But Van Ness was also penniless. Van Buren accepted, in lieu of the expected loan, a pinch of snuff from the jeweled box of the poor dandy. Within twenty-four hours Van Buren had enough silver in his pocket to pay the expenses of Van Ness as well as himself. Van Ness did not inquire where Van Buren obtained the loan; and the two set out for Rensselaer's county seat, Van Ness mounted on a splendidly caparisoned steed from his father's stable, and Van Buren astride a borrowed nag; for his father did not possess even a work horse. The Van Burens plowed with oxen.

Van Buren was lionized at the caucus, and his vote for Van Ness's nomination was greeted with loud huzzas. Van Buren canvassed for Van Ness, who was elected. Shortly thereafter the new Congressman married a rich girl. He advised Mat to leave Silvester and finish his clerkship in a New York office, under some good Republican. He told Van Buren to count on him, now that he had a wealthy wife, for any money he might need during his clerkship.

Van Buren, grateful for this generous offer, acted upon the advice, and arrived in Manhattan in the fall of 1801. Billy Van Ness found him cheap lodgings in Catherine street. Unable to find him a clerkship, Billy took him into his own almost-clientless office until Van Buren could find a more remunerative preceptor.

The first week or so in the city was a period of investigation for Van Buren. It was all dazzling. He saw several carriages. He was pleased to know that all New York turned out to see the

Patroon when he came from Albany in his carriage, just as they did in Kinderhook when the equipage with outriders and postilions passed through. He was not astonished that the Patroon excited this interest, for New York was still preponderatingly Dutch. And although the majority of the fashionables worshiped at Trinity, Grace Church, and St. Paul's, a goodly number attended the Old Middle Dutch Church on William street, where Colonial troops died from cold, hunger, and vermin, during the British occupation of the city. He went there to hear a service in his own tongue, but was disappointed. Save on rare occasions, the services had been conducted in English for years. The change was necessary to hold the growing generation, as most of the younger people knew only the language of the Yankees. Then he recalled how like Kinderhook was New York in many respects: save for a little stretch of narrow brick pave on Broadway near St. Paul's, there were the same dirt walks; the few cobblestones did not hinder the pigs and cows who wandered the streets; Dutch was spoken in streets and in many shops; Dutchmen smoked long clay pipes outside their doors; and the floors of the taverns were sanded.

On a fine afternoon he stood on the steps of the City Hall at Nassau and Wall streets and watched the beauty and ton file by. Kinderhook boasted nothing like this, which could be equaled only at the Battery on a clear Sunday, when vari-colored silks and satins and velvets shone like brilliant jewels in the sun, and where powdered wigs and curls were as commonplace among the men as frizzled locks among the young girls. Here one saw dandies of an earlier day walking more erect than their sons, the sword at their side clutched by a gloved hand half hidden under lace ruffles. No poor man—at least no man poorly dressed—strolled through the arbored walks at the Battery; nor could one see a woman outside the fashionable world, save some bedizened and venturesome member of the frail sisterhood.

Up at the other end of the city, the northern end of the Park, stood the almshouse, the Bridewell, and the Debtors' Prison. From the grated windows of the last of the melancholy group, those whose crime was poverty dangled ropes to attract the charity of the few who passed that way. At the end of these ropes were crude baskets large enough to hold a loaf of bread. In the winter the

Quakers provided these unfortunates with wood for their fires.
There was little, save morbid curiosity, or politics, or amusement,
to take any one there, as the place was so far away from the scene
of things. When there was talk of building a new City Hall in the
Park, the proposal was received with laughter. Those with an eye
for beauty, seeking the architect's drawings, knew that to view
the contemplated triumph of Colonial architecture, in proper
perspective, a vista such as only the Park afforded, would be
adequate. All were agreed, when the Hall was planned, that the
city would never extend beyond it, which accounts for the cheap
brownstone forming the rear wall, now concealed underneath
successive coats of white so as to make it resemble the marble
façade and side walls.

The Debtors' Prison served one useful purpose: its porticoed
tower was paced by a watchman whose lantern, suspended from a
long pole, indicated the direction of a fire after an alarm was
sounded. Across from the gloomy group was the slave burying
ground. Far to the north were the country homes of the rich.
On Richmond Hill, a mile or so away, near where Varick and
Charlton streets now intersect, lived Aaron Burr. The Park—it
was always capitalized in the old days—was the open-air forum of
the city. No permit was required, and no public official dreamed
of misusing his authority to silence a speaker in the Park or
elsewhere. The stifling of free speech was confined to the mobs.

Many thousands could be assembled in the Park, which was
then an irregular triangle, its lines formed by Broadway, Chambers street, and Park Row. The lower end of the Park, where
Park Row and Broadway meet, had not yet been turned over to
the Post Office Department as a site for an architectural horror.

Not long after Van Buren began his clerkship with Van Ness
a youth of his own age, Philip, the eldest son of Alexander Hamilton, went to the Park for an evening's amusement. Young Hamilton was accompanied by another lad of nineteen named Price.
Their destination the theater—there was only one then and it had
no designation; but later it was called the Park Theater—on Park
Row between Ann and Beekman streets. The date was Friday,
November 20, 1801.

Long before playgoers of our day sit down to dinner, young
Hamilton and his companion were in their seats. There was pre-

sented that evening "a celebrated Comedy called The West Indian
. . . to which will be added, A Grand Pantomimical Drama, interspersed with Songs, called Obi; or Three-Fingered Jack,
Founded on a Fact which occurred (A.D. 1789) in the Island of
Jamaica." To quote further from the advertisement in the *Evening Post*, which young Hamilton's father had established only
four days before: "The doors will open at ½ after 5, and the
curtain [will] rise at ½ after 6 o'clock. It is earnestly requested
that no person will carry a lighted Segar into any part of the
Theatre, or attempt to renew the dangerous practise of smoking
[*sic!*] either in the Lobbies or in the presence of the audience."

Hamilton and his friend occupied part of a box. They sat immediately behind George I. Eacker, senior member of the law firm
of Eacker and Van Slyck. Eacker was a Republican—a Burrite.
The two youths found little amusement in the performance, and
boy-like, began to amuse themselves. Young Hamilton remembered
that Eacker had spoken at the last Fourth of July celebration,
and—in the language of the *Spectator*—"pointed ridicule upon
the oration delivered by Eacker."

Eacker overheard the remarks. To return to the *Evening
Post:* "Eacker . . . asked Hamilton to step into the lobby; Price
followed—here the expression *damned rascal* was used by Eacker
to one of them, and a little scuffle ensued; but they soon adjourned
to a public house:—an explanation was then demanded, which of
them the offensive expression was meant for; after a little hesitation, it was declared to be intended for each. Eacker then said,
as they parted, *I expect to hear from you;* they replied, *you shall.*"

Eacker was about thirty years of age. In the tavern he observed the extreme youth of the two he had challenged. But such
were the customs of the times that age was no barrier to this
socially recognized form of maiming and murder.

Hamilton and Price consulted with their friends who agreed
that the retaliation of Eacker had been so violent that it would
be impossible for either not to notice the matter further; but
as young Hamilton had given the first offense his message should
be conciliatory, and merely call for "some explanation of the
offensive expression."

Eacker, out for blood, replied: ". . . the expressions I made
use of toward Mr. Hamilton at the Theater Friday night last

were produced by his conduct on that occasion; I thought them applicable then, and I think so still."

Young Price and Eacker were the first on the dueling ground at Weehawken. Four shots were fired without effect when the affair was brought to an end by the seconds.

The interview between Eacker and Price occurred Sunday, two days after the incident at the theater; and the next day young Hamilton faced Eacker on the same field. Hamilton and Burr were soon to meet each other here.

At the command "Fire!" Eacker discharged his pistol, the ball plowing through the boy's intestines. Young Hamilton fell mortally wounded. In falling, his pistol was discharged in the air. The following morning the lad expired in his father's arms.

Robert Troup, a veteran of the bar, and a life-long friend of the elder Hamilton, wrote a fortnight later: "Never did I see a man so completely overwhelmed with grief as Hamilton has been. The scene I was present at, when Mrs. Hamilton came to see her son on his deathbed . . . and when she met her husband and son in one room beggars all description! . . . At present Hamilton is more composed and is able again to attend to business; but his countenance is strongly stamped with grief. Eacker [*sic!*] has not since made his appearance at the bar. There is a general current of opinion agt. him, except amongst the violent democrats."

The father of the slain youth was opposed to dueling on moral and religious grounds. The *Evening Post*, in a temperate editorial, thus voiced his views:

Reflections on this horrid custom must occur to every man of humanity; but the voice of an individual or of the press must be ineffectual without additional, strong and pointed legislative interference. Fashion has placed it upon a footing which nothing short of this can control.

Van Buren shared the horror of the rest of the community over the duel. There were, as Troup had written to Rufus King, Republican extremists who condoned the slaying; some even approved it. Van Buren viewed the custom with contempt; but Billy Van Ness held opposite views.

A week after the duel Van Buren's funds were at low ebb.

He was beginning to despair of finding a clerkship in a law office where clients waited in the reception room. Such places were obtained, as Van Buren said, only by those with powerful family connections, and it was his boast that he had none of these.

Billy Van Ness could see no occasion for alarm. It was only a question of time when his bag would be filled with briefs. Was not his friend, Aaron Burr, Vice President of the United States?

There was no denying the intimacy between the youthful Billy Van Ness and Burr. Van Buren was to see many proofs of it in his visits with Billy to the Vice President's home on Richmond Hill. Van Ness was a political lieutenant of Burr. A short time after Van Buren's arrival in the city, Van Ness and thirty others who were propertyless, and therefore unable to vote, clubbed together and bought a house, thus technically qualifying as electors for the municipal elections held in the month of November. All of Van Ness's associates in this novel undertaking were young lawyers, law students, and mechanics. The votes of these thirty-one turned the close election in the Fifth Ward, and elected a Republican member of the Common Council. One of the "owners" of the house in the Fifth Ward was Daniel D. Tompkins, a future Governor of the State.

This evasion of the election law was the beginning of a wide-spread system, and the Federalists were not slow in copying the device, whose inventor was probably Burr or his friend and biographer, Matthew L. Davis, Grand Sachem of the Society of Tammany.

Billy was prolific in promises. But Van Buren could not live on words. He had never before known the fear of hunger, a fear unknown on a farm; for there one always has enough to eat. If Billy's brother, the Honorable John P. Van Ness, M.C., were only in the city! It was hard to ask for a loan in a letter; but the Congressman had told Van Buren to draw on him for any sum he might require until his clerkship was finished. At last he gathered enough courage to write.

He wrote his first appeal for funds on December 3. He waited ten days in patience, and at the end of another ten days he was beginning to believe that the Member of Congress from the Sixth New York had completely forgotten his promise to assist him financially.

Christmas Day found Van Buren poorer than ever. The continued silence of Congressman Van Ness put his boasted sanguine temperament, ardent disposition, and high and buoyant spirits to an acid test. How unreal the day seemed! It was not like Christmas. Once he believed that by singing to St. Nicholas the good holy man would put on his best cloak and ride to distant climes for things he wanted. On December 27 he wrote his second letter to Van Ness.

At last an answer came from Washington enclosing twenty dollars. Van Buren's two letters are lost; but in the rich archives of the Division of Manuscripts of the Library of Congress, the answer is preserved, revealing, as though we had Van Buren's pleas before us, how he masked his avowal of poverty with a request for counsel. Van Ness, in six pages of script, the once jet black ink now brown with age, advised him to move only in the best society; to be moderate in attending the theater lest he become addicted to it; to avoid vice and idleness; to improve his mind by constant study. Then he added: "I have no doubt you will (reflecting and considering that your future prospects are principally founded upon your attention to the improvement of that mind and those talents, with which you are blessed) neglect no opportunity of accomplishing this desirable object to such a degree as to render you an ornament and an honor to your friends and your country."

That last phrase of Van Ness's was fraught with prophecy. But it stirred no greater aim in Van Buren's mind than a place on the Supreme Court bench, the dream of all law students. The Congressman was right about improving his mind and talents: Van Buren heartily agreed with this. And then, as all through his life, he vowed to devote less time to political journals and pamphlets, and more to books to which he was a total stranger. He could not help envying Billy Van Ness, who could quote Latin poetry, and recited some of the Horatian epistles by heart. There were two bits of advice which Van Buren followed through life: to be moderate in his theater-going, and to move only in the best circles.

# CHAPTER VII

THE hardships of Van Buren in New York were compensated by the study he made at close range of politics and those who pulled the strings. The visits to Aaron Burr were the bright spots in his long dreary months in the city. Burr was pleased with the youth; his staunch Republicanism delighted him; and he showed him the courtly consideration he bestowed on men of affairs. But Van Buren could not have helped observing that the Vice President showered a wealth of affection on Van Ness denied to other visitors at the house lying between the city and the village of Greenwich. And Van Ness, in turn, venerated Burr. But these relations brought no clients to the law office of William P. Van Ness, Esquire. Because of this, Van Buren acquired the habit of living on little. An extra dollar was so seldom in his purse that he developed a spirit akin to niggardliness.

Burr stood in need of the loyalty of Van Ness and other steadfast friends at the beginning of 1802. Long menaced by Hamilton, his professional and partisan rival, he was now confronted by a still greater peril within his own party. These new foes were *the Livingston family*—as the faction headed by Chancellor Robert R. Livingston was designated—and the Clintonians. The venerable Governor Clinton was nominally the leader of this wing of the Republican party. The actual control was wielded by his nephew, the brilliant De Witt Clinton, then in his thirty-third year, and a member of the United States Senate.

This powerful combination declared war on Burr on the pretext that he had intrigued with the Federalists to rob Jefferson of the Presidency for himself. A plausible *prima facie* case was established to support this charge of treachery. Contrariwise, it was not difficult to cite circumstances tending to show that the powerful combination was animated solely by a desire to elect a Clinton or a Livingston to the highest office in the land. This could not be done while Burr was in its way.

48

A more powerful coalition could not have been effected in New York. The Livingstons were scions of the house of Callender, their most noted ancestor being Sir Alexander Livingstone— thus he spelled the name—who was appointed by the estates as one of the two regents during the minority of James II of Scotland. The first Livingston in this country was Robert, who married Alida, widow of Dominie Nicolaus Van Rensselaer, and sister of Colonel Pieter Schuyler. Robert, although born in Scotland, was in speech a Dutchman, his father, a minister, having been exiled in 1663 for his non-conformity. Father and son, the latter then a child of nine, went to the Netherlands where the victims of religious persecution of all lands found asylum. On reaching his majority he sailed for Rensselaerswyck, and in time became a patroon. His manor began some five miles south of the present city of Hudson, extending south on the east bank of the Hudson for twelve miles, and stretched out eastward like a fan until it touched the Massachusetts line, where its length was twenty miles. The tract embraced nearly a quarter of a million acres. The Livingstons were Dutch, in everything but name; and were related by blood or marriage to nearly every family of distinction in the State. They were distantly related to General Philip Schuyler, father of Elizabeth, wife of Alexander Hamilton.

The first of the American Clintons was a son of a cadet in the family of the Earls of Lincoln, whose estates were sequestrated for espousing the cause of Charles I. This son, Charles, in the year 1729, at the age of forty, followed by his family, some neighbors, dissenters all, sailed from Dublin Bay for Massachusetts. They landed on bleak Cape Cod, but not liking the land or the climate, came to New York two years later, and settled some sixty miles up the Hudson, in a place they named Goshen.

These two families, like every one of note in public life, had distinguished records in the Revolution. All the resources at the disposal of the Clintons and Livingstons were used in their warfare on Burr; even the Bank of Manhattan, which Burr surreptitiously brought into existence through a joker in a bill to supply the city with water following the yellow fever epidemic of 1798. This was the only financial house controlled by the Republicans; and at the first meeting of the managers of the bank after hostilities began, Burr and John Swartwout were turned out of the directorate. Swartwout had been Burr's colleague in the State Assembly when the Bank of Manhattan joker was slipped into the water bill.

Swartwout's only sin lay in his friendship for Burr; and he voiced his affection by saying that De Witt Clinton had planned the war on the Vice President because of selfish and other unworthy motives. Clinton was imperious. When fresh from college he was appointed secretary to his uncle, then Governor of the State. He had served as an Assemblyman and State Senator before going to the United States Senate. When he learned of Swartwout's remarks he denounced him as "a liar, a scoundrel, and a villain." Offensive phrases rolled readily from the tongue of Clinton in discussing his political opponents. Swartwout demanded a retraction of the unwarrantable epithets; Clinton agreed provided Swartwout would withdraw his reflections on Clinton's opposition to Burr. Swartwout refused, and then the barbarous code duello was invoked.

Clinton, as he said in the course of the duel, had no personal enmity toward Swartwout. Three shots were exchanged without either being hit. After each fire Clinton's second, Richard Riker, the District Attorney of New York, inquired: "Is your principal satisfied?" Each time Swartwout shook his head, whereupon his second would announce: "He is not." The fourth shot hit Swartwout in the leg.

Riker, who had hoped that the duel would end without bloodshed—he had tried to prevent the meeting—concealed his annoyance and disappointment as he asked: "Is your principal satisfied now?" We can sympathize with Riker, for he was the officer sworn to prosecute crime in all Manhattan.

"He is not," replied Swartwout's second for the fourth time, after receiving his cue.

For the fifth time the two men faced each other. Swartwout fell as the smoke cleared, the ball taking effect in the same leg.

"Is your principal now satisfied?" asked Riker in saddened tones.

"No!" shouted Swartwout as his seconds urged him to yield, while surgeons made ready to probe the wounds.

"Well! well!" said Clinton meditatively. After a few seconds' reflection he angrily threw his pistol to the ground, and exclaimed: "Then he may go to the devil, for I will fight no more."

Clinton strode off the field, followed by his friends.

The war continued, the passions of its leaders and their followers being kept at a fever heat by their personal organs. Burr's newspaper was the *Morning Chronicle*, edited by Dr. Peter Irving, and in its columns the charge was first publicly made that the Clintons and the Livingstons warred on Burr to realize their ambition to elevate a Clinton or a Livingston to the Presidency. In this journal Washington Irving, a younger brother of the editor, made his literary bow over the signature of Jonathan Oldstyle. Another contributor was Van Buren's preceptor, Billy Van Ness. The opposition was represented by the *American Citizen*, whose chief contributing editor was the versatile De Witt Clinton himself; but the scurrilities were written by the reckless James Cheetham, whose pamphlet, "A View of the Political Conduct of Aaron Burr," is his *chef-d'œuvre* in the strife.

Whatever hope had been entertained by the friends of the leaders of the two factions of stopping their private war perished with the appearance of the Cheetham work, which was answered with one of the most venomous pamphlets in our history. Not for years was it known that Billy Van Ness was the American Junius who had dipped deep into the well of hate to impeach the public and private character of the Clintons and the Livingstons. Edward Livingston, now Mayor, scoffed at the thought this his former law clerk had any hand in it. Van Ness masked his identity behind the name of Aristides. A more appropriate pseudonym would have been Callimachus. Van Buren, one of the few who knew that Van Ness was the author, kept the secret; but years later he was falsely charged with having betrayed the confidence to Burr's enemies.

This war had its beginning in the preceding year, when the Clintons and Livingstons divided the principal offices in the State among the members of their own families, and placed their followers in lesser places. The most important appointment at the disposal of the Governor was the New York Mayoralty. As a Clinton was Governor it was only fitting that a Livingston should be Mayor, and accordingly this office, the richest in the State in fees and in patronage, was bestowed on Edward, son of Chancellor Robert R. Livingston. To Brockholst Livingston, son of Governor Livingston of New Jersey, and a cousin of Edward, went one of the two vacancies on the Supreme Court, which paved the way for his elevation to the bench of the United States Supreme Court. Morgan Lewis, son of the Signer, was made Chief Justice of the State court. This was not because of his ancestry, but because he was the husband of Gertrude Livingston, sister of Edward. Chancellor Livingston, no longer competent for the office because of his age, resigned, and was appointed Minister to France by Jefferson, with the approval of the Senate and the approbation of the Clintons.

In the division of offices one of the Livingstons lost a job. This exception was John Armstrong. He, too, had married into the family. He was then United States Senator. It was agreed that Armstrong should be succeeded by a Clinton. So Armstrong obligingly retired that De Witt Clinton might be elected to the United States Senate. All the Republican members of the Legislature, including the Burrites, voted for him, open hostilities not having yet begun. To atone for this sacrifice, another Livingston by marriage, Dr. Thomas Tillotson, who had espoused another sister of Edward, was appointed Secretary of State of the State of New York.

With the two Clintons filling the offices of Governor and United States Senator, they had no choice in giving the Livingstons the lion's share of the remaining important offices. William Stewart, a brother-in-law of Governor Clinton, was appointed District Attorney of Tioga and other counties in the Southern Tier. This was one of the strongholds of the Clinton faction outside of New York City. Sylvanus Miller, their political lieutenant in Kingston, was appointed Surrogate of New York.

There was criticism of this last appointment. No one found fault with the talents or character of Sylvanus Miller; and this was true of all the appointments. It was said, however, that it was not proper to go eighty-nine miles from the city for a surrogate when there were many men of equal worth born and living within the city's walls.

Scarcely an important office went to a Burrite. If Burr could be deprived of political strength in his own State, he would, automatically, cease to be a figure in national politics. The Clintons and the Livingstons were slowly, but effectively, destroying Burr's political organization while building their own.

Burr had no family connections in the State, but he had intensely loyal friends in every section. They were zealots all; and friend and foe alike called them the Little Band. Burr's well-earned fame as the greatest of lawyers before a jury made him the idol of a large following in the city. A drama in its home opposite the Park did not hold the attraction of a trial in which Burr was counsel. He was primarily an advocate; and always histrionic. His client was ever pictured by Burr in the robes of innocence; and invariably he persuaded juries to his view. He was an actor, and knew every legal stratagem; some he invented. As defense counsel in a murder trial he protracted his cross-examination of the key witness for the prosecution until after dusk had fallen. When the candles were lighted Burr intensified the accusatory note in his embarrassing questions. The witness was honest. But who would not falter under such an ordeal? At a prearranged signal a clerk handed him a lighted candle. Burr then strode to the witness chair, and holding the flame close to the face of the man whose testimony he could not break down, cried to the jury: "Behold the murderer!" And the jury returned a verdict of "Not Guilty!"

Lawyers feared to oppose Burr before a jury, for his charm too often outweighed the evidence. To break down his hold on the popular mind was no child's task, as his opponents knew. But it had to be done if a Clinton or a Livingston was to be New York's choice in a Presidential nominating caucus.

Burr and his followers realized the strength and determination of the opposition and acted accordingly. Nearly every secret move made by a Clinton or a Livingston became known to the leaders of the Little Band, and of this group none was more youthful, dashing, daring, and unforgiving, than Van Buren's preceptor.

Van Buren saw that the Clintons and Livingstons in buttressing their opposition to Burr were doing something novel. They removed from office Federalists who were not ready to support them, and filled their places with Republicans. Hitherto, party workers, in the main, were inspired by principle, or emotion. Now the driving power was money, and nearly every penny came out of the public treasury in the form of fees and salaries. Judges with the power over life and property, who should be utterly removed from the prejudices of partisan politics, directed the various units of this vast corps of electioneers. There was not a township without its organization, compact and efficient, and all reporting to the Clintons or the Livingstons. Burr, too, had his machine, but it was the old model, composed of men who admired him and believed in the things he preached, and making up in zeal what they lacked in numbers. He had nothing to give.

Both sides relied heavily on newspapers and pamphlets for propagating their cause, and the printer had for ally the letter writer who proselyted by post, or kept the wavering ones steadfast.

The country looked on in astonishment at this innovation of the Republicans of New York. They could not but contrast it with what was happening in the national government where Jefferson, in his first sixteen months as President, had removed only sixteen office holders without assigning a reason. He was publicly opposed to using offices of government to attain partisan ends. This article of his faith was scorned by his followers in New York where thousands of worthy men were removed from office because of their devotion to Burr. There were more than five thousand fee or salary jobs in the State which were filled by factional partisans. But the assault on New York's civil list was infectious, and toward the end of Jefferson's first administration the disease spread to Washington, although not with the violence known in New York.

Nominally, and in law, the removals and appointments were made by the Council of Appointment, but, in fact, the active agent was Governor Clinton. This body was the executive counterpart of the Council of Revisions with whose legislative-judicial functions we are familiar. Both were designed by the framers of New York's Constitution to keep the entire control of the State government in the hands of a few.

The Council of Appointment consisted of the Governor and four members of the State Senate, who represented the landlords. The four Senators were chosen annually by the Assembly, which was elected by the small freeholders. And the rest of the all-men-

who-are-created-free-and-equal were just people. Hamilton called
them "a great beast"—the least of his offenses against democracy.
We should no more judge him by these utterances than we would
Euripides for scourging with thongs one who reflected on his
breath, or the greatest of the Livingstons by his one misstep.

This misfortune befell the Clinton-Livingston faction in the
summer of 1803. Until then everything was going against the
Burrites. Now Edward Livingston, Mayor of New York, and
United States Attorney for the entire State, had fallen. These
two offices he administered simultaneously. Jefferson had appointed him to the Federal berth after he resigned from Congress.
It was not unusual for a man to hold more than one high office at
the same time. The perquisites of the two places netted Livingston more than $20,000 annually. This was a princely income in
those days. Like men who care little for money, he was generous
to a fault. As Mayor he had to entertain lavishly; and as a proud
scion of the house of Callender he must play host in manorial
fashion.

When the yellow fever visited the city, in July of this year,
the rich fled to the country. Livingston remained at his post and
called at the homes of the stricken after his work was done.
Madeira, the most expensive of wines, was prescribed for sufferers,
and in the epidemic of 1803, even the poor did not lack this stimu-
lant or other luxuries of the sick room. Livingston saw to that.

In the midst of his ministrations to the afflicted Livingston
was stricken with the fever. While he was convalescing the government demanded an accounting of the moneys he had collected as
United States Attorney, and of which he was custodian. A shortage
was disclosed. While government investigators were trying to
determine the precise deficiency, which was later shown to be
$43,666.21, Livingston confessed judgment to $100,000. He
transferred all his property, save his clothes, to a trustee, to be
sold for the benefit of the government, and resigned both offices.
This was in the middle of August.

At the age of thirty-nine, Livingston, with a brilliant record
as a statesman and lawyer, set sail for New Orleans, to start life
anew; and to earn enough to square his account, which he did.
In his voluntary exile, some twenty years after, he flashed upon
an admiring world his famous Louisiana Code. The General As-

sembly of Louisiana had retained him to recodify the ancient welter of Spanish and French laws. He produced a code wherein man, for the first time in jurisprudence, was made transcendent to property. The Czar of Russia joined in the universal tribute to the exile; the King of the Netherlands had a gold medal struck in his honor; Napoleon's former Marshal, from his Swedish eminence, paid his homage to the American; Victor Hugo wrote: *"Vous êtes du nombre des hommes qui ont le plus et le mieux mérité de l'humanité dans ce siècle"*; and Jefferson, from whom Livingston had been estranged since the affairs of 1803, unconsciously paraphrased Hugo with: "It [the Code] will certainly arrange your name with the sages of antiquity."

This Code, which was translated into nearly every civilized tongue, has been the main source of all reform in our treatment of criminals. The ax, the musket, and the halter, to use Kent's phrase, were banished from the realm of punishment. Sentimentalists have seen in this great work an expression of a contrite heart. Livingston's record as Mayor is a story of active interest in the less fortunate. One reform he planned was the establishment of municipal workshops to relieve suffering in times of industrial depression. On a parity with this attempt to account for the Code is the acceptance by his apologists of a vague and tardy tale of an unnamed and obscure clerk embezzling $43,661.21 in the care of the most humane and one of the most sagacious lawgivers of our age.

Following the resignation of Livingston as Mayor there was a meeting of the Livingston and Clinton families. It would not do to appoint another Livingston to this place; that would have made for too much criticism by the Federalists and the Burrites. So a Clinton was named, De Witt Clinton, who resigned the more exalted station of United States Senator to sit in New York's City Hall. And John Armstrong resumed the seat he had vacated to make way for Clinton. It did seem to some that even the Clintons and the Livingstons might have refrained from playing battledore and shuttlecock with a toga.

If Van Buren had been another Adams! But he kept no diary, and there is no reference to this tragedy in any of his papers which fill sixty-one massive solander cases. That he was moved to pity there is every reason to believe, as there is to assume that

his preceptor gloated in the downfall of Burr's enemy, for he
had written under his nom de plume of Aristides that the rule of
life followed by the Livingstons had been summed up in that
cynical maxim of the respectables of thiefdom:

"... Rem, facias rem[,]
Si possis recte, si non quocunque modo, rem."

But after all, even the house of Callender should not have
patronized the house of Kidd.

Dark and malignant has the spirit of Billy Van Ness been
called; it was basically cowardly as well, as Van Buren was soon
to know. But Billy's clerk continued to be more interested in where
he would find next week's meals and lodgings than in the ups and
downs of New York's ruling families. Evidence that he made at
least three appeals for loans in 1803 is extant in the archives at
Washington. One is a reply from his half-brother, John I. Van
Alen, who sent enough from time to time to keep Mat from starving; the others are letters from Billy's brother the Congressman.
These were dated November 3 and 11. We will quote from the
first of the notes written by the politician who had promised to
finance Van Buren's two years in the city:

I have long been in hopes that I would have been able to answer
your letter with a One Hundred Dollar Bill, but innumerable disap-
pointments prevent—by God, my friend, Cash is out of my power;
but if my note for a hundred dollars at Twelve, or if necessary, at
Six months will answer your purpose let me know, and it is at your
service.

Van Buren's days of worrying over shelter and sustenance
were drawing to a close when he wrote to the Congressman, for
he was admitted to the practice of law about three weeks before
attaining his majority.

He returned to Kinderhook with little delay, for he had not
seen the snow on the hills of his childhood in more than two years.
It seemed longer since he had seen that shy, frail little girl, a distant kinswoman of his mother, Hannah Goes, or as it came to be
spelled, Hoes. Hannah was probably the last to welcome the
prodigal home; for she loved him and, maiden-like, showed it by

concealing it. Kinderhook saw a changed Martin Van Buren. The boyish slouch was gone, and in its stead was an erect carriage, peculiar to soldiers and men who are small and slender. Van Buren was not quite five feet six, and remained slight of figure until he was well on in years. His long, curly, yellow hair was parted over the right temple and combed back in wavy masses, hiding the ears, but revealing a forehead of extraordinary proportions. Deep-set eyes, big and blue, and always laughing, looked out at one with boyish frankness from under heavy eyebrows. His nose was long and aggressively Roman. His upper lip was a perfect Cupid's bow, the nether one full and inclined to protrude ever so faintly. The determination in the jaw was lost sight of in his constant smile. But it was not a gay smile: suffering had given a wistful turn to the corners of his mouth. The mother, as she looked at Martin, could not but recall a time when she felt that it had been unjust for her, a penniless widow with three small children, to marry the struggling, improvident tavern-keeper. She no longer thought so; for it was through the self-denials of one of those three—she attributed much to her prayers—that Martin was enabled to finish his clerkship in New York. And Mine Host Van Buren forgot their struggles as all sat down to the well-scoured table of white pine. He had eyes and ears only for Martin, and it was with pride that he watched his first son devour the *oli-koekjes*, those sweet cakes our Dutch forefathers took with their wine. The children always had their share of the koekjes, which have been Anglicized phonetically as cookies.

# CHAPTER VIII

VAN BUREN'S return to Kinderhook marked the actual beginning of his career in public life. The honor accorded him as a youth in choosing him a delegate to the Congressional district caucus in Troy was largely a gesture of affection. He had reached his majority on December 8, 1803, and would cast his vote in the spring elections for Governor, Lieutenant Governor, and other candidates. He had resolved to enter politics, knowing that prestige and clients come through activity on the hustings and in the party caucuses. Politics, however, was to be secondary to his practice, for he and his half-brother, James I. Van Alen, had a hard road ahead. He had seen how young Billy Van Ness's time had been consumed almost entirely by his passion to play the rôle of Burr's defender, and in turn, the defamer of the Clintons and the Livingstons.

All the political gossip centered on the impending battle between the Republican factions. Burr, still Vice President, had added to his reputation of being the most surprising political strategist of his day by announcing through his friends, early in January of 1804, that he did not want to be a candidate again for the Vice Presidency; but would reënter State politics as a nominee for Governor. Burr reasoned that by capturing the State he would make short shrift of his enemies, and place himself in line for the Presidency four years thence. There was another motive behind Burr's temporary abandonment of the national field: Jefferson's friends in Congress—and legislative caucuses named State and national tickets in those days—had determined not to renominate Burr for Vice President, and to select Governor Clinton as Jefferson's running mate. It was manifest to Burr that the President was as anxious as the Clintons and the Livingstons to retire him to private life.

In the early part of February the Republican members of the State legislature, under the direction of Burr's opponents, nominated Chancellor John Lansing for Governor. In the preceding election the Federalists had polled such a small vote in the

State that their leaders agreed that it would only be a waste of time and money to make a contest. Accordingly a number of them met secretly in the dining room of Lewis's tavern in Albany on the night of February 16 to consider whether it would be better strategy to support Lansing or Burr. Their only logical course was to support Burr, thereby widening the scissure between their enemies. But Burr was personally disliked by many of the prominent Federalists, notably Hamilton, who urged the gathering to support Lansing. "The principal part of his speech," reads an account of the meeting in the *Morning Chronicle*, "went to show that no reliance is to be placed on Mr. Burr." Hamilton, however, was in a minority. The report of this meeting was obtained by two Burrites who had concealed themselves under a bed in a room adjoining that used by Hamilton and his associates.

The next day Chancellor Lansing announced that he would not be a candidate for Governor. This was playing into the hands of Burr, whose followers in the Legislature caucused the subsequent afternoon and nominated him for Governor.

The Clinton-Livingston Republicans were thrown into a ferment by the march the Burrites had stolen upon them, and two days subsequent to Burr's nomination, they held a legislative caucus and nominated a Livingston, Chief Justice Morgan Lewis, for Governor.

Burr had many staunch followers in Kinderhook, as Billy Van Ness was one of his campaign managers. Billy was writing vitriolic articles for the press, and sending letters to his friends to enlist them in Burr's cause.

Van Buren was one of the few in the village not championing the cause of Burr. Worshipers of Jefferson throughout the State were supporting the candidacy of Morgan Lewis; and likewise the personal following of Hamilton in the Federalist ranks. The Livingston-Clinton faction were as pleased as they were astonished with Hamilton's aid.

All Republican opposition to Burr up to February 25 was inspired by the belief that he had intrigued with the Federalists to steal the election from Jefferson during the preceding national campaign. This belief was transmuted into knowledge by the alchemy of the Republican Congressional Caucus which met that day in Washington and nominated Governor Clinton for Vice

President. Thenceforward all devout Jeffersonians interpreted Burr's rejection as convincing evidence of the charges lodged against him.

Van Buren's brother—so let us call his law partner, for Van Buren never referred to him otherwise—was a candidate for the Assembly. He also canvassed for Lewis, who was nominated, it should be noted, by a preponderating majority of the Republican members of the Legislature, and hence was more representative of the party than Burr. And because the legal firm of Van Alen and Van Buren supported Lewis, the Van Nesses, the Van Schaacks, and the Silvesters, and the rest of the *bon ton* of Kinderhook and nearby, heaped abuse on the firm and its members. Van Buren was their particular target, because he had been entertained by Burr in his home, and had studied law in the office of Burr's youthful champion and friend. They were persistent in their efforts to convert him to the cause of Burr, for he was an idol among the Republicans. Van Alen was not much of a spouter, and lacked the indomitable energy of his junior partner. Billy Van Ness, on being apprised of the situation, used the post to woo Van Buren back to Burr. This letter was written on Washington's Birthday, and arrived at Kinderhook after the village learned that Jefferson, through the Congressional Caucus, had pronounced anathema on Burr.

There is a cold formalism in Van Ness's letter; and even the address and signature breathe hostility. There is also in the note a reflection of the attitude of Burr's supporters, who regarded him as the object of a treacherous conspiracy directed by the Clintons, Livingstons, and Hamilton. The letter reads:

Dr Sir

I have been informed since my arrival in this part of the Country that you have become a zealous advocate of the Clintonian party, those traitors * to the Republican interest & the general welfare—In addressing you it is unnecessary to enter into a discussion of this subject —You know that Mr Burr is the intended victim of villany and persecution against which it is the duty of every friend to freedom to sustain him—I hope you will not suffer my sentiments to influence you upon this occasion, but that you will pursue faithfully the honest

* Here I have supplied the word, which is mutilated in the original.

convictions of your mind—I should be much gratified however to be informed of the principles upon which your decision has been made —if they are correct, I assure you that no one will more readily applaud your conduct—As I esteem you much be careful I beseech you that you are not influenced by motives that will hereafter dishonor you— I wish you to reflect maturely before you take a side—and when you do never change—I write in great haste, which I hope you will pardon —I could not omit it, as I feel much interest in your respectability and welfare. Your friend & very humb. Servt

W. P. Van Ness

In Van Buren's reply we see the cautious leader of later years. He studiously disclaims passing judgment on the charges of treachery against Burr, and professes partiality for him, and a "pure and disinterested affection" for Van Ness and other "intimate friends" of the man he is opposing; he speaks of the abuse visited upon him and his brother by the Burrites of Kinderhook; he vigorously and paradoxically defends his course because it is inspired by expediency and purity of motives; and truthfully observes that most men are not scolded out of their opinions. The reply itself is not extant, but Van Buren made a draft of it. Time and ill-usage have worn holes in the two sheets on which Van Buren copied his earliest political paper, but fortunately only obvious words and parts thereof are lost. The letter reads:

Dr Friend:

I Received a Letter from you some time ago upon the subject of the ensuing election, but have been prevented by absence from answering it—

The sentiments of liberality and magnanimity which it contains are such as from a knowledge of your character and the qualities of your heart I had a right to and did expect—Possessed of strong personal prejudices for Mr. Burr and feeling a pure and disinterested affection for some of his most intimate friends amongst whom it is with pleasure that I name you as first in my esteem—the Controversy which exists up[on this] momentous occasion was to me of [the utmost] delicacy—Upon the most matur[ed and] passionate reflection, however, I am fully impressed with the conviction that the support of Col. Burr would not under existing circumstances be expedient and in giving this opinion to you I wish to be understood as not at all embracing the truth or falsity of the charges, I do not conceive myself

called [to pass] upon that question, and knowing as I do the purity
of my intentions and motives I feel persuaded they will never prove
a source of dishonor to myself or regret to my friends—I might enter
much more minutely into the grounds upon which my resolution has
been formed, but as a discussion of this subject *cannot now* be productive of one salutary consequence I forbear—I flatter myself that
impair
a difference in opinion on the subject will not at all affect the friendly
relations which have heretofore existed between us—for my part I
can say it will not. If however contrary to my most confident expectations such should be the case regret on my part would be the only
consequence.

My Brother & myself have received much abuse from your friends
in this Town, in their illiberal & unmanly remarks with respect to me.
Your name has been made use of I feel confident unauthorisedly—
My attempts to check the fury of some of [Mr. Burr's] enemies, are
now pretended to be construed by *some persons* who then sanctioned
and authorized the attack on Mr. Burr & his friends in all its parts,
into duplicity—My hearts [*sic!*] acquits me of the charge—They do
not however by conduct of this kind promote Mr. Burrs [*sic!*] election in this place—most men are not to be scolded out of their opinions—I hope you will excuse this scrawl I write in great haste, as
her[etofore] your sincere friend—

M. V. BUREN

Billy Van Ness's brother, the Congressman, paid a visit to
Kinderhook shortly thereafter and tried his powers of persuasion.
When he discovered at the end of several days that Van Buren
was more zealous than ever for Morgan Lewis, he stopped him
one morning in the street and exclaimed with feeling:

"I see, sir, that you are determined upon your course."

"Yes, sir!" retorted Van Buren with equal heat. "I told you
so at the beginning."

The Congressman with the rich wife looked hard at the poor
tavern keeper's son, and abruptly ended the interview and their
friendship with a curt:

"Good morning, sir!"

On the first morning of the three days of election, Peter Van
Schaack, his patriarchal features framed in a mass of silver hair,
and the venerable father of Billy Van Ness, were standing, arm
in arm, in front of the poll clerk's table as young Van Buren

approached to cast his first vote. Odd company, thought Van Buren as he saw the man who commanded a regiment in the Revolution linking arms with the most notorious Tory in all Kinderhook. Van Buren also noticed the son of Peter Van Schaack, haughty and proud of mien like his father, standing beside them. Presently all three advanced toward Van Buren, and young Van Schaack challenged his right to vote.

The astonished inspectors declared themselves satisfied with Van Buren's qualifications; he was white; of lawful age; possessed of freehold of the value of £100 or more; and had never been convicted of a felony. Surely no one would question any of these; the freehold was duly recorded in his name. But it was equally true, although not susceptible of proof, that he was only nominally the owner.

Young Van Schaack, resplendent in rich apparel, his elders nodding their approval, persisted in the challenge, thus compelling Van Buren to submit to the indignity of taking oath that he was not a felon, and was otherwise qualified to exercise the privilege of suffrage. He cast his vote. The Van Schaacks and General Van Ness then departed. But at the next election Van Buren waited until young Van Schaack entered the tavern to cast his vote, and then he retaliated by forcing the young dandy to go through the same humiliating performance.

Some five or six weeks after Burr's defeat by Lewis, gossip reached Burr that Hamilton had said things concerning him. Billy Van Ness, as Burr's friend, carried to Hamilton letters reminiscent of the style of his Aristides pamphlet. And one morning in July all Kinderhook was startled by the intelligence that Hamilton and Burr had met on the gory dueling ground at Weehawken. And like his slain son, Hamilton fired his pistol in the air after he received his mortal wound. It was hard for the people of Kinderhook to believe that Billy Van Ness had been the Vice President's second in the tragic interview.

Van Buren was saddened on hearing the melancholy news. Soon after he heard that Billy Van Ness was in hiding in his father's home. Van Buren was not long in doubt, for Billy sent him a confidential note urging him to visit his place of concealment. He wanted to go to Albany, but feared arrest for his part in the duel, and sought Van Buren's opinion on his right to bail.

The Van Ness home was a brisk half-hour's walk south of the village. Over the dusty Albany post road on this sweltering July day Van Buren trudged toward the big house, which was set far back from the highway, in the center of a semi-circular driveway. As he ascended the wide steps of the porch he observed that the upper half of the double-door was open wide, revealing the back of the snow-haired head of Billy's father, who was seated in a chair, hidden by the lower half of the door, reading a newspaper.

As the old man heard the sound of footsteps he turned his head, and seeing Van Buren—they had not laid eyes on one another since young Van Schaack had challenged Van Buren's privilege to vote—he resumed the reading of the journal. Van Ness had not forgotten, nor forgiven, the youth's opposition to Burr.

Van Buren paused for a fraction of a second after receiving the snub. Then advancing, he stretched his hand over the head of the old man and his newspaper, and seizing the rapper of the knocker, pounded it lustily against the brazen breast of the staring goddess which was affixed to the dead center of the opened half of the paneled door. As Van Buren put forth his hand, he cast a shadow on the newspaper. But the old man gave no sign that any one was near him. Van Buren had an excellent view of the right side of the old patriot's face, and lost a little of his anger as he saw that his lusty pounding had forced a smile. Van Buren then stood stock-still, awaiting developments. Presently Billy came to the door, whispered to his father, who rose, and without turning around, entered the drawing room immediately on the left. Billy then pulled the chair his father had sat in to one side, and unlatching the lower half of the door, admitted his former clerk.

Billy took Van Buren's arm and escorted him down the wide hall, and through the back door. Outside, Billy apologized for the incident, saying that he had forgotten the relations between the two. Billy laughed as Van Buren recounted all that happened. The two walked to a brook, where they could not be seen from the road. It was a stream where other Van Burens had fished and bathed, being part of the original purchase made by Martin Van Buren's American primogenitor, who had borne the same name. The property, a rough two hundred acres, remained in the family

until the close of the Revolution, when the distant relation of
Martin's father, as lacking as the tavern keeper in the capacity
to hold on to what he had, sold it to pay his debts. Thus it came
into possession of the Van Nesses, who had torn down the old
wooden farm house and erected the stately pile of brick in its
place. On the bank of the stream the two talked over Van Ness's
plight, and when they parted with fervent handclasps, Van Buren
assured Billy of his unwavering devotion.

There was more than a tribute to Van Buren's legal attainments in Van Ness's appeal for his assistance; there was recognition of his former clerk's political leadership and the influence
of the law firm of Van Alen and Van Buren. Van Alen, who had
been elected a member of Assembly in the April elections, had been
appointed Surrogate of the county shortly after Morgan Lewis
was inaugurated Governor on July 1.

Toward the end of the summer Van Buren began to pay his
debts to his brother, and started saving a little for the rainy
day. The clients of the prospering firm were all small landholders,
and Republicans. The magnates of the county, as Van Buren described them in his spoutings on the hustings, all Federalists,
retained Elisha Williams or some other lawyer who rejected the
Jacobinical teachings of Jefferson. Williams alone created apprehension in Van Buren. Like Burr he mesmerized juries; but there
was this difference: Williams depended solely on his well-nigh
matchless eloquence. Van Buren was better than Williams on
appeal.

# CHAPTER IX

Now that Burr was out of their way, it was only natural that the Clintons and the Livingstons would war on each other. A rupture was inevitable. There was no end of able and well qualified Livingstons, many of them, like the exiled Edward, scholars and politically ambitious. On the other side was George Clinton, elected Vice President to succeed Burr. De Witt Clinton had resigned from the United States Senate solely for the vast patronage that went with the Mayoralty in order to augment his strength as a party leader. His appointment of men of influence in groups to which he was alien helped. All this meant additional votes. There were also at his disposal licenses for street occupations which were filled by those who possessed no land, and consequently did not vote. These men were scavengers, porters, cartmen, carriers, criers, carmen, and scullers. Marshals also plied their trade by grace of the Mayor. Tavern keepers opened and closed their doors at the will of the Mayor.

The tavern keeper represented the most influential class in the list enumerated. All were treated as men of the world by the jolly host, whose wares made even those not entitled to vote, believe in the reality of democracy. After a few drinks the poorest man thought himself as good as the Mayor himself, or even the Governor, or the President, or anybody else. Sometimes poor men acquired these moods without cost to themselves. On these occasions they could drink anything in the place. They were always forewarned of these joyous days. The time to begin drinking was carefully calculated. After filling up they would march to meetings to cheer or boo the speakers; or shout aye, or no, when a resolution was offered. Leaders directed their actions. This was easy work, and money sometimes went with the drink. Not infrequently they were called upon to perform more strenuous tasks, such as storming a meeting and pitching all who did not flee into the night. On these evenings of strife the proletaires met in one of the larger taverns, called Long Rooms from their size, and at the appointed time sallied forth to perform their duty.

De Witt Clinton made use of the taverns and every other recruiting agency of popular expression throughout his political career. But in so doing he was following an ancient royal precedent.

Almost immediately after the election of Lewis a coolness developed between him and Clinton. In the fall all relations ceased when Lewis appointed his brother-in-law, Maturin Livingston, Recorder of New York City. The Federalist newspapers denounced the appointment; but they did not remain long with Clinton.

The Federalist supporters of Governor Lewis were more of a hindrance than a help to him. They were destroying themselves with their tactlessness far more effectively than the Republican opposition. This reacted on Lewis and the whole Livingston clan. In the summer of 1805, the Common Council of the city of Albany, composed almost wholly of Federalists, in making provision for the celebration of the Fourth of July, adopted a resolution barring the reading of the Declaration of Independence. The specious plea on which this unwise and uncalled-for action was taken, was that the reading of the immortal document served only to perpetuate prejudices and hostile feelings against Great Britain. More properly might Parliament forbid the printing of the Magna Charta because it recited, in the form of a confession, some threescore counts of royal wrongs. One is a people's indictment of a monarch; the other a plea of guilty by one who can do no wrong; and each is an unanswerable impeachment of divine right.

The Livingstons now felt the need of Edward. But he was far away in Louisiana. There were older and wiser heads among them, but none possessed the particular talent needed to cope with the political machinations of De Witt Clinton.

Lewis continually made capital for the Clintons. He had a glorious record in the Revolution; and in common with most survivors of the fight for freedom, foresaw another war with Great Britain. He was constantly ordering out the militia in the various counties of the State. We must not be unprepared. These brigade parades were not pleasing to militiamen, for to most of them it meant absence from work for three days.

An incident which for refinement of cruelty is unequaled in

our annals, was basely turned against Lewis by the Clintonians. A teacher in Otsego County brutally whipped a little girl until she fell in a huddled heap on the floor. Even then the rain of blows did not cease. The child's offense lay in her refusal to spell a word pronounced by her assassin. An indictment for murder was found, and conviction followed. On the day set for the execution thousands thronged Cooperstown, the county seat, where a gallows had been erected. A cheer went up from the multitude as the condemned man was brought from his cell and the solemn march to the scaffold began. The prayers of the clergymen were audible to the inner fringe of the throng.

On the staging, beside the noose, stood a man whose face was concealed by a grimy black mixture of grease and soot. He was the hangman. He quickly tied the hands of the schoolmaster behind his back. The sheriff then asked the condemned if he wished to address the people. The doomed one nodded, and began a prolonged muttering. Suddenly the sheriff stopped him, and drew from his pocket a document which he read aloud. It was a reprieve. The reprieved man fell in a faint. The mob, whose appetite had been whetted for the sight of a human being squirming at the end of a rope, set up a shout of disappointment. Above the uproar could be heard hysterical laughter and ribald curses. There were some who would have hanged the Governor had he been there.

This incident was kept alive for months; Lewis's enemies untruthfully accused him of having directed the sheriff to stage the scene of horror. The local official performed this exquisite bit of torture as a protest against what he regarded as the Governor's wanton interference with justice.

Clinton, in his opposition to Lewis, made use of the same charge he and the Livingstons had raised against Burr: the Livingstons, one and all, were traitors to the Republican party. Here it should be noted that De Witt Clinton's younger brother, George, who added junior to his name to distinguish him from their uncle, was chosen in February, 1805, to fill an unexpired term in the House of Representatives, and later reëlected to a full term.

Van Buren, hard at his law practice, and almost as hard at the game of politics, took the Clinton end of the row. This was

but natural; he was of the small independent farmer class, and
they, almost to a man, were out to wreak vengeance on the manorial families. Although the Livingston manor had been partitioned
shortly after the Revolution, the ancient bitterness which had
led to uprisings among the tenant-farmers throughout the entire
Hudson River valley in the middle of the eighteenth century,
survived. In Kinderhook the feeling was perpetuated by the unjust claim of the Patroon that the village and the farms surrounding it were originally Van Rensselaer property. The only
results were costly litigation and class consciousness. The defense
had been in the hands of the venerable Peter Van Schaack since
1772, but his years were telling on him now, and the freeholders
of Kinderhook and vicinity, the Van Schaacks among them, retained Van Buren and his brother to defend the cause. This
change in counsel occurred shortly after Governor Lewis's
election.

The Clintonians at a secret meeting in Manhattan effected
a combination with the Burrites in the month of December. This
made Clinton all-powerful in New York City, where the Martling
men, staunch Burrites, and loyal to their leader in his exile, controlled the majority of the city's representatives in the Legislature.

In the legislative elections the following April this newly
formed amalgamation triumphed. De Witt Clinton was elected
a Senator from New York City, where he continued to serve as
Mayor.

The politicians and statesmen in Virginia, who had helped
the Clintons and the Livingstons in their war on Burr, now lent
a helping hand to the Livingstons. This solidarity, later called
the Virginia Dynasty, dominated the aristocracy founded on the
slave society of the South, and was jealous of the growing power
of the New York oligarchy, rooted in the feudal manorial grants.
The Virginian aristocrats did not fear the third social division
in the country, comprising the merchant and farmer class of
New England. These were so intensely Federalist as to be a negligible factor in the country's politics. But New York, Republican
like the South, and not lacking in men of great attainments, was
menacing the Old Dominion's control of the nation. To render
New York impotent, the Virginians, by devious means, fed the

fires of dissension among the Republicans of the Empire State.

When the Legislature elected in the spring of 1806 convened, the Assembly, following its usual custom, chose the Council of Appointment. All, of course, were Clintonians, headed by De Witt Clinton himself. This done, the new Council of Appointment removed Maturin Livingston from the office of Recorder of New York City, replacing him and other members of the Livingston family and its followers, with their own. Governor Lewis voted against these replacements, but his vote was only one of five.

The Livingstons were dwindling as a political power. And now the Virginia Dynasty, following its practice of aiding the weaker side of the New York factions, assailed Clinton in its organ, the Richmond *Enquirer*. The basis of the attack was that Clinton was Mayor of New York, a State Senator, and a member of the Council of Appointment at one and the same time. A like charge could have been made not so far back when Jefferson's appointee to the office of United States Attorney for New York was also the city's Mayor. But then the Virginians were aiding the Livingston-Clinton coalition in its war on Burr. The statesmen of the Old Dominion were not doing anything novel; they were playing a game known to the ancients. But they had improved on the methods employed by the tyrant of Corinth twenty-four centuries earlier in ridding himself of "overtopping citizens." The particular head topping the rest of the political cornfield in the year 1805 A.D. was that of Vice President Clinton, whose candidacy for the Presidency was being openly espoused by the major faction of the New York Republicans.

One of Clinton's first acts as Senator was to introduce a resolution to expel Ebenezer Purdy from the Senate. Purdy had taken a bribe from the sponsors of the Merchants Bank of New York, which obtained its charter the preceding year—for a price. Purdy resigned his seat the day before the Senate met to act on the Clinton resolution. Clinton could not endure a corruptionist. He contemplated prosecution of Purdy, but abandoned his design when he discovered no law on the statute books against bribery of public officials.

Richard Riker, Clinton's second in his duel with Swartwout, and now a member of the Assembly, hastened to correct this deficiency, and prepared a measure to make it impossible for another corrupt legislator to escape criminal prosecution. The bill was introduced March 31, and seven days later Governor Lewis's signature made bribery punishable by not more than two years' imprisonment and a fine of one thousand dollars.

In the spring elections of the following month the Federalists, in counties where they were in the minority, voted for candidates for the Legislature who wore the quarterings of the Livingstons. In the new Legislature the Federalist-Livingston forces had a majority in the Assembly. In New York City, in the municipal election that year, the Federalists and the Livingstons elected a majority to the Common Council. Instantly all followers of De Witt Clinton who held office at the pleasure of the local body were removed.

This amalgamation with the Federalists alienated a considerable body of Republicans from the Livingstons, who were now dubbed Quids, as the followers of John Randolph of Roanoke had been. Toward the close of 1806 the Quids found that their alliance with the Federalists, which gave them scant control of the Assembly, was worthless in a party caucus: here the Clintonians marshaled a preponderating majority. As the traditional method of nominating a Governor was at a closed meeting of the party's representatives in the Senate and Assembly, the Quids held a sparsely attended meeting in New York City on New Year's day and renominated Lewis. When the Legislature met, the Quids, aided by the eighteen Federalists in the Assembly, elected a Council of Appointment committed wholly to the fortunes of the Livingston family. At once reprisals on the Clintonians were made, which were capped with the removal of De Witt Clinton as Mayor of New York.

These removals were made on Monday afternoon, February 16, 1807. They did not come unexpectedly, for the legislative elections of the preceding spring foreshadowed what would happen unless the Clintonians were ready to capitulate. In the appointment of Marinus Willet, an old ally of Burr, and a distinguished patriot, as successor to Clinton, an excellent and popular choice was made. Other Burrites were given place by the anti-Clintonian Council of Appointment. The reappointment of Maturin Livingston as Recorder of New York, and his brother-in-law, Dr. Tillotson, as Secretary of State, served only to emphasize the charge of the Clintonians that the Livingston family were hogging the principal offices of trust and emolument in the State.

On the evening of the same day the Republican members of the legislature caucused and nominated Daniel B. Tompkins for Governor. We met him earlier when he and twenty-nine others joined with Billy Van Ness to evade the election law by buying a house in Manhattan that they might qualify as voters. Tompkins was now a circuit judge of the Supreme Court. Far abler men could have been named to oppose Lewis, and had the Clintonians followed precedent and nominated a factionist of State-wide fame, and of recognized talents, their choice would have been limited to De Witt Clinton and his brother-in-law, Judge Ambrose Spencer. But these two were unavailable because De Witt Clinton wanted to keep alive the charge that the Livingston family were selfishly ambitious. They also sought to capitalize the ill-feeling against the Livingstons among the small independent farmers who, with the small tradesmen, constituted the bulk of the Republican electorate.

In nearly every partisan effusion, written or spoken, the Clintonian nominee was referred to as "the farmer's son." Van Buren canvassed unceasingly for "the farmer's son," save during the week-end immediately following the nomination. A short time before Van Buren had been sworn in as the counselor of the Supreme Court. In those early days a lawyer had to practice in the inferior courts four years or more before being permitted to undertake the weightier problems of his profession. And almost immediately thereafter he proposed to the fair Hannah Hoes —he called her in their own tongue, Jannetje—and on the Saturday morning following the naming of Tompkins, Van Buren and his childhood sweetheart were married in the village of Catskill. Both wished to avoid the boisterous celebration which would have followed a wedding in Kinderhook. This mutual wish for privacy entailed a round trip of twenty-five miles over the snow-covered roads and the frozen Hudson. Van Buren was twenty-five years old, and his bride a year his junior.

In the ensuing weeks Kinderhook's newest benedict paid more attention to politics than to the domestic hearth. He was on the hustings day and night. He covered the distances on horseback, speaking in taverns and at the cross roads. When he visited a public house he stood treat for all who lined up before the bar with him, taking his own share of whatever was served.

The election wrote *finis* to the political control exercised by the Livingston family as effectively as the election of Lewis three years before did to the public career of Burr. The duel was only a confirmation.

There was not much excitement in Kinderhook until late one evening in August when word was received that anchored off Clermont, the seat of Chancellor Livingston, was the invention perfected by Robert Fulton, a Livingston by marriage. Clermont, after which the first steamboat was named, was a generous twenty miles down the river. Fulton's modest report of the trip reads:

I left New York on Monday at one o'clock, and arrived at Chancellor Livingston's seat at one o'clock Tuesday—time twenty-four hours, distance one hundred and ten miles. On Wednesday I departed from the Chancellor's nine A.M., and reached Albany at five P.M. The sum is one hundred and fifty miles in thirty-two hours, equal to nearly five miles an hour. Returning I made it in thirty hours—just five miles an hour.

The *Clermont* passed Kinderhook Landing on her maiden voyage in the middle of the afternoon. And on the shore as the *Clermont* steamed by, with sparks belching from her smokestack, was all Kinderhook. What had been *Fulton's Folly* two days before, was now a miracle materialized.

# CHAPTER X

VAN BUREN had an anxious concern in the new Council of Appointment chosen on February 1, 1808. The Council proceeded immediately to eliminate all Livingstons from office and restore the Clintonians to their old places, De Witt Clinton, of course, being reappointed Mayor of New York City. Throughout the State, sheriffs, mayors, justices of the peace, and other local officers who were beholden to the Livingstons or suspected of loyalty to the cause of the fallen house of Callender were displaced. Officers of the militia suffered a like fate. In all these appointments the wishes of the Republican members of the Senate and Assembly were consulted. Thus, with few exceptions, the new appointees were partisan rather than personal appointees. In the third week of March Van Buren was appointed Surrogate of Columbia County to succeed his brother. Van Alen had no flair for politics, and sought office only to promote the interests of the law firm.

At the caucus in the National Capitol in January, Vice President Clinton, New York's choice, received three votes, a like number being cast for James Monroe, while the other Virginian, James Madison, was nominated by a vote of eighty-three. Clinton was again named for second place. In those early days Presidential campaigns were of ten to twenty months' duration.

The nomination of Madison was not unanimous. Seventeen Republican members of Congress, including De Witt Clinton's brother, protested. The Clintonian press also disapproved the choice. Articles in the Albany *Register* were typical of the outbursts of Clintonian rage. This journal, while declaring its confidence in Mr. Madison, insisted that the nomination for the Presidency rightfully belonged to Vice President Clinton, and voiced the truth in charging the politicians and statesmen of Virginia with cherishing an opinion that only a Virginian was fit to be President.

These protests of the Clintonians had their constructive side: they were paving the way for De Witt Clinton's ambition to be President. Four years hence his uncle would be of an age which traditionally disqualifies men for the highest office in the land; the nephew would be fifty-three. Van Buren enlisted early in this campaign, giving, as he gave to all things associated with a canvass, every surplus ounce of energy.

These political endeavors of Van Buren raised a host of implacable foes in his county. South of Kinderhook lay part of the old Livingston manor, where the venerable Chancellor and many of his kin resided; to the north and east were the lands of the Van Rensselaers. On the west lay the Hudson. Sometimes he felt that there was more friendship for him in the river than on its banks. But he was seldom downcast.

Van Buren cultivated a quiet disdain for his political foes. He believed himself more than a match for them in a fair fight. His principal asset was a cheerful disposition. His smile and ready wit dominated the gatherings in the court room when the judge was not on the bench; and in the little social gatherings where law and politics were taboo, he was looked up to; in the less formal assemblies in the tavern his jovial nature was marked, and he was not above partaking a sling. The base of that thoroughly democratic loving cup was rum, Schiedam, whiskey, or brandy, as fancy dictated. Into the largest tumbler in the tavern was poured a full gill of spirits; and to this was added cold water, and sugar to taste. The mixture was then stirred until it foamed. He who ordered sipped a little and passed it to the next, who likewise took a small drink and coasted it to his neighbor; and so until all had drunk from the same glass: when emptied, some one else would stand treat. Van Buren was temperate. He rarely drank to a point where he lost the caution for which he was noted. His readiness to mingle with tavern frequenters when occasion required counted heavily in his favor.

In the spring Van Buren made his first visit to New York since leaving it nearly five years before. This, too, marked his first appearance before the highest tribunal of the State, the Court for the Correction of Errors, a most august and anomalous body, in which all three divisions of government commingled. It was composed of the Governor, the Lieutenant Governor, the Chancellor, the five justices of the Supreme Court, and the thirty-two Senators. And if Billy Van Ness was in town during this

May term of the Court, Van Buren called on him, for Burr's second was seeking a restoration of his civil rights which he lost because of his part in Burr's duel with Hamilton. It was due to Van Buren's efforts that Governor Tompkins removed the bar to Van Ness's exercise of the suffrage and to holding office. Van Buren was fond of his impetuous preceptor who was now compiling his two-volume work, much consulted by the lawyers of his day.

In New York Van Buren heard much criticism of the Clintons. The Vice President himself was charged with secretly opposing Jefferson's Embargo Act, a most unpopular measure with the merchants, whose trade it paralyzed.

Van Buren studied this question; he copied extracts of the violations of the law, and their prosecution. The ineffectiveness of the act was becoming apparent to analytical observers as the Presidential campaign drew nigh. But Jefferson, unwilling to confess that he had been worsted in matching wits with Pitt and Napoleon, let the law remain on the books, and the Burrites and the Livingstons, who were holding on grimly and hoping for a better day, charged the Clintons with playing false to the idol of American democracy.

This charge was a half-truth. The Clintons had been, like many other Republicans, opposed to the Embargo, but as early as the beginning of the year De Witt Clinton publicly renounced his old belief and declared himself in favor of the Embargo. This, too, was Van Buren's stand.

In the Electoral College which chose Madison for President and reëlected Clinton Vice President, six of New York's Electoral votes were cast for Clinton for President, and three New York Electors voted for Madison for Vice President. New York was formally serving notice on the Virginia Dynasty.

Sometime in December, 1808, or not long after the New Year, Van Buren and his family moved to Hudson, now the county seat; and here, in the month of February, he presided at the first of a series of meetings to counteract the anti-Embargo rallies of the Federalists. Extremists among the latter saw only the defects of democracy, and favored a monarchical form of government. Many were for a return of British rule, and like Hamilton, believed that the government of the mother country, as it existed before the Reform Acts of 1787, was "the best in the world."

At this first meeting in Hudson Van Buren drafted resolves upholding Jefferson, and breathing defiance to France and England alike, and asserting that the Embargo Act was one of three courses left us as a nation, the other two being war or "submission to European despots." At a second assembly in Hudson, Van Buren again drafted the resolutions which read:

> Resolved, as the sense of this meeting, That the decrees and orders of France and England are the real cause of the interruptions to our commerce and the consequent embarrassment of our citizens; and that our Government, by submitting to these decrees and orders, would have destroyed the independence and surrendered the sovereignty of the American nation.
>
> Resolved, That the members of this meeting . . . do solemnly engage to support the Government in measures to obtain redress for our national injuries, and protection to our national rights; that they will never be driven from a fair and manly support of this resolution by the power of our enemies or the threats of factions, and that, should the Government be forced to abandon the pacific policy it has pursued and unsheathe the sword, they will be found at their posts ready and willing to sacrifice their lives and fortunes in their country's cause.

Similar meetings were held throughout the State. When the Legislature of 1809 was in session four days, De Witt Clinton introduced like resolutions pledging support to the National government. In moving them, he condemned the rabid opposition of New England to the Embargo Act; denounced the policy of the Federalists in Massachusetts as tending to a division of the Union and declared that the Eastern Federalists, like Milton's fallen angel, held that it was "Better to reign in Hell than serve in Heaven."

The purpose of these February meetings which Van Buren called, and similar efforts of Republican leaders elsewhere, was to support Jefferson in the closing weeks of his career as President. But they did not avail, for one of Jefferson's last acts was to sign a measure repealing the Embargo, thus leaving the incoming President a choice—to use Van Buren's phrase—of war or submission to European despots.

# CHAPTER XI

FOR the first two years of Madison's administration Surrogate Van Buren led a more or less eventless life. His law practice was constantly increasing; his quarrels with the Federalists and the anti-Clintonian faction in the county grew in like measure. He made frequent visits to Albany, sometimes appearing before the Court for the Correction of Errors. In his visits to Albany he was invariably accompanied by Sheriff John C. Hogeboom, the Republican overlord of Columbia County. When Hogeboom's fees were branded as extortionate by the Federalists, Van Buren defended him in letter, handbill, newspaper advertisement, and on the hustings.

In the spring elections of 1810 the Federalists elected a majority to the Assembly. This victory was due to the hostility of the merchants to the National administration, and the continued opposition of the Martling, or Tammany, men to De Witt Clinton. Again Clinton lost the Mayoralty of New York. But in another twelvemonth the Republicans regained control, and the new Council of Appointment restored Clinton to his old office; and in the same April balloting he was elected Lieutenant Governor of the State. Clinton, now an active candidate for the Presidency, was the target of the Virginia Dynasty which was advocating the renomination of Madison. Clinton had spent the $90,000 he had received in fees as mayor of New York in financing pamphlets, editors, and political aides to promote his candidacy. What little he had besides went the same way. In a word he was broke. But only his intimates knew this.

During the spring elections Van Buren had his first political clash in the open. Jacob Rutsen Van Rensselaer, one of Columbia County's representatives in the Assembly, was a candidate for re-election on the Federalist ticket. It was reported and believed in the district that Van Rensselaer had said in a debate in the Assembly that the tenants of the Manor were not fit to govern themselves and "deserved to have a master." Accompanied by Elisha Williams, Van Rensselaer called on Van Buren, explaining that while he had no suspicion that Van Buren had even countenanced the canard, which was doing him unmerited harm, he was confident that a word from him would effectually counteract this unfair campaigning.

Van Buren replied that he would gladly publish a card denying the report, provided Van Rensselaer would repudiate equally untruthful stories about Van Buren which were at that very moment being published by the local Federalist press, although he was not running for office. In making this stipulation, Van Buren observed that these calumnies against him had not met with any criticism from Van Rensselaer or his friends.

Van Rensselaer was unwilling to do this; and finding Van Buren insisting on a *quid pro quo*, announced that he would call a meeting of the people of the Manor towns and accuse Van Buren of having written to Reuben Whallon, an Assemblyman from Washington County, urging him to withhold action on a petition of the tenants for relief, that the delay might adversely affect Van Rensselaer's candidacy. Van Buren hotly branded this charge as untrue. Van Rensselaer admitted that he had not any proof. He had been informed that such a letter existed; anyway he would call a meeting of the people of the Manor towns and make the charge since Van Buren would not comply unconditionally with his demand.

Van Buren wrote to the chairman of the meeting recounting what had occurred between him and Van Rensselaer. He specifically denied the charge about to be made. He sent the communication by a trusted aide who requested that the letter be read to the audience.

This request for fair play was rejected. The people only heard the impeachment of Van Buren, who promptly denied the charge in handbills and cards in the newspapers. He next called a meeting of the Manor towns. On the night of his meeting, Van Buren observed Van Rensselaer in the rear of the room. Beside him stood Elisha Williams and several Livingstons.

In his rapid declamatory delivery, in which nothing was left to the imagination, Van Buren denied all that Van Rensselaer had said of him, and read duly certified copies of his correspondence with Assemblyman Whallon supporting his disavowal. Van Buren then invited Van Rensselaer to maintain the charge in the face of all this, if he could.

Van Rensselaer smiled as Van Buren finished. Van Buren had played into his hands. All that he had said were self-deserving declarations. He had avoided giving the lie, even indirectly, and Van Rensselaer would capitalize this in the campaign. Van Rensselaer and his friends were satisfied, and the scion of the great Patroon held his peace. Van Buren remained standing in silence for two or three minutes. When the audience grew restless, he stretched forth his hand for quiet. Then, in his loud voice he declared that the silence of Van Rensselaer could be construed as nothing less than a confession that his charges were untrue.

Van Rensselaer, his face flushed as he heard his veracity impugned, strode forward angrily to the platform where Van Buren awaited developments. Van Rensselaer merely defended his original charge, and pledged to deposit five hundred dollars in court if Van Buren would sue him, agreeing to forfeit the money if his accusations were not actionable and he could not prove the truth of them. The words used by Van Rensselaer were chosen with such nicety as not to be actionable.

When Van Rensselaer finished, Van Buren told his hearers that he would accept the challenge, and asked them to remember his prediction that the five hundred dollars would not be deposited. Van Rensselaer did not prove the charge.

Throughout the summer Van Buren made efforts to have him make good his pledge. In a letter dated August 24, 1811, Van Rensselaer briefly wrote, tongue in cheek, that he was no longer bound by his promise, saying that Van Buren should have commenced action before the April elections were held.

Van Buren, whose unexpected moves were a constant source of dismay to his opponents, published the correspondence between himself and Van Rensselaer. This further widened the gulf between Van Buren and the county's aristocrats, and the ill-will they bore him was magnified by toadying retainers whenever opportunity offered.

At the fall term of the Supreme Court the long-drawn-out action of the Van Rensselaers to dispossess the people of Kinderhook from the homes they and their ancestors had honestly held for more than a century and a quarter, came to trial. Van Buren, as chief counsel for the defendants, attacked the credibility of a surveyor formerly in the employ of the defendants. This occurred on Friday, November 22, during Van Buren's summing up. Van Buren had previously served notice on the counsel for the other side of his intention to impeach their witness. Counsel for the Van Rensselaers included Elisha Williams, his brother-in-law, Thomas P. Grosvenor, then a member of Assembly and later Congressman, and John Sudam of Kingston, a prominent Federalist on the other side of the Hudson, and in after years a distinguished member of the State Senate. Sudam was very young and very impetuous.

During the impeachment of the surveyor's credibility, Sudam interrupted Van Buren with offensive personal references. Van Buren, who had not yet acquired the capacity of ignoring attacks that recoiled on their makers, answered in language equally abusive. There the matter rested. At Saturday's session the case went to the jury without any untoward circumstance. The incident of the day before was forgotten.

On Sunday, Van Rensselaer—the same Jacob Van Rensselaer who had the encounter with Van Buren—gave a dinner at his mansion in Claverack, to which were invited the counsel in the case and other leading members of his party who were stopping in Hudson for the November term of court. The Livingstons came from their ancient seat to grace the gathering. Wine flowed freely, and friend and foe entered into the hilarious conversation. Naturally there were unpleasant criticisms made of Van Buren. Just what was said at this dinner concerning Van Buren is not known; but the next morning, while Van Buren was seated in court waiting for a case to be called, Elisha Williams's brother-in-law called him out and, announcing that he was acting as the second for Sudam, presented him with a challenge and generously offered to try to compose their differences.

Van Buren, smarting under the continued partisan assaults, just and otherwise, which had been visited upon him since he was a boy in Francis Silvester's law office, thanked Grosvenor, and said that he had passed the point of endurance, and that he would make a formal reply through his friend, George Morell, who, he was certain, would serve as his second.

Van Buren had a total disregard of consequences once he had

embarked on a given course. He seldom gave quarter to a partisan foe; and never asked for any. He did not believe in the code duello, but to decline the challenge would have called for more moral courage than he possessed; ancient tradition sanctioned the custom, and good society approved it. These considerations outweighed conscientious scruples, religious beliefs, and love of family: in this regard he was another Hamilton. Besides his frail little wife there were two others now looking to him for support; the older one, named after Mine Host Van Buren, was not quite four years old; then there was John, who was beginning to pronounce an occasional word intelligibly, Dutch or English, as infant whim dictated. Then there were the old folks up in Kinderhook. Van Buren went through the day without any one knowing what was passing in his mind. He was being forced to the wall. Well, he would face them and fight back.

After court adjourned he asked Morell to serve as his second. Morell agreed. He then sat down and wrote a formal acceptance, which is preserved with his papers. The last word of his acknowledgment of the challenge, legible that November evening beneath the blob of ink, is now indecipherable. The acceptance reads:

Sir,

Your communication has been handed to me by Mr. Morell he is authorized to make arrangements contemplated and [word blurred]
Your hble svt
M. V. Buren
Nov 25 1811

J. Suydam [*sic!*]

That date!—Monday, November 25, 1811: his firstborn would be four years old on Wednesday, only two days off!

The small, narrow sheet of note paper was handed to Morell. Van Buren then went home.

The next morning Morell returned with word that Grosvenor, who had been roundly scored by his brother-in-law and his friends for delivering the challenge, had withdrawn as Sudam's second. Morell had gone to Sudam, who declined to receive Van Buren's acceptance, insisting that it must come through Grosvenor.

Van Buren, his fighting blood up, dispatched Morell to Sudam with a verbal proposal that they select others to act as seconds. Back from Sudam's hotel came Morell: under the circumstances Sudam could not dispense with Grosvenor's services.

Van Buren, unsatisfied, sat at his desk, carefully selected the broadest quill, and wrote on a large sheet of paper. In another minute he was on his way to Sudam's hotel, where he posted Sudam as a coward.

The threatened encounter ended with Van Buren, Sudam, and their seconds being bound over to keep the peace.

For years Van Buren and Sudam did not speak, although the latter made several indirect overtures for peace. One day, when unexpectedly seated opposite each other in a tavern during the noon recess of court, Sudam, recovered from his astonishment, asked Van Buren to pass the bottle of wine. The better class of taverns always placed a bottle of native wine on the dining tables. Van Buren, instead of passing the bottle, asked Sudam if he would drink a glass with him. After toasting each other they returned to court together arm in arm.

# CHAPTER XII

THE aborted duel between Van Buren and Sudam gave him his first public prominence outside of the Dutch counties. Newspapers reprinted the articles from the local papers; and because of the prominence of the Federalists at the dinner in Jacob Rutsen Van Rensselaer's home on the eve of the challenge, Van Buren was regarded by many as the intended victim of blind Federalist rage. We must do justice to the memory of those who dined with the impetuous and wine-fired Sudam. The conduct of Elisha Williams and other guests of Van Rensselaer in persuading Grosvenor to withdraw as Sudam's second, leads to the conclusion that there had been no talk of a duel in Van Rensselaer's home, unless, possibly, between Grosvenor and Sudam. Van Buren received letters approving his conduct from Richard Riker and other leaders of his party.

Shortly after Riker's letter reached Van Buren at his home in Hudson—it bore the date of February 17, 1812—he was visited by Billy Van Ness, now the lord of his father's manse. Billy was ambitious to run for State Senator against Edward P. Livingston, the Federalist nominee, then representing the district. Van Buren replied that he wanted Sheriff Hogeboom to canvass against Livingston. He said that Hogeboom's services to the party entitled him to the nomination. Billy thanked him for the frank answer and went his way.

Van Buren and Sheriff Hogeboom went to Albany a few days later. On the way Van Ness joined them and all three entered the city together. Hogeboom and Van Buren were there a few days when they learned that Billy was intriguing to name his own man for State Senator if he himself could not get it.

Through Van Buren's mind flashed a panorama of his relations with the Van Nesses: his aiding Billy's brother to obtain a seat in Congress; the latter's failure to make good his promise to assist him in those trying two years in Manhattan; Billy's threatening letter when he learned Van Buren was opposing Burr; the subsequent humiliation inflicted on him at the polling booth

by Billy's father and Peter Van Schaack and the latter's son;
his successful efforts to restore Billy's citizenship. He owed
the Van Nesses nothing: they were in his debt. And now Billy was
adding another black mark to the record.

Posthaste to Hudson returned Van Buren and Hogeboom.
On this short trip Van Buren received a fresh surprise. Hogeboom
informed him that many of the leading Republicans in the district
wanted Van Buren to make the race, and capped it by announcing
that De Witt Clinton was of like mind, adding that his business
affairs would not permit him to run; and he spoke so earnestly
that Van Buren agreed to make the contest provided Robert
Jenkins did not seek the place. Robert was a brother of Elisha
Jenkins, Secretary of State, and Seth Jenkins, Jr. Their father
was Seth Jenkins, Sr., who, with his brother, Thomas, wealthy
Quakers from Rhode Island, purchased the site of Hudson as a
settlement for their families and others of their faith the year
after Van Buren's birth. Robert was Mayor of Hudson, as his
father had been before him. Van Buren believed that if the Mayor
wanted the honor, it was only fitting that he should have it, rather
than a newcomer in Hudson like himself.

On reaching Hudson Van Buren invited Seth Jenkins, Jr.,
and two others, who constituted the local delegation to the Senatorial Convention, of which he was chairman, to meet at his home
in the evening. When all were assembled Van Buren repeated his
conversation with Sheriff Hogeboom. He spoke of his own disinclination to run, and of his intention to support Mayor Jenkins
if he sought the nomination. From the ensuing conversation Van
Buren inferred that he had been mistaken in assuming that the
Mayor was a candidate. Moreover, they concurred with Hogeboom that Van Buren should be the nominee.

Following this conference Van Buren issued the call for the
convention. A few days later, a country justice of the peace
named Wagner called at Van Buren's office and observed that
Hudson was to have the Senatorship. Van Buren coyly replied
that that seemed to be the plan. The plain-spoken countryman
blurted out that he meant Mayor Jenkins and no one else. Van
Buren replied that he was in error. The rustic insisted he was
right, and that within the hour Seth Jenkins, Jr., asked him to
support his brother, and that when he said he had heard talk of

Van Buren, Jenkins had said Van Buren's youth—he had celebrated his twenty-eighth birthday less than three months before—
and his recent removal to the city disqualified him.

Van Buren at once addressed invitations to Seth Jenkins,
Jr., and the other two delegates from Hudson, to a second conference at his home. Without parley he informed the three what
he had heard. Jenkins confirmed the correctness of the information. It should be borne in mind that Van Buren was of pure
Dutch stock, and boastfully proud of this to his last hour; contrariwise, he always regarded the descendants of the English
in common with the Dutch of the day, as not only a race apart,
but in the finer qualities inferior to his own people. Among the
descendants of the settlers of the New Netherlands there still
persists the tradition that the Dutch gave the name of Yankee
to the English settlers back in 1642 when a British officer likened
the petty quarrels between the Dutch and the English in Connecticut to two dogs snarling over a bone. Snarler in Dutch is
*Janker;* and Yankee is obviously a mild corruption of this word.
Van Buren demanded with considerable warmth why Jenkins
had treated him so ungenerously. Jenkins was to him a Yankee,
and in relating the incident, he observed that "Mr. Jenkins had
many of the good qualities of his race."

Because of his faith, Jenkins could not take an oath, but he
affirmed that he was not inspired by unfriendly motives, but was
governed by circumstances which he would some day reveal.
He assured Van Buren that neither he nor his friends would
complain of whatever course Van Buren might elect to pursue
in the convention. He protested that any appearance of unkind-
ness or disingenuousness on his part did him an injustice. But
what had wrought the change in him? Angry as he was, Van
Buren could not quarrel with such an opponent. He told Jenkins
that henceforward he was out to get the nomination; and as a
parting shot, assured them he was certain to triumph over his
foes.

At the convention Van Buren was opposed by the Jenkinses,
the Republican members of the Livingston family, and the
friends of Billy Van Ness. As he had suspected, Robert Jenkins
and Billy Van Ness had an understanding; but it was long after
that he learned that Van Ness had pledged Jenkins to secrecy

while the contest lasted. Van Ness's scheme was to combine forces, and after defeating Van Buren to let the convention decide between Van Ness and Jenkins. Van Buren was nominated on the first ballot.

Until after the State Constitutional Convention of 1821, New York was divided into four Senatorial Districts, the Southern, Middle, Eastern, and Western Districts; so that a candidate for the upper branch of the State Legislature had to canvass one-fourth of the commonwealth. The Middle District embraced the Dutch counties on either bank of the Hudson and all the Catskill Mountains region. This was the arena in which Van Buren contested for supremacy with one of the Livingstons. Van Buren's adversary not only was the regular nominee of the Federalist Party, but had a spurious Republican nomination to boot. The old friends and supporters of Burr, led by Billy Van Ness, worked zealously to defeat Van Buren. A powerful group of New York financiers also aided Livingston. These were trying to bribe the New York Legislature to create a successor to the Bank of the United States, whose charter had failed of renewal in the United States Senate by the casting vote of Vice President Clinton.

Livingston openly advocated a charter for the Bank of America, as the contemplated successor of the Philadelphia institution was known. After Van Buren had been nominated, and while the bill chartering the Bank of America was before the Senate on second reading, Governor Tompkins prorogued the Legislature from that day, March 27, until May 21.

In his message to the Legislature Tompkins justified this drastic action by saying he had sufficient proof to convince him that the applicants for a charter had used, or attempted to use, corrupt means to gain their ends.

The Governor's resort to this relic of royal prerogative convulsed the State. That bribers had been employed was beyond question. Solomon Southwick, editor of the Albany *Register*, was almoner for the charter applicants. His chief assistant in bribing legislators was David Thomas, the State Treasurer.

Livingston's advocacy of the bank charter, and the opposition of the Federalists to the Republican demand for war with England, were capitalized by Van Buren. To wear a red ribbon on one's watch fob meant a mauling. That the color was part of a Republican dandy's apparel mattered not to his fellow Jeffersonians: to most of them it was the secret badge of a Tory. So watch ribbons of red went out of favor before the election was over.

Towards the end of the campaign Vice President Clinton died. When the returns began to come in Van Buren conceded Livingston's election by a small majority. Many normally Republican counties were carried by the Federalists' nominees for Assembly, thereby giving them control of the lower house. Van Buren would forget his defeat in his law. He packed his bag, and threw his references and notes into his green bag preparatory to leaving for New York to attend the May term of the Court for the Correction of Errors. It would be easier for him to forget the election if the Federalists in the hotel across the street would only be quiet. They had been singing constantly since noon, and their songs grew louder and less tuneful as the afternoon progressed. Every one in the hotel seemed to be singing—and drinking. He could see one or two of the celebrants watching his door through a window of the tap room. It was common knowledge that he was taking the New York boat that afternoon.

Van Buren, weighted down by his luggage and papers, strode out of his office. As he stepped into the street, the merriest of the lot, with grins that would have been a credit to Silenus, sallied forth on the piazza of the hotel and bestowed their broadest grimaces on Van Buren. They uttered not a word. They just swayed to and fro and leered at him.

On the steamboat, Van Buren met Ebenezer Foot, also bound for the May term of court. Foot had been one of the foremost Republicans until the recent campaign, and pretended to sympathize with Van Buren. Two hours later, as the steamboat was pulling out of Catskill, Van Buren saw the tall figure of Moses I. Cantine, his brother-in-law, towering above the crowd on the wharf, frantically pointing to a small sail heading for the steamboat. Presently the little craft hove alongside, and a packet addressed to Van Buren was thrown on board. As Van Buren read the enclosure his face lighted: Cantine had given him the official returns from Delaware County, which varied several hundred from the unofficial canvass,—and in Van Buren's favor. The corrected figures gave Van Buren so pronounced a lead over Livingston in that western extreme of the Middle Senatorial District that his election was assured.

Van Buren showed them to the sympathizing Foot. He smiled as he saw Foot's countenance drop the mask and reveal the disappointment that suddenly possessed him. The official canvass was: Van Buren 5,993; Livingston 5,800. It was a slender majority; but large enough to make him a member of the Court for the Correction of Errors before which he would appear on the morrow. It was a pleasing prospect.

When he reached New York City he learned that the two Clintonian nominees for Senate had defeated the candidates of the Martling men by substantial majorities. A queer lot the Martling men; held together by the mummeries of a pseudo-Indian ritual; chartered by the Legislature as a benevolent organization, but in fact a compact political body, not numerically powerful, but at times capable of deciding close elections. Their one hate was Clinton.

# CHAPTER XIII

VAN BUREN stopped at the most fashionable boarding house in New York. This was kept by Mrs. Rosa Keese at No. 1 Wall street, on the south corner of Broadway, facing Trinity Church. Here the élite of the bar from the country districts forgathered and talked law and politics. They were now talking war, and their talk was marked by a violence that the most impassioned advocate would hesitate to use before a jury.

The Senator-elect from the Middle District proved an excellent audience. He saw old friends sit down to discuss the threatened conflict and part in silence. In the language of Dr. James Renwick, "the only true question was, whether Britain or France should be selected as an enemy, for both had been equally guilty." Madison would not be renominated if he did not consent to declare war against England. Henry Clay and other Republican leaders in Congress threatened to desert him if he did not remain faithful to the teachings of Jefferson, which were now reduced to: peace with France and war with England.

He heard the Martling men curse Clinton as a traitor to his party and to his country. His treason lay in his seeking the Presidency and in his supposed opposition to a war with England. It was rumored that Ambrose Spencer, who married a sister of De Witt Clinton, was ready to take the field against his brother-in-law.

Van Buren was beginning to understand with horrifying clearness how his own little village had been divided against itself in the Revolution. Those who were decrying the talk of war were not all Anglophiles; some had shed their blood in 1776. Their hatred for their old foe had not abated with the years. They also loathed the thought of a conflict that might wreck the experiment which all Europe wanted to destroy. This divided sentiment was not peculiar to New York. It was general.

Federalist papers for two years had been denouncing the suggestion of war. Distinguished ministers of the Gospel thundered anathema at France and all who cried for war with England. David Osgood, from his famed pulpit in Medford, preached:

> The strong prepossessions of so great a proportion of my fellow citizens in favor of a race of demons and against a nation of more religion, virtue, good faith, generosity, and beneficence, than any that now is or ever has been upon the face of the earth, wring my soul with anguish, and fill my heart with the apprehension and terror of the judgments of heaven upon this sinful people.

Osgood was neither a sensational pulpiteer nor an impetuous talker; seventy-five years made him cautious; a bachelor's degree from Harvard and a theologian's training made for conservatism. He was professedly pro-British, and violently opposed to France. Osgood was typical of most Federalist leaders. Rational men, who tried to avoid taking sides, asked themselves if a declaration of war against England would not spell civil war at home.

Madison was made to see the crisis through the eyes of Jefferson and Clay, and on the day following the reconvening of the prorogued Legislature in Albany, the Republican Congressional Caucus met in Washington and renominated him. Only eighty-three of the one hundred and thirty-three Republican members of Congress attended the Caucus. Madison was not popular with his party. After Madison was nominated war ceased to be a debatable issue: war henceforth was only a question of time.

Almost immediately after the Legislature reconvened a majority of Federalists and Republicans, as Tompkins knew in advance, combined and passed the charter of the Bank of America. Some lawmakers were for the charter because they had friends interested in the promotion of the bank; some were bought. The charter out of the way, the Republican members of the Legislature met on May 28, six days after Madison's nomination by the Congressional Caucus, and nominated Clinton for President.

A silent spectator at the caucus was Clinton's brother-in-law, Chief Justice Spencer of the Supreme Court. He had Clinton's interests at heart, and with war a certainty, believed that Clinton would have no chance with Madison pictured as the unselfish, patriotic redresser of the country's wrongs. He urged him not to jeopardize his brilliant prospects. Another four years would not be long to wait. But Clinton saw victory ahead. He had regarded Madison as a personal enemy ever since a former clerk of the President attacked him in the Washington *Monitor;* and the unceasing criticisms of himself and family by the press of the Virginia Dynasty only whetted his desire for the contest. Clinton, in permitting the Federalists to acclaim him as "the Peace President," wrecked his campaign almost before it was under way. As we shall see later, he lost the campaign through the defection of a single State.

On June 18 war was declared. Clinton's Republican supporters in the New York Senate, anticipating that they would be charged in time to come with disloyalty in opposing a war President, adopted resolutions before word had reached Albany of the momentous decision at Washington, pledging "to support such measures as shall be adopted by the General Government for the vindication of our violated rights and honor." The Federalist members of the Senate offered an amendment declaring that "neither the honor nor the interests of the United States require that a war should be declared against either of the belligerent countries." This was voted down.

The War of 1812 was far from being a popular conflict. The division in the House of Representatives on the bill declaring war was seventy-nine ayes and forty-nine noes. Most of the Republican members from New York were Clintonians and voted against the war. Clinton's spokesman in the United States Senate, Obadiah German, voted and spoke against it.

On the eve of war the people of Boston held a town meeting in Faneuil Hall at which Thomas Dawes was moderator. Resolves drafted by a committee of eminent citizens including William H. Sumner, Harrison Gray Otis and Gamaliel Bradford were unanimously adopted, and published as broadsides. We quote a few phrases: ". . . the inhabitants of this town sincerely deprecate a war with Great Britain, as extremely injurious to the interests and happiness of the people, and peculiarly so, as it necessarily tends to an alliance with France, thereby threatening the subversions of their liberties and independence. That an offensive war against Great Britain alone would be manifestly unjust, and that a war against both of the belligerent powers would be an extravagant undertaking, which is not required by the honor or interests of the nation."

Two days after war was declared the *Federal Republican,* published in the National Capital, but printed and distributed in Baltimore, violently assailed the motives of the administration:

Without funds, without taxes, without an army, navy or adequate fortifications . . . our rulers have promulgated a war against the clear and decided sentiments of a vast majority of the nation. . . . We mean to represent . . . that it is unnecessary, inexpedient, and entered into from partial, personal, and as we believe, motives bearing upon their front marks of undisguised foreign influence which cannot be mistaken. We mean to use every constitutional argument and every legal means to render as odious and suspicious to the American public, as they deserve to be, the patrons and contrivers of this highly impolitic and destructive war . . . We shall cling to the rights of a freeman both in act and in opinion, till we sink with the liberty of our country, or sink alone. . . . We are avowedly hostile to the presidency of James Madison, and we will never breath [*sic!*] under the dominion direct or derivative of Bonaparte, let it be acknowledged when it may. . . .

The editor of this Federalist organ was Alexander C. Hanson, friend of General "Light Horse Harry" Lee, one-time Governor of Virginia, and of another old hero of the Revolution, General James Lingan.

Two nights later a mob surrounded the plant of the *Federal Republican* in Baltimore. Edward Johnson, Mayor of Baltimore, watched the mob destroy the building and its contents.

Hanson, at his home in the country, heard of his loss the following evening. The next day he arrived in Baltimore, and made arrangements to revive the paper. The editor learned that he could not hope for any protection from the State or municipal authorities. Hanson left Baltimore vowing never to return until he could return prepared to assert his rights as a freeman and a journalist.

A month later he returned to Baltimore accompanied by eight friends determined to maintain the rights of person and property, and the freedom of the press. These eight were Generals Lee and Lingan, Captain Richard S. Crabb, Peregrine Warfield, Charles K. Kilgour, Otho Sprigg, Ephraim Gaither, and a young actor named John Howard Payne who lived to write *Home, Sweet Home.*

On Monday, July 27, the first issue of the revived paper was distributed. That evening two of Ephraim Gaither's brothers, William and Harry, and a Major Musgrove joined Hanson and his party in the new office of the *Federal Republican* on Charles street. An hour or so later some twenty residents of Baltimore, some of them strangers to Hanson, joined the defenders. The owner of the house, his son, and his son-in-law, asked Mayor Johnson to protect the building from mob violence. The Mayor replied he would not interfere. The Mayor then left town.

Hanson and his friends finished their evening meal in peace and the gathering twilight. When darkness fell the mob arrived. It was at first timorous, but as its numbers increased, it grew emboldened and collected under the windows of the house. General Lee called upon the mob to disperse, warning that any attack would be repulsed with arms.

The mob retreated to the opposite side of the street and began to bombard the house with stones. This lasted for two hours. By that time there was not a window sash left in the front of the house. The sidewalk was a mass of stones, bricks, splintered glass, broken shutters, and shattered window frames. Some of the missiles fell inside the house, causing Hanson and his companions to abandon the front rooms. The mob was having everything its own way.

It was nine o'clock when the mob began to hurl stones at the house. At eleven o'clock some one gave the word to stop the stone throwing and to force the front door. A rude battering ram was found and the door gave way. As the door fell the mob instinctively paused.

This momentary pause gave the mob an opportunity to glimpse the entry hall, dimly lighted by candles on the second landing. They could make out massive pieces of furniture in the hall; desks, tables, and chairs, all roped together elaborately. The rope lent an ominous note to the inanimate pile. Above the top of this barricade, on the upper steps of the stairs, could be seen the legs of men who did not move. This took but a second to envision, and the mob retreated to the middle of the road. But they remained there only a moment.

After the door was rammed, General Lee commanded that three pistols, without ball, be fired from the upper story. These shots had the desired effect. The mob dispersed. When they discovered that blank shots had been fired, the mob reassembled. Some of the hoodlums were armed with pistols.

A well-dressed member of the mob, a Dr. Gale, harangued his fellows, who instantly stormed the house. None passed the threshold of the gaping doorway. A volley discharged from the staircase dropped them. Simultaneously the defenders fired from the windows into the brown of the mob, which seethed forward, cursing, shouting, and firing pistols. But the fire from the windows and staircase was effectual. Dr. Gale was dead, a big hole in his head. Several others were wounded. Only one of the defenders was hit. The mob now beat a disorderly retreat, carrying their dead and wounded with them.

Shortly after their attackers had fled, Hanson and his defenders heard the distant ruffle of a drum. They breathed easier, confident the militia had been ordered out. But this drum was slung over the shoulders of one of the mob. At first only a handful marched behind him. Through the darkened streets the weird procession wended its way. Some of the marchers carried lighted candles. A little after midnight, with hundreds of new recruits, the mob reassembled near the *Federalist Republican.*

Cautiously, in groups of four and five, the mob returned to the house. "Light Horse Harry" Lee, whose kindly face and silver hair were known to all Baltimore, thinking that a word to these early arrivals would avoid further bloodshed, addressed them from behind the barricaded doorway. One of his listeners pointed a pistol at the old hero's breast and fired. The flint flashed in the pan.

There was no parleying with the mob, which resumed its stoning of the house, attacking it front and rear. But now the stone throwing was carried on beyond the reach of pistol shot.

Inside the besieged house every man was at his post, pistols loaded and primed, and naked dirks where they would be most serviceable in an unlooked-for hand-to-hand conflict. One of the defenders, Ephraim Gaither, was bleeding profusely from the wound received in the attack of three hours before. Lest he be relieved of his guard, Gaither made no complaint. It was now two o'clock in the morning.

Suddenly there was heard the rhythmic clatter of horses'

hoofs on the paved streets. The mob ceased its attack and listened. Then some one cried: "The troop is coming!" The cry was reëchoed as the hoof beats grew louder, and in a moment a small troop of cavalry drew rein where the mob had been seconds before. The commander of the militia, Major William Barney, overtook a few of the mob a short distance from the besieged house, and told them that there must be no violence done either to person or to property, and that he was there to prevent both, and "to secure the party in the house."

Barney had blundered. This he realized when some began to wrangle with him, and demanded by whose authority he came. He showed his order, and so placated them that they gave him three loud huzzas. Many of these cheers were from men who had abandoned the taverns at the sound of the drum. The mob took courage from their drunken companions, who boisterously asserted their rights as free-born men. Major Barney replied with soft words to these misguided freemen, who frequently boasted that they would wreak vengeance on the accursed Tories. This singular scene continued for half an hour in front of the doorless and windowless house, where a handful of resolute men continued silently at their posts. They could hear Barney assuring the mob from time to time that he was their personal and political friend.

Barney ceased speaking as he beheld a large body of men approaching with measured slowness. There were at least a thousand in the irregular formation. As they advanced an erratic rumble as of a heavy weight being dragged over the paving stones, grew louder. From his mount Barney observed that in the center of the advancing horde was a gap which neither increased nor diminished as the silent men plodded onward.

The officer kept watching that perplexing void. As the mob neared the house the enigma was solved. The gap was a field piece. This cannon was a nine-pounder, and had been seized at the gun house of one of the city's artillery companies.

Barney leaped from his horse, and throwing the reins to a trooper, ran toward the new menace and pleaded with the men to retire. But he might as well have talked to a stone wall. They surged forward, Barney a straw in the human stream. The men with the cannon halted twenty-five yards from their objective.

At the command of one of its leaders, the mob in front of the cannon opened up like the blades of a pair of shears, and Major Barney was swept to one side. In another second the cannon, which had been loaded earlier with its deadly charge, was trained on the house. They had battered down the door; now they would batter down the walls.

As the order to fire was given, Barney was before the gaping mouth of the gun. His hands outstretched so that the cannoneers could see that he was unarmed, Barney appealed to them not to fire, saying that if they did, they would fire on him and his men, who were drawn up in front of the house. The officer reminded the mob that he and his men were their fellow townsmen, and to drive this home, added that they were their friends. The plea was successful, but only for a short time. New hands seized the cannon and were about to apply the match when Barney, with a total disregard of consequences, thrust his breast against the muzzle of the field piece. Many times during the night this scene was reënacted, and each time Barney's reckless heroism turned the mob from its purpose.

At six in the morning Mayor Johnson, who had been summoned from the country by messengers, arrived at the scene. With him was Brigadier General John Stricker, a banker of the town, a veteran of the Revolution, and commander of the local militia. After a parley with Hanson and his defenders, the two were admitted to the house.

Stricker was calm. He represented the inflamed mind of the public, and the practical impossibility of protecting Hanson and his friends against a force which might soon come to the aid of the mob. Johnson was choleric. Turning to Hanson, with great agitation, he said: "We are impressed with the belief that a civil war is inevitable, and I consider this a party thing and the commencement of it."

The purpose of the visit was to ask Hanson and his defenders to submit peaceably to arrest. He was answered that none of them ever had any thought of resisting the authorities; and all they asked was their protection, and this having been denied them, they sought to protect themselves. Stricker assured them an adequate guard.

A little after eight o'clock, Hanson, Lee, Lingan, and their companions, marched out of the shambles that had been the office of the *Federal Republican.* A heavy escort of cavalry and foot was drawn up in the street, deserted save for the militia. On the march to the jail a few stones were thrown, slightly injuring some of the soldiers. Meanwhile the mob was permitted to demolish the vacated house.

The jail was a new structure, and sturdy as a medieval castle. The prisoners were lodged in a large common pen. This room had a door of heavy iron grill. This was not locked. To reach this place of confinement the imprisoned had to pass through a corridor with double-barred doors at either end.

By noon a threatening mob massed outside the jail. An hour later a regiment of infantry, two troops of cavalry, and two companies of artillery, were ordered out. Some of Hanson's companions did not like the thought of the door of the room in which they were confined being unlocked. They sent for the turnkey and asked him to lock the door, and to pass the key to them through the bars, reminding him that they were not ordinary prisoners accused of crime, but were taken because they had defended their persons and the freedom of the press. The jailer said that his keys were in the front room—the office of the jail—and that he would comply with their request.

Immediately after, General Stricker, several magistrates, and the Mayor, entered the pen and spoke with the prisoners. Three rudely dressed men also accompanied the Mayor. These three men did not speak, but directed their attention to the dress and features of the prisoners. One remained after the Mayor and the rest of his party left. This man was John Mumma, a butcher of the town. Mumma stood silently at the door of the pen continuing his observation for some minutes. He then took his departure. Mumma also dealt in human flesh, for he was a stealer of slaves.

The militia arrived at the jail while the Mayor and his party were inside. The mob was not molested. The orders merely called for the parading of the forces at the prison. The Mayor said that on his arrival at the jail he found "a number of persons assembled, the much greater part of whom were peaceable and orderly citizens; those of different temper of mind upon being remonstrated with, appeared to yield to the admonitions of the others and to be appeased with the assurance given that the party in gaol should not be bailed or suffered to escape during the night." This fiction is from the official report of the investigating committee appointed by the common council of Baltimore.

After Mumma the butcher left the jail, Hanson and Lee and Lingan again sent for the turnkey and repeated their request that the door of their pen be locked and the key given to them. Again the turnkey promised, and, again, failed. They were now apprehensive for their safety. If they could only lock that door! They had four pistols which they had smuggled in on their persons, and a dirk or two. Throughout the afternoon the prisoners reiterated their requests of the turnkey, but without avail.

News traveled slowly in those days. The first intelligence Boston had of the events in Baltimore on the last Monday and Tuesday of July was published in a broadside the following Sunday afternoon by the *Gazette*. The story was headed: "Madison's Mob!" One of the subheadings of the caption read: "This morning's mail gives us a few particulars of a most barbarous riot in Baltimore, instigated by the friends of the Administration, and completed by French Democracy." The story opened with: "Extracts from a letter from Baltimore dated July 28. The reign of Terror and Proscription has raised its hideous form once more amongst us." After briefly relating some of the events with which we are familiar the correspondent, commenting on the passivity of Mayor Johnson, exclaimed: "Oh that we had a De Witt Clinton here—an end would soon be put to these iniquities and abominations."

New York, Philadelphia and cities not so remote heard of the horror a day or two earlier. Even the most rabid Federalists in these cities doubted the truth of part of the correspondence, as for example, that the Mayor ordered the militia to be removed from the jail during the course of that tragic afternoon. Let us quote again from the official report of the Mayor's own friends: "It became the prevailing opinion about the prison that no mischief would be attempted that night, in consequence of which, and of the insufficiency of the force [the mob] assembled, the military, by order of the General with the approbation of the Mayor, were dismissed, and many persons left the prison and went to their homes."

Nowhere in this texture of truths, half-truths, and false-hoods is there any reference to the remonstrances made by Major Heath against the dismissal of the soldiers. Heath was overruled.

Generals Lingan and "Light Horse Harry" Lee looked at one another as they heard the familiar commands in the street outside. To their inquiring companions they explained that the militia was abandoning them to the protection of the jailers—and themselves. Again they sent for the turnkey and urged him to lock the door and pass the key to them through the grill. Once more he treacherously promised to comply with their pleading.

When darkness fell that evening, Mumma and other worthies of Baltimore joined the mob at the jail. There were many ardent Republicans there, as zealous in their devotion to the teachings of Jefferson as their unworthy Mayor. These, on seeing the temper of the mob, warned the Mayor. But he refused to order out the militia. Instead he went to the jail. Before he reached the prison the mob battered the front door, but did not force it.

The appearance of the Mayor served as a signal for a second assault upon the jail. "The Mayor with the aid of a few persons," reads the conniving official report, "succeeded for a time in preventing the prison door from being forced open; . . . overpowered by the increased numbers and violence of the assailants, the Mayor was forced away, and the door having been previously battered, and again threatened, was opened by a turnkey."

The exultant roar of the mob as it gained entrance to the prison told "Light Horse Harry" Lee and his companions that they were trapped. They could hear the mob battering at the doors at the further end of the corridor. The persistent pounding on the more distant door, and the cries of disappointment, revealed that the treacherous turnkey had not unlocked this door. If he had only locked them in and given them the key, as they had so often urged him, they could make a stubborn last stand. But it was no time for regrets. They gathered hope as the shouts continued to be muffled by the two doors the mob would have to force before they could reach the pen.

As they looked at one another in the dimly lighted pen—their only illumination came from flickering candles stuck on the shelves with their own wax—one thought was dominant: the militia would return to the jail before the mob could batter down the remaining doors. Infantry, cavalry, and artillery had escorted them to the jail in the morning; some of these troops would be back again before long. "Light Horse Harry" Lee put his arm around the shoulder of General Lingan, who alone found it difficult to keep awake. Lee was anything but a youth himself, but he was firm and erect, unlike his companion of the Revolution. Why had they permitted Lingan to join them? He was so noticeably old and infirm. And he was very poor too. He had long ago solved the problem of supporting a family on the income of a day laborer while maintaining an appearance comporting with his rank.

For fifteen minutes hope was high in the hearts of all. Then the door attacked by the mob was either unlocked or battered down. Now Lee and his companions considered what their course should be if the mob forced the second door before help, in the shape of the militia, reached the jail. Some proposed that those armed with pistols fire into the assailants, and in the ensuing confusion, try to make their escape.

Lee and Hanson counseled against this, saying it would only add to the fury of the mob. Their counter-proposal, which was agreed to, provided that when the mob forced the second door, at a given signal, the candles in the pen were to be snuffed, and then all were to rush out, extinguish the lanterns in the hall, crash into the mob, and trust to the sudden darkness and confusion to enable some of them to escape. All were reminded that the moment the candles were snuffed it would be each man for himself.

Mumma the butcher was not with the members of the mob who forced the first door and were now at the second. He was standing beside the grate in the entrance of the lobby where he could see all who passed in and out. Several evil-looking fellows stood beside him, their ugly faces illuminated by the light of many candles.

The second door did not long remain between the mob and its prey. The bolts were thrown back by the turnkey after a few blows had been rained upon it.

The dominant characteristic of a mob is cowardice. Between this mob and the unlocked door of the pen was a short stretch of hall. Nothing intervened. The mob, apprehensive and timorous, halted in the passageway. Captain Murray, who had been "Light Horse Harry" Lee's chief aide, was quick to notice this. He and John Thompson, who was the nearest to him of the other three armed with firearms leveled their pistols at two who made bold to peer into the pen.

"My lads," said Murray, "you had better retire; I can shoot either of you."

Lee and Hanson commanded Thompson and Murray not to fire. They obeyed. The ruffians in the rear, shouting encouragement, pushed and forced their fellows into the pen.

As the first of the mob entered, the prearranged signal was given, and the candles extinguished. Lee and Lingan led an advance which is not considered in books on the conduct of battles. It was a silent precipitate advance intended for a retreat. The sudden darkness created the confusion that had been counted upon, and mobster and hero were indistinguishable.

At the far end of the corridor was Mumma the butcher. He turned questioningly to his companions as he heard the crash of falling lanterns in the passageway and saw the sudden onrush past him of a score or more men who piled through the main door and down the steep flight of steps to the street in an indistinguishable mass.

Mumma was too astonished to remember his rôle. He had missed quite a few. But not again was he to be caught napping. He was big and powerful, and in the next two or three seconds had felled by a hand long used to slaughter "Light Horse Harry" Lee, Lingan, and Hanson. None save those struck by Mumma were molested by his aides, who kicked the unfortunates as they lay in the lobby of the jail, pulling them to one side as more were knocked down by Mumma's blows. The victims who looked dead were carried to the door and pitched out into the street by Mumma and his assistants, whose hands were red with blood. Six others besides Lee and Lingan and Hanson were thrown into the same heap in front of the entrance to the jail. Four others were taken a short distance away by the assassins. One of these was tarred and feathered and carted around town, while his torturers made slits in his tarred flesh, and then thrust lighted matches into the wounds.

Mumma and his companions, now that they had cleared the jail of the Tories, turned their attention to the pile of bodies in the street outside. Most of these assassins carried lighted candles to examine the mangled faces of their victims. One of their tests for detecting the presence of life was to open the eyelids and drop hot candle grease into the eyes. Another was to jab penknives into the bleeding faces. Sometimes they were merciful and merely pricked a hand.

Some of the supposed dead had never lost consciousness. These, numb from their mauling, simulated death as the mob dropped hot candle grease into their eyes or pricked them with their knives. "Light Horse Harry" Lee had lost consciousness, and when he raised his head, one of Mumma's aides slashed his  nose, and the General's head fell back to earth. A moment later the old hero tried to rise again. This time another knife thrust gashed his cheek, and in a paroxysm of pain, the former Governor of Virginia rose almost to a sitting position, and then fell over, face downward, on Hanson's breast.

General Lingan regained consciousness while Mumma's butchers were moving among the victims. His first thoughts were of his family. He would plead for them. In a plaintive voice he recalled that he had fought for freedom; that he was now old and infirm, and that he had a large and helpless family dependent on him.

An assassin armed with a cudgel, danced on Lingan's chest as he struck him, and shouted "Tory!" Lingan moaned that he wanted to live that his family might not want; he was not concerned about himself. Each phrase was greeted with blows of the club on head and face. "This damned old rascal is hardest dying of all of them!" exclaimed the assassin as the hero of the Revolution made his last appeal for mercy, a mute one, a vain uplifting of almost lifeless hands. Another blow and the hands fell.

One who walked amid the lifeless forms was a man of consequence. He carried a walking stick with which he prodded the helpless ones, and suggested that they be emasculated. Others proposed casting the bodies into the cesspool of the jail. Some were for throwing them into Jones's Falls, a stream which flowed in front of the prison. They were all lifeless-looking enough now, but some of Mumma's apprentices wanted the throats of all slashed to make sure that none would live.

While these fiends flitted around in the dark with their lighted candles a surgeon of the city, a Dr. Hall, accompanied by several other citizens of the town, appeared. Instantly the assassins blew out their candles and fled. Under the direction of Dr. Hall the unfortunates were carried back into the jail. Lingan ceased to breathe a few minutes after his removal. "Light Horse Harry" Lee's fate was typical of the majority of the survivors: he never wholly recovered from his wounds.

Mumma and several others were indicted for murder, but a petit jury found them innocent of any crime: it was not an offense to kill one who sympathized with a Federalist editor. Maryland somewhat atoned for this blot on her escutcheon by sending Hanson to represent her in the Senate of the United States.

While the mob was storming the jail, leaders of the Federalists in New York were planning another sort of storming under the leadership of the Patroon himself, now General Stephen Van Rensselaer, commander-in-chief of New York's militia in the field. The objective of the Patroon and his men was Canada. A brother of Martin Van Buren, Lawrence, his junior by four years, abandoned the plow at Kinderhook to join the colors. He entered as an enlisted man and was discharged a major.

Van Buren was more concerned with the war of the politicians. In the early part of July he was attending the circuit of the Supreme Court in Auburn where Judge Spencer was presiding. Both were seated on a piazza in the cool of the evening when their mail was brought to them announcing the death of Matthias B. Hildreth, Attorney General of the State. Turning to Van Buren, Spencer said: "You ought to be Hildreth's successor." When Spencer followed with a promise of support, Van Buren observed that as he had not yet reached thirty years, older men might feel slighted. Spencer scoffed at his objections. Van Buren wrote to Richard Riker, Clinton's confidential agent in political matters, who replied that he approved his candidacy.

A special meeting of the Council of Appointment was called for August 12 to fill the vacancy. Van Buren was confident that he would be appointed until a short time before the members of

the Council, all Clintonians, assembled in Albany. Learning that
Senator William W. Gilbert, of Manhattan, an intimate of
Clinton, was adverse to discussing the subject with Riker, he
gracefully retired. Thomas Addis Emmet, brother of the mar-
tyred Irish leader, was appointed Hildreth's successor.

Emmet was one of the ablest lawyers of his day. Like many
leaders of his race who came here in those early days, he had
studied at Dublin's ancient Elizabethan pile. He was a physician
as well as a lawyer, and had sat in the Senate-hall of his native
land. After the downfall of the revolution of 1798, he and several
other Fenian leaders were seized as prisoners of State. No indict-
ments were returned against them. Many of his fellows in misfortune, like himself, were men of unusual attainments and large
fortune. The British Government professed a willingness to
permit these State prisoners to emigrate to the United States,
but Rufus King, resident minister at the Court of St. James's,
succeeded in preventing their coming to these shores for four
years, and consequently, kept them that much longer in an
English prison.

Emmet and his family landed in New York on November 11,
1804. He first visited Washington where he was admitted to
practice in the United States Supreme Court, and this without
any action on his part. The Clintons caused the Legislature to
pass a special act permitting him to practice in the courts of
New York State. Legislative action was necessary because
Emmet was not a citizen. He was at once welcomed into the city's
social set. His success was immediate and his clients numbered
the Pintards and other wealthy merchants of the town.

On the eve of the preceding National campaign, when Rufus
King was the Federalist candidate for Vice President, Emmet in
a series of open letters to King helped the cause of Madison while
paying off an old score. In these epistles Emmet accused King
of having conspired with English officialdom to keep him and his
fellow compatriots in jail, and from emigrating to our shores.
King remained silent, suspecting that his accuser was awaiting
a denial to hurl at him proofs of his guilt from the correspondence
of Lord Castlereagh. But Emmet had not these incriminating
documents which the Viscount incorporated in his memoirs. Republican meetings were held in New York and Albany at which

resolves were adopted predicated on Emmet's unanswerable charges. These were given country-wide circulation in Republican newspapers and broadsides. Pretending to regard King's silence as evidence that King thought him unworthy of notice, Emmet wrote:

> Yet in fact, sir, I do not clearly see in what consists your superiority over myself. It is true that you have been a resident minister at the court of St. James's; and if what I have read in the public prints be true, and if you be apprised of my near relationship and family connexion with the late Sir John Temple, you must acknowledge that your interference as resident minister at the court of St. James's, against my being permitted to emigrate to America, is a very curious instance of the caprice of fortune. But let that pass. To what extent I ought to yield to you for talents and information, is not for me to decide. In no other respect, however, do I feel your excessive superiority. My private character and conduct, are, I hope, as fair as yours —and even in those matters which I consider as trivial, but upon which aristocratic pride is accustomed to stamp a value, I should not be inclined to shrink from competition. My birth certainly will not humble me in the comparison; my paternal fortune was probably much greater than yours; the consideration in which the name I bear was held in my native country was as great as yours is ever likely to be, before I had an opportunity of contributing to its celebrity. . . . Circumstances which cannot be controlled, have decided that my name must be embodied into history. From the manner in which even my political adversaries and some of my contemporary historians, unequivocally hostile to my principles, already speak of me, I have the consolation of reflecting, that when the falsehoods of the day are withered and rotten, I shall be respected and esteemed. You, sir, will probably be forgotten, when I shall be remembered with honor, or if, peradventure, your name should descend to posterity, perhaps you will be known only as the recorded instrument of part of my persecutions, sufferings, and misfortunes.

This fragment of the resolutions adopted at the Albany Coffee-House shows how the unilateral controversy was turned to the advantage of the Republicans: ". . . and it is moreover evident that King's only objection to the emigration of the Irish state prisoners emanated from a belief that they would unite with the republicans, who were then opposing, with the weapons of argument and reason, that mad career of federalism, which,

under the career of John Adams, had well nigh subdued the spirit
of freemen by systematic oppression, and by attempts, with a
standing army, to overawe and silence public opinion."

Emmet was an intimate of De Witt Clinton, and to this
Van Buren ascribed the appointment. He felt injured that Clinton
had not told him of his intention to have Emmet named. When
Clinton informed Van Buren over a cup of tea at his home that
he had no hand in the appointment, Van Buren was skeptical.

Van Buren lost out solely on the score of youth. Governor
Tompkins, who had succeeded in having Thomas, the State Treasurer, and Southwick, the editor of the *Register*, indicted for
attempting to bribe a Senator and the Speaker of the Assembly
to pass the charter of the Bank of America, wanted the older
and more experienced man for the task. But although a perfect
case was presented to the trial jury, these twelve men, hypnotized
by the eloquence of Elisha Williams and Ebenezer Foot—Van
Buren's hypocritical sympathizer—returned verdicts of not
guilty.

# CHAPTER XIV

AFTER the appointment of Emmet, Republicans throughout the country, many of them politically unfriendly to Madison, tried to induce Clinton to withdraw as a candidate for the Presidency. They argued, as Spencer had argued, that the country being at war, a second Republican contending for the place would divide the people still further, and that his election would be regarded by Europe as a popular repudiation of the war. Here it should be noted that many of Clinton's supporters believed he would prosecute the war more efficiently than Madison was doing.

These overtures were made by General William King, of that part of Massachusetts then known as the province of Maine, to Spencer, and an old friend of the Clinton family, Judge John Tayler, of Albany, a member of the State Senate. "No event would exalt Mr. Clinton higher than a surrender of his pretensions to the presidential chair," wrote Tayler and Spencer to Riker. And they added, on the representations of King, that Massachusetts would support Clinton in 1816.

Spencer and Tayler had written in confidence to one whose political judgment Clinton valued above all others. Riker replied that the people had made Mr. Clinton their candidate and had the right to his name. And as for King's suggestion that Massachusetts would support Clinton four years hence if he would withdraw now, that could not be considered for even a moment, as bargains between politicians are inconsistent with the purity and dignity of republicanism. This last, from a practical politician, was amusing.

These two letters were published in the newspapers early in October at Clinton's behest, and caused an open rupture between the brothers-in-law. Clinton lampooned Spencer in the *American Citizen*, under savage satires entitled *Ambrosiad*.

Ambrose Spencer lodged at Mrs. Keese's boarding house. Here Van Buren met him after the third of Clinton's pasquinades had appeared. The Chief Justice made no effort to conceal the wounds made by his brother-in-law's venomous quill. John Armstrong, now Madison's Secretary of War, who was stopping at Mrs. Keese's, poured the salt of sympathy into the wounds made by the ancient enemy of his family. Armstrong had pamphleteered against Clinton, and said his ruddy countenance was the product of the vine.

Van Buren listened to the outpouring of Spencer and Armstrong and that evening called on Clinton at his home in an effort to repair the breach. He prefaced his peacemaking with an avowal of loyalty, and declared that when the Legislature met he would vote for Presidential Electors committed to Clinton's candidacy, volunteering that the spring legislative caucus left no Republican in the state any other choice. Van Buren was an orthodox partisan. He brought up the subject of the *Ambrosiads*, and said that Spencer was pained by the separation as much as he was by the satires in the *American Citizen.* Clinton was pleased with Van Buren's pledge of support, but confessed ignorance of the authorship of the lampoons. He discounted the thought that Spencer was pained by their separation, and said his brother-in-law had joined the Madisonians to subserve his own personal ends.

Van Buren returned to his original proposition, saying that no good could come from a continuance of the *Ambrosiads*, and urged Clinton to use his influence with the editor of the *American Citizen* to suppress the *Ambrosiad* advertised for appearance on the morrow, and to prevent further publication of the articles.

Clinton, after repeating his opinion of his brother-in-law's motives, said he would try to persuade the editor to suspend publication of the *Ambrosiads* long enough to convince Van Buren that forbearance with Spencer would prove useless.

At breakfast the next morning Van Buren, Spencer, Armstrong, and other political leaders were seated at the common table. William Ross, a lawyer of Newburgh, who two years later was elected to the State Senate, joined them when they were half through the meal. Ross had been at the barber shop, as his appearance indicated, and when asked what that unfailing medium of intelligence produced, replied that the advertised *Ambrosiad* was not in the *American Citizen,* and that no reference was made to the omission.

Van Buren was delighted.

"What is in it?" asked Armstrong, who did not share Van Buren's happiness at the cessation of hostilities.

Ross answered that the paper published a letter from Riker to Spencer and Tayler, which was not lacking in severity.

"Ah, only a change of dish!" exclaimed Armstrong gloatingly. "Good policy that! To-morrow we shall have the *Ambrosiad* again!" ·

This was designed to irritate Spencer to utterance. It succeeded, the Chief Justice remarking with frigid formality that it was immaterial whether the *Ambrosiad* appeared or not, as Clinton had already gone too far to make his future course of any consequence to him.

Armstrong finished his breakfast in happy mood.

At the breakfast table there sat one of those scavengers of politics who follow in the wake of men in power as gulls follow a ship. Scraps of intelligence these fellows pick up are carried to those whose success dazzles and defiles them. Some politicians cultivate this type; but not a few are self-appointed, seeking no return save the abased emotion of spying. All Spencer said was retailed to Clinton. The deferred *Ambrosiad* appeared within a few days renewing the strife which lasted three years.

In the Presidential years when Electors were chosen by the Legislature, the two branches convened on the first Tuesday in November. The session lasted only long enough to transact this quadrennial duty, which the aristocracy of New York would not submit to the people: even the sister State of New Jersey had transferred this privilege to the electorate some five years back.

In 1812 this Tuesday fell on the third of the month. Winter, which sometimes comes early in this part of the State, was unusually early that year, and a heavy blanket of snow covered the hilly streets of Albany.

Van Buren's arrival in Albany was anxiously awaited by Clinton's intimates. Van Buren, who looked forward to playing the silent and attentive rôle of a first-year member of the Legislature, was astonished when told that the Clintonians were looking to him for leadership in the caucus. They were confessedly without a plan.

This dilemma arose from the division of the parties in the

two houses. In the spring election, as we have seen, the Federalists elected a majority to the Assembly. The respective partisan strength, excluding three members who were absent, was: Federalists, fifty-eight; Republicans, fifty-one. The Republican Assemblymen were in turn divided thus: Clintonians, twenty-nine; Madisonians, twenty-two. Among the thirty-two Senators, nine were Federalists, and of the remaining twenty-three, the Madisonians counted four. Ordinarily there would have been nothing to worry the Republicans, as on joint ballot of the Senate and Assembly the vote would have been: Republicans, seventy-four; Federalists, sixty-seven. But the party schism put a complexion on the situation which baffled the veterans. The Clintonians wanted victory without Federal support, if possible.

Van Buren marveled that the older heads had not conceived the simple solution which readily occurred to him. He soon learned that the average political leader is lacking in invention. They had done what they had been doing before: bought up such papers as they could with money or promises, closing the columns of these journals to the Madisonians. They had made a most effectual job of it in Albany, where the supporters of the President had to use handbills to tell of their meetings. We have one before us recounting a meeting "at the house of Jared Skinner, inn-keeper," wherein is related that "the only paper in this city which was the organ of our communications, has ceased to express our sentiments,—Therefore, Resolved, that the foregoing preamble and resolution be published in handbills, in the *Aurora* of Philadelphia, *Public Advertiser* and *Plebian* of New York, *Boston Patriot*, and *Pittsfield Sun*."

When the Republicans assembled in caucus, Van Buren, always fond of the dramatic, surprised most of his colleagues by nominating for chairman, Senator Tayler, the ally of Spencer. Of course, Tayler was unanimously elected. There was tact in Van Buren's choice as chairman, as the selection of an avowed Madisonian made the minority feel more kindly disposed to the blue-eyed young man with the shock of yellow locks who had suddenly emerged as the Clintonian leader. And it was Van Buren's rôle of peacemaker a few weeks before which commended him to Clinton.

Van Buren next proposed that the two factions be repre-

sented on the Presidential ticket in proportion to their respective
strength in the Legislature. This would have given Madison nine
electors and Clinton twenty. On the face of it, the proposal was
fair. But it was doubtful if the Clintonians, in a State-wide vote,
could have mustered a majority on the issue raised against Clinton by the Madisonians—that Clinton's election would be a
repudiation of the declaration of war. The followers of Madison
noisily spurned the offer.

Van Buren, unmoved by clamor, which was directed by Senator Erastus Root, refused to budge. He knew the Clintonians
could carry this or any other proposition he advanced. He declined every counter proposal. If the Madisonians would not
accept his proposal, he intended to give them nothing.

Seeing that nothing could be accomplished by protracting
the discussion interminably, and determined not to compromise,
Van Buren moved that a ticket composed entirely of Clintonians
be nominated. This motion was as unfair as it was audacious.
This was tyranny of the majority. Van Buren was essentially
partisan. No one in the room was stirred more by the move than
the chairman. He beckoned Van Buren to his side, and inquired
if he intended to persist in his motion.

"Certainly, unless the Madisonians will accept a reasonable
portion of the ticket," replied Van Buren.

The aged jurist became silent with rage. Seizing his broad-
brimmed hat, he rose, and forgetting that he was in an assemblage where the last word in decorum was observed, clapped his
hat on his head, and without a word, strode out of the room. As
the door closed behind him he was heard to cry out: "Lew! Boy!"
A few seconds later the chairmanless caucus knew that Senator
Tayler had found his servant, for the merry peal of sleigh bells
was heard as he was driven to his home. Van Buren next proposed that Senator Reuben Humphreys be chosen chairman.
This was carried. He then pressed his motion for a complete
Clintonian ticket. This, too, was adopted. At the joint session
of the Legislature some of the Madisonians voted for the ticket,
while twenty-eight of them cast blank ballots. But the Federalist
votes more than made up the deficiency. This ended the Presidential election in New York, as it was not until twelve years
later that Electors were chosen by direct vote of the people.

Clinton received the votes of all the New England States except Vermont. New Jersey also voted for Clinton, as did Delaware. Of Maryland's eleven votes, six went to Madison, and five to Clinton, who carried the entire North with the exception of Ohio and Pennsylvania. Had Madison lost Pennsylvania's twenty-five votes, Clinton would have won the election, the tally in the Electoral College being Madison, 128; Clinton, 89.

The reëlection of Madison was a bitter dose for Van Buren to swallow. Many of the Federalists continued to oppose the war, even to the extent of rejoicing at the defeat of American arms. Madison, to many of them, was the choice of a mobocracy. The invasion of Canada in the first months of the war was characterized by some as a bandit enterprise. This campaign added luster to the names of the War-Federalists, notably that of the Patroon, whose impoverished kinsman, Captain Solomon Van Rensselaer, at the battle of Queenstown, was seen "in a gallant charge at the head of his troop, shot through the body, the blood oozing from his lungs, still smiling with complacency." Six musket balls had ripped their way through this Van Rensselaer's body. It was not a new experience: back in 1794, when a captain of Dragoons, he was shot through the body in an Indian charge. Many Federalists, however, refused to follow the flag across the border, maintaining that the militia was only a home-defense organization.

The example of these militiamen was applauded by the ultra-Federalists, who denounced Madison and the war in pulpit, forum, and press. Van Buren, an omnivorous reader of partisan publications, found a bit of verse in a Federalist journal which struck his fancy. It is the only bit of rhyme in Van Buren's hand extant, and thus he transcribed it:

The day is past—the election o'er
And Madison is King once more!
Ye Vagabonds of every land, cut-throats & knaves a patriot band—
Ye Demagogues lift up your voice
Mobs & Banditti all rejoice.

On the same sheet of paper he wrote: "The rogues march was played under the window of the man who drew the declaration of Independence." His use of the small *d* is typical of his manuscript. He was constantly copying political opinions of all sorts, and in these, as in all his writings, he was equally scornful of punctuation and capitals. He had assistance in preparing his public documents.

When the Legislature reconvened after the first of the year Van Buren found the world a little topsy-turvy. Clinton, as Lieutenant Governor, appointed him to serve as chairman of the Senate Committee to draft a reply to the Governor's speech to the Legislature. Here was a signal honor, hitherto accorded to men who could readily quote Horace and Virgil and Sallust. And again Van Buren resolved to study.

Van Buren's selection was due to his known capacity to reduce political questions to homely language having a direct appeal to the people rather than to the cultured few who led them. The country was at war, and all men who are created free and equal and able to shoulder a musket were to be appealed to: the property restrictions of the voting places were alien to the recruiting office. This ability was first brought to the attention of party leaders in the resolutions Van Buren had drafted at Republican meetings three years before.

The reply to the Governor's speech was a spirited defense of the war, and a counterblast to the attacks of Federalism in the Assembly, where Elisha Williams boldly defied the Government with: "I will not furnish the administration with the means for carrying on this war; I would starve them into peace with all my heart. The Government dare not impose taxes, because they are conscious that the war is unjust and unnecessary. They know, and we know, that the people will not bear taxes for such a cause."

In the selection of the successor to United States Senator John Smith, whose term would expire on March 4, 1813, Van Buren's leadership was again put to the test. The Federalists nominated Rufus King. The Federalists were secretly boasting that King would be elected. Van Buren made inquiries, and heard enough to convince him that the Federalists and some of Clinton's friends were intriguing to elect King. There was not a Martling man in either house who was not ready to whisper the charge. At once Van Buren suspected that Clinton himself might be

directing the intrigue in return for the Federalist support in
the Presidential campaign.

He related the rumors to Clinton and said that if any Clintonian legislators voted for King or any other Federalist when
it was in the power of the Republicans to elect one of their own,
it might well be said by his enemies that he had promised the
Federalists the United States Senatorship on condition that they
support him in the canvass for the Presidency.

Clinton allayed Van Buren's suspicions. State Senator John
W. Wilkin was the choice of the Republicans. Wilkin had presided at the legislative caucus in the preceding spring at which
New York proclaimed Clinton her favorite son for the Presidency; moreover, Wilkin and Clinton were old personal friends.

The two houses of the Legislature met in joint session in
the Assembly Chamber Tuesday noon, February 2, to elect
Smith's successor. Ruggles Hubbard, one of the stalwarts among
the Clintonians in the Senate, asked Van Buren to write the name
of Wilkin on his ballot and to accompany him to the ballot box
to see that he deposited it. Van Buren knew that Hubbard also
entertained the suspicions that had been his before he had talked
with Clinton, so he at once assured him that his apprehensions
were groundless, and that Wilkin would win.

"I ask you but a small favor," said Hubbard solemnly, "and
I hope you will not refuse to grant it."

Van Buren wrote out Hubbard's ballot and walked with him
to the ballot box.

When the result of the vote was announced Wilkin had
sixty-one votes and King had sixty-eight! Rufus King, Federalist, was elected to the United States Senate by a Republican
Legislature! Politics was a strange game, filled with surprises.

After the vote was announced the members of the Senate
returned to their chamber to continue their routine labors. Van
Buren was thinking hard when Clinton approached him and said:
"I hope you no longer entertain the suspicions you spoke of?"
Van Buren quickly replied: "No!" Clinton, highly gratified that
Van Buren did not include him in the conspiracy, for its existence
was now a matter of record, started toward his seat on the rostrum. Van Buren halted him. "Mr. Clinton," said Van Buren,
stressing each syllable, "you must not misunderstand me. My

suspicions have become convictions. I know that the men I pointed out to you have done this deed."

Clinton, taken aback by the boldness of the speech, in an agitated voice answered that he was convinced that Van Buren was mistaken, and was doing his friends a grave injustice. The conversation was ended when one of Clinton's clerks informed him that everything at the desk was in order. Clinton then reconvened the Senate.

Now there is another and a more plausible explanation of this treachery than that held by Van Buren and Clinton's old foes, the Martling men, who alone circulated the rumor that Clinton's friends had conspired with the Federalists. A weak *prima facie* case could be established against Clinton on the basis of his alliance with the Federalists. He was still working with them, as we shall presently see. But that he could be so base as to play traitor to Wilkin, who more than any one else made his Presidential canvass possible, is improbable in view of Clinton's reputation for fair dealing, which, with this exception, is above suspicion.

A far more tenable explanation of this treachery is that Thomas and Southwick, who bribed members of the Legislature of 1812 to grant a charter to the Bank of America, in paying bribes to the corrupt Republicans who voted for the charter, committed them also to vote for a Federalist for United States Senator in 1813. The Federalists in Congress, almost without exception, were for renewing the charter of the United States Bank. This institution had its paid agents in every quarter of the country; it had not given up the fight. Wilkin, who fought the Bank of America, attributed his defeat to bank influence.

On the Thursday evening following the election of King, the Republicans held their State caucus. Although they had not spoken for two days, Van Buren, who was indebted to Clinton, could not avoid discussing the evening's program with one so deeply concerned. After an exchange of courtesies Clinton asked Van Buren what he thought the caucus would do. Van Buren replied that an attempt would be made to nominate Senator Tayler in Clinton's place. Clinton next inquired what Van Buren thought would result from the attempt to name the Madisonian. Van Buren answered that if Clinton did not object he would

renominate him for Lieutenant Governor, adding that he apprehended that the feeling in the party over the election of King
was such that Tayler would be nominated. Quick as his tongue
could frame the question, Clinton demanded if Van Buren would
submit to the nomination of Tayler. "Certainly, if it is fairly
made," replied Van Buren.

Clinton could not trust himself to speak. He made a deep
bow, signifying the interview was over, and returned to his seat
on the rostrum. So ended the political friendship of Clinton and
Van Buren: the Martling men had gained a formidable recruit.

This caucus of February 4, 1813, was one of the most
sparsely attended in the history of the party. Cowardice kept
some twoscore members outside the closed doors. And cowardice
reigned behind the bolted portals. For some time no one spoke
above a whisper. Finally some brave anti-Clintonian moved the
joint nomination of Tompkins for Governor and Tayler for Lieutenant Governor; just the bare motion; not a word in support of
the rejection of Clinton.

The burlesque was made complete when Van Buren rose and
nominated Clinton in a speech intended to destroy whatever
chance Clinton had. He spoke of the rancor in the party over
the election of Rufus King; he shared the feeling; by inference,
he charged Clinton with having conspired to defeat Wilkin; but
the Republican party was as magnanimous as it was powerful;
he was nominating Clinton because that distinguished gentleman
had long held honorable place in the party's councils, and before
the country; but he would not nominate him if he was not convinced that Clinton would not act with the party in the future!

There was a seconding speech and then the vote, which gave
thirty-two to Tayler and half that number to Clinton.

The next business was the appointment of a committee to
draft the party's annual appeal to the electorate. Van Buren
was honored with the chairmanship of this select group. This
document, the first public one of length from Van Buren's hand,
was called by Chief Justice Spencer, who was overjoyed with
Van Buren's desertion of Clinton, the Second Declaration of
Independence. As it went to the people it was substantially as
Van Buren had written it, save that more knowing hands had
knocked off the rough edges. The opening paragraph reads:

Fellow-Citizens—It is not to the arbitrary mandates of despotic power, that your submission is demanded; it is not to the seductive wiles and artful blandishments of the corrupt minions of aristocracy, that your attention is called—but to an expression and discussion of the wishes and feelings of your representatives.

After setting forth the wrongs inflicted upon the country which led to the declaration of war, Van Buren sought to destroy the influence of the Federalists with the merchant class.

"What are the causes for which this war is waged, and which have hitherto embroiled us with the nations of Europe?" asked Van Buren, who answered: "They are the violation of our commercial rights, and the impressment of our seamen!" Then he added: "The oft-exploded, the ten-thousand-times-refuted tale of *French influence*, is ever and anon brought upon the carpet. It would be insulting to your understandings to detain you by a discussion of this odious and insulting insinuation. Was it evidence of French influence on the adoption of every measure of commercial restriction, to place both France and England on the same footing? Was it evidence of French influence to cause it to be officially notified to the court of St. James's, on the adoption of each of those measures, that in case they rescinded their orders in council, the United States would assume a hostile attitude towards France? Was it evidence of French influence to embrace the earliest opportunity to conclude the arrangement with Erskine—leaving our affairs with France in a hostile attitude? If not, where, then, is the evidence to support this impudent censure? Is it to be found in a similarity of manners, of language, or of feeling? When an Englishman visits your country, is he not received with the familiarity, and cherished with the hospitality of a friend? Is a Frenchman ever treated by you otherwise than as a stranger? Away, then, with those whining, canting professions, of fears and apprehensions of the danger of French influence. Intelligence must reject, and integrity abhor them."

The Federalists were appealing to the war-weary as the party of peace. The war-fever must be kept at a high temperature, so Van Buren wrote:

But to crown this picture of folly and of mischief, they [the Federalists] approach you under a garb which at once evinces their contempt for your understanding, and their total want of confidence in your patriotism; under a garb which should receive the most distinct marks of your detestation; they are *"the friends of peace!"* While our enemies are waging against us a cruel and bloody war, they cry "Peace." While our western wilds are whitening with the bones of our murdered women and children—while their blood is yet trickling down the walls of their former habitations—while the Indian war-whoop and the British drum, are in unison saluting the ears, and the British dagger and the Indian tomahawk suspended over the heads of our citizens,—at such a time, when the soul of every man who has sensibility to feel his country's wrongs, and spirit to defend her rights, should be in arms—it is that they cry *peace!* While the brave American tar, the intrepid defender of our rights, and redeemer of our national character, the present boast and future honor of our land—is impressed by force into a service he detests, which compels a brother to imbrue his hands in a brother's blood—while he is yet "tossing upon the surface of the ocean, and mingling his groans with those tempests less savage than his persecutors, that waft him to a returnless distance from his family and his home,"—it is at such a period, when there is no peace, when there can be no peace, without sacrificing every thing valuable—*that our feelings are insulted, the public arm paralyzed, and the public ear stunned, by the dastardly* and incessant cry of *peace!* . . . Can any man be so stupid as not to perceive that it is an appeal *to your fears, to your avarice,* and to all the baser passions which actuate the human heart? That it is approaching you in the manner in which alone those puny politicians who buz about you, and thicken the political atmosphere, say you are accessible, *through your fears and your pockets?* Can any American citizen be so profligate as not to spurn indignantly the base libel upon his character?

The phrase in the last sentence but one, *puny politicians . . . say you are accessible through your fears and your pockets,* is a variant of a line of Alexander Hamilton, sacredly cherished by Van Buren throughout his political career. To have used the phrase in its original purity would have left him open to the charge of invading the sanctity of the tomb. So by changing the word *interests* to *pockets* and making other slight changes, he avoided this charge.

But it is not enough to accuse the leaders of the opposition with materialism: they must be made odious; and what would be more serviceable in this respect than to identify the Federalists of 1812 with the Tories of 1776? And thus Van Buren did it:

Fellow-citizens—should those political witlings, who are not only ignorant themselves of the leading points of controversy in our disputes with the belligerents, but who are uniformly assailing you as men destitute at once of spirit and of judgment—should they point to the wars which agitate and have convulsed Europe, as arguments against the prosecution of that just and necessary one which has been forced upon us, we know that you will indignantly repel the unfounded suggestion. The wars of Europe are waged by monarchs, to gratify their individual malice, their individual caprice, and to satiate their lawless ambition. Ours is in defence of rights which must be defended, or our glory as a nation will be extinguished—the sun of our greatness will set forever. As well might it have been said during the revolution, that war should not be waged, because wars had desolated Europe. *The same rights you then fought to obtain, you must now fight to preserve—the contest is the same now as it was then—and the feelings which then agitated the public mind, which on the one hand supported, and on the other sought to destroy, the liberties of the country, will be seen and felt in the conduct of the men of this day.*

He again displays an acquaintance with world politics in:

We solicit the honest men of *all parties*—to remember that ours is the last republic—that all the influence of the crowned heads of Europe has been exerted to propagate the doctrine, that a government like ours can never stand the rude shock of war; to reflect that this is the first occasion in which this government has been engaged in a war, and that the great and interesting questions, whether man is capable of self-government, whether our republic must go the way of its predecessors, or whether, supported by the hearts and arms of her free citizens, she shall deride the revilings, and defeat the machinations of her citizens, are *now to be tried.*

After using the argument of the Madisonians in their successful fight against Clinton a few months before, that the issue is "who is for his country or against his country," and that all Europe is watching the polls, he ended his appeal with:

*To the polls,* then, and by a united and vigorous support of the candidates we submit to you, discharge the great duty you owe to

your country, preserve for your posterity the rich inheritance which
has been left you by your ancestors,—that future ages may triumphantly point to the course you pursued on this interesting occasion,
as evidence that time had not as yet extinguished that spirit which
actuated the heroes of *Breedshill* and of *Yorktown;* of those who fell
at *Camden,* and of those who conquered on the plains of *Saratoga.*

But while Van Buren was showered with praise by the enemies of Clinton for writing the appeal, his old friend from
Columbia County, Sheriff Hogeboom, drove to Albany through
the snow when he read of the latest honor thrust on Van Buren.
Hogeboom told Van Buren that a decent respect for the old
friendship between him and Clinton, in which Van Buren shared,
required that Van Buren play the part of a neutral in the campaign. Tompkins, whom Clinton had made Governor, as he had
made Van Buren Surrogate, inspired the attack on his patron.
Tompkins wanted to be President.

Van Buren weakly replied that the support of Tompkins
meant the support of the war. In high dudgeon the honest old
Dutchman abruptly ended the conversation and their friendship,
and forthwith began a warfare on Van Buren that did not stop
with politics, but extended to Van Buren's clients, and lasted
for several years.

A few days after Clinton's rejection, the Federalist Council
of Appointment removed Van Buren as Surrogate. This did not
surprise him: it was part of the game. And had he held the
Attorney Generalship—he still believed Clinton kept him out of
this place—he would have been displaced, as Emmet had been.

The Federalists were relying on the support of Clinton's
friends and sympathizers in the spring elections. The Patroon
was their candidate for Governor, and they hoped his war
record would win him thousands of Republican votes. Their confidence was increased when forty-one leading Republicans—Clintonians all—including United States Senator German, publicly
assailed the Madison administration, and decried Tompkins and
Tayler as mere partisans and tools of Madison. Reports from
the country districts where Clinton had a large following indicated victory for the Federalists, who had not elected a Governor
since 1799.

The New York election held the attention of the country.

The New England States were opposed to the continuance of the war, and fears were entertained that a Federalist triumph in the Empire State might force the Government to make a disgraceful peace. The Patroon had condemned the National government for its handling of the campaign on the Canadian border in resigning his command. The Government was without credit. A resolution empowering the State to lend five hundred thousand dollars to the Government passed the Senate, but was defeated by the Federalists in the Assembly; every measure in support of the war which passed the Republican Senate was defeated by the lower house. A disgraceful peace was not an idle fancy.

No one in Albany worked harder in support of these war measures than Van Buren. All who had business at the State capitol thronged into the Senate when Van Buren, or Morgan Lewis, the former Governor, or Erastus Root, was speaking. An attentive follower of Van Buren's war speeches was the silver-haired Senator from Schoharie County, Henry Hager, who bore wounds received on the battlefields of the Revolution. After Van Buren finished an unusually moving address, Hager, his eyes filled with tears, walked over to Van Buren's seat and embracing him, kissed him on both cheeks. And again the chamber rang with applause.

There was gloom among the other Republicans in the Legislature as they received advices from their homes; old-line Republicans, tired of the war, or the way it was being bungled, were openly working for the Patroon. When the votes were counted it showed that the Federalists still controlled the Assembly, but that the Republican candidates for Governor and Lieutenant Governor were elected by the bare majority of 3,606 votes.

Van Buren's leadership was strengthened.

## CHAPTER XV

In March of 1813 Van Buren sat for the first time in the Court for the Correction of Errors. This highest tribunal, for the convenience of the majority of its members, held its sessions in Albany during the legislative session. In common with others brought up in the country Van Buren regarded the Debtors' Prison as the most abominable institution existing in the Republic. Outside of New York City a debtor was lodged in the same jail which immured felons. He noted that this relic of barbarism was perpetuated by his own profession, and unscrupulous merchants who persuaded the poor to make purchases beyond their means and trust to the sympathy of the neighbors of the unfortunate to pay the debt to get him out of jail. Thurlow Weed, speaking of his boyhood in the village where Van Buren was married, described the lot of one of these unfortunates with tears:

In those days, hard as it may seem now, poor men, however honest, lived in dread of *Imprisonment!* My father was one of a class whom ill-fortune tracked through life. He worked hard, but never prospered. His horse was always sick, or lame, or was backing the cart off the Dock. The Debtors' Prison, therefore, was ever staring us in the face. But there was this blessed mitigation of the horrors of a Debtors' Prison. There were Gaol Liberties connected with the prison, of which a debtor, with a reputation for honesty, and a wealthy friend who would sign his bond to remain upon the "Limits," might avail himself. The Limits, accurately defined, extended to business parts of the Village, so that a poor man stood some chance of keeping the wolf from devouring his wife and children. This, however, was not the full measure of the Law's humanity. On Sunday the debtor was free! And on these days of jubilee I used to roam with my enfranchised father down to the "Point," over to the Shad Fishery, or up to Jefferson, with a deep sense of gratitude that he was permitted, one day in the week, to walk God's earth, and breathe His atmosphere, unrestrained. Creditors were on the watch, always, for truant debtors, who sometimes failed to return to the Limits before twelve o'clock on Sunday night.

In Van Buren's first sitting in the Court for the Correction of Errors, one of these cases was up on appeal. A short time before, the Legislature had softened the lot of the debtors to the extent of permitting them to be liberated on bond, the "liberties" or "limits" in country districts being a fixed radius of which the jail was the center. In this particular case the debtor was a poor farmer. While at "liberty" pasturing his only cow, the bovine wandered "four, six, or ten feet" beyond the imaginary line. The farmer followed his cow for "four, six, or ten feet" beyond the "limits," and immediately returned within bounds. His vigilant creditor was at hand and sued to recover the amount of the bond. A justice of the peace held that there was an "escape" and decided for the creditor. The Supreme Court, James Kent presiding—the author of the *Commentaries* did not rise to the dignity of Chancellor until 1814—affirmed the harsh decision of the lower court.

Van Buren, in an opinion reversing the findings of the lower courts, showed his intense feeling by characterizing, inferentially, Kent and all others who held to the strict letter of the law, as wanting in intelligence, reflection, and philanthropy. He said:

Coeval with the authority of imprisonment for debt, have been the exertions of men of intelligence, reflection and philanthropy, to mitigate its rigor; of men who viewed it as a practice fundamentally wrong, a practice which forces their fellow creatures from society, from their friends and their agonized families, into the dreary walls of a prison; which compels them to leave all those fascinating endearments, to become an inmate with vermin; which confines them within the same walls which contain the midnight incendiary and the ruthless assassin; not for crimes which they have committed; not for frauds which they have practised on the credulous and unwary; (for such distinctions are not made;) but for the misfortune of being poor; of being unable to satisfy the all-digesting stomach of some ravenous creditor; of men who looked upon the practice as confounding virtue and vice, and destroying the distinction between guilt and innocence, which should unceasingly be cherished in every well regulated government.

Van Buren's enemies said that he never rose above the stature of a pettifogging country lawyer. The fragment we have culled from his decision in the case of Barry *vs.* Mandel destroys this least of the canards circulated by his foes. A month later he introduced a bill entitled "An Act for the Relief of Small Debtors" which the Senate passed, as a gesture of friendliness to him, knowing that even were the Assembly Republican, it would be doomed there, as neither the legal profession nor the merchant class was prepared to grant any further concessions toward debtors. In succeeding sessions he introduced similar measures, capping them in 1818 with "An Act to Abolish Imprisonment for Debt and to Punish Fraud." This also passed the Senate and died in the Assembly.

Toward the end of the session of 1813, the agents for the Bank of America performed a feat without parallel for many years. In order to give those who voted for the bank's charter an excuse for their constituents, the institution had agreed to pay a bonus of $400,000 to the common school fund. A bill was introduced reducing the bonus to $100,000. This meant an outright gift to the bank, in which, of course, the corrupt legislators would share.

Van Buren and Root led the opposition to this audacious measure. Daniel Paris, who was serving his fourth year in the body, was presiding during the debate. The opponents and friends of the measure were violent in their language. Excitement ran high; and while Van Buren was in the midst of his attack on this particular iniquity of the lobby whores—they were not called lobbyists until shortly before the Civil War—Senator Paris rose, reeled, and fell back in his chair in a faint.

The bill passed, and went to the Council of Revision, which included the judges of the Supreme Court. One of them, Judge William W. Van Ness—sometimes confused with Van Buren's preceptor and Burr's second, who was also a judge, having been appointed to the United States Circuit Court a few months back —received $5,000 for favoring the measure. This same judge, some years earlier, while an Assemblyman, was the agent of the Merchants Bank, when it bribed the Legislature. In the granting of the bank charters the Governor had no voice.

In this session Van Buren exposed the sham of the banking system of the day, a system which was little short of legalized robbery. Van Buren's speech was on his motion to reject the bill chartering the Catskill Bank. He bared the sordid corruption of the banks in obtaining their charters, and in robbing the public. He labored long on the eight pages of closely written notes he held in his hand as he denounced the great evil, which he was destined, a quarter of a century later, to destroy.

. . . The very manner in which our banks go into operation, on what is called foreign paper, shows that the idea of redemption by specie is not indulged in at their very inception. . . . At the commencement of the banking business, it was confined to men of high notions of credit; confidence must of necessity be destroyed by throwing the management of it, with chartered privileges, into the hands of everybody.

Meantime, what is the situation of the State? First, specie is driven out of circulation; next, trade becomes extensive in the proportion in which the amount of supposed cash has been extended. But the value of everything bears a proportion to the value of your money. The good-sense of the community must ultimately impair confidence in bank paper; the failure of a single bank would consummate it. And when paper-money is all the money we can depend upon to answer the purposes of trade, a depreciation in its value not only produces a like depreciation in the value of property, but an entire stagnation in business.

Against only the sources of danger thus far delineated, what are the inducements to continue the accumulation of banks? Can any one doubt but that the increase of banks must, some time or other, lead to their destruction? Can any one say or expect that there will be a more fit opportunity to stop than now? . . .

When the Legislature adjourned in the middle of April, Van Buren returned to Hudson, stopping at Kinderhook to visit his parents as he had done on week-ends during the session when the roads were not too high in snow. He was glad to get home; he now had three children, all boys, and the third, some four months old, was named for him.

During the summer he did considerable horseback riding between Hudson and Kinderhook. His father, now retired and living the life of a country squire, was sixty-eight, and the devout little woman looked little more than fifty, although she was only two years her helpmeet's junior. She was always recalling little incidents of Martin's boyhood, pleasant ones all, for somehow she had forgotten all the hardships of those early years.

It now seemed as though they had never wanted for anything; but then no one ever does who has trust in the Lord. This was her simple faith. But there was little of the objective religious note in Van Buren. He has left us only two quotations from the Bible, one a brief line, and the other five verses from the Acts. These occurred to him as he watched Madison deriving advantage by dividing his political foes, as Paul had done to escape from his enemies.

This part of Acts 23 is the guide of many political leaders; but to get the full flavor that Van Buren found in the five verses he cited, it is necessary to summarize the events leading up to the scene described in the quotation. A mob in Jerusalem had seized the Apostle and was about to slay him when he was rescued by soldiers of Cæsar, who took him before the high priest Ananias. And Paul said that he had lived in good conscience before God, whereupon Ananias commanded that Paul be smitten on the mouth. And the free-born man of Tarsus cried out: "God shall smite thee, thou whited wall; for sittest thou to judge me after the law, and commandest me to be smitten contrary to the law?" The reviling of their high priest incensed the people. Now follows the passage which guided Van Buren in his struggle for place and power:

6 But when Paul perceived that the one part were Sadducees, and the other Pharisees, he cried out in the council, Men and brethren, I am a Pharisee, the son of a Pharisee: of the hope and resurrection of the dead I am called in question.

7 And when he had so said, there arose a dissension between the Pharisees and the Sadducees: and the multitude was divided.

8 For the Sadducees say that there is no resurrection, neither angel, nor spirit: but the Pharisees confess both.

9 And there arose a great cry: and the scribes that were of the Pharisees' part arose, and strove, saying, We find no evil in this man: but if a spirit or an angel hath spoken to him, let us not fight against God.

10 And when there arose a great dissension, the chief captain, fearing lest Paul should have been pulled in pieces of them, commanded the soldiers to go down, and to take him by force from among them, and to bring him into the castle.

With the coming of the New Year Van Buren made preparations for another legislative session. Although war was raging, much of the talk on Capitol Hill was of the Presidential election of 1816, a good two years away. Governor Tompkins, confident that the nomination would come to New York, considered himself the heir-apparent of Madison, now that Clinton was out of the way; and he was making friendly overtures to all of the leading Clintonians. Tompkins did not regard the candidacy of Armstrong as formidable. The Secretary of War was a Livingston; that would alienate the needed Clintonian strength from his cause. And by the time another year or so had passed, Tompkins hoped to make his peace with Clinton.

Van Buren missed the aid of John W. Taylor of Saratoga, a man of his own years, who had been most helpful to him in the lower house. Taylor was in Congress now. It was Taylor who said that he "never knew a man who had fixed his hopes upon the presidency who would not sacrifice all his personal considerations, and all pre-existing friendships to attain his object." Taylor served his State many years in the National Capitol, and was several times elected Speaker. He was only citing the record in uttering this cynical truism. Taylor was a regular correspondent of Van Buren, and kept him informed of the political moves in Washington.

The Legislature convened Tuesday, January 25. The Federalists resumed their policy of obstructing all war measures. They were but paralleling their partisans in Congress where another Elisha Williams had distinguished himself a week the Friday past in opposing the enlistment bounty bill. He was younger than Williams, and represented New Hampshire in the House of Representatives. His name was Daniel Webster. He answered the charge that Federal opposition was responsible for the failure of the war by saying that that was not a new strain. Then he added:

"It has been sung a thousand times; it is the constant tune of every weak or wicked Administration. What Minister ever yet acknowledged that the evils which fell on his country were the necessary consequence of his own incapacity, his own folly, or his own corruption? What possessor of political power ever yet failed to charge the mischiefs resulting from his own measures, upon those who had uniformly opposed those measures?"

And then he proved, by the logic now used by the Madison administration, that Lord North had not lost the American Colonies to England, but that the fault lay with those who had forewarned him that his disastrous policy would disaffect the Colonies: Chatham, with his impertinent boldness; Fox, with his idle declamation; and Barré, with his unseasonable sarcasm.

Webster painted the horrors of civil war with a few bold strokes in his reference to the Canadian campaign: "Canada, they [the Americans] know, is not to be conquered but by drenching its soil in the blood of its inhabitants. They have no thirst for that blood. The borderers, on the line, connected by blood and marriage, and all the ties of social life, have no disposition to bear arms against one another. Merciless indeed has been the fate of some of these people. . . . In some of the affairs which we call battles, because we have nothing else to give the name to, brother has been in arms against brother. The bosom of the parent has been exposed to the bayonet of his own son. Sir, I honor the people that shrink from a warfare like this."

The failures of the campaigns, Webster truthfully asserted, were not due to want of natural resources. "The Northern States alone are able to overrun Canada in thirty days, armed or unarmed, in any cause which should propel them by inducements sufficiently powerful. Recur, sir, to history. As early as 1745, the New England Colonies raised an army of five thousand men, and took Louisburg from the troops of France. On what point of enemy's territory, let me ask, have you brought an equal force to bear in the whole course of two campaigns? On another occasion, more than half a century ago, Massachusetts alone, although its population did not exceed one-third of its present amount, had an army of twelve thousand men. Of these, seven thousand were at one time employed against Canada. A strong motive was then felt to exist. With equal exertion that Commonwealth could now furnish an army of forty thousand men."

Webster recalled that our troops had been able to drive the enemy back to their own line each time they invaded us, but that our arms did not pass that line, because they did not choose to pass it. This was to support his utterances that "the world will not ascribe the issue to want of spirit or patriotism in the American people."

In his long public career Van Buren met and quarreled with many: all were forgiven save Webster; for him he cherished an undying hate; and not without cause. It was to be years before these two Titans were to meet.

There were other days when Webster and other ultra-Federalists sat silent in their seats. These were the occasions when the atrocities committed by Indians and British on the Western frontier were recounted. New York's legislative session of 1814 was well-nigh fruitless. All war measures were killed by the Federalist Assembly. Only two bills of moment became law. One legalized lotteries for the aid of Union College, Columbia College, and two other institutions of learning now no more. Union College received $200,000 of the amount raised. Everybody gambled. Investigations of a later day disclosed that the public had little or no chance in these lotteries. The big prizes generally went to secret representatives of influential politicians. The second bill provided that children of the poor might attend the common schools without cost on a majority vote of the district trustees.

Almost simultaneously with the opening of the session, Winfield Scott, then a Colonel, arrived in Albany after conferences with Madison and his Secretary of War. "At this dark period of the war," wrote Scott, "Albany, rather than Washington, was the watchtower of the nation." Scott was under orders to remain in Albany until his commission as Brigadier General reached him, when he was to return to the Canadian frontier.

Scott's mission to Albany was political as well as military. In the day he supervised the dispatch of military trains from the arsenal to the Canadian frontier, and performed other work of a soldier. At night he was in conference with Governor Tompkins and other Republican leaders "on high political and military matters." Ambrose Spencer, the most conspicuous war Republican in the North, was at these gatherings, and "Van Buren—then emerging into distinction, . . . now began to mix a little in the reunions alluded to."

Scott was twenty-nine, two years younger than Van Buren, and they became fast friends. Scott, no mean politician himself, complimented Van Buren by predicting that he would round out his career as President. Scott is silent on Van Buren's reply.

Then came the happy morning in the middle of March when

the post brought Scott his commission. There were few things remaining to be done in Albany before he could start for the Niagara frontier. After leaving the post office with the precious parchment, he met Van Buren on the street. Van Buren congratulated Scott on hearing the news.

"General," added Van Buren, "we must celebrate this happy event. Come to my house this evening; I'll invite a few friends, and we'll take a glass of wine and a few oysters together."

Scott promptly accepted. As he did so, Van Buren suddenly remembered that he was host to one well-nigh penniless, and by many regarded as a traitor. Betraying a little embarrassment, he hastily added:

"General, I forgot something which I ought to have mentioned before asking you to my house. Colonel Burr is stopping with me for a few days. Have you any objection to meet him?"

"Any gentlemen, Mr. Van Buren, whom you think proper to present me to, I shall be happy to know," replied the soldier.

Burr had returned to his native land nearly two years before, after his self-exile in Europe. Many of his old acquaintances cut him on the street, and Burr, on seeing an acquaintance of happier days approaching, would glance furtively out of the corner of his eye: and if he apprehended a snub, he would look the other way. The Madison administration was hostile to Burr, and this was in the mind of the ever cautious Van Buren when he apprised Scott of Burr's presence in his lodgings.

After the oysters and wine had been served, Scott, Van Buren, and Burr sat down to a game of whist with a fourth man, unnamed by Scott. Burr was Scott's partner and they got on famously.

"General Scott, I have seen you before," said Burr as a trick was taken.

The younger soldier remembered the occasion well: it was at the trial of Burr for treason at Richmond. He was visibly embarrassed as he stammered:

"Have you, Colonel? And where was it?"

The courteous Burr, whose piercing brown eyes were fixed on Scott, played a card, and in his courtly yet careless tone, and with his characteristic short, sharp phrases, answered:

"At Richmond; in the court room; at my trial. You stood on

the lock of the door above the crowd. I noticed you at the time:
it was on the first day."

The massive lock of wrought iron was again under Scott's
feet as Burr revived the scene in the court room. Scott was tall,
and the added height of his perch had attracted the attention of
the prisoner at the bar. Scott was impressed with the detached,
impersonal manner of Burr in discussing his trial: he might have
been talking of the cause of a client; and Burr was pleased with
the marvelous memory and delightful conversation of his partner.
Scott had an eye and ear for everything: the picture painted by
Parton of the scenes inside and outside the court, the demeanor
of the judges and lawyers, and of Burr himself was from the
imprint of Scott's recollections.

While they talked of politics and the war, Burr exclaimed:

"There is a man in Tennessee to whom Jimmy Madison will
not give a commission because he is a friend of mine; but he is
equal to any service. I mean Andrew Jackson. If they give him a
commission, things will go better in the western country."

This recalled to Scott a vivid scene in Richmond during the
trial. He was in a crowd gathered around a fiery speaker whose
rostrum was the steps of a grocery. The orator was defending
Burr as the victim of a political conspiracy, and accused Jefferson of being his persecutor. Scott asked a bystander the name of
Burr's champion.

"A great blackguard from Tennessee, one Andrew Jackson,"
he was told.

It was a late hour when Scott said good-night, or good-
morning, to his amiable host and his delightful guest. Ten weeks
later Madison commissioned Jackson a Major General in the
regular army.

Burr was in Albany attending the Court for the Correction
of Errors. On learning this, Van Buren invited him to his lodgings by way of returning the hospitality shown him at Richmond
Hill.

As in 1813, Van Buren drafted the Senate's reply to the
Governor's address to the Legislature, and again he wrote the
party's appeal to the voters. Seven of the eight Senators elected
this spring were Republicans. Among them was Moses I. Cantine,
Van Buren's brother-in-law. The Republicans also elected a ma-

jority of the Assembly, giving them control of both branches of the Legislature for the first time since the war started.

Early in July, Van Buren, who had been watching the campaign on the Canadian frontier with redoubled personal interest, was heartened by the victorious charges of Scott and his men at the battles of Lundy's Lane and Chippewa. After routing the British with an inferior force in the latter engagement, Scott was carried from the field with an ugly musket wound in his shoulder.

This news from the Niagara frontier offset the intelligence that a powerful British fleet was operating in Chesapeake Bay and menacing Washington. And from New York came word that Clinton, once more Mayor, had appealed to citizens without respect to condition or party to lend their services and their wealth for the defense of the city.

Clinton's appeal was published Tuesday, August 2. On Saturday all organized groups in the city, with descriptive banners planted beside them, began throwing up earthworks at strategic points. The crafts engaged were enumerated in a jingle of the day from which we quote:

> Plumbers, founders, dyers, tinners, tanners, shavers,
> Sweepers, clerks, and criers, jewelers, engravers,
> Clothiers, drapers, players, cartmen, hatters, nailers,
> Gaugers, scalers, weighers, carpenters, and sailors.

Schoolboys able to swing a pick and shovel did the work of men, while lads of tenderer age carried dirt on fire shovels and shingles. When the work was done, Samuel Woodworth stirred the town with a poem addressed to the enemy which ended with the stanza:

> Better not invade; recollect the spirit
> Which our dads displayed and their sons inherit.
> If you still advance, friendly caution slighting,
> You may get, by chance, a bellyful of fighting.
>     Pick-axe, shovel, spade, crowbar, hoe and barrow;
>     Better not invade; Yankees have the marrow.

No one in the city had been more zealous in preparing the city and its environs against attack of a marauding fleet than Clinton. From the very beginning of hostilities he was foremost in rendering real aid to the State and Federal governments in their prosecution of the war. At his initiative the city raised the funds to pay the militia quartered within its boundaries. He applied to the Governor for a command. Tompkins, raised from obscurity by Clinton, declined to grant this request; and unblushingly gave as his reason that Clinton was opposed to the war.

Clinton ignored the rebuff. The city's credit was good, and he loaned the State $300,000; and advanced $1,400,000 through the State to the National government as United States Treasury notes were regarded as almost worthless.

To make this second loan effective, it was necessary for Tompkins, as Governor, to indorse the United States notes before the banks would accept them as collateral. An agent of Clinton obtained the promise of Tompkins to indorse them; but when he called on him, the Governor said that he must hasten to Albany as Mrs. Tompkins was about to be accouched. Later, when pressed to sign the collateral, the Governor denied ever making the promise.

At this moment of national peril Rufus King asked Tompkins to indorse the Treasury notes. Tompkins replied that he would have to act on his own responsibility and would probably be ruined.

"Ruin yourself if it becomes necessary to save the country, and I pledge you my honor that I will support you in whatever you do," said King.

Tompkins signed the notes.

Still there was much concern over the arrival in American waters of England's veterans of the Napoleonic Wars, and the burning of the National Capitol by the enemy in the middle of the month was not forgotten in the repulse of the invading troops at Baltimore. Armstrong, made the scapegoat for the Washington disaster, resigned from the Cabinet. Tompkins was now New York's only favorite.

Early in September fourteen thousand British troops crossed the St. Lawrence and invaded New York. A naval force flying the crosses of St. Andrew and St. George, coöperated, and sailed into Lake Champlain—each drop of this long narrow body of water lay in the United States, the eastern shore being part of Vermont's western boundary line. On the morning of September

11 the land and sea forces of Great Britain began their offensive, the guns of his Majesty's ships opening up the two-and-a-half-hour performance on the lake.

The American squadron lay in the harbor of Plattsburg, under command of Thomas MacDonough, a pious Gael of thirty years. Before the battle he gathered his officers around him on the deck of the *Saratoga* and all knelt in prayer. MacDonough's flagship was supported by a brig, two schooners, and ten galleys or gunboats. Commander Downie's opposing force was superior by two sloops and two gunboats.

One of the first shots of the invading squadron struck a hen coop on MacDonough's flagship, releasing a young game cock, the mascot of the ship. The bird crowed lustily throughout the battle from a gun slide. A rhymester thus described the incident:

> O, Johnny Bull, my Joe, John,
>      Behold on Lake Champlain,
> With more than equal force, John,
>      You tried your fist again;
> But the cock saw how 'twas going, John,
>      And cried "cock-a-doodle-doo,"
> And MacDonough was victorious, John,
>      O, Johnny Bull, my Joe.

Two weeks after the battle of Plattsburg, the Legislature met in a special session at the call of the Governor. Van Buren drafted the bill calling for conscripting twelve thousand troops. This act, which Benton described as "the most energetic war measure ever adopted in this country," became law on October 24.

Other war measures raised the pay of the State militia; created twenty companies of sea fencibles for the defense of the port of New York; authorized the raising of two regiments of blacks to serve for three years, slaves to join only with the consent of their masters, and to be manumitted when honorably discharged; empowered associations to engage in privateering.

In this special session Van Buren played what is euphemistically called practical politics. Solomon Southwick, who had waxed fat on that ancient perquisite, State printing, knowing that the Senate was about to name Jesse Buel State Printer, wrote in protest to Van Buren. Buel was owner of the Albany *Argus*. Southwick charged him with having loaned type to counterfeit United States Army bills. "That Buel committed this base and infamous crime is certain," wrote Southwick, "and if the Senate with the record of it on their journals can vote for his appointment,—Amen!" Van Buren pocketed the letter, and Buel was appointed.

This act would stamp Van Buren as dishonest in business; but in politics a man is an honest man if he is not personally corrupt. Moreover, Southwick was not making the charge because of purity of motives: he was Buel's rival for the place. Then again, Southwick was no longer serviceable to the politicians; for he had been caught passing them bribes. Van Buren was honest. But he was ambitious, and to use the language of a contrite thief of later days, he knew that "a politician in coming forward takes things as they are." Van Buren was as yet a politician.

Some of the war measures reënacted into law were criticized by Chancellor Kent. Samuel Young, the brilliant speaker of the Assembly, under the pseudonym, *Juris Consultus*, made reply in Buel's journal. Kent, under the pen name of *Amicus Curiæ*, answered with another series of letters. When these two worthy foemen had their turn, Van Buren entered the lists. His friends at first were apprehensive of the consequences to his reputation, but his contributions to the controversy, under the nom de plume of *Amicus Juris Consultus*, raised his legal stature.

While the Federalist legislators voted against every war measure, they did not send any representatives to that ill-conceived gathering, the Hartford Convention. The legislatures of Massachusetts, Connecticut, and Rhode Island sent delegates; two counties in New Hampshire, and one Vermont county, were also represented. The twenty-six New Englanders who met in Hartford on the second Thursday in December, and adjourned *sine die* on the first Thursday in January, were held up by the Republican press as a subcommittee of the Houses of Parliament. Harrison Gray Otis was the special target of the opposition. Among the delegates were jurists of the first rank such as James Hillhouse and Zephaniah Swift; men of affairs and philanthropists saw their spokesman in Daniel Waldo; George Cabot, a mere novice in politics, presided over the convention;

and more than ordinary patriotic flavor was given the assemblage by three officers who fought under Washington—Samuel
Ward, Hodijah Baylies, and Daniel Lyman.

There were men in New England who wanted their States
to secede from the Union. But Massachusetts chose Cabot to head
her delegation because of his opposition to "the young hot-
heads," as he called the extremists. The ambiguous language of
the resolutions adopted, and the impenetrable secrecy thrown
around the proceedings for nearly nineteen years, gave rise to
the wildest conjectures. History is replete with men who have
been indifferent to the falsehoods circulated by their adversaries:
Van Buren is a conspicuous example. But the Hartford Convention is the only public assemblage whose entire membership exercised a concerted contempt for public opinion. This is at once
glorious and grotesque. During the better part of two decades
the delegates let it be thoroughly fixed in the mind of the people,
and in the books written of the period, that their proceedings
were treasonable. They ignored challenges to publish the journal
of their deliberations: when it suited the twelve who remained of
the original delegation, the innocuous minutes were given to the
world.

Each delegate to the Hartford Convention was a fanatical
believer in State rights. Its remonstrance against the conduct
of the war, and the charges that the administration of Madison
had violated the Constitution, were predicated on this theory of
State sovereignty. Phrases like the following abound in the report
of the convention: ". . . if the Union be destined to dissolution, by
reason of the multiplied abuses of bad administration, it should,
if possible, be the work of peaceable times, and deliberate consent . . . a severance of the Union by one or more states, against
the will of the rest, and especially in a time of war, can be justified only by absolute necessity . . . in cases of deliberate, dangerous, and palpable infractions of the constitution, affecting
the sovereignty of a state, and liberties of the people, it is not
only right but the duty of such state to interpose its authority
for their protection, in the manner best calculated to secure that
end."

The New Englanders, in preparing this ideal brief for the

cause of the slave society of the South, snuffed the flickering candle of Federalism.

Three days after the Convention made public its report, Jackson won the Battle of New Orleans and a niche in the New World's Pantheon. At that moment, the treaty of peace, which had been signed on Christmas Eve, was on the high seas. The first news the people of the United States had of the success of the mission of Albert Gallatin, John Quincy Adams and their associates, was published in a special edition of a New York journal herewith reproduced:

### PEACE

Office of the New-York Gazette,
Saturday Evening, 11th Feb., 9 o'clock P. M.

It has pleased the Almighty to restore to us the blessings of peace.

We have just seen Henry Carroll, Esqr, Secretary to the American Legation. He informs us that he has arrived on the British Sloop of War *Favorite,* with the Treaty of Peace signed by the American and British Commissioners on the 24th of Dec. and that he is to depart for Washington in the morning. The vessel is below, and will be up to-morrow.

The special edition was printed in large type which filled one side of a sheet of octavo size. It was more like a small handbill than a newspaper. A tavern brawl has been spun to the dimensions of a novel; the conquest of a people has been told in three words.

# CHAPTER XVI

WHEN the news of peace reached Albany Van Buren was in the midst of preparations for a war that was to keep him embroiled for nearly half a century. He was venturing in Presidential politics. There was a likelihood that he would succeed where the Clintons and Livingstons had failed—in ending the sway of the Virginia Dynasty. The statesmen and politicians of Virginia seemed submissive to the inevitable. Madison himself had shown the way by inviting Governor Tompkins to accept the office of Secretary of State, a post which had led to the Presidency since the days of Washington. The tender carried with it the understanding that Monroe would be made Secretary of War after resigning as heir-apparent. Tompkins responded that he could be of better service to the nation as Governor of New York.

Of immediate moment was the election of a successor to United States Senator German, whose term would expire March 4. The Livingstons, hoping to restore their shattered political fortunes, backed Armstrong. Clinton's brother-in-law had been his chief sponsor. But now Spencer was allied with Van Buren who was working quietly to keep the Livingstons down. When the Republicans met the contest lay between Spencer and Nathan Sanford. The latter was a lawyer and a crony of Van Buren, and he passed the word that Tompkins favored Sanford.

Spencer, not being a member of the Legislature, was not present at the caucus. But his friends were there, and when Van Buren announced that he did not believe Spencer wanted the nomination, which was equivalent to election, the Spencerians truthfully replied that Van Buren was in error. This Van Buren knew, but he was inventing a means to enable Spencer's friends to withdraw his name. They declined the suggestion, and challenged the word of Van Buren by moving the appointment of a committee to wait on Spencer and request him to inform the caucus if he would accept the nomination. This was opposed by Van Buren, who asked that the caucus ballot immediately on

Sanford and Spencer. The Spencerians called for a vote on their motion, which was carried.

The friends of Spencer did not dare push his claim beyond the point they had. It would not do to fly in the face of Tompkins, who was more than Governor: he was the State's choice for the Presidency. His wishes could not be brushed lightly aside on the eve of a national campaign, and when the caucus reassembled the committee reported that Spencer was not a candidate "because he would not put himself in competition with so young a man as Mr. Sanford." This naïve thrust at the candidate of Van Buren and Tompkins carried with it the noted jurist's acknowledgment that the patronage and power they wielded insured their control of the caucus. Sanford was elected.

Spencer felt that he had been ungenerously treated by Van Buren. He had vainly tried to have Van Buren appointed Attorney General three years before. Van Buren was now a candidate for the place, which was held by a Federalist, Abraham Van Vechten, successor of Emmet. Spencer, jealous of Van Buren's growing power, and chagrined by his defeat, threw his influence behind John Woodworth, Van Buren's rival.

The Council of Appointment met on February 17. Two of the four Senators voted for Woodworth, and two for Van Buren. In this situation the Governor cast the deciding vote for Van Buren, who after the manner of the day, held both offices.

Until this day, Van Buren's high legal talents were known only to the bar. But to the people the Attorney General of the State, by virtue of his office alone, was a great lawyer. His predecessors, without exception, were men of recognized worth: Van Vechten, Emmet, Hildreth, Spencer, Josiah Ogden Hoffman, Lewis, Aaron Burr; and Burr's predecessor, Egbert Benson, first Attorney General.

Not long after his appointment, Van Buren moved his family to Albany, which was his home for the next fourteen years. His slave, Tom, did not get along with the other blacks in the State capital, so he became a runaway. Van Buren made no effort to get him back. He replaced him with a hired man, a free negro.

On Washington's Birthday Albany celebrated the signing of the Treaty of Peace. Wine flowed freely. At the Eagle Tavern where the Tammany legislators lodged—they were no longer be-

ing called Martling men, as they had their own Wigwam—a
transparency was hung, which read: Tompkins and Crawford.
Thus did Tammany, which paid tribute to Van Buren, acknowledge its fealty to the Governor. William H. Crawford, their
choice for Vice President, was United States Senator from
Georgia, and a Virginian by birth. And countless toasts were
drunk to Van Buren, Tompkins, and Crawford.

The patrons of the Eagle Tavern were grateful to Van
Buren and Tompkins because they were enemies of De Witt
Clinton. After the April elections, when the Federalists elected
a majority of the common council in New York City, the Tammany men and their up-State allies pressed for the removal of
Clinton as Mayor. For many months past Clinton had been sat-
irized in a number of brilliant articles signed *Abimaleck Coody*,
who professed to be a humble maker of women's shoes. The author
was Gulian C. Verplanck. Clinton replied in a series of letters
signed *Traveller*. Clinton, unequaled in political polemics, in one
of his responses said that Verplanck "has become the head of
a political sect called the Coodies, of hybrid nature, composed
of the combined spawn of Federalism and Jacobinism, and gen-
erated in the venomous passions of disappointment and revenge,
without any definite character; neither fish nor flesh, nor bird nor
beast, but a nondescript made up of all monstrous, all prodigious
things." Thenceforward anti-Clintonians were called Coodies.

The faction of the Coodies led by Verplanck and Spencer
wanted Peter W. Radcliff, State Senator, appointed Mayor of
New York. The Tammany men pressed the cause of John Ferguson, their Grand Sachem. Tammany, whose membership increased considerably because of its zealous advocacy of the war,
could not be ignored. Radcliff was vastly superior in talents to
Ferguson and had been Mayor under a Federalist Council of
Appointment in 1810. Van Buren strove to please both sides,
so a bargain was struck to name Ferguson Mayor until a Federal office with patronage could be obtained for him. Ferguson
was Mayor but a short time, the Madison administration appointing him Surveyor of the Port of New York, and Radcliff
succeeded him.

They had a reason, of course, for removing Clinton: he had
not been loyal during the war! And that his brother-in-law would

have part in his removal on such a malicious pretext is baffling only to those unacquainted with the hatreds engendered by partisan politics. Van Buren had offered a mild protest to Tompkins against Clinton's removal. He regarded the displacement as impolitic—nothing more.

The sentiments of the people were voiced by Emmet and Dr. William J. MacNeven, when they wrote, on behalf of a vast majority of their race: "We prefer the moment of your retreat from office for the expression of our deep sense of your manifold and important services to the public." As this is the only time we shall see these two Fenian leaders together, let us visit St. Paul's churchyard, where two obeliscal cenotaphs flank the house of worship which Washington attended when New York was the seat of the new Republic. MacNeven lies in the family burying ground on Long Island, and Emmet sleeps in a vault in St. Mark's in-the-Bouwerie. These monuments loom high above Broadway, and dwarf their fellows in this resting place of not a few of the country's illustrious ones. The curious will be repaid by a walk around these obelisks; for the epitaphs are graven in Gaelic, in English, and in faultless Latin. The inscriptions in the Roman tongue are the product of William A. Duer. There were hundreds of other minor politicians who could have done the work of Duer.

Base as was Spencer's part in the removal of Clinton, the Governor's complicity was far more reprehensible. Tompkins owed all to Clinton. It was Clinton who had him appointed to the Supreme Court, and it was Clinton who brought about his nomination for the Governorship. But Tompkins had Presidential aspirations.

The Council of Appointment made Ruggles Hubbard Sheriff of New York County. Hubbard, a member of the State Senate, resided in Troy, a full day's journey from New York. Tompkins and Van Buren had precedent for appointing him; the Clintons in 1801 imported Sylvanus Miller from Kingston to be Surrogate of New York County. Miller was talented and honest. Hubbard was a drunkard, dissolute, and corrupt: this was known to every one in Albany. Tammany welcomed Hubbard, and elected him Grand Sachem, but Hubbard did not remain long in the city. He fled on August 15, 1817, to escape arrest, his accounts being short thousands of dollars.

Before the two houses adjourned *sine die* on April 18 the Legislature met in joint session to elect a Regent of the University of the State of New York. Hitherto all who had held this office were men with degrees, or of recognized scholarship. A precedent was established in conferring this honor on Martin Van Buren.

In the spring elections the people showed their resentment over the removal of Clinton by electing many Federalist candidates for the Assembly in Republican districts; and the two parties, for the first time in the history of the State, were evenly divided in the popular branch. One of the Senators chosen from the Southern District was Jacob Barker, the most influential banker in New York City. Barker was overlord of Tammany, and always a friend of Van Buren.

The removal of Clinton had strengthened him with the voters, many regarding him as a martyr. For five years he had labored, without reward, aided by the Patroon and others, to unite the Great Lakes with the Hudson River, by means of a canal. Tammany by formal resolutions had denounced the idea as "so visionary and absurd that no rational man for one moment, could seriously entertain it."

Tompkins was an implacable foe of the canal. At the preceding regular session of the Legislature, unknown to the friends of the proposed improvement, Van Buren and others had a joker slipped into the supply bill repealing the authority of the Canal Commission to borrow the needed money to construct the inland waterway.

# CHAPTER XVII

At the close of the legislative session of 1815, Van Buren had served three of his four years' term as Senator. He had become thoroughly acclimatized to the intrigue-laden atmosphere of legislative halls. But he was to learn more of the base designs of factious partisanship. The Virginia Dynasty was secretly opposing the candidacy of Tompkins and espousing that of one of its own, James Monroe, Madison's Secretary of State. Crawford, recalled from his embassy to France to serve as Secretary of War, was striving for first place, unwilling to be the choice for Vice President.

The pre-caucus campaign divided the New York Republicans into three factions. Clinton forgot his hatred of the Virginia Dynasty and joined hands with them to have revenge on Tompkins: he was for Monroe. Spencer supported Crawford. Van Buren and Tammany were for Tompkins.

Van Buren was puzzled. Early in December he went to Washington to look over the field. As he had suspected, Tompkins did not have a chance for first place. The New York members were in a quandary. One of them, Jabez B. Hammond the historian, asked Van Buren whom the New York delegation should support. He and Representative James Birdsall craned their heads forward as Van Buren meditated.

The question was obviously unpleasant. But Van Buren could not dodge it, so he replied: "We say Tompkins, of course." Instantly he turned the conversation into other channels. This was a favorite artifice with him.

When he left them, Hammond and Birdsall commented on his coldness to the candidacy of the Governor. They repeated his brief reply with the peculiar intonation he put on the last two words: "We say Tompkins, *of course.*" They could not resolve it; they were confessedly mystified.

The New York State Legislature convened on the last Tuesday of January. The Assembly was no longer evenly divided.

145

Three of the one hundred and twenty-six members of the lower house had passed on, and the opening roll-call showed sixty-two Republicans and sixty-one Federalists in their seats.

One of the Republican seats was held by Peter Allen through an election fraud committed by the County Clerk of Ontario. William A. Duer, then serving his second term as a Federalist member from Dutchess County, presented a petition praying the Assembly to unseat Allen and declare Henry Fellows, Federalist, duly elected. After Duer's plea was read, no one doubted that Fellows should be seated. But Van Buren and Governor Tompkins had secretly ordered to perpetuate the fraud long enough to give the Republicans, with their dishonest majority of one, sufficient time to choose the four Senators to serve with the Governor on the Council of Appointment during the ensuing year. If Fellows were seated before the Council was chosen, Van Buren would be removed as Attorney General, and nearly six thousand other Republicans holding civil office at the pleasure of the appointing power would be replaced with Federalists.

As set forth in Duer's petition, the clerk of Ontario County had wrongfully deprived Fellows of forty-nine votes in the town of Pennington. The inspectors of election had filed a certificate with the clerk of the town that Henry Fellows had received these votes. In the duplicate, sent to the county clerk, the candidate's name was written Hen. Fellows. The county clerk rejected these ballots, giving Allen a false majority of nineteen; and this corrupt official then certified that Allen had been elected.

Van Buren canvassed the Republicans in the Assembly who wanted to do the honest thing and seat the Federalist. He argued that if the situation had been reversed, the Federalists would do what he was counseling: to keep Allen in his seat and let him vote on every measure until the Council of Appointment was selected; once that was done, Fellows could be seated. Meanwhile, Van Buren cautioned the timid ones, they must vote against considering the petition of Duer until the Republicans had stolen the Council of Appointment from the Federalists.

Van Buren was seldom off the floor of the Assembly until the Council of Appointment had been chosen. So brazenly did he circulate among the wavering Republicans, that Peter A. Jay, a son of John Jay, pretended that he could not recall the name of a Republican Assemblyman with whom Van Buren was at that moment talking, said: "I mean the gentleman who always speaks with the Attorney General at his elbow." Van Buren blushed as the Federalist members applauded the sally, and presently Van Buren left the floor.

For eight days the Republicans kept Fellows out of his seat, and Allen voted on all measures. Every corrupt motion made by Henry Leavenworth, the Republican member from Delaware County who directed the sorry farce, was sustained by Daniel Cruger, the Republican Speaker. After the Council of Appointment was chosen by the Republicans, the house acted on Duer's petition, and with only one negative vote, seated Fellows. And until adjournment on April 17 the Federalists had a majority of one vote in the Assembly; but the Republicans had the Council of Appointment.

Allen was given a dinner before he left Albany. This was the only price he received for his harlotry.

On February 14 the Republicans in caucus instructed their partisans in Congress from New York to support Tompkins for the Presidency. Tompkins had no chance, and there was no harm in letting him have the honor. Six days later the Republicans held another caucus to nominate a State ticket. Tompkins was renominated for Governor. The Federalists named Rufus King to oppose him.

During this session Tompkins and Van Buren, intent on the political annihilation of Clinton, struck at him through the Erie Canal. This was done in the Governor's speech to the Legislature, delivered by Tompkins, but written by Van Buren. The Canal was essentially an enterprise for the State of New York to carry through. Tompkins, without committing himself one way or another, suggested that the Western States and the State of Vermont coöperate with New York in "any judicious plan" for linking the Great Lakes with the Hudson, and in turn, with the Atlantic. Such a plan would delay the work indefinitely. The fleeting references by Tompkins to this great project follow:

It will rest with the legislature, whether the prospect of connecting the waters of the Hudson with those of the Western Lakes and of Champlain, is not sufficiently important to demand the appropriation of some part of the revenues of the state to its accomplishment, without imposing too great a burthen upon our constituents. The first route being an object common with the states of the west, we may rely on their zealous coöperation in any judicious plan that can perfect the water communication in that direction. As it relates to the connecting the waters of the Hudson with those of Lake Champlain, we may with equal confidence, count on the same spirited exertions of the patriotic and enterprising state of Vermont.

It was now obvious that the inland waterway, destined to make New York the center of wealth and the greatest seaport in the Western World, would be delayed while Van Buren and Tompkins played politics with the Canal. Meetings of merchants were held throughout the State to force them to action. The meeting held in New York City led to Clinton's political restoration. This gathering, one of the most important assemblages of men of affairs held in years, was presided over by William Bayard. Resolutions were adopted favoring the construction of the Canal, and directing Clinton to draft and present a memorial to the Legislature.

This sent Clinton to Albany in a dual capacity: as Canal Commissioner and agent of the New York merchants' meeting. As an official, Clinton, in dealing with politicians, displayed a hauteur in speech and manner that made him enemies. The average politician, unless Clinton knew otherwise, was to him corrupt or potentially corrupt. But in this new rôle he was pleading for a project that was his very life. As a suppliant Clinton won the hearts of the new members, and restored friendships broken in the fight for place.

As a result of Clinton's mission all the old laws referring to the Canal were repealed, and one of Clinton's device was passed entitled: "An Act to provide for the internal navigation of this state." And the Patroon, and Clinton, and three other friends of the Canal were appointed to the new Canal Commission which possessed adequate powers.

In the elections the Republicans won by large majorities, capturing more than two-thirds of the Assembly seats. Van Buren was returned to the Senate, and Tompkins and Tayler were reëlected Governor and Lieutenant Governor. Tompkins, too, was to be the Republican choice for Vice President, the Vir-

ginia Dynasty having decided on him as the running mate of
Monroe. This meant that Tompkins would resign as Governor
sometime before March 4, 1817, as even the most sanguine Federalist conceded the election of the Republican ticket.

Clinton was being hailed as the coming man in the State.
The Canal was restoring him to the high place he had held before
the war. Van Buren was growing weary of it all. He was not yet
thirty-four, and was without a peer among the younger lawyers.
Tompkins, who had started the fight on Clinton a year ago, had
yielded to the public clamor, thus paving the way for Clinton's
return to public favor. Why should he bear all the kicks? He
could make more money practicing law, unencumbered by the
offices of State Senator and Attorney General, and the hatreds
these places were making for him. He discussed it with his wife,
and with his friends. None outside his family took him seriously
when he talked in this way. His prospects in the political arena
were too alluring: he could not mean what he said. But he had
fared well in a worldly way. He had his own carriage. As Attorney General he received $5.50 a day, and a little more than half
that as a Senator for each legislative day. In addition, he received
traveling expenses and other perquisites. But these were poor
returns for the work performed. The game was not worth the
candle. He would resign at the end of the next legislative session
and find peace and ample remuneration in his profession.

One day as he was preparing to leave Schenectady, where he
was on business, he found Aaron Burr at the hotel inquiring
for a conveyance to Albany. He offered Burr a seat in his carriage. While driving to the State Capital, Burr, who had drunk
deep of the dregs of the bitter cup, was indulging in his usual
satirical observations on men and things. Suddenly he changed
his tone and began to speak in high terms of Van Buren's political future. What was Van Buren's ambition? Van Buren astonished him by answering that he intended to quit politics and practice law exclusively. Why? After listening to his reasons, Burr
meditated awhile before pronouncing this dictum:

"Sir, you have gone too far to retreat! The only alternative left to you is to kick or be kicked; and as you are not fool
enough to prefer the latter, you will not resign!"

Van Buren did much kicking that fall, and for many winters,

and summers, and springs as yet unborn; and he received many kicks in return. Time and again he would renew his resolve to start a new life with the coming of spring. But the words of Burr always proved prophetic, even when his tortured spirit was crying aloud for the peace of private life. The peace for which he thirsted was not to be his while life lasted.

## CHAPTER XVIII

THE fall term of court in 1816 was held in New York City. A small dinner was given in the last week of October by Senator Barker in his home on Beekman street. Van Buren and his friend Smith Thompson, of Schenectady, Chief Justice of the Supreme Court, were invited. Another jurist attending the dinner, who also lived at Mrs. Keese's boarding house, was Joseph C. Yates, later Governor of the State. So far as any of the three of them knew, the only other guest was to be Ambrose Spencer to whom Barker had been greatly devoted for years.

Sauntering up Broadway Van Buren asked Yates and Thompson whom they expected to meet at Barker's besides Spencer. Knowing that Van Buren must have something in the back of his head to put the question, they mentioned several names. To all their guesses Van Buren muttered a no, and then he named De Witt Clinton. Both Thompson and Yates chorused: "Why, Spencer is to be there!" "That's the very reason!" exclaimed Van Buren, who saw no other purpose for the dinner.

They had not heard of any change in the strained relationship between the distinguished brothers-in-law. It was Van Buren's surmise that Barker was trying to effect a rapprochement. De Witt Clinton was growing in popular favor. And Clinton was an amateur in pulling wires compared with Spencer or Van Buren. Before reaching Barker's home Van Buren outlined his suspicions: Spencer was indispensable to Clinton; Barker was a friend of Spencer and Clinton before he was a politician; and now he was playing the rôle of peacemaker.

Knowing the brothers-in-law, all agreed that the overtures for peace would have to come from Spencer. Clinton was too obstinate to yield first. Then, too, he was now penniless, and his inordinate pride was magnified by his poverty. It was only fitting, therefore, that Spencer should make the advances.

As they entered Barker's home the only guest who had arrived was Clinton. He greeted all three of them most warmly. Van

Buren, who had been a Beau Brummel ever since his boyhood lecture on the importance of dress from his first preceptor, the courtly Francis Silvester, was struck by Clinton's plain and careless attire. He had just come in from his country seat.

A few moments later Spencer entered the room, bringing an atmosphere of embarrassment with him which all felt. There was no look of recognition by Clinton. Spencer, older and wiser, took no notice of his brother-in-law's failure to greet him. At dinner neither Clinton nor Spencer addressed the other directly; but they conversed through the medium of the other guests. Their remarks on these occasions were in noticeably conciliatory tones.

Some days later Van Buren learned that Clinton and Spencer met again that same evening at the home of Dr. John A. Graham, another mutual friend, and renewed their old relations.

On the Friday following, the first of November, Thompson told Van Buren that although court would not adjourn until the morrow, Spencer had taken leave of his fellows on the bench at the noon recess with the explanation that he was leaving for Albany in the afternoon.

Van Buren needed no other word. He was opposed to the return of Clinton to power. He instantly packed his trunk, called his carriage, and was driven posthaste to the steamboat landing.

As he had anticipated Spencer was on the boat. Clinton was with him. He had not counted on this. Clinton disembarked at Newburgh to return to his country house. Spencer invited Van Buren to a private talk in a cabin on the after deck. Now, thought Van Buren, Spencer would lay all his cards on the table. He did. Spencer proposed that Thompson and Clinton be named Presidential Electors-at-Large, Van Buren to say which should take rank. He pledged that Clinton would vote for Monroe for President and Tompkins for Vice President.

Van Buren had expected all this. He knew, when Thompson told him that Spencer had suddenly headed for Albany, that the sole purpose of the trip was to canvass the Republican members of the Legislature who had been summoned to meet on Tuesday to choose the Presidential Electors.

Spencer was moved almost to irritation by Van Buren's refusal. He declared that Van Buren's unwillingness to confer a mere formal distinction of this character on Clinton betrayed a

violence of factional feeling that he had not expected from him.
Van Buren quietly replied that he would not be adverse to conferring the honor if he were not convinced that this was Spencer's
opening move in an effort to make his brother-in-law Governor
when Tompkins would resign to take office as Vice President on
March 4. Van Buren had divined his intentions. Van Buren added
that Spencer would consider him weak indeed if he did not oppose
this preliminary move to promote Clinton to the Governorship.

Spencer ignored Van Buren's observations and turned the
conversation back to the main question, again urging him to
agree to Clinton's election as a Presidential Elector-at-Large. He
was rapping his snuffbox excitedly as he perceived that he was
not making headway. The interview was brief and ended amicably.
Not until the boat neared Albany did Spencer make any further
reference to the subject. Once more he vainly sought to obtain
Van Buren's consent.

This was one of the busiest week-ends in the lives of Van
Buren and Spencer. They called on every Republican in Albany,
Spencer appealing for pledges for Clinton, and Van Buren implor-
ing that Clinton be kept off the Electoral ticket. Frequently one
would be in the room of a legislator when the other called. Which-
ever happened to be the unintentional intruder would gracefully
retire.

On Monday, the day before the Electors were chosen, the
Republicans, observing the ancient usances, met in caucus.
Spencer encountered Van Buren shortly before this decisive meeting, and after giving him a pinch of snuff, boasted that he had
a majority of twenty for Clinton. Van Buren knew that if the
legislators were left to their own wishes there would be more than
a majority of twenty for Clinton; but he had wielded the party
lash in his informal interviews, and intended to apply it with even
greater severity in the caucus.

Van Buren replied to Spencer's boast by asking if he would
be in the Senate chamber on the morrow when the Electors were
duly chosen in accordance with law. Spencer replied that he
would.

When the caucus was organized, Van Buren made two motions: first, that each Congressional District name an Elector;
second, that the two Electors-at-Large be selected from the

Southern and Western Senatorial Districts. There was no objection to either proposal. Samuel Chipman, of the Western District was unopposed. Clinton and his rival, Henry Rutgers, were both from New York.

Clinton's friends in the caucus were not concerned, for Rutgers was comparatively unknown outside of the city. They were relying on votes from the Eastern, Western, and Middle Senatorial Districts to offset the almost unanimous vote that they knew would be polled in the Southern District for Rutgers, or more precisely, against Clinton.

Van Buren was a master of surprise, which is the very essence of intrigue. After the peaceful choice of the district Electors, Van Buren moved that the members from the Western District select one of the Electors-at-Large and the representative from the Southern District elect the other Elector-at-Large.

Instantly every Clintonian in the room was on his feet denouncing this manifestly unjust proposition. How could Van Buren, in fairness, propose that Electors-at-Large, representing the people of the entire State, be chosen by members from a single district? The Southern District was almost a unit against Clinton. Why this mockery? Violent speeches by the score were made condemning the unjust and unfair motion. The Clintonians offered an amendment for the election by ballot of the Electors-at-Large by the entire State.

Van Buren's friends sat silent. They wondered how their leader would meet the just, albeit caustic and frenzied criticisms of his motion.

When the Clintonians had spent themselves, the object of their invectives took the floor. His first remark put the Clintonians on the defensive: they should have shown him the common courtesy to explain the motion before they had so grossly assailed it and him. The rumbling ceased. Perhaps they had misjudged him. Then he indulged in subtle, fallacious arguments to show how unfair his critics had been. All he desired was a vote on his proposal to test Clinton's strength. If carried, it would mean that the meeting did not want Clinton as an Elector-at-Large; if defeated, he would submit to the wishes of the majority and accept Clinton. What could be more fair? Let the test be taken, not by ballot but by a *viva-voce* vote.

This proposal was fair on its face; but Van Buren knew that if the caucus voted by ballot, which would enable all present to vote secretly, the promises made to Spencer could and would be kept, and Clinton would be chosen by a majority of twenty. But by calling the roll and making each one vote in the open, as he proposed, he was confident that there would be enough weak sisters to switch to Rutgers. And thus he argued.

Ordinarily he would not object to voting by ballot, although it was preferable that one should always vote in the open. No one could doubt that when all present were elected, the constituencies which sent them to the Legislature were decidedly opposed to Clinton. And if they were to choose Clinton as an Elector-at-Large, without consulting the people, there would be great excitement throughout the State and the people would think that the Legislature had stolen a march on them and the party; and in justice to the members who wanted to avoid suspicion of betraying their constituents or their party, he wanted each man to do the manly thing and vote in the open so that those who were opposed to Clinton could be saved from the consequences of the acts of others.

There was more in the same strain, and Van Buren's appeal to the fears and interests of his hearers was successful, and the caucus sustained him. Rutgers was elected the following day. But Spencer was not in the Senate as he had promised. He saw Van Buren later and told him that the fight had only begun, and that it would not cease until Clinton was Governor. Van Buren accepted the gage of battle.

Spencer could not but admire the manner in which Van Buren had defeated Clinton. It was grossly unfair, but it was within the rules, and, moreover, masterly. He was learning. There was everything to fear from Van Buren in a caucus, where each representative was dependent upon the whim and caprice of Van Buren for the passage of his legislation. He was invincible here.

It occurred to Spencer that five years back, when Clinton was in the saddle and the controlling genius of the caucus, the Tammany men had sought to abolish this system of nominating State officers, and to substitute therefor the convention method. Their arguments were unassailable. In a legislative caucus voters in districts represented in the Legislature by partisans of opposing faith, had no voice whatever in the nomination of the Governor and Lieutenant Governor. This was emphasized by the Tammany men in pleading for a State convention. But Clinton, unwilling at the time to disturb his absolute sway, had turned a deaf ear to his factional opponents. Now, with Spencer directing things, the demand for abolishing the undemocratic caucus was revived.

The Spencerian plan for a State convention provided that in counties represented in the Assembly by Federalists, the Republicans, at their town primary meetings, were to elect delegates, and these, in turn were to select from their number a quota equal to the county's representation in the Assembly. These secondary selections were to sit with the Republican members of the Legislature in the proposed convention, and have equal voice with the lawmakers in nominating the candidates for Governor and Lieutenant Governor.

The Tammany men, who were comparatively few when they raised the cry, and almost entirely without allies outside of New York City, could not now turn their backs on the proposal they had advanced with such persistency when Clinton was supreme.

The Clintonian leaders everywhere talked nothing but State convention and Clinton. Foremost among them was Joseph C. Yates, a member of the Supreme Court, who carried the message on his circuit. Within two months the State was converted to the convention system.

By the time the Legislature reassembled for the regular session which began January 14, Van Buren realized that his only hope lay in some adroit handling of the convention. The legislators who had voted against Clinton for Elector-at-Large saw the handwriting on the wall and were apprehensive. The voters wanted a State convention—and Clinton.

Van Buren turned to Tompkins for help. But Tompkins, who would be inaugurated Vice President of the United States on March 4, was thinking of still higher honors, and had washed his hands of the factional contest. Van Buren must fight alone. He had, in the language of Burr, gone too far to retreat: it was a case of kick or be kicked.

Tompkins was aware that the driving power behind Clinton was the Canal. The country was proclaiming its worth. Tompkins could not hope to fight the people of the nation and still expect to be chosen their President four or eight years hence. He intended to remain Van Buren's friend, but he had no thought of warring further on Clinton.

The Legislature had been sitting about two weeks, when the machinery for a State convention was set in motion. This was done on Tuesday, February 4, at a meeting in Albany. Resolutions were adopted giving counties represented by Federalists in the Assembly representation in the convention, which would be held in the capital, March 25.

The Clintonians, emboldened by the desertion of Tompkins, set out to capture the Council of Appointment, and succeeded at the caucus of Republican Assemblymen on February 13. The Senators chosen from the Middle, Eastern, and Western Districts were adherents of Clinton. Only in the Southern, where the Tammany men controlled, was an anti-Clintonian elected to the patronage dispensing machine. This could have been prevented by Tompkins, to whom Van Buren appealed in vain. Clinton was again in full control. But Van Buren did not concede defeat. He labored unceasingly to stem the Clintonian tide. He induced Judge Yates, friend and advocate of Clinton, to be a candidate for the nomination against Clinton.

While Van Buren was making preparation to oppose Clinton in the convention, he was hoping that this would not be necessary. He had recourse to a new device. He would persuade Tompkins to serve out his term as Governor after he had been sworn in as Vice President. Van Buren contended that neither the State nor the Federal Constitution prevented him from acting in this dual rôle. Tompkins accepted the contention, but insisted that he could not afford to subject himself to the criticism which such a course would provoke. A few days before March 4 Tompkins resigned, and Lieutenant Governor Tayler automatically succeeded as Governor until a successor could be elected.

Van Buren next resorted to another artifice. Under the State Constitution of 1777, still in force, the Governor was elected for three years, his term beginning on the first day of July succeeding the April election. Tompkins had been elected in the preceding April, and his term would not expire until noon of July 1, 1819. Van Buren now advanced the theory that Tayler was Governor *de jure* until the end of the period for which Tompkins had been chosen. He cited in support of his proposition the second clause of Article XX of the State Constitution which reads: "And in case of the impeachment of the Governor, or his removal from office, death, resignation, or absence from the state, the lieutenant-governor shall exercise all the power and authority appertaining to the office of governor, until another be chosen, or the governor absent, or impeached, shall return, or be acquitted."

The Clintonians answered with the first provision of Article XVII which reads: ". . . the supreme executive power and authority of this state shall be vested in a governor, and that statedly, once in every three years, and as often as the seat of government shall become vacant, a wise and discreet freeholder shall be, by ballot, elected . . ."

Van Buren, who had advanced the proposal in his desperation, abandoned it, and strove to hold steadfast his majority of partisans in the Legislature, for by hook and crook he had rounded up the bulk of the Republicans as convention time neared. He planned to exclude all representatives chosen at the primary meetings who were not legislators. There was no law governing the nomination of officials, and he was counting on the precedent of years to support him.

A Senator he tried hard to win over was Peter Swart, a placid Dutchman of the old school and a distant kinsman of Van Buren. Swart spoke English with a pronounced accent. Van Buren, when excited, also showed a trace of the mother tongue. Swart was fond of his young relative; but people who thought they could get him to desert Clinton were just "tam" fools.

A few days before the convention Van Buren called on Smith Thompson. Van Buren's fourth child, a boy like the rest, and born on January 16, was named for the Chief Justice. Van Buren told Thompson he suspected that Spencer would persuade Yates at the last moment to decline to make the race. Thompson assured Van Buren that he misjudged Yates.

On the very eve of the convention Yates invited Van Buren to visit his chambers. When the Senate leader entered, Yates said that he must decline to be a candidate. He began to give his reasons, but Van Buren, concealing his indignation, interrupted and said that he need not go to any further trouble. In the same breath he added that no one would be embarrassed by the withdrawal of Yates as he had the written consent of General Peter B. Porter to place his name before the convention. And without giving the abashed jurist time to utter another word, Van Buren departed. Van Buren was not easily caught napping.

The declension of Yates had a disquieting effect on Van Buren's following. They had seen Clinton capture the Council of Appointment, and knew that Tompkins was neutral. Men who had been pledged to support Van Buren in his war on Clinton began offering the most specious excuses for their contemplated desertion. The Tammany men alone remained faithful. They were wrathful at the very suggestion of the possibility of Clinton's nomination. Senator Darius Crosby, speaking for the organization, asked Van Buren to bolt the convention if the Clintonians mustered a majority, and nominate Porter in a convention of their own. Van Buren replied that if they were to retire merely because they were outnumbered they would go the way of other disgruntled factions. His advice was: submit to the decision of the convention and bide their time. He was convinced that Clinton would let Federalists influence his administration. This would alienate the Republicans who now made him a power. Of course, if the Clintonians committed a palpable outrage, such as rejecting properly elected delegates, he would bolt, and appeal to the electorate through the nomination of Porter. Van Buren by this time was forced to give up all thought of trying to exclude delegates who were not legislators. He appreciated the situation as beyond his control: why fight Fate?

No outrages were committed by the Clintonians. They elected Van Buren's kinsman, Senator Swart, chairman. Clinton was nominated on the first ballot, the vote being: Clinton, eighty-five; Porter, forty-one. The delegates voting included ninety-three legislators, of whom Clinton had sixty; and of the thirty-three civilians, twenty-five were for Van Buren's foe.

The following day the Tammany men appealed to Van Buren and asked him to join with them in nominating Porter. They called on him when he was thoroughly disgusted with politics, politicians, and political intrigue. He gave them short answers, and they left him in high dudgeon.

Outside of New York City there was little opposition to

Clinton. There Tammany voted for Porter, and printed his name on ballots which they sent to their allies up-State, where they received but small help. The Federalists did not hold a convention: they supported Clinton in the general election. And Clinton, as his contemporaries put it, may be said to have been elected without opposition.

# CHAPTER XIX

ONE of Clinton's first public acts as Governor was to convene the Council of Appointment in special session on August 27. Two Tammany men were removed from office. Clinton assigned no reason, but allayed the fears of thousands of office holders by announcing that there would be no general removals: it was high time that public office ceased to be a pawn in politics.

Unknown to the public, Clinton did a generous thing: he sent the Adjutant General of the State, Solomon Van Rensselaer, whom he met at the Battle of Queenstown, on a peace mission to Van Buren. Van Rensselaer told Van Buren that there was nothing unfriendly in the Governor's feelings toward him, and that it was Clinton's hope that they could get along amicably. Van Buren responded that he reciprocated these sentiments with much cordiality, and begged Van Rensselaer to say that all he asked of the Governor was an administration which would satisfy all that he desired to sustain the Republican party. It was Van Buren's turn to go further and call on the Governor; but this he did not do. He even remained away from the inaugural ceremonies in accordance with a pact with Smith Thompson, who, next to Van Buren, was the leading anti-Clintonian of the State. Thompson, without informing Van Buren of any change of mind, attended Clinton's inauguration, and there was considerable comment over Van Buren's absence. Thompson never volunteered an explanation, and Van Buren sought none.

The first actual work on the Canal was done this summer. And when the fall came Clinton issued a proclamation setting aside Thursday, November 13, as a day of thanksgiving and prayer. This feast had been traditional in the New England States since the landing of the Pilgrims; but it had been attempted only once in New York, in the year 1795, when Jay was Governor. Jay's opponents denounced the proclamation as a bid for the support of the clergy, and a violation of the spirit of the State Constitution, which was so pronounced in the policy of the

161

separation of church and state that Article **XXXIX** voiced the democratic doctrine that "ministers of the gospel are, by their profession, dedicated to the service of God and the cure of souls, and, therefore, no minister of the gospel, or priest of any denomination whatsoever, shall, at any time hereafter, under any pretence of description whatever, be eligible to or capable of holding, any civil or military office or place within this state."

No one revived the captious cry which had greeted Jay some two decades earlier, and the custom spread until it embraced the entire country.

Clinton's first six months were peaceful. But it was apparent when the Legislature convened on January 27 that it was to be war to the knife between him and Van Buren. Hammond, no longer a member of Congress, took his seat in this Senate. It was not long before he found Clinton "cold, if not vindictive, towards Mr. Van Buren and others, who had opposed his elevation." Van Buren and his followers "reciprocated these feelings and were filled with determination to excite prejudices and jealousies against the governor, to render him unpopular with the Republican members of the Legislature, and to embarrass him in the discharge of his executive duties, and thwart him in his measures."

All the Tammany legislators, with the exception of Cadwallader D. Colden, were openly and persistently hostile to Clinton. In the Assembly, the Tammany leader was the brilliant Michael Ulshoeffer, lawyer, writer, and jurist. Ulshoeffer it was who denounced the Governor's speech in the Legislature as a "remnant of royalty," and demanded that the Republican method of communicating with the two houses in writing be adopted. The seed sown by this son of a Hessian soldier who deserted his regiment at Trenton took root, and eventually Presidents, as well as Governors, printed their annual messages which were read by the clerks of the local and national law-making bodies. It was not until our own time that the "remnant of royalty"—the speech from the throne—was revived.

On the first day of the session Clinton had majorities in both houses. Before the Legislature was twenty-four hours old, Van Buren's magic had changed these majorities into minorities. He began with the Assembly. Here he labored with the aid of the older members who remained loyal to him to elect a Council of Ap-

pointment secretly opposed to Clinton. To Van Buren the control
of this body meant more than patronage: it meant that "those
who feed men, and enjoy the privilege of dispensing the public
bounty, will in a greater or less degree, influence and control
them." The phrase is Van Buren's, and was voiced in the State
Constitutional Convention September 6, 1821.

Only one avowed anti-Clintonian was elected to the new
Council of Appointment. He was Peter R. Livingston, of the
Southern District, the choice of Tammany, and he embodied the
combined prejudices and hatreds of his family and his organization for the Governor. The three up-State districts elected men
with the Clinton label: Henry Seymour, from the Western; Hammond, from the Middle District; Henry Yates, Jr., from the
Eastern District.

Yates was a brother of Judge Yates. Van Buren had secretly
contrived his election. It was Van Buren's intent to work on Yates
by confiding in him that he still hoped to make his brother Governor. Hammond was so unswervingly Clintonian that his presence on the Council disarmed suspicion. Seymour, father of New
York's Civil War Governor, was merely an acquaintance of Van
Buren: this was the general understanding. After Seymour's selection Van Buren wrote to Billy Van Ness—they were again
friends:

"All is safe. Seymour! Seymour! Seymour!"

To begin with, Van Buren had Livingston and Seymour.
Yates would follow soon, and with these three he would render
Hammond and Clinton powerless in the Council.

After the council was chosen the Senate was presented with
a contested election on all fours with the Hen. Fellows *vs.* Peter
Allen case in the Assembly two years ago. In the Eastern District in the preceding election there were two contests: one for a
full term of four years and another for a short term of one year.
Dr. Jedaiah Prendergast received a total of fifteen thousand and
eighty-six votes and Isaac Wilson fifteen thousand and nine votes.
Wilson was elected to the short term, and Prendergast to the
long term. But Van Buren decided otherwise because Prendergast
was a Clinton man and Wilson was a Van Burenite.

This theft of a four-year term was achieved with the aid of
the Bible. Among the ballots cast for Prendergast were ninety-

one written Jedidiah Prendergast, and ten where the voters abbreviated the given name to Jed. Forty-two voters who had either misspelled or abbreviated the first name, swore before the Senate investigating committee that they had voted for Dr. Jedaiah Prendergast. Testimony adduced that there was no Jedidiah Prendergast in the district. Some of the witnesses who had abbreviated Dr. Prendergast's first name to Jed. further testified that they had never heard of the name Jedidiah.

An able coadjutor of Van Buren in the Senate was Samuel Young, former Speaker of the Assembly. He was versed in the Bible, and after the friends of the Governor asked that Dr. Prendergast be given the full term, Senator Young rose and demanded if they wanted to fly in the face of Holy Writ. Had they not heard the Scriptures say: "And he sent by the hand of Nathan the prophet; and he called his name Jedidiah, because of the Lord." Let those who questioned consult the very verse he had just read to them: the doubting Thomases would find it in the twelfth chapter of the Second Book of Samuel, verse twenty-five. No one save an infidel would agree with the witnesses who swore that they had never heard of Jedidiah, the other name for the wisest man of all time.

Van Buren and his brother-in-law Cantine, and three of the four Senatorial members of the Council of Appointment, voted with the majority who pretended to be swayed by the Scriptural citation of the sanctimonious Young. Van Buren's other kinsman, Senator Swart, voted with the Clintonians. Hammond, alone of the council, voted against this fraud. There was no longer any doubt that Van Buren was Clinton's master in the Council of Appointment. The last council was controlled by Clinton, and Van Buren was not removed as Attorney General through the grace of the Governor. He need no longer fear his foe, at least for another year.

Hammond, because of his talents and inclinations, was acquainted with many in the State who were of scholarly bent. One of these was the youthful John C. Hamilton, a son of Alexander Hamilton. Hammond learned that young Hamilton wished to be appointed a commissioner of deeds. There was a little honor, and some small fees in this office. Hammond had to make a personal appeal to each of his associates on the Council of Appointment, from the Governor down, before he could obtain this pittance of a job. Clinton was timorous of appointing Federalists: the Van Burenites were constantly proclaiming that he was secretly allied with them.

On February 15 Van Buren threw politics to the four winds and hurried to Kinderhook where his mother was seriously ill. He reached there in time. She had been grieving since the previous April, when Van Buren's father passed on. Beside him sleeps his wife. Two pieces of Parian marble mark their places of rest in the village cemetery. On one of them Van Buren had carved:

Sacred to the memory of Mrs. Mary Van Buren, relict of the late Capt Abraham Van Buren; she died on the 16th day of Feb. AD 1818 in the 71st year of her age.

Her long life was adorned by domestic virtues of the most useful kind. The early profession of the religion of a crucified Jesus which she made she sustained to the end with that undeviating fidelity which proved its foundation to have been laid in the heart. And her life and conversation characterized her piety by bringing forth abundantly fruit meet for repentance.

> Earth has an overcoming power,
> It triumphs in the dying hour
> Christ is our life, our joy, our hope,
> Nor can we sink with such a prop.

Van Buren did not take his wife with him to Kinderhook, although she had wanted to go. He had not been pleased with her own health ever since the birth of their last child. She had a cough that stayed with her, and he took extra precautions to keep her indoors during the cold weather.

The session ended on April 21. The rivalry of the Van Burenites and the Clintonians consumed more of the attention of the lawmakers than did the affairs of State. Clinton attempted reprisals by proposing a legislative investigation of the manner in which banks had obtained their charters. The Assemblymen, who are elected annually, did not dare oppose the measure. But in the Senate Van Buren rallied a majority against the inquiry. He was personally clean; but many of his colleagues were not. The boys must be protected.

The restrained language of the Assembly report hints at

the real menace of the political banking system of the times. "Their [the bankers'] influence too frequently . . . assumes a species of dictation altogether alarming . . . Senators and members of the Assembly will be indebted to the banks for their seats in this capitol, and thus the wise ends of our civil institutions will be prostrated in the dust by the corporations of our own creation." The same horrible truth could be said of the seats in Congress. But it remained for Van Buren to say it and to destroy the evil.

There had been much talk during the session in the rooms of the members of the need of following the example of other States and abolishing the property restrictions on voting. Van Buren frowned on all this red republicanism. Six days after the Legislature adjourned he wrote to his friend Gorham A. Worth: "We have had brought upon us a greater degree of rampant Jacobinism than ever this State was cursed with." Worth, a former Albany banker, was now the cashier of the Cincinnati branch of the United States Bank, which had been rechartered during Madison's administration. He was a warm admirer of Clinton.

In the April elections the Republicans held their ground in all counties save one. And a vast majority of the Republicans were Clintonians. In Rensselaer, William L. Marcy, journalist, Recorder of Troy, and later Governor and United States Senator, nominated his own ticket when the Clintonians outvoted the Van Burenites in the county convention. The result was a Federalist victory. Marcy, who always worked with Van Buren, was removed from office by the Council of Appointment at its next sitting on a charge of party treachery.

The Van Buren factionists were being designated Bucktails, an appellation originally applied to the partisan foes of Clinton in Manhattan. In the early days of Tammany, its meetings were held subject to calls published in the daily press. On patriotic occasions the calls—we are quoting from one in the *American Citizen*—would end with: "Each member will wear a Buck's tail in his hat, the distinguishing badge of Tammany, in honor of the day." Thus, through the press, the people who had never seen a Tammany celebration, knew that the buck's tail was the badge of "the sons of Tammany"—a phrase also used in the official announcements. Van Buren, although not a member of the organization, was the Bucktail leader of the state.

He was getting his fill of State politics, and was looking for some way out. He could not expect to continue as Attorney General after the first or second month of next year unless he made his peace with Clinton, which he had no intention of doing. The Governor's friends were certain to control the Council of Appointment, as most of those who had deserted to Van Buren were denied renominations in the up-State Republican strongholds and men of unquestioned loyalty to Clinton named and elected in their stead. He could not repeat his strategy of the session past: Clinton would prevent it.

The cry of the Bucktails was that Clinton was truckling to the Federalists. Van Buren himself was guilty of the very political crime he laid up to Clinton. But he managed to keep his offense dark.

On November 9 Smith Thompson ceased to be Chief Justice of the New York State Supreme Court upon his appointment as Secretary of the Navy. When the Cabinet place was offered him by Monroe, he asked Van Buren's advice before accepting it. Thompson's elevation left a vacancy on the State bench. On Christmas Day, Thompson, anxious to advance Van Buren to the Supreme Court, wrote that the Federalists would be for him "if they can't get one of their own." Van Buren was the second choice of the Federalists!

From this letter it is evident that there was more than mere talk in the whispered story that Van Buren was secretly committed to the reëlection of Rufus King as United States Senator, whose term would expire on March 4. After asking Van Buren who would be the next Senator, Thompson wrote:

"The great object you ought to keep in view is to avoid the least semblance of an understanding or bargain with the Federalists. This is the rock on which Mr. C[linton] is to split." Thompson also warned him not to let the Legislature reappoint King as "it would disarm you of the most powerful argument you have against your adversaries—Federalism and Federal coalition."

Van Buren and Marcy were secretly plotting to reëlect King, who owed his seat in the Senate to the defection of corrupt Republicans who had been bribed by Southwick and Thomas. Yet the legislators on arriving in Albany for the session of 1819 were greeted with the canard that Clinton was for King.

The first matter of importance was the election of a Speaker of the Assembly. Van Buren was for William Thompson, of Seneca County. Thompson's chief recommendation was a violent hatred of Clinton. The day before the opening of the Legislature the Republicans caucused. The Bucktails were there to the last man. The Clintonians were not fully represented, and the minority faction outvoted them. Too late the majority faction discovered that every Bucktail in the Assembly was present. Van Buren had issued orders directing his followers to be on hand. The Clintonians had taken no such precaution, trusting to the law of averages to equalize the absentees.

Under caucus rules, the minority is bound by the vote of the majority. In this case the numerical strength was obtained through trickery, and the Clintonians refused to abide by the result. Obadiah German, whom we have met as a member of the United States Senate in 1812, was their candidate for Speaker. There is no gainsaying his vast superiority over Thompson; but the Clintonians would have made more capital for their cause by submitting to the decision of the packed caucus. German, as we have seen, voted against the declaration of war and spoke against it. His selection by Governor Clinton was impolitic.

At the organization of the Assembly the Bucktails, of course, voted for Thompson. The Clintonians cast their ballots for German, as did Federalists, and their combined strength—as the Van Burenites put it—defeated the honest choice of a Republican legislative caucus.

Clinton vainly denied that he had bargained with Federals of high or low degree; and circumstances bear this out. The active director of the Federal forces in New York was William Coleman, editor of the *New York Evening Post*. The support given to the Clintonians by the Federalists was in accord with a plan outlined by Coleman, a little more than two years before, in a confidential letter to Charles Miner, a journalist of Philadelphia. "Generally speaking," wrote Coleman, "I feel disposed, in common with the leading Federalists here, to stand perfectly still, and wait for events to happen, as Jefferson says, we know not when. Something may come from the quarrels of opposite sections of the Democratic factions, and I think the most we can do is occasionally to *fan the embers.*"

Acting in accordance with their policy of fanning the embers, the Federalists, after the Speakership was out of the way, turned round and helped Van Buren openly by lending him a sufficient number of votes to elect his man Seymour to the Canal Commission, whose members were chosen by the Legislature. The selection of Seymour gave Van Buren control of the construction of the Canal—Clinton's project. There was considerable patronage at the disposal of the commission, and formal notice that Clintonians need expect neither appointments nor contracts was given in Buel's Albany *Argus*. "A majority of the canal commissioners are now politically opposed to the Governor and it will not be necessary for a person who wishes to obtain employment on the canal as agent, contractor, or otherwise, to avow himself a Clintonian."

Common friends of Clinton and Van Buren sought to patch up their differences. The foremost of these was Barker, who informed Van Buren that Clinton was willing to nominate him to the Supreme Court vacancy. Clinton had promised John Woodworth, brother-in-law of the Patroon, to support him for the office. The Patroon and others tried to induce Woodworth to release Clinton from his word, but Woodworth remained obdurate. Clinton kept his word and appointed Woodworth.

Barker did not give up hope. He next proposed that the membership of the Supreme Court be increased by two additional justices, and give Van Buren one of the new places. This proposal met with the objections of the five Supreme Court justices, and was abandoned. Clinton had frankly hoped that by elevating Van Buren to the bench, his troublesome foe would be removed from the arena of politics. Van Buren was not averse to the proposal: he was more tired than ever of political management.

As in the February past, Van Buren made a journey through the snows to Kinderhook. This time his wife was with him. There was no further need of protecting her from the cold of winter. On the sad ride to the village where they had been born, Van Buren must needs recall another February day, only twelve years back, when he and Jannetje—as he always called her

—set out through the snows to be married in Catskill. And his tribute to her memory is carved on her headstone: "Sacred to the memory of Mrs. Hannah Van Buren, who departed this life on the 5th of February, A.D. 1819 in the 36th year of her age. She was a sincere christian [*sic!*], dutiful child, tender mother and most affectionate wife; precious shall be the memory of her virtue."

The loss of his wife was the great tragedy in Van Buren's life. He was devoted to her, and no other woman ever filled the void in his affections. Her passing embittered him. He did not return to Albany for days, although the session was in full swing, and there were plots and counterplots afoot. He remained in Kinderhook among the scenes that were now hallowed by the memories of his parents and his wife.

On Saturday, February 12, he was still in the little village. A letter written the evening before by his brother-in-law, Cantine, told him all that had happened in his absence. One bit of gossip was that the Council of Appointment had met and removed him as Attorney General. This evoked a contemptuous sniff from Van Buren. On his return to Albany he learned he had not been removed. His removal had not even been considered.

Few of the Bucktail legislators were in their seats during the last week of February. Andrew Jackson was visiting New York. Van Buren had seen the hero of the Battle of New Orleans on his first visit to Washington after the short session of Congress convened in December, 1815. Van Buren would have liked to be with his Bucktail braves, but sorrow and legislative routine held him in Albany.

The Bucktails, to the last man, were at the dinner given to Jackson in Tammany Hall on Tuesday evening, February 23. The freedom of the city had been presented to the Tennesseean in a gold box. Tammany hoped that the presence of the hero of New Orleans in their Wigwam would destroy what support was left to Clinton on the island of Manhattan and weaken him elsewhere in the State.

The Bucktails were jubilant as Jackson sat down to their festal board. They had outstripped Clinton. They were entertaining the hero. And when the wine had flowed long, the toast to the guest of the evening was given: "To General Jackson; so long as the Mississippi rolls its waters to the ocean, so long may his great name and glorious deeds be remembered."

Amid loud huzzas and maudlin shouts, Jackson rose to respond to the toast. Confusion to Clinton and all other foes of Tammany! Some such sentiment would Jackson voice. The Bucktails beamed as Jackson raised his glass. They were also standing, glass in hand. Presently in tones which warriors had heard above the din of battle the hero of New Orleans pronounced the response:

"De Witt Clinton, Governor of the great and patriotic State of New York!" For a moment there was deadly silence. Jackson alone drank the toast. As he emptied his glass the Bucktails crashed their wine-filled glasses to the floor. Threats and imprecations were heard above the din. While the pandemonium was at its height, Jackson, irate and defiant, left the banquet.

Jackson was a snake in the grass, and his name became a thing to sneer at in the inner circles of the Wigwam. The incident gave rise to many verses in the daily and weekly press. One that was copied and recopied by newspapers throughout the country was Fitz-Greene Halleck's "The Secret Mine Sprung at a Late Supper." One stanza reads:

> The songs were good, for Mead and Hawkins sung 'em,
>     The wine went round, 'twas laughter all and joke,
> When crack! the General sprung a mine among 'em,
>     And beat a safe retreat amid the smoke.
> As fall the sticks of rockets when we fire 'em,
>     So fell the Bucktails at that toast accurst,
> Looking like Korah, Dathan, and Abiram,
>     When the firm earth beneath their footsteps burst.

After the Jackson dinner Van Buren conceived a plan for uniting the Bucktails and the Clintonians. This called for Clinton's resignation as Governor, and his acceptance of a foreign post. In a jocose way he submitted his terms of peace to Speaker German, Clinton's legislative leader. The old statesman replied in like manner. Van Buren did not expect any serious discussion of the subject then, and let German treat the proposal lightly. He knew that German would realize before long that his jesting tone masked an earnestness, and that Clinton would soon know what was in his mind. With the Secretary of the Navy and the Vice President his friends, Van Buren had no doubt that they could induce the President to end the factional strife in the State by this simple means.

The Legislature adjourned *sine die* on April 13 without electing a successor to Rufus King. The two factions of Republicans were divided on the Senatorship, as on nearly everything else, the Bucktails supporting Young, and the Clintonians Spencer. The Federalists, of course, were for King, and had high hopes of seeing him reëlected when the next session convened. They were counting on Van Buren; and their enmity to Clinton for restraining his followers from voting for King, was as deep as Van Buren's.

Following his example of the year before, Van Buren, a few days after the lawmakers returned to their homes, sat down and poured out his soul to his banker friend in Cincinnati. This communication to Worth is a dramatic speech wrapped up in a letter. Now Van Buren is the Moor in his last grand moment; and he declaims, in his own fashion: "I have done the state some service, and they know it." Again he is Cassius; but as he speaks his lines, we are reminded at times of Madelon and Cathos. New York must be saved from Cæsar.

There is contempt for Clinton's failure to put down factions, and masked envy for his rival's lettered mind. Peace, as he intimates, can be purchased. But he will not pay the price, as he has not yet learned to eat toad for breakfast. This boast, indirectly made, is not an idle one, for Van Buren never knew fear of man or place. He shows his scorn of Clinton for "stooping to kiss the rod which has chastized him." He does not conceal that it is his intention to destroy Clinton and all Clinton's "supporters, aiders, and abettors." When the Governor is overthrown, Van Buren will attend to the Virginia Dynasty. This will be done by pursuing a course which "will give New York her due weight in the union."

This document is all Van Buren. Nothing else that he has written shows so much of this rare man as he really was. In it he lives again. No alien hand has polished his punctuation, changed his orthography, corrected his mistakes in grammar, clarified his obscurities, or emended his misquotations. The letter as it left Van Buren's hands, follows:

Dʳ WORTH

    Your last epistle on the subject of New York politics has served only to add demonstration to my previous conviction that you are totally and deplorably ignorant not only of Mʳ Clinton (I mention him first out of complaisance to you) but of the State, her political interests and the Sentiments and views of her citizens, & that when you meddle at all with politics you are, as I have frequently told you wholly out of your element. This blunt sincerity may not flatter your vanity but that I am not bound to do you good alone is what I wish to promote. A man to be a sound politician & in any degree usefull to his country must be governed by higher & steadier considerations than those of personal sympathy and private regard—I will not suffer your unmerited censures or the *kind reproaches* of your *"Intelligent men from all quarters"* who have so kindly taken our political interests into their secure keeping, to drive me to say of Mr. Clinton what his political demerit would abundantly Justify—his fallen and falling fortunes are calculated to excite other sentiments than those of reproach or exultation and the man who ever for a moment entertained the Idea, that in the opposition which I have been constrained by an imperious sense of Duty to make to him I was actuated by a single inducement of a personal nature or that I ever ceased to regret that his political infidelity had lead & was leading to the frustration of his personal weight & influence in the State, knew nothing of me or my views— Had I the least idea that you was serious in your declamatory remarks upon this subject I would sorely regret that I had been so much misunderstood by a friend who I dearly love and for whose good opinion I have always entertained so high a regard—In the name of all that is decent where is the evidence of that towering mind & those superior talents which it has been the business of myriads of puffers and toad eaters to attribute to him & who with their never ending hallelujahs to his *"Stupendous greatness"* have stunned the public ear & nauseated the public taste—he has spent the best part of half a century in the acquisition of general knowledge & the improvement of his mind, uninterrupted by the necessity of applying to business and I ask again for the evidence of those talents, for opposition to which we are to be burnt as heretics or denounced as Jacobins by *"people of information from every part of the Union who congregate at Cincinnati"*—who utterly ignorant of the State & its political interests and wholly destitute of the means necessary to a correct Judgment have the presumption to accompany their volunteer opinions with reproaches on the conduct of men whose sole objects are the interests & honor of the State and who can proudly say that they have "done her some service & that she knows it"—That Mr Clinton is a man of *ordinary strength* of mind, of considerable acquirements and that he writes very well is cheerfully conceeded—all beyond is gratuitous assumption & nothing else—when has M^r Clinton in times of peril stood forward in the Senate & by the powers of eloquence or even argument sustained the Interests of his country & hushed the clamours of faction, *never*—but you may say that that is not his fort & every man cannot be an orator —when has he originated & carryed through any measure of interest to his country, which required penetration, industry, fortitude talents & perseverance ~~never~~, say you but be careful what you say of the Canal. When has M^r Clinton when beset with difficulties shewn that presence of mind, that fertility of invention that fortitude in suffering & that vigour and perseverance & controlling & removing difficulties which are the inveriable indicia of a great mind—*never* on the contrary recently when danger pressed and the storm of public indignation howled about him, when a great man of correct views would not have consented for any earthly object to stoop to his political enemies, still less to receive a favour at the hands of him who had contributed most to his overthrow at such a time & under such circumstances "ere he arrived at the point proposed he was heard to cry "Help me Cassius or I sink", and when the fever of apprehension was on him to exclaim "Tirtinius give me some drink like a sick girl"—not only this but he consented to be supported by Judge Spencer who had persecuted him & to be by him held up to the people as *a penitant,* thus stooping to kiss the rod which had chastized him—was this a course deserving the approbation of my high-minded, honorable & spirited friend G A Worth Es^qr. was it by this *Christian act* of humbling himself that he might be exalted that he became the object of M^r Worths Idolatry—If in these things he has not shewn the great man in what has he—I have always understood that under all governments one of the strongest traces of a capable ruler was to be found in the peace & *harmony* of his subjects or citizens—M^r C. has not yet been Governor two years and our State is distracted and our councils disturbed to an extent beyond all precedent—speak not of the *tammany men,* they are but a drop in the waters of bitterness—the whole State is in motion—from Montauck point to Buffalo—& from the St Lawrence to the Atlantic one continued sentiment & expression of deep rooted & settled discontent is felt & heard—nor is this confined to the democratic party, the most respectable although not the most numerous of the federal party openly express their contempt for an administration which has disappointed the hopes of all—how do you account for this, M^r Clinton came into the government at the most auspicious period—admit that there was a violent party agt him in New York, good conduct & the exercise of only a small portion of his "great talents" would have put that opposition to shame & draw upon them the execration of the community as the causeless disturbers of the public peace & general harmony— has it been so—no but on the contrary as I have before stated every section of the State is filled with reproach & Complaints—his re-election put out of the question—can all this be & yet M^r Clinton be that sound patriot & great statesman you would make him to be—or are the people of this State those people who sustained the Gen^l Government during the late war, those patriotic Citizens who never shrunk in the hour of peril, who submitted to all manner of privations for their countries good, who with their characteristic magnanimity in an evil hour consented to blot out a volume of errors & to select as their ruler a man who had so lately forfeited their confidence, are such a people I ask rather than question M^r Clinton's talents or patriotism to be stigmatized by the "Intelligent men from all quarters who visit Cincinnati" as a lawless race of disorganizers and unprincipled Jacobins—I think not, I highly value the tender solicitude of your citizens for our welfare, their object is no doubt pure but I think they carry it a little too far.

I have always supposed that an other distinguishing trait in a good administration is that it ralleys round the governmental standard the good the virtuous & the capable now it is a fact too palpable to be denied & which is virtually admitted by yourself that so far from that being the case with us, there is not an Instance on record in which any administration has embodied in its support so great a number of dissolute, abandoned & broken down politicians as that with which according to you we are blessed—but I have done—I have violated the resolution with which I commenced this letter already—it is not a pleasant subject to me & once for all I must assure you that foolish, wicked & deluded as you and your "intelligent persons" may suppose us to be, we have resolved, irrevocably resolved to drive from power the present State administration & all its supporters, aiders & abettors & that that resolution will be carryed into complete effect is certain as fate that whatever strangers may wish or suggest we value too highly the Interest & honor of a State of which we are Justly proud to be Citizens, to sacrafice them to courtesy, sympathy or any such feeling —we now have for the first time in *ten years all our enemies in front* & we will give them such an overthrow and after that pursue a course

that will give to New York her due weight in the Union and silence
the calumny "That her wide walks encompassed but one man" under
whose "huge legs" we "peep about" to find ourselves dishonorable
graves.

You must not for a moment think that any thing you have said
has cooled the ardour of my attachment for you, that is impossible—
it is built on too solid a base to be so easily shaken—the beam is in
your eyes & you are searching for the mote in mine, there lies all the
difficulty—Write me often, make my best respects to M^rs Worth and
believe me to be your

Firm friend in great haste

M. V. Buren

April 22^d 1819

G. A. Worth Esq^r

N. B. Your friend Dudley will succeed for the Senate over *your
friend Jenkins* Remember that this is for your perusal only.

M V B

The Dudley in the postscript is Charles E. Dudley, who, as
Van Buren foretold, was elected State Senator from the Middle
District a few days later. This letter to Worth is also noteworthy in that it contains more classical allusions than are to
be found in everything else that he has written or spoken combined. One source of his strength lay in his knowledge of his
limitations.

# CHAPTER XX

In the early spring of 1819, a twelvemonth in advance of the triennial gubernatorial election, Van Buren began planning to make it impossible for Clinton to be reëlected Governor. Such pretensions on the part of any other man in the State would have been laughed at by Clinton and his following. But Van Buren was different. He was shattering all precedents. The son of a tavern keeper and small farmer, without family, and un-lettered, yet he was the acknowledged leader of men of scholarly attainments and of distinguished ancestry. No one could make the same telling appeal to the mass. His ignorance of books was compensated for by his knowledge of men. To cap it all, he had an invention which made him matchless in intrigue. He could not be ignored.

Clinton's brother-in-law sent a message to Van Buren asking for an interview. Van Buren was to name the place. He chose Spencer's home, and a whole evening was spent in the Spencer library, the door locked to prevent interruptions and vainly the older man made a second effort to effect a truce. As they were about to separate, Spencer mentioned, disclaiming any menace in the reference, that great pressure was being brought to bear upon the Governor to remove Van Buren from the office of Attorney General, solely because he was directing the opposition to Clinton.

Van Buren answered that he would continue to oppose Clinton; that the Governor could not, in fairness, attempt to coerce him into submission by a threat of removal, as the same power which placed Clinton in the Governorship had made him Attorney General; that he had held his office before Clinton was elevated to his high estate. Yet, continued Van Buren, in the practice which had grown up in party control, the principle advanced by Spencer had resolved itself into an academic abstraction. Van Buren approved it, adding that if their positions were reversed, he would probably remove Clinton. Moreover, ever since Clinton had had it in his power to replace him, he had looked upon the loss of the Attorney Generalship as an inevitable consequence of his opposition to the Governor's reëlection.

Spencer replied that although they had not accomplished anything, their conversation could not fail to infuse a milder tone into the future differences.

During the first week of July the Council of Appointment was sitting in New York. German was there. Van Buren met German on his return from the city. He inquired if a new Attorney General had been named. No action had been taken yet, answered German, voicing the hope that he could persuade Van Buren to end the factious strife which was embittering the party. Van Buren responded in most serious fashion, that he would apply to Washington for an ambassadorship for Clinton if he would accept it and retire from State politics. German had evidently repeated Van Buren's earlier conversation to the Governor, for he immediately responded with an unequivocal "No! No!"

The suggestion that a Governor resign his office, quit his State and country, coming from a member of the Legislature who held an exalted State office at the pleasure of the Executive, moves us at once to amazement and admiration.

When Van Buren heard German's refusal, he delivered an ultimatum: Clinton must submit to banishment to a foreign post or fight. He gave German his reason: a truce between him and Clinton was impossible because it would spell public discredit to both sides; the people would suspect a bargain. If Clinton was unwilling to accept the offer, it would be war without quarter, to end only after one side was destroyed.

Clinton was sitting with his Council of Appointment in New York when Van Buren's uncompromising attitude and fantastic proposal were retailed to him. This was July 8. Immediately Van Buren was removed. The new Attorney General was Thomas J. Oakley.

Oakley was a lawyer of note, a Federalist, and high in his party's councils. His selection would serve as a counter to Van Buren's intrigues with Oakley's partisans. Only on the score of politics could there be criticism of Van Buren's successor. But Van Buren could not very well raise this cry, as he, too, had truckled to the Federalists. But his followers raised a row. The

Livingstons organized a Republican meeting in Oakley's home county to denounce Van Buren's removal and his replacement by a Federalist. Similar meetings were held throughout the State.

Washington was helping Van Buren, who brought all the prestige of the National government to his support by inducing Vice President Tompkins to run for Governor.

Shortly after Van Buren's removal, and when it was known that it was his intention to draft Tompkins, Archibald McIntyre, Comptroller of the State, a Clintonian, charged Tompkins with a shortage in his accounts with the State of some $110,000 to $120,000. The charge was made public in an open letter to the Vice President. Corruption was implied.

The accusation would probably never have been made if Tompkins had not been known to be the choice of the Van Buren-ites for Governor. The existence of the shortage had been known for three years. In the previous session a law was enacted allowing Tompkins commissions on the loans he obtained during the war on his signature as Governor. This act was passed to enable him to balance his account with the State, and the debate on it was conducted so as to conceal the defalcation. But McIntyre refused to make the settlement, as Tompkins demanded $25,000 in excess of the sum he owed the State.

Hammond, who listened to the debate and had first-hand knowledge of the incident, thus systematically accounts for the shortage:

This deficiency was supposed to be, and I believe it to be, owing, not to an intentional appropriation by him of the money of the state to his own use, but to the casual loss of vouchers; to the payment of money, in many cases, when, in the hurry and bustle of the times, no vouchers at all were taken; to the infidelity and knavery of agents; and, perhaps, as he mingled his own money with that of the public, to his sometimes expending for domestic purposes more than his income, and thereby, unintentionally, using for private purposes the public funds.

McIntyre's letter embodying the ugly implications of personal dishonesty on the part of the second officer of the National government was printed in pamphlet form as well as in the columns of the Clintonian and Federalist press.

On reading the charges against Tompkins, Van Buren hurried to the Vice President's home on Staten Island: the village which grew up around it is called Tompkinsville. Van Buren, like all the intimates of Tompkins, believed that the Vice President could not be guilty of deliberate dishonesty. McIntyre's effective attack must be answered. Tompkins gave Van Buren the keys to the desk containing his private papers. These would prove that he was not a defaulter, Tompkins declared.

The search began with Tompkins's letter book covering the early months of the war. The first thing Van Buren encountered was a letter to Thomas Addis Emmet urging him to accept the office of Attorney General after Hildreth's death in July, 1812. Book in hand, Van Buren hastened to the garden and, showing Tompkins the copy of the letter, exclaimed:

"Vice President, I find here that you were the author of an appointment that I have always attributed to Mr. Clinton."

Tompkins nodded as he replied: "Governor Clinton knew nothing of the matter. I wanted to have Thomas and Southwick convicted of the bribery they practiced on the passage of the bill to incorporate the Bank of America, and thought you too young for that service. And I knew, besides, that you would come to the office early enough."

Well, Van Buren was out of the office now, through the act of Clinton; but this could not make him forget how he had doubted Clinton when he said that he had had nothing to do with the appointment of Emmet. And during all these seven years he had unjustly believed that Clinton had prevented him from getting the office, which he had sought at the suggestion of Spencer.

The discovery was not a pleasant one. Van Buren was distressed. He regretted the many injustices he had committed against Clinton: acts inspired by his unjust conclusion. He resolved that henceforth he would not trust solely to inferences in important matters. But now was not the time to make amends, as the war was on between him and Clinton. With more vain regrets, Van Buren dismissed the incident from his mind and went on examining the papers.

The Secretary of the Navy, whose son, Jonathan Thompson, was married to a daughter of the Vice President, had a summer home near the Tompkins place. Smith Thompson was absent when

Van Buren arrived, but in the course of two or three days they met. The Secretary's first inquiry concerned the examination. Van Buren replied that so far he found the condition of Tompkins's account good, and added: "But there is another matter that has afflicted me more." He asked Thompson if he had observed that the Vice President was becoming intemperate. Tompkins was drinking, and drinking heavily, all during Van Buren's stay. Thompson answered that he believed the drinking was due to worry, and would wear off when his accounts were adjusted.

Van Buren was thinking not only of the well-being of their friend, but he could not go ahead with his plan to nominate Tompkins, although he was the most popular man in the State, barring Clinton, if he became a drunkard. While it was a time of hard drinking, the people demanded at least the outward appearances of sobriety in their public servants. Thompson promised to let Van Buren know if the drinking threatened to become a habit. Van Buren was so upset by his fears that he wrote a letter in a disguised hand counseling the Vice President not to drink hard. He put the letter in his pocket intending to mail it when he reached New York, but could not bring himself to the point of posting an anonymous note, even though it was intended to serve a good purpose.

The reply of Tompkins, which Van Buren drafted, brought forth a rejoinder from McIntyre; and the whole country took up the question, and the Federalist press kept up the controversy which was to remain alive for many months.

Tompkins was drinking far beyond the point called hard drinking; occasional intoxication would not have alarmed Van Buren. We find one of the Livingstons also concerned over the Vice President's habits. Van Buren was never without his glass of wine at table, and that it was not an ungenerous glass is evident from a letter to Jesse Hoyt, a lawyer formerly of Albany, then resident in New York, and for many years a handy man in political and other matters to Van Buren.

"I want," wrote Van Buren on November 17, "about fifteen or twenty gallons of table wine—say prime Sicily, Madeira, or some other pleasant, but light and low wine to drink with dinner. I wish you would get Mr. Duer, who takes this, to select it for me, and buy and send it up. Get me also a box of good raisins and a basket of good figs, and send them with the wine."

This was a small order, for not long after he bought sixty-three gallons of wine from Domenick Lynch—all choice wines were purchased from this New York society leader and introducer of opera to America—as instanced by a note to Hoyt in the following August: "You will oblige me by presenting the above draft to Mr. Kaufner, and the within check at the City Bank, who will, of course, give you the money for it, which pay to Domenick Lynch, Esq., for a half pipe of Wine I bought of him some time since."

While the honesty of the Vice President was being debated in every part of the nation, Van Buren, who regarded the sending of an anonymous letter, even in a meritorious cause, as an unprincipled act, sat down in the quiet of his Albany lodgings and wrote an anonymous pamphlet. His friend Marcy polished the phrases and supplied the proper punctuation and paragraphing. This document, unique in our history, was an appeal to the Republican members of the Legislature to reëlect Rufus King, the leading Federalist of the country, to the United States Senate. Van Buren masked his authorship behind the subscription: One of your Colleagues.

A few of Van Buren's intimates knew that he had written this eulogy of King, which omits all references to King's early opposition to the War of 1812, and recalls only the aid he rendered when the nation's "coffers were kept empty and her armies unrecruited by the ruthless efforts of faction." He sums up King's patriotism thus:

At this momentous crisis, which applied the touchstone to the hearts of men, when many of the stoutest were appalled and the weak despaired of the Republic, Mr. King was neither idle nor dismayed. His love of country dispelled his attachments to party. . . . He remonstrated in his correspondence with the leaders of the opposition in this State and in the East, on the folly, the madness and the mischief of their course; he contributed largely of his means to the loans of government; he infused confidence into the desponding, and labored to divest the timid of their fears; he sought Governor Tompkins . . . and to him Mr. King communicated the patriotic ardor with which he himself was animated. . . .

Anticipating the charge of bargaining, Van Buren observes that "it is certainly very extensively believed that our legislative halls have in repeated instances been made the theatres of the most exceptionable and unprincipled political bargains and coalitions; of coalitions in which men acted, not from the honest dictates of their consciences and with a single eye to the public interests, but from the unworthy motives of personal aggrandizement, not only disconnected with the public good, but in direct hostility to it." He notes that "in proportion as those charges have been credited abroad, the character of our State has sunk in the estimation of our sister States."

It is not his intention to discuss the truth of these charges, but it will "doubtless soon become necessary to probe them, as well as other transactions of a deeper cast, and still more injurious in their effects upon our public character, to their inmost recesses; to separate the innocent from the guilty; to vindicate the great body of our citizens from the charge of participating in the profligacy of the few, and to give rest to that perturbed spirit which now haunts the scenes of former moral and political debaucheries to the end that this great and otherwise flourishing State may no longer be retarded in her march to that respectability and influence, to which she is so eminently entitled."

All this last was intended for the consumption of the constituencies of the Republican legislators who were to be forced into line for the generalissimo of the Federalist forces. Van Buren knew the people. They must be flattered. What does the anonymous author of the appeal for the reëlection of Rufus King promise? "to vindicate the great body of our citizens from the charge of participating in the profligacy of the few." No one then, or before, or since had accused "the great body of our citizens" of sharing in the corruption of their leaders. But doubtless, reasoned Van Buren, they would not be keen enough to realize this; and by such phrases he hoped to induce them to believe that the masked author of the pamphlet was thinking chiefly of their good name. Consequently he was their friend.

The great guile of Van Buren is displayed not only in his sophistry, but in the time of the publication of his appeal for King. The pamphlet appeared less than a fortnight before the Legislature would be convened. In that short time the subtle deceptions of the anonymous document could not be properly answered, and it was his plan to force the issue immediately after the two houses had organized. Tammany was solidly behind him in his scheme. His appeal, therefore, was intended chiefly for the up-State Republicans who were wavering in their faith between the Clintonians and the Van Burenites. He must assuage their fears that voting for King would be high treason. To these he directs these closing paragraphs of his print:

> It is, as I have already stated, apprehended by several honest men, whose devotion to the Republican cause, and whose good opinion I hold in the highest regard, that the support of Mr. King, at this time, might expose us to the suspicion of being influenced in our determination by the single view of securing the coöperation of a sufficient number of Federal members to effect the various legislative objects at the next session, for which parties generally, as it is natural they should, feel considerable solicitude.

> This is the matter fairly and plainly stated. Now, strong as my desire is that we should confer on Mr. King our support; sensible as I am of the tendency of such a measure, to repel and to put to shame the volumes of calumny and scurrility which have been heaped on us by those who deceive themselves with the hopes of breaking down the free spirit of a great party, and grateful as I know it would be to the feelings of distinguished Republicans in our sister States, still, if I believed there was adequate cause for such apprehensions, I would on that ground forego its adoption. For it is not so important that we succeed soon, as it is that, when we do so, we proceed in a manner the most unexceptionable. But I know well that those fears are groundless.

> Our party, in the first place, is not liable to suspicions of this kind. We have throughout sustained a character which has, and will continue to exempt us from them. We are not a "personal party." We have no individuals amongst us who claim and exercise the right of stipulating for our acts; nothing is done for us, that is not done by the will of the majority, and which is not well understood to be in unison with the general sentiments, and consonant to the wishes of the people. With a party so organized, and thus acting, motives so justly deprecated can seldom, if ever, operate, and, of course, the suspicion of their existence is not likely to arise.

In the passages quoted we see Van Buren not only pleading for King, but praising Tompkins, and by indirection, assailing Clinton. Yet the note sounded throughout is the harm done to the

State by "moral and political debaucheries" in New York's legislative halls. He was an omnivorous reader of the press. These abuses were being magnified in a systematic onslaught on our experiment in democratic government by the whole monarchial press of Europe. In England, where a part of the people were on the verge of revolt against the archaic and unfair electoral system, the ruling class, in and out of Parliament, constantly criticized America in an attempt to divert the attention of the disgruntled.

In their assaults on our electoral system, and the misuse of patronage that went with it, the English critics were fair, limiting their criticisms to New York and Pennsylvania, and, as a noted Philadelphian publicist observed, "it happens that those are precisely and notoriously the parts of the Union, in which the game of state politics . . . bears the worst character and appearance. In them, there is more perhaps, of what, as long as human nature is not perfect with us, must exist in a certain measure in the rest,—I mean paltry intrigue for petty offices, and interested effort to influence votes."

But these assaults did not stop here. It was necessary that the entire nation be made odious and all our institutions cried down. That species of conditional white slavery, the traffic in redemptioners, as the farmers and merchants of Europe who were too poor to pay their own passage were called, was largely a British enterprise, carried on by British ships manned by British crews. Yet this traffic in mortgaged whites was described by the English writers as an example of American brutality.

The trade in blacks and the kidnaping of free negroes were the subject of appropriate strictures, yet they were silent on the shameful part played by their own rulers in fostering the theft, purchase, and sale of human beings, or the refusal of the directors of the Sierra Leone Company to permit the transplanting of American freed slaves at the instance of Washington, acting on the application of the Legislature of Virginia. Rufus King represented the United States in this praiseworthy effort of 1802.

These attacks were answered by American writers with quotations from official reports of special committees of the House of Commons where the cause of the poor was, too infrequently, the object of much humane concern. The kidnaping of free negroes in the United States was more than outweighed by the buying and kidnaping of boys and girls by the master chimney sweeps in England. The lot of these unfortunate children was tragically portrayed in a report which would defy the credence of the modern reader if we did not remember that the child slave is still employed in our own factories under the color of law. We quote a part:

> Children are sometimes sold by their parents to master chimney sweepers, and oftentimes they are stolen. These children are very liable to cough and inflammation of the chest, from their being out at all hours, and in all weathers: these are generally increased by the wretchedness of their habitations, as they too frequently have to sleep in a shed exposed to the changes of the weather, their only bed a soot bag, and another to cover them, independent of their tattered garments.
>
> They are very subject to burns, from their being forced up chimneys while on fire, or soon after they have been on fire, and while over-heated; and, however, they may cry out, their inhuman masters pay not the least attention, but compel them, too often with horrid imprecations, to proceed. They are sometimes sent up chimneys on fire.
>
> It is in evidence before your committee, that at Hadleigh, Barnet, Uxbridge, and Windsor, female children have been employed.
>
> It is also in evidence, that they are stolen from their parents, and inveigled out of workhouses; that, in order to conquer the natural repugnance of the infants to ascend the narrow and dangerous chimneys, to clean which their labor is required, blows are used; that pins are forced into their feet by the boy that follows them up the chimney, in order to compel them to ascend it; and that lighted straw has been applied for that purpose; that the children are subject to sores and bruises, and wounds and burns on their thighs, knees, and elbows; and that it will require many months before the extremities of the elbows and knees become sufficiently hard to resist the excoriations to which they are at first subject.

But it was largely to matters such as the hardships of chimney sweeps that the House of Commons directed its attention. The sufferings of the workers and other major problems were ignored. The mass, there, as here, was then inarticulate. But as in all times, even under the most tyrannical governments, leaders were found among the more fortunate, and while Van Buren was beginning to concern himself with the tangled accounts of Tompkins, the attacks of the monarchists on our popular institutions were stayed by the hand of tragedy, a tragedy which was to rouse the lawmakers of New York to a realization that they could not much longer deny the ballot to the people.

# CHAPTER XXI

THE evils under which Britain suffered were brought to a head by the Corn Laws, not inaptly called the Starvation Laws. France had taxed the people for light and air: England was taxing them for bread. The tragic manifestations of the English reform movement in 1819 were to advance the cause of manhood suffrage and progress generally in New York and elsewhere.

The tragedy in England had its origin during the American Revolution when a number of "the gentry, clergy, and freeholders of Yorkshire," of "the first consideration and property in the county, if not in the kingdom" assembled at York. A petition to the House of Commons was drafted protesting against the burdens of taxation placed on the land to carry on "a most expensive and unfortunate war"; against the squanderings of public moneys; against the creation of sinecures "with exhorbitant emoluments" for favorites; against unmerited pensions; against the great and unconstitutional influence which the Crown had acquired, "which, if not checked, might soon prove fatal to the liberties of this country."

But nothing was done save to tell the people how inferior our republican institutions were to the political excrescences of the House of Hanover and to enact more irksome laws. The movement for reform continued until the clique surrounding George III had a law passed known as the Seditious Meetings Act. This was designed to stifle the protests of the people, and to handicap the judiciary, which, in the main, was opposed to the suppression of free speech and the right of peaceable assembly. The hands of the judges were tied by the suspension of the Habeas Corpus Act. This was in 1794. These repressive measures were repealed and restored from time to time.

The clamor increased with the enactment of the Corn Laws in 1815, intended solely to enrich the comparatively few large landowners. The House of Lords was made up exclusively of this class, and this same minority dominated the House of Commons, where "five hundred of the seats . . . are articles of purchase, and always go to the highest bidder." The sale of seats "is as notorious as the sun at noonday." And "the gentry, the clergy, and the freeholders" voiced these and similar truths in the summer of 1819.

At Birmingham, on July 11, the workers, who had no vote, and a sprinkling of the gentry, clergy, and the freeholders, who exercised the privilege of suffrage, did a novel thing. The town was without a seat in the House of Commons, so Sir Charles Wolseley was elected "Legislatorial Attorney" to represent the people of Birmingham "amid the thundering acclamations of one undivided multitude." And he was instructed to present himself to the bar of the next Parliament for admission.

The defiant thunder of this meeting reverberated in Buckingham Palace and in the lowliest fisherman's hovel. Seventeen days later Sir Charles Wolseley addressed a smaller meeting at Stockport, where only four or five thousand people attended. Some of them carried flags and banners. One read: "Universal Suffrage." Another: "Election by Ballot." Other demands depicted included "Annual Parliaments" and "No Corn Laws." One of the flags was surmounted by the red cap of Liberty.

Sir Charles said that "he was a most determined friend of the people, and should remain so while there was a drop of blood in his heart. . . . He was proud to say that he had been at the taking of the Bastile in France, and would be happy to be at the taking of a Bastile in England. Were all hearts but as firm in the cause as his own, they would soon put an end to the present tyranny and corruption. They should be firm and united, for in a few weeks the struggle would be made and ended."

Another speaker was the Reverend J. Harrison. He won his plaudits when he contemptuously referred to Lord Sidmouth's refusal to present the people's petition to the Prince Regent— George III was in his last days. "There was a barrier between the throne and the people which must be removed either by force from heaven or hell, in order that they might see whether a man or a pig was upon the throne," said the clergyman.

Two days later the Regent issued a proclamation calling on the magistrates of the land to put down "insurrection against his Majesty's authority" and to bring to justice all "who had been or may be guilty of uttering seditious speeches and harangues."

This did not silence the movement, and many more gatherings were held. In Manchester the reformers advertised a meeting in St. Peter's Field for Monday, August 16, "to consider the propriety of adopting the most effectual means of obtaining a reform in the Commons House of Parliament."

This was the largest meeting held by the reformers up to that time. Banners bearing legends similar to those seen at Stockport were borne by the marching thousands as they proceeded to St. Peter's Field, where between sixty thousand and eighty thousand were congregated when Henry Hunt, leader of the movement, arose to address them. Hunt is described by Francis Place as "in almost all respects the best mob orator of the day, if not, indeed, the best which had ever existed." His hustings was a wagon, and around this rude rostrum were massed many of the silken standards, some of them reminiscent of the French Revolution. One read: "Liberty and Equality." On a black banner was written in large characters: "Equal Representation or Death." Towering over all was a staff supporting a Phrygian cap of crimson velvet on which was embroidered: "Liberty."

It was a peaceful gathering. Hundreds of women and children were scattered throughout the earnest mass of men. Not one of the sixty to eighty thousand was armed. The people assembled in compliance with the existing laws.

As Hunt began speaking two things happened simultaneously. One was observable to the throng. This was the arrival on the outskirts of the crowd of a troop of cavalry, their drawn sabers flashing in the sultry sun. The second was the issuance of warrants by magistrates, who sat in near-by houses. The illegal instruments called for the arrest of Hunt and his associates. The only pretense on which the judges acted was the proclamation of the Prince Regent, which did not make law. These orders for arrest were served peaceably. Among the prisoners was the correspondent of the London *Times*. The officers assumed that the journalist, being well dressed, and close to Hunt, was one of the "reformers."

The *Times* account of the wanton tragedy which immediately followed relates that after the peaceful arrests "a cry was made by the cavalry, 'Have at their flags!' In consequence, they immediately dashed not only at the flags which were in the wagon, but those which were posted among the crowd, cutting most indiscriminately to the right and left to get at them." In another part of the field stood Samuel Bamford, who thus described the subsequent events:

The cavalry were in confusion; they evidently could not, with all the weight of man and horse, penetrate that compact mass of human beings; and their sabers were plied to hew a way through naked held-up hands and defenseless heads; and then chopped limbs and wound-gaping skulls were seen, and groans and cries were mingled with the din of that horrid confusion. "Ah, ah!" "For shame!" "For shame!" was shouted. Then "Break, break; they are killing them in front, and they cannot get away"; and there was a general cry of "Break, break!" For a moment the crowd held back, as in a pause, then was a rush, heavy and resistless as a headlong sea, and a sound like low thunder, with screams, prayers, and imprecations from the crowd-moiled, and saber-doomed who could not escape. . . . On the breaking of the crowd, the Yeomanry wheeled; and dashing wherever there was an opening, they followed, pressing and wounding. In ten minutes from the commencement of the havoc, the field was an open and almost deserted space. The sun looked down through a sultry and motionless air. . . . The hustings remained with a few broken and hewed flagstaves erect and a torn and gashed banner or two drooping; whilst over the whole field were strewed caps, bonnets, hats, shawls, and other parts of male and female dress, trampled, torn, and bloody. The Yeomanry had dismounted; some were easing their horses' girths; others adjusting their accoutrements; and some were wiping their sabers. Several mounds of human beings still remained where they had fallen, crushed down, and smothered; some were still groaning; others, with staring eyes, were gasping for breath; and others would never breathe more.

More than five hundred men, women, and children, were wounded and eleven slain outright. A grim wag, meet to be jester to the gods, having in mind the epic written on the field of Waterloo, dubbed the saber charge in St. Peter's Field the Battle of Peterloo, which the more sober changed to the Peterloo Massacre. All England took up the phrase—all save Lord Sidmouth, secretary to the Prince Regent, who in the name of his Royal Highness, expressed "high approbation" of the soldiery on this occasion, and told the Manchester magistrates of the "great satisfaction derived by his Royal Highness from their prompt, decisive, and efficient measures for the preservation of the public tranquillity."

Tranquillity prevailed only among the slain; for from one end of England to the other, the people assembled to protest against this shameful and unprecedented assault upon their liberties. Many of these meetings were presided over by the nobility. In the castle yard at York, "the independent inhabitants of Yorkshire" were addressed by the Duke of Norfolk and Earl Fitzwilliam. These, with Lord Milton and Lord Cowper, had signed the call for the assembly. For espousing the cause of the people, Earl Fitzwilliam was dismissed as Lord Lieutenant of the West Riding of Yorkshire.

Processions were held in the streets with bands playing funereal music. Forty thousand assembled near Halifax and marched to the meeting place to the strains of "Scots wha hae wi' Wallace bled" and the "Dead March in Saul."

When Hunt arrived in London after his release from prison, more than three hundred thousand, the *Times* estimated, turned out to greet him. A banquet was tendered him, and the London Common Council adopted resolutions calling upon the Regent "to institute an immediate and effectual inquiry into the outrages that have been committed, and to cause the guilty perpetrators to be brought to signal and condign punishment."

The Regent curtly told the representatives of London that they were unacquainted with the circumstances and "incorrectly informed"; and that if laws were violated, the ordinary tribunals of the country were open for redress. The courts were functioning. Several of the leaders of the movement were sentenced to terms of imprisonment ranging from one to two and one-half years for pleading for reform.

Almost a generation later, Carlyle, speaking of the continued demand of the people for relief, said: "These Chartisms, Radicalisms, Reform Bill, Tithe Bill, and infinite other discrepancy and acrid argument and jargon that there is yet to be, are *our* French revolution; God grant that we, with our better methods, may be able to transact it alone." Carlyle prayed not in vain

# CHAPTER XXII

THE Legislature of 1820 was convened on January 4. Four days later the two houses, by joint ballot, reëlected Rufus King to the United States Senate. Three uncompromising Republicans in the Assembly alone voted against him. Clinton, who had been also playing with the Federalists, made no opposition, seeing how successful Van Buren's appeal of the previous month had been. New York anticipated the Era of Good Feeling by some months. King was at his home in Jamaica, Long Island, when word reached him of his election. He wrote to his son John to thank William A. Duer for his constancy and friendly exertions, and added:

> The part taken by Mr. Van Buren has indeed been most liberal, and as I conceive at the risk of impairing his high standing and influence among his political friends; do not fail therefore to inform him that I can never be insensible of his generosity & that no occasion can arrive, that I shall not be ready to prove to him the personal respect & esteem with which he has inspired me.

King knew the danger Van Buren incurred in espousing his cause. It was to plague Van Buren in later years; but Van Buren was desperate in his determination to crush Clinton. And he was hopeful of Federalist support.

In his annual message to the Legislature, Clinton recommended that a convention be called to consider amendments to the State Constitution which the Legislature would designate. He especially urged that the Council of Appointment be abolished. There was a demand among many, both Federalists and Republicans, for a revision without any restrictions by the Legislature, and the lawmakers, unable to agree on the scope of the call, deferred action for another year.

The real rub lay in the apprehensions of friends of the members of the judiciary that the delegates, if permitted uncontrolled sway, would report an amendment removing the judges from office because of their political activities. The people were complaining of the partisan acts of their higher judges, both on and off the bench, to which they were appointed for life. The voters felt that wearers of the ermine, possessing the power to make one man rich and another poor, to deprive this one of his liberty, and that one of his life, should not debauch themselves in the orgies of partisan passions.

In the first month of the session, William W. Van Ness, a justice of the Supreme Court, was accused of bribery in a resolution moved by Erastus Root. Van Ness took $5,000 for a favorable vote on the charter of the Bank of America in the Council of Revision. Van Ness was a supporter of Clinton. The Clintonians, with a sufficient number of Federalists, marshaled by Elisha Williams, successfully opposed his impeachment. Williams had been counsel for the bank. But the attendant disgrace shattered Van Ness's health; and he paid for his wrong with his life.

While the legislators were factiously discussing in the lobbies Van Ness's knavery, Assemblyman Henry McNeil, of Oneida County, introduced a resolution instructing New York's representatives in Congress "to oppose the admission, as a state, into the Union, of any territory . . . without making the prohibition of slavery therein an indispensable condition of admission." Some weeks before, Missouri in applying for statehood, exhibited her constitution which contained a clause tolerating slavery. James Tallmadge, a New York member of the House of Representatives, raised objections to this section. The Assembly unanimously adopted the McNeil resolution instructing his associates to support him.

On January 20 the resolves reached the Senate, and Van Buren and every other member voted for them. A call for a public meeting in Albany to protest against the further extension of slavery was also signed by him. By this time Van Buren had a second thought: there was Clinton to defeat, and there were slaveholders and pro-slavery men in the State. He must not antagonize them. Although New York in 1817—this was one of the last acts Tompkins signed as Governor—abolished slavery in the State after 1827, there was considerable sentiment in the Hudson River counties, where slavery was an established institution, against the manumission movement. Van Buren did not attend the meeting; and declined to sign the anti-slavery resolutions adopted. This would have made him too conspicuous: he had gone far enough.

While Van Buren was plotting Clinton's end, a survey of the Middle District indicated that he himself would be defeated if he sought another term in the Senate. He would not be an office holder after June 30. But he was remaining in politics until he succeeded in retiring Clinton.

Meanwhile he busied himself with unifying the Republican and Federalist opposition to Clinton. Ten days after King was returned to Congress, the Van Burenites, or Bucktails, met in caucus and nominated Tompkins for governor.

The return of the Bucktails to the caucus system of naming candidates for State office, which they had condemned when they were a minority in the Legislature, was denounced by the Clintonians, who met in open convention and renominated Clinton and Taylor.

In an unsigned letter, Van Buren informed Tompkins of the nomination, dispatching the note by Tompkins' son-in-law, Jonathan Thompson, who had instructions from Van Buren to converse freely with Tompkins "on the state of things here." Tompkins was wavering, fearful that his unsettled accounts, with the implied charge of defaulting with $110,000 to $120,000 of the State's money, might be disastrous to him in an election. Van Buren sought to dispel these fears, but being prepared for a refusal from Tompkins, he ended his letter with a proposal that if Tompkins declined, an effort be made, "through the interference of our friends at Washington," to induce Smith Thompson, Secretary of the Navy, to make the race. Tompkins reluctantly accepted.

Van Buren next wrote to King and asked him to advise the Federalists to support Tompkins. King's son, John A. King, a member of the Assembly, also vainly appealed to his father.

In the various private letters he wrote to his intimates, Van Buren always declared confidence in the election of Tompkins. Had he been frank, he would have said, as the Patroon did to Solomon Van Rensselaer: "The Vice President, it is said, will be too heavy a load . . . I think it very doubtful who will succeed."

On January 19, before Tompkins had agreed to run, Van Buren wrote to Rufus King: "He is unambitious & for himself wishes nothing so much as retirement; he has long been balancing in his own mind as to the propriety of asking the place of Collector of New York."

In this same letter we see the outline of the plan of a nation-wide spoils system which Van Buren was to inflict upon the country. He wrote: "It appears to me that to check Mr. Clinton's career is a matter of as much interest to our sister states as to us; he has collected around him a set of desperadoes, who, instigated by the hope of official plunder, will never be content to limit their depredation to the boundaries of this State, but would, if successful here, without doubt, extend their incursions abroad."

There was no basis for this ugly charge against Clinton; but Van Buren wanted all possible aid in his fight on Clinton— the whole nation if he could get it. There was no justification for the suggestion that Clinton was seeking the Presidency at this time; for neither Clinton nor any one else had any hope of depriving Monroe of a renomination. Having made this accusation to inspire fears in the Virginia Dynasty, he made bold to ask King to induce the President to force Thompson to be a candidate if Tompkins declined. "I cannot but hope," wrote Van Buren, "that Mr. Monroe would under suitable explanations interest himself to prevail upon Mr. Thompson to comply with our wishes."

Van Buren's anxiety ended on Washington's Birthday when Tompkins arrived and formally accepted the nomination. He "was escorted by the Military, and a great concourse of the Citizens from the ferry to his lodgings," King wrote to his father, "and upon leaving the sleigh, was greeted by three cheers from the surrounding multitude. A meeting of between eight hundred and one thousand persons met at five in the Capitol, and there ratified the acceptance of the Vice President and nominated openly General Moers [*sic!*] from Plattsburgh as a candidate for Lieut. Governor. A well written address and Resolutions were then submitted by Mr. Van Buren, the Chairman of the meeting, and were adopted with long and repeated cheering." Benjamin Mooers, the running mate of Tompkins, had been nominated and elected the preceding April as a Clintonian. The price for his desertion was this nomination.

Van Buren grew more and more apprehensive over the outcome. He presented a report as chairman of a special committee of the Senate asserting that the Comptroller ought to have allowed premiums of twelve and one half per cent on $1,050,000 to Tompkins, which would produce $131,250, giving the Vice President not only a certificate of character, but $11,870.50 above his admitted shortage. He introduced a bill carrying out this recommendation, and made the only speech in support of, or against, the proposed law and his committee's report.

Hammond recorded that this speech, which lasted two and a half days, was the "most ingenious, able and eloquent speech" he had ever heard. All were moved by Van Buren when he depicted the Vice President as the victim of persecution; Jeremiah Lott, who was elected the following month to represent Brooklyn in the Assembly, burst into tears and was led from the Senate Chamber. Van Buren's arguments had to be ingenious, because Tompkins had no just claim against the State; his claim for premiums on the loans—if he had any at all—lay against the National government. The Senate passed the bill by a vote of two to one.

In the Assembly, where Clinton ruled supreme, the measure was referred to a special committee of which Attorney General Oakley was chairman. Oakley's committee reported to the Assembly that the Comptroller in refusing to settle the accounts had acted correctly, and recommended that Van Buren's bill be amended to require the Comptroller to bring suit against the Vice President to recover the shortage if the balance due the State was not paid by August 1. The report was adopted and its provisions carried out by the Clintonian majority, leaving the question as unsettled as when the shortage was first discovered in 1816, and making it an issue in the coming campaign. Had a suit been brought against Tompkins it would have availed nothing: he was broke.

On April 14, the closing day of the session, the wealth and the brains of the Federalist Party, as represented by forty-eight signatories to the letter, made a public appeal to their fellow partisans to vote for Tompkins. This document was ready early in March, as we learn from a letter of John A. King to his father. Another son of Rufus King, Charles, with William A. Duer, and the latter's brother John, and two sons of the late Alexander Hamilton, John C. and James A. Hamilton, had been active for weeks in obtaining the signatures of the other forty-two members of the Federal *altezza*.

Their principal objection to Clinton, as set forth by the forty-eight, was that his faction partook of the character of a personal party; that he favored those who praised him, and that his advisers were men lacking in independence and possessed of a suppleness of disposition, "disgusting to the feelings of all truly high minded and honorable men who entertained a decent self-respect." They further averred that the Federalist Party no longer existed, and therefore they threw their lot in with Tompkins, and urged all of the old faith to do likewise.

Clinton did not stoop to abuse or answer these "high minded" men; instead, he used their own unfortunate phrase to ridicule them, and called them the High Minded Federalists—a name which stuck to his Federalist opponents for many years. The Clintonian press stressed the phrase in the few days left them, usually capitalizing or italicizing High Minded.

Clinton won by the slimmest of majorities—a bare 1,457 votes. But the Van Burenites carried a majority of the Assembly.

Had Clinton been defeated, Van Buren would have quit politics and moved to New York. Five weeks before the election, Van Buren's law partner, Benjamin F. Butler, also a native of Kinderhook, who had studied law under him at Hudson, wrote to Jesse Hoyt: "I do not yet precisely know what are Mr. Van Buren's expectations, nor do I believe he knows himself. It is very probable that he will spend the summer in settling up his affairs in this part of the state and in Columbia [county]." In the month of February Butler informed Hoyt that Van Buren had asked him to hold himself in readiness to move to New York in the spring.

Butler at this time—March 17, 1820—had been away from the law for two years, trying the rôle of president of a wild-cat bank established by Jacob Barker at Sandy Hill, now Hudson Falls. But the institution was soon to close its door with thousands of dollars of its worthless scrip unredeemed. A month after Clinton's reëlection Butler arranged to rejoin Van Buren in partnership on June 15. And Van Buren thus accounts for the change in his plans in a letter from Albany to Worth, under date of June 1:

I had intended to have left here for New York this fall, in the event of the War being ended, but as it is, my desire to serve your dear friend *the Great Clinton* will keep me here a few years longer— I have not the remotest objections that you should stick to him . . . but for gods [*sic!*] sake give us no more puffing in verse, I assure you solemnly that it will no longer pass current here—that Mr Clinton owes his election to a community of various interests hopes & fears is well known & that he is in no sense the favourite of this State is as certain as it is true that he does not deserve to be—but I will vex you no more—

If we did not have this and other indisputable proofs of Van Buren's deep hatred for Clinton, a hatred verging on obsession, it would be difficult to believe that a man of his attainments and years would alter his plans to so great an extent that he would remain in Albany to carry on "the War" against the Governor. Van Buren was now approaching his thirty-ninth birthday. His exhortation was provoked by the predilection of Worth to write in rhyme on almost every conceivable subject. Some of his rhyming was in praise of Clinton; hence Van Buren's "for gods [*sic!*] sake give us no more puffing in verse."

There are two letters of Van Buren written to Hoyt in the latter part of the month which show his dislike of imposition by borrowers. The first, dated the twenty-first, informs Jesse that a nephew of Sheriff Hogeboom had "borrowed $10 under a promise to send it up, which he has not done; and from what Mr. Hogeboom tells me I apprehend he did not intend to do it. I wish you would see him and make him pay it to you." Some nine days later he wrote: "I am afraid you will begin to think me a very troublesome friend—but I am constantly the victim of imposition—that man Plimpton who owns the *Aboliva*, borrowed five dollars of me under a promise to send it up. If you happen to fall in with him I wish you would —— him—he is a graceless dog."

These letters in themselves give the impression that Van Buren was niggardly. He had toiled for all he had; he had paid for it in brain and brawn and bone; and he wanted it back. His early life had taught him the value of a dollar. Yet in his own quiet way Van Buren was charitable to the deserving.

# CHAPTER XXIII

On the first day of July Van Buren was a private citizen. He held no public office. He was, however, the acknowledged leader of the major faction of the Republican Party. He controlled the Legislature. He had organized the political machine of which he was the head with a thoroughness previously unknown.

He felt free for the first time in years. His children were living with relatives, and he and his partner Butler boarded in Gilbert Stewart's house, 132 State street, a short walk down the hill from the State Capitol. Across the street was their law office. His only concern now was his law practice—and Clinton.

A picture of Van Buren's law office is left us by his partner Butler. On a summer day he wrote to Jesse Hoyt, whose brother, Lorenzo, had just been taken in as a law student. Lorenzo had been manager of Barker's bank at Sandy Hill. "Take it all together," said Butler, "we have the pleasantest establishment in the city, if not in the state. We occupy the whole lower floor. . . . Mr. Van Buren has the front room, with the library. I keep my office in the back room, which is cool and pleasant, besides being better adapted for study than the other. We have two students besides Lorenzo. A young man, a brother of Caldwell, (Gourlay's son-in-law) who has been eighteen months in our office, and a sedate, attentive, and I expect, useful clerk—and a son of the loud talking Pugsley, who is a wild fellow, and whom I keep on condition of good behaviour. So far, he has not forfeited. If Lorenzo remains with Mr. Van Buren, I will, with great pleasure, pay particular attention to him. He is digging away at Blackstone, which I shall permit him to continue until I get my books from Sandy Hill; then I will set him about reading a course of history and studying the Latin grammar."

It was not a small office: three clerks were busy copying the forms under Butler's direction. Butler was very busy at the summer term of court, held in Albany, over which Spencer was presiding. In a second letter to Hoyt, dated August 17, he revealed that a lawyer's gray hairs meant something on motion day.

"I have done nothing more than oppose a motion, in which I was successful," Butler tells Hoyt, "but to-morrow expect to make some provided I can get a *hearing*. I attempted it last week, but His Honor, the Chief [Spencer], in his mild way, told me to wait until my seniors had been heard; and as I was the youngest Counsellor at the Bar, perhaps this was right; but it excited a great deal of observation among the bar, and is generally spoken of as not *very* liberal nor proper. I really don't know how it is; but I am considered, by some persons, as possessed of a remarkable degree of forwardness, &c., &c., merely because I am unwilling to remain forever at the foot of the professional ladder. However, if my life is spared, I shall grow older every day, and therefore, sometime or other, will be entitled to a hearing."

All during this summer the Bucktails held banquets in every town and city of the State—to toast Van Buren. The generalship was concealed.

Butler's activities enabled Van Buren to give considerable attention to his war on Clinton. On October 7, the Bucktails met in Tammany Hall and formally recommended that a State Constitutional Convention be called, the delegates to have unlimited power to propose amendments.

This roused the few who still clung to the old order and were unwilling to accept a radical political change. The reform urged most by the advocates of a convention with unlimited powers was universal manhood suffrage. "Would you admit the populace, the patron's coachman, to vote?" asked an American Tory. "We would rather be ruled by a man without an estate than by an estate without a man," replied his fellow on a Republican paper.

The meeting of Bucktails was held at this time to impress the Legislature which would meet in special session on November 7 to choose Presidential Electors and to consider such matters as the Governor brought before it. Monroe was to be unopposed, the only President outside of Washington to be accorded this honor.

When the Legislature assembled Van Buren, although no longer a member, was on hand to direct its deliberations. Clinton's message was read to the lawmakers, who listened listlessly to his recommendations for a Constitutional Convention and the enactment of a law giving voters the privilege of choosing Presidential Electors at the polls, to continue in force until the United States Constitution should require their selection by districts—as had been advanced by a Southern State.

The recommendation of this proposed reform, which was in practice in several of the States, was used by Clinton as a peg on which to hang a veiled charge that the officers of the National government had interfered in State elections. Justifiable jealousy was displayed in our early days at any interference by the Federal authorities in a State canvass. To quote part of the message:

> The apprehensions which some of our wisest statesmen entertained, at the formation of the constitution, that the state governments would constantly encroach on the powers of the national government, appear not to have been realized. The practical tendency has been in the opposite direction. The power of the general administration has increased with the extension of its patronage. And if the officers under its appointment shall see fit, as an organized and disciplined corps, to interfere in the state elections, I trust that there will be found a becoming disposition in the people, to resist these alarming attempts upon the purity and independence of their local governments: for, whenever the pillars which support the edifice of the general government are undermined and prostrated, the whole fabric of national freedom and prosperity will be crushed in ruin. I have considered it my solemn duty to protest against these unwarrantable intrusions of extraneous influence, and I hope that the national legislature will not be regardless of its duty on this occasion.

This was Clinton's surprise for his foes. Had Clinton made a direct charge, it would probably have been ignored. But his accusation by inference confounded his enemies. They assumed that he lacked proof of interference by Federal officials "as an organized and disciplined corps" in New York's election. But they bided their time before taking official notice of it.

One of the first measures considered wiped out the debt of more than $100,000 that Vice President Tompkins owed the State. This same bill, which was approved by the Council of Revision, gave Tompkins some $11,000 additional.

The bill convoking a Constitutional Convention was considered next. This was reported by a special committee of the Assembly of which Michael Ulshoeffer was chairman. Ulshoeffer's

bill demanded a convention with unlimited powers and the submission of the proposed amendments in gross to the people.

This bill passed the two houses and went to the Council of
Revision for its action. While awaiting the verdicts of this body,
the Senate adopted a resolution calling upon the Governor for
any information he possessed supporting his implied charge
against officers of the Federal government. The answer was brief
and ironical. It reads:

### TO THE SENATE

Gentlemen—Fully appreciating the patriotic solicitude of the
senate to prevent all unwarrantable intrusions in the political affairs
of the state, I have received their application for information on this
subject with great pleasure, and I shall, in due time, make them a
communication, which, I trust, will be satisfactory in its nature and
salutary in its tendency.

De Witt Clinton.

It was known that the Legislature would adjourn on the
twentieth, five days after the Senate asked Clinton for proofs of
his charge. On the morning of the final day the Council of
Revision returned the bill for a convention disapproved. Under
the State Constitution of 1777, it required a two-thirds vote in
both houses to override a veto.

Chancellor Kent wrote the veto message. He admitted that
the Constitution needed revision, but denied that the Legislature
had authority to create a convention with unlimited power, and
further, asserted that the bill should have required the convention
to submit the amendments separately.

On both points of law the august body erred. The chief
concern of the judges, who were appointed for life, and remov-
able only upon charges by a court of impeachment, was to prevent
Van Buren from carrying out his known intention of having the
convention abolish the existing system in order to get rid of
Chief Justice Spencer. This, rather than the popular demand
for reform, motivated Van Buren. Three weeks before the Legislature convened Van Buren's partner wrote to Hoyt: "The city
has been full of farmers, &c., these two days—at a cattle show—
but I have seen nothing of it myself. Chief Justice Spencer
delivered a speech on the occasion, by the way, as I suppose, of

preparation for the period when he will be compelled to retire to the shades of private life."

The bill was rejected by the Council of Revision by the casting vote of the Governor. There were four others present, and it was understood, if not agreed, that Chancellor Kent, Chief Justice Spencer, and Judge Woodworth would vote against it. This would leave the vote of Judge Yates the only voice in its favor. This would not have called for a vote by the Governor. But to the astonishment of his colleagues, Woodworth voted for the bill, compelling Clinton to break the tie. Woodworth's brother-in-law, the Patroon, and nearly all his kin, were opposed to a convention of unlimited scope. Woodworth, who owed his appointment to Clinton, never explained his sudden change.

It was charged that Woodworth gave his vote "in the hope, or in accordance with a secret understanding with the party in the majority in the Senate [the Van Burenites], that that majority would decide that the judgment rendered against him in the Supreme Court should be reversed." Judgment was rendered for several thousand dollars on a note Woodworth had indorsed. As we have seen, the Senate, with the judges of the Supreme Court, and the Chancellor, composed the Court of Errors, and the six votes of the judges were outweighed by the thirty-two votes of the Senators on all appeals brought before this highest tribunal.

As the bill was returned on the day set for adjournment, Ulshoeffer, as chairman of the committee which reported the measure, moved to table it until the Legislature met again in January.

That night, a few moments before the Senate adjourned, Clinton not having replied to its request for information, Van Buren's majority in that body adopted the following resolution:

In Senate—Nov. 20, 1820.—Whereas his excellency the governor, in his reply to the call of the senate for information, relative to the general government, or its officers, as an organized corps, interfering in our elections, has not furnished the senate with any evidence in support of such charges. And whereas it is highly improper that the chief magistrate of the state should criminate the administration of the general government, without ample testimony in his possession, by reason whereof the good people of this state may have their confidence in the general government greatly impaired. Therefore,

Resolved, That the senate repose the strictest confidence in the patriotism and integrity of the general government, and will not change such opinion, or yield to any insinuations against such administration, but upon full and satisfactory testimony.

Most of the Senators were homeward bound the following morning when Clinton sent them a brief word that he would notice their resolves when the Legislature reconvened in January, and expressed regret that "any branch of the Legislature should, in so unprecedented a manner, lose sight of the respect due to itself, and the courtesy due to a coördinate branch of the government."

Meanwhile Clinton was being held up as a vilifier of the Monroe administration, and this continued until January 17, when Clinton sent a message to the Assembly, accompanied by affidavits and letters showing that high administrative officers, including at least one member of Monroe's Cabinet, had used the influences of their offices in an attempt to defeat him for reëlection the previous April. So voluminous were these documents that they were delivered to the Assembly in a green bag.

One of the letters was written by Van Buren almost a month before the election, asking for the removal of four postmasters. This missive was addressed to Henry Meigs, a Member of Congress from New York, a relative of Return J. Meigs, the Postmaster General. Van Buren demanded the instant removal of four postmasters—"Rascally P. Masters" he called them. They were rascally because they were Clintonians. "Unless we can alarm them by two or three prompt removals, there is no limiting the injurious consequences that may result from it. If anything is done, let it be done quickly." Two of the postmasters were instantly removed.

Clinton, on receiving a copy of Van Buren's letter from Washington, wrote to Solomon Van Rensselaer, then serving his first term in Congress, and thus commented on it: "It is equally offensive to grammar and truth."

Other documents included in the famous Green Bag Message showed that electors employed in the Brooklyn Navy Yard were marched to their polling places behind a marine band. Van Buren's letter to Rufus King asking the President himself to interfere, remained inviolate in King's keeping.

The Legislature appointed a joint committee to consider Clinton's charges of Federal interference. While the inquiry was on, Van Buren made the final arrangements for the Republican caucus at which a successor to Nathan Sanford, United States Senator, would be chosen. Sanford, a Republican, and free of faction, was justly entitled to reëlection; but Van Buren had other plans. He controlled sixty-four of the ninety Republican votes in the two houses, and he had decided that these votes should be cast for himself.

The caucus met on Thursday evening, February 1. Senator Young, who had invoked the Bible to support him in his theft of a four-year term from Dr. Prendergast, presided. Van Buren's friends, who had lists of those pledged to him, noted that six were not in attendance. But this was of no consequence. One of Sanford's friends was also absent. John King, now a Republican, left us the only report of what happened behind the locked doors. This is embodied in a letter to his father, which reads in part:

Mr. [Samuel B.] Romaine from New York then nominated Mr. Sanford, and Mr. [Caleb] Eldred from Otsego, Mr. Van Buren. Mr. [Clarkson] Crolius then rose and asked [the] gentlemen to offer some reason for the nomination of Mr. Van Buren in opposition to Mr. Sanford against whom no charge or complaint had been made. If there was cause for dissatisfaction he should be glad to know it, and if it was well founded he would be the first to oppose his reëlection; if however it should be satisfactorily proved that he had been an undeviating republican and a faithful senator in the councils of his Country, that he should then rely upon the support of every man in the Meeting and by an unanimous vote re-nominate Mr. Sanford as a candidate for the Senate of the U. S., of which body he had been so long a distinguished member. He was followed by Mr. Romaine, who, in an animated speech, called upon gentlemen to pause before they sealed the political usefulness of Mr. Sanford, before they passed a vote of censure upon the long and unimpeached services of that gentleman, by giving their support to Mr. Van Buren. If Mr. Sanford should fail to receive a majority of the votes of this meeting the consequences would be the destruction of his political character in the public estimation, and a suspicion that he had either neglected the duties of his high station or had fallen from the faith which he had so long professed. He mentioned among other instances of a reëlection your own case, able and experienced and a friend to your country as he admitted you to be. Still that you were a federalist, and if in such a case Republicans could consent to a reëlection how much more were they bound to return a gentleman, an acknowledged Republican, against whom no charge was made and to whose public services all were willing to bear testimony.

Young, in a pointless reply, ignored the argument made by Romaine. There was no need of an answer: Van Buren had the votes. With one ballot blank, the vote stood: Van Buren, 58; Sanford, 24. The following Tuesday Van Buren was elected by the Legislature. Some thirty-odd Federalists stood by him. The tally was: Van Buren, 86; Sanford, 60. The Federalists decided the election. King's debt to Van Buren was wiped out.

New York's junior Senator-elect had eleven months to wait before he could take his seat, as his term would not begin until March 4, the day after the Sixteenth Congress was to adjourn. This pleased him, as many things in Albany needed looking after, notably the Council of Appointment, which was beginning to make a clean sweep of all Clintonians.

One of the first removals was Archibald McIntyre, the Comptroller, whose revelation of the Vice President's debt to the State was responsible for the reëlection of Clinton. His place went to John Savage of Salem. Many of Van Buren's followers vainly protested against the removal of McIntyre, who had administered the office of Comptroller with distinction for fifteen years. This office of watchdog of the State's finances had hitherto been regarded as above politics. Van Buren was ruling with an iron hand.

Attorney General Oakley of Poughkeepsie was replaced by a devoted aide of Van Buren, Samuel A. Talcott, of Utica. Jonas Platt, a member of the Supreme Court, commenting on the youth of the new Attorney General, observed that this was the age of young men. Van Buren made it a practice to cultivate the younger generation, chiefly because they expected less than those who were older and wiser.

Benjamin Knower, a hatter of Albany, succeeded Gerret L. Dox as State Treasurer. Knower was qualified because he was father-in-law of William L. Marcy.

Solomon Van Rensselaer, who, save for the year 1809, had continuously held the office of Attorney General under successive Governors since 1801, was removed to make way for Marcy, who boldly attempted to justify this sort of thing in an amazingly frank speech on the floor of the United States Senate some ten years later—a speech which would have been forgotten had he not said: "to the victor belongs the spoils."

Van Buren was working the spoils system to an extreme unknown even in the days when the Livingstons and the Clintons fought for control of the State. Hitherto all military officers, although holding their commissions at the pleasure of the Council of Appointment, were not disturbed. But now one after another was removed from his command to satisfy the thirst for place of a follower of Van Buren. Two of the most noted military men in the State, General Anthony Lamb, the commissary general, and Colonel Gilead Sperry, commander of a regiment of cavalry, were replaced. Mayors, sheriffs, district attorneys, county clerks, surrogates, justices of the courts of common pleas, justices of the peace, notaries public, and commissioners of deeds, were removed where the least suspicion existed of disloyalty to Van Buren.

The previous August, Van Buren's brother-in-law, ex-Senator Cantine, was made State Printer after becoming owner of record of the Albany *Argus*. Van Buren, the real owner, assumed responsibility for the payments to Jesse Buel, from whom the paper was purchased. Van Buren's former law partner and half-brother, Van Alen, was appointed to his old berth which Van Buren also had filled, that of Surrogate of Columbia County. Van Buren's partner, Butler, was named District Attorney of Albany County. A full brother of Van Buren, Abraham, was chosen Clerk of Columbia County. Other relations of Van Buren were appointed to lesser places. He was copying the Livingstons.

Clinton records that there were "thousands and thousands of office seekers" besieging the Council for places. One of its acts was disgraceful. This was the removal of Gideon Hawley as State Superintendent of Common Schools. In his place was named Welcome Esleeck, "a mere collecting attorney." This was the first blow suffered by the public school system, which had been instituted in 1805 under the patronage and direction of Clinton, the first President of the Public School Society of New York. This organization owed its existence to two Quakers, John Murray, Jr., and Thomas Eddy, who interested Clinton, then Mayor of New York. Clinton drafted the application for a charter. Governor Lewis featured the request in his annual message to the Legislature in 1805, and recommended a general system of common schools. When the charter was granted, Clinton and Frederick Depeyster made a house-to-house canvass of their friends and obtained $4,910 to carry on the work of public education. Clinton then obtained from the Common Council a grant of the old arsenal for a school, and an appropriation of $2,000. The following year, he induced the State to vote $12,000 outright and an annual subscription of $1,500.

Albany and Troy quickly followed New York's lead. When the system spread, Hawley was made superintendent. Hawley was a pedagogue. He had no interest in politics. He had been appointed on Clinton's recommendation; and that, now, was enough to condemn him.

Protests against Hawley's removal made no impress on either Van Buren or his Council of Appointment. Almost the entire Legislature was incensed at this assault on the public schools, whose worth had already been demonstrated. The legislators could not override the Council and restore Hawley. But they were determined that a scholar and not a sciolist, should direct the instruction of the children of the State.

They achieved their purpose by introducing a bill making the Secretary of State, ex officio, the State Superintendent of Common Schools. The measure passed both houses unanimously, and accordingly the wise and benign influence over the teaching of the rising generation was continued by the talented John Van Ness Yates.

The joint committee, to which the charges of Federal interference in the preceding State election had been referred, reported on March 15 that the National government had never interfered in any State elections. Perjured depositions denying the truth contained in the affidavits submitted by Clinton in his Green Bag message, accompanied the legislative report, which deceived only its authors.

The Legislature again passed a bill for a Constitutional Convention to be held in August, the delegates to be chosen in June, provided the voters at the annual April election approved the proposal. Once more the lawmakers wrote in a provision that the delegates should have unlimited power to propose amendments.

This time the Council of Revision did not dare to reject the measure. The Bucktail press had likened their disapproval of the first convention bill to the Tories who were denying the ballot to the people of England. The major criticism was visited upon Clinton; and typical of the newspaper attacks was the following: "His Excellency cannot retain the gentry, the judges, and the manors in his interest without he opposes, either openly or clandestinely, every attempt to enlarge the elective franchise."

The efforts of the manorial interests to frighten the freeholders into believing that the extension of suffrage to the propertyless workingman and the tenant-farmer would injure them or their property were vain; for the electors by a vote of more than three to one approved the call of the convention. The returns showed 109,346 for, and 34,901 against.

# CHAPTER XXIV

AFTER the April elections Van Buren found himself in an unenviable position. It was announced that King would be a candidate for delegate from his own Assembly District in Queens. Van Buren knew that he had not one chance in a thousand of being elected from a single Assembly District either in Columbia County, where he was born, or in Albany County, where he resided. The removal from the office of Adjutant General of the invalided hero of two wars, Solomon Van Rensselaer, had enraged the people of Albany, the hub of the Manor of Rensselaer. Mass meetings of protest had been held, and sympathy extended to the popular and impoverished relative of the Patroon. And the old General was not without friends and kin in Columbia County. While both counties had given decisive majorities in favor of the convention, they were Dutch to the core, and resented this harsh treatment of a scion of the first of the Patroons.

There were ten counties in the Middle District represented by Van Buren in the Senate for eight years. Eight of these were among what were known as the Dutch counties; and the feeling in Albany and Columbia pervaded the counties of Sullivan, Orange, Greene, Ulster, Schoharie, and Schenectady. Delaware County had so many of the original Dutch stock in it that it would have been playing with fate for Van Buren to seek election as a delegate from either of its two Assembly Districts. The remaining county, Otsego, which was of recent settlement, was composed largely of British stock; and so Van Buren, leader of the Republican party of the State of New York—for Clinton now headed only a minor faction of the party—was forced to seek a nomination there. The safest of the five districts in Otsego was chosen; and he was elected.

The other delegates from Otsego were Joseph Clyde, David Tripp, Ransom Hunt, William Park. All were farmers. From the biographical information compiled by the secretary of the convention, we learn that both of Tripp's parents were English;

211

Park's were Scotch: Hunt's were Irish: Clyde's mother was English and his father was Scotch. Odd company for Van Buren to seek, he was reminded by his waggish colleagues, who were aware of the traditional solidarity of the Dutch.

The convention was opened in the Assembly Chamber at noon on Tuesday, August 28. One of the delegates from Staten Island was Vice President Tompkins, and to him was accorded the honor of presiding over the body. He was a tragic figure. Although comparatively young, the disgrace attending the review of the shortage in his accounts had prematurely aged him; and as Van Buren had feared two years ago this very month, Tompkins was habitually seeking solace in drink. He was poor; for he entertained up to the last penny that came in. He was low in health because of his habits. Both health and habits were to grow worse with the years; and his closing days were to be spent in trying to keep up appearances while wondering who, among his relatives, would provide the money for next week's living. Had he been dishonest, he could have made several fortunes in the high offices he had held.

The Assembly Chamber was a long rectangular room running north and south. Tompkins sat on a dais flanked by two winding stairs of four narrow steps. The semi-circular seat with its bowed back carried out the line of the graceful handrail supported by banisters, squared and slender. Instead of the ordinary newel posts, the master of cabinetry had made a slight convolution at the base on each balustrade. The two flights of steps were wide apart on the floor, and almost met at the dais. Each stair swelled outward to complete the simple harmony of gentle curves.

The desk of the presiding officer was imbedded in the floor. The lower half of its paneled front served as the back of a seat at which a clerk sat; and before him was a small square-topped table whose pedestal partook of the simple lines of the desk. This masterpiece of a forgotten craftsman was set apart from the rest of the room by a low platform whose outer line formed a half-circle.

When the unknown engraver made the floor plan showing the seating of the delegates, he incised this majestic rostrum which, we feel confident, was of mahogany. The drapery on the wall above was, we are equally certain, of crimson velvet.

The seats were arranged in a semicircle. The delegates sat

facing the east. On their extreme right and left were massive fireplaces. There were four sections of seats, which made five aisles, including those at either end. On the most southerly aisle sat Erastus Root, the third seat from the front. In the same section, but on the inside aisle, in the first row, was Nathan Sanford. Directly across the aisle was his former colleague, the white-haired Rufus King. Two desks behind sat Chancellor Kent; and in the same row, the third seat in, was the Patroon. In the next section, on the aisle seat in the first row, was Van Buren's first preceptor, Francis Silvester, of Kinderhook. His hairs were now silvered; and he was still the same dandy as of yore; but he did not excel in sartorial elegance his old pupil to whom he had lectured years back on the importance of dress. Two rows behind Silvester, also on the aisle, was seated Chief Justice Spencer, his back to the most eloquent member of the convention, Elisha Williams. In the next and last section, in the second row on the aisle, Van Buren had his place.

There were other men of note in the semi-circle: Jacob Rutsen Van Rensselaer, Peter A. Jay, Judge William W. Van Ness, Peter R. Livingston, and James Tallmadge. Van Buren's brother-in-law, Cantine, also had a place within the bar: he was official stenographer to the convention.

While the Bucktails were in the vast majority, it became apparent to Van Buren, even before he began to fraternize with his partisans that he could not dictate to them as he did to the political hacks who were sent to the Legislature. They were of a different type; but he intended to do what he could with them.

Tompkins appointed seven committees to which would be referred proposed amendments dealing with the principal sections of the Constitution, and an eighth to consider all measures not classified.

Several of the most eminent men in the Convention, irreconcilable Clintonians or Federalists, were ignored by Tompkins in making appointments to the four important committees. Among those slighted were Chancellor Kent, Chief Justice Spencer, Elisha Williams, and Peter A. Jay. These committees were to report measures affecting suffrage, the judiciary, the Council of Appointment, and the Council of Revision.

The first important committee to report was the last named.

It recommended that the Council of Revision be abolished, and the veto power vested in the Governor. There were few friends of this archaic combination of the executive, judicial, and legislative branches of government. The convention supported the recommendation. Van Buren did not vote for the proposal on these grounds alone. Thus he explained his vote: "I object to it because it inevitably connects the judiciary, those who, with pure hearts, and sound heads, should preside in the sanctuaries of justice, with the intrigues and collisions of party strife; because it tends to make our judges politicians, and because such has been its practical effect. I am warranted by facts in making this objection." He had a minor objection: he was opposed to judges who were appointed for life, and therefore no longer responsible to the people exercising a veto on legislation passed by men who were elected annually and quadrennially.

Van Buren, as the chairman of the committee dealing with the spoils distributing machine, the Council of Appointment, was the next to report. He recommended that this other relic be abolished.

All were agreed on this. Likewise there was unanimity for the recommendation that the 8,287 military officers, with the exception of the adjutant general, the major generals, and the brigadier generals, be elected by the privates and officers of the various commands.

With as little discussion the convention also voted to empower the Legislature to elect, in joint session, the Secretary of State, the State Treasurer, Comptroller, and other heads of the various departments of the State government.

Van Buren, in submitting his committee's findings, explained that he differed with the majority who favored the election of sheriffs and justices of the peace: he was opposed to the election of any judicial officers. This was the voice of Van Buren the machine leader, not Van Buren the statesman. As he said during the debate which lasted for days on his report, these minor courts heard five times as many cases as all the other courts combined. Consequently the justices of the peace met five times as many people, and, if politically minded, could sway many. And sheriffs, through their deputies, reached into every corner of the State.

During the session of Wednesday, October 3, Van Buren

defended the proposal to create a Council of Appointment consisting of the Governor and six members to be elected from as many districts in the State. And answering the proposal that justices of the peace and sheriffs be elected by the people, he said: "The further this power could be removed from the people the better."

The convention voted down the new type of Council of Appointment, which Spencer said would be worse than the old one.

King was also opposed to the election of sheriffs. He held that as executive officers they should be appointed by the Governor. The justices of the peace, he contended, should be elected. The convention compromised, and decided that justices of the peace should be appointed by the boards of supervisors and the county judges, and that the sheriffs should be elected by the people. Mayors were to be appointed by the common councils of their respective communities, and hundreds of other officers were to be appointed by the local authorities. Those not so disposed of were to be appointed by the Governor, by and with the advice and consent of the Senate, or in such manner as the Legislature might direct.

After shearing the judges of their vast powers as members of the Council of Revision, the Convention took up the question of abolishing the existing judiciary. The majority were for this drastic step, but the Patroon, Rufus King, and others among the more conservative members of the body, opposed it. When Van Buren's ally, Erastus Root, moved an amendment to the judiciary committee's report to remove Spencer and his associates, Van Buren joined the ultra-conservatives in voting down Root's proposal.

The explanation for this action of Van Buren, which astonished his followers, is found in a letter he had written to King praising the Patroon, and urging King to wean him from Clinton and induce him to cast his lot with the Bucktails. The Patroon had been apprehensive alike of the Convention and those who were demanding it. "Although I have not taken a lead in this convention business," wrote Van Buren, "being somewhat timid in all matters of innovation, still I am convinced thoroughly that temperate reform & that only is the motive of those of our friends who urge it most strenuously." This was palaver for the Patroon.

Root hated Clinton and his brother-in-law as much as Van Buren did. Of like cast was Young. So when Matthew Carpenter, friend of Young and Root, a farmer from Tioga County, ignorant of the law, brought in a plan to abolish the old court, and create a new one, all suspected Root and Young of using Carpenter as their agent.

The deep-seated dissatisfaction with the judiciary was voiced by Peter R. Livingston on Saturday, November 3, when he said:

On the proper establishment of our judiciary depend the life, liberty, and prosperity of this community. . . . When the Council of Appointment was under discussion you found a ghost in every corner; and there was not a man to be found that would advocate its cause for a moment. When the Council of Revision was under review there were ghosts equally numerous; and no man dared defend or advocate its cause; but when the judiciary is under review, the ghost does not appear, but you find the gladiator in every corner, ready to protect and defend it.

I admire the judiciary as much as any other man, when it is worthy of esteem; and I am as willing to assail it when there is just ground for attack. Sir, this State has been degraded and disgraced by the debates which have been had upon this floor. . . . What has disgraced us? Some gentlemen tell us it has been a shuffling and scuffling for office. Not so, sir! It has proceeded from another source. Characters have been permitted to remain in your judiciary department who have been implicated with attempts to procure corrupt laws. It has been that department which has prevented the passage of wholesome laws which the public good required. It has been that department which has given sanction to laws unfriendly to the public good. It has been some of that department who have become notorious in every part of your State in electioneering campaigns; who have repeatedly attended political meetings, and spoken in them over and over again.

I now make an appeal, and an awful appeal it is, to the professional gentlemen of this Convention, whether it has not been the case, that when a man in the country, of any political standing, has had a suit depending at a circuit court, he has not consulted with his counsel, to know what judge was to preside at the circuit; and whether he has not been frequently told, that a political judge was to preside, and it would not do to let the cause come on? Can there be a more *awful picture imagined,* than such a state of things presents?

The Convention created a new judiciary system.

The suffrage question was the major concern of the Convention. To understand Van Buren's attitude on the extension of the ballot during the debates, let us peer into a confidential letter he wrote to John A. King in the last weeks of the deliberations: "I have had at various times to come in severe contact with three distinct interests in the Convention, viz The old Federalists & Clintonians, the New York delegation and the high minded gentlemen and a small number of Mad-caps among the old democrats who think nothing is wise that is not violent, and flatter themselves that they merit Knighthood by assailing everything that is venerable in old institutions."

If Van Buren had named the "Mad-caps" he would have placed Livingston at the top of the list. Van Buren at heart was as thorough a democrat as any extremist on the floor; but he was cultivating the Patroon and Rufus King; and so must needs play the ultra-conservative. Consequently we shall see him advocating a removal of the freehold qualifications of voters, but insisting on certain restrictions on the proletaires, such as the performance of military service or other public work, or the payment of a personalty tax.

During the deliberations on the suffrage extension no one excelled Van Buren in his broad and intimate knowledge of the subject. Not only had he studied the constitutions of the various States, but he was familiar with the intricacies of the British system.

When the suffrage committee recommended the removal of the property qualification with the restrictions enumerated, Chief Justice Spencer, backed by the old Federalists and Clintonians, offered an amendment to keep the election of Senators exclusively in the hands of freeholders. They argued that as the members of the Senate constituted the major part of the Court for the Revision of Errors, property owners should have sole voice in selecting them as had been ordained in 1777.

Spencer, in moving his amendment, said that the sober sense of the community had not demanded the removal of the freehold qualifications, and characterized the proposal as a deep and dangerous innovation.

By removing these guards we repress industry, frugality, temperance, and all those exertions to the acquisition of landed property, which make good citizens. Are we not jealous of property that we should leave it unprotected? To the beneficence and liberality of those who have property we owe all the embellishments and the comforts and blessings of life. Who build our churches? Who erect our hospitals? Who raise our school-houses? Those who have property. And are they not entitled to the regard and fostering protection of our laws and Constitution? . . . Let us take care, whilst we nominally give the right of voting to a particular description of our citizens, that we do not in reality give it to their employers. The man who feeds, clothes, and lodges another has a real and absolute control over his will. Say what we may, the man who is dependent on another for his subsistence is not an independent man, and he will vote in subservience to his dictation. . . .

Here it would be profitable to look to that country from which most of us are derived; I mean England. Independently of the rotten boroughs, which send fifty or sixty members to Parliament, and which are owned by individuals, there are districts containing from one hundred to five hundred electors, and sending upwards of one hundred members to the House of Commons, who notoriously and publicly buy their seats by different modes of corruption and bribery. In some places the electors have long been habituated unblushingly to receive for their votes a fixed and standard price. In others, it is managed with more decency; but the corruption is gross and palpable; and who has not heard and read, of the tumults, the riots, the mobs, and the murders attending their elections? At no very remote period, when luxury and vice shall have extended their empire among us, as they assuredly will, may we not expect, if we admit the mass of our adult male population to vote for every branch of the government, to see these disgusting scenes acted among us?

Numerous supporters of Spencer reëchoed his words. Chancellor Kent said that universal suffrage when applied to the legislative and executive departments of government, had been "regarded with terror by the wise men of every age." There was no doubting his sincerity. He wanted to preserve the Senate for the landed interest. "I wish them [the Senators] to be always enabled to say that their freeholders cannot be taxed without their consent." Then he went on:

The apprehended danger from the experiment of universal suffrage . . . is too mighty an excitement for the moral constitution of men to endure. The tendency of universal suffrage is to jeopard the rights of property and the principles of liberty. . . . The growth of the city of New York is enough to startle and awaken those who are pursuing the *ignis fatuus* of universal suffrage. In 1773 it had 21,000 souls; 1801 it had 60,000 souls; 1806 it had 76,000 souls; 1820 it had 123,000 souls. It is rapidly swelling into the unwieldy population, and with the burdensome pauperism, of an European metropolis. . . . In less than a century, that city, with the operation of universal suffrage, and under skillful direction, will govern this state.

We are destined to become a great manufacturing as well as commercial State. We have already numerous and prosperous factories of one kind or another; and one master-capitalist, with his one hundred apprentices and journeymen and agents and dependents, will bear down at the polls an equal number of farmers of small estates in his vicinity, who cannot safely unite for their common defense. Large manufacturing and mechanical establishments can act in an instant, with the unity and efficacy of disciplined troops.

It is against such combinations, among others, that I think we ought to give to the freeholders, or those who have interest in land, one branch of the Legislature for their asylum and their comfort.

However mischievous the precedent may be in its consequences, or however fatal in its effects, universal suffrage never can be recalled or checked but by the strength of the bayonet. We stand, therefore, at this moment on the brink of fate, on the very edge of the precipice. If we let go our present hold on the Senate, we commit our proudest hopes and our most precious interests to the waves.

Van Ness, too, stressed the fear that the future growth of the cities would menace the safety of the State under universal suffrage, and added: "And what will be the condition of their population? By an irrevocable decree of providence, it is pronounced, 'the poor ye have always with you',—people who have no interest in your institutions, no fixedness of habitation, no property to defend." Others invoked Holy Writ to show that discrimination against the poor was divinely ordained. And Young, whom we have seen citing Scripture to steal a Senate seat, answered these trespassers on his preserves.

"Whom do the gentlemen mean by the epithet poor?" he demanded. "The paupers? They are excluded by every proposition that has been made. Or do they intend to describe that intermediate class of society, between the very poor and the very rich? If they mean the latter, I am prepared to say, and that too with emphasis, that they ought not to be excluded. They are the soundest, the most honest and incorruptible part of your population."

Much was said by the old order against Jacobinism and the condition into which it had plunged France. Livingston could answer that: he had been there when the Chancellor was minister to that country.

"France has been alluded to," said Livingston. "The French Revolution has produced incalculable blessings to that country. Before that revolution one-third of the property of the kingdom was in the hands of the clergy; the rest in the hands of the nobility. Where the interest of one individual has been sacrificed, the interests of thousands have been promoted.

"After dining with that friend of universal liberty, the patriotic La Fayette, he once invited me to walk upon the top of his house, that commanded a view of all the surrounding country. 'Before the revolution,' said he, 'all the farms and hamlets you can see were mine. I am now reduced to a thousand acres, and I exult in the diminution since the happiness of others is promoted by participation.'

"This, sir, is the language of true patriotism; the language of one heart, larger than his possessions, embraced the whole family of man in the circuit of its beneficence. And shall we, with less ample domains, refuse to our poorer neighbors, the common privileges of freemen?"

Others of like mind declared that the people had demanded this extension of suffrage, and that the delegates were in duty bound, by virtue of the action of their constituencies, to vote to abolish the freehold qualification. This gave Elisha Williams an opportunity to mock the apostles of democracy. Said he:

Gentlemen say the people have settled this matter in their primary assemblies. *Vox populi vox dei.* But the worshipers of this deity have certainly a right to know his commands; and they cannot reasonably be censured for hesitating to obey injunctions of which they are ignorant. . . .

One argument which has been pressed upon this committee, I confess I never expected to hear in this hall; it is, that "the people demand this right." . . . Sir, if it be just and safe to confer this right it should be bestowed gratuitously; nothing should be yielded to this menacing demand. If this demand were presented in a different shape—if you were called upon to bestow so much of your freeholds upon these unqualified demandants as would enable them to vote against you, would you advocate that claim? Would you yield to it?

I know, sir, that one honorable gentleman [Livingston] has pointed out the blessings which would flow from yielding this boon to our brethren in distress. He has witnessed the exultation of the patriot La Fayette, in the victory of republicanism over his own property. The honorable gentleman was taken by the noble marquis to the terrace of the splendid château of Le Grange. Before him, as far as the eye could see, lay the rich domain. "But yesterday," exclaimed the imperial Republican, "this vast territory was my property; it was dotted with cottages filled with my vassals. Mark the blessings of *la grande révolution;* those who were then hewers of wood and drawers of water, the vassals of my estate, are now the legitimate sovereigns of republican France, the lords of their own soil."

How long, Mr. Chairman, if we yield to this demand, will it be, in all human probability, before those who now modestly ask no more than a right to govern our property—they have none but themselves to engross their attention, or require their care—will appear armed with the elective power of the State to consummate to us, the rich blessings conferred on the vassals of Le Grange by the French revolution?

Williams could not let the opportunity pass without a fling at Jefferson, knowing that this would goad the opposition, especially Van Buren, who was ever quoting him. George Bancroft, in his campaign sketch of the public career of Van Buren, said: "Williams . . . had insulted the name of Jefferson." Bancroft, when he penned this unjust charge, was writing a partisan life of Van Buren, and like all engaged in this sort of work, he depicted a lopsided view of the man, omitting highly important incidents that would reflect on the character of his subject, and altering the written word to make his image seem real. Williams had his faults, but they were not the qualities of a cad. His references to Jefferson follow:

Mr. Jefferson has said, sir, that great cities were upon the body politic great sores. In mentioning the name of this illustrious statesman with commendation, I am aware that I may fall under the lash of the honorable gentleman from Richmond [Tompkins] for most certainly I have never been an admirer of the gunboat system. But however that may be, his old adherents and universal admirers, cannot object to his authority, because he may be cited by one who has not assented to all his views; and adopting his sentiment as already expressed, I would not, certainly I would not, if I could prevent it, carry by absorption, the absorption of those sores through the whole political body.

Williams, too, could be unfair; and he was in his strictures on the cities; for when he had cited Jefferson he added:

These cities are filled with men too rich, or too poor, to fraternize with the yeomen of the country; and I warn my fellow freeholders of the dangers which must attend the surrender of this most inestimable of privileges—this attribute of sovereignty. . . . When dangers threaten to whom must you look for support? Is your militia called for, he who has no interest in your soil swings his pack and is away, leaving the farmer and the farmer's son to abide the draft, and defend the life, liberty, and the property of themselves and the community.

Van Buren reacted as Williams anticipated, and answered in language which would lend a little color to Bancroft's charge. "Sir," said Van Buren, "it is grating to one's feelings to hear a man who had done his country the greatest service, and who at this moment occupies more space in the public mind than any other private citizen in the world, thus spoken of. But no more of this."

Van Buren's main speech on suffrage was made on Tuesday, September 25. He had waited until all of the chief actors in the drama had spoken their big lines. One of his great assets was his capacity to riddle the arguments of an antagonist; another was to develop in dramatic fashion the thought, simply expressed, of another, and make it his own.

The convention stenographer, in transcribing his notes, sometimes wrote as he recorded the words; again he would summarize; and frequently he would report in the third person. He did the last in putting down Van Buren's replies to Spencer and Kent. Answering the Chancellor, he said:

If he could possibly believe that from an extended suffrage there could result any portion of the calamitous consequences which have been so feelingly portrayed, he would repeat the acknowledgment of his respect and regard, he would be the last man in society to vote for it. But believing, as he conscientiously did, that those fears are altogether unfounded, hoping and expecting the happiest results from the abolition of the freehold qualification, and hoping, too, that caution and circumspection will preside over the settlement of the general right of suffrage which was hereafter to be made, and knowing, besides, that this State, in abolishing the freehold qualifications, would be but uniting herself in the march of principle which has already prevailed in every State of the Union, except two or three, including the royal charter of Rhode Island, he would cheerfully record his vote against the amendment.

Replying to the apprehensions of the Chief Justice that manufacturers would influence the vote of their workers, Van Buren said: ". . . it was a sufficient answer to the argument, that if they were so influenced, they would be enlisted on the same side, which it was the object of the amendment to promote, on the side of property. If not—if they were independent of the influence of their employers, they would be safe depositories [*sic!*] of the right."

This is unmistakably Van Buren. But the historian turned partisan altered the record and made Van Buren say: "If they are so influenced, they will be enlisted on the side of property which you propose to promote; if they are independent of their employers, they will be safe depositaries of the right."

Van Buren ably answered Spencer's fears that England's rotten boroughs would follow in the wake of an extension of suffrage. Bancroft states Van Buren said: "The cause of those corruptions is this: the representation of Great Britain is a representation of territory, not of men." We prefer what Van Buren said, so we will quote him, as the official stenographer did; sometimes in the first, and again in the third person; and leaving the V. B.'s we found there in lieu of Van Buren:

The honorable gentleman from Albany [Mr. Spencer] had next directed their attention to the borough elections in England, as evidence of the consequences which might be expected from the non-adoption of his amendment. Mr. V. B. said he could not, in his view of the subject, on the most mature reflection, have selected an argument better calculated to prove the amendment to be unwise and improper, than the one on which the gentleman mainly relied for its support.

What, sir, said he, was the cause of the corruptions which confessedly prevailed in that portion of the representation in the Parliament of Great Britain? Was it the lowness of the qualifications of the electors, in comparison with the residue of the country? No. In many of the boroughs a freehold qualification was required; in most, that they should be burgage holders and in all that they should be freemen, paying scot and lot. Compare, said Mr. V. B., these qualifications with those required in Westminster, and it will be found that the lowest of the former are equal to the latter.

It would not be necessary for him to say, that if the will of the people prevailed in any election in England—if patriotism and public spirit was sure to find its appropriate reward anywhere in that country it was at the Westminster elections. The qualifications of the electors, was not the cause, except it was in some instances where the election was confined to a very few, as for instance, to the Mayor and common council of the borough.

But I will tell you, sir, what is the cause: it is because the representation in question, is the representation of things, and not of men; it is because that it is attached to territory, to a village or town, without regard to population; as by the amendment under consideration, it is attempted here to be attached to territory, and to territory only. Suppose for a moment, that the principle upon which the report of the select committee is based, and which the amendment opposes, should be applied to the representation in the parliament of Great Britain, that instead of the present representation it should be apportioned among all their subjects who contribute to the public burthens? Would you hear any complaints from that country on the subject of their rotten boroughs? No, sir; but on the contrary that reform in Parliament would be at once obtained, for which the friends of reform in that devoted country have so long contended, and which they probably never will obtain except—to use the language of the gentleman from Albany—at the point of a bayonet. He could not therefore, but think that the illustration resorted to by the honorable mover of the amendment was most unfortunate to his argument, nor ought he to withhold his thanks for these suggestions.

Van Buren's speeches were like his letters, prolix, yet incisively thorough. He began his argument on suffrage with a mocking reference to the fears of the opposition. He singled out the venerable Chancellor, whose "known candor and purity of character would forbid any one to doubt that he spoke the sentiments of his heart"; and strengthened his followers with this bit of satire:

If a stranger had heard the discussion on this subject, and had been unacquainted with the character of our people, and the character and standing of those who find it their duty to oppose this measure, he might well have supposed that we were on the point of prostrating with lawless violence one of the fairest and firmest pillars of the Government and of introducing into the sanctuary of the constitution, a mob or a rabble, violent and disorganizing, as were the Jacobins of France; and furious and visionary as the radicals of England are, by some gentlemen supposed to be.

Van Buren then took his hearers through every State of the Union, showing how most of the States lacked freehold qualifications for electors, and that only in South Carolina was a distinction made between the two branches of the Legislature such as that proposed by Spencer.

He showed by the census figures of seven years earlier that of 163,000 electors, more than 75,000 owned freeholds of less than $250, and inquired if this class, composed of professional men, small landholders, and mechanics, should be excluded from representation in the upper house, which had equal power to originate bills, had a negative on all measures, and as the court of last resort, was entrusted with the life, liberty, and property of all citizens. It was to relieve this injustice, he added, that the Convention had been called.

And we will again cite the stenographic record:

There were two words, continued Mr. V. B., which had come into common use with our Revolutionary struggle; words which contained an abridgment of our political rights; words which, at that day, had a talismanic effect; which led our fathers from the bosoms of their families to the tented field; which, for seven long years of toil and suffering, had kept them to their arms, and which finally conducted them to a glorious triumph. They were, taxation and representation; nor did they lose their influence with the close of that struggle. . . .

Apply, said he, for a moment the principles they inculcate to the question under consideration and let its merits be thereby tested. Are those of your citizens represented whose voices are never heard in your Senate? Are those citizens in any degree represented or heard in the formation of your courts of justice, from the highest to the lowest? Was, then, representation in one branch of the Legislature, which by itself can do nothing—which instead of securing to them the blessings of legislation, only enables them to prevent it as an evil, anything more than a shadow? Was it not emphatically keeping the word of promise to the ear and breaking it to the hope? Was it not even less than the virtual representation with which our fathers were attempted to be appeased by their oppressors? It was even so; and if so, could they, as long as this distinction was retained, hold up their heads, and, without blushing, pretend to be the advocates for that special canon of political rights, that taxation and representation were, and ever should be, indissoluble? He thought not.

In whose name and for whose benefit, were they called upon to disappoint the just expectations of their constituents, and to persevere in what he could not but regard as a violation of principle? It was in the name and for the security of farmers that they were called upon to adopt this measure. This is, indeed, acting in an imposing name, and they who use it knew full well that it was so! It was, continued Mr. V. B., the boast, the pride, and the security of this nation that she had in her bosom a body of men who, for sobriety, integrity, industry, and patriotism, are unequalled by the cultivators of the earth in any other part of the known world. Nay, more: to compare them with men of similar pursuits in other countries was to degrade them. . . . He could not, he said, yield to any man in respect for this invaluable class of our citizens nor in zeal for their support; but how did this matter stand, inquired Mr. V. B., was the allegation that they were violating the wishes and tampering with the security of the farmers founded in fact, or was it merely colorable? Who, he asked, have hitherto constituted the majority of the voters of the State? The farmers—Who had called for and insisted upon the convention? Farmers and freeholders!

He then declared with truth that Spencer's amendment offered no additional security to property, and that its only purpose would be to excite jealousy in those who had no freehold property. Sound policy, he suggested, would dictate the abandonment of restriction. "I believe," he said, "with that elegant and modern writer 'that constitutions are the work of time and not the invention of ingenuity; and that to frame a complete system of government, depending on the habits of reverence and experience, was an attempt as absurd as to build a tree or manufacture an opinion.'"

The debate on suffrage went on intermittently for an entire month. When Spencer's amendment was defeated, Jay moved to include free blacks among the electors. Van Buren opposed this, but finally compromised by admitting negroes with freeholds of the value of $250 or more to the privilege of suffrage, and exempting from taxation all of their race who could not qualify as voters.

Numerous other extensions were attempted. Root offered one which was regarded as a preliminary to another which would have bestowed suffrage on every male citizen above the age of twenty-one who was not a pauper.

Two days after he made his big speech on suffrage Van Buren declared, without qualification, that he was opposed to universal suffrage. It was necessary that he cater to the prejudices of Rufus King, who with emphasis declared that "such an extent of the elective privilege would be in the highest degree dangerous: no government, ancient or modern, could endure it." The old order had faith in itself.

"We had already reached the verge of universal suffrage," said Van Buren. "There was but one step beyond. And are gentlemen prepared to take that step? We were cheapening this invaluable right." He added that he was disposed to go as far as any man in the extension of "rational liberty," but he could not consent "to undervalue this precious privilege, so far as to confer it with an Undiscriminating hand upon every one, black or white, who would be kind enough to condescend to accept it."

The following day the stenographer recorded that "Mr. Van Buren occupied the floor for some time in expressing his sentiments decidedly against the amendment and against universal suffrage."

Bancroft, who pictured Van Buren as an exponent in the convention of "the government of all by all," does not make a single reference to these strictures on universal suffrage.

There were minor changes also made in the Constitution: the term of the Governor was cut down from three to two years to balance the grant of the exclusive power of veto. This was to make him more responsible to the people. On motion of Livingston, Ulshoeffer's objections to "the speech from the throne" were written into the basic law, by ordaining that the Governor communicate with the Legislature by message.

In reducing the Governor's tenure of office it was provided that the next term would begin on January 1, 1823. This, as had been intended by his foes, shortened by six months the term to which Clinton had been elected.

Van Buren pretended to King that he believed that the

amendments would be defeated; and King, writing to his son John before the voters passed judgment on the work of the Convention, said:

> Van Buren never was zealous, nay has doubted whether the amendments wd. be adopted. In this he has not only been sincere, but individually disinterested, and should the Constitution fail it will possibly create more joy than grief.

It was Van Buren's boast that he studied the currents of public sentiment, and that to encounter them recklessly was inconsistent with the character of a prudent statesman. He had this quality; and he was neither astonished nor grieved when the electors ratified the new Constitution by the overwhelming vote of 75,422 to 33,925.

But the people were not satisfied with the restrictions placed on suffrage and agitation led to the granting of universal suffrage five years later. And nothing but words were exchanged in achieving this great reform; in a monarchy mere agitation for it led to riots and bloodshed.

## CHAPTER XXV

THE Convention adjourned without delay on November 10; and on the first Monday in December Van Buren took his seat in the Senate of the United States. His activities in the Senate during his first year might be summed up in saying that he attended the sessions regularly and that he seldom missed a meeting of the two important committees of finance and judiciary to which he had been appointed. It was not long before he was elected chairman of the latter, a post he held throughout his career in Congress. But he was more occupied than most of his colleagues. He mingled with every one of importance, called on all the Representatives from New York, and paid especial attention to the followers of Clinton. One of the first he visited was Solomon Van Rensselaer, who had been unanimously elected to the House of Representatives after his removal from the office of Adjutant General by Van Buren's Council of Appointment.

Although Monroe's successor was not to be chosen for another two years, Washington talked little else. Van Buren held his counsel: no one knew where he stood. Some suspected he inclined to John C. Calhoun. Yet in a letter to Johnston Verplanck, in the latter part of December, he did not even mention Calhoun as a possibility: he foresaw the country divided on John Quincy Adams, William H. Crawford, and Henry Clay.

"The present prospect," he wrote, "is that the East will be for Adams the West for Clay & the South for Crawford & it will be for New York by & by to rally enough of them upon the old ground & save the party. To do this with effect it is highly important that she be kept out of the contest as long as that can be done without exposing herself to the danger of distraction at home or subjecting ourselves to the imputation of being governed by selfish motives. How long that can be done I confess I am not prepared to say . . ."

Van Buren's concern is to wait until things have so shaped themselves that New York can dictate the nomination, without, of course, appearing selfish. The New York Legislature carried out Van Buren's thought, and adopted resolutions that it was inexpedient to act on the Presidential election.

In the middle of December it was gossiped among the New York members that the financial affairs of Solomon Southwick were in bad shape. Southwick, although disgraced in the eyes of the average man after he had been pilloried as a corruptionist, had not lost caste with some of the politicians, who had him appointed Postmaster of Albany. Van Rensselaer learned that the Postmaster General had demanded that Southwick make good the shortage immediately under penalty of removal.

The day after Christmas Van Rensselaer wrote to the Patroon: "Van Buren is very civil, he and all the Bucktails have been to see me. I am on very good terms with them all. . . . The office of Post Master at Albany will become vacant unless he [Southwick] makes deposits to a large amount in the State Bank without delay. . . . The Post Master General is my decided friend, I will also have the support of the Secretary of War [John C. Calhoun]. I think also all the members from our State in our House, Ohio, Kentucky and Tennessee will vote that office to me; and if a strong recommendation comes from Albany, and you write to King and Van Buren in such terms as the occasion will warrant, I think by abandoning politics, with strict regard to my duty, I may sit down in comfort, peace and quietness with an affectionate family the rest of my precarious days."

If the old soldier could get this berth he could, as he put it, sit down in comfort, peace, and quietness for the rest of his days. Southwick had a fixed salary of $2,000, he employed four clerks, two of them at $300 each, another at $800, and a fourth at $150. The last two places were held by sons of Southwick, one a small boy. Van Rensselaer had grown-up sons and daughters who could do some of the work.

On New Year's Eve twenty-two of the twenty-eight Representatives from New York signed a petition to the Postmaster General recommending the appointment of Van Rensselaer on his merit, and because of "an ardent wish that a brave and wounded soldier may be sheltered from the storms of adversity, and may with his family find a solace to his afflictions in the gratitude of his country."

Four days later, when Van Buren learned of these efforts, he and Rufus King wrote to Postmaster General Meigs asking him to delay making an appointment until "all concerned" could be heard. Meigs called on President Monroe and said that he had made up his mind to appoint Van Rensselaer unless he had objections. Monroe replied that he had none, but would like to consult the Secretary of the Navy, Smith Thompson.

Thompson, after he heard the President, objected strongly, but Monroe looked for more than a mere objection. Thompson immediately informed Van Buren and Vice President Tompkins of his conversation with the President. And—as Adams wrote in his diary—Tompkins later in the day "broke out into the most violent language against the President himself, and in the presence of a person who he must have known would report all he said to him."

The following day Meigs replied briefly to Van Buren and King, intimating strongly that he would appoint Van Rensselaer "without delay." Instantly Van Buren, King, and the Vice President held a council of war: Van Buren was determined that he was to dictate all Federal appointments in New York State as he did all local appointments at home.

Under the law, the President had no voice in the appointment of Deputy Postmasters. This was exclusively within the province of the Postmaster General. It should be also borne in mind that officially the President knew nothing of the affair. But at this council the trio were resolved that the President must be dragged into the case and the administration stampeded into forcing Meigs not to appoint Van Rensselaer. Accordingly all three signed a letter to Meigs requesting delay, and adding: "Should you think proper to comply with our request we propose two weeks as the requisite time, and in that event you will please inform us whether the consideration of the question is still with the President, in order that the citizens of Albany may be informed to whom their communication may be addressed. We request the favor of your answer in time to enable us to make the requisite communication by the next mail."

Never before had a Vice President of the United States and two United States Senators made an issue of a minor appointment. The President, on being shown the letter, summoned his

Cabinet to meet immediately. The heads of all the departments of the government on reaching the President's office were relieved to learn that there were no other hostilities impending than the Clinton-Van Buren war.

At the Cabinet conference Meigs gave the President his reasons for deciding on Van Rensselaer. He further said that no other candidate had been presented for his consideration. Thompson, Secretary of the Navy, inquired if John Lansing, New York's former Chancellor, had not been recommended to him. Meigs answered no, and observed that Lansing was nearly seventy years of age. Meigs spoke the truth. Van Rensselaer had stolen a march on Van Buren.

Adams, then Secretary of State, inquired if there would be any inconvenience in delaying the appointment for a fortnight. Meigs said there would; that Southwick would in the meantime be receiving the money of the public, and the longer he remained in office the greater would be the amount of his delinquency. Adams asked if his deputy could not be authorized to act in the interval. Meigs said his deputy was of his own family and would be under his control. Meigs then left the room and the President said that "he thought it very questionable whether he ought to interfere in the case at all."

A heated discussion followed. Thompson insisted that Van Rensselaer should not be appointed. Wirt declared with equal vigor that this was the era of good feeling, and that there were no political divisions in the land, and that there were no parties. The meeting adjourned without any decision being reached.

The Cabinet meeting was held on Friday, January 5. On the same day Van Buren wrote his aides in Albany directing them to shower memorials on the President protesting against the appointment of Van Rensselaer. The first on Van Buren's list of correspondents is Knower, Marcy's father-in-law. One memorial is to be signed by the citizens of Albany, and is to "state simply the respectability &c. of the chancellor, and the desire to see him provided for." A more elaborate petition is to be prepared by the Republican members of the legislature. Van Buren reveals his motives in opposing Van Rensselaer with Lansing, saying:

We thought proper to present the name of Chancellor Lansing. By we I mean the vice-president, Mr. King, and myself. The President being personally acquainted with the chancellor, and entertaining a personal regard for him we thought it the most likely mode to defeat the appointment of V. R. . . .

Van Buren directs that the memorial shall stress "that whatever may be deemed a fit course at this time on the question of removing federalists from office on the ground of their politics, you think that all other matters equal, a republican should be preferred for a new appointment on that ground only."

He is emphatic that this be done, adding: "I would present that question distinctly to the president, that we may know hereafter what we are to expect." He cautions them not to be offensive in their language, and to phrase the petition "with the utmost delicacy and respect." This, he notes, is extremely important; for "if the petition should in the least degree wear the aspect of threatening or scolding, it would be ruinous." Yet, at the same time, he directs that the Republicans in the Legislature speak with firmness, and as if conscious of their rights and regardful of their duties.

Van Buren also wants letters sent to the Bucktail members in Congress protesting "in such terms as are not offensive" against their recommending Van Rensselaer for the place. "By this means I propose we may defeat V.R.'s appointment," continues Van Buren. He is anxious that Knower show Southwick the correspondence with Meigs so "that he may know that we had not sought his removal."

The next night Van Buren called a meeting of the Republican Congressmen from New York. He protested against their signing Van Rensselaer's petition, and persuaded eleven to sign an appeal addressed "To the President of the United States" asking for delay. And Van Buren the same day informed Knower that he and Tompkins were prepared to prevent the appointment by a personal appeal to the President "and put the question on such political ground that the people of the United States may distinctly understand what principles prevail in that department of the government, and may take measures necessary to a wholesale reform. . . . I am for taking the bull by the horns at once, and if our friends at home sustain us, we will effect it." Van Buren would "reform" the Post Office Department in the interests of the spoils system.

234 An Epoch and a Man

The following morning the President washed his hands of the sordid scramble for place in a short note to Van Buren. Monroe wrote that the law did not contemplate that the President should have any agency in the appointment of deputy postmasters, and that he deemed it "improper to interfere." Meigs appointed Van Rensselaer.

Van Buren felt that his prestige had been hurt by the incident. He would not let it rest. In a letter to Charles E. Dudley, marked private, dated January 10, he directed that public meetings be held in Albany to protest against the action of Meigs, and to center all their fire on him, but not to criticize any other officer of the National government. Attacks were immediately made on Meigs. The tone of them is reflected in this line from Dudley to Van Buren: "No other atonement can be made, in my opinion, to the injured feelings of the republicans of this state than by the president's removing the post-master-general [*sic!*] from office."

Four nights after the Van Burenites held their meeting, the Clintonians held one at which Lieutenant Governor Tayler and others spoke. Philip S. Parker said, "That Mr. King, a high-toned federalist and ci-devant leader of the party, should object to the appointment of General Van Rensselaer because he was a federalist is truly remarkable." Parker added that it was "a fact very notorious, in this city and state, that the vice president and Mr. Van Buren . . . contributed much to the election of Mr. King to the senate of the United States, notwithstanding he was a Federalist."

After reading the Bucktail attacks on the administration, Calhoun told Walter Patterson, a New York member, that they were disgraceful. Patterson, writing to Van Rensselaer, said: "Van Buren is determined, if possible, to remove the Post Master General but he has not the *power*, though he possesses the *will*."

Van Buren was planting the seeds of New York's spoils system in the Nation's Capital; but the night air of several winters must nurture this singular and noxious plant to make it bloom in the larger field.

# CHAPTER XXVI

THE setback to Van Buren's political prestige made him none the less welcome socially. His courtly manner, short stature, and yellow locks were familiar to every drawing room in Washington. A widower, not yet forty, well-to-do, and a member of the Senate, is a highly desirable addition to the invitation list of the most discriminating hostess.

"There is here," wrote Rufus King in a gossipy letter to his son John, "a Miss Randolph, granddaughter of Mr. Jefferson; about whom the young members of Congress collect, and with them V. B."

Of course V. B. was none other than his yellow-haired colleague from New York. But to let King continue the gossip:

"She is intelligent and more interesting for her education and literature than for beauty, or the manners of good society."

The truth is that she shocked King by asking the Marine Band to play a popular song of the day at a quadrille party at Colonel Henderson's. Van Buren with his yellow locks was there. And thus King described the dreadful *faux pas:*

"During a few days since at Col. Henderson's, the Marine Band was present, and Miss Randolph, requested to name the music, called for the Yellow-haired Laddie &c, &c—"

When King reached the second &c he was mute at the thought that the daughter of a Governor of Virginia, and the granddaughter of a President of the United States, could so forget the conventions. The very title of the ballad pointed to King's colleague. There was a suggestion of playful raillery of Van Buren in her request; for the song concerned a love-sick rustic, and fickle to boot. The first two verses ran:

In April, when primroses paint the sweet plain,
And summer approaching rejoiceth the swain,
The yellow-hair'd laddie would oftentimes go
To wilds and deep glens, where the hawthorn trees grow.

> There, under the shade of an old sacred thorn,
> With freedom he sung his loves, evening and morn;
> He sang with so soft and enchanting a sound
> That Sylvans and Fairies unseen danc'd around.

The sprightly miss who made King wonder what the growing generation was coming to, was Ellen Wayles Randolph, one of the gracious daughters of Martha Jefferson and Thomas Mann Randolph. She and her two sisters, Mary and Cornelia, who never married, and their parents, were frequently guests of Van Buren; and the Randolphs often played host to the yellow-haired laddie.

Van Buren grew enamored of Washington society. When Root inquired if he would accept the office of Chief Justice of New York's Supreme Court, he replied, a day or so after the party at Henderson's: "To your question respecting the Chief Justice (with proper impressions of your friendly feelings in the matter) I answer no. The situation in which by the favor of the state I have been placed is perfectly satisfactory to me, and whatever others may from time to time have for mischievous purposes suggested, I have not had, nor have I now, the least disposition to change it. . . ."

The same thought is repeated on February 18 in a letter to Worth: ". . . *I have an entire aversion to the place of Gov^r.*—I have seen enough of state politics for many years—*I have made my debut here and am abundantly satisfied*—The situation I occupy is precisely the one which at this moment is most agreeable to me & I am determined not to quit it voluntarily." Even the Governorship could not lure him from Washington and its gay society.

In the middle of March Van Buren journeyed to Richmond to visit Governor Randolph, the father of the sprightly Ellen. Politics, chiefly, was the subject of the interview.

This visit was noted in the Washington dispatches to the metropolitan press. The New York members of Congress, in letters home, made the trip the basis of a report that he was affianced to one of Jefferson's granddaughters. Spencer, a week or so after Van Buren returned to Washington, wrote: ". . . Rumor with her hundred tongues says that you are going to Europe; that you are going to be married &^c. I suppose both are equally true."

Almost simultaneously he received a letter from Michael Ulshoeffer which began with a reference to the trip to Virginia and then continued: "Whilst the politicians asserted that you had undertaken that journey with views of a political aspect, others circulated a report that you had gone to consummate a matrimonial scheme. One set believed that there was a great plot to revive the republican party (which they vainly hope cannot be sustained on the old grounds) and that Jefferson & Madison are to be engaged in it. The others said that the object of your journey, was a beautiful & accomplished young lady, not distantly related to the Governor of Virginia, and that an alliance of portentous consequences was thus to be formed between the 'ancient dominion' and this 'great state,'—But whatever may have been the dreadful design of your visit, I rejoice at your safe return . . ."

Van Buren was too busy with politics to think of love; but he was fond of Ellen, of whom he speaks twice in his political memoirs. In the following January he was conversing with her at a party given by the French minister when Rufus King, seeing her shoe-string trailing, dropped on his knee and retied it. Van Buren felt ashamed at his own "unprompt gallantry." In describing this incident, Van Buren refers to her as "a very interesting young lady—the granddaughter of Mr. Jefferson and my warm friend."

The other reference concerns his visit to Monticello with his political ally, Senator Mahlon Dickerson, later Governor of New Jersey. After speaking of their first day at the home of Jefferson, he says: "On the next and subsequent days, leaving the Governor [Dickerson] to be entertained by our host's granddaughter, an accomplished and very agreeable lady, now Mrs. [Joseph] Coolidge, of Boston, (whose future husband paid his first visit to her while we were at Monticello) we employed our mornings in drives about the neighborhood."

Before the session ended Van Buren found himself deep in Presidential politics. But no one was certain just where he stood. The Patroon, from his seat in Congress, wrote to his predecessor on April 9: "Col. [John] Williams [Senator from Tennessee] is in favor of Crawford, he is the favourite at present, being a Virginian; that State will be in his favor unless they see a prospect for Clay as President. V. Buren was, when he arrived here, a Calhoun man. . . . Governor Clinton I think is rising in public estimation the more they appreciate his character. I have endeavored to remove their objections; they represent him as an intriguer, and as dangerous a man as *Burr* was. If he retires a few years, his weight of character will be acknowledged and he will rise."

Congress adjourned on May 8 to the first Monday in December. Van Buren's only speech of moment was in opposition to a disputed Louisiana land claim on February 12. On his return to Albany he reformed friendships with many who had been estranged by his conduct in the matter of the postmastership; and in time he and Solomon Van Rensselaer shook hands.

In the first week of July there was a turtle feast at Cruttenden's tavern, Albany's largest inn. Edward Livingston, Senator from Van Buren's district, "sat between Mawne [Harmanus] Bleecker and Mat. Van Buren, and received from the latter sundry protestations &c." From another letter of Livingston to Hoyt we learn that "Gibbons the butcher wants to be mayor of Albany, and Southwick governor." Which caused the irrepressible Edward to exclaim: "Huzza for universal suffrage!" And he expresses the fervent wish that it be mixed with a little universal knowledge and honesty.

Southwick was not nominated by the Republicans; but that did not prevent him from nominating himself. He obtained only a handful of votes against Judge Joseph C. Yates, who had the united support of the Clintonians and the Van Burenites.

Clinton, of course, had no choice but to retire, as Van Buren controlled the nominating machinery. Van Buren, in short, was master; only a moral issue, ably presented to the people, could overcome the thoroughly drilled corps of electioneers at Van Buren's call.

All that remained to Clinton in the shape of public place when the hour of midnight was tolled on December 31, 1822, was his office as Canal Commissioner. There was no money in this for him. The Patroon, too, served without pay. The other Commissioners were paid for their services.

Clinton accepted his fate cheerfully. He could always make a living. He would have more leisure now for his literary and scientific work. He was president of these learned bodies: the

Academy of Fine Arts, the Literary and Philosophical Society, and the New York Historical Society. His enemies could not cry down his talents, so they ridiculed them, and nowhere with more effect than in the *Opera Minora of the Poetae Bucktailici*, which had made its appearance in the winter of 1819-1820. To quote a fragment:

> 'Tis Dr. Clinton, our State's chief reliance,
> A paragon of learning, wit and science,
> Skilled in all arts, the Crichton of our day . . .

This volume, familiarly known as *The Bucktail Bards*, was all the more effective for having a semblance of impartiality. In the introduction we read: "Corruption has erected her court on the heights of the Hudson, in the avenues of Albany, in the lobby of the legislature. . . . Her throne was the lobby—the ermine her cloke [*sic!*]—banks were her playthings—bribes were her sugar plums." When the book came out Van Buren was asked by Johnston Verplanck to distribute them in Albany "to annoy Clinton." The authors—the work appeared anonymously—were Gulian Crommelin Verplanck and John Duer. They penned the first bit of verse on Van Buren in the following couplet:

> What schemes to Master Clinton's ruin,
> The fertile brain of Mat was brewing.

Shortly before Clinton retired from the Governorship he answered his critics with a volume of letters which had appeared periodically in the New York *Statesman*, and entitled: "Letters on the Natural History and Internal Resources of the State of New York." The book was what its title indicated. Yet it was more: manners and customs were described, and throughout its pages were interspersed subtle assaults on his foes, literary and political.

Following the custom of the times, Clinton concealed his identity behind a nom de plume. He assumed the rôle of a visitor from Ireland, and signed himself *Hibernicus.*

"I hardly understand the nomenclature of parties," wrote Clinton. "They are all republicans, and yet a portion of the people assume the title of republican, as an exclusive right, or patent monopoly. They are all federalists, that is, in favor of a general government—and yet a part arrogate to themselves this appellation to the disparagement of the others. It is easy to see that the difference is nominal—that the whole controversy is about office, and that the country is constantly assailed by ambitious demagogues for the purpose of gratifying their cupidity. It is a melancholy, but true reflection on human nature, that the smaller the difference the greater the animosity. . . . I have often asked some of the leading politicians of this country, what constituted the real points of discrimination between the Republicans and Federalists, and I never could get a satisfactory answer. An artful man will lay hold of words if he cannot of things, in order to promote his views."

And then this biting observation on the High Minded: "There are some who are continually oscillating between parties . . . In order to cover their turpitude, they assume high sounding names, and are in verity political partisans, laying claims to be high minded, and like Jupiter on Olympus, elevated above the atmosphere of common beings. And what adds infinitely to the force of these pretensions, is to find the most of these gentry to be the heroes of petty strife, and the leaders of village vexation, the fag ends of the learned professions, and the outcasts of reputable associations."

He praised the occasional productions of America's scientific men, who are attacked immediately "by the witlings, the poetasters, and the sciolists of the country, who unite to run down merit which they cannot imitate. . . . Dr. [David] Hosack has been assailed by the low buffoonery of literary punchinellos and shallow-pated coxcombs. When in company with the savants of my native country . . . I never heard the names of [Gulian Crommelin] Verplanck and . . . [John] Duer . . . until I landed on these shores."

The immediate purpose of these letters was to show how the Canal would lessen the cost of transportation, thereby benefiting not only the State, but the nation. And this he hurled at the foes of the project: "To see the profligate attempts to arrest this great system of public improvement, in order to elevate obscure pettifoggers, and miserable drivellers, is really calculated to excite more than common sensibility."

Had Clinton been as thorough a politician as he was a philosopher, he would not have retired before Van Buren. But throughout his public career he mocked his enemies in phrases that stung and lacerated. In his retirement he could find consolation in the last line of the twenty-sixth letter of his *Hibernicus:* "A combination of smatterers in literature, of sciolists in knowledge, of pretenders to public spirit, and of all that is little and contemptible, against all that is great and respectable can never prevail in an enlightened and patriotic country." Clinton had more than one proof of the truth of this: he was to have more.

# CHAPTER XXVII

VAN BUREN began his second session in Washington with concerns for his political machine in New York. Reports reached him that Governor Yates was inclined to be independent. Rumors reached Yates that Van Buren had boasted he would dictate the policy of the Governor. Yates was angry. Van Buren denied that he had voiced any such sentiment. In the same letter he recommended that the Governor appoint Jacob Sutherland and William A. Duer Associate Justices of the new Supreme Court. He made no suggestion regarding the office of Chief Justice, which Spencer was holding until the reorganized judiciary took office on August 10.

Yates threw the recommendations into the waste paper basket, and sent to the Senate the names of three of the sitting judges, including that of Chief Justice Spencer, Clinton's brother-in-law. Van Buren had no personal feeling against Spencer. They corresponded regularly. But it was war to the knife against all Clintonians. Nor had he any ill-will toward the other nominees, Jonas Platt and John Woodworth. Van Buren could not control Yates, but he did control the Senate, which promptly rejected the Governor's nominations by a vote that was almost unanimous.

Yates learned a lesson quickly. The next day he sent to the Senate the names of two of Van Buren's aides, Sutherland and John Savage, together with one of his own selection, Samuel R. Betts. Savage, who was State Comptroller, he named for the place of Chief Justice. The Senate confirmed the two Van Burenites, and rejected Betts.

Yates thought this unfair; he had given the lion's share to Van Buren, whose followers did not seem willing to let him have even a crumb. He had resolved not to name Duer. Knowing that Van Buren was cultivating the friendship of the Patroon, Yates nominated the Patroon's brother-in-law a second time. The Senate had Van Buren's permission to confirm the appointment.

Duer, who had invoked Van Buren's aid, again writes to him. He is now seeking a place on the circuit bench. He complains that the Van Burenites had raised the cry "against the high minded" —he had been one. "Even your friend [Levi] Beardsley I hear is against the high minded appointments," said Duer. He believes that if he will solicit aid among the Senators he may be confirmed, as Yates, anxious to appoint men of capacity, will send in his name. This grandson of the Earl of Stirling, who cast his lot with the Revolutionists, shrinks from begging for the place, much as he wants it, and gives this reason: "To me the indelicacy of electioneering with Senators is insurmountable . . . perhaps you may be disposed to exert your influence in my behalf with your friends in the Senate."

Van Buren did the work from which Duer shrunk and made him a judge in the last week of April. He also permitted the Senate to confirm Yates's friend Betts as a circuit judge.

While Van Buren was being solicited by his followers in New York for jobs, his brother-in-law, Moses I. Cantine, died. This left the editorship of the *Argus* vacant, the official organ of Van Buren and his immediate aides, who were becoming known as the Albany Regency. Van Buren asked Hoyt to seek a suitable successor to Cantine. "Under no circumstances," he wrote, "ought any one to be appointed who is not a sound, practicable, and above all, discreet Republican. Without a paper thus edited at Albany we may hang our harps on the willows."

The chief of Van Buren's editorial corps in New York City, Mordecai M. Noah, then editing the *Advocate*, sought the place of State Printer, which Cantine held. On encountering considerable opposition, Noah protested to Hoyt. "I am not so certain that I can be defeated—but if so, I am willing to hazard a defeat, reserving to myself the right of spreading the facts before the world, and exhibiting the system of peddling away the patronage of the State," wrote Noah.

The main opposition to Noah came from the Republicans in his own city. Ulshoeffer and other Tammany leaders were annoyed by his dictatorial manner. Ulshoeffer confidentially inquired at this time if Noah was authorized to say "as he does in his paper, that all who are not his friends had better stay at home or not offer their names at Albany this winter."

Noah was not appointed State Printer; and he did not spread
before the world the system of peddling away the patronage of
the State—nor did any one else. Van Buren mollified him by
having him nominated for Sheriff of New York, a place to which
he had been appointed before his patron left for Washington.
He was the last Sheriff under the appointive system. He was an
able editor, and the first of his race to attain high distinction in
the field of journalism in this country. He had a good style and a
ready wit. When objections were made to his being appointed
Sheriff on the pretense that it would not be fitting for a Jew to
hang a Christian, Noah retorted: "Pretty Christians to require
hanging at all!" A few months after he was defeated for Sheriff,
Tammany elected him Grand Sachem, thanks to Van Buren's
friendly offices.

There was a streak of the grotesque in Noah. He professed a
belief that the Indians were the descendants of one of the lost
tribes of Israel. In September, 1825, during one of his droll
moments he decked himself out in crimson and ermine, hired a
band, and led a procession through the streets of Buffalo, and
thence to Grand Island. There, with much ceremony, he laid the
corner stone of what he said would be a new city, which he called
Ararat, in commemoration of the landing of the earlier Noah on
the Assyrian mountains after the deluge. But the editor of the
*Advocate* was unable to persuade either his own people, or the
Indians, to carry out his fantastic scheme for a new Jerusalem
of which he was to be king, with a capital on an island in the
river above Niagara Falls.

To the *Advocate* all Washington turned in the early part of
1823 to see if Noah was saying anything new about the Presidency. No one could get a word from Van Buren, but from the
persistency with which Noah advocated the nomination of Crawford, and his attacks on all who showed a contrary preference, it
was assumed that Van Buren was for Crawford.

There was considerable demand for a Northern man, as
Virginia had monopolized the office since the formation of the
Republic. Vice President Tompkins was out of consideration; but
the other New York member of the administration, Secretary
Thompson, was quietly eyeing the grand prize.

On the night of February 1 Thompson called on Van Buren

at Bradley's boarding house, and together they visited King, who also lodged there. They talked of the news from Albany, and then Thompson asked if it was not time that the New York Legislature showed an interest in the next President. Van Buren responded that the legislators showed a clear opinion in favor of delay at the last session, and in taking a definite stand now, with the campaign a year away, they might be charged with inconsistency. Thompson replied that several States had actually nominated candidates since that time, and that there was no analogy between last winter and the present. Van Buren declined to assent to this, and displayed a disinclination to continue the discussion. Thompson changed the subject.

Van Buren left the room for a minute. Thompson turned to King and said: "When you shall ascertain Van Buren's preference among the candidates, you must let me know it." Thompson recalled that Noah's paper was constantly talking Crawford, and that every one in Washington believed Noah reflected Van Buren's opinion. When they heard Van Buren returning Thompson hurriedly repeated his request that King tell him where Van Buren stood on the Presidency, adding that Van Buren continued to keep his preference dark. As Van Buren entered, King said: "We are speaking of the *Advocate's* being the index of your opinions and preferences." Van Buren was not to be caught. He continued them in the dark.

After Thompson departed, Van Buren, who had been reflecting on Thompson's urging that New York take a stand on the Presidency, observed that Thompson seemed willing to be a contender for the office. King agreed, and suggested that Van Buren talk the subject over with his old friend.

Two days later, which was the first Sunday in February, Van Buren told King that he had thought much on the subject; that he did not see his way clear; and that he never engaged in anything which he could not see his way through.

Congress adjourned on March 3. The following day Van Buren told Thompson frankly the contest lay chiefly between Crawford and Adams, and that if he sought the Presidency he would find opposition in his own State; but that he might aspire, with some degree of success, to the Vice Presidency. Thompson replied that he might succeed Brockholst Livingston on the

United States Supreme Court Bench. Livingston was nearing the end.

That night, it being the end of the session, much wine was consumed in Bradley's boarding house. One of the diners was the son of Thomas Tillotson, who had sat in Van Buren's seat in Congress. Young Tillotson and Van Buren had more than their share of the wine.

The wine had robbed Van Buren of his usual caution. Tillotson chid Van Buren with being unfriendly to his cousin, Edward Livingston—who had sat between Mawne Bleecker and Van Buren at the turtle feast last July, and listened to sundry protestations from the latter. And Livingston's kinsman then declared that Edward was sure to be reëlected to the State Senate, let Van Buren do as he would.

Van Buren bristled up at this challenge. He denied that Livingston could succeed against his influence—even in Columbia County. Van Buren recalled how he had helped Tillotson's kinsman to be elected to the State Senate; yet, when Van Buren's brother was a candidate for the nomination for Surrogate of Columbia County, and he sought delegates in Livingston's own town, Livingston was neuter.

Van Buren was very rarely in this condition. He was probably very contrite on awakening in the morning; for he did not oppose Livingston when he was reëlected that fall, the new State Constitution having moved the election of legislators forward.

On his return to New York the dispatches told of the passing of Associate Justice Livingston. He advised Thompson to accept Livingston's place if it were offered to him. Thompson replied that his health would not endure the cloistered atmosphere of the bench; and if Monroe offered it to him, he would recommend Van Buren for this high honor. Van Buren's heart beat faster. Other correspondence passed between the two; and on the night of Good Friday, Van Buren called on King at Jamaica for aid and advice. All that remained, according to Thompson's last letter, was Van Buren's acceptance of the offer when the President appointed him.

Van Buren was accompanied by Ulshoeffer. Both listened while King dwelt on the importance, authority, dignity, and independence of the office; and stressed that this high place precluded expectations of ulterior advancement, and demanded complete divorcement from party or personal politics. King then recalled that all knew that Van Buren was engaged deeply in party politics, and that if he succeeded Livingston he must dissolve all political ties.

Van Buren was confident that he could do all this. Still King was not satisfied. He emphasized that the dissolution of all contacts with the political world must be absolute; that entering the temple of justice was like taking the vow and veil in the Catholic Church; and unless Van Buren was confident that he had the strength to do this, he must not consider the Supreme Court for a moment.

Ulshoeffer concurred. Van Buren in assenting expressed confidence in his firmness to renounce the political world on taking the oath of office of a member of the United States Supreme Court.

Van Buren and Ulshoeffer remained with King over night. King promised to see Van Buren in the city on Easter Sunday, but a snow storm prevented his making the trip. It was not until Tuesday, April 1, that King kept the appointment.

Van Buren in the meantime had answered the last letter of Thompson; but in accordance with a promise to King, he withheld posting his reply until the older man had seen it.

King was not satisfied, and altered the letter so as to exclude the thought that Van Buren was seeking the office. In it he acknowledged his acti. 'ty in party politics, and avowed himself ready to sever all political ties when offered the appointment. To induce an early decision Thompson was reminded that the Presidential question would soon assume a distinct shape, and that Van Buren, from his standing in the party, could not avoid this under present circumstances.

At Van Buren's suggestion, King wrote letters to the President and to the Secretary of State. King dispatched his brief note to Adams immediately: the second half of it reading: *"The appointment would not only be good, but better than any other which could be made from this State. In other respects, the measure will be important, and, if elected without delay, may perhaps be decisive. This communication could not be delayed."*

In the italicized sentence King emphasized that Van Buren

was worthier of the office than Thompson, Spencer, and other New Yorkers mentioned for the place. The next phrase pleased King, who observed as he read it over: "If Mr. Adams has a good nose, he can be at no loss for my object."

It did not require even a good nose to sense that Van Buren's appointment would give Adams a great advantage in New York by removing from the political arena Crawford's ablest ally in the East. Adams, who always spoke his mind, recorded in his diary that in a conversation with the Patroon he said that "Mr. Van Buren was a man of great talents and good principles, but he had suffered them to be too much warped by party spirit."

King's praise of Van Buren, in his letter to the President, reads: ". . . Men of all parties agree that Mr. Van Buren possesses superior talents, much legal acumen, and great public experience; that on difficult occasions he has shewn uncommon sagacity and decision of character; in affairs, in which the purity of men's motives has sometimes appeared doubtful, the disinterested, open, and decided proceedings of Mr. Van Buren have constantly protected his integrity from suspicion; so that in this respect no man stands on higher ground, and in all other respects, no one is better qualified for a high and difficult judicial station."

King added that Van Buren possessed the prudence which might be required "in reconciling and adjusting the powers of the General and State Governments—a reconciliation that from year to year becomes more critical; and which can be effected by no other means than by the prudent exercise of the powers of the national Judiciary."

He noted that appointments to this high court should be made with the utmost caution; and observed that this had not always been the case. After dwelling on the importance of the bench in its relation to the preservation of the public liberties, he added:

"We must not forget that the wisdom of other Departments is inadequate to supply a defect of the Judiciary. We are therefore all responsible, and the President and Senate above all others, that the Supreme Court be so composed, that the Master Spirit of the Chief Justice may not die, but by the appointment from time to time of able & prudent men, may be rendered perpetual. With these views, in a matter that so deeply concerns the public welfare, I offer no apology in urging you with earnestness and sincerity to name Van Buren as the successor of Mr. Livingston."

On April 6 Thompson wrote to Van Buren: "I submitted to the President confidentially your letter. He informed me that no appointment would be made in some time: as it could not be made in time for the Spring Courts, there was no necessity for acting at present. He said nothing from which I could gather his intentions in relation to the appointment. I think he is quite undecided and means to take due time for consideration."

The next day Adams wrote to Rufus King that Thompson had not communicated with the President on the subject, and King at once transmitted the information to Van Buren.

Something had gone wrong in Washington. Van Buren saw through it at once and wrote Thompson pointedly: "If you will excuse me for troubling you further on this subject I will be glad to be informed, whether your declension has been definite & whether Mr. Monroe so understands it."

Adams, who agreed with all that King had said of Van Buren's talents and availability, was the first to suspect that Thompson was deceiving Van Buren. Van Buren hinted at the same suspicion in a letter to King, written the day before he addressed Thompson: "Habitual indecision and intercourse with court parasites make great havoc in the capacity of a man to behave well on special occasions."

Adams was thoroughly disgusted with the course of Thompson. Adams, who was kept constantly advised by King, went directly to Monroe and asked if Thompson had given him a definite answer to his tender of the appointment to the bench. This was a month after Thompson had written to Van Buren that he had declined and had recommended him in his stead. The President replied that Thompson had not.

Adams when he next saw Thompson told him what the President had said. Caught in this web of his own weaving, Thompson penned a weak explanation to Van Buren. It was now clear to Van Buren and his friends that Thompson had changed his mind and wanted the place for himself.

The incident was now closed with Van Buren, save to tender his thanks to King. He could not write to Adams, as he was acting as a friend of King. In expressing his gratitude Van Buren said:

". . . If as you seemed to think you owed any duty to the public in relation to this mater [*sic!*] it appears to me that what you have already done amounts to a full discharge of the claims of private friendship. With the President I do not see that any further communication can with propriety be had, & M^r. A^s. disposition needs no improvement. The conduct of the latter gentleman [Adams] has made a most favorable impression on my mind of which I hope one day to be able to give him suitable proof. . . ."

In the middle of the summer Van Buren received this brief note from Thompson: "Nothing has as yet been definitely decided relative to the filling of the vacancy on the Bench of the S. Court. My present object is to enquire of you whether after what has passed between you & myself on the subject you think I could with propriety, as it respects yourself, take the office?"

Van Buren, following King's advice, made a most reserved reply. He again told Thompson, as he had early in the spring, to accept the place; and prefaced a profession of friendship with this barbed line: "This opinion, and this advice, my dear sir, are not changed by anything that has since taken place between us." And Thompson, after whom Van Buren had named his last child, was appointed Livingston's successor.

Thus ended another of Van Buren's dreams of renouncing the world of politics.

## CHAPTER XXVIII

Some four weeks before Van Buren received Thompson's letter, he took his two oldest children to Jamaica, leaving the younger with Rufus King's family, where he lived while attending school in the Long Island village. The guest of the Kings was John, now in his thirteenth year, destined to be the Prince John of his and his father's enemies. Godkin truly said that Prince John could sway a popular audience almost better than any man of his day. His brother, Abraham, three years his senior, was being indulged a bit by his father before he began his studies at West Point.

We will leave the two boys and return with Van Buren to Albany. His law practice required his attention, and yet he must canvass for Crawford. Van Buren was anticipating an indecisive vote in the Electoral College which would throw the election of Monroe's successor into the House of Representatives: he had predicted its possibility to both Thompson and King early in the year.

He was determined, however, that New York's Electors would be pledged to Crawford. To effect this he sought the nomination of candidates for the Assembly and Senate favorable to a Congressional Caucus. The anti-Crawford men were against the Caucus.

Hard-thinking men everywhere were beginning to see that the nomination of candidates for President and Vice President by a caucus of national legislators and the naming of Presidential Electors by State legislators menaced the Republic. In a letter to his son John, King characterized the system as irregular, and said that if continued, it might "bring about a pernicious change in favor of a hereditary Presidency. . . . We must choose the electors by the people or the public liberties will be lost."

Through some secret channel this thought of King—though not ascribed to him—went through the State like wild-fire, and was made the sole article of faith of a new political group, the

People's Party. Among some of the Van Burenites, now derisively called the Regency Party, groundless fears were entertained that the object of the new party was to project Clinton for President.

Candidates both for the Senate and for the Assembly were nominated by the new party; and many who received their nominations from Republican conventions pledged themselves to support a law giving to the people the privilege of choosing the Presidential Electors.

In New York City the Republican candidates were defeated by the People's Party nominees, who were supported by the Clintonians. A majority of the Assembly was pledged to the reform. But in the Senate, where only one-fourth of the membership changed each year, the people were unable to make their voices effectively felt through the polls. One of the new Senators chosen, and pledged to vote for the popular measure was Silas Wright.

Van Buren departed for Washington at the end of November. He left a plan in the hands of his regents to defeat the popular will in the matter of choosing Presidential Electors when the subject came before them. The Albany Regency, now in its second year, consisted of Roger Skinner, United States District Judge; Talcott, Attorney General; and Edwin Croswell, who succeeded Cantine as State Printer; Knower, Marcy, and Butler. With the exception of Croswell, all had been members since its organization a year earlier.

The first Monday in December in the year 1823 marked the beginning of the month. On Tuesday Congress listened to a brief message from the President which has gone down in history as the Monroe Doctrine. The two Senators from Tennessee did not hear this immortal document read; they did not take their seats until Friday. The junior member was Andrew Jackson. Eyes were politely turned on the new member, who had been placed in nomination for the Presidency some seven months ago by a mass-meeting in his own State. His colleague was his friend and biographer, John H. Eaton, who had entered the Senate with Van Buren.

Jackson was not a stranger in the halls of Congress. When Tennessee had but one member of the House of Representatives, he constituted her entire delegation. This was in 1796, when Philadelphia was the capital. The next year he was elected to the

Senate, but in April of 1798, after six months in the Upper House, he was excused from sitting the remainder of the term. Worries over financial embarrassments and dislike of the life inspired his return home. He resigned soon after.

Van Buren was now the acknowledged leader in the nation of the Crawford campaign; and to use his own words, he now "made his début in the art and business of President-making." It was an art and business which he was to develop to a state defying improvement—or reform. But he was now only getting his hand in the national game, and he described his first essay as "a rough and tumble Presidential Canvass."

The New York delegation was concerned with what Governor Yates would say in his annual message in recommending an immediate change in New York's election law. In the second week of January a newspaper containing the communication arrived at Bradley's boarding house as Van Buren and his friends had finished dinner. The Patroon had joined the distinguished mess over which Rufus King presided at the beginning of the session; and others who sat at the table included Andrew Stevenson, then a member of the House, and the spokesman of the Virginia Dynasty in its campaign to elect Crawford; and Louis McLane, Delaware's lone Representative, who also looked to Van Buren for direction.

King asked that the Governor's message be read aloud. Yates had shown a certain degree of independence of the Regency, and it was confidently expected that he would recommend the popular election of Presidential Electors. Stevenson was chosen to read the message. King, his face beaming with smiles of anticipation, spread out his embroidered handkerchief on the tablecloth, and rested his arms on it, as was his custom. But as the Virginian proceeded, the smiles gave way to a fixed frown of dismay. "No practical remedy probably does exist," read Stevenson, "competent to remove the evil effectually, except by an amendment to the national Constitution." And there was more of the same tenor, which could be thus summed up: "I recommend that the State law remain as it stands."

King suspected what all Albany at that very moment was saying: Yates had been promised the Vice Presidency by the Regency. Knower, the Chief Regent, was credited with having persuaded the Governor to abandon the people and embrace the Regency. When Stevenson finished reading, King turned to Van Buren with: "I think, Mr. Van Buren, that Mr. Crawford's friends ought to send the Governor a drawing of the Vice President's chair."

This was more than Van Buren had expected, and fencing for time, he inquired the reason.

"Because," said King, whose temper had now risen in protest against the evasion, "I presume they have promised its possession to him."

Knower, who accomplished some things without Van Buren's knowledge, had achieved this by way of a pleasant surprise to the Director of the Albany Regency. Van Buren in the same respectful tone used by King, but with voice also surcharged with suppressed anger, replied that he could not say what allurements had been held out to Yates by friends of other candidates, but that he was quite sure that Mr. Crawford's friends had not made any promises. This was a weak rejoinder, but the best he could make in the circumstances.

"I hope so," said King incredulously.

"I know so!" exclaimed Van Buren heatedly.

King picked up his handkerchief, and walked out of the dining room without uttering another word. He remained incommunicado in his room the rest of the evening, and absented himself from the breakfast table the following morning. Toward evening he was in a forgiving mood, and conscious that he had, in a measure, provoked Van Buren, made his apologies.

Van Buren saw that the chances of Crawford would be poor unless Clay could be induced to take second place on the ticket. He made efforts to this end through his friend and colleague from Missouri, Senator Thomas H. Benton, related to Clay by marriage. Failing here, he adopted Pennsylvania's most distinguished citizen, Albert Gallatin. This alliance, he hoped, would turn Pennsylvania to Crawford.

Van Buren did not regard Jackson as a formidable candidate: he was the son of penniless emigrants from Ireland, of little schooling, and without diplomatic or Cabinet experience. The only assets he possessed which the others did not have, were a reckless courage, and golden spurs won on the field of battle.

Crawford's greatest strength was his indorsement by the Virginia Dynasty; but Van Buren would have liked to have Monroe outspoken in his preference for his Secretary of the Treasury. The President made no attempt to dictate.

At the very outset of the session Van Buren told Calhoun what his course would be. He had tried to induce Clay to accept second place on the Crawford ticket, so that he was not regarded as hostile in the Clay camp. And if Clay and Calhoun failed, as he apprehended Crawford would, he was on intimate terms with Adams. With the exception of Jackson, no one regarded any of the other dozen or so contenders as worthy of consideration. And Jackson, in Van Buren's opinion, lacked the means to acquire the republican purple.

There was weakness, as well as strength, in Van Buren's choice for second place. No worthier citizen did the land boast than Gallatin; yet he was foreign-born, the scion of *la plus ancienne famille de Genève*—as Voltaire said in a letter introducing Gallatin's father-in-law to the Comte d'Argental in 1761, the year of Gallatin's birth. Soldiers were these Swiss Gallatins, of whom Voltaire wrote: "They have shed their blood for us from father to son since the time of *Henri Quatre*."

Gallatin lost his parents when a child; and was brought up by his grandmother, Madame de Gallatin-Vaudenet. When he was nineteen she announced proudly that she had obtained a commission for him in the army of the Landgrave of Hesse-Cassel. "I won't serve a tyrant!" exclaimed the youth, who after recovering from a box on the ears emigrated here with a very small fortune. He made Massachusetts his home, and embraced the cause of the Revolution. A brief residence in Virginia was followed by his settling in Pennsylvania, whose Legislature, in February, 1793, elected him to the United States Senate.

His political adversaries raised the cry that he was not technically a citizen of the United States under the laws of Pennsylvania, and induced the Senate, by a vote of 14 to 12, to declare his election void. This unjust act was committed February 28, 1794. The following year he was elected to the House of Representatives, where no question was raised of his citizenship. He continued as a member of the House until 1801 when Jefferson appointed him Secretary of the Treasury.

Gallatin was a financier. He held the Treasury post until the spring of 1813 when Madison sent him abroad to negotiate a treaty of peace with England. Before his departure, finding the Treasury empty, he saved the nation from bankruptcy by making terms with the banking house of Parish and Girard, through the aid of John Jacob Astor. After the signing of the Treaty of Ghent, Gallatin was appointed Minister to France.

He had returned with his family to the United States in the preceding June. He married the daughter of an American naval officer, Commander James Nicholson, grandson of Sir Francis Nicholson, a Colonial Governor of Virginia and of Maryland. Gallatin's long career in public life prevented him from making the fortune to which his talents entitled him. And because he held offices of great trust he once said at the family table: "A man holding the position I have must not die rich." He might have known poverty if his wife had not inherited a little money.

This rigid honesty was the dominating note of Gallatin's life. Astor several times tried to induce him to quit politics and reënter business. Once Astor offered to take him into partnership with a fifth share in a business then netting $100,000 a year. Gallatin respected Astor, and always felt indebted to him for the big part he played in saving the country from bankruptcy, but he confided to his family that he could never place himself on the same level with Astor.

The first of the Astors was a trial to the Gallatins. They dreaded the evenings he dined with them. From the diary of Gallatin's son we learn that on one occasion Astor horrified the family by poking peas into his mouth with a knife; and to show his dexterity, he followed this by eating his ice cream with the knife. This was in America. But in France Astor outdid himself. It was on the day that the daughter of the Gallatins, Frances, was given a lesson by her dancing mistress in "how to curtsy and to back without tumbling over." Her delightful brother, who noted his sister's preparations for her début at court, also wrote in his diary:

Really Mr. Astor is dreadful. He came to déjeuner to-day; we were simply en famille, he sitting next to Frances. He actually wiped his fingers on the sleeves of her fresh white spencer. Mamma in discreet tones said, "Oh, Mr. Astor, I must apologize; they have forgotten to give you a serviette." I think he felt foolish.

Gallatin's admirer, Walter Lowrie, the senior Senator from Pennsylvania, was the most active advocate of the venerable diplomat. Van Buren made his decision respecting Gallatin immediately after New Year's, and Gallatin arrived in Washington almost simultaneously with the printed reports of Yates's message.

Gallatin found Congress immersed in the approaching canvass. The most important measures before the two houses involved proposed amendments to the Constitution affecting the election of President and Vice President: four were in the Senate; one of these was sponsored by Van Buren. His proposal varied in two particulars from the existing law.

One novelty ordained that if the Electoral College did not make a choice on the first ballot, it should vote again, confining its selection to the two highest. This was intended to eliminate the House of Representatives as a factor in deciding a Presidential contest, a device "deemed objectionable by all the States, on the ground that it jeopardizes the purity of the election, and exposes the whole system to danger by affording facilities to the corruption of a part." In advocating his plan Van Buren endeared himself to the South as an extreme State-rights man, and defined the Union as a league of sovereign States upon equal terms.

The second change proposed was offered by Van Buren to give his Regency an excuse for refusing to invest the people with the power of choosing New York's Presidential Electors. Van Buren's amendment would confer this grant on the voters of the country,—after the impending Presidential election was a matter of history.

In five other States the Legislatures also chose Presidential Electors. Van Buren was for this reform; but he did not want any change while the present canvass was in progress. His objection to immediate reform in New York was fear of Jackson at the polls. Clinton had declared for the hero of New Orleans; and he would return to power if he could carry the State for Jackson, provided the Tennesseean did the seemingly impossible by defeating the field. The people could not be controlled with the ease with which intriguing men sway legislatures; hence the temporary halt of the march of progress.

Van Buren was flying in the face of popular wrath. But he had nothing immediately at stake. His term would not run out for three years. The danger menaced only the members of the Assembly who would follow the Regency's dictation, and the Senators whose tenure of office expired that year. He was not so much concerned over the Governor: he had not proven tractable. And Van Buren was hoping, after the manner of politicians, that the anger of the electors could be diverted from the Regency. It is easy to erect a scarecrow.

The clamor against the Congressional Caucus was growing. Van Buren was also for this change,—but not for the present, as it would likewise interfere with his plans. In the preceding year the Legislature of Tennessee had adopted resolutions condemning the evil, and transmitted a copy to the Senate of the State of New York.

This was, of course, a subtle plea for Jackson's candidature, to which Van Buren's organ, the *Argus*, responded: "He is respected as a gallant soldier, but he stands, in the minds of the people of this State, at an immeasurable distance from the Executive Chair."

Van Buren answered the clamor against the Congressional Caucus defiantly on February 6, by issuing a call for one to be held in the Representatives' Chamber on the evening of Valentine's Day. This call bore the signatures of six Senators and five Representatives from as many States. Simultaneously appeared a card signed by twenty-four members of Congress, representing fifteen of the twenty-four States of the Union in which it was asserted that of the two hundred and sixty-one members of Congress there were at least one hundred and eighty-one who deemed it "inexpedient, under existing circumstances to meet in a caucus" to nominate a national ticket. The preponderating majority in the opposition represented Adams, Calhoun, Clay, and Jackson.

Van Buren and his supporters were dubbed the Radicals, or Rads; and on the day named in the call, the *Republican*, a Washington journal favoring Calhoun, published a column of amusing jingle ridiculing the caucus. The metrical satire opened with:

> Wend you with the Rads to-night—
> Sixty-five perchance they'll muster—
> There will be none of mind or might,
> But some three score in a fluster.
> General Chandler will be there—
> Tough as steel and bold as Hector—
> Basset, with Virginia air—
> Van the Albany Director.
> Forsyth, with his foreign graces—
> Edwards, Williams, in a stew—
> Plotting brains and dirty faces,
> With the blushes reddening through—
> Shallow knaves, with forms to mock us,
> Straggling, one by one, to Caucus.

The poet had predicted in his second line that "sixty-five perchance," would be at the Caucus. There were sixty-six present; two were represented by proxies. The smallness of numbers made some, who fancied that more could be mustered if they had time, move to adjourn for six weeks. Van Buren successfully opposed the motion. It would not do to have the entire sixty-eight for Crawford. Accordingly two were cast for Adams, one for Jackson, and one for the dean of Senate, Nathaniel Macon, of North Carolina.

In the balloting for Vice President the same ruse was observed, Gallatin receiving fifty-seven; two to Root of New York, and the other seven were scattered among as many candidates.

This Congressional Caucus was the least representative of its kind. Of the sixty-eight who attended or were represented by proxy, forty-eight were from four States: New York, Virginia, North Carolina, and Georgia. Its last act before adjournment was to adopt the traditional resolutions recommending the nominees to the suffrage of the voters.

It was, as Van Buren characterized it, a rough and tumble canvass, and nowhere more so than in his own State. And he whose boast it was that he never entered upon anything unless he could see his way through, could only blunder in the general direction of his goal.

Good news continued to come from Albany: the Regency was holding the Senate firm against the bill empowering the people to choose Presidential Electors. The Assembly had passed the measure with only five votes recorded against it.

The Senate did not dare defeat the measure outright; but deferred action until the Legislature met again on the first Monday in November to choose Presidential Electors.

The Assemblymen who were members of the People's Party met on April 7 and issued a call for a convention to be held in Utica to nominate a Governor and Lieutenant Governor.

Two days later the Clintonians held a mass meeting in New York City at which Jackson was nominated for President.

And Yates, who had incurred the resentment of the people by advocating the Regency's recommendations to let the electoral law remain, suddenly found himself rejected by the combination at a legislative caucus which nominated Senator Young for Governor. Yates, who had had the promise of the Vice Presidency whispered in his ears a few short weeks back, now found himself the scapegoat of the Regency. Yates maintained an ominous silence.

On April 12, the last day of the session, the Regency, drunk with power, introduced a resolution removing Clinton from the Canal Board. Clinton had but three friends in the Senate; they alone voted against this wantonly cruel measure.

When the proposal reached the Assembly, the Lower House became a bedlam. The Regency had done some fine work among the representatives of the People's Party in the popular branch of the Legislature: it had assiduously spread the false report that the new party was Clinton's personal machine, and its leaders were secretly working to make him President.

Two Assemblymen occupied singular positions: they belonged to no party; they had nominated themselves. One was John Crary of Washington County; the other was Henry Cunningham of Montgomery County. They led the opposition to Clinton's removal.

Cunningham had never attended a school of any sort, but he had a native eloquence that gripped his audience. He described the Senate resolution as born of black ingratitude and base design, and engendered in the feelings of malice. He referred to the unimpeachable character of Clinton, whose reputation could not be destroyed by a few leading partisans of the day. Then he continued:

When the contemptible party strifes of the present day shall have passed by, and the political bargainers and jugglers, who now hang round this capital for subsistence, shall be overwhelmed and forgotten in their own insignificance—when the gentle breeze shall pass over the tomb of that great man, carrying with it the just tribute of honor and praise which is now withheld—the pen of the future historian, in better days and in better times, will do him justice, and erect to his memory a proud monument of fame as imperishable as the splendid works which owe their origin to his genius and perseverance.

Sir, I have done—and I have only to beseech every honorable gentleman on this floor, to weigh and consider well the consequences of the vote he is about to give on this important question. It is probably the last that will be given this session, and I pray God it may be such as will not disgrace us in the eyes of our constituents.

The Regency had its way, and Clinton was retired to private life.

In the language of Hammond, "the news of this outrage operated like an electric shock on the whole community." Newspapers not directly controlled by the Regency voiced the spirit of the State. "We very much doubt," said the *Daily Advertiser*, "whether the annals of party spirit, in the most impassioned period of their violence and rancor, contain so unworthy an act as this . . . which not merely disgraces those by whom it was adopted, but degrades and discredits the character of the State." And this in the *Evening Post* of April 15: "The envenomed malignity . . . must cause the cheek of every honorable man who calls himself a New Yorker to glow with a blush of shame and indignation."

No one was more grieved or surprised than Van Buren. Judge Skinner, who had an intense personal dislike for Clinton, was the author of the plot.

As the session of Congress neared its end, King, who was inclined to favor Adams, wrote to his son John: "V. B. says all things are going well for Crawford, but he sees what I cannot." And this on Jackson: "Jackson continues to observe & maintain the dignified course which he has done throughout our session, and has certainly given not a few proofs of his firmness and capacity beyond what was anticipated." This was praise from Cæsar.

Congress adjourned May 27. And Van Buren's legislative record was a little less uneventful than in his previous sessions. The most controversial measure considered was the protective tariff, which Clay, from his vantage as Speaker of the House, placed on the statute books under the label of "The American System." Van Buren voted for it. A proposal to permit Great Britain to search ships flying the Stars and Stripes to put an end to this subterfuge by slavers, was defeated in the closing days of Congress. Again Van Buren was with the majority.

One measure revealed to his colleagues a side to Van Buren unknown outside of New York. It was in the last weeks of the session. Henry M. Johnson, of Kentucky, had introduced a bill abolishing imprisonment for debt: it was in essentials the same measure Van Buren had introduced as a new member of the Senate of the State of New York.

For another nine years Johnson fought for this humane bill before it was enacted into law. Van Buren was ever his staunch ally, and, largely through his influence, it became part of the Federal Code.

Instead of going on to New York at the close of the session Van Buren made a pilgrimage to Monticello. He was accompanied, as we have seen, by Senator Dickerson. Jefferson received them both with "unaffected cordiality," concealing the suffering that debts inflict on a sensitive mind. Jefferson was almost penniless. He recalled the tempestuous times of Adams's administration, —the Reign of Terror—when Dickerson, then Recorder of Philadelphia, walked arm in arm to prison with Dr. Thomas Cooper, the educator, a victim of the Alien and Sedition Laws.

What impressed Van Buren most forcibly about his "beau ideal of thorough patriotism and accomplished statesmanship" was the utter absence of any partisan or personal prejudices in Jefferson's reminiscences of his political battles. In discussing the Bank of the United States, Jefferson animadverted on the decisions of the United States Supreme Court in this institution's favor, which, he held, tended to subvert the republican principles of the Government. Van Buren heard him denounce the life tenure of the offices of members of the court as an error.

Jefferson's remedy was the annual appointment of the justices, which prevailed in the New England States: he would be content with tenures of four or even six years, trusting to experience for future reductions.

Van Buren could not subscribe to these views, which he thought extremely Jacobinical, but he lived "to subscribe to their general correctness."

Jefferson was then in his eighty-first year, and Van Buren was forty-two. Thirty years later, in reverting to Jefferson's strictures on life-terms for judges, he wrote:

The experience of ages proves that with exceptions too few to impair the rule, men can not be held to the performance of delegated political trust without a continued and practical responsibility to those for whose benefit it is conferred. The theory of the independence of the Sovereign in the case of the Judges in England, which we have copied, entirely fails when applied to us. There they are rendered independent of the Crown to secure their fidelity to the public against the influence of the power to which they owe their appointment; here their life-tenure renders them independent of the People for whose service they are appointed. Irresponsible power of itself excites distrust, and sooner or later causes, on the part of its possessor, an impatience of popular control and, in the sequel, a desire to counteract popular will. The only effectual and safe remedy will be to amend the constitution so as to make the office elective, and thus compel the Judges, like the incumbents of the Executive and Legislative departments, to come before the people at stated and reasonable periods for a renewal of their commissions.

There was much discussion of other days and other men. In Jefferson's estimation, John Adams, father of John Quincy Adams, was the most effective orator of the Revolution; and he instanced the omission of his name from the list of blanket pardons which George III tendered to the revolting Colonists in corroboration.

In discussing partisan differences he would say "the Republicans" did this, and "Hamilton" did that. To him Hamilton was the head and heart of the Federalists. Once he roundly condemned an act of the opposition, and when Van Buren inquired if Hamilton was responsible, Jefferson replied: "No! He was above such things!" Jefferson spoke of Hamilton as more anti-republican than any of his contemporaries, and "as a man of generous feelings and sincere in his political opinions."

While in the ample library Van Buren saw a volume entitled: "Libels." Taking it from the shelf he noted that it consisted of attacks on Jefferson clipped from newspapers. Jefferson laughed heartily as his guest exhibited the volume, and observed that it was his good fortune to be, in an unusual degree, indifferent to the groundless attacks to which men in public life are exposed. Van Buren was of the same mold.

As they were leaving, Jefferson pressed them to stay several days longer. Van Buren replied that he must return to Washington to attend the opening session of the special committee of the House which was investigating charges that Crawford had culpably mismanaged the public funds. Ninian Edwards, of Illinois, who had resigned his seat in the Senate during the session to accept the mission to Mexico, had originally made the accusation in a series of anonymous newspaper articles the year before; and while en route to Mexico he sent these stories to the Speaker of the House of Representatives with a letter acknowledging the authorship. He said that the charges could be proven if the House investigated. Jefferson knew the keen interest of both in the investigation, and said that he would take the liberty of an old man to give them some advice on the subject of being in a hurry. Van Buren thus recorded it:

The first fifty years of his life had been harassed by the habit of thinking it indispensable that things should be done at a certain time and engagements kept to the moment; but upon summing up results he had found that his punctuality had proved a losing business and that in a thousand instances things would have gone on rather better if he had given himself more latitude and that subsequently he had adopted a different, and as the result had satisfied him, a wiser rule.

After an affectionate farewell Dickerson and Van Buren started on their journey.

In accordance with a promise he made, Van Buren forwarded a pamphlet to Jefferson, who in thanking him, repeated in writing what he had said to Van Buren of the feelings of himself and other old Republicans toward Washington, and of the efforts of the malevolent to persuade the first President that Jefferson entertained ill-will toward him. "He," wrote Jefferson, "lived too short a time after and too much withdrawn from information to correct the views into which he had been deluded, and the continued assiduities of the party drew him into the vortex of their intemperate career, separated him still further from his real friends, and excited him to actions and expressions of dissatisfaction which grieved them but could not loosen their affection from him. They would not suffer the temporary aberration to weigh against the immeasurable merits of his life, and altho' they tumbled his seducers from their places they preserved his memory embalmed in their hearts with undiminished love and devotion, and there it forever will remain embalmed, in entire oblivion of every temporary thing which might cloud the glories of his splendid life."

## CHAPTER XXIX

VAN BUREN might well have wished himself on the Supreme Court bench, or anywhere else than in politics, when he returned to New York. The State was in a turmoil. Clinton's removal from the Canal Board had made a martyr of him. Meetings of protest had been held throughout the State, and more were planned. In New York City ten thousand assembled to voice their indignation and to groan: "Regency! Regency! Regency!"

He met men on the streets wearing vests on which were printed in wood blocks the features of their choice for President. Most of these novel campaign standards were of silk, and those least able to afford them wore silken waistcoats stamped with the likeness of Jackson. There seemed as many Adamses as Crawfords; and Clays were also popular. The Calhouns were a drug on the market, the South Carolinian having withdrawn from the contest.

The barroom of nearly every tavern in the State had pasted on its walls a printed list of the names of the seventeen Senators whose votes prevented the people from choosing the Presidential Electors. Under the names of the seventeen was a legend reciting how Livingston, in moving postponement, had said that the demand did not come from the people, but from barroom politicians.

If the people had only stopped with printing lists of the seventeen and pasting them on barroom walls Van Buren would not have minded; but they took old clothes and stuffed them with straw, and labeled them Silas Wright, Edward P. Livingston, or any other name of the seventeen which struck their fancy. Some of these stuffed Senators were hanged, and some were burned. Many of these effigies wore waistcoats with the face of Crawford printed on them. These were not burned: they dangled ignobly from branches of trees on the public highways until cut down by partisans. And on many a farm the swaying scarecrow in the cornfield had a card stitched to its ragged coat on which was written "Regency!"

In the midst of all this Yates dropped his rôle of the placid scapegoat and turned avenger by issuing a proclamation convoking the Legislature in extraordinary session on August 2 to consider the Presidential Electors bill. After reciting the history of the measure, he said that the people were justly alarmed by having "their undoubted right" withheld from them; therefore, to enable their representatives to carry their wishes into effect, he had summoned the lawmakers to undo the wrong.

Van Buren in replying to Jefferson's letter, from which we have quoted, wrote: "Our Gov$^r$. has utterly ruined the little standing he had left, and unintentionally rendered us essential service by his proclamation. . . . The Legislature will do nothing that they ought not to do."

Van Buren could speak for the Senate, which could negative any act of the Assembly. The Legislature met in accordance with the Governor's proclamation; and after listening to his message, the Senate adopted resolutions censuring the Executive for convoking the Legislature to consider a measure on which they had acted at the regular session. A second resolve called for immediate adjournment.

The Assembly concurred in the censure of the Governor, but by a vote of seventy-five to forty-four, adopted a resolution demanding that the popular demand be met. But on this there could be no agreement, and on the fourth day of their sitting, the Legislature adjourned to meet in November to choose the Presidential Electors.

Meanwhile a steady campaign was being waged in the opposition press directed at Crawford's running mate because of his foreign birth. This unjust attack on Gallatin was an appeal to the prejudices of the native-born.

These same journals then turned around and appealed to the passions of the foreign-born by reprinting a puerile passage from a report submitted by Crawford in 1816 to President Madison telling of his department's efforts to civilize the Indians. The much quoted excerpt reads:

If the system already devised has not produced all the effects which were expected from it, new experiments ought to be made; when every effort to introduce among them [the Indians] ideas of exclusive property in things real as well as personal shall fail, let intermarriages between them and the whites be encouraged by the Government. This cannot fail to preserve the race, with the modifications necessary to the enjoyment of civil liberty and social happiness. It is believed, that the principles of humanity in this instance, are in harmonious concert with the true interests of the nation. It will redound more to national honor to incorporate, by a humane and benevolent policy, the natives of our forests in the great American family of freedom, than to receive, with open arms, the fugitives of the old world, whether their flight has been the effect of their crimes or their virtues.

In Pennsylvania, where the people elected the Presidential Electors, the turbulent John Binns, with a view to rousing his fellow Irish against Crawford, printed this humorous explanation of Crawford's plan: "Possibly the gentleman is for an amalgamation of the wild Irish with the tame savages to produce fit subjects for his reign when he becomes President."

Crawford made no reply. Attacks made on his rivals were likewise received in silence. It was not the custom then for a man seeking high office to campaign for votes, all being governed by that admirable dictum of Aristotle: "Nor is it right that any one who is found worthy of the office should be obliged to make a personal canvass, as the right man ought to fill the office whether he wishes or not." This precept, while observed, generally permitted issues to be discussed, and prevented personalities from affecting the decision of the people. But the campaign of 1824 was without an issue: it was a contest of personalities. Theoretically the era of good feeling still existed; there was only one national political party, but there were many factions.

Politics were forgotten for a brief time when La Fayette landed at the Battery and began a triumphal tour throughout the country as the guest of the nation. Old now was this hero of many battles, and there was a perceptible limp in his walk: that old wound he received at the Battle of Brandywine was bothering him. It was not as a Marquis of France that he was welcomed, but as a General of the American Revolution.

The latter half of the third week in September he arrived in Albany, where Spencer, no longer Chief Justice, was Mayor. Solomon Van Rensselaer, as marshal of the day, received the Revolutionary hero; and on the last evening of his stay, La

Fayette, escorted by dragoons and infantry, visited the home of De Witt Clinton who had a residence at the capital. Here he remained an hour. This honor was accorded Clinton because La Fayette and Clinton's uncle had been brothers-in-arms. Then he called at the home of the Patroon's poor kinsman, where the widow of another Van Rensselaer, who had fought beside him, was expecting the call. And he reminded the old lady—as though she could have forgotten it!—of a bitterly cold winter day in 1778, when both were very young. The snow covered the ground, and she was distressed to see him wearing a pair of white silk stockings and silver-buckled shoes: he would freeze if he did not wear some warm woolen *koussen*. She smiled gratefully as he repeated the Dutch word she had used that wintry day nearly half a century ago; and remembered vividly his pulling the coarse thick woolen hose, which she had knitted, over his silk stockings.

Escorted by horse and foot, La Fayette went to the home of John Tayler, the former Lieutenant Governor, an old Revolutionary hero too. To Cruttenden's tavern La Fayette went next, where he received a deputation of his Royal Arch brethren; and his last visit was to the house of Governor Yates.

Long after La Fayette waved his hat as the steamboat bore southward, the tar barrels which lined Albany's streets were blazing, the lurid flames lending fantastic tones to the flowers and greens festooned from the windows of the houses.

The following Tuesday the People's Party met in convention at Utica, and chose John Tayler president. The delegates were elected by the people at informal primary meetings to nominate a Governor and Lieutenant Governor pledged to reform the electoral law. James Tallmadge, a relation of Clinton by marriage, was placed in nomination for Governor, but the convention could not agree on him. John W. Taylor, of Saratoga, sometime Speaker of the House of Representatives, was next proposed, but a neighbor of his read a letter saying that he would not accept a nomination.

There was strong support for Clinton among the hundred and twenty-two delegates; but the New York City delegation and the People's Party men in the Legislature were opposed to him. The metropolitan supporters of Clinton were largely Jackson men.

It was known to all, although no formal announcement had been made, that Clinton would run for Governor regardless of what the Utica convention did. His platform would read: "Reform the Electoral Law; Banish Caucus Nominations." That, too, would be the appeal of the choice of the People's Party.

Toward the end of the second day delegates who did not share the hatred of Clinton that envenomed the former New York Bucktails, put his name before the convention, and nominated him by a large majority. Tallmadge was chosen as his running mate.

Twenty bolted and held a rump convention. But they were faced with a most unusual situation. They did not want Clinton, and they could not support Young, the Regency candidate, who had been nominated at a legislative caucus, a procedure which was formally and unanimously condemned by resolution after Tallmadge had been named. They could not, without leaving themselves open to a charge of treachery to the cause of election law reform, place a third candidate in the field. So they contented themselves with adopting a protest against Clinton's nomination and indorsing Tallmadge for Lieutenant Governor.

The Nativism campaign bore its fruit shortly after the nomination of Clinton, and following a series of conferences with Lowrie and other intimates, Gallatin wrote to Lowrie declining the nomination for Vice President, and forwarded copies to Stevenson and Van Buren. The letters were dated and posted October 2.

In his letter of self-effacement, Gallatin made no reference to the clamors of the mob which drove him from the field. He was willing to stand if Van Buren and Lowrie and Stevenson thought his withdrawal "may prove . . . injurious to the success of the Republican ticket."

He wrote that the time being short, they need not consult with him further, but were to use their discretion in making public his declension. They did not wait long; Gallatin's home State, which Van Buren had counted on carrying because he was on the ticket, was almost solidly for Jackson for President.

On the morning of Election Day a small crowd were waiting outside the polling place where Van Buren was to cast his vote. As he approached the group, he was received with the cry of

"Regency! Regency! Regency!" Van Buren set his jaws; his face crimsoned at the affronts.

Into the polling place he went and nearly a score followed, still shouting: "Regency! Regency! Regency!" Before he could cast his ballot there were a dozen challenges of his vote. The Clintonian watchers tried to persuade their angry partisans to withdraw the protests which were predicated on the absurd ground that he was not a *bona fide* resident. But not one could be induced to withdraw his challenge, even when reminded that Van Buren represented the State in the United States Senate. For the second time in his life Van Buren was forced into the humiliating position of taking the prescribed oath before he could vote.

Van Buren retired that night a little downcast. No such manifestation as he had encountered at the polls could be ascribed to local feeling: it was, as he believed, a reflex of the sentiment of the State. The next morning at breakfast, Judge Skinner brought returns which confirmed his worst suspicions.

Van Buren went on eating, but listlessly. Skinner was not in any mood to talk, and without removing his cloak, he went to the window and looked out on the passers-by on State street. His heart was sad, not so much at the Regency's defeat, but with Clinton's victory. Why had he removed him from the Canal Board? He had made him a martyr, and he was responsible for Clinton's triumph. Clinton was dead politically in April; but he had brought him back to life.

Similar thoughts were running through Van Buren's mind as he watched Skinner playing a mournful monody on the window pane with his gloved fingers. Skinner stopped suddenly as Van Buren gave vent to his long pent-up feelings by exclaiming:

"I hope, Judge, you are now satisfied that there is such a thing in politics as killing a man too dead!"

Skinner stung to the quick, said not a word, and immediately left the room. Van Buren seized his hat and hurriedly throwing his cloak over his shoulders, hastened after his friend and found him at his lodgings, and humbly begged his forgiveness. Skinner never recovered from the sorrow wrought by Clinton's victory, which gradually undermined his frail health; and one evening, some three years later, he expired in Van Buren's arms.

The defeat of the Regency and the election of Clinton astonished the nation. He was chosen Governor by the unprecedented majority of a few votes less than seventeen thousand. The Regency candidates for Assembly were defeated in a vast majority of districts, and only two of the Regency nominees for Senator were elected. It was a political revolution which placed Clinton in line for the Presidency.

This triumph of the popular will in a State where the forces of reaction were more firmly entrenched than elsewhere in the nation, had a salutary effect on the entire body politic.

# CHAPTER XXX

THE Legislature was to meet in Albany on Tuesday, November 2, to choose Presidential Electors. But as the polls in the State election did not close until the following night, most of the legislators did not start for the capital until the last of the ballots in the Clinton victory had been counted.

It was apparent as the two houses began balloting separately that Crawford could not get one of New York's thirty-six Electors save by intrigue. The Regency was prostrate, and Van Buren said he was as completely broken down a politician as his bitterest enemies could desire.

In the Senate, "the immortal seventeen" who had been hanged and burned in effigy voted for a Crawford ticket. This was a bare majority. Seven Senators voted for Adams, and an equal number for Clay. But in the Assembly the ranks of the Regency broke. Here only sixty out of one hundred fifty-six stood by Crawford. The opposition was divided between Clay and Adams supporters, fifty for Adams, and thirty-two for Clay. The supporters of these two had a combined strength in the two houses of ninety-six. The Regency could muster only seventy-seven. The inevitable followed: a coalition of the Clay and Adams men.

The respective strengths of the Clay and Adams supporters were fifty-seven and thirty-nine. Under a generous division of the thirty-six Presidential Electors, generous in the apportionment to Adams, Clay would have had fourteen and Adams twenty-two. But after the amalgamation, the magic of intrigue, on which the record is silent, gave Adams twenty-five. If the remainder had gone to Clay, the Kentuckian, and not the Georgian, would have been one of the three highest in the Electoral College, and under the Constitution, Clay and not Crawford, would have been balloted for in the House. Hammond and other contemporary commentators on New York politics hold to the opinion that had Clay been justly treated in Albany, he would have been elected President.

273

A secret pact was undoubtedly formed between the Regency and the Adams men after the two houses met in joint ballot. This premise is supported by the nomination on Saturday, November 13, of the Adams Electoral ticket, not by an Adams man, but by Oran Follett, a Regency Assemblyman from Genesee, and its support by many members of the Crawford party. Livingston offered a diversion on the same day by presenting a Clay ticket, which was rejected, and a Jackson ticket, which received only twenty-eight votes. "Many," wrote the *Evening Post's* Albany correspondent, "voted for the Jackson ticket who never seriously meant to support it."

By the following Tuesday when the Electors were chosen, the art of the Regency magicians had been so potent that the first ballot resulted in the election of only thirty-two of the thirty-six Electors, of whom twenty-five were for Adams and seven for Clay. A second ballot showed the extent of the betrayal of the Clay party by the Adams men, for the remaining four were Crawford Electors.

These four votes sealed the fate of Clay. The Electoral College which met in Washington on December 1, gave Jackson ninety-nine; Adams, eighty-four; Crawford, forty-one; Clay, thirty-seven. A shift of four votes from Van Buren's candidate to Clay would have eliminated Crawford from the contest. As it was, Crawford had lost two of the New York votes, one being cast for Adams and one for Jackson.

When the latest example of legislative legerdemain was over, Van Buren, downcast, and designedly alone, set out for Washington. At the dining table on the steamboat to New York he found himself sitting beside James Jones, and his sister, the wife of De Witt Clinton. During the meal Jones lowered his voice as he said to Van Buren: "Now is the time admirably fitted for a settlement of all difficulties between Mr. Clinton and yourself."

Van Buren was more in a mood to fight than to make peace— with any one. But he concealed his real feeling by replying that his political fortunes were at a low ebb, but that when they had improved, he would remember the generous proposal; so they talked commonplaces.

On reaching New York Van Buren's intention to continue his journey to Washington alone had not changed. He was not in any mood for company. Hitherto he and Rufus King had made the trip together. But Van Buren was through with King because of his support of Clinton, and for the further reason that he was an Adams man. He felt that King's indebtedness to him was not discharged, and that he should have supported Crawford.

At the city he found the Patroon waiting for him. The Patroon knew the depths into which Van Buren's spirit had been plunged by Clinton's unprecedented victory. He wanted to companion him on the way. Van Buren was touched by this gentleness, and after paying off his election losses he set out with the grand old Dutchman for Washington.

King overtook them at Philadelphia. This proved more embarrassing than meeting Mrs. Clinton and her brother; for King inquired why Van Buren had not called at Jamaica. This interrogation was put in the most amusing form of diplomatic circumlocution. "William had inquired," said King, "why it was that Mr. Van Buren had, for the first time, passed on without calling." William was King's servant, and venerable and courtly as his master. King added that he had told William he knew of no reason, and did not believe that a good one existed. Van Buren was even more diplomatic: he made a wordy reply which signified nothing.

On reaching Washington, Van Buren and the Patroon, who had abandoned his old friend King to be with Van Buren in his misery, rented a furnished house. They shared it with McLane of Maryland, who had been in the King-Van Buren mess in other years, and Alfred Cuthbert, a new Representative from Georgia.

There was a little good-humored chaffing of Van Buren by his friends in Congress after the vote in the Electoral College was announced. Calhoun was elected Vice President on the first ballot, but Georgia cast her nine votes for Van Buren for Vice President. But the matter did not end here; for Charles King, son of Rufus, published in his (New York) *American*, the following paragraph flattering on its face, yet destined to work mischief by making Van Buren more obnoxious than ever in the eyes of the supporters of Jackson and Clinton:

The apparent question now before the public is, "Who shall be our next President?" but the real question is, whether Martin Van

Buren shall be President of the United States on and after March 4th, 1833? At that time the great State of New York having never furnished a President, will have irresistible claims to that honor. If any of her citizens are now qualified, the blossoms of eternity, fast gathering upon their heads, will have fallen; they will be superannuated— that is, they will have passed the age of sixty years, that gloomy period when the Constitution of New York declares that judges lose their senses, and that all flesh is grass. In that day Mr. Van Buren will be in the full strength of life, the only New Yorker fit for the Presidency.

Clinton on March 4, 1833, would be sixty-four years of age, and Van Buren slightly over fifty. This would also eliminate the hero of New Orleans, as he would then be sixty-two years old.

Van Buren's mind was taken from "the art and business of President making" by a letter which reached him while the Christmas spirit was at its height. It was from A. G. Hammond, a farmer of Rensselaer County, who wrote that his runaway slave, "Tom," was in Massachusetts. "There is yet some time before he is free," the letter ran, "as he is of that class which will be free July 4th, 1827. He was when young a slave of my father and I think I can induce him to be of some service to me if I own him."

The children were mere toddlers when "Tom" ran away, and their mother was still with them. Hammond wanted "Tom" for "a small compensation." Money was little to Van Buren, but he put a stiff price on the slave—$50—and added an impossible provision: "Tom" must be recovered without violence. "Tom" remained free.

Van Buren was giving all his thoughts to the Presidential election, which would be decided in the House on February 9. On January 22 the Patroon wrote to Solomon Van Rensselaer: ". . . Mr. Clay has taken his ground in favor of Adams, this will insure his election without doubt it is said on the first ballot; but I doubt this, the second or third certainly. . . . We may be divided in our delegation at first. . . . I feel inclined for 'Old Hickory' myself. . . ."

One of Clay's friends, Francis Johnson, a Representative from Kentucky, called on Van Buren and told him of Clay's intention to unite his forces with the Adams supporters. He urged Van Buren to join them, adding that they believed it possible to elect Adams without the assistance of the Crawford party.

Van Buren replied: "I think that very possible; but, Mr. Johnson, I beg you to remember what I now say to you—if you do you will sign Mr. Clay's political death warrant. He will never become President, be your motives as pure as you claim them to be."

Clay was Speaker of the House. Van Buren regarded him as the greatest orator of the day, and always read his printed speeches. But they were never allies, and this visit of Johnson, made in the week ending on January 22, the date of the Patroon's letter, was the first effort to bring the two together.

"During this week," King noted in a memorandum, "rumours circulated that Mr. Clay would, contrary to the instruction of the legislature of Kentucky which requests the Reps. of that state in Congress to vote for Jackson, use his influence in favor of Adams. Saml. Swartwout who was very active in East Jersey to promote the choice of Jackson's Electors in that State, about this time appeared in Washington, and it is understood proposed a reconciliation between Jackson & Crawford, towards which purpose Mrs. Jackson made a visit to Mrs. Crawford, who returned it without delay."

But nothing came of Swartwout's endeavors, and the following Monday Clay publicly avowed himself for Adams. Clay's intimates had been expecting this for months: he had confided his intentions to some of his Kentucky neighbors in November, before he set out for Washington. His reasons he repeated in a letter to Francis P. Blair on January 8, and again in a communication to Francis Brooke, twenty days later. To Brooke he said:

I have pursued, in regard to it, the rule which I always observe in the discharge of my public duty—I have interrogated my conscience as to what I ought to do, and that faithful guide tells me that I ought to vote for Mr. Adams. I shall fulfill its injunction. Mr. Crawford's state of health, and the circumstances under which he presents himself to the House, appear to me to be conclusive against him. As a friend of liberty, and to the permanence of our institutions, I can not consent, in this early stage of their existence, by contributing to the election of a military chieftain, to give the strongest guaranty that the Republic will march in the fatal road which has conducted every other republic to ruin.

Many, like Clay, objected to Jackson because they feared his elevation to the Presidency would incline the Republic from its wholesome civilian character. Jefferson, himself, held to this language. "I feel much alarm at the prospect of seeing General Jackson President," said Jefferson. "He is one of the most unfit men I know for the place. He has had very little respect for laws and constitutions, and is, in fact, an able military chieftain. His passions are terrible . . . he is a dangerous man." Jackson had advocated hanging the members of the Hartford Convention. He had been a strict, harsh, military disciplinarian, and Binns had printed thousands of the Coffin Handbills, on which the story of the wanton execution of the six militiamen was revived in all its horror with the aid of graphic wood blocks and blood-curdling phrases. And then there were the stories of his almost countless duels and brawls, not lessened in the telling. All these had been told against him.

Now the friends of Crawford and of Jackson, especially the latter, turned accuser, and the ugly charge of offering a Cabinet seat in return for the Presidency was whispered by venomous tongues. Four days after Clay's public announcement of his advocacy of Adams, an anonymous letter, evidently written by a member of the House, repeated the rumor in the *Columbia Observer* of Philadelphia:

> For some time past, the friends of Clay have hinted that they like the Swiss, would fight for those who would pay best. Overtures were said to have been made by the friends of Adams to the friends of Clay, offering him the appointment of Secretary of State, for his aid to elect Adams. And the friends of Clay gave this information to the friends of Jackson, and hinted that, if the friends of Jackson would offer the same price, they would close with them.

Clay answered with a card in the *National Intelligencer* on Monday, suggesting that the letter was a forgery, and if it were not, he stigmatized the member, "whoever he may be, a base and infamous calumniator, a dastard, and a liar."

Thursday's issue of the *Columbian Observer* contained a letter signed by George Kremer, a Representative from Pennsylvania, in which he admitted authorship, and asserted that the accusations could be supported by competent proof.

Clay immediately moved for a House investigation. When invited to appear before the committee of inquiry, Kremer denied its power to interrogate him. Official action ended here. Kremer named several as his informants, and most of them promptly repudiated him. Kremer and his charges were thereupon discredited by all save the more ardent Jacksonites.

On the morning of February 9, when the House convened to elect a President, Van Buren had no misgivings about the result; but he was confident that he could prevent the House from electing Adams on the first ballot by dividing the New York delegation so that there would not be a majority for any of the three candidates. There were then twenty-five States, and it took thirteen to elect.

Adams was sure of twelve votes: the six New England States, Maryland, Louisiana, Kentucky, Missouri, Ohio, and Illinois. Besides his own State, Jackson had New Jersey, Pennsylvania, North Carolina, Alabama, Mississippi, and Indiana. Crawford had only three States in addition to Georgia: Virginia, Delaware, and North Carolina.

These Jackson and Crawford States were regarded as invulnerable. Van Buren intended to deadlock the House on the first two ballots to compel the Adams men to appeal to him for New York's deciding vote.

Before the Patroon left for the Capitol he called on Van Buren and told him that he was considering voting for Jackson. This was of no import, as all Van Buren had planned was to keep any of the Jackson or Crawford members of the New York delegation from voting for Adams. The Adams men numbered seventeen. This was precisely half of the number of the Representatives from New York: they needed another New York Congressman to make a majority. Van Buren told the Patroon that the only effect of his vote for Jackson would be to subject himself to the imputation of fickleness. The Patroon assented to this and said he would stand by Crawford.

But before the Patroon took his seat he was ushered into the Speaker's room where Clay pleaded the cause of Adams, ably supported by Daniel Webster. How could he reply to the mesmerizing arguments of these two masters of eloquence and dialectics? Clay had fresh in his mind the words he had written to

Brooke but five days before: "He [Thomas Ritchie] ought to recollect that he is struggling for a man, I for a country—he to elevate an unfortunate gentleman [Crawford] worn down by disease, I to preserve our youthful institutions from the bane [militarism] which has destroyed all the republics of the old world. . . . All attempts . . . to induce me to give up the defense of our institutions, that we may elect a sick gentleman, who has also been rejected by the great body of the nation, are vain and utterly fruitless. Mr. Ritchie ought to awake, should be himself again, and love Rome more than Cæsar." Both told him that the question of election or no election depended on his vote, and spared no words in depicting the disorganization in governmen which might ensue from a protracted contest such as occurred in 1801.

The Patroon left Clay's office with his intention to vote for Crawford shaken. He went into the House and told McLane of his indecision, urging him to get Van Buren to come from the Senate side of the Capitol at once. McLane sent word through William S. Archer of Virginia. Van Buren replied that the great disparity in their ages, and the sacredness of the moment, forbade any attempt on his part to influence the venerable Patroon, whom he had grown to love as a father. Archer agreed. But the Patroon was not satisfied with the message, and returned word that it was urgent that he talk with Van Buren.

Van Buren assented; but resolved that he would not introduce the subject of the election: the Patroon must do that. It turned out that there was no need of discussing anything with the Patroon, who had meanwhile assured the fourth member of their mess, Cuthbert, that he would not vote for Adams on the first ballot. While this circumstance was being communicated to Van Buren at the entrance to the House, a drama was being enacted inside which would have enraptured Milton. The Patroon was the entire cast.

Van Rensselaer was deeply devout. So was Adams, who never went to bed without saying aloud the simple prayer he had learned at his mother's knee:

> Now I lay me down to sleep,
> I pray the Lord my soul to keep;

> If I should die before I wake,
> I pray the Lord my soul to take.

When the Patroon's predecessor in Congress had a narrow escape from death when the stage from Philadelphia was overturned, he wrote his kinsman that he had offered thanks to God on learning of his safety.

A cardinal tenet of the Patroon's faith was never to enter upon any great or important undertaking without first invoking the aid of the Deity. After he told Cuthbert that he would not vote for Adams on the first ballot, the solemn arguments of Clay and Webster recurred to his mind, perplexing him more than ever.

The balloting had begun. Now, as never before, the Patroon felt the need of divine guidance. He bowed his gray head on the edge of his desk and prayed. When he removed his hand from his eyes he saw on the carpet at his feet one of the three printed ballots that a few moments before had been with the rest of his papers. The ticket bore the name: John Quincy Adams.

This was the answer to his prayer. The Patroon picked up the ticket and dropped it in the box.

Thus was the sixth President of the United States elected, and so ended Van Buren's plan of dramatizing New York's importance in shattering the Virginia Dynasty's hold on the Presidency.

It was several days before the Patroon told Van Buren why he had voted for Adams. Meanwhile Van Buren was charged with deception by several of Crawford's friends, notably his fellow lodger, McLane, who informed Charles F. Mercer, a Representative of Virginia, that he felt uncomfortable living under the same roof with so base a deceiver.

Van Buren bore this calumny in silence. He could not betray  the sacred confidence of the Patroon.

Not a note of partisanship entered into any of Adams's appointments, which were made solely on merit. The nomination for Envoy Extraordinary and Minister Plenipotentiary to Great Britain was omitted from the list. Adams had publicly invited De Witt Clinton to accept the honor, which Clinton declined in like manner, saying he could not retire as Governor of New York until he had an ample opportunity of evincing his gratitude and devotion to the interests of his constituents.

King was not sitting in this special session for his term of office had expired on March 3, and having reached the allotted threescore years and ten, he was looking forward to an honorable retirement. He was still in Washington, but planned to depart on the 6th. The night before he left, the President called unexpectedly at his lodgings and asked him to round out his public career in this important post he had filled when he and the country were both young.

"His first and immediate impulse was to decline it," wrote Adams. He spoke of King's exceptional qualifications for the office, and the satisfaction his acceptance would give to the old Federalists, and thus aid in harmonizing the feelings of the people. King promised to consider the offer; some weeks after he accepted.

On the seventh the Senate confirmed the nominations. Some of the friends of Crawford, and Jackson and his supporters, voted to reject the appointment of Clay as Secretary of State. Van Buren, unwilling to put a stigma on Clay or Adams on the basis of a groundless charge of bargain and corruption—many of the enemies of Adams regarded the nomination of Clay as conclusive proof of the accusation—voted with the majority. Van Buren also knew that Adams had privately offered this place to Clinton before tendering it to Clay.

The seeds of hatred sown by Kremer were already bearing fruit. In Crawford's home state, the minority led by John Clarke, sometime Governor of Georgia, had adopted Van Buren as their stock candidate for lowly offices, some real and some the product of their crude humor. During the organization of the lower house of the Georgia Legislature, the Clarkeites opposed the majority candidate for doorkeeper with Van Buren. Outvoted, they nominated him for dog-whipper in derision of the State's nine Electoral votes cast for him for Vice President.

This jeering jest of the Clarkeites was carried on with mock solemnity. They had ballots printed with various designations of their mock candidate. He was "Little Van," "Whiskey Van," "Blue Whiskey Van," and the like. These tickets were adorned with crude caricatures depicting Van Buren as part fox and part man, half snake and half mink, and in other hybrid forms.

The Clarkeites were giving Van Buren a foretaste of the bitter cup which Fate was preparing for him.

# CHAPTER XXXI

VAN BUREN's return to Albany was followed by a trip to Kinderhook to rest and to get away from politicians and newspapers. It was impossible to pick up a journal and not read of some new demand of the people of this or that State for a canal or highway. And every account, save in the rabid Bucktail press, must refer to Clinton and the Canal, whose final link, from Buffalo to the Great Lakes, would be completed in the fall. Clinton was a national hero. In the spring the citizens of Philadelphia tendered him a banquet at which the Mayor presided. A little later Ohio and Kentucky invited him to visit these States. He accepted; and his journey was made a triumphal tour. The merchants of New York City subscribed $3,500 for a pair of silver vases in recognition of his services to the city.

The spontaneity of these testimonials alarmed the friends of Adams and Jackson. Clinton was outstripping them in popular favor. Jackson, who had again resigned from Congress, was once more proposed by the Tennessee Legislature as a candidate for the Presidency.

Clinton was Jackson's supporter, yet Adams had offered him the first place in his Cabinet and most important diplomatic post at his disposal. Van Buren was Clinton's enemy, yet Adams worked like a Trojan to elevate him to the United States Supreme Court. These strange alliances were passing, and with them the Era of Good Feeling, which produced them. In May of this year, Adams revealed his change of heart toward Van Buren. He confided to Samuel L. Southard, his Secretary of the Navy, "of the transactions and correspondence which preceded the appointment of Smith Thompson as a Judge of the Supreme Court of the United States . . . and the distant and disguised graspings of Van Buren, both at that office and a mission abroad." The foreign mission was the ministry to the Court of St. James's. Adams now bracketed Van Buren with Webster: "a combination of talent, of ambition, of political management, and of heartless injustice."

The "heartless injustice" was confined to the realm of partisan or factious politics. Van Buren had also turned against Adams because of his partiality to Clinton. His future lay in opposing Adams. This would probably mean an alliance with Jackson; and in New York, Jackson spelled Clinton, unless Clinton were defeated for reëlection in 1826.

Mutual friends of Clinton and Van Buren arranged a meeting between them; but failed to compose their political differences. Their relations, however, became friendly. In midsummer Van Buren found himself a passenger on the boat for Albany with Clinton. He had a letter from Dr. Cooper—the same Cooper with whom Senator Dickerson had walked to jail upon his conviction under the Alien and Sedition Laws—in which the old Jeffersonian, now head of Columbia College in South Carolina, discussed the possibility of Clinton for President. Cooper admired Clinton; but he believed that Clinton would come under the domination of the clergy. This apprehension was based on Clinton's recent address before the Bible Society. Van Buren handed Clinton the letter, who colored as he read it. As he returned the communication, Clinton smilingly observed that Cooper's fears were groundless.

Then came the second day of November when a cannon thundered its welcome to the waters of the Great Lakes as they flowed into the Canal. Big guns were placed within sound of each other along the entire length of the waterway, and on the banks of the Hudson. Each piece was fired after its fellow to the north was discharged, until the people of New York City were made aware of the union of the waters of the Great Lakes and the Atlantic by the booming of the field piece at the Battery.

Every one of importance in the State, save Van Buren, accompanied Clinton and his party from Buffalo to New York; Van Buren could not, as the State's representative in Congress, avoid joining the party somewhere along the route. This he did at Albany. Clinton remembered, when they reached Manhattan, the stricture of the Bucktails on him and the Canal: "a ditch fit to bury its author in." This was years ago, when he first proposed it. The ditch opened the West to settlers.

It was altogether an eventful month. On the last Monday of November the country had its first taste of opera, when Van

Buren's wine seller presented the famed Garcia family at the Park Theater in *Il Barbiere di Siviglia.*

The beginning of the next week saw Van Buren in Washington. Until this session his career had been as colorless as that of the average timeserver. More than once, in statesmanlike speeches, he displayed a knowledge indicating a life-long study of the subject in hand. Those who shared his confidence knew that he was utterly ignorant of many of the questions he discussed so profoundly until he began his painstaking research of the documents bearing on the matter. This ignorance was a carefully guarded secret: the first to detect it was Jackson.

Before Van Buren left for Washington he had instructed his son, John, not yet sixteen years old, to visit their kin and friends at Kinderhook before spending the Christmas holidays with the Duers at their home in Greenbush, across the river from Albany. He wrote reprovingly to the boy, who was studying at Yale. In this, the first intimate family letter of Van Buren's extant, he bares a grief which we cannot but share; and reveals how he tried to take a mother's place in the lives of his children.

My dear Son

I am as you supposed somewhat surprised to hear that you went direct to Greenbush. I wrote you advising you to go to Kinderhook & to visit Albany from thence. I know the kindness which induces Mr & Mrs Duer to wish to have you at their house, & approve your taste for being pleased with the good society you meet there, but I fear your Kinderhook friends will think themselves neglected as I think they well may. You know the pain it gives me [to] express dissatisfaction with your conduct, but I would do injustice to both, were I not to say that the amount you give me of your expenditures is far from satisfactory.

You say you have spent $150 in six weeks, & instead of giving me an account of it, or even speaking of its absolute necessity, you tell me of the expenditure of other boys, & the declaration of [Js. Backner?] as to how much he had spent. You have nothing to do with the expense of other Boys—when I proposed to make you the depository of your funds, I did so (you know) agt. the opinion & advice of others—My wish was to excite your ambition to shew that you was free from the weakness of other boys in this respect, & more deserving of confidence than they too often are. I endeavored to impress you sensibly on this point, and assured you solemnly, that the moment I had reason to apprehend that my confidence was not safely placed, I would withdraw it. I will not judge you definitively until I hear [from] you, but if the amount you give me of your disbursements is not such as it should be, I shall assuredly, promptly, & peremptorily change my course, & leave it to M^r Croswell to advance you from time to time what money you may want—Let me therefore hear from you directly upon this subject.

I sincerely hope you will be able to explain to me this matter fully as I shall be uneasy until you do so—

The money is the least, by far the least, of my concern.

Make my most affectionate regards to Mr & Mrs Duer & all the children.

Your affectionate father<br>M. V. Buren

Mr John V. Buren

At this early age the habits of this exceptionally brilliant youth were fixed. These traits were to provoke this characterization from Godkin: "aristocratic in his bearing, in his habits, in his training and tone of thought."

On the second day of the session Adams informed Congress that an invitation had been accepted to send ministers to the Congress of American Republics on the Isthmus of Panama to participate in its deliberations "so far as may be compatible with that neutrality from which it is neither our intention, nor the desire of other American States that we should depart."

Back of this movement, as the documents exhibited to the Senate in Executive session disclosed, was the first step toward a close defensive confederacy of the American Republics,—a step further than the Monroe Doctrine contemplated. Under the Senate rules all documents communicated to it by the President shall be kept secret. Van Buren sought to circumvent this by having the Senate adopt an innocent-looking resolution reading:

Resolved, That upon the question whether the United States shall be represented in the Congress of Panama, the Senate ought to act with open doors; unless it shall appear that the publication of documents, necessary to be referred to in debate, will be prejudicial to existing negotiations.

Resolved, That the President be respectfully requested to inform the Senate whether such objection exists to the publication of the documents communicated by the Executive, or any portion of them;

and, if so, to specify the parts, the publication of which would, for that reason, be objectionable.

"Delicate and ensnaring," observed Adams, in noting that "these resolutions are the fruit and ingenuity of Martin Van Buren." And thus he analyzed the design of the resolves: "The limitation was not of papers the publication of which might be injurious, but merely of such as would affect existing negotiations; and this being necessarily a matter of opinion, if I should specify passages in the documents as of such character, any Senator might make it a question for discussion in the Senate, and they might finally publish the whole, under color of entertaining an opinion different from mine on the probable effect of the publication."

In answer to the resolution Adams said:

Believing that the established usage of free confidential communications, between the Executive and the Senate, ought for the public interest, to be preserved unimpaired, I deem it my indispensable duty to leave to the Senate itself the decision of a question, involving a departure, hitherto, so far as I am informed, without example, from that usage, and upon the motives for which, not being informed of them, I do not feel myself competent to decide.

This indirect reflection on the motives of the Senate rankled in the breasts of many. After several days of secret sessions, the Senate adopted a resolution lifting the seal of secrecy from its debates on the propriety of sending envoys to the Congress.

Van Buren appealed to the fears of the Senators supporting the administration—and they were in the majority—by reminding them that supporters of the first Adams had imposed their will upon the early Republicans, and that these triumphs of the Federalists were but forerunners of their self-destruction. And the President they were supporting now, he intimated, had been one of the detested Federalist Party. He denounced the Mission as unconstitutional and violative of Washington's admonition against entangling alliances.

Answering the argument that a confederacy of American Republics was necessary to counter the aggressiveness of the Holy Alliance, Van Buren said:

Wherein consists our objections to the Holy Alliance? Because they confederate to maintain governments similar to their own, by force of arms, instead of the force of reason, and the will of the governed. If we, too, confederate to sustain, by the same means, governments similar to our own, wherein consists the difference, except the superiority of our cause? What is their avowed motive? Self-preservation and the peace of Europe. What would be ours? Self-preservation and the peace of America. . . .

I detest, as much as any man, the principles of the Holy Alliance. I yield to no man in my anxious wishes for the success of the Spanish American States. I will go as far as I think any American citizen ought to go, to secure to them the blessings of free government. I commend the solicitude which has been manifested by our Government upon this subject, and have, of course, no desire to discourage it.

But I am against all alliances, against all armed confederacies, or confederacies of any sort. I care not how specious, or how disguised; come in what shape they may, I oppose them. The States in question have the power and the means, if united and true to their principles, to resist any force that Europe can send against them. It is only by being recreant to the principles upon which their Revolution is founded; by suffering foreign influence to distract and divide them; that their independence can be endangered.

But happen what may, our course should be left to our choice, whenever occasion for acting shall occur. If, in the course of events, designs shall be manifested, or steps taken in this hemisphere by any foreign power, which so far affect our interest or our honor, as to make it necessary that we should arm in their defense, it will be done: there is no room to doubt it.

Van Buren had no more staunch ally than Senator Randolph of Virginia,—John Randolph of Roanoke, as he usually signed himself. Genius had set her chaplet on his brow a bit awry. No one approached him in eloquence in the Senate: Webster was still a member of the House. He had wealth, broad acres, a large stable; he raced his horses and bet on them; he played cards and gambled on them. Clay gambled; Jackson gambled; every one in their class gambled. George Poindexter, Senator from Mississippi, told Jackson and Van Buren of holding an unbeatable hand in a game of brag with Clay. The Secretary of State had lost heavily, and driven desperate by his losses, Clay bet, or bragged, his hotel and lands at Cincinnati against a named sum. Clay would be ruined financially if Poindexter saw his brag. **Poindexter** laid down his invincible hand. Often Clay would remind Poindexter that he once had him in his power—the only man, he would always add.

Randolph had opposed Van Buren's resolution requesting the President to indicate the parts of the documents which could be published without prejudicing the pending negotiations. But after Adams replied, the attitude of the Virginian underwent a violent change.

Randolph of Roanoke had been drinking heavily. Bottled porter was his chief tipple at this session. Under its stimulus his erratic nature was whipped into extremes which knew no curbing. Appeals had been made to Calhoun to call Randolph to order, but he pleaded that he was without power. "This was tolerated by Calhoun," wrote Adams, "because Randolph's ribaldry was all pointed against the Administration, especially against Mr. Clay and me, and because he was afraid of Randolph." Replying to those who wanted him to hold his liquorish tongue in leash, Randolph, in a speech on the Cumberland Road bill, said:

A good deal has been said, sir, about the dignity of this Assembly; about its being improper to talk vernacular English here—we must speak so superfine and mincing that nobody but an accomplished lady from a female seminary can understand us. Is that the case in the House of Commons, or even in the House of Peers? . . . have not assertions, not the most delicate, been made on the floor of both Houses of Parliament, in the House of Peers, with all its robes and wigs, and everything else? Was it not broadly insinuated, over and over again, that there was an adulterous intercourse between the Dowager Princess of Wales and the Earl of Bute, the favorite? Is this very delicate? Is this very sentimental and refined?

Ten days later, on March 30, Randolph, ribald as before, began an oration—drunk or sober he was eloquent—which stands alone in deliberative bodies. Quiet reigned as he rose. Many who blushed at the things he said, remained lest they might miss some phrase worth cherishing.

Before Randolph had proceeded far, it was evident that he intended to make his attack on the Panama Mission a vehicle for personal abuse of the President and the Secretary of State. He

said that the proposal was patterned on the abortive attempt by
Webster two years earlier to send a mission to Greece, and a
resolution offered at the same time by Clay, which asserted that
this country would not see, "without serious inquietude, any forcible interposition by the allied powers of Europe to restore the
South American Republics to Spain."

In the concomitance of these circumstances on January 20,
1824—a resolution by Webster of Massachusetts, and another
by Clay of Kentucky—Randolph saw "an alliance . . . between
old Massachusetts and . . . young Kentucky, not so young, however, as not to make a prudent match, and sell her charms for
their full value."

Many were hoping that Randolph, who believed the charge
of bargain and coalition, would stop here. Randolph then took
his audience to England, where he had spent the summer of that
year, and returned to Washington in time for the deadlock when
—this with fine sarcasm—"the knowing ones [were] . . . intriguing about the Presidency; trying perhaps, to make some
dirty bargain about the Presidency, when the question was settled
as far back as January, 1824."

Later he referred to "the mover of this resolution . . . about
South America [Clay], to whom it does not become me to allude."
Followed some prurient allusions, and then:

Sir, in what book is it—you know better than I—in what parlia-
mentary debate was it, that, upon a certain union between Lord
Sandwich, one of the most corrupt and profligate of men in all the
relations of life, and the sanctimonious, puritanical Lord Mansfield,
and the other ministerial leaders—on what occasion was it, that Junius
said after Lord Chatham had said it before him that it reminded him
of the union between Blifil and Black George?

There was no mistaking that Randolph was comparing the
President to Lord Mansfield and to the canting hypocrite in *Tom
Jones;* and his Secretary of State to Lord Sandwich and to Field-
ing's debased character.

Next he drew on *Gil Blas* for invidious comparisons, and
then this: "I say I will prove . . . that the President has dropped
an extinguisher on himself . . . by the aid of this very new ally.
I shall not say which is Blifil and which is Black George."

There were gasps at this. He followed with the charge, which had no other foundation than his copious draughts of porter, that the Spanish documents sent to the Senate by the President, had been forged in the office of the Secretary of State. "My suspicious temper may have carried me too far—if it has, I will beg pardon—but will show enough—not a handkerchief—not to justify the jealousy of Othello—yet I believe that the jealousy might have been pardoned to the noble Moor, certainly by me, had he not been a black man; but the idea to me is so revolting, of that connection, that I can never read that play with any sort of pleasure—see it acted I never could."

Then he bared an old hate for all the Adamses. He began deriding the second Adams as "an apostle of universal liberty," and condemned the first Adams as "an apostle of monarchy." "I was in New York when he [John Adams] took his seat as Vice President," he went on. ". . . I was a schoolboy at the time, attending the lobby of Congress when I ought to have been at school. I remember the manner in which my brother was spurned by the coachman of the then Vice President for coming too near the arms blazoned on the escutcheon of the vice-regal carriage. Perhaps I may have some of the old animosity rankling in my heart, . . . coming from a race who are never known to forsake a friend or forgive a foe."

Having made this avowal and reference to his descent from Pocahontas, Randolph sketched his course against Van Buren in the secret session; and after reading that part of Adams's answer—the dirty lines, he called them—to Van Buren's resolutions which impugned the motives of the Senate, he exclaimed: "The innuendo was that our motives were black and bad. That moment did I put, like Hannibal, my hand on the altar, and swear eternal enmity to him and his, politically." Adverting to the closing hours of the secret session, he said: "After twenty-six hours' exertion, it was time to give in. I was defeated, horse, foot, and dragoons—cut up—and clean broke through—by the coalition, unheard of till then, of the Puritan with the blackleg."

Randolph spoke another quarter of an hour. But no one followed him save the stenographer. It was impossible, because the ears of all were ringing with the phrase: "the coalition, unheard of till then, of the Puritan with the blackleg." Clay gambled, recklessly as we know; but blackleg—he was not that.

A newspaper account erroneously quoted Randolph as saying that he held himself personally responsible for all that he had said.

Adams ignored the vilification. Clay, on the assumption that the newspaper had done justice to Randolph, immediately challenged.

The day following Randolph's speech was Friday. General T. J. Jesup, bearing Clay's note, was unable to find Randolph at his lodgings until Saturday. Jesup opened the interview by announcing the position he occupied, adding that he was aware that no one had the right to question him outside of the Senate for anything said on the floor, unless he chose voluntarily to waive the privilege. Randolph replied that he would never take advantage of any subterfuge, and proposed that the General take back his answer. Randolph had forgotten, in his excited state, the punctilio of the occasion. Jesup recalled it by reminding him that he should consult with friends before taking so important a step.

"You are right, sir!" exclaimed Randolph, seizing the hand of Clay's second. "I thank you for the suggestion. But as you do not take my note, you must not be impatient if you do not hear from me to-day. I now think of only two friends; and there are circumstances connected with one which may deprive me of his services, and the other is in bad health: he was sick yesterday and he may not be out to-day."

Jesup assured him that any reasonable time which he found necessary would be satisfactory.

Randolph had in mind Edward F. Tatnall, a Representative from Georgia, and Senator Benton. Both were experienced in such matters. Benton and his younger brother Jesse had exchanged shots with Jackson and his friend, Colonel Coffee, at Benton's hotel in Nashville, some thirteen years back. Jackson fell at the first exchange, his left shoulder shattered. When the pistols were emptied, dirks were drawn. One of these was wielded by Stokely Hall, another friend of Old Hickory. Hall had seen Jesse's fire bring down Jackson. Drawing his sword cane, he lunged, the point striking a button on Jesse's coat with such force that the blade splintered as though made of glass.

Jesse, who had been recently shot in the buttocks in a duel with William Carroll, another fire-eating friend of Jackson, fell in the onslaught. While on his back he received several gashes on his arms before he was rescued by a peaceable Tennesseean. Coffee and Alexander Donaldson closed in on the elder Benton; their dirks inflicted five flesh wounds before the encounter was ended by several men of peace.

To the elder Benton, whose tirades against Jackson for acting as second to Carroll in the duel with Jesse had led to the affray in Nashville, Randolph repaired after Jesup had left him. Benton knew nothing of the challenge when Randolph entered. Was he a blood-relation of Mrs. Clay? was his visitor's first remark. On learning that he was, Randolph said that that put an end to a request he was about to make. Imposing inviolable secrecy, he confided that it was his intention not to return Clay's fire.

This was in keeping with the tall, gaunt, erratic Virginian. He could not deny Clay satisfaction; but he must not return Clay's fire: to do so would be to concede a point he would not yield, the right of any one to question him on a speech in Congress. ". . . and for any Speech or Debate in either House they shall not be questioned in any other Place." Thus ends Section 6 of Article I of the Constitution. This thought Randolph stressed in the acceptance which reads:

Mr. Randolph accepts the challenge of Mr. Clay. At the same time he protests against the right of any minister of the Executive Government of the United States to hold him responsible for words spoken in debate, as a senator from Virginia, in crimination of such minister, or the administration under which he shall have taken office. Colonel Tatnall, of Georgia, the bearer of this letter, is authorized to arrange with General Jesup (the bearer of Mr. Clay's challenge) the terms of the meeting to which Mr. Randolph is invited by that note.

The seconds entered into an exchange of letters and interviews which lasted a week, in the hope that Randolph could be induced to offer an explanation that would satisfy Clay. But Randolph proved unyielding. Accordingly, the afternoon of Saturday, April 8, was agreed upon. The field of honor was a bit of Virginia on the right bank of the Potomac above the Little Falls Bridge.

There was a law against dueling in Virginia. Randolph, who was not a lawyer, believed that he would not violate the law by standing, a pistol in hand, to receive Clay's fire! And he had insisted on the interview taking place in Virginia that his State might receive his blood if he fell.

At noon on the day of the duel Benton called at Randolph's lodgings. His seconds were busy making codicils to his will. Benton's errand was to learn if there had been any change in Randolph's sentiments. He could not ask a question which would cast doubt on Randolph's word. But he found a way: he spoke of visiting Clay's home the night before, of seeing Mrs. Clay, tranquil and smiling, and the youngest child of the Clays asleep on a couch, and reflecting, as he viewed the peaceful scene, how different all might be the next night.

"I shall do nothing to disturb the sleep of the child or the repose of the mother," commented Randolph.

At that moment Randolph's servant Johnny entered with the information that officers of the local branch of the United States Bank said they had no gold.

"They are liars!" exclaimed Randolph. "Johnny, bring me my horse."

Benton waited while master and man galloped to the bank, Johnny riding forty paces in the rear, after the manner of the times. Randolph demanded all he had on deposit, and not bills, but money. Some four thousand dollars were to his credit.

"Have you a cart, Mr. Randolph, to put it in?" asked the teller, politely, as he began lifting sacks of silver to the counter.

"That is my business, sir," was the reply.

The cashier, attracted by the scene, learning the cause of Randolph's annoyance, explained that the wrong answer had been given to the servant. This appeased Randolph, who departed with nine gold pieces—his servant's original request—in the left pocket of his breeches. He was now ready to meet Clay.

On his return Randolph handed Benton a slip of paper on which he had written that if he fell, Benton was to take the nine gold pieces from his pocket, keep three, and give the same number to his seconds. He also delivered to Benton a sealed envelope to be returned to him if he survived.

As the hour approached, Randolph and his seconds, Colonel Tatnall and James Hamilton, Jr., a Representative from South Carolina, drove to the dueling ground in a carriage. The faithful Johnny, mounted on one of his master's thoroughbreds, served as outrider. In a second carriage sat Randolph's surgeon. Benton, who had been granted permission to be present, followed on horseback.

Benton was the last to reach the clearing in the forest where the seconds were carefully measuring ten paces. Randolph, who was sitting in his carriage waiting for the summons, called to Benton.

"Colonel," he said, "since I saw you, and since I have been in this carriage, I have heard something which may make me change my determination. Colonel Hamilton will give you a note which will explain it."

Benton needed to hear no more. He understood too clearly. One of his seconds had told Randolph something which might make him change his determination not to shoot at Clay. But the manner in which Randolph had stressed the word *may* indicated that he had not yet made up his mind.

Here a word of explanation is necessary. When the duel had been decided upon, the seconds threw dice for choice of position. Tatnall won. Consequently, this gave to Clay's second the privilege of counting off the time. It was agreed by the seconds that there was to be no practicing by their principals; and in the hope of further reducing the possibility of a tragedy, Jesup assented to giving the word in the quickest possible time.

Early that morning Jesup informed Tatnall that Clay would not consent to the word being given quickly. "If you insist upon it, the time must be prolonged, but I should very much regret it." Clay insisted. This is what Randolph had heard on his drive to the forest clearing. Tatnall cautioned his principal to fire quickly and carefully, and informed him that he would set the trigger on hair. Randolph answered that he did not want this. Tatnall argued, but to no avail. Randolph had not told his seconds of his resolve not to fire at Clay.

Within a few moments after Benton left Randolph the principals were called to the field. As they took their positions, still unarmed, Clay facing the slowly setting sun, they courteously saluted one another.

Presently Hamilton handed Randolph his pistol. Randolph called to Clay's second to repeat the word as he intended giving it when all was ready. This strange duel was opening in a manner characteristic of all things involving Randolph. And Jesup thus complied:

"Fire! One! [There seemed to be an eternity between the two words!] Two! [How long it took him to call it out!] Three! [Why couldn't he count faster?] Stop!"

There was no longer any doubt that Jesup intended giving the word slowly. Ordinarily Randolph would have been satisfied; but this was an unusual moment; so he asked Jesup to give the word again.

Jesup had about completed the request when a deafening explosion silenced his voice. Randolph, in adjusting the pistol butt to the palm of his hand, had accidentally touched the trigger.

Senator Josiah Johnson, of Louisiana, one of Clay's seconds, was carrying a loaded pistol to his principal. He stood stock-still when Randolph's pistol was discharged. Jesup was standing nearer Clay, and Tatnall was occupying the same relative position to Randolph. The surgeons of the two antagonists had assumed their positions, and the servants were partly concealed among the trees. Benton, too, was in the forest.

All turned toward Randolph, whose pistol at the moment of discharge was pointing almost straight downward. The ball had plowed a small furrow near his feet.

"I protested against that hair trigger!" exclaimed Randolph before the others had recovered from their alarm.

Tatnall, who was in duty bound to protect his principal from sacrificing himself, shamefacedly took the blame.

This unusual incident was at once the subject of an inquiry into its cause by Clay's seconds, which Clay ended with:

"It was an accident! I saw it."

The pistol was reloaded. The accidental fire preyed on Randolph's sensitive feelings. The generous remark of Clay only intensified his chagrin. He was fairly beside himself; but outwardly his emotions were under control.

Soon all was ready. The principals and their seconds were at their respective places, and Jesup slowly gave the word. Both men exchanged their fire simultaneously. Randolph, an excellent shot, had fired at Clay! Fortunately the bullet missed Clay's legs. Clay's bullet had torn a hole through the skirt of Randolph's coat.

Benton, who had been invited to the field as a mutual friend, strode quickly to the dueling ground and offered his services as mediator.

"This is child's play!" exclaimed Clay, with an imperious wave of the hand, a gesture to which he was prone. He demanded another fire. Randolph echoed the demand.

While the seconds were reloading, a slow, punctilious process under such conditions, Benton prevailed on Randolph to leave his post, and pressed on him to yield to some accommodation. But Randolph was angry with himself: first for the accidental discharge, which could be interpreted by the world at large to his dishonor; and again, because in the ensuing excitement he had fired at Clay. Randolph had taken deliberate aim at Clay's legs, below the knees, intending merely to foul his aim. He now regretted having done this; for after talking to Benton in his carriage he had renewed his resolution not to shoot. Who would believe this now, save the very few who knew him well? By this really unintentional shot he had violated the law of his State and admitted Clay's right to question him for words said in debate. In his disturbed state he showed impatience at Benton's kindly intentions and returned to his post.

This time the word was given by Tatnall. Clay fired. His bullet passed through Randolph's pantaloons. After receiving Clay's fire, Randolph discharged his pistol in the air, threw it to the ground, and rushed toward Clay, exclaiming:

"I did not fire at you, Mr. Clay."

Clay had followed his example and they shook hands midway on the field.

"You owe me a coat, Mr. Clay," said Randolph, as he laughingly pointed to the rent made by Clay's bullets. He had not noticed the hole in his pantaloons.

"I am glad the debt is no greater," said Clay fervently.

Benton joined the group and unbosomed all that Randolph had confided in him the preceding Saturday. And Randolph added: "I came upon the ground determined not to fire at you, but the accidental discharge of my pistol, with the circumstances attending it, for a moment changed my mind."

That evening Randolph, Benton, Tatnall, and Hamilton regaled themselves at Randolph's lodgings. The sealed envelope was opened: it directed Randolph's interment among his patrimonial oaks. Instructions were also enclosed to have seals made out of the gold coins in Randolph's pocket.

"But Clay's bad shooting shan't rob you of your seals," said Randolph. "I am going to London and have them made for you."

The measure which led to the duel was passed with four votes to spare. The slavery issue was not involved in the Panama Mission. The opposition was predicated almost wholly on factional grounds. Some of the objectors, in the course of the debate, did say that there could be no discussion in any foreign assembly of the country's settled policy of not interchanging diplomats with Haiti, then ruled by blacks. But this was chicane. Nine of the twenty-one Senators from the South who were present when final action was taken, voted for the Mission.

Into the same realm of factious fiction must be consigned the remark attributed to Van Buren after the bill was passed: ". . . if they had only taken the other side and refused the Mission, we should have had them." The secretary of the Mission was William B. Rochester, of New York, whose father had been a business partner of the father-in-law of Clay. Van Buren made a note of this.

But the caution displayed by Van Buren was thrown to the winds by his Regency while the seconds of Clay and Randolph were exchanging notes and interviews. No one in Washington misunderstood Van Buren's intentions toward the administration; yet on April 3, the leading editorial in the Regency's organ, the *Argus*, advocated a non-committal stand with respect to Adams and his program. Edwin Croswell, editor of the paper, advised Van Buren not to be surprised at the tone of the leader, and added: "Whilst there is a great aversion towards Mr. Adams amongst the Republicans of this State, there is a great aversion on their part to any collision with the administration which shall drive them to the support of Mr. Clinton, or that shall force them to encounter the hostility of both. They prefer, for the present at least, to stand in the capacity of lookers on, believing that the natural hostility between A[dams] and C[linton] will be certain of shewing itself, and the sooner if we afford them no other ailment than themselves."

The administration newspapers charged Van Buren with having written or dictated the non-committal editorial. The country rang with the charge, and many stories were invented to build up an image of non-committalism. The word *vanburenish* crept into the jargon of the day. Van Buren, who never took the trouble to deny the accusation, enjoyed some of the vanburenish anecdotes.

One of the stories, at which Van Buren laughed heartily, concerned a wager made by two of his friends that he would not answer any question definitely. Accordingly one asked Van Buren —so the yarn went—if he concurred in the general opinion that the sun rose in the east. Van Buren replied: "I presume the fact is according to the common impression, but as I sleep until after sunrise, I cannot speak from my own knowledge." This passed current for truth among many.

There was nothing more definite than Van Buren's opposition to the measures of the Adams administration, an opposition based almost entirely on partisan grounds. Clay was the great apostle of internal improvements. He was Van Buren's senior by three years. He had entered Congress as a member of the Senate seventeen years before. Van Buren in 1822 and 1823 had voted for toll gates and repairs on the Cumberland Road. But the next year, on the eve of the Presidential election, he introduced an amendment to the Constitution which struck at Clay.

This amendment would empower Congress to make appropriations for internal improvements under restrictions safeguarding the sovereignty of the States. The money from the national Treasury was to be dispensed by the State or States building the road or the canal; but no enterprise could be undertaken without the consent of each commonwealth affected.

In his efforts to injure Clay by holding him up as an anti-State-rights man, Van Buren overlooked that his proposal was in essence a negation of State sovereignty, as the States not benefited by the improvement would have to share the cost.

While opposing the Panama Mission, which was more Clay

than Adams, Van Buren introduced a resolution whose major resolve read: "Resolved, That Congress does not possess the power
to make roads and canals within the respective States."

Van Buren's resolution left to a select committee the task of
working out an amendment which was to be subjected "to such
restrictions as shall effectually protect the sovereignty of the
respective States, and secure to them a just distribution of the
benefits resulting from all appropriations made for that purpose." There was more of crafty politics than statesmanship in
this. The resolution died aborning.

He was consistent in this session. After the Randolph-Clay
duel he opposed administration measures providing appropriations for work on the Cumberland Road, surveys for canals and
roads, and for subscriptions by the government to two quasi-
private canal enterprises. In voicing his objections to the government buying stock, Van Buren reminded the Senate that there
was little analogy between this and an investment by an individual.

"Where an individual subscribed for stock," said Van Buren,
"he had a personal, a direct interest, which caused him to move
with caution, and to see that his interests were properly attended
to . . ." He added that where aid was granted in the form proposed, abuses would creep in, and in nine cases out of ten, deception would follow.

While the partisan view of the issue largely governed his
attitude, he never resorted to the harsh word. He expressed his
guiding principle in debate at the beginning of the speech just
quoted from, when he said that he did not wish to entertain feelings of asperity toward those who differed from him.

But he contrived to differ with every measure of moment
advocated by the administration. He pictured himself and his
followers as the defenders of State rights, and popular government. He made it impossible for any one to take personal umbrage,
interspersing his speeches with such professions as: "Different
views are taken on this subject by persons who are pure and
honest."

Until this year the members of the United States Supreme
Court attended circuits, and lived in their respective jurisdictions.
The administration proposed to increase the number of circuits—
no one could cavil at this—and to constitute the Supreme Court

a court of appeals, as it now exists, and relieve the judges of the revisory body of the arduous labors of the circuit.

In arguing against relieving the judges of the Supreme Court from circuit work, he said that "the whole business of the Justices of the Supreme Court will be done here, and sooner or later, they would, in the natural course of things, all move to, and permanently reside at the seat of government." This was the intent of the bill.

Van Buren was for the additional judges, but no more. In this he was sincere: he was fundamentally opposed to centralized government. Had the proposed reform emanated from an administration he was loyally supporting, it would have met with the same vigorous opposition.

In Van Buren's masterful speech against the change, he quoted, without indicating the author, Jefferson's objections to the life tenure of judges, and the strictures uttered by the sage of Monticello on Van Buren's visit, against the impotence of the power of impeachment to remove an unworthy member of the court.

"I know well," said Van Buren, "that the opinion that the tenure of the office of justices of the Supreme Court is the rotten part of the Constitution, is entertained by men who have established for themselves imperishable claims to the character of saviours of their country, and benefactors of the human race."

This was Jefferson; but Van Buren disavowed these as his sentiments, explaining that his early and constant connection with the courts may have biased him. In arguing against the permanent residence in Washington of the members of the Supreme Court, and their separation from their brethren on the circuits, Van Buren made use of Jefferson's belittlement of the impeachment power.

"It is impossible, with the best intention on the part of the Executive branch of the Government, to avoid bad appointments," said Van Buren. "Influence and favoritism sometimes prevail, and to a want of correct information the Government is always exposed. Incompetent men, therefore, will sometimes be appointed."

This incompetency, he reasoned, would be shielded by the capacity and learning of the able men on the Supreme Court bench, but if all had to face the "public ordeal" of holding circuit, bad appointments were less likely to be made. Then he added:

"There is a power in public opinion in this country—and I thank God for it: for it is the most honest and best of all powers —which will not tolerate an incompetent or unworthy man to hold in his weak or wicked hands the lives and fortunes of his fellow-citizens. This power operates alike upon the Government and the incumbent. The former dare not disregard it, and the latter can have no adequate wish that they should, when he once knows the estimation in which he is held. This public ordeal, therefore, is of great value; in my opinion, much more so than what has, with some propriety, been called the scare-crow of the constitution— the power of impeachment."

In mild periphrasis, Van Buren accused the court of encroaching upon the rights of the States under cover of the provision prohibiting the enactment of "any law impairing the obligations of contract." It had been explained that this clause was inserted in the Constitution, he said, to negative the acts adopted between 1783 and 1788 by Virginia, South Carolina, Rhode Island, and New Jersey as reprisals for Great Britain's refusal to comply with the stipulations of the treaty of peace. The measures, although general in scope, were designed to prevent the collection of debts by Britishers.

Van Buren, without vouching for the correctness of the explanation of the origin of the clause, uttered this grain of wisdom: "if it be true that such was its object, . . . it adds another solemn proof to that which all experience has testified, of the danger of adopting general provisions for the redress of particular and partial evils." That Van Buren believed that this was the true explanation is evident from his speech.

Under the broad interpretation of this clause, the court has taken jurisdiction over acts of the State in which contracts are not expressed, "but implied by law, from the nature of the transaction." He continued: "Any one conversant with the usual range of the State legislation will at once see how small a portion of it is exempt, under this provision, from the seven judges of the Supreme Court. The practice under it has been in accordance with what should have been anticipated . . . if the question of conferring it was now presented for the first time, I should unhesitatingly say that the people of the states, might with safety, be left to their own legislatures and to the protection of their own courts."

He observed that it had been said that "there exists not upon the earth, and there never did exist, a judicial tribunal clothed with powers so various and important" as the Supreme Court. It decides whether or no the laws enacted by Congress are "pursuant to the Constitution, and from its judgment there is no appeal." Thus it could veto nine-tenths of the laws passed at each session.

"Although this branch of its jurisdiction is not that which has been most exercised," he continued, "still instances are not wanting in which it has disregarded acts of Congress, in passing upon the rights of others, and in refusing to perform duties required of it by the Legislature, on the ground that the Legislature had no right to impose them."

But his grievance did not lie in this direction, but in the nullification of "statutes of powerful States, which had received the deliberate sanction, not only of their legislatures, but of their highest judicatories, composed of men of venerable years, of unsullied purity, and unrivaled talents . . ."

There was courage in this speech, and Van Buren was not unaware of it. He said: ". . . a sentiment, I had almost said, of idolatry, for the Supreme Court, has grown up, which claims for its members an almost entire exemption from the fallibilities of our nature, and arraigns with unsparing bitterness the motives of all who have the temerity to look with inquisitive eyes into this consecrated sanctuary of the law. So powerful has this sentiment become, such strong hold has it taken of the press of this country, that it requires not a little share of firmness in a public man, however imperious may be his duty, to express sentiments that conflict with it."

He would unqualifiedly concede so much of the "high-wrought eulogies" as credited the members of the court with "talents of the highest order and spotless integrity." And he sincerely believed that "that uncommon man who now presides over the court [John Marshall] is, in all human probability, the ablest judge now sitting upon any judicial bench in the world."

"But to the sentiment which claims for the judges so great a share of exemption from the feelings that govern the conduct of other men, and for the court the character of being the safest depository of political power, I do not subscribe," he continued with feeling. "I have been brought up in an opposite faith, and all my experience has confirmed me in its correctness. . . . I believe that the judges of the Supreme Court, great and good men as I cheerfully concede them to be, are subject to the same infirmities, influenced by the same passions, and operated upon by the same causes that good and great men are in other situations."

Van Buren knew that the majority of the lawyers of the Senate shared these views, and that in his strictures on the bench, mostly by innuendo, he was voicing the sentiments of a goodly number of the Senators who were not of the law. Randolph, the day before his duel with Clay, spent two hours denouncing the court, and on Randolph's return from the field of honor, Senator John Rowan, from Clay's own State, indulged in a savage tirade against the bench.

"The Constitution now exists," said Rowan, mockingly. "The six courts and three judges created by that bill do not now exist. And yet, it will no sooner have passed into a law, than it will be asserted that these six courts and three judges, which will be created by the act, were created by the Constitution. The whole corps will assert it. The Bank of the United States will back the assertion with all its influence—with all its metallic intelligence . . ."

Few dared to talk about the Bank as Rowan did: its tentacles reached into the very halls of Congress, into editorial sanctums, into merchants' counting rooms, and to the hearths of the newest settlers on the nation's frontiers. Mortgages, loans, paid advertisements, retainers, and outright bribes,—these were the sources of its vast influence. It was the savings bank of the poor and the Treasury of the government. It made leaders, and destroyed them. Rowan received his cue from Governor Joseph Desha, who in his message to the Kentucky Legislature, in the preceding November, had denounced the Bank and all banks as hostile to the powers and rights of the States.

In the closing days of the session two select committees, appointed solely to keep alive the old animosities against Adams, and to create new ones, made their reports to the Senate. Benton was chairman of both, and Van Buren their directing genius.

The first report consisted of an amendment to the Constitution, recommended with all solemnity, although few in the entire Congress really believed in it. This provided for the direct election of President and Vice President. The Electoral College would be abolished; but its essential feature was retained by dividing each State into districts coequal with the number of Congressmen from the State. The candidate receiving the largest number of votes in each district would receive the district's vote in the tally made in Congress. A second clause provided that in the remote event of a tie, the two candidates receiving the highest number of district votes would again go before the people at a subsequent election to be held in December; if the seemingly impossible were to happen, and neither received a majority the contest was to go into the House.

Van Buren said that it was too late to act upon the resolution now, but that if he lived, he would press it to a conclusion at the next session; for on no one point were the people more united than "upon the propriety, not to say the indispensable necessity, of keeping the election of the President from the House of Representatives." His sole purpose in advocating the measure was to provide those who had voted for Jackson, Crawford, and Clay with fresh fuel to fire their abating anger.

The second report was accompanied by six bills aimed at an old evil. One deprived the President of designating newspapers for government subsidies in the shape of advertisements and gave the distribution of largesse to the members of Congress. Three others dealt with the country's fighting forces: two transferred the appointment of cadets and midshipmen from the President to the Congressmen; a third prevented a President from dismissing officers of the Army and Navy without just cause.

The remaining two struck at the root of the evil of Federal patronage. One was designed to keep honest collectors and disbursers of revenue in office during their good behavior by mandating the appointing power to inform the Senate of the reasons for removals of men holding places of public trust. The sixth bill provided for Senatorial confirmation of postmasters receiving a salary in excess of a sum to be determined. The attendant publicity, it was believed, would reduce the use of the Post Office Department for political purposes to a negligible factor.

By innuendo Adams was accused of all the wrongs which the measures sought to correct. The report of the select committee, having in view the covert attacks made by Randolph and others on Adams as a monarchist in disguise, said that the names of rulers meant nothing: the first Roman emperor was called the Emperor of the Republic: the late French emperor had a similar title: and if the patronage of the President of the United States was not curbed, and the press freed of the bribery of government advertising, the people might awake some morning to cheer the Emperor of the Republic of the United States.

This report was a fitting prelude to the disgraceful campaign of 1828.

# CHAPTER XXXII

VAN BUREN returned to Albany happier than when he had left it in the fall. His plan of attack on Adams had been successful. But it might turn out to be so much labor for Clinton. He had found at Washington considerable sentiment for his old foe, due largely to the completion of the Canal. If Clinton were reëlected Governor, he would be New York's favorite for the Presidency. And Van Buren, more than once, pictured himself managing Clinton's campaign.

The fiftieth anniversary of the birth of the nation was observed July 4. Van Buren retired that night not knowing that the day was made more memorable by the deaths of John Adams and Thomas Jefferson. They had served on the committee of the Continental Congress charged with drafting the immortal document to which Jefferson's name is forever attached; both had directed the nation in its early years. These and like recollections were mentioned reverently at meetings held wherever the Stars and Stripes floated, when the stages brought the tidings. And many saw the interposition of Providence in the singular coincidence.

Toward the end of the month a sudden change came over members of the Regency. During the past winter they had told Clinton that he would not be opposed for reëlection. Van Buren was agreeable to this; but Silas Wright and other aides of Van Buren could not endure Clinton. Van Buren made no effort to stem this sentiment, lest he distract the party. He did not want a conflict, as he did not want to jeopardize his return to the Senate when his term expired on March 3.

On September 21 Clinton was unanimously renominated at Utica. The Regency was for naming William Paulding of Westchester County, and called a convention for this purpose at Herkimer on October 4. Two or three days before the meeting Van Buren summoned Wright and other aides to a conference in Albany and told them that deep as was his respect for Paulding

he had strong objections to running him against Clinton. One
was that Paulding and most of his county had been opposed to
the construction of the Erie Canal; another was that their choice
had a monomania regarding his physical perfections, believing
himself strong as Hercules and handsome as Adonis. Van Buren
recalled that this vanity of Paulding was common gossip in the
State, and reminded his hearers of Clinton's powers of ridicule,
and pictured Paulding laughed out of the campaign by Clinton's
sallies.

Van Buren revealed a plan which amazed even these intimates, who knew him as a master unapproachable in the realm of
intrigue. He sketched the history of the last election, when the
coalition of the Clinton-Jackson faction with the friends of
Adams and Clay had contributed heavily to the overthrow of
the Regency. He reminded them that it was public property that
Adams had privately offered the first post in his Cabinet to
Clinton, and upon his declension had appointed Clay; and it
was a matter of record that Adams had tendered the highest
diplomatic honor to Clinton. Consequently, Adams, Clay, and
Clinton were one in the public mind, and the supporters of the
Administration would vote for Clinton unless the Regency named
a man closely identified with Adams and Clay, and thereby gave
his nomination the appearance of being dictated by Washington.

Van Buren had the man: William B. Rochester, Secretary
to the Panama Mission, and, as we also know, son of a business
partner of Clay's father-in-law.

Rochester was nominated, and the Regency spread the report
that the National Administration had forced his nomination. No
denial of this fiction came from Washington, and the deceit
worked as Van Buren anticipated. Tens of thousands of votes
which would have gone to Clinton were cast for Rochester.
Enough Van Burenites were elected to the Legislature to return
him to the Senate. The vote for Governor was close, but every
indication pointed to the defeat of Clinton. For four days after
the polls closed the result was still in doubt.

Clinton and his wife were members of the Presbyterian
Church. Van Buren sometimes attended Clinton's church, a habit
he had acquired through his wife, who in her closing days embraced its teachings. Marcy visited Van Buren on the Sunday fol-

lowing Election Day. Both were discussing the belated returns when the siren announced the arrival of the steamboat from New York.

A minute later a friend of Clinton ran past Van Buren's window in the direction of the Governor's residence. No one but the bearer of good news would be in such haste, observed Van Buren to Marcy as he pointed out the messenger. Marcy suggested that his friend was needlessly alarmed.

On their way to church Van Buren predicted that the mystery would be solved when the Clintons came to service: if the messenger brought word of victory, the Governor and his wife would be late, as they would entertain the visitor; if bad news, they would hasten to church. Never was Van Buren more distracted at his devotions. He was noted for his vigorous voice during the congregational singing, but his thoughts were not upon hymns now. His attention was on the pew reserved for the Governor, which remained unoccupied until the services were well under way. Van Buren and Marcy were seated across the aisle. As Mrs. Clinton settled herself in her seat she glanced triumphantly at her husband's enemies.

"The election is indeed lost," Marcy whispered mournfully to Van Buren as the Governor's wife turned her gaze from them.

Clinton had won by the narrow margin of three thousand, six hundred and fifty; Henry Huntington, nominee for Lieutenant Governor, was defeated by Nathaniel Pitcher, the Regency candidate.

The election was a distinct shock to the Regency. All had expected Clinton's defeat by at least ten thousand. Van Buren, anxious to make up his losses on his bets in the election of two years before, had wagered heavily, and on the very eve of the balloting he wrote to Churchill C. Cambreleng, one of New York City's Congressional delegation: ". . . Dont forget my bets. I cannot think of letting this election go by without making up for most losses. If you cant bet on ten thousand you may on nine or a suit of clothes or 8. thousand."

The Regency reluctantly agreed that Clinton could not be ignored as a Presidential possibility. Not a word passed between Clinton and Van Buren; but after the latter left for Washington, the Governor learned from one of the Regents—Knower, Marcy's

father-in-law, maintained friendly relations with the Governor—
that Van Buren "would place him on an equal footing with his
compeers in the Presidential canvass." Marcy sent Van Buren a
summary of political happenings in which he noted: "Gov Clinton
has said that Gen Jackson's popularity is on the decline and that
you would be convinced of it when you got to Washington. Is
that so?" The reply is missing, but several incidents indicate that
Clinton thought Van Buren was with him; for in the Legislature
Clinton's friends voted for Van Buren's reëlection.

But Van Buren had made up his mind in favor of Jackson
at least three days before he was reëlected to the Senate as evidenced by a letter introducing to Jesse Hoyt a subscription
solicitor of the *Telegraph*, recently established at Washington
in the interests of Jackson. "Any assistance you can give him in
promoting his object will be gratefully remembered by the editor
and oblige your friend," wrote Van Buren.

Jackson's popularity was not declining. Aiding Van Buren
in directing the canvass for Old Hickory were Edward Livingston, New York's quondam Mayor, and now, after five years of
service in the House, a member of the Senate from Louisiana;
Jackson's old foe—and older friend, Senator Benton; the unscrupulous Samuel Swartwout; Duff Green, editor of the *Telegraph;* and William B. Lewis, husband of a niece of Mrs.
Jackson.

After Congress adjourned on March 3, Van Buren, accompanied by Cambreleng, made a short political tour of the South
on behalf of Jackson. At a dinner given at Raleigh to his
colleague, Senator Robert Y. Hayne, of South Carolina, he spoke
on State rights. He visited Crawford at his home in Georgia, to
obtain first hand—his enemies later charged—the whispered
story that Calhoun, while Secretary of War under Monroe, had
proposed at a Cabinet meeting that Jackson be punished for his
high-handed acts in the Seminole War.

On May 12 Van Buren paid Adams a morning call; and the
President entered in his diary: "Van Buren is now the great
electioneering manager for General Jackson, as he was before
the last election for Mr. Crawford. . . . His discourse with me
this day was upon the late Mr. Rufus King, his history and

character, and upon Mr. Monroe and his affairs; also upon the Petersburg horse-races, which he has been attending."

The next day, Sunday, Van Buren started homeward with Cambreleng. It was generally reported that Jackson, if elected, would make Van Buren his Secretary of State, would support him for President at the end of his term. The campaign of 1832 was already well under way.

An editor supporting Adams applied to James Barbour, the Secretary of War, for a copy of the order of execution of the six militiamen which Jackson had signed. Adams told Barbour that compliance would be considered a measure of hostility to Jackson, and suggested a refusal. When a Jackson editorial supporter joined in the request the next week, Barbour thought it would now be proper to make public the documents; but Adams remained of the same mind: he did not want a second term through unfair means.

Jackson was campaigning with a reckless zest. On June 5, nearly two years after the Bargain and Corruption calumny had been refuted, Jackson revived it. He wrote to Carter Beverly of North Carolina that "a distinguished member of Congress" had proposed, in the name of friends of Clay, to vote for him in the House if he would declare that Adams would not be continued as Secretary of State; and that he had replied that before he would sit in the President's chair through bargain and corruption "he would see the earth open and swallow both Mr. Clay and his friends and himself with them!"

This was not a difficult thing for Jackson to fancy, believing, as he always did, that he had been robbed of the Presidency by Clay and Adams. In this letter Jackson insinuated that the proposition had been made to him at the instance of Clay, and added that immediately after he had refused to bargain, Clay came out for Adams.

Jackson's word was challenged. He replied that the "distinguished member of Congress" was James Buchanan, then in his third term in the House of Representatives. The future President of the United States, an ardent supporter of Jackson, failed to sustain the General's charge. He said that he had gone to Jackson as his friend, and not as the agent of Clay or any one else;

and that he did not believe or suspect that Jackson thought otherwise until he saw the revival of the charge in print.

As the summer waned, and after Clinton was nominated for President by meetings in Virginia, Ohio, and elsewhere, an article appeared in the *Evening Post*, declaring that Clinton was not a candidate for this high office, and that his choice was Jackson. Clinton realized that the best he could hope for was second place, as Jackson's nomination had long ceased to be in doubt.

Although the election was a year and some months away, the partisans of Jackson and Adams were canvassing with an intensity usually reserved to the last weeks of the most stubbornly contested struggles. It was a campaign of scurrilisms of which the least vile was Jackson's revival of the Bargain and Corruption calumny. The supporters of Adams replied with more of the coffin broadsides and attacks on the good name of Mrs. Jackson. The General's friends published a defense written by Judge John Overton, who knew all the circumstances of Jackson's courtship of Rachel Donelson Robards. Quickly followed attacks on the honor of Adams, which plumbed the depths of the original mud when it was said that he had surrendered an American servant girl to Czar Alexander, "*e più volte carnalmente la cognobbe.*" Charges of wasting public funds, and of defrauding the Government while Minister to the Russian Court, which could have been disproved by citing the record, Adams treated with the same contemptuous silence.

Van Buren was of Adams's mind on this. On September 14 he wrote to Nashville advising the General to refrain from issuing any more defensive publications. He began by saying that Jackson's election could be prevented only "by some indiscretion of our own." Then he struck at Clinton with: "For four-fifths of the time since 1800 the old Republican Party has possessed the power of this state. It does so now to a greater extent (the Gov. alone excepted) than it has done for many years." Then followed the advice:

One word more & excuse me for the liberty I take in referring to it. I can well appreciate your feelings under the torrents of malignant vituperation to which you have been exposed, & I am sensible of the difficulty of avoiding replies to direct applications which are (sometimes with the best intention but not unfrequently from mere

vanity on the part of their authors) made to you from different parts
of the Union. But I think I hazard nothing in saying that for the
future the case must be an extreme one that can make full explanation from you personally necessary. The obvious design to bear you
down by calumny has produced a great reaction, & I am quite certain
that they have so much overacted their parts as to render their past
as well as future vituperation entirely harmless. Our people do not
like to see publications from candidates. It is a singular fact that in
almost every case in which they have (with us) been attempted on the
eve of an election they have operated agt. the cause they were intended to serve.

Knowing how peppery Jackson was, Van Buren added: "Do
not infer from this that it is my intention to complain of the
past. On the contrary I am clearly of [the] opinion that all that
has been done was not only proper but unavoidable and has been
useful." Van Buren's advice was followed.

Van Buren believed in campaign literature—of the right
sort. He directed the preparation of numerous pamphlets and
like contributions. Hamilton—Alexander's son, James A.—also
penned at least one laudatory tribute to Jackson's personal
character. These effusions, before being given to the public, were
gone over carefully by Van Buren and his "board of censors"—
as he described his Regents in a letter to Cambreleng.

A word on one of the calumnies of this campaign. The most
baseless of all is still repeated. The day Van Buren called on
Adams after his Southern electioneering trip, Adams entered in
his diary: "He [Van Buren] is now acting over the part in the
affairs of the Union which Aaron Burr performed in 1799 and
1800; and there is much resemblance of character, manners, and
even person, between the two men." Adams is occasionally peri-
phrastic.

Van Buren resembled Burr in manner as did any other
courtly citizen of the day. The chief characteristic of Burr's
private life—his affairs with women—was absolutely lacking in
Van Buren. They were adepts in the art of political intrigue,
and great lawyers; but Van Buren was Burr's master in each field.
In person they were alike in one respect only: their smallness of
stature. Here all physical comparisons cease. Burr, stood five
feet six, and was a little taller than Van Buren. Van Buren had

yellow hair; Burr's was brown; Burr had dark hazel eyes; Van Buren's were blue; Van Buren had a Roman nose; Burr's was pronouncedly retroussé.

In Parton's *Recollections of Winfield Scott* occurs: "Speaking of Martin Van Buren, for whom General Scott had a great regard, he alluded to the popular tradition that the ex-President was the son of Aaron Burr. He gave a decided denial to the scandal, and adduced convincing reasons for rejecting it."

With more plausibility the pothouse politicians might have said that Van Buren was the son of Napoleon; for there was an undeniable kinship in noses.

During the summer and early fall, Van Buren remained most of the time in Albany, receiving county leaders, and directing affairs outside the State by post. Hamilton was enlisting old Federalists of substance in Jackson's cause. Before this missionary work began, which was mainly carried on by letter, Van Buren wrote to Hamilton: "Does the old gentleman have prayers in his house? If so, mention it modestly." Van Buren kept a check on the newspapers, and when the Jacksonian press blundered, he hastened to correct the error, as is instanced by the following to Cambreleng:

I am sorry to see that a paper of so much real promise as the Courier should fall into so great a mistake as to speak lightly of the Morgan affair. Depend upon it that this course may do us much injury. There never was in any part of the world a more deep & general solicitude upon any like subject than now pervades the western counties in relation to the fate of Morgan. You will see by the Argus of today that last week there was a meeting of 3000 persons in one County. The editors are also mistaken as to the fact. There is no rational doubt that Morgan is dead & has perished by violence. Speak to them. . . .

The Morgan affair was then in its infancy. William Morgan had been dead for about a year. There was a hidden drama in his death which fired the imagination; and none, save his slayers, knew how he died, or how they had disposed of his body. And no one knew who had killed him, save his executioners, and they were not talking. Clinton, as Governor, had offered a reward of $2,000 —a princely sum in those days—for the apprehension of the guilty, and appointed a special prosecutor.

All that is definitely known is that on September 11 Morgan was seized at his home in Batavia, in the western part of the State, and taken by a company of men to Canandaigua on a petty criminal charge. He was acquitted of the count and immediately rearrested on a civil process for a small debt. Upon judgment being obtained he was committed to prison. The following night the debt was paid and he was taken from the prison by those who had obtained his release and thrust into a carriage and taken to Fort Niagara, where he was imprisoned in the magazine.

What happened after is not a matter of record: that he was slain is beyond question.

Before Morgan's abduction his neighbors knew that he was engaged in publishing a book purporting to reveal secrets of the first degrees of Free Masonry. Local Masons were accused of having abducted Morgan, and subsequent investigation revealed that the disappearance of Morgan was not known to any man, Mason or non-Mason, outside of the two western counties of Genesee and Monroe, until after search of him had been instituted.

When Van Buren wrote to Cambreleng, the affair was being capitalized by petty politicians who raised the cry that the entire Masonic fraternity was behind Morgan's abduction, and that Governor Clinton, as Grand High Priest of the Grand Chapter of Royal Arch Masons, had ordered the execution of Morgan! Van Buren was not concerned in Clinton, but he was in Jackson, who was also a prominent Mason, and whose name was being linked up in the mysterious disappearance of Morgan.

Van Buren realized that the Jacksonian press, in view of the General's lifelong affiliation with the order, must not deny the known facts. In the western part of the State, many who were not Masons, were demanding proscription of all Masons. A candidate for State Senator in the Western District was rejected because he was a Mason, and T. H. Porter, a non-Mason, nominated in his stead. In this obscure convention was the germ of an organization which was to introduce bigotry into American politics on a national scale.

Early in October Van Buren, whose moods are often reflected in his letters, asked Cambreleng to collect a debt from an unnamed Colonel. "You have really disappointed me in getting the money from the Col. so soon," wrote Van Buren on October 22. "If you will come & live with me I will make you my Collector General." Then he added, with his usual disregard for punctuation: "Why dont I get the wine. Let me have it before Thursday at least the dozen that has been drawn of[f] on that [day] I give a dinner to all the young Jackson Blood in the city." That he practiced the rigorous economy he preached to his son is evident from the following: "I wish to stay at your house but I cannot afford to pay $2 a day for a room nor will it do for me to be stuck up in a garret." He was not seeking luxurious couches as his next line indicated: "When I was there in the Summer I had N°. one with a cot in [it] & was comfortable. . . ."

On Thursday, November 25, Van Buren complimented John on his progress at Yale, and urged his son to take his fair prospects as a stimulus to continued and renewed exertions. "I leave here on Tuesday for Washington in indifferent health but good spirits," he wrote John. His good spirits were due not only to the reports of John's improvement in his studies, which tended to belie the reports he had heard of John's fondness for the tavern, but to the progress of the campaign. The Jacksonians had elected a majority to the Legislature; gains were reported in other States.

# CHAPTER XXXIII

No happier man than Van Buren answered the opening roll call of the first session of the Twentieth Congress. Another fifteen or eighteen months and the Senate would know him no more. John would have his degree by then. They would practice law together. But Fate had planned otherwise. Van Buren was soon to plead his last cause in court, and his Congressional career was to end with the present term.

For the first two months Van Buren paid more heed to the campaign than to legislation. His first speech of any length was on January 28 on the bill giving half pay to officers of the Revolution. But not until the debate on the vain efforts to clothe the Vice President with power to call a Senator to order did Van Buren take a stand on any controversial question. In leading the opposition Van Buren characterized the proposal as violative of the Constitution and referred to the Bank of the United States as "the first of Constitutional encroachments."

This speech was delivered on February 11. That day Clinton had been at his office in New York's Capitol, and read his mail, heavy with letters praising him for the reference in his annual message to the wanton attacks on Mrs. Jackson. After dinner that evening, while seated in the library talking to his two sons, his head fell forward in eternal sleep. Within the week the news reached Washington. Clinton was not quite fifty-nine years old.

Two days passed. On the evening of the 18th, Representative Thomas J. Oakley, who succeeded Van Buren as State Attorney General, wrote to Van Buren that there would be a memorial meeting of the New York delegation in the Capitol the following morning. Oakley said that Nathaniel Sanford—shelved to make way for Van Buren—who had been elected to fill King's seat, would be present, and added: "I suggest, whether, under existing circumstances, *you* ought not to take the lead in this business—with some appropriate resolutions and remarks—Such a step will be well received in our State."

317

Van Buren's speech that morning showed that the death of the Governor had dazed him. He said little. He referred to Clinton's talents; to the Canal—"the greatest public improvement of the age"; and then: "For myself, sir, it gives me a deep-felt, though melancholy satisfaction to know, and more so to be conscious that the deceased also felt and acknowledged, that our political differences have been wholly free from that most venomous and corroding of all poisons—personal hatred." This might have better been left unsaid. But we must remember that he was speaking extemporaneously and under intense emotion.

"In other respects," he continued, "it is now immaterial what was the character of those collisions. They have been turned to nothing, and less than nothing, by the event we deplore." His heart now began to speak, and after a few words more he said:

"I, who whilst living, never,—no never, envied him anything, now that he is fallen, am greatly tempted to envy him his grave with its honors."

When Jefferson died, debts swallowed his estate. Clinton, too, died penniless; and while the people mourned, the sheriff sold the roof over the heads of Clinton's widow and children.

Van Buren was now without a rival in New York.

As the session progressed it was apparent that Van Buren was determined not to alienate votes from Jackson by speeches on doubtful subjects. Another Cumberland Road appropriation gave him an opportunity to declaim on State rights. But this and his reference to the Bank were his only ventures into the realm of the controversial.

The debate on the most important economic measure introduced in Congress since its beginning, started May 5. This was Clay's "American System" with a list of imposts objectionable to the South. The Southern Senators sought to destroy the bill by adding oppressively high duties, so that the bill became known as the "tariff of abominations." Early in the year the New York Legislature had instructed its Senators to vote for a duty on wool. Van Buren, who before long was to espouse free trade, interpreted the instructions with extreme liberality and voted for the entire tariff. During the entire three weeks of debate he uttered not a single word, save to announce his vote.

This silence, in view of Van Buren's acknowledged leadership of his party in both houses, was unprecedented and remains unparalleled. Two years earlier he had voted against the repeal of the impost on salt. Local motives then governed, as New York taxed its own salt production to pay for the Canal. At the same session he also voted to reduce the duties on wines, teas, and coffees. The division on the "tariff of abominations" was sectional. Sixteen of the seventeen Southern votes were cast against the bill. The only other opposition came from five New England Senators. The entire delegations from the Middle Atlantic and Western States with six New England Senators and one from Louisiana supported the tariff. It was this division, together with the rôle he played as campaign manager for Jackson, which dictated the silence of Van Buren.

When the debate was at its height Van Buren was made downcast by reports from Yale. Briefly he wrote his son: "It has given me great pain to receive a letter from the President of the College informing me that he was instructed by the faculty to inform me that your conduct in not attending at the chapel in the morning was cause of dissatisfaction & that it would be necessary *to increase* your exertions greatly to enable you to succeed with any thing like credit at the examination in July. I hope it can only be necessary to inform you of the circumstances to secure your prompt and indefatigable exertions." A month earlier, he had written to the youth: "I send you a check for the $200 but am bound to say that taken in connexion with the amount previously advanced your expenses for the last six months are unreasonably high. Send me the items that I may not suspect you of the folly of extravagance."

On his return to Albany Van Buren made his last appearance as a lawyer. This was in the case of Varick *vs.* Jackson before the Court for the Correction of Errors. When Van Buren finished, the court turned to Burr, the senior counsel. Burr announced he could add nothing to what his assistant had said.

Had Clinton lived, he would have been renominated for Governor, and the union of the Clintonians and the followers of Van Buren would have meant a clean sweep in the State for the Jackson electors. Most of the Clintonians joined the Adams following. The Bucktails must nominate their most outstanding man for Governor; they had agreed to retire Nathaniel Pitcher,

Governor since the death of Clinton, because he had not shown
sufficient subserviency to the Regency. Late in the spring Van
Buren decided to make the race himself.

This was political expediency at its worst. If Jackson were
elected, Van Buren would be Secretary of State, so that he could
not serve as Governor more than two months and three days:
his running mate, Enos T. Throop, would serve the remainder of
the term as Governor.

The Anti-Masonic party was extending itself, and nominated
Francis Granger for Governor, and John Crary for Lieutenant
Governor. This party of proscription was against Jackson
because Jackson was a Mason.

The Adams convention in New York nominated Smith
Thompson for Governor. This was the first time that a member
of the United States Supreme Court permitted his name to be
dragged through the mire of a State campaign; for he did not
resign from the bench. There was a working arrangement between
the Adams delegates and some of the leaders of the Anti-Masonic
party, and Granger was named for Lieutenant Governor. The
leaders of these two anti-Jackson groups hoped to unite forces,
carry the State for Adams, and defeat Van Buren and Throop.

Crary agreed to decline the Anti-Masonic nomination for
Lieutenant Governor after Granger tendered his declension of
the major nomination. Crary, for a reason never explained, failed
to live up to his part of the agreement. In vain it was urged
upon him that an Anti-Masonic ticket would only divide the
Adams vote for Governor and would result in the probable election of Van Buren and Throop. Then the real character of the
backers of the movement was revealed when the corrupt Solomon
Southwick was named for Governor in Granger's stead.

Thompson was made the target of the Jackson party, who
recalled that the people in ratifying the State constitution,
had declared that a judge holding office during his good behavior
ought not to be a candidate for elective office. This legally only
applied to the State judiciary; but, morally, it applied with even
greater force to the highest court in the land.

Van Buren was elected as a result of the division created in
the ranks of the opposition by the Anti-Masonic party. He polled
136,783 votes, three thousand less than the combined votes of

Thompson and Southwick, who received 106,415, and 33,335, respectively. Jackson carried eighteen of the thirty-four Congressional districts, which assured him twenty from New York in the Electoral College, as the majority would choose the Electors-at-Large.

In this campaign the Adams men called themselves National Republicans; the Jacksonians styled themselves the Democratic-Republican party.

The Friday following election Van Buren wrote to Hoyt: ". . . We shall . . . have enough votes to put Jackson's election out of all question, and what is over is only important on the score of bets." The next week he went to New York to collect his winnings. While in the city he wrote to the President-elect —whom he addressed as "My dear General": ". . . We lost two or three Districts by the disgraceful direction given to the excitement growing out of the Morgan affair. But we have enough and to spare. I will not harass you by a description of the virulence that has characterized the contest in this State."

One of the canards which waddled through New York's campaign was a droll bird. It was said that Van Buren sprayed his side whiskers with *eau de Cologne* and gave up part of each morning and evening to posing before his mirror.

While working on his message to the Legislature, a bit of gossip concerning himself gave him much amusement. Suspecting Cambreleng, he wrote him: "You rogue you—you have put me in a peck of trouble—Throughout *my* dominions—The story is that I am to be married to Mʳˢ. O. S. in a few weeks & all upon your authority— . . . If Gen. Jackson has any regard for me I hope he will let me try and execute you under the seccond [*sic!*] section & I shall ask no farther favour from him. . . . & if you speedily give me a detailed account of all the sayings & doings of Washington as well in the female as political departments I may forgive you for bringing all the young & old & middle aged women in the State upon my back. . . ." This is the only reference we have seen to the mysterious Mrs. O. S.

Van Buren was inaugurated Governor on January 1, 1829. In his few weeks he accomplished more than many executives who served their full terms. In his annual message he recommended several noteworthy reforms. He urged the choice of Presidential

Electors by general ticket, instead of districts; he advocated a law limiting the use of money in elections to printing. This was also enacted into law; but was permitted to remain a dead letter. A third recommendation urged the separation of State and National elections. This desirable reform was opposed by his Regents. He did not press it.

Another admirable proposal, which was almost immediately carried into effect, protected the public from wildcat banks. There were forty banks in the State, with aggregate deposits of $30,000,000, and a paid-in capital of half that amount. This financial reform created a "safety fund"—hence the name given to the innovation—to be maintained by contributions from the banks not to exceed more than half of one per cent annually on their capital. This fund, designed to redeem dishonored notes of member banks, was guaranteed by the State, so that henceforth the scrip of a defaulting institution would be taken up by the commonwealth. The idea of the "safety fund" was suggested by Joshua L. Forman, of Syracuse, but perfected by Van Buren and two friends. In his message, while disclaiming authorship, he proudly proclaimed himself its sponsor.

He paid a gracious compliment to the achievements of Clinton; he reviewed the accounts of the State's finances, its public works, its institutions of learning and benevolence; and philosophically adverted to the lamentable virulence of the campaign: "These excesses are the price we pay for the full enjoyment of the right of opinion, which is emphatically the birthright of the American citizen."

There were clamorous demands for more canals. Impressive petitions had been submitted to Van Buren by the advocates of these projects. He could not, without hurting his party in the State, avoid mention of these applications in his message. He talked at length about them, but the nearest to a recommendation was his declaration that the State ought to apply such portion of its means as could be spared from other necessary objects on works on internal improvements. But he did not say when, nor did he commit himself one way or the other on the merits of any of the various proposed canals. "Non-committalism," commented his adversaries.

On January 15, Charles E. Dudley, of Albany, was elected

Van Buren's successor in the United States Senate. A less competent man would have been hard to find. Dudley's qualification, which he displayed as a member of the State Senate, was his absolute subserviency to the Regency. He could not make a speech, and was so shy that he could converse only with difficulty.

Marcy was broke. He needed a well-paying job badly. Van Buren appointed him to the Supreme Court and made Silas Wright State Comptroller.

The cries of the faithful for patronage were heeded with few exceptions. Behind one of his refusals is the Van Buren of private life. Tammany demanded all the places in the State Health Department's Quarantine Station on Staten Island. Why they did not get one place is explained by Van Buren in the following apologetic message to Hoyt: "I cannot dismiss Dr. [Joseph R.] Manley. His extraordinary capacity is universally admitted; and his poverty, and misfortune in regard to the new Medical College which he brought into existence but failed to get a place in it, has excited a sympathy for him with medical men in all parts of the State of unprecedented extent. Mr. Clinton was so sensible of it that he once actually nominated him for health officer, and was upon the point of doing it again the very week when he died. His removal if made could only be placed on political grounds." Hoyt was the New York representative of New York's spoils system, now on the eve of being made a national institution.

The formal tender of the first place in the Cabinet was made on February 15. On its receipt five days later, Van Buren accepted. Not until March 12 did he resign as Governor. His followers in both houses immediately adopted resolutions approving his acceptance of the place in Jackson's Cabinet. Senator William H. Maynard protested, saying that the resolves could not be adopted with propriety, as Van Buren, in consenting to be a candidate for Governor, gave an implied pledge that if elected, he would serve the full term of two years,

## CHAPTER XXXIV

IT was dark when Van Buren reached Washington. On alighting from the stagecoach he was followed into his hotel by a swarm of office seekers. He was weak from illness and the fatigue of his trip. He showed it. But that did not deter the office-hungry horde from trooping after him into his room, grouping themselves round him when he threw himself upon a sofa. He listened to their pleas for an hour, committing himself to nothing. Then he excused himself—as he had apprised them he would—to pay his respects to the President.

As the door of the White House opened, Van Buren found himself in a vestibule lighted by a solitary camphine lamp. In his weak condition his first impression was one of gloom. In the President's office he again saw a single light, a glimmering candle on the desk. His morbid feelings vanished in the warmth of Jackson's greeting; and then he noticed the glowing logs in the fireplace.

Jackson's health was also low. He still grieved over the loss of his wife. He believed that her death in the previous December was hastened by the shameful attacks upon her in the campaign. Discovering that his visitor was in no shape for a protracted interview, Jackson told him to return to his lodgings and rest, and come back on the morrow.

Van Buren's political pamphleteer of the recent campaign, James A. Hamilton, had been Acting Secretary of State since March 4. Van Buren quickly picked up the threads of the office. From Hamilton and other friends he heard the gossip which had not found its way into the newspapers. All the New York delegation was talking of the visit to the White House of Solomon Van Rensselaer, who knew that Chauncey Humphry and at least three other Van Burenites were trying to displace him. After a cordial greeting by the President, the Albany postmaster, instead of making his exit through the East Room, seated himself on one of the sofas. Here Jackson saw him when the rest of his visitors had departed, and was about to engage him in conversation when Van Rensselaer blurted out:

"General Jackson, I have come here to talk to you about my office. The politicians want to take it from me, and they know I have nothing else to live upon."

Before Jackson could reply, the old soldier excitedly began to remove his coat.

"In heaven's name what are you going to do?" asked Jackson. "Why do you take off your coat in this public place?"

"Well, sir, I am going to show you my wounds which I received in fighting for my country."

Van Rensselaer's coat was now off.

"Put it on at once, sir!" commanded Jackson. Remembering the older man's years, and his excitement, he added softly: "I am surprised that a man of your age should make such an exhibition of himself."

Jackson averted his head as he said good-by to the old man, whose first commission, "Captain in Squadron of Light Dragoons," bore Washington's signature. Jackson's eyes were suffused with tears. Van Rensselaer did not lose his place while Jackson was President.

There was another side of Jackson. When Joseph L. White, delegate from the Florida Territory, inquired why twelve officials in Florida had been displaced by men "most of whom could be shown fitter candidates for the treadmill than public office," Jackson passionately replied he had been abused from Dan to Beersheba for the removals, but that not a single man had been removed except for oppression or defalcation. White repeated Jackson's remark to Van Buren and demanded that he particularize the acts of oppression or defalcation. "The President's recollection must be at fault," replied Van Buren. "We give no reasons for our removals." And he wrote in similar tone to a clerk in his own department.

Van Buren's hand is evident in the case of John McLean, a Methodist minister, who had served as Postmaster General under Monroe and Adams. When McLean refused to be party to the removal of postmasters solely on political grounds, Jackson got rid of him by appointing him to the United States Supreme Court. William T. Barry of Kentucky was then placed at the head of this department, the principal source of the spoilsman. Barry did what was expected of him.

Van Buren early saw the possibility of building up a political machine with the aid of the Post Office Department. We have seen him trying his hand at it in 1822, when he wrote to Knower, Marcy's father-in-law, that the Post Office Department was "one of the most interesting departments of the government, and instead of spending our time in small matters, I am for taking the bull by the horns at once . . ." He explained that he hoped to induce President Monroe, with the aid of Vice President Tompkins, to convert the department, in so far as it affected New York, into a spoils machine. There was no Monroe to hinder him now.

The evidence, documentary and otherwise, all points to Van Buren as the originator of the extension of the New York spoils system to our national government. Before he left Albany for Washington the removals were under way: but he had written to Hamilton: "If the General makes one removal at this moment he must go on. Would it not be better to get the streets of Washington clear of office holders first in the way I proposed? . . ." When Van Buren attempted to enlist the entire Monroe administration in his fight against Clinton nearly ten years before, we recall that he wrote to Rufus King: ". . . he [Clinton] has collected around him a set of desperadoes, who, instigated by the hope of official plunder, will never be content to limit their depredation to the boundaries of this State, but would if successful here, without doubt, extend their incursions abroad . . ."

Clinton was dead; the set of desperadoes that existed then only in Van Buren's fancy were now alive in the flesh, and conducting their incursions with a cruelty and thoroughness that shocked and astonished the country, which remembered that Adams had removed only two men, and both for cause. And it was plunder—to use Swartwout's word—that many of them were after. Samuel Swartwout, Jackson's political majordomo in New Jersey, wrote to Jesse Hoyt while Van Buren was en route to Washington: ". . . I hold to your doctrine fully that no damned rascal who made use of his office or its profits for the purpose of keeping Mr. Adams in, and Gen. Jackson out of power, is entitled to the least lenity or mercy, save that of hanging. So we think both alike on that head. Whether or not I shall get any thing in the general scramble for plunder remains to be proven; but I rather guess I shall."

Swartwout was seeking the biggest plum at the disposal of the administration, that of Collector of the Port of New York, with its revenues of $10,000,000, and perquisites sufficient to enrich a man in four years. He was not a resident of the State, but was well known to the politicians, and his reputation was very unsavory.

Van Buren had his allies throw several obstacles in Swartwout's path. Samuel D. Ingham, of Pennsylvania, Secretary of the Treasury, also opposed Swartwout. In April Van Buren wrote to Cambreleng: ". . . Mʳ Ingham has advised me to request you to get some fifteen or twenty of our strongest men to write to the President directly setting forth (mildly and kindly of course) but firmly and distinctly the objections to Swartwout's appointment. . . . Neither my name or [*sic!*] Mr. Ingham's must under any circumstances be mentioned in this matter except to Mʳ Walter Bowne [Mayor of New York City]. . . ." In this same letter Van Buren avowed his intentions to continue the proscription of Clinton's friends. The factional war had extended beyond the grave.

Swartwout was appointed because he was one of Jackson's "original friends"—to use Van Buren's phrase. Whereupon Cambreleng wrote Van Buren: ". . . if our collector is not a defaulter in four years I'll swallow the Treasury if it was all coined in coppers." Swartwout stole $1,222,705.69 from the Custom House receipts and fled to Europe with the plunder. He was indicted. When most of his money was gone a friend of his happier days met him in a drinking place in Algiers. Presently Swartwout burst into tears and sobbed that he could never return to his native land.

High and low felt the axe of the spoilsman. The hundreds of clerks in Washington, old men many of them, some carrying the honorable scars received in battle, suddenly found themselves without the jobs they had worked at for years. These, for the most part, were the shabby genteel of the land: There was the graybeard who had seen better days; the superannuated teacher or preacher distinguished by the worn coat, threadbare pantaloons and the immaculate white stock; the paterfamilias from the coun-

try, lured by the glamour of the Capital and the better schools
the vicinity afforded; the typical clerk, happy in his work, and
asking only to be let alone. These, or their types, had been here
since the seat of Government was moved from Philadelphia. Administrations came and went, but these humble ones were undis-
turbed till now.

"I turned out six clerks on Saturday," wrote Amos Kendall
in a letter to his wife. Kendall had just been made an auditor
in the Treasury Department. "Several of them have families and
are poor. It was the most painful thing I ever did. . . . Among
them is an old man with a young wife and several children. I
shall help to raise a contribution to get him back to Ohio."

There was a veritable Reign of Terror in the various departmental offices. Spies abounded who repeated anything said
in the least critical of the administration. The identity of the
members of the espionage corps was jealously guarded; consequently everybody suspected everybody else. Men who had been
longest in these small jobs dreaded their loss the most. They had
become accustomed to their groove. They could not move outside
of it. In Van Buren's own department a clerk went crazy at the
thought that he might be removed from his accustomed rut. In
the War Department, another unfortunate, similarly obsessed,
concealed his madness until he had slashed his throat from ear
to ear.

The case of Elbridge Gerry, son and namesake of the Signer
and Vice President, showed that the spoilsmen drew no distinctions. He was well on in years. The family fortunes were low.
His mother and four unmarried sisters lived with him. All were
dependent on his income as Surveyor of the Port of Boston. It was
not much, but it enabled them to keep up appearances. The Gerrys
and Adamses were friends for generations; naturally he supported
Adams in the campaign. Pocketing his pride he confessed to Jackson his political offense and his need of a job. Jackson promised
to keep him. Nine months later he heard that he was to be removed. He arrived in Washington as Jackson sent the name of
his successor to the Senate. Jackson flew into a rage when reminded of his promise. He denied making it, and ordered Gerry
from the White House for circulating a report that he had.

This is not the only instance of Jackson's broken promises

during the degrading orgy of removals and replacements. But he was distracted by intrigues, within and without his official family. No administration was so beset by storms. Jackson bore the brunt of them.

An occasional Adams supporter was temporarily continued in office. One of these was Van Buren's friend, John Duer. A few others equally well-connected in New York were also permitted to remain. Jesse Hoyt wrote to Van Buren a few days after the latter's arrival in Washington that he had found him a valet, who had previously been in the employ of William B. Astor, son of John Jacob Astor.

Hoyt was in a violent mood when he penned this letter. The heads of Duer and all others who had supported Adams must drop into the basket. Hoyt, who was seeking Duer's place, was offered the office of District Attorney of New York County through Van Buren's influence. This he spurned, and in his protest to Van Buren said: "I will hold no office from any political party that will keep Mr. Duer in his present station." Hoyt gave Van Buren a week in which to remove Duer from the office of United States Attorney of the New York district. If this were not done Hoyt said he would write a pamphlet on *The Life and Adventures of John Duer* "to hand in person to every member of the Cabinet." And Hoyt hurled covert abuse at Van Buren, as he had in an earlier letter.

"I never expected," answered Van Buren, "to see the day when I should be constrained, as I now am, to address you in the language of complaint. Nothing but my strong conviction of the extent and sincerity of your friendship could sustain me in resisting the belief that you have a settled purpose to quarrel with me. Here I am engaged in the most intricate and important affairs, which are new to me, and upon the successful conduct of which my reputation as well as the interests of the country depend, and which keep me occupied from early in the morning until late at night, and can you think it just to harass me under such circumstances with letters, which no ordinary man of common sensibility can read without pain? Your letter to me at New York contained many truths, for which I was thankful, and reflections which I thought just, but the whole were expressed in terms so harsh, not to say rude, as to distress me exceedingly. I have scarcely recovered from the effect of so great an error in judgment, to say nothing else, when I am favored with another which transcends its predecessor in its most objectionable features. I must be plain with you. I have all my life (at least since I have known you) cherished the kindest solicitude for your welfare, and have manifested at least my good will towards you, and should be extremely sorry to have occasion to change those feelings, but it is due us both that I should say, that the terms upon which you have seen fit to place our intercourse are inadmissable. . . ."

The salt was washed out of the wound with the subscription: "Your friend and humble servant in extreme haste, M. V. Buren." But Hoyt was not to be appeased with words. He reminded Van Buren that he had labored twelve years in the city of New York "to advance your reputation as a man, and your integrity as a politician" and not without success. And he had no intention of changing his sentiments, expressed in his letters or elsewhere. He softened all he said by signing himself: "Yet, as I ever have been, your friend, J. Hoyt."

Van Buren never let a friendship of long standing be sundered by a display of ill temper. Hoyt was unscrupulous,—and serviceable. There was a phrase in the last letter which characterized him far more than volumes could. He was hurt by Van Buren's charge of rudeness, and rudeness, he observed, "always detracts from the gentlemanly deportment I am most anxious to preserve." Van Buren had unintentionally torn through the veneer. Hoyt was mollified later when Duer was supplanted by James A. Hamilton.

In the midst of these scrambles for office Van Buren found himself thrown into intrigues unlike anything he had before encountered. One was his undoubted duty to solve. This was the dread of Jackson which had been assiduously nurtured by the Bank of the United States, both here and in England where a large part of its stock was owned by the aristocracy. Jackson's election was regarded as ominous of war by the people of England, whose leaders, inspired by the holders of Bank shares, went to King William with their alarms.

Van Buren ended these apprehensions by inviting Sir Charles R. Vaughan, the British Ambassador, to become well-acquainted with Jackson as the surest way of assuring himself of the utter falsity of this prevalent opinion. Vaughan was soon convinced of his error. Jackson, in his first message to Congress, changed the tone of England by observing that "with Great Britain, alike distinguished in peace and in war, we may look forward to years of peaceful, honorable, and elevated competition . . ." And to preserve these "cordial relations" was his avowed purpose.

Van Buren extended similar invitations to the rest of the diplomatic corps. The tact Van Buren had displayed in the political squabbles in New York, he was now successfully applying to world affairs.

There was one member of the diplomatic corps who was not a foreigner—to Van Buren. This was the Chevalier A. de Bangeman Huygens, Minister from the Netherlands. Van Buren would go, uninvited, to the home of the Huygenses to forget the cares of state in the charming company of the Chevalier and his lovely wife. Here he would gladly forego his customary glass of wine for Schiedam, which he sipped as he puffed away at a long clay pipe. Tender memories of the little tavern at Kinderhook were revived as they talked in the language that, as a lad, he knew better than English. He always greeted Huygens as "my Dutch brother."

In sharp distinction were his relations with his fellow Cabinet members. Although all were personally pleasant toward him, he was looked down upon because he had come into Jackson's camp in the eleventh hour. They felt the superior talents of Van Buren, a feeling which always rankles small minds. Save Van Buren, Jackson had selected mediocrities to head his departments.

Besides Barry and Ingham, Van Buren's colleagues were: John M. Berrien, of Georgia, Attorney General; John Branch, of North Carolina, Secretary of the Navy; and John H. Eaton, of Tennessee, Secretary of War. They were sycophants all. Jackson, although he arrived in Washington nearly three weeks before his inaugural, did not pay his respects to Adams, who retaliated by leaving only a servant to welcome Jackson to the White House. Jackson's conduct was inspired by his belief that Adams was behind the scurrilous attacks on Mrs. Jackson. Eaton, Branch, Ingham, and Barry felt that they must also snub Adams.

Van Buren had been in Washington a few days when he called on Adams, who noted in his diary: "Of the new Administration he is the only person who has shown me this mark of common civility. . . . All the members of his [Jackson's] Administration have been with me upon terms of friendly acquaintance, and have repeatedly shared the hospitality of my house. I never was indebted for a cup of water to any of them, nor have I given one of them the slightest cause of offence. . . . Ingham is among the basest of my slanderers, Branch and Berrien have been among the meanest of my persecutors in the Senate. Among them all there is not a man capable of a generous or liberal sentiment towards an adversary, excepting Eaton; and he is a man of indecently licentious life."

The Eaton imbroglio had its beginning three months before Van Buren arrived in Washington. Eaton, then a member of the Senate, married the beautiful Margaret O'Neale Timberlake. Peggy O'Neale, as she was then familiarly known, had been the wife of Purser J. B. Timberlake, U.S.N., until the preceding summer, when he made her a widow by taking his own life. The accepted reason for Timberlake's act was his jealousy of Eaton, who lived at the tavern which Peggy's father kept, and where his daughter tended bar. It was a popular inn, and here, too, in his brief Senate career, Jackson lived. Two other reasons were advanced for the suicide: his fear of a drunkard's grave, and the shortage in his accounts. Eaton was now oftener in Peggy's company; gossip grew louder; and before his appointment, Eaton discussed the scandal with Jackson, who agreed with him that marriage would silence the talk.

When Van Buren reached Washington the members of the Cabinet and their wives, with the exception of Barry and Mrs. Barry, were holding aloof from Mrs. Eaton. The appointment of her husband as Secretary of War brought Mrs. Eaton a new name—an allowable pun—Bellona. A detractor, with a knowledge of Italian, prefixed the bellicose soubriquet with the definite article, ordinarily applied to a singer or a strumpet. La Bellona did not sing. Besides Barry, La Bellona had a stout friend in Jackson, who went far afield in his efforts to induce his official family to accept Mrs. Eaton.

On his arrival in Washington Van Buren's mind was made up: he would treat all members of the Cabinet and their families on equal terms,—an easy solution for a widower. This further endeared him to Jackson, who packed off his private secretary,

A. F. Donelson, and Mrs. Donelson, who was Mrs. Jackson's niece, when the latter refused to visit La Bellona.

The first snub given to La Bellona by the wife of a member of the Administration came from Mrs. Calhoun, the wife of the Vice President. And it also happened that before Van Buren was in Washington a month the movement to make Calhoun Jackson's successor had spread to New York. Calhoun was in Van Buren's way as Mrs. Calhoun was in La Bellona's way. Jackson was perhaps the only person in Washington who believed that an open rupture with his Cabinet could be avoided. Van Buren saw the hopelessness of it when he failed to persuade Mrs. Donelson to change her course, if for no other reason than the President's sake. Mrs. Donelson presided over the domestic circle of the White House. Her husband was working secretly for the political advancement of Calhoun.

The genius of Van Buren could not have invented an intrigue to approach in excellence the one he found ready made. Only a master would have remained unappalled in contemplating the situation or dared to give it direction. Van Buren was capable of both.

Jackson found recreation in the saddle. His companion on these rides was Van Buren. On these excursions into the neighboring countryside the two talked of everything in the world save the Eaton imbroglio—until a pleasant November afternoon. It was eight months since his administration began, and he had not as yet given the traditional Cabinet dinner. Jackson confided that he was fearful of declensions from all save Barry. When the ride was over Jackson had thrown off his fears. The invitations went out and all the Cabinet members and their wives attended, and no one snubbed La Bellona. It was obvious, however, that only the presence of Jackson himself prevented some untoward scenes; for the conversation at the table was rigidly formal, and the party broke up at a very early hour.

Van Buren now assumed direction of this unique affair. Many feared it would not end before some one was sent to join the unfortunate Timberlake. The President having shown the way, Van Buren, as the ranking member of the Cabinet, issued cards for a Cabinet dinner. As Van Buren lived alone, and the Secretary of the Treasury was the next ranking officer of the Cabinet, it

would not do to let this avowed enemy of La Bellona preside at
the table. Van Buren's ingenuity found a way out: he gave the
dinner jointly in honor of his Cabinet and Mrs. Thomas Mann
Randolph. Every one in Washington reverenced this sole sur-
viving daughter of Jefferson, now a widow. No one dared protest:
further, there was no occasion for objection. Mrs. Randolph and
all the members of her family had been fond of Van Buren from
the early days of their acquaintance. Van Buren had made her
son-in-law, Nicholas P. Trist, Jackson's private secretary. Mrs.
Randolph readily entered into Van Buren's plans, impelled by
those all-controlling qualities, ever present in woman, the love of
adventure and intrigue. She was curious to meet La Bellona, who
could crush an adversary with a toss of her Botticelli head, or
an almost imperceptible movement of the lips.

Ingham and Branch accepted for themselves, the latter coldly
informing Van Buren that "he is requested to say on behalf of
Mrs. Branch and the young ladies [their daughters] that circumstances unnecessary to detail deprived them of the pleasure
of dining with him." Berrien and Ingham sent excuses for their
wives. In declining on his own behalf, Berrien pleaded the traditional prior engagement. Barry and Eaton attended, but La
Bellona and Mrs. Barry remained away, taking refuge behind
suddenly acquired poor health.

This dinner was a choice morsel of gossip in the homes and
in the anti-Administration press throughout the country. But
still choicer morsels were in the making. Van Buren's intimate,
Sir Charles Vaughan, also a bachelor, gave a reception and ball
which La Bellona attended. Then Van Buren gave a second party,
and invited most of official Washington. Van Buren's cards were
hardly out before an article appeared in a local journal accusing
Van Buren and Sir Charles of intriguing to force La Bellona
on Washington society. The writer, who masked his identity behind Tarquin—the circumstances lent an unpleasant connota-
tion to the pseudonym—urged the ostracism of Van Buren for
his championship of La Bellona.

When the dancing commenced, Van Buren took advantage
of the distraction as his guests filed into the ballroom to snatch
a few minutes' repose on the lower floor. By so doing he missed
seeing an exciting encounter between La Bellona and the wife of

Major General Alexander Macomb, Commander-in-Chief of the United States Army. They had accidentally brushed one another with the elbows, whereupon each accused the other of willful assault, and displayed resentment in other ways.

The party was followed by one given by Baron Krudener, the Russian Ambassador. He, too, was a bachelor, and did not hesitate to invite La Bellona. And Van Buren was accused of having inspired the invitation which gave offense to so many. Mrs. Ingham, of course, absented herself, making the wife of the Secretary of War the ranking American woman present. Baron Krudener gave his arm to La Bellona, and together they led the guests—save two—into the dining room with its famous gold service. The exceptions were the Huygenses. The Baron, aware of the determination of the wife of the Dutch Ambassador not to break bread with La Bellona, had tried to persuade her to relent. But she remained obdurate, and departed with her husband.

With the coming of the New Year, gossip had it that Madame Huygens had consulted with the wives of the Cabinet members who would not associate with La Bellona, and that all four would give receptions from which the wife of the Secretary of War would be excluded. On January 6 the home of the Dutch Ambassador opened its doors to all official Washington save the proscribed lady. And rapidly followed similar parties at the homes of the Secretary of the Treasury, the Secretary of the Navy, and the Attorney General. Jackson, who had earlier doubted the reports, now believed that Madame Huygens and Mistresses Ingham, Branch, and Berrien had conspired to drive the Eatons out of Washington society and Eaton from the Cabinet.

In the last days of January Jackson sent for Van Buren. They talked over the events of which La Bellona was the pivot. Jackson did most of the talking. He was for dismissing the offending members of his Cabinet after he had sent Chevalier Huygens his passports. Jackson must first obtain proof of the conspiracy, which he reduced to an attempt to punish him for appointing Eaton.

Van Buren on returning to his office sent a note to his Dutch brother saying that he desired to see him on business, but as it would also be necessary to communicate with Madame Huygens, he would call at their house at their convenience. There was the usual affectionate greeting when Van Buren called, and he was at once invited to a pipe and Schiedam.

The Huygenses knew the object of the call, but being diplomats both, waited for their friend to speak his piece. Van Buren stated that the President disclaimed any intent or right to meddle with their social relations, and had no concern in whom they invited to their home; and then he repeated the gossip of the conspiracy. Madame Huygens declared she had been too long in diplomatic life to lend herself to such an enterprise. Van Buren waited only long enough to hear her disclaimer, as he was anxious to make a written report to Jackson, who replied: ". . . I am happy Madame H. has stated they are not true as far as she is concerned. . . ." This was dated the same evening as Van Buren's note, January 24, 1830.

This, of course, prevented Jackson's dismissing the Calhoun members of his Cabinet. They had never been other than mere departmental heads to Jackson. From the beginning of his administration he had depended on the advice of a group consisting of Amos Kendall and two other editors, Duff Green and Isaac Hill, and Jackson's artful neighbor, Major Lewis. They were all secondary to Van Buren. This was the Kitchen Cabinet.

Lewis alone approached Van Buren in guile; and long before the Eaton imbroglio was under way he had set out to destroy Calhoun. But it was not until January, 1828, when Van Buren dispatched his aide, James A. Hamilton, on an electioneering tour, that the dream began to materialize. Save for the presence of the son of Alexander Hamilton in this intrigue, the hand of Van Buren is nowhere visible. Hamilton's intimacy with Van Buren, in itself, is sufficient warrant for assuming that the master himself at least knew all that was going on. Lewis instructed Hamilton to see Crawford and what to say to him. Hamilton, failing to see Crawford, entrusted the mission to Forsyth, who under date of February 8 wrote to him that Calhoun had tried to have Jackson censured for his conduct in the Seminole War. Jackson had lured two Indian chiefs to an American ship flying the British flag, and hanged them. Equally reprehensible was his hanging of the aged Alexander Arbuthnot, a British subject who had spent many years trading with the Seminoles, and Robert Ambrister, a former lieutenant in the Royal Marines. To cap all this he took possession of Florida, then the territory of Spain, with which we were at peace. These highly censurable acts occurred three years after the Battle of New Orleans, and when Calhoun and Crawford were members of Monroe's Cabinet.

All this was kept dark by Hamilton, Forsyth, and Lewis until November, 1829, when the Eaton imbroglio was given momentum by Jackson's Cabinet dinner. A banquet to ex-President Monroe at the White House afforded the plotters the opportunity they had been seeking since the early fall when the Kitchen Cabinet decided that Jackson must run again in order to solidify the party. Eaton was now dragged into the conspiracy against Calhoun. After the coffee had been served, Lewis and Eaton discussed the letter from Forsyth to Hamilton so near to Jackson that the President overheard. Jackson asked questions.

Calhoun was doomed that night. He always distrusted Van Buren, and had appealed to Jackson not to appoint him to the Cabinet. After Jackson was satisfied that Calhoun had attempted to tarnish his military record, a story, inspired by Jackson, appeared in Van Buren's New York City organ, the *Courier and Enquirer*, advocating Van Buren for President if Jackson did not run again. The *United States Telegraph* replied that such talk was premature. Duff Green, Calhoun's sole ally in the Kitchen Cabinet, edited the *Telegraph*.

On December 31, twelve days after the *Courier and Enquirer* opened the war between the Van Buren and Calhoun editors, Jackson wrote Judge Overton lauding Van Buren as worthy not only of his confidence, but of that of the nation. "Van Buren was not an intriguer, but frank, open, candid, and manly; an able and prudent counselor, pleasant, and well qualified to fill the highest office in the gift of the people, who in him will find a true friend and a safe depository of their rights and liberty." And then this Jacksonian thrust at Van Buren's adversaries: "I wish I could say as much for Mr. Calhoun and some of his friends."

This letter was suggested by Lewis, who wanted Jackson's indorsement of Van Buren on paper, lest Jackson die suddenly: his health had been poor for months.

Jackson determined to destroy the "monster"—the Bank of the United States. Calhoun was silent on this. Jackson was for enforcing the tariff which South Carolina was opposing. Calhoun had encouraged the resolutions which the Legislature of his State had adopted: he had not yet propounded his defense of nullification, the right of a State to oppose by force of arms any act of the Union infringing upon her sovereignty.

During the first days of 1830 Van Buren directed his Regents to have the Jacksonians in the Legislature adopt resolutions urging Jackson to be a candidate for renomination. On February 13 his wishes were carried out. The following month Lewis had the Pennsylvania Legislature appeal to the President to serve his country another four years. He enclosed the appeal he wanted signed, and counseled his correspondent to secrecy, observing that it would not help to have it known that Jackson's friends in Washington were behind the movement.

Then came the first Jackson Day banquet. This was Calhoun's idea. On Monday, April 12, the day before the celebration, Van Buren visited Jackson, as he believed Calhoun and his supporters intended to conduct the proceedings at the dinner in a manner "portentous of danger to the Union." There had been gossip that nullification would be thrust to the fore, and Van Buren's recollections of his conversations with Calhoun during the enactment of the "tariff of abominations" lent credence to the reports. He was apprehensive that Calhoun's stand would make him the outstanding defender of the ultimate of State rights. Perhaps he might follow the example of the Governor of South Carolina and give for his toast: "The right to fight!" Van Buren and Jackson planned to stop Calhoun before he got started. For some time they worked on their toasts; and they parted confident of nullifying anything the great nullificationist might say.

On the following evening the first volunteer toast called for was the President's. A tense silence pervaded the assemblage as Jackson arose. Van Buren, who was at the second table, stood on his chair so that he might see over the heads of those in front. Jackson, in copying the toast he and Van Buren had agreed upon, omitted one word, so that when he read it, the diners heard:

"Our Union—it must be preserved."

Robert Y. Hayne, one of South Carolina's Senators, rushed to the President and requested him to insert the word *Federal*. This was the word Jackson had omitted. He assented, and the toast as published, reads:

"Our Federal Union—it must be preserved."

There was no intent on Jackson's part to wound any one's feelings wantonly, ready though he was, as he implied in his toast, to put all the forces of government behind the tariff which South Carolina opposed.

The Vice President was next called upon. Calhoun's great weakness was an incapacity to confess error, a common complaint of public men. Instead of bowing to the inevitable he gave as his toast:

"The Union—next to our liberty the most dear; may we all remember that it can only be preserved by respecting the rights of the States and distributing equally the benefit and burden of the Union."

Then came Van Buren with: "Mutual forbearance and reciprocal concessions; thro' their agency the Union was established —the patriotic spirit from which they emanated will forever sustain it."

This was the prologue to the epic drama on which the curtain was rung down at Appomattox.

The last week in June Van Buren wrote to his son John, now practicing law in Albany, warning him against drink. "What you may regard as an innocent & harmless indulgence will take you years to overcome in the public estimation. . . . The light & vain feeling of desiring to be regarded as a dashing fellow is surely gratified at too great an expense in this way. Washington is full of reports at your expense. It was no longer ago than last evening that I was informed by a friend—well meaning but fond of gossip —that Major Fane should have said here that you had been twice carried drunk from the race course. I knew of course that this was untrue."

A few days later Van Buren returned to New York for the first time since he had resigned the Governorship. Jackson had also left Washington for a rest. On July 12, from the Hermitage, he made veiled reference to the new slanders which were being circulated about him: now it is that he has more than a fatherly interest in La Bellona. ". . . I cannot speak with certainty," he wrote Van Buren, "but do suppose during next winter will live quite a batchellors [*sic!*] life, would to God I had commenced it with my administration, it would have prevented me from much humiliation

& pain that I have experienced, and have prevented much injury to the innocent, by the secrete [*sic!*] slanders circulated here & fed from the city—time will unfold the authors."

Van Buren's vacation ended early in September. The last week or so was spent in New York. On Thursday, September 2, his son John, evidently on his way back to Albany, bade his father farewell. Van Buren did not sleep that night. In a letter to John, written the following evening, he gave the reason: ". . . I only regret that I must always part with you with mortification, but [it] seems to be unavoidable. My reflections on the course of life which you appear to have marked out for yourself, & in which eating, and drinking, & dressing appear to be most important, not to say least exceptionable of your persuits [*sic!*], have given me a feverish & sleepless night. . . ."

The sorrow that was gnawing at his heart was softened as he resumed his labors and his rides over the Georgetown hills with Jackson. On one of these Old Hickory advanced the most audacious proposal of its kind in our history. The President, some six or seven months earlier, had convinced himself that Calhoun had proposed his arrest or reprimand for his high-handed acts in the Seminole War. Although the public was not aware of it, Jackson had severed all relations with Calhoun. Jackson led up to his daring plan without intimating its nature. He spoke of his resolution not to serve more than one term. Of course that resolve had been undone by circumstances. But Jackson had thought of a middle course. He would run again; and Van Buren must be the candidate for Vice President. Both would be elected. Jackson's years and health dictated his retirement. He would resign as President after serving a year, or two at the most, and Van Buren would automatically carry on his work.

Van Buren was pleased beyond measure at this evidence of Jackson's faith in him. But he was dumbfounded by the childishness of the proposal. He must check this madness before it went further, but without wounding Jackson's sensibilities. Van Buren began with voluble thanks, and confessed his ambition to be President some day. He dwelt on the purity of Jackson's motives, but reminded him how his enemies would blacken them. They would say that Jackson had smuggled Van Buren into the Presidency to gratify his resentments against Calhoun and his friends.

Van Buren thought that he had won Jackson from his idea, which probably had its genesis in 1828 when Van Buren smuggled Throop into the Governorship of New York. But a year later, as we shall see, Jackson, in two letters to Van Buren, revealed that he had not abandoned his wild idea.

In October word came that Louis McLane, now Ambassador to the Court of St. James's, had successfully paved the way for reopening to American shipping British ports in the West Indies which had been closed since December 1, 1826, by an Order in Council. This was the culmination of eleven years of retaliatory measures by both countries. Gallatin had vainly tried to break the diplomatic deadlock in 1827.

Van Buren instructed McLane to open his negotiations with the British by stressing that the election of Jackson was a rebuke by the people to the Adams administration, whose attitude resulted in the deadlock, and that the United States was ready to comply with the Act of Parliament of 1825, which established the terms on which nations might trade with her colonies. After the Adams administration blunderingly ignored the Act, Clay sent Gallatin to England to concede "that the President acquiesced on the decision taken by the British Government that the Colonial trade shall be regulated by law." The British ministry, resentful at what they regarded as contumacy, declined to negotiate.

In the spring, Congress, anticipating a settlement of the question, had empowered the President to declare the retaliatory measures repealed when England treated American shipping in West Indian ports on the same terms as her own. In November the war of discriminatory duties and other reprisals ended.

This was the crowning act of Van Buren's settled plan to effect harmony between England and America. The merchants and shippers, especially of New England and the Middle Atlantic States, hailed the recovery of the profitable trade with the West Indies as a triumph of Jackson, and the administration press reëchoed their praises. The few who made a study of our foreign relations, knew that the credit belonged to the Secretary of State. In December the first non-political honor conferred on Van Buren was awarded him by the New York Alpha Chapter—

Union College—of Phi Beta Kappa, which elected him an honorary member.

Congress was in session now and it was whispered that a row was impending between Jackson and Calhoun; but it was not until February that Calhoun published his pamphlet exhibiting the correspondence between him and the President over the Seminole War controversy. Calhoun followed this with a communication to Duff Green, who published it in his paper, charging Hamilton with acting dishonorably in the affair. The joint purpose of the letter and pamphlet was to fasten the plot on Van Buren. Calhoun, while not naming Van Buren, was sufficiently pointed in all he said to indicate him. Van Buren publicly denied in the Calhoun organ that he had sought "to prejudice the Vice-President in the good opinion of General Jackson." In the same issue Duff Green gave the lie direct to Van Buren. Whereupon Van Buren returned to his old policy of silence. Green next charged Van Buren with having directed the Eaton imbroglio as part of the conspiracy to destroy Calhoun. The anti-Jacksonian press repeated it. Van Buren remained silent.

Van Buren became the country-wide medium through which the Calhoun forces attacked Jackson. New names were hurled at him. He was no longer the spoilsman, the political juggler, the manager; they now called him the great magician, the red fox of Kinderhook, and the Flying Dutchman.

The problem was unique. Its solution called for a factor, novel and unprecedented. Van Buren had it. He would resign. He confided this to his eldest son, Abraham, who had been living with him since he won his epaulettes at West Point. He would submit his resignation to Jackson on one of their rides. It was early spring. One day when overtaken by a heavy thunderstorm they sought shelter in a tavern. Jackson suddenly became unusually serious. Van Buren left him to his thoughts, and conversed with a farmer who had also found shelter at the inn. When the rain ceased Jackson and Van Buren spurred their horses to a brisk canter, as the skies were still threatening. Without warning Jackson's horse slipped. Van Buren seized the bridle and prevented a spill. "You have possibly saved my life, sir!" exclaimed Jackson. Van Buren responded that he did not regard the danger so

gravely, but congratulated himself on having been of the slightest
service. Jackson half muttered that he was not certain that his
escape from death, if it was one, was worthy of congratulation
under existing circumstances.

Van Buren had started on this ride determined to tender his
resignation as Secretary of State. But this accident upset his
plans. On their next ride, Jackson, in a happier frame of mind,
epitomized his hopes for an end of the internal strife with: "We
shall soon have peace in Israel." Van Buren took this as his cue.
"No, General, there is but one thing can give you peace." "What
is that, sir?" "My resignation."

Earnestly Jackson looked at Van Buren as he said with impressive solemnity: "Never, sir! Even you know little of Andrew
Jackson if you suppose him capable of such a humiliation of his
friend by his enemies."

The two continued their ride. A quarter of a century later
Van Buren resumed the story thus: "I thought I could satisfy
him that the course I had pointed to was perhaps the only safe
one open to us. He agreed to hear me but in a manner and terms
affording small encouragement as to the success of my argument.
I proceeded for four hours, giving place only to brief interroga-
tions from him, to present in detail, the reasons upon which my
suggestion was founded, extending to a careful and, as far as I
was able, a clear review of the public interests and of our own
duties and feelings involved in the matter." Jackson inquired what
he intended to do if he accepted his resignation, and Van Buren
replied he would return to the law. Jackson then suggested the
English mission, having in mind his intention to have Van Buren
run for Vice President the following year.

We can only conjecture what arguments Van Buren used,
as he is silent regarding them. Van Buren was attracting assaults
on the Administration because he was known as Jackson's successor; the friends of Calhoun and other rivals for the Presidency
formed a combination and had already rejected some of Jackson's
appointments and were menacing his legislative program; his resignation would end the hostility, and thus pave the way for the
enactment of laws in the interest of the public. These arguments
we can read into the maze of ambiguities which Van Buren sub-

sequently published; and these are undoubtedly the propositions he advanced to Jackson.

He did not mention that his resignation would inevitably force Eaton to resign. These two resignations would leave Barry and the three friends of Calhoun in the Cabinet. Jackson would not long endure such a situation. But Van Buren was not the first Secretary of State who had Presidential ambitions.

The attacks on Van Buren were directed at him largely because he was the champion of La Bellona and the head of the conspiracy against Calhoun. And Van Buren, in not making these things clear to Jackson, imposed upon the guilelessness of the President.

Van Buren relates that the discussion was resumed the following morning at the White House, and continued in the afternoon while they were horseback-riding. That night Jackson consulted Barry, Eaton, and Lewis. All were in agreement with Van Buren. The following afternoon all five foregathered at the President's office; subsequently Eaton, Lewis, and Barry repaired to Van Buren's house for supper. As they entered, Eaton exclaimed: "Why should you resign? I am the man about whom all the trouble has been made." Three or four days later Jackson had Van Buren's and Eaton's resignations in his hands, Eaton's being dated prior to Van Buren's, as agreed.

The resignations of Berrien, Branch, and Ingham were demanded; but two months elapsed before the Cabinet was dissolved. Barry alone remained. Butler was informed of the circumstance confidentially, and under date of April 22 he answered Van Buren: ". . . I see no objection to your being brought forward for the V. Presidency . . . and *you* with your present reputation would again make that office what the older Adams & Jefferson found it—the nearest & most direct avenue to the higher station. . . ."

Noah had broken with Van Buren because he did not get the job he was after, and he editorialized: "Well indeed may Mr. Van Buren be called the great magician for he raises his wand and the whole Cabinet vanishes."

Van Buren left Washington before Eaton sought to meet Berrien, Branch, and Ingham on the dueling field. He was succeeded by Edward Livingston, now an idol of the world of learning. New York's former Mayor was sixty-seven years old, and as he countersigned Van Buren's commission as minister to England, he musingly recalled the days when his brother, the Chancellor, had filled the same post: then it went by the name of Department of Foreign Relations.

# CHAPTER XXXV

Van Buren remained in New York two months before sailing for England. The dissolution of the Cabinet created a greater storm than he had anticipated. Much was made of the charge of Ingham, the ousted Attorney General, that Richard M. Johnson, United States Senator from Kentucky, had said to him "that the President had finally determined on our removal from office unless we agreed at once that our families should visit Mrs. Eaton, and invite her to their large parties." Many circumstances supported Ingham's story, although Johnson denied that he had used the threatening language. In Pendleton, South Carolina, at a dinner to Calhoun, the toast to the President was omitted. Several reflecting on Van Buren, in which his name was not mentioned, were given, but before the dinner ended, this one was drunk:

"Martin Van Buren—
    'Ah! that deceit should steal such gentle shape,
    And with a virtuous visor hide deep vice.' "

On August 16 Van Buren sailed on the packet ship *President*, accompanied by his son John, an attaché of the Legation. They were met in London by Washington Irving, who had been appointed Secretary of the Legation by Van Buren two years earlier at the behest of Captain John B. Nicolson, U.S.N., a common friend. After his formal presentation to King William, Van Buren was a guest at the palace, and on one occasion the King had a heart-to-heart talk about Jackson. He described the extent of the alarm created among "all classes of his subjects" by Jackson's election. "But I kept myself free from those alarms," confided the King; "for I have made it a rule through life never to condemn an untried man; and in respect to other matters, I regarded Mr. Jackson as placed in that position. I said to those who addressed to me their apprehensions: 'I will judge Mr. Jackson by his acts.' I have done so, and I am satisfied that we shall have no reason to complain of injustice at his hands."

Irving had resigned before Van Buren's arrival, but instantly formed a warm attachment to the new Minister, and agreed to serve under him. They became fast and lifelong friends, and this is Irving's measure of the man: "The more I see of Mr. Van Buren, the more I am confirmed in a strong personal regard for him. He is one of the gentlest and most amiable men I have ever met with; with an affectionate disposition that attaches itself to those around him and wins their kindness in return."

The author lived with Van Buren, who leased a large house on Stratford Place, a quiet street in a fashionable part of town. This cost him $2,500. His servants and their keep took $2,600 out of his pocket, and he lavished $1,550 on the latest in coaches, although he had taken his own carriage with him. Irving, who knew England well—and he was not a stranger to Kinderhook, having found the originals of Ichabod Crane and other characters there while tutoring the children of Van Buren's old preceptor, the late William P. Van Ness, dead now some five years—played guide to Van Buren in a tour of old castles, ancient abbeys; they ate boar's head "crowned with holly" and drank wassail in the Yule log's warmth in quaint taverns of hallowed memory; and watched mummers, morris dancers, and listened to glee singers.

On his return to London from this holiday jaunt Van Buren found that politics had not changed in the States since he had left them. Cambreleng was sending the gossip, and Van Buren was ever begging for more. ". . . Your last," he wrote to the faithful correspondent, "was written with the freedom, and in the spirit I desire. It was committed to the flames, as I shall do all that speak in the same way of men and things, for it is useless to keep them on file. Therefore speak on. . . ."

The fanatical Anti-Masonic party had met in national convention in Baltimore and nominated William Wirt, of Maryland, for President and Amos Ellmaker, of Pennsylvania, for Vice President. They stole a march on the old parties by innovating the representative method of naming national candidates. Jackson on December 6 wrote: "Everything is going on well at present. Nullification and antimasonry are both declining fast, & will ere long be *buried in oblivion*, doing no harm, but carrying with it the promoters, exciters, and supporters." Calhoun is "an ambitious demagogue." The new Cabinet is harmonious, but he misses

Eaton and Van Buren "very much." In this same letter Jackson referred to the proposal he made during one of their rides together: that Van Buren run on the same ticket with him, and after serving a year, he would resign and make Van Buren President. "I do hope," wrote Jackson, "that in the *selection of a vice president*, I may be placed in such a situation at the time I have heretofore sugested [*sic!*] to you to withdraw to the peaceful shades of the Hermitage, from the busy scenes of public life—on this subject, I will write you fully in a few months."

Jackson was still in feeble health: hence his wish to surrender the office to Van Buren. He felt, as did all his advisers, that he must run again to keep the opposition down. In an earlier letter, dated September 18, Jackson begins with his usual complaints of the abuse and slanders which are being heaped upon him daily, and reverts to his intention to resign in Van Buren's favor: "How disgusting this is to a virtuous mind, & how I long for retirement to the peaceful shades of the Hermitage, for I assure you the depravity of human nature which is daily unfolding itself, by the slanders of the wicked part of the opposition have truly disgusted me. I therefore wish how soon I may be able, with honor to resign the trust committed to me to another & a better hand." Thirteen days earlier, Jackson ends a seven-page letter with: "I cannot close without again repeating that I hope circumstances will occur to enable me to return to the Hermitage in due season and set an example worthy to be followed and give an evidence to my country that I never had any other ambition than that of serving my country when she required it, and, when I know it could be better served by others, to open the door to their enjoyment; *you will understand me.*"

While Van Buren was enjoying the glamorous life of London, Calhoun, Clay, and Webster were concocting a scheme for his destruction. As Van Buren's had been a recess appointment, Jackson, on December 7, sent his name to the Senate. Rumors reached Jackson that the opposition was considering rejecting Van Buren. On December 12, the National Republicans, after the example set by the Anti-Masons, met in national convention in Baltimore, and nominated Clay for President, and John Sergeant, of Pennsylvania, for Vice President. Five days later Jackson told Van Buren of the nominations and of Calhoun's attack on Van Buren for his success in his negotiations over the Northeast boundary and fugitive slave questions. Next he referred to the plot: "The opposition would, if they durst, try to reject your nomination as Minister, but they dare not,—they begin to know if they did that the people in mass would take you up and elect you Vice President without a nomination. Was it not for this, it is said, Clay, Calhoun & Co. would try it."

On January 13, three days after Senator Littleton W. Tazewell, of Virginia, for the Committee on Foreign Relations, favorably reported Van Buren's nomination, Senator John Holmes, of Maine, moved to investigate the causes leading to the dissolution of the Cabinet "and also, whether the said Martin Van Buren, then Secretary of State, participated in any practices disreputable to the national character, which were designed to operate on the mind of the President of the United States, and calculated to smooth the way to his appointment to the high office to which he has been nominated." This motion was tabled. When the nomination was called up the vote was a tie; and Calhoun left the Vice President's chair and by his casting vote tabled the nomination. The junior Senator from New York was William L. Marcy. On January 24 Marcy moved that the Senate resume consideration of Van Buren's appointment. The next day, again by the casting vote of Calhoun, the way was paved for an indictment of Van Buren on the following counts:

1. The instructions drawn up and signed by Mr. Van Buren as Secretary of State, under the direction of the President, and furnished to Mr. McLane, for his guidance in endeavoring to reopen the negotiation for the West India trade.
2. Making a breach of friendship between the first and second officers of the Government—President Jackson and Vice-President Calhoun—for the purpose of thwarting the latter, and helping himself to the Presidency.
3. Breaking up the Cabinet for the same purpose.
4. Introducing the system of "proscription" (removal from office for opinion's sake), for the same purpose.

A *prima facie* case, at least, could have been made out against Van Buren on the second and third counts. He was unquestionably guilty of the fourth. But the first charge in the indictment was puerile. Yet it was on this that the opposition, led by Webster and Clay, made its principal attack. The hollowness of this charge, which they hoped would rouse the country, lay in the fact that Van Buren's instructions to McLane had been before the Senate for more than a year, and no one questioned them during the months Congress was in session; and all these nine months Van Buren was serving as Secretary of State.

In instructing McLane to remind the British that there was a new administration in power, Van Buren wrote: "I will add nothing to the impropriety of any feelings that find their origin in the past pretensions of this Government to have an adverse influence upon the present conduct of Great Britain." Webster, as he quoted this, and more of the same tenor preceding it, exclaimed, tongue in cheek: "Sir, I would forgive mistakes; I would pardon the want of information; I would pardon almost any thing, where I saw true patriotism and sound American feeling; but I cannot forgive the sacrifice of this feeling to mere Party. I cannot concur in sending abroad a public agent who has not conceptions so large and liberal, as to feel, that in the presence of foreign Courts, amidst the Monarchs of Europe, he is to stand up for his country, and his whole country; that no jot and tittle of her honor is to come to harm in his hands; that he is not to suffer others to reproach either his Government or his Country, and far less is he to reproach either; that he is to have no objects in his eye but American objects, and no heart in his bosom but an American heart; and that he is to forget self, to forget party, and to forget every sinister and narrow feeling, in his proud and lofty attachment to the Republic whose commission he bears."

Clay made a speech also fit for the hustings, from which we quote: "On our side, according to Mr. Van Buren, all was wrong; on the British side, all was right. We brought forward nothing but claims and pretensions; the British Government asserted, on the other hand, a clear and incontestable right. We erred in too tenaciously and too long insisting upon our pretensions, and not yielding at once to the force of their just demands. And Mr. McLane was commanded to avail himself of all the circumstances in his power to mitigate our offense, and to dissuade the British Government from allowing their feelings justly incurred by the past conduct of the party driven from power, to have an adverse influence towards the American party now in power. Sir, was this becoming language from one independent nation to another? Was it proper in the mouth of an American Minister? Was it in conformity with the high, unsullied, and dignified character of our previous diplomacy? Was it not, on the contrary, the language of a humble vassal to a proud and haughty lord? Was it not prostrating and degrading the American Eagle before the British Lion?"

Calhoun spoke through Hayne who said: "From facts and circumstances which have fallen under my own observation, many of them notorious to the whole country, as well as from information derived from sources on which I implicitly rely, I have arrived at the following conclusion; that when Mr. Van Buren came into the Cabinet, he found a state of circumstances here that opened a door to the establishment of an influence favorable to his personal views; that, instead of exerting himself to remove the causes of discord and dissention by which the executive was unhappily surrounded, he dexterously availed himself of them, and wielded them for the promotion of his own personal and political interests, and for the advancement of his friends and supporters to office, to the exclusion of almost all others."

One phrase born in this bitter debate has become almost a household saying. During Marcy's denial of the charge of intrigue against his chief, and his plea of guilty to the last count in the indictment, he said: "It may be, sir, that the politicians of New York are not so fastidious as some gentlemen are as to disclosing the principles on which they act. They boldly preach what they practice. When they are contending for victory they avow their intention of enjoying the fruits of it. If they are defeated, they expect to retire from office; if they are successful, they claim, as a matter of right, the advantages of success. They see nothing wrong in the rule that to the victor belongs the spoils of the enemy."

Marcy's rendering of the Brennic "Woe to the conquered!" grated harshly on the ears of his confrères. The spoilsman was caught unawares. In the excitement of the occasion he had forgotten that Jackson had attempted a defense of the wholesale removals in a message to Congress with a more palatable phrase: "rotation in office."

This debate lasted two days. A dozen set speeches against Van Buren were matched with impromptu rejoinders by Marcy, Forsyth, Bedford Brown, of North Carolina, and Samuel Smith, of Maryland. These were Van Buren's only defenders. Even Benton, his friend, companion, and political bedfellow, was silent. He probably thought he would profit by what might happen. Jackson was not mute. Through Smith he told the Senate that Van Buren's instructions to McLane were his own.

On January 26, by Calhoun's casting vote, Van Buren was rejected as Minister to the Court of St. James's. Some friends of the South Carolinian doubted the wisdom of rejecting Van Buren. But the Vice President silenced their doubts with: "It will kill him, sir, kill him dead. He will never kick, sir, never kick." But he lacked the profundity of Van Buren, who had said to Judge Skinner: "There is such a thing in politics as killing a man too dead."

Marcy divided the enemies of Van Buren into two groups: the friends of the Adams administration who voted to reject him because he "denounced the government to a foreign power and invoked favors upon party considerations"; and the friends of Calhoun. Of them he wrote to the recalled Minister: "Calhoun and his little band . . . came to the aid of Webster and Clay but the grounds were very different. You had seduced they represented—not a woman—but the President—made a breach between him and our worthy presiding officer—you were a great intreguer [*sic!*]—the author of sundry plotts [*sic!*]—&c &c."

Marcy also informed Van Buren that he would be made the candidate for Vice President. "Gen. J[ackson] is advanced in life & to be frank with you is in feeble health. I must say, however I may wish otherwise, that I think the chances are against his lasting five years longer. With the best of those now spoken of for Vice Prest. at our head as chief Magistrate we should be in a miserable situation. This consideration has had great influence with our wisest friends in bringing them to the conclusion that you should in all events be a candidate for V. P."

Immediately the Regency had the New York Legislature address a memorial to Jackson protesting against the indignity to her favorite son. Jackson replied in like spirit, and repeated what Smith had said in his behalf to the Senate; professed his incapacity to tarnish the pride or dignity of that country whose glory it had been his object to elevate; denied that Van Buren had been party to the rupture between him and Calhoun; asserted that he had asked Van Buren to serve as Secretary of State to meet the general wish and expectation of the Republican party and because of his own respect for Van Buren's great private and public worth and integrity.

Van Buren was too far away to be more than a pawn in the game which he could play so well. But the players were not amateurs: Marcy, Lewis and Cambreleng were making the moves. Meetings of protest were held in Tammany Hall in the last two days of January, and these were followed by like gatherings in villages and cities up-State.

Van Buren was ill in bed when the news reached him. An unusually large batch of letters was brought to him with his breakfast. He sifted them until he recognized an envelope in the familiar manuscript of Cambreleng. "I most sincerely congratulate you on your rejection by the Senate—23 to 23 and by the casting vote of the Vice President," Cambreleng's letter began. ". . . Poor Hayne has laid himself on the grave of Calhoun— and Webster & Clay die in each other's arms. . . . you will be made V. P. in spite of yourself—and you will ride over your adversaries, or rather drag them after you *à l'Achille.* Come back as quick as you can—we have not triumphal arches as in ancient Rome, but we'll give you as warm a reception as ever Conqueror had."

This letter effected a complete recovery: he had planned to stay in bed all day. He dressed hurriedly, but with his usual care, went downstairs, and surprised Washington Irving at the breakfast table. He handed the author Cambreleng's communication, which cheered Irving; for he had just read the meager news in the *Times.*

Van Buren told Irving that he regarded his presence at the Queen's Drawing Room imperative in view of his rejection. Irving agreed, provided it did not involve too great a sacrifice of feeling. Van Buren was not concerned over that. When he reached the Palace, Lord Palmerston took him aside and said that he had received an intimate picture of what had happened from the British Chargé at Washington, and had transmitted it to the

King. Early in the morning the King had sent for him and commanded him to assure Van Buren that His Majesty was satisfied the rejection had been inspired by partisan consideration, and while it was far from the King's habit or inclination to meddle in the purely domestic affairs of other governments, he felt it due to the President and Van Buren to say that his respect for him was unimpaired. And there were more gracious and considerate sentiments expressed by the King. As the company, preceded by the diplomatic corps, passed through the Throne Room, the King halted the procession to express his regrets personally to Van Buren.

Van Buren waited until another mail arrived before making any move. Cambreleng again advised him: "I think on reflection that I would endeavor to arrive in this Country about the 11ʰ of May about 2 or 3 weeks before the meeting at Baltᵒ." Lewis was for an even longer stay: he recommended his entry after the Baltimore convention. Jackson, knowing the difference in opinion among his political managers at home, told Van Buren to use his own discretion. Van Buren decided that it would look better if he did not return until after he had been nominated, and made his plans accordingly.

Late in March he was received by the King and Queen at Windsor, and the beginning of the second week of April found him in Paris. He made a trip to Germany, where his stay was equally brief; but he spent nearly a month in the land of his ancestors. He was received by the King of the Netherlands, William I, who suggested that they were distantly related, saying that his title of Count Buren came from an ancestor who married the Countess of Buren, then head of an ancient family, now no more, whose castle was in the old town of Buren. Van Buren replied that all he knew of his family was that the first American ancestor "came over in 1633." Van Buren, as we know, was in error by two years, as he was in believing that the family name was Buren. But there was no Holland Society in those days, and no one was especially concerned over the old Dutch records in and around Albany.

Early in June Van Buren and his son sailed for home. On July 5 they landed at New York, where Van Buren learned, as he had anticipated, that the Democratic-Republican National

Convention had nominated him on May 21. Jackson was not nominated at the convention; this had been already done by the State Legislatures; the convention merely indorsed Jackson's nomination.

A periodic visitation of the cholera was raging in New York when Van Buren arrived. Demonstrations had been planned in his honor, but he declined to attend them. His enemies charged him with cowardice. As usual, he made no explanation; but one is found in a letter from Jackson, which was directed to him at the ship, requesting him to come immediately to Washington.

To understand the dramatic scene awaiting Van Buren at the White House, a word of explanation is in order. The renewal of the Charter of the Bank of the United States was the dominant issue before the people. Although its grant would not expire until 1836, the question had been before Congress for more than a year. The convention which nominated Clay had declared in favor of a renewal. The delegates who nominated Jackson and Van Buren had been silent on this and all other questions. They were content to adopt a brief resolution praising Jackson. And on Jackson's desk, at the time Van Buren reached Washington was the bill extending the life of "the monster."

The letter which Jackson had sent to meet Van Buren's ship was written three days after the bill had passed the Senate, and while it was still before the House. It was a pitiful cry for help from a very sick man. We quote from it: ". . . The coalition are determined to press upon me at this session the Bank, and a few more internal improvement bills—I am prepared to meet them as I ought—but I want your aid—The able heads of Departments, except Woodbury and the Attorney General, are all in favor of the Bank—Let me see you as early as you can."

On arriving at the White House Van Buren was shown to Jackson's bedroom. The President was emaciated and pale, reminding Van Buren of a specter. But there was an unquenchable fire in his blue eyes. He took Van Buren's hand, wearily ran his free hand through his white locks, and in an even voice, utterly devoid of passion, said: "The Bank, Mr. Van Buren, is trying to kill me; but I will kill it."

Jackson vetoed the bill July 10. In the remaining few days of Congress, Webster, Clay, and other friends of the Bank tried to muster the necessary two-thirds to override the President's veto. But Van Buren was flitting around the corridors of the Capitol to prevent them. Clay met him, and in ending a speech, informed the Senate that he had just shaken hands "with our late Minister to England, Mr. Van Buren, and was gratified to find him in excellent health and appearing to great advantage in his English dress."

Clay did not know, or he would also have made a point of it, that Van Buren brought more than clothes from England; his ultra-modish English coach came on the same ship with him.

## CHAPTER XXXVI

THE type of campaign waged against Jackson and Van Buren is illustrated by a broadside issued by the Massachusetts National Republicans pretending to be an order for a procession and dinner at Haverhill, and signed: "Per order of the Kitchen Cabinet, Van Buren, Auctioneer." One of the toasts read: "By an incipient Tory: 'The Greatest and Best.' The *greatest* robber, the *best* distributor of the spoils. Overture to the Forty Thieves." Jackson, of course, was the Tory. Another ran: "By Black Hawk: '*Mrs. Eaton.* Handsome Squaw, big petticoat cover up all old man's sins. Tune *An Old Man Went a Wooing.*'" The *Old Man* was Jackson also. There was a thrust at Jackson's ancestry in this: "Gentlemen who take part in the procession may be assured that the Irishmen and members of *Infant Schools* will be removed so that nothing shall remain to annoy the senses of the most fastidious Tory."

But the writers of broadsides and pamphlets, with their allies on the venal journals, had overdone their tasks in the campaign of 1828. They made little impression, one way or another. And the espousal of the Bank by the opposition, with the suspicion—well founded—that some of the supporters of Clay were in the Bank's pay, outweighed the talk of spoils and Mrs. Eaton and the Kitchen Cabinet. Francis P. Blair, who supplanted Duff Green as chief of the Jackson editorial corps after the Calhoun scissure, wrote to Van Buren: "The Bank cannot buy the majority of the nation." Webster had obtained $32,000 from the Bank in "loans." One was a sum of $10,000, surreptitiously paid by the President of the Bank, Nicholas Biddle, the Monday following Webster's speech against Jackson's veto message on the Bank's charter. The speech was worth it. Congress, in March, knew that Webster was $22,000 "in debt" to the bank, and that other members of Congress were also in its clutches. The list of these Congressional beneficiaries of the Bank was embodied in a minority report of the Clayton Committee, which had investi-

gated the corrupt acts of the Bank. The report was sent to the
Government printer, who, for a reason never explained, suppressed it. "Czar Nicholas," as Biddle was known, only partly
complied with the demand of Congress to enumerate "the loans
made by the Bank and its branches to members of Congress,
editors of newspapers, or persons holding office under the general
government." In *The Globe* of August 23, Blair charged Webster
with corruption in his relations with the Bank; but Webster and
Biddle remained silent to the end of their lives. The Bank, at its
expense, circulated Webster's $10,000 speech as a Clay campaign
document.

After leaving Washington Van Buren journeyed through
New York, visiting leaders on both sides of the river on his way
to Albany. The State seemed safe enough, but he did not want
to leave anything to chance. When he reached Kinderhook the
birds were singing counter to the melancholic monody of the
katydids, whose first notes are still regarded by the inhabitants of
the Dutch counties as an unfailing sign that frost will be with
them six weeks later to a day. The early asters were beginning to
blossom along the roadsides, another indication that summer was
on the wane. He had been in the village little more than a day
when he thought it was time to call on Peter Van Schaack. Ever
since he had become a power in the State Van Buren had never
returned to Kinderhook without calling on him. Van Buren had
tramped that part of London where Van Schaack had lived
during his banishment, noting every change in the neighborhood.
All this had been for the delectation of the man who had challenged him at the polls when about to cast his first vote. That
was well-nigh a generation ago.

As Van Buren was about to start, young Van Schaack
called and said that his father was waiting for him as it might be
their last time together. When Van Buren entered the library the
dying Tory raised himself on the bed and extended his hand.
He was happy to hear Van Buren's voice again; he knew his
tread; he had learned to recognize the footsteps of his friends
during the past twenty years: he had been blind that long. Van
Buren was saddened to see his bed moved into the library, as it
was Van Schaack's wish—all his friends knew it—to die amidst
his books. After the exchange of greetings, Van Schaack volun-

teered that he was going through the last change. Van Buren
was voicing the hope that such might not be the case when the
old man cut him short with a vigorous "No!" He calmly added
that death was inevitable, and a part of life; he had lived the full
measure of his days—eighty-five years in all—and was thankful
to God that his mental faculties remained unimpaired to the end.
Blindness was nothing. Van Buren let him finish and then talked
of Van Schaack's retreat in London, and of the changes there.
And then they gossiped of the village, of their friends, and of
the law-suits they had tried together.

It was now growing late. The sun had dropped behind the
Catskills. A servant lighted the candles. It was time to depart.
Van Schaack held Van Buren's hand in their last good-by. "I am
happy, sir, to think," said the old man slowly, "that we have
always been——" No! that was not so; he had been Van Buren's
enemy once: he could not say they had always been friends. He
had never been guilty of duplicity; he had suffered for opinion's
sake; he could not, even unintentionally, begin now. Through his
mind surged recollections of bitter party strife, beginning with
that Election Day twenty-nine years earlier, when he challenged
Van Buren's vote. He still held Van Buren's hand, as lawyer-like
he rephrased his utterance: "I am happy, sir, to think that you
always came to see me when you visited Kinderhook." This was
Van Schaack; and he inclined his head graciously as Van Buren
bowed and said farewell.

The survey of the State, and the work done by Van Buren,
left no doubt as to the outcome. The western counties, where
Anti-Masonry had its birth, were overwhelmingly against him and
Jackson. There were reports of money being used by the Bank
throughout the country. Subsequently it was proven that the
Bank spent $80,000 in pamphleteering alone: how much was used
in bribery and vote buying is a matter of speculation. Isaac Hill
wrote from New Hampshire: ". . . we may be relied upon giving
a decisive majority for Andrew Jackson. Yet the Bank is scattering its thousands here to affect us." Aaron Ward, Van Buren's
lieutenant in Westchester County, wrote: "I fear the Bank
influence more than anything else. I have no doubt that the Bank
managers will expend a large sum of money in this county."
Blair wrote to Van Buren: "We cannot & ought not to employ

money to bribe voters. . . . The Bank cannot buy the majority of the Nation. . . ."

In spite of the Bank the election of Jackson and Van Buren was foreshadowed long before Election Day. The Hickory Clubs were more potent than the Bank and its branches. Jackson, under date of August 30, wrote from the Hermitage that he was about to return to Washington, and asked Van Buren for advice on his message to Congress. "I wish your views not only that my course may be consistent, but that if any accident should befall me, that the Government may continue to be administered as we have commenced it, and the Government brought back & adminis-tered agreeable to the true reading of the constitution." This letter also revealed that Jackson was inclining from the tariff.

On October 4, replying to an inquiry from a meeting at Shocco Springs, North Carolina, Van Buren set forth his views on the tariff. Explicit was Van Buren's characterization of his sentiments to his interrogators; but a vaguer letter Van Buren never penned. On the same day that Jackson had written him, J. Grant, Jr., of Raleigh, North Carolina, had warned him to be • wary of the seemingly friendly address from Shocco Springs. Van Buren did not need the warning: he replied he was for a more equitable adjustment of the tariff; that he was opposed to oppres-sive inequality or imposts designed to benefit one section of the country to the disadvantage of another; that he favored a reduc-tion of the revenue to the wants of the government; and expressed a preference for encouraging manufactures essential to the national defense, and extending protection to industries adapted to our country and of which the raw material was produced by ourselves. These "explicit" views stamped him as either an ultra-protectionist, or a tariff reformer: you could take your choice. But there was nothing equivocal in his attitude on the Bank, internal improvements, and nullification: he was against all three.

In another public letter written in the close of the campaign, Van Buren spoke of the unceasing hatred and contumely that had been visited upon him by his political enemies since his en-trance into public life. Other men in official life had been attacked, but they had had respite, while he had never known a moment's peace. He consoled himself by observing that there had been scarcely a man who had been the victim of unwarrantable obloquy who had not risen in public estimation in exact proportion to the intensity and duration of the abuse.

The victory for Jackson and Van Buren was more decisive than it had been for Jackson and Calhoun four years earlier. Jacksonian Governors and Jacksonian Legislatures were elected in most of the States. In New York, Marcy was chosen Governor by 13,000 majority; his seat in the Senate was later filled by Silas Wright. Twenty-three of the States had adopted the system of choosing Presidential Electors by popular vote; South Carolina alone clung to the undemocratic method of leaving this privilege to the Legislature, a practice maintained until 1860. South Carolina was going it alone, in more ways than one: it nominated John Floyd, of Virginia, for President, and Henry Lee, of Massachusetts, for Vice President, and gave them its eleven Electoral votes. Pennsylvania had nominated a Jackson ticket, but in obedience to the Bank, had chosen Electors pledged to William Wilkins, of Pennsylvania, for Vice President. Vermont went Anti-Masonic. Jackson received 219 of the 286 votes in the Electoral College, and Clay 49; Van Buren 189; the difference represented Pennsylvania's vote for Wilkins.

Van Buren on arriving in New York to collect his election bets found himself a social lion. Hone recorded, after meeting him at several parties: "Mr. Van Buren . . . is all the fashion at present. . . . he must be more or less than a man if he can avoid exultation when he assumes the Vice-President's chair, vacated by the man who gave the casting vote in the Senate which recalled him from his honorable station abroad."

He was more sought after than Signora Edelaide Pedrotti— he always heard her called La Pedrotti—the prima donna of the Italian opera company, which opened the season at the old Richmond Hill Theater in the last week of September. Of all the socially prominent families, the Hones alone failed to invite the soprano to their home. Hone made her acquaintance at the John Delafields', on Park Place, the night following his dinner with Van Buren at the Marches. She had sung that evening the title rôle in Mercadante's *Elisa e Claudio*. She was very tired. She had responded with generous encores to the enthusiastic bravas and the cries of *"Bis! Bis!"* All begged her to sing just a little bit. She curtseyed her thanks in declining. Still the Delafields and their guests were hopeful. "And she refused to sing, too, after Mrs. [Henry] Parish and Helen McEvers had kindly set the example," observed the incensed Hone. "If she did not sing, why was she there? And then the elegant amateurs of Italian music pretend to compare this woman to Fanny Kemble; nay, pretend to say that, independently of her singing, she plays better and has more grace!" Thenceforward La Pedrotti's glorious eyes, as dark and mysterious as night, were "staring"; her Venus-like figure was "immense" and "vulgar"; her modest dress "tawdry."

There was some truth in Hone's criticism of the admirers of La Pedrotti: New York's society found more witchery in her than in "the greatest Juliet of her day" because she was from the Continent: Fanny Kemble could only boast England as her birthplace. Everything European was worshiped and imitated by the *élite* of the Metropolis. Even Hone went into ecstasies when his set began giving elaborate luncheons and called them by the French equivalent for a substantial breakfast. "A *dèjeuner à la fourchette* is something of a novelty in this country, and the last imitation of European refinement," wrote Hone. "This series of breakfasts given by Mr. William Douglas at his fine mansion, corner of Park Place and Church Street, can hardly be called an *imitation;* for in taste, elegance, and good management it goes beyond most things of the kind in Europe. . . . The company assembles at about one o'clock, and remains until four. Breakfast is served at two o'clock, and consists of coffee and chocolate, light dishes of meat, ice-cream and confectionery, with lemonade and French and German wines. The first two floors, elegantly furnished, of this spacious house, are thrown open; the dining room opens into a beautiful conservatory, in which, amongst other pleasant objects, is an aviary of singing-birds, the delicate notes of the canary mingling sweetly with the shrill pipe of the foreign bullfinch, and the whole concert regulated and stimulated by the great leader of the feathered orchestra, our own native mocking-bird. A band, also, of a more commercial nature, plays at the head of the stairs during the whole time of the entertainment, and after the young folk have partaken of their breakfast-dinner, cotillions and waltzes are danced until the hour of reluctant departure. . . ."

La Pedrotti, in declining to entertain the Delafields and their guests, was not following custom. When the wine had mellowed all, those with accomplishments the least out of the ordinary, contributed to the entertainment of the occasion. It was a rare gathering which did not number a celebrity. Charles Kemble, who played Mercutio before the public, at these dinner and supper parties would frequently play Romeo to his daughter's Juliet. And their own Edwin Forrest seldom needed a bidding to declaim his favorite passages from Lear, Othello, Macbeth, and other dramas which made him wealthy and famous. Irving, who was of their own circle, never failed them for a story. Domenick Lynch needed no importuning to sing the latest French or Italian air. But the favorite was Charles Matthews, the comedian, who always played to crowded houses on his visits to this country. His days were numbered; but he concealed his doom from his audiences. In private homes he sang and recited, and told stories of Daniel O'Connell "and other eloquent Irishmen in order to illustrate the different kinds of Irish brogue." And when he died in England in the early 30's, Hone said: "Few men of the present age have contributed so much to the amusement of others. . . . I have seen him at my own table delighting and surprising the company with stories, songs, and imitations, himself the only person whose heart was not light and joyous by the merriment he caused."

No entertainment was complete without dancing and wine. Hone had two wine closets to supplement his cellar. And when, toward the end of Van Buren's term as Vice President, he sold his house at Park Place and Broadway, and moved almost a mile to the north—to Broadway and Bond street—he inventoried 2,180 quart bottles and 254 gallon bottles of Madeira and sherry. Hone's cellar was modest, as the cellars of Gotham's fashionables went.

Van Buren's social graces astonished those who met him for the first time. They had expected to find a typical farmer's son: they had forgotten that Albany, too, boasted a society of which the Patroon was the acknowledged leader, and that while the ballrooms were few in the seat of Knickerbocker New York, dancing masters made annual visits even to the smallest villages of the Dutch counties. They saw that Van Buren not only danced the plain waltz and the hop waltz, but was as lively as the next in the spirited gallopade, and could lead a cotillion. But he was deficient in two of the accomplishments of the dandies of the day: he played neither the flute nor the guitar; and he was a stranger to the pianoforte.

Van Buren's round of entertainments ended Monday, November 26, when Tammany observed the anniversary of the evacuation of the city by the British. It was only fitting that the venerable and beloved Morgan Lewis, one of the few heroes of the Revolution left, should preside. Lewis, before leaving to meet his old enemy in the War of 1812, informed his many tenant-farmers that those who took up arms or sent a son to the war need not worry about any rent then due or which might be due in the future: instantly Lewis's income from his tenants was reduced to almost nothing. In introducing Tammany's guest, the son of the Signer recalled his words to Van Buren in the spring of 1814 when Van Buren was finishing his second year in the State Senate: "Being a much older man than yourself, you will excuse me for saying it to you, that should you retain your talents and integrity, the first honors of your country will await you." And Van Buren had lost neither his integrity nor his talents; and part of Lewis's prediction was fulfilled.

There was more cheering when Van Buren rose to speak; and after he finished he gave the scheduled toasts. The first was to the memory of the Signers. The glasses were emptied while the orchestra played "Oft in the Stilly Night." As they drank to the memory of Washington, the musicians sounded the noble and elegiac strains of Pleyel's Hymn. Lewis had selected this number. Its significance was not lost on the Masons present. In the preceding year Lewis had been elected Grand Master of the Craft.

From his seat on the dais Van Buren had an excellent view of the hundreds who were crowded into the Long Room of the Wigwam. All were well dressed; but there were many who were obviously out of place. These were the keepers of pot-houses and waterfront grog shops. They were beginning to make themselves felt in the two political organizations of New York. They controlled the votes of fellows more debased than themselves. But no one imagined that within a decade they were to be entrenched in the political councils of New York and other large cities. They fattened on misery in the mass. A few weeks back, while Van Buren was in the midst of the campaign, newspapers told of the alarm felt by officials of Canada and the United States over the unprecedented emigration of the poor from the British Isles. This great flow was caused by "the distress of the lower classes in England and Ireland." In the five months following the opening of navigation of the St. Lawrence in the spring, 49,569 debarked at Quebec alone. "A large proportion find their way into the United States destitute and friendless." There were countless hundreds entering daily the ports of Boston, New York, and Philadelphia. Most of them remained in these congested centers, and there was no organized effort to relieve their distress. Thousands had already gravitated into the network of crooked streets immediately to the north of where Van Buren was being entertained by Tammany. Here lived the very poor, in wretched hovels. Whole families, native born and foreign stock, lived in the cellars of these rude shacks unfit for cattle. In the mornings the little children of these unfortunates came out into the fresh air. Some —many of them little girls of eight and nine years—carried brooms. With these they swept the crossings on Broadway and other main streets. The less ambitious begged for pennies. Other little ones sought refuge from hunger in crime. Their elders— when they had the price—purchased momentary forgetfulness in the grog shops, whose keepers, on Election Day, dictated their votes at the polls. Before many years had passed, these harpies of politics were to occupy the seats of honor now occupied by Van Buren, Lewis, and their kind.

In returning to Albany Van Buren passed many farms, and envied the peace of those who tilled them. He was looking forward to the day when he would cast the cares of office and return to the quiet of a farm in Kinderhook. The village had none of the city's splendor; and it had its poverty, too, as he himself could bear witness; but no one went hungry, and squalor was unknown.

Calhoun did not serve out his term; for his State at a popular convention, presided over by Governor Hamilton—Randolph's second in the duel with Clay—declared the tariff laws passed by Congress in 1828, and in July of the current year, null and void. Secession was one step removed. Jackson answered immediately by ordering two war vessels to Charleston, and troops within striking distance of South Carolina's border. The newspapers of December 12 published Jackson's proclamation to the people of South Carolina. There was fatherly advice in it, and this: "I consider the power to annul a law of the United States, assumed by one State, incompatible with the existence of the Union, contradicted expressly by the letter of the Constitution, unauthorized by its spirit, inconsistent with every principle on which it was founded, and destructive of the great object for which it was formed."

These sentiments shocked all State-rights theorists. Nathaniel Macon, in honorable retirement after a lifetime of service in Congress, wrote to Van Buren that a State had the right to secede. All knew that the proclamation was beyond the power of Jackson, and Hone wrote: "Whoever shall prove to be the author has raised himself to imperishable glory." One of Hone's predecessors in New York's City Hall, the framer of the Louisiana Code, had written it. Three days after Christmas Calhoun resigned the Vice Presidency, and was elected to the Senate to succeed Hayne; and from the floor of Congress disavowed any hostility toward the Union. Calhoun personally feared Jackson, who had threatened to hang the nullifiers; and in letters to Van Buren Jackson expressed the wish to lead a *posse comitatus* into South Carolina and arrest Calhoun and his immediate lieutenants.

Van Buren remained in Albany during the first two months of the legislative session. There were two United States Senators to be chosen; one to fill the unexpired term of Governor Marcy, and another to succeed Dudley, whose tenure of office ended March 3. Silas Wright was chosen without opposition for the first place. The Regency was divided on a successor to Dudley, some demanding Jacob Sutherland, a Supreme Court Justice, who had married a Livingston, and others, led by Knower, advocating Nathaniel P. Tallmadge, of Poughkeepsie, a State Senator, and an avowed protectionist.

Wright was elected on January 4. Van Buren sent him posthaste to Washington with a letter commending him to Jackson. And Jackson waited for another communication from Van Buren. In his annual message to Congress, which was read in both houses on a month to a day before Wright's election to the Senate, Jackson had informed Congress of the situation in South Carolina, of his views on the tariff and the Bank. Legislatures in other States had commended him for his stand, but New York remained silent. Then came Jackson's special message on South Carolina's bellicose acts "which manifest a determination to render inevitable a resort to those measures of self-defense which the paramount duty of the Federal government requires . . ." Congress heard it on January 16. Jackson waited nine days longer to hear New York's Legislature approve his attitude, and growing impatient, wrote to Van Buren: ". . . whispers and innuendoes . . . are circulated, to injure you, carrying out the idea, that you wield the Legislature & thro fear of results are silent. Friendship dictates that I should let you know that such is the course of your enemies—and the silence of the Legislature gives a colouring to these false suggestions."

Van Buren did fear the results. He wanted to avoid taking a stand, if possible. He did not agree with the negation of State rights involved in the doctrine pronounced by Jackson, originally voiced by the Federalists. The survivors of this party, led by Webster and Harrison Gray Otis, had been foremost in organizing meetings to approve Jackson's course. The erratic John Randolph of Roanoke was tearing up and down Virginia shouting —ardent Jacksonian though he was—that Jackson "had disavowed the principles to which he owed his elevation to the Chief Magistracy . . . and transferred his real friends and supporters, bound hand and foot, to his and their bitterest enemies, the ultra Federalists, ultra tariffites, ultra internal improvement and Hartford Convention men—the habitual scoffers at State rights, and to their instrument, the venal and prostituted press."

The exaggerated language of Randolph voiced the sentiments of the extreme State-rights theorists. It would not do for Van Buren to slight them; and he could not ignore Jackson. Consequently he wrote a report to please both. He catered to the State-rights men with: ". . . the states must be regarded as parties to the compact . . . it is a Constitution established by 'the people of the United States,' not as one consolidated body, but as members of separate and independent communities, each acting for itself, and without regard to their comparative numbers." He praised Jackson for his stand on the Bank, on the tariff, and spoke on nullification in a way to avoid offense to either side: "It is a thorough conviction, that anarchy, degradation, and interminable distress will be, must be, the unavoidable results of a dissolution of the union of these States. . . . We may differ as to the time, the manner, or the extent of the measures to be employed, whether of conciliation or coercion. . . . If every man looks only to his own interest, or every State to its own favorite policy, and insists upon them, this Union cannot be preserved." And there was more praise for Jackson and more conciliatory talk; but no specific mention of South Carolina. This report was adopted in the Legislature Thursday, January 31.

Conciliation was also practiced by Van Buren in the election of Dudley's successor. His choice was his old law partner, Benjamin F. Butler; but the majority of the Regency were for Tallmadge. He had his way in the matter of Marcy's successor. Van Buren was living at Congress Hall, where Tallmadge also resided during the session. They visited each other in their rooms; but Van Buren never broached the Senatorship. Tallmadge gathered courage to say that his name had been mentioned as a successor to Dudley. Van Buren resorted to his favorite artifice of turning the conversation and inquired if Tallmadge had read George Canning's recently published work. Hearing a negative, Van Buren said he would send him the volumes, and left the room. The books were faithfully delivered, but Tallmadge had little heart for reading until the pressure of the Regents forced their Director to give his assent to Tallmadge's election.

Van Buren reached Washington on the last Tuesday in February. The following Monday he was inaugurated Vice President, the oath being administered by Chief Justice Marshall, who a few moments before had sworn in Jackson. Congress having adjourned the preceding Saturday, Van Buren had no work to do as Vice President until the Senate convened the following December. His stay at the White House was far from pleasant. Blair and Kendall had won over Jackson to their scheme of removing the Government funds from the Bank. When Kendall broached the subject to him, Van Buren heatedly said that the resolution adopted on March 2 in the House of Representatives declaring the deposits safe in Biddle's institution should have ended the agitation. Kendall answered that the recharter of the Bank before the next Presidential election was certain unless it was crippled by this blow. The Government's deposits exceeded those of all private depositors; and Kendall argued that the Bank would use the power that went with the deposits to corrupt Congress, and once rechartered, the opposition, aided by the Bank, would elect the next President of the United States. "I can live under a corrupt despotism as well as any other man by keeping out of its way, which I shall do," said Kendall, who threatened to lay down his pen if the deposits were not removed. But before leaving Washington Van Buren told him: "I had never thought seriously upon the deposit question until after my conversation with you; I am now satisfied that you were right and I was wrong."

Jackson and his intimate advisers had believed that Biddle, through his Bank, was aiming at control of the government. The record revealed Biddle as a petty pattern of Louis XVI, against whom, during his trial before the National Convention, was hurled: "All kinds of corruption were employed by you: you paid the expenses of publishing libels, pamphlets, and journals, which tended to pervert the public opinion . . ."

James Gordon Bennett was having a hard time this spring keeping the *Pennsylvanian* alive. He sent five begging letters to Hoyt in an effort to induce Van Buren to advance him money. First he suggested $10,000, then dropped to $2,500. When he obtained nothing he talked of the ten years he had worked "day and night for the cause of Mr. Van Buren and his friends," and of his hopes that he could find a friend "somewhere between heaven and earth" to enable him to carry out his "fixed purpose in favor of Van Buren and his friends." His failure to find this angel he blamed on "the Vice President himself." Bennett then indulged in a little polite blackmail: "I am beset on all sides with importunities to cut him [Van Buren]—to abandon him—what can I do? By a word to any of his friends in Albany he could do the friendship I want as easily as drink a glass of Saratoga water at the Springs. What shall I do? I know not. . . . I do not know whether it is worth while to write to Van Buren or not —nor do I care if you were to send him this letter."

He followed this with an appeal to Van Buren; but Van Buren declined to submit to blackmail. He informed Hoyt from his retreat at Saratoga Springs: ". . . I cannot directly or indirectly afford pecuniary aid to his [Bennett's] press . . . If he cannot continue friendly to me on public grounds and with perfect independence, I can only regret it, but I desire no other support. Whatever course he pursues, as long as it is an honest one, I shall wish him well." A month after this incident, Jackson, under date of September 19, said that "the Bank had bought up Bennett."

All through the summer Van Buren and Jackson corresponded on the Bank question. McLane, because he opposed the removals, had been transferred from the Treasury to the Department of State, vacant through the appointment of Livingston as Minister to France. William J. Duane, of Pennsylvania, son of the noted editor of the *Aurora*, was given McLane's place in expectation that he would give the orders for depositing the government moneys in the various banks, chartered by the States. Roger B. Taney, Attorney General, prepared a paper advocating the removals because of the Bank's duplicity in its dealings with the Government, its political activity, and its unconstitutionality. This was read by Jackson to his Cabinet on September 18. He disavowed any attempt to dictate to the Secretary, who was charged by law with control of the deposits, but assumed the responsibility of deciding that no more public money should be placed in the Bank and the Government's funds therein drawn out and deposited in State banks. Duane refused to sign the order and was dismissed. Taney succeeded him; and the removals commenced. Van Buren had his old law partner made Attorney General; but Butler, who knew he could make more money in private practice, took the post reluctantly.

All of Jackson's Cabinet, with the exception of Taney, were opposed to the removals, at least during the recess of Congress. This was Van Buren's attitude. Once Jackson had determined on his tempestuous course—wholly justified by the acts of aggression of the Bank—Van Buren was for the measure. This violent blow at the Bank's credit could only have been given by one of Jackson's mold, just as it took the cautious and calculating mind of Van Buren to find not only a substitute, insofar as the Government's needs were concerned, but a preventive against the revival of the Bank. This he was to accomplish a few years later. Historians have assumed, on the basis of erroneous conclusions of contemporaries of Jackson and Van Buren, that there was a temporary break between them over the removal of the deposits, and that Taney for a time was Jackson's closest adviser. Van Buren remained in New York until the middle of October, when the heavy assaults on the Bank had been under way for a fortnight. This and information gleaned from a fragmentary part of the correspondence between Jackson and Van Buren would tend to support these false assumptions. But the complete exchange of letters between Jackson and Van Buren shows that the friendship —there has been nothing like it in our political history; for Jackson loved Van Buren as a father does a son—continued unbroken, and that had Van Buren held out against a removal of the deposits during the recess of Congress, Jackson would have implicitly followed his advice.

Jackson was pitiably sick this summer. Only the excitement kept him up. On July 29, before leaving Washington for the Rips Raps, he penned, with obvious bodily pain, a four-page letter to Van Buren, wherein he recounted the reasons why the deposits should be removed. And he added this qualification: "Still as my health is feeble, & life uncertain, and the administration of the Government on my death must devolve on you, I would not wish to do an act of such importance, without having your full views upon this subject." Two days before the removals began Jackson wrote Van Buren: ". . . my duty to my country, & the perpetuity of our happy republican government dictated the course which I have adopted & if the people do not sustain me, then indeed a private station is the part of honor."

These removals were followed by many abuses. Three New York banks had been selected, and two of them Jackson described as the Macanics [Mechanics] and the M Hattan [Manhattan]. Taney, said Jackson, wanted Van Buren to name the fourth. Van Buren knew that any one who meddled in the selection of these banks stood a chance of being tarred. He resolved to keep clean in this, as he had done throughout his career in all matters involving money. "I have no choice," Van Buren answered. He said that he had "mentioned Mr. Taney's wish in respect to the additional bank to Mr. Cambreleng & requested him to confer with his associates in Congress from this city." The selections of the State banks to act as Government depositaries were made on recommendation of the politically powerful; hence their name— pet banks.

Meanwhile the Bank mustered all its forces for the fight, which was waged with renewed and desperate vigor in the press; and anticipating the convening of Congress on December 2, sought "to force a restoration of the deposits, and . . . extort a renewal of its charter" by trying to create a financial panic, as Jackson charged in his annual message. "It must now be determined whether the Bank is to have its candidates for all offices in the country, from the highest to the lowest, or whether candidates on both sides of political questions are to be brought forward, as heretofore, and supported by the usual means," Jackson said to Congress.

Van Buren arrived in Washington toward the end of the second week of the session, it being traditional for the Vice President to absent himself until the Senate committees had been appointed. On taking the chair on Monday, December 16, he made his first public utterance as the second officer of the land. It was short and one such as others before and after him have made; totally devoid of significance. It provoked no comment; but the coach he had brought over from England did. The adverse journals described it as an English coach of state—"a very splendid carriage, drawn by two beautiful blood-horses, their heads and tails full of a great deal more of intellect, passion, feeling, and sublimity than their owner. . . . It is of a dark-olive hue, with ornaments elegantly disposed, shining as bright as burnished gold," and "far more superb than the equipages of royalty."

Scarcely a day passed without Clay, Webster, or some of the lesser lights of the Senate presenting a memorial from some city telling of the distress of the people, and protesting against the removal of the deposits. These memorials were written by the same hand, or from a pattern supplied by agents of the Bank. Some of these meetings were undoubtedly of spontaneous origin; but their direction was singularly the same. In 1811, when the Bank attempted to extort a recharter from another unwilling Congress, it had resorted to similar means. Then it lost by the casting vote of Vice President Clinton.

On March 7, after Webster had presented a memorial from a meeting of building mechanics in Philadelphia, and moved its publication, Clay, rising to second, appealed to Jackson's supporters in the chamber to urge the President to retrace his steps, and abandon his fatal experiment. And then apostrophizing Van Buren, Clay said: "No one, sir, can perform that duty better than yourself. You can, if you will, induce him to change his course. . . . Go to him and tell him, without exaggeration, but in the language of truth and sincerity, the actual condition of his bleeding country. Tell him it is nearly ruined and undone by the measures which he has been induced to put in operation. . . . Depict to him, if you can find language to portray, the heart-rending wretchedness of thousands of the working classes cast out of employment. Tell him of the tears of helpless widows, no longer able to earn their bread, and of unclad and unfed orphans who have been driven, by his policy, out of the busy pursuits in which but yesterday they were gaining an honest livelihood. . . . Tell him of the ardent attachment, the unbounded devotion, the enthusiastic gratitude, towards him, so often signally manifested by the American people, and that they deserve, at his hands, better treatment. Tell him to guard himself against the possibility of an odious comparison with that worst of the Roman emperors, who, contemplating with indifference the conflagration of the mistress of the world, regaled himself during the terrific scene in the throng of his dancing courtiers. If you desire to secure for yourself the reputation of a public benefactor, describe to him truly the universal distress already produced, and the certain ruin which must ensue from perseverance in his measures. Tell him that he has been abused, deceived, betrayed, by the wicked counsels of unprincipled men around him. . . . Entreat him to pause and to reflect that there is a point beyond which human endurance cannot go; and let him not drive this brave, generous, and patriotic people to madness and despair."

Van Buren drank in every word of Clay's appeal. Long before he entered Congress he had read every speech of the Kentucky statesman he could lay his hands on. To him, Clay's oratory was matchless. He never took his eyes off the face of his foe during the delivery of this splendid specimen of histrionics. When Clay took his seat Van Buren surrendered his chair to a Senator, and with all eyes focused on him, he stalked slowly over to Clay's seat and whispered. Clay, somewhat astonished, complied with the request by offering Van Buren his snuff-box. Van Buren took a pinch of the rose-scented snuff—Clay always used the finest maccaboy Martinique produced—and walked away.

Clay's purpose was to cast part of the odium of the panic and its consequences on Van Buren. And the Bank agents arranged a meeting in Philadelphia at which resolutions were adopted asserting "that Martin Van Buren deserves, and will receive, the execrations of all good men, should he shrink from the responsibility of conveying to Andrew Jackson the message sent by the honorable Henry Clay, when the builders' memorial was presented to the Senate. . . ."

Three weeks later Clay introduced a resolution censuring Jackson for removing the deposits, holding that he had "assumed upon himself authority and power not conferred by the Constitution and laws, but in derogation of both." The resolution was adopted by a vote of 26 to 20. Benton at once served notice that he would move to expunge the resolution of censure from the Senate journal, which he did at the next session.

These attacks were having their effect. In New York City, Jackson's greatest stronghold in the north, the opposition, now calling themselves Whigs, carried a majority of the Common Council in the April elections. Cornelius Van Wyck Lawrence, the Jackson candidate for Mayor, was elected by the slim margin of one hundred and seventy-nine votes. The Jacksonians resorted to violence in their efforts to carry the city, as they were apprehensive of its effect on the gubernatorial election in the fall. Preserved Fish, Abraham LeRoy, and George D. Strong, and other blue bloods in Tammany incited the Irish to drive the Whigs from the polls. Not much persuasion was required, as the opposition to Jackson had cried down his Irish ancestry. On the third and last day of the election, Thursday, April 10, pitched battles occurred in the streets. Stones, cudgels, and dirks were freely used. When Gideon Lee, the Mayor, led a large body of watchmen to quell the rioting, the warring partisans turned on the police and routed them, injuring many; eight policemen were taken to the hospital. Then the battle between the Americans and the Irish—as the anti-Jacksonian press always designated the factions—was resumed, lasting until word reached them that a troop of cavalry and a regiment of infantry were on the way.

Although the Jacksonians elected their Mayor, the New

York election was distinctly a Whig triumph, as all the officials received their appointments from the Council. The following Tuesday the Whigs celebrated at Castle Garden, consuming 1,512 quarts of wine, and 40 barrels of beer. Food was also served. The victory in New York was the excuse for Whig jubilations elsewhere. These were jointly promoted by Whig leaders and agents of the Bank. A week after the Castle Garden meeting, a multitude was feasted on the outskirts of Philadelphia. Tens of thousands came from adjacent States. "The whole number congregated was supposed not to be less than fifty thousand. . . . Many cattle and other animals had been roasted whole, and there were 200 great rounds of beef, 400 hams, as many beeves' tongues, &c., and 15,000 loaves of bread, with crackers and cheese, &c., and equal supplies of wine, beer, and cider. . . . Strong bands of music played at intervals, and several salutes were fired from the miniature frigate, which were returned by heavy artillery provided for the purpose."

At these meetings Van Buren received "the execrations of all good men," and the comminations were continued in the Senate. Congress sat until the end of June. On the 23d of the month the Senate rejected the nomination of Andrew Stevenson, seven years Speaker of the House of Representatives, as Minister to England to succeed Van Buren. Jackson decided to help them in their efforts to make themselves ridiculous by letting it be known that he would not send in another name for this most important post. As both Jackson and Van Buren were avowed friends of England, this could be done without offense. It was not until the close of Jackson's term in 1836 that the Senate gave its assent. This affront to the President was followed by another: the rejection of Taney as Secretary of the Treasury.

With the view of hurting Van Buren in the South it was said that he favored freeing the slaves by act of Congress. In a letter to Stephen Gwin, of Clinton, Mississippi, a fortnight after the adjournment of Congress, Van Buren not only nailed this lie but proclaimed himself a staunch advocate of the slave-owning States. ". . . The subject is, in my judgment, exclusively under the control of the State Governments; and I am not apprised, nor do I believe, that a contrary opinion, to any extent deserving consideration, is entertained in any part of the United States.

. . . I do not see on what authority the General Government could interfere, without a change of the Constitution, even at the instance of either or of all the slaveholding States."

The deadliness of this falsehood lay in the fresh impetus given to the manumission movement by the Act of Parliament in the preceding year freeing some 800,000 blacks in the British West Indies. William Lloyd Garrison, who had been firing the North for the past four years with his uncompromising demand for immediate emancipation without compensation to the slave-owners —England indemnified the former owners of slaves—had become a living nightmare to the South. His *Liberator* was proscribed below the Mason and Dixon Line: the Legislature of Georgia offered $5,000 reward for the arrest of any one circulating it.

At the beginning of 1834, the little band of fanatics which gathered round Garrison when he began his labors in Boston, had swelled to considerable proportions. In New York the Abolitionists held several meetings, some in churches where the pastors and congregations went bodily into the movement. These gatherings had been attended throughout by considerable turbulence. On July 11 the anti-Abolitionists went to the homes of Lewis Tappan and his brother Arthur, two of the wealthiest and most conspicuous Abolitionists in the metropolis, broke the doors and windows, destroyed the small pieces of furniture, and hurled the large pieces to the street and made a bonfire of them. Then they marched through the city, attacking several churches, and were finally driven off by a regiment of infantry. John Quincy Adams —now in his third year as a member of the House of Representatives—and other conservative antislavery men, looked upon Garrison and the Abolitionists as incendiaries, and equally dangerous to the peace of the Union with Calhoun and his nullifiers.

The following month several hundred men, dressed as for a masquerade ball, assembled in the shadow of the unfinished Bunker Hill Monument. The hour was midnight. Many carried torches, others axes, and a few shouldered muskets. They marched in orderly ranks to their objective. The most dispassionate description of what happened thereafter, and its cause is found in Hone: "A most disgraceful riot occurred on the night of Monday, August 11, at Charlestown, near Boston. The populace having been deceived by ill-designed persons into an erroneous belief that a young lady was confined against her will in the Ursuline Convent, a highly respectable seminary under the charge of the Roman Catholics, made an attack upon the convent, a noble edifice, and the other buildings belonging to the sisterhood, and burned them to the ground with all the valuable furniture, desecrated the cemetery, and committed every species of outrage." There were about sixty young women in the convent when the mob, crying "No Popery!" gave the nuns a scant few minutes to leave the building with their charges. The firemen were driven off by the mob. At a meeting in Faneuil Hall, Harrison Gray Otis, Josiah Quincy, and others denounced the outrage. A committee of investigation appointed at this meeting disclosed the facts. The ringleaders were arrested; all save a youth were acquitted, and he was pardoned by the Governor of Massachusetts. The temper of the State was reflected in the refusal of the Legislature to indemnify the sisterhood for its loss.

Bigotry had been taught the generation by the politicians during the Anti-Masonic excitement.

Mobs next arose in Philadelphia, sacking and burning the homes of the freed blacks, destroying thirty buildings including two churches during the three nights of rioting. A negro asleep in his home was thrown through the window to the street below.

The State campaigns were waged on national issues. It was the prelude to the Presidential campaign of 1836. Van Buren wrote the address to the people of the Democratic-Republicans of New York State; he supervised the preparations of pamphlets, the speeches on the hustings, urging especially that ridicule be heaped on the Whigs, who were to be asked by what name they would be known in another year. The Whigs had made the spoils system and the Bank the dominant issues. The Van Burenites ignored the first, but answered the second with "Down with the Aristocracy!" and "The Rich Against the Poor!"

A new member was added to the Regency at the beginning of the campaign. Although only twenty-four years of age, he was regarded by Van Buren as possessed of more ability and undeveloped capacity than any other member of the Regency. The latest acquisition was his son John. He had sown the wildest of his wild oats; he still drank, but not more than the average youth in his set. He was an inveterate gambler, and, like his associates, given to profanity. His chief task was tabulating the predictions made by the various subordinate leaders in the machine, State and national.

John had lost heavily in stocks following the transfer of deposits: he had guessed the stock market the wrong way. He called on Washington Irving with a long face in the spring and bemoaned his losses. All his earnings from his law practice were wiped out. He vainly tried to borrow $1,000 from his father, but was able to raise funds somewhere to stay in the market. Most of his trading was done through Jesse Hoyt. When John gave him an order to buy and enclosed none of the wherewithal, Hoyt wrote back for money, provoking this response from John: "Why G—d d—n you Jesse! buy my stock and draw upon me at sight. You must be poor bitches down there, if you cannot raise this two penny sum. If the stock has gone up, let it go to Hell. The Bank will come against the Safety Fund Banks, and depress stocks—the Governor's message will eventually relieve the country."

The reason for John's anger was Hoyt's failure to understand that when he gave him the original order on Friday, March 22, 1834, he had information that Marcy would send a message to the Legislature recommending that the State extend its credit to the Safety Fund Banks to the extent of five to six million dollars. In his letter asking Hoyt to buy he wrote: "I fear stocks will rise after Monday. . . . There will be something done here [Albany] Monday. . . ." It was not until Tuesday that John heard from Hoyt. Marcy's message was then twenty-four hours old, and the necessary legislation to enable the State banks to continue specie payments, and extend their loans, was being drafted. Hoyt bought the stock on receipt of the second letter, but at the beginning of the fall campaign John was again in poor straits as the opening sentence of a letter to Hoyt revealed: "For God's sake send me my over coat—my underclothes are all worn out, and I'm a beggar."

Toward the close of the State election, in which John recouped most of his stock losses, Van Buren went to Kinderhook where the Whigs were making a desperate struggle so that their organs might publish: "Van Buren Defeated in His Native Village." From here, when confident of victory, Van Buren wrote to Hoyt: "I almost begin to pity the poor Whigs. Their next cognomen will be *Democrats*—mark what I say." The winnings of John totaled more than $9,000 in cash through Hoyt. Early in September he began placing wagers on Marcy's majority, on the fate of various candidates for Congress, and on the results in Ohio, Maine, and Pennsylvania. He could not lose, and knew it. "If you can," he wrote Hoyt three weeks before election, "get me an even bet against Marcy to any amount less than Five Thousand Dollars. . . . I consider Marcy's election, by from 7,500 to 15,000, as sure as God." Marcy defeated William H. Seward, "the young man with the sandy hair," by 11,000. In addition to cash Hoyt collected wagers consisting of fire-wood, wheat, hams, barrels of apples, bales of cotton, a $7 pair of boots, a $10 hat, and cases of champagne. John Duer lost a suit of clothes costing $50; Alexander Hamilton, Jr., $250 cash; John A. King, $100; Charles L. Livingston, $100; John Hone, the diarist's brother, $150. How much Van Buren himself won on the election is not disclosed.

Van Buren resumed the Vice President's chair with the opening of Congress. His opponents, disappointed over the results of the State elections, were downcast. They had used the very arguments they were counting on to win the next Presidential election, and had failed to impress the nation. Some were despondent; others desperate. The extreme of their desperation was revealed after Benton had made public his letter to Wiley Davis, of Mississippi, declining the nomination for President by its State convention, and citing the reasons why Van Buren should be nominated. Benton's colleague, Poindexter, who had voted for the resolution censuring Jackson, now became embittered toward Van Buren. The brilliancy of Poindexter's intellect was dulling under the effects of drink, dissipation and domestic embroilments. He was reckless in conversation and debate. Men feared to cross him. Within a few days of the publication of Benton's letter Van Buren learned that Poindexter intended to quarrel with him over some official trifle, and shape therefrom a situation which would lead to a duel or a beating, and thereby render Van Buren an object of scorn. Doubts as to the accuracy of his information vanished after the New Year when he received the prelude to a challenge. Poindexter's carefully phrased letter read in part:

The unusual punctuality, with which you attended, as the Presiding officer of the Senate at the commencement of the present session of Congress, has been attributed by certain newspapers edited by your friends and supporters, to considerations having a direct personal relation to myself. . . . I refer especially to an article in the Newburg Telegraph, which has been copied into other kindred prints, and cannot have escaped your observation:

The President of the Senate was in his chair at the opening of the session and thus preserved it from being disgraced by "that bloated mass of corruption—Poindexter."

. . . I will not permit myself to believe that in taking your seat at the opening of the session, you were actuated by the unworthy motives, which your friends have so indiscreetly attributed to you, until you manifest a disposition to place yourself in that attitude. I should much prefer for your own sake, and that of the august body over whose deliberations you have been called to preside, to regard your early attendance as an evidence of the promptitude and industry, with which you were anxious to discharge your public duties. It is now in your power, to give me this assurance which I consider *absolutely* necessary to avert the consequences of an opposite conclusion.

That evening there was a conference at the White House, with Forsyth and Silas Wright present as consultants to Van Buren and Jackson. All agreed that Poindexter intended to resort to violence. Meanwhile the conferees decided on this reply:

Washington Jan$^y$ 6$^{th}$, 1835.

SIR;

You are quite correct in not permitting yourself to believe that the official act to which you allude, in your letter of yesterday, was designed to arrogate to myself the right of deciding upon the propriety of the Senate's choice of their President pro tempore, or to interfere with the relations in which you or any other member, may stand to that body, and to the country.

Your very proper and explicit disclaimer of all idea of holding me responsible for the commentaries or constructions of the public press has enabled me so far to respect the official relations existing between us, and to which you refer, as to give you this answer.

I am Sir, your humble servt

M. VAN BUREN.

To the Hon$^{ble}$ George Poindexter.

Next morning, when Van Buren ascended the Vice President's chair he had a pair of pistols, loaded and cocked, concealed on his person. This was the first time that he had gone armed in his life. Less than four weeks later an incident occurred which convinced Jackson that Poindexter was bent on slaying him as well as Van Buren. While he was descending the east front of the Capitol after attending the funeral services for Representative Warren Ransom Davis, of South Carolina, a house painter named Richard Lawrence fired two pistols point-blank at Jackson. Both flashed in the pan. A local politician charged that the attempted assassination had been instigated by Poindexter. Jackson, in his morbid state of mind and body, believed the falsehood. Poindexter demanded an investigation by the Senate, and was exonerated. Lawrence, unquestionably crazy, was acquitted, and remanded to custody as insane. Poindexter did not carry out his intentions. Van Buren regarded the change in Poindexter's attitude toward him as having been dictated by Henry Clay, who learned of the Mississippian's mad design after the exchange of letters.

In February the Massachusetts Whigs nominated Webster for President. The election of 1836 was twenty-one months off, but the campaign was a month old, as Jackson's own State had nominated Hugh Lawson White, Jackson's successor in the Senate. White was a State-rights Whig. Webster had no strength outside of his own State. The Whigs of other Northern States were planning to make Major General William H. Harrison, the hero of Tippecanoe, their candidate. Harrison was rounding out his life on his farm at North Bend, Ohio, making ends meet with his little salary as clerk of the county court.

When the gavels fell in both houses on March 3, all eyes turned anxiously toward Baltimore, where on May 20, the Democratic-Republicans would hold their national convention. On this third Wednesday in May delegates from every State in the Union excepting Alabama, South Carolina, Illinois, and Tennessee, were in their seats when George Kremer, as temporary chairman, presented a clergyman to offer up prayer. Tennessee was absent because White was her candidate. Alabama had made the cause of White, and that of John Tyler, his running mate, her own. South Carolina, still playing a lone hand, had a candidate for President in Willie P. Mangum, of North Carolina; and supported Tyler for second place. There was more than personal feeling in White's candidacy for President: his supporters were Cotton Whigs, who agreed with their partisans of the North only in believing that Jackson had violated the Constitution. They differed with them on the Bank, the tariff, internal improvements, and State rights. Tennessee disapproved of national conventions, holding that the party in power would dominate their deliberations with "village politicians and placemen."

Although this was the first of the national conventions made up of place holders and others beholden to a Federal administration, it was not as thoroughly drilled as others that followed. When Romulus M. Saunders, of North Carolina, as chairman of the Committee on Rules, offered the undemocratic unit and two-thirds rules, he was outvoted, 231 to 210. The two-thirds rule had been adopted four years before to make Van Buren's nomination for Vice President all the more impressive. On the following day, there was a reconsideration of the vote by which the majority rule had been adopted; and the two-thirds and unit rules were substituted in its stead.

Andrew Stevenson was chosen permanent chairman. On announcing that the next business of the convention was to nominate a candidate for President, he filled the convention with smiles. Van Buren received the unanimous vote of every delegation present, as well as the fifteen votes of absent and unrepresented Tennessee! But one of the fuglemen found a native of Tennessee named Edward Rucker in town; and Rucker was recognized as the "delegation" from Jackson's home State. Rucker was obscure and unknown; but this piece of political magic gave him an unenviable prominence, and enriched the political argot of the day with the verb "to rucker."

The convention balked when the party managers moved the nomination of Senator Johnson of Kentucky. Had the Tennessee delegation—which did not exist save in the fancy of the convention—not been recognized, Johnson would not have been nominated. With the imaginary fifteen votes from Tennessee the total number of accredited delegates was 265; actually there were only 250 delegates present. Under the two-thirds rule, had the fictive fifteen been omitted from the reckoning, it would have taken 167 votes to nominate. The opposition to Johnson mustered 87, three more than the required number to block a nomination. But the fraudulent votes from Jackson's own State saved the day for Johnson, as he received 178 to the 87 cast for William C. Rives of Virginia. The opposition to Johnson was unanimous in the delegations from Maine, New Jersey, Virginia, Georgia, and North Carolina; and ten of the fourteen votes from Massachusetts went to Rives. But all save Virginia agreed to support Johnson. The Virginians adopted a resolution declaring that the Old Dominion had no confidence in either the principles or character of Van Buren's running mate; and chagrined with Van Buren, whom they held responsible for the admission of the non-existent Tennessee delegation, the Virginia delegates also placed on the record that they came to the convention to support principles, not men, and had wandered sufficiently far afield in voting for Van Buren.

On Friday the convention adjourned after an address to the electorate was drafted. No platform was adopted.

Van Buren had remained in Washington during the deliberations of the convention. In his letter of acceptance, Van Buren avoided discussing a single issue. "I am not aware," said he, "that there is any point of interest in the general policy of the Federal Government, in respect to which, my opinions have not been made known by my official acts—my own public avowals, and by the authorized explanations of my friends. If there be any such, however, you may rest assured of my ready disposition to comply, on all suitable occasions, with the wishes of my fellow citizens in this regard."

This letter has been condemned as inane and prolix. It was prolix, but not inane: there were eighteen months of campaign ahead, a hostile Congress, hostile State legislatures, a hostile press, and designing and resourceful enemies. These things he had in mind; and he intended, as the canvass progressed, to discuss new "points of interest" when raised, but only on "suitable occasions": and his foes did not select the occasions. He paid this tribute to Jackson: "I content myself, on this occasion, with saying, that I consider myself the honored instrument, selected by the friends of the present administration, to carry out its principles and policy; and that, as well from inclination as from duty, I shall, if honored with the choice of the American people, endeavor to tread generally in the footsteps of President Jackson —happy, if I shall be able to perfect the work which he has so gloriously begun."

He set the fashion for future nominees by protesting that he had not sought the nomination. He reminded the country of the apprehension entertained by the ruling cliques of the old world that the divine right of kings must give way before the sovereignty of the people. "We hold an immense stake for the weal or woe of mankind, to the importance of which we should not be insensible," he said. "The intense interest manifested abroad in every movement here, that threatens the stability of our system shows the deep conviction which pervades the world that upon its fate depends the cause of Republican Government. The advocates of monarchical systems have not been slow in perceiving danger to such institutions in the permanency of our Constitution, nor backward in seizing upon every passing event by which their predictions of its speedy destruction could be in any degree justified. Thus far, they have been disappointed in their anticipations, and the circumstances by which they were encouraged, however alarming at the time, have in the end only tended to show forth the depth of that devotion to the Union, which is yet, thank God! the master passion of the American bosom."

Every device was employed by the doomed order in its conflict with the inevitable. Less than five years before, a week after the Revolution of July, La Fayette, who had defended his faith in republics with his blood at Brandywine, presented Louis Philippe to the people, with: "We have done a good work. This is what we have been able to make most like a Republic." The monarchists debased this into: "Behold the best of Republics." So widely and zealously was this perversion propagated that it was accepted as truth years later by France's noblest writer. Hugo, too, had fought for freedom. But he missed La Fayette's disclaimer to General Bernard as this passage in his masterpiece indicates: "The 221 made Louis Philippe king, and La Fayette undertook the coronation. He named him *the best of Republics*, and the Town Hall of Paris was substituted for the Cathedral of Rheims." And the bourgeois King's successor, who proclaimed himself Emperor while President of the Republic, was the tool used by Europe to attempt the destruction of the Union by setting up the ill-starred Empire to the south of us when secession had become a reality. Van Buren had foreseen it; but in 1835 his adversaries translated his warning into an artful, self-serving appeal to the electors: they had heard the politician so long that they were deaf to the statesman.

The summer boded little good to Van Buren's candidature. The Abolitionists were flooding the Southern mails with incendiary broadsides and pamphlets. It was charged that the intent of these extremists was to incite a servile revolt. Color was lent to the accusation by the unbridled tongue of George Thompson, imported from England by the fanatics, who said that the slaves ought, or at least had the right, to cut the throats of their masters. The South searched the mail bags for the antislavery literature, which was burned publicly, or ceremoniously cast in the water. Slaves suspected of complicity with Abolitionists were summarily hanged. Two gibbets were erected in front of Garrison's home in Boston; and he was manhandled by a mob who were bent on wreaking vengeance on Thompson, who made his escape on a sailing vessel.

A postmaster in Calhoun's State, hoping to enmesh the administration in the fanaticism of the Abolitionists, and thereby hurt Van Buren in the South, placed the question before the Postmaster General. Kendall, who had held this place since May, after it had been shown that the Department under Barry had lost money through jobbery by mail contractors and others, avoided the pitfall by intimating that matter prohibited by State laws should not be transmitted through the mails. While the tumult was at its height Van Buren rested at Saratoga Springs, calm and unruffled, a plenteous supply of wine at his table: for he followed the custom of the day in sending a bottle to the tables of friends and acquaintances.

Toward the end of the summer three campaign biographies of Van Buren were on the presses. Two were the work of friendly hands: one of pamphlet size, by William Emmons; and a more pretentious volume by William M. Holland. The third was by David Crockett, one of the most picturesque and heroic products of the early American frontier, whose crude Falstaffian wit had made him a national figure before he left the Tennessee Legislature to serve his State in Congress. From a loyal Jacksonite, he had become a violent partisan of White. A more scurrilous document has not been penned against a candidate for the Presidency. To quote: "Van Buren is as opposite to General Jackson as dung is to a diamond. . . . He has no pedigree that I can trace back farther than his sire. During the war of the revolution, his father was considered on the *Whig* side, while his uncle, his father's brother, was a Tory, and it was said, occasionally aided, as a guide to British scouting parties. I state this fact merely to show the *breed*. . . . he is what the English call a dandy. When he enters the senate-chamber in the morning, he struts and swaggers like a crow in the gutter. He is laced up in corsets, such as women in town wear, and, if possible, tighter than the best of them. It would be difficult to say, from his personal appearance, whether he was man or woman, but for his large *red* [*sic!*] and *gray* whiskers."

Crockett, in his blind partisanship, believed the worst of the stories invented when Rufus King was reëlected United States Senator through the covert influence of Van Buren. After a fair summary of the extraordinary events leading to the Federal leader's choice by a Republican Legislature, Crockett wrote: ". . . Mr. King was well known to possess high-toned aristocratic feelings; and that he would not mix or associate with such men as Mr. Van Buren and me, who were nothing but the sons of little, petty, country tavern-keepers, unless it was his intention to make use of such folks as we were; and for such use he was willing to *pay*; and, unfortunately, in Mr. Van Buren he found a person not less willing to *receive* than he was to *pay*." Van Buren did not answer this untruthful and unsupported charge. He did not believe in defensive publications. Then, too, if he had any thought of replying at the beginning of the spring of 1836, he had waited too long, as a candidate for office cannot attack a man whose exit is made glorious by the glamour of heroism. After the publication of his book, Crockett joined Colonel James Bowie at the Alamo; and when Santa Anna's vastly superior numbers took the old Spanish fort, Crockett and five others alone were living of the little band of defenders. The six prisoners were taken before the Mexican leader, at whose throat Crockett sprang with bare hands when the frown of Santa Anna transformed the swords of his soldiers into the knives of butchers.

Following a rest at Saratoga, Van Buren visited Niagara Falls, and while on his way back, a letter from William Schley, of Athens, Georgia, brought forth a fresh disavowal from Van Buren that he entertained "views and opinions that are justly obnoxious to the slaveholding States." He recalled his expressed conviction denying that the Federal Government could interfere, and added: "I should poorly requite the candor with which I have hitherto been treated by the great mass of my fellow-citizens at the South, were I to allow myself to apprehend that those who would otherwise be disposed to give me their confidence could, under such circumstances, suffer me to be prejudiced in their opinion by the unsupported assertions of my enemies, however reckless or vehemently persisted in."

On his return to Washington Van Buren found a vast accumulation of mail. J. M. Van Buren, a cousin, wrote that he had been teaching since he graduated at Union College in June, when "for the special gratification of the Citizens of that Dutch place [Schenectady] I delivered my oration in the Holland, my vernacular language. . . . At Dr. [Eliphalet] Nott's levee he seemed to take uncommon satisfaction in complimenting the Dutch orator. . . ." He had abandoned pedagogy to study at the Theological Seminary at Auburn. He recalled occasions when Van Buren had helped him; and told of having an essay in the July number of the *North American Quarterly*. The subscription, *Yours affectionately*, and the address, *Honored and Respected Friend*, charmed; for there was no mistaking the gratitude and sincerity of the seminarian, who had lost his parents at an early age, and had been brought up by the Hogebooms at Kinderhook. Van Buren had advised him to practice law. "You will excuse me for taking the Ministry instead of Law, my conscience & feelings would not permit me to do otherwise," he explained; and reasoned that since mankind, "generally conceded th[e Minis]try * to be the most honorable calling, it certainly must be so in the sight of God." Van Buren cherished this letter, and at the bottom noted: "Sent him $30."

* Torn.

A letter from Marcy brought him back to his orbit with an inquiry as to what should be said on slavery in his annual message to the New York Legislature. Van Buren's response, although missing, is indicated by Marcy's condemnation of the conduct of the Abolitionists as tending to disturb the harmony of the Union by creating sectional jealousies.

Van Buren also had the papers of Jackson to supervise. The annual message to Congress must also discuss the Abolitionists and the far more pressing question of the nation's claims against France, which had almost led to war in 1834. These claims, arising out of the aggressions on our shipping under the despotic reign of Napoleon, had been a subject of fruitless negotiation for twenty years. European countries had collected similar debts, and Jackson's stern message of the previous year was justified by the advices from Livingston and France's failure to pay the initial instalment of one and one-half millions of francs in accordance with the terms of the treaty signed in the first year of the reign of Louis Philippe. France had agreed to pay twenty-five million francs, a paltry part of what was really due; the United States, in turn, was obligated to settle the claims of French citizens totaling one and one-half million francs. Congress had voted three million dollars, or three-fifths of the sum France owed us, for coastal defense.

We see Van Buren in such lines as these in Jackson's message: ". . . when France was overwhelmed by the military power of united Europe . . . whilst other nations were extorting from her payment of their claims at the point of the bayonet, the United States intermitted their demand for justice, out of respect to the oppressed condition of a gallant people, to whom they felt under obligations for fraternal assistance in their own days of suffering and peril. . . . The conception that it was my intention to menace or insult the Government of France, is as unfounded, as the attempt to extort from the fears of that nation what her sense of justice may deny, would be vain and ridiculous. . . . The people of the United States are justly attached to a pacific system in their intercourse with foreign nations. . . ."

Nowhere was there a withdrawal of a word previously uttered; instead, there was a spirited, yet, inoffensive, defense of what had been said and done. This message was read December 8. On

January 18 Jackson informed Congress that France had demanded that the United States make certain explanations or apologies in writing in terms which she shall dictate, "and which will involve an acknowledgment of her assumed right to interfere in our domestic councils." And, added Jackson, "she will never obtain it."

This second message would have been a preliminary to a formal declaration of war but for the conciliating counsel of Van Buren. Now the President recommended that the importation of French products and the entry of French ships be prohibited until she made "the tardy and imperfect indemnification . . . solemnly agreed upon by the treaty of 1831 . . ." On February 8, when the breach seemed wider than ever, the country learned through another message to Congress that England had offered to mediate. Two weeks later the country was apprised that the friendly offices of our ancient enemy had been successful. Jackson paid high tribute to "the elevated and disinterested part" England had played.

Van Buren's intimates knew that it was his hand which guided the pen of Jackson. Washington Irving, writing to Van Buren on February 1, said: "Much has been calculated on here from your moderation and discretion in this delicate matter, to temper the old General's 'heady valour' into true magnanimity." On February 24 Irving wrote Van Buren: ". . . By heaven you have brought us nobly through this affair and placed the country on a high footing abroad. I have been much pleased with the manner in which all the Messages this year have spoken on this subject. They have corresponded with the tone of some observations which dropped from you in the course of one of our conversations at Washington, and on which I founded hopes of a magnanimous and pacific course of policy. . . . I am inclined to give you great credit for the happy management of this matter, and for the able manner in which the *Collisions* between the two countries have been prevented from *striking fire*. I am happy to find the same opinion is entertained even by those who are usually disposed to gainsay your merits and misrepresent your actions. . . ."

But there was no such happy solution of the problem raised by the Abolitionists. Jackson recommended the enactment of a law to "prohibit, under severe penalties, the circulation in the Southern States, through the mail, of incendiary publications intended to instigate the slaves to insurrection." The opposition still controlled the Senate. A special committee was appointed to consider Jackson's recommendation. Calhoun dominated the deliberations of his associates which submitted a report, as well as a bill, intemperate, unrestrained, and certain to widen the breach between the North and South. It set forth that the States were sovereign and independent communities, and were united by a compact. This, in a word, was nullification. The report assumed that the South was menaced. Typical of the sentiments expressed are the following: ". . . Setting out with the abstract principle that slavery is an evil, the fanatical zealots come at once to the conclusion that it is their duty to abolish it regardless of the disasters which must follow. . . . The inevitable tendency of the means to which the abolitionists have resorted to effect their object must, if persisted in, end in completely alienating the two great sections of the Union. . . ."

The measure accompanying the report went further than Jackson intended. Calhoun demanded that the proposed law, known as the Incendiary Bill, be enacted under pain of secession, not merely of South Carolina, but of the entire South. "If you refuse coöperation with our laws," he said, "and conflict should ensue between your and our law, the Southern States will never yield to the superiority of yours. We have a remedy in our hands, which in such events, we shall not fail to apply. We have high authority for asserting that, in such cases, 'State interposition is the rightful remedy'—a doctrine first announced by Jefferson, adopted by the patriotic and republican State of Kentucky by a solemn resolution in 1798, and finally carried out into successful practice on a recent occasion—ever to be remembered—by the gallant State which I, in part, have the honor to represent." Calhoun was out-Garrisoning Garrison.

Those on the inside knew that the measure had no chance of passage, as at least six Senators from slave-holding States were opposed to the vicious principle of making a censor of every post-office employee in the land. Clay led the opposition; but he was not averse to Calhoun's plot to make it appear that Van Buren alone was responsible for its defeat: this was to be accomplished by throwing the fate of the bill into Van Buren's hands. Calhoun succeeded in effecting a tie vote of eighteen to eighteen to engross the bill: there were twelve absentees. When the vote was taken, Van Buren was out of the chair. Calhoun loudly demanded the presence of the Vice President, calling upon the sergeant-at-arms to produce him. Van Buren was pacing up and down behind the colonnade back of his desk. He let Calhoun enjoy a moment's thought that he had deliberately absented himself, and then took his seat, rising, a moment later, to give the casting vote for the engrossment. Calhoun's plan to inflame the South against Van Buren failed. The measure was defeated later by twenty-five to nineteen, New York's Senators, Wright and Tallmadge, voting with the minority.

Congress adjourned July 4. The disorderly campaign was then approaching its peak. The disorganized Whigs saw no hope save a division in the Electoral College which would throw the election into the House. Van Buren was making the campaign in his own way. Before the adjournment Adams, who had been a member of the House of Representatives since December, 1831, thus appraised, and justly, Van Buren and his principal opponents: "Van Buren's personal character, however, bears a stronger resemblance to that of Mr. Madison than to Jefferson's. These are both remarkable for their extreme caution in avoiding and averting personal collisions. Van Buren, like the Sosie of Molière's Amphitryon, is 'l'ami de tout le monde.' This is perhaps the great secret of his success in public life, and especially against the competitors with whom he is now struggling for the last step on the ladder of his ambition—Henry Clay and John C. Calhoun. They indeed are left upon the field for dead; and men of straw, Hugh L. White, William H. Harrison, and Daniel Webster, are thrust forward in their places. Neither of these has a principle to lean upon. Van Buren's principle is the talisman of democracy, which, so long as this Union lasts, can never fail."

But Van Buren was not "the friend of all the world." Biddle could testify to that. The charter of the Bank expired on March 4; and before its expiration, Van Buren, answering an invitation to be the guest of a partisan gathering in Cincinnati to celebrate "the deliverance of our country from the thralldom of the Bank of the United States," reviewed the various devices to which Biddle's institution resorted to extort a renewal of its charter from Congress, and said: "The people triumphed in that open contest, but before time had been allowed for seasonable celebrations of that triumph—even since your festival has been appointed, and before the day arrived for the expression of your joy—the same power, fighting under the same panoply, but changing altogether its approach, has again entered the field and gained a victory over the popular will . . . But how changed the mode of warfare in this last effort! Instead of commercial distress, public and private embarrassment, and all the concomitants of an uncontrollable panic in the public mind, plenty and even profusion pervaded the city of the Bank, while its noiseless approach to the legislative power was characterized by a dispatch altogether unprecedented in so important a matter in the history of legislation."

These cryptic utterances referred to the granting of a charter to the Bank by the Pennsylvania Legislature, after $400,000 had been mysteriously spent by Biddle's institution: this was unquestionably the price paid to the Pennsylvania lawmakers for extending the life of "the monster." He called the Bank "this aristocratic institution" which "mistook the character of that people whose stubborn necks it proposed to bend to its selfish and sinister designs." He had now reached the fullness of his years; and his belief in the people was no longer disturbed by doubtings.

Before starting for New York he reiterated his views on slavery in replying to six partisans of the town of Jackson, North Carolina, who inquired specifically if he believed Congress had the power to interfere with or abolish slavery in the District of Columbia. Congress at this time was being deluged with petitions from Abolitionists and other anti-slavery groups to prohibit slavery in the national capital. A plain categorical response to this inquiry would have lost him the South, as he would have had to answer: Yes. So he began the reply with repetitions of his avowals on slavery which had endeared him to the South, following them with the expression that "I have not been able to satisfy myself that the grant to Congress, in the Constitution, of the power of 'exclusive legislation in all cases whatsoever' over the Federal District, does not confer on that body the same authority over the subject that would otherwise have been possessed by the States of Maryland

and Virginia; or that Congress might not, in virtue thereof, take such steps upon the subject in this District, as those States might themselves take within their own limits, and consistently with their rights of sovereignty."

As a matter of law there was no doubting the power of Congress to abolish slavery in the district; but as a matter of equity, the national lawmakers should not disturb the existing situation. As Van Buren observed, the cession of the land comprising the seat of government would not have been made by the slave-holding States of Maryland and Virginia had the present agitation been foreseen, except on the express condition that Congress should not exercise this power; "and that with such a condition the cession would, in the then state of public opinion, have been readily accepted." But the rub of the letter lay in this: "I must go into the Presidential Chair the inflexible and uncompromising opponent of any attempt on the part of Congress to abolish slavery in the District of Columbia, against the wishes of the slave-holding States; and also with the determination equally decided, to resist the slightest interference with the subject in the States where it exists." And the high level on which Van Buren sought to keep the campaign was exemplified in the subsequent sentence: "In saying this, I tender neither to them nor to you any pledges, but declare only settled opinions and convictions of duty."

When one of Clay's lieutenants, Sherrod Williams, a Representative from Kentucky, tried to force Van Buren to answer a series of questions before Congress adjourned, he publicly replied he would not reply until after adjournment. Harrison had answered the queries promptly; but Van Buren in declining to do so, said that he would not permit an avowed partisan foe to pick his own time and place to interrogate him; and further, he might, as Vice President, be called upon to vote on some of the matters involved. Williams said these reasons were wholly unsatisfactory. Van Buren curtly responded that Williams must wait. The Kentuckian, openly supporting Harrison, had asked the two chief candidates if they approved of: 1, A distribution of the surplus revenue of the nation among the States according to their population for such uses as they might appoint. 2, A like distribution of the proceeds of the sale of public lands. 3, Federal appropriations to improve navigable streams above ports of entry. 4, Another charter for the Bank if it should become necessary to preserve the revenue and finances of the nation. 5, Expunging records of proceedings of either House of Congress. Harrison had answered the first four in the affirmative, and the fifth in the negative.

Van Buren's answer to the first of these questions, if we had no other record before us, in itself gives the quietus to the oft-repeated line of writers of the period that he was "an echo of Jackson." This related to the proposed distribution of the surplus of $35,000,000 in the national treasury to begin on January 1, 1837. Jackson, who first objected to the measure, signed the bill when it reached him. The financial stringency was being felt everywhere with growing intensity, and the Distribution Act was popular. Van Buren replied that he was opposed to this legislation, insisting that Congress lacked the power to raise money for distribution among the States. "I hope and believe that the public voice will demand that this species of legislation shall terminate with the emergency that produced it." He also disapproved the distribution of the moneys from the sale of public lands to the States, holding that the funds should be applied to the general wants of the Treasury. In this he was one with Jackson. He also opposed, as did Jackson, appropriations for improvements of rivers above ports of entry save for expenditures for lighthouses, buoys, beacons, piers, and the removal of obstructions to navigation. If the people wanted a President who would approve a new charter for the Bank, or any other bank, they must elect some one else, as he was irrevocably opposed to the proposal; he added that it was high time the Federal Government confine itself to the creation of coin and that the States afford it a fair chance for circulation. Answering the last question he said the President would have no voice in expunging proceedings in Congress, but that he believed the adoption of Benton's expunging resolution would be "an act of justice to a faithful and greatly injured public servant, not only constitutional in itself, but imperiously demanded by a proper respect for the well-known will of the people."

The campaign of the opposition was a mild repetition of Jackson's first campaign. Van Buren was "the mistletoe politician, nourished by the sap of the hickory tree." Calhoun stigmatized the followers of Van Buren as "a powerful faction (party it cannot be called) held together by the hopes of public plunder, and marching under the banner whereon is written: 'to the victors belong the spoils.'" The *American,* still edited by Charles King, editorialized on October 28: "Mr. Van Buren . . . consorts most naturally with the degraded and the vile—for among them he is a superior." Six days later: "The good we desire we may not be able to attain: but the evil we dread, the great and menacing evil, the blighting disgrace of placing Martin Van Buren, illiterate, sycophantic, and politically corrupt, at the head of this great republic, and Richard M. Johnson, the husband of a negress and the father of a motley brood, in its second seat of honor; that evil and disgrace, by united exertion, we *can avert* and such a consummation is surely worth some trouble and the sacrifice of personal predilections." This also was fed to its readers: "Gen. Harrison was received with enthusiasm at Columbia, the old military station at the Points of Fork. At night, the citizens procured a tar barrel and several of them proceeded to light it with candles. At the moment of ignition, out popped a snake which had found a residence in the barrel. It was pursued by shouts of 'Van Buren! Van Buren! Here he goes! Put it to him!' amidst an uproar of mirth and applause."

Throughout the closing months of the canvass Van Buren remained in Albany, making occasional visits to lieutenants in other parts of the State who had not found it convenient to call upon him at Saratoga Springs—where he spent most of August— or at his home. Here he received news of his victory, his popular vote being 762,678, to the 735,651 for all his opponents. In the Electoral College the vote was: Van Buren, 170; Harrison, 73; White, 26; Webster, 14; Mangum, 11. Van Buren carried Maine, New Hampshire, Rhode Island, Connecticut, New York, Pennsylvania, Virginia, North Carolina, Alabama, Mississippi, Louisiana, Arkansas, Missouri, Illinois, Michigan; Harrison swept Vermont, New Jersey, Delaware, Maryland, Kentucky, Ohio, Indiana; White polled the votes of Georgia and Tennessee, Webster those of Massachusetts, and Mangum won South Carolina's eleven. Had Van Buren lost his own State, Pennsylvania, or Virginia, the Whigs would have thrown the election into the House, where Harrison would have probably been chosen, as the Whigs and opposing members of the Democratic party—as the party was now generally known—mustered a majority. The Electoral College now consisted of 294 votes, requiring 148 to elect. Virginia, after voting for Van Buren, cast her twenty-three votes for William Smith of Alabama for Vice President. This defection left Johnson with only 147 votes. This threw the contest into the Senate; but here the Van Burenites had a majority, and Johnson was chosen on the first ballot.

Van Buren reached Washington late in November. He spent much time with Jackson; and on learning that John Quincy Adams had reached the capital, immediately paid him a formal visit, which the ex-President returned on December 10. Abraham Van Buren, who had been promoted to a captaincy of dragoons in July, was again aiding his father in the rôle of amanuensis. Yet Van Buren still wrote letters of a personal nature in his own hand; one penned three days before Christmas showed a side known only to his chosen intimates. It also revealed a kindliness of spirit on the part of Marcy on which the record is otherwise silent. This letter, which is addressed to John Van Buren, leaves much to the imagination. It is evident from the letter that a friend of Van Buren, now very old, and too poor to go to Washington to see Van Buren inaugurated, had been inveigled into an absurd election bet by Marcy so that the old man would have the means to gratify his wish. The aged gambler's name is not mentioned by Van Buren, only his initials, V. W.; and we may assume that he was a Van Winkle, a Van Wagenen, or one of the other Van W——'s who were determined to see the first Dutchman inducted into the Presidency. Van Buren wrote: "Gov. M[arcy] suggested to me that our friend V. W. so arranged it with him (by way of a bet) that he was to pay something toward fitting * out Mr. V. W. for Washington to witness the Inauguration, & that he had been requested to suggest to me a contribution, which I cheerfully agreed to make & intimated to him that I would have word with you upon the subject. I have not heard of any thing else & have nothing else in my power. I wish therefore that you would advance him $30 for me to be applied to that object, or if he should when the time comes think the sight not worth the trouble, to any other purpose that suits him better. He is a good natured man . . . but I am sure when he takes into considera-

\* Van Buren erroneously wrote *filling*.

tion the time of the year &c he will be inclined to think that he can upon the whole make better use of his money. Advise him frankly what is for his best."

New Year's Day witnessed the distribution to the States of the first instalment of the surplus in the Treasury. This took $9,367,000 from the "pet banks." For a fortnight or so there was no appreciable effect on the strained financial situation of the country, which had been growing more tense since the summer of 1834. Later in the month, after two days' debate, Benton succeeded in having the censure passed upon Jackson three years earlier for removing the Government's funds from the Bank, expunged from the Senate journal.

Van Buren took his leave of the Senate on January 28. King was elected President pro tempore for the remaining five weeks of the term.

When Van Buren began to prepare his message to Congress, the clouds, which were to overshadow his entire administration, began to gather. On Friday, February 10, placards appeared on the dead walls of New York City reading:

BREAD! MEAT! RENT! FUEL!
Their Prices Must Come Down!
*The voice of the people shall be heard and will prevail.*
The people will meet in the Park, *rain* or *shine,* at
4 o'clock Monday Afternoon,
To enquire into the cause of the present unexampled distress, and to devise a suitable remedy. All friends of humanity, determined to resist monopolists and extortionists, are invited to attend.

| | |
|---|---|
| Moses Jacques, | Daniel Gorham, |
| Paulus Hedl, | John Windt, |
| Daniel A. Robertson, | Alexander Ming, Jr., |
| Warden Hayward, | Elijah F. Crane. |

*New York, February 10th, 1837.*

Some of the newspapers carried the same intelligence as paid advertisements. The signers were leaders of the Equal Rights party, composed of radicals who had withdrawn from Tammany two years before as a protest against the control of the organization by Wall Street bankers. Van Buren, who was soon to go further than even the Equal Rights men had planned for themselves, had attempted to compose these differences. But the Equal Rights men, or Loco-focos, as they were derisively called, were determined to clean house in their own way, and nominated a State ticket headed by Isaac L. Smith of Buffalo. Dr. Moses Jacques—he was prominent in the medical profession—was candidate for Lieutenant Governor. It was he who headed the list of signatories for the meeting in the Park. A similar one had been held three weeks earlier in the old Broadway Tabernacle.

At the appointed time the Park was thronged with several thousand men and women. Mayor Lawrence watched the proceedings from the windows of his office. Hundreds in the assemblage came from fuelless and foodless hovels immediately to the north of the City Hall. There were many undernourished boys in the throng. These, or such of them as had homes, lived in the Sixth Ward, the most poverty-stricken section of the city. Present also were many small merchants and professional men who sympathized with the purposes of the meeting. All cheered the attack on the dealers in wheat, who were asking $15 a barrel for flour which a short time before brought $8. "Fellow citizens," said one of the speakers menacingly, "Mr. Hart has fifty-three thousand barrels of flour in his stores. Let us go and offer him $8 a barrel, and if he does not take it—" A friend tapped the speaker on the shoulder, warning him to be careful. "And if he does not take it," he continued, "we shall depart from him in peace."

These last words were uttered in a tone which instantly transformed a small part of the peaceful gathering into a mob, which marched down snow-covered Broadway to Dey street, where it turned west; and in another two or three minutes it was storming the iron doors of the warehouse of Eli Hart. One of the doors was forced, and thirty barrels of flour rolled on the street before Hart returned with a body of policemen. They were instantly charged by the rioters; but by good fortune the police managed to get into the warehouse and drove out the comparatively few who had usurped possession. By this time Mayor Lawrence arrived and addressed the mob.

While he was talking the rest of the hungry or determined ones who had been listening to the speeches in the Park appeared, increasing the number of rioters by many hundreds. They showered the Mayor with snowballs, and as he fled, the handful of policemen were put to rout. Now the mob began its work in earnest: barrels of flour thrown from the upper floors exploded like bombs as they struck the pavement. Six hundred barrels went this way, and more than a thousand bushels of wheat.

Women, covered from head to foot in flour, walked off with their aprons bulging, and the more provident, who brought baskets or boxes, filled these from the street, now knee-deep in flour.

The mob next stormed and took the warehouse of S. H. Herrick & Company, but before they had hurled a hundred barrels of flour to the street, the city's entire police force, with the troops not far behind, drove them off. Many were arrested and sent to prison for long terms, but no attempt was made to apprehend Dr. Jacques or his aides. The convicted men, jobless workers all, save two boys, were fortunate, for they had food and warmth in jail, while many of their fellows, unable to find work, or food, or fuel, died of starvation or were frozen to death. Horace Greeley, who headed the relief committee in the Sixth Ward, was so moved by the scenes of suffering, that he openly embraced the Communistic teachings of Fourier while maintaining his political integrity as a Whig.

The troops stopped the sacking of the flour warehouses, but not the suffering. Van Buren did not relish reading the accounts of starving women risking a shot from a soldier's musket the night of the riot to gather up handfuls of flour from the sidewalks. His inauguration was only a fortnight away. But Jackson was in the seventh heaven. On March 2 the General wrote to Nicholas P. Trist: "On the 4th I hope to be able to go to the Capitol to witness the glorious scene of Mr. Van Buren, once rejected by the Senate, sworn in by Chief Justice Taney, also being rejected by the factious Senate." The next day Captain Abraham Van Buren resigned his commission to accept the post of secretary to the President.

# CHAPTER XXXVII

No⊤ since its foundation had Washington known a more pleasant inauguration day than fell on the first Saturday of March, 1837. The sun beamed down with summer splendor. Only the snow on the hills and a nipping breeze remained to remind one that winter had not yet departed. After breakfast Van Buren drove to the White House, which he had insisted must remain the residence of Jackson until he had recovered his health. A little before noon, against the advice of his physician, Jackson took his seat beside Van Buren in the new phaeton, made from wood of the frigate *Constitution,* a present from Tammany to the retiring President. At the crack of the whip the four dappled grays turned out of the grounds and up Pennsylvania avenue, escorted by a small body of cavalry and infantry and a large contingent of civilians. The cheers of twenty thousand greeted their arrival at the Capitol. The crowd parted for them as they made their way up the steps. Reaching the Senate Chamber the procession was formed; and "Van Buren, attended by the ex-President, the Members of the Senate, of the Cabinet, and the diplomatic corps, led the way to the rostrum erected on the ascent to the eastern portico." N. P. Willis described the ensuing scene: ". . . the ex-President and Mr. Van Buren advanced with uncovered heads. A murmur of feeling rose from the moving mass below, and the infirm old man, emerged from a sick chamber, . . . bowed to the people, and still uncovered in the cold air, took his seat . . . Mr. Van Buren then advanced, and with a voice remarkably distinct, and with great dignity, read his address to the people. . . . I stood myself on the outer limit of the crowd, and . . . his words came clearly articulated to my ear."

The address is unmistakably Van Buren; no alien thoughts find lodgment there; but throughout the finishing touches of Butler and of his sons Abraham and John are noticeable. Save for a few sentences, the five thousand words in the document constitute a spirited defense of our experiment in democracy; nay,

400

more, a pæan to the triumph of the test. But this was overlooked by the Whig journals, which riddled an occasional poorly constructed sentence, notably the observation that he was the first President born under the Stars and Stripes: "Unlike all who have preceded me, the revolution that gave us existence as one people was achieved at the period of my birth; and while I contemplate with grateful remembrance that memorable event, I feel that I belong to a later age, and that I may not expect my countrymen to weigh my actions with the same kind and impartial hand." His birth, and not the Revolution, was the memorable event he had in mind, pedantically observed Charles King in the *American.* With Van Buren's capacity for dramatization, what would he have done, had he but known that, two hundred years before to a day, the first of his ancestors of whom there is record landed on Manhattan Island, bringing back his bride, the fair Catelijntje, who hugged their infant child closer as they made their way to the rude wooden church under the sheltering guns of the fort?

The whole tenor of the address was to effect an understanding between the North and the South; and so successful was his effort that Calhoun and his nullificationists acknowledged his leadership. The conversion of Calhoun was credited to his ambition to succeed Van Buren. Clay, on the Senate floor, recalled that the South Carolinian had once compared Van Buren to "the most crafty, most skulking, and the meanest of the quadruped tribe." Clay testified to his own high appreciation of the personal quali-  ties of Van Buren: "I have always found him . . . civil, courteous, and gentlemanly; and he dispenses . . . a generous and liberal hospitality. An acquaintance with him of more than twenty years' duration has inspired me with a respect for the man, although I regret to be compelled to say, I detest the magistrate." The Abolitionists charged that he had sold himself to the South; yet he thus animadverted to the attacks on them, and to similar manifestations of mob spirit: "Occasionally, it is true, the ardor of public sentiment, outrunning the regular progress of the judicial tribunals, or seeking to reach cases not denounced as criminal by the existing law, has displayed itself in a manner calculated to give pain to the friends of free government, and to encourage the hopes of those who wish for its overthrow. These occurrences, however, have been far less frequent in our country than any other of equal population on the globe. . . ."

He noted that the Republic had passed through experiences which the foes of democracy had predicted would mean the wreck of the experiment, especially the extension of its domain, the multiplication of sovereign States, and the increase of population. "Our system was supposed to be adapted to boundaries comparatively narrow. These have been widened beyond conjecture; the members of our confederacy are already doubled; and the numbers of our people are incredibly augmented. . . . Overlooking partial and temporary evils as inseparable from the practical operation of all human institutions, and looking only to the general result, every patriot has reason to be satisfied. . . .

"The last, perhaps the greatest, of the prominent sources of discord and disaster supposed to lurk in our political condition, was the institution of domestic slavery. Our forefathers were deeply impressed with the delicacy of this subject, and they treated it with a forbearance so evidently wise, that, in spite of every sinister foreboding, it never, until the present period, disturbed the tranquillity of our common country. Such a result is sufficient evidence of the justice and patriotism of their course; it is evidence not to be mistaken, that an adherence to it can prevent all embarrassment from this, as well as every other anticipated cause of difficulty or danger . . . the least deviation from this spirit of forbearance is injurious to every interest . . ."

He regarded his election as an indorsement of his opposition to every attempt on the part of Congress to abolish slavery in the District of Columbia against the wishes of the slaveholding States, and gave added assurance that he would veto any such measure if it came before him. Once more he referred to the mob attacks on the Abolitionists; this time as terrifying scenes of local violence. Again he was optimistic of a happy settlement; for "neither masses of the people nor sections of the country have been swerved from their devotion to the bond of union, and the principle it has made sacred. It will ever be thus. Such attempts at dangerous agitation may periodically return . . . That predominating affection for our political system which prevails throughout our territorial limits, that calm and enlightened judgment which ultimately governs our people as one vast body, will always be at hand to resist and control every effort, foreign or domestic, which aims to overthrow our institutions."

Jackson's deep affection for Van Buren was whole-heartedly returned, and his fine tribute to the ailing old man who sat bareheaded, happy in leaving the Presidency, and happier that Van Buren was entering it, was also seized upon by the Whig journals as meet for ridicule. Jackson knew the deep, filial love Van Buren bore him, and we can see his pallid cheeks glow as he hears the sincere voice ring out his praises, which are followed by a prayer that ends with a blessing. "In receiving from the people the sacred trust twice confided to my illustrious predecessor, and which he discharged so faithfully and well," said Van Buren, "I know that I cannot expect to perform the arduous task with equal ability and success. But, united as I have been in his councils, a daily witness of his exclusive and unsurpassed devotion to his country's welfare, agreeing with him in sentiments which his countrymen have warmly supported, and permitted to partake largely of his confidence, I may hope that somewhat of the same cheering approbation will be found to attend upon my path. For him I but express, with my own, the wishes of all—that he may yet long live to enjoy the brilliant evening of his well-spent life; and, for myself, conscious of but one desire, faithfully to serve my country, I throw myself, without fear, on its justice and its kindness. Beyond that I only look to the gracious protection of the Divine Being, whose strengthening support I humbly solicit, and whom I fervently pray to look down upon us all. May it be among the dispensations of His providence to bless our beloved country with honors and with length of days; may her ways be ways of pleasantness, and all her paths be peace."

When Van Buren finished his address, Taney, Chief Justice of the United States Supreme Court, whom the Senate had rejected as Attorney General, administered the oath of office to the eighth President of the United States. Jackson's happiness was now complete. The scene restored his health, and in the evening he attended the inaugural ball at Carusi's.

What Van Buren's emotions were as he returned that evening to the house which had been his home during the past four years we can only fancy. Thirteen years earlier he had made his début as a Warwick of democracy, a circumstance due, in no small measure, to the advice given him by Burr a decade earlier as they rode from Schenectady to Albany. Burr was now at rest in the family plot at Princeton. He had died penniless the preceding September, the object of charity of a woman who had known him in his days of prosperity. Others, who had had great expectations of Van Buren, had also set forth on their last adventure. He could not avoid thinking of her who had never doubted his greatness as he saw their four children gathered round him; all save the youngest had voted for him: Smith Thompson had lacked two months of his majority when the balloting was on.

Before the summer was out Van Buren started to finish what Jackson had commenced: the divorce of the bank and state. This was to be accomplished through the establishment of a depository for the nation's funds, the Sub-Treasury, the great achievement of his administration. The power that had been Biddle's was not destroyed: it had merely been transferred to the host of state banks in which the government had placed its money. These "pet" banks had labored for Van Buren's election; their opposition would have spelled his defeat. To oppose this vast aggregate of wealth, with the tremendous influence that went with it, took courage.

Jackson had advantages in his fight on the Bank on which his successor could not count: the glamour of glory won on the battlefield; a prosperous people who had long venerated him; and powerful allies in the very institutions Van Buren would have for foes.

Jackson had sufficiently regained his health to start for the Hermitage three days after the inauguration. Van Buren accompanied him to the station of the new railroad, where the Orestes and Pylades of American politics took an affectionate leave of each other. Van Buren was deaf to Jackson's plea that he did not want a doctor to travel with him; but Van Buren was President, and the Surgeon-General of the United States Army was under his orders; so the old hero smilingly accepted the medical officer as a traveling companion on his way home.

At the outset of his administration Van Buren learned that he need expect not even the suggestion of a fair deal from the opposition press. His very utterances were distorted. His most implacable foe among the Washington correspondents was

Matthew L. Davis, the literary executor of Burr, then working on the latter's life and letters. That we may not have an unjust measure of Davis, who signed his articles in the *Morning Courier* and *New York Enquirer* "The Spy in Washington," this story should be retold: He was showing a friend hundreds of love letters to Burr, some signed by women of wealth and position. When Davis's companion observed that these billets-doux could enrich a blackmailer, Davis cast them into the open fire. Yet in describing Van Buren's reception to the diplomatic corps, Davis wrote that the President was flurried, ill at ease, and blunderingly addressed them as the Democratic corps. In commenting on the President's address in the same issue of March 10, the journal, addressing the Chief Magistrate as "Mr. Matty Van Buren," said: "As for the Presidency's being 'the highest of all marks of the country's confidence' we are compelled to say that the fact of your election utterly overturns that idea."

Van Buren made only one appointment in the Cabinet, naming Joel R. Poinsett, an uncompromising Union man from South Carolina, Secretary of War to succeed Lewis Cass, whom Jackson named Minister to France. John Forsyth, of Georgia, was Secretary of State; Levi Woodbury, of New Hampshire, Secretary of the Treasury; Mahlon Dickerson, of New Jersey, Secretary of the Navy; Amos Kendall, of Kentucky, Postmaster General; and his old law student and partner, Benjamin F. Butler, was prevailed upon to continue as Attorney General. Although the Cabinet, with the exception noted, was named by Jackson, it was largely of Van Buren's selection; and all were friends of long standing save Kendall. As Cabinets go, it was far above the average in ability and capacity.

But no group of men, however able, could check the financial panic which distressed the nation shortly after the adjournment of Congress. It has been the fashion to attribute the upheaval to Jackson's fight on the Bank. His specie circular of July 11, 1836, is regarded by those who hold this view as an immediate cause of the crash. These were minor factors. The panic had its genesis in the opening of the Erie Canal in 1825. This started the country on a career of canal and road building, followed by the construction of railroads and steamboat lines. These improvements led to the settlement of new villages and towns. All this called for the extension of credits. Until the speculator entered the field, the expansion had no effect on the resources of the country's financial institutions. The speculator projected improvements which included villages, towns, and even cities, for which there were neither settlers nor demand. The unprecedented prosperity attracted European capital, and conservative business men were ensnared by the mania for speculation, which reached its peak in 1835. The sales of public lands afford us the best indicia of the extremes into which the unwary had plunged. In 1834 the sales of public lands amounted to $4,500,000; in the ensuing two years $39,500,000—mostly paper signed by favorites of the banks—was invested in these unproductive lands. To check this evil the Treasury Department ordered that payments for public lands be in specie. An exception was made of bona fide settlers, who were granted an additional six months' grace. As the nation sold its land for $1.25 an acre, the actual tiller of the soil was not hard pressed, as he owned little, and had little to find. The speculating frenzy extended into every realm of trade and commerce, the total loans and discounts of all the banks being increased from $354,000,000 in 1834 to $457,000,000 in 1836.

Two weeks after the adjournment of Congress Hone noted: "The prospects in Wall street are getting worse and worse. . . . The accounts from England are very alarming; the panic prevails there as bad as here." On March 28 the New York merchants, seeing ruin staring at them, drafted a letter appealing to Biddle to save them. They might as well have asked the mill wheel to stem the stream which turned it. Within the next ten days ninety-eight New York business houses went bankrupt, and thereafter the failures were so numerous that count was lost of them. Land at Broadway and 100th street, which had sold seven months before for $480 a lot, now changed hands for $50. This was symptomatic of what was happening in other commercial and industrial communities.

At the end of April the New York merchants met in Masonic Hall and appointed a committee to urge Van Buren to repeal the specie circular and call an extra session of Congress. This had been Biddle's advice. Hone thus appraised the situation: "No man can calculate to escape ruin but he who owes no money. Happy is he who has a little, and is free from debt."

While the committee was vainly importuning Van Buren one of the New York banks failed. The next evening, May 9, all the New York banks agreed to suspend payment in specie. The paper they offered in lieu of gold and silver had greatly depreciated. "Where will it all end?" asked Hone, who answered: "In ruin, revolution, perhaps civil war."

A packet brought intelligence that fears were entertained for the stability of the Bank of England. Hone, who regarded Jackson and Van Buren as the cause of the distress, ironically observed: "Markets continue extravagantly high; meat of all kinds and poultry are dear as ever. The farmers (or rather the market speculators) tell us this is owing to the scarcity of corn; but the shad, the cheapness of which in ordinary seasons makes them, as long as they last, a great resource for the poor, are not being bought under seventy-five cents and a dollar. Is this owing to the scarcity of corn, or are the fish afraid to come into our waters lest they be caught in the vortex of Wall street?"

The suspension of the New York banks led to bank suspensions throughout the country. Many shared Hone's alarm of revolution or civil rage. The suffering among the laborers and mechanics in the cities now extended to the ranks of clerks, professional men, and merchants. The only classes which did not feel the pinch of want, or the absence of customary luxuries, were the very rich and the farmers: the panic did not affect the fecundity of the soil, the fertility of the hens, or the productivity of the cattle.

The effrontery of Biddle, whom Van Buren regarded as a contributory cause of the panic, was shown by his visit to the White House. Van Buren received him and talked about everything save banking and commercial distress. Biddle published a card informing the public of Van Buren's silence "upon the great and interesting topics of the day." This was followed by an editorial by Bennett in his *New York Herald* reading: "The first symptoms of the mania which has produced the present revolution, developed themselves in the Spring of 1829, when Mr. Van Buren, a common country lawyer, who began life by trundling cabbages to market in Kinderhook, perfumed with Cologne water, and his yellow whiskers arranged *à la Paris*, presented the famous Safety Fund scheme of banking in Albany. . . . Martin

Van Buren and his atrocious associates form one of the original causes of the terrible moral, political, and commercial desolation which spreads over the country. . . . Nicholas Biddle . . . is such an aristocrat as you will find in heaven—Martin Van Buren such a democrat as you will discover coiled up in any burning corner in the other place— . . ." A blackmailing snob makes a contemptible foe.

On May 15, less than six weeks after Van Buren had declined to call an extra session, the demand became so general that he issued a proclamation convening Congress on the first Monday in September. This gave him three and a half months in which to formulate a remedy, or at least a palliative, for the crisis. Two days later, Abbott Lawrence, head of the largest cotton and woolen commission houses in the country, told a mass meeting of fellow Bostonians that no other people were so abused, cheated, plundered, and trampled upon by their rulers as Americans. He advanced sinister counsel: no overt act should be committed by the people until the laws of self-preservation compelled a forcible resistance; "but the time might come when the crew must seize the ship." In New York, where the Whigs had been triumphant in the April charter elections, Van Buren's refusal to repeal the specie circular was described as "a more high handed measure of tyranny than that which cost Charles the First his crown and his head—more illegal and unconstitutional than the act of the British ministry which caused the patriots of the Revolution to destroy the tea in the harbor of Boston—one which calls more loudly for resistance than any act of Great Britain which led to the Declaration of Independence."

The friends of the administration countered with meetings equally large and fiery. Thousands of Philadelphians commended Van Buren's course, and adopted resolutions wherein occurred: "We hereby pledge our lives, if necessary, for the support of the same." A Baltimore gathering denounced the demand for the repeal of the specie circular as "the senseless clamors of the British party." Down with paper currency! and Give us hard money; were the passwords of the Van Burenites. The Whigs responded by printing debased paper currency and coining tokens in tin, lead, brass, and iron adorned with caricatures of Van Buren and Jackson. Many establishments in all parts of the country issued tokens with real value. Scrip, too, was printed by business houses of all sorts.

Webster and other Whig leaders thundered at Van Buren from the hustings. But Van Buren was as silent under these attacks as he was to the strictures of their journalistic supporters. He intended to meet the crisis in his own way and at a time and place of his own selection. With his son Abraham he took daily rides over the roads he and Jackson had traveled. On May 23, in a letter to Jackson, he said: "I have sent by the same vessel that conveys to you the *Constitutional Carriage* a quarter cask of old & excellent gold sherry, which has been ordered for me by our friend Capt Nicholson. I find it to be of superior quality, & beg you to accept of it, & shall feel most highly honored to be occasionally remembered by yourself and friends in the use of it." Van Buren himself drank Madeira, or the rarer product of the hills between Caserta and Naples, the exquisite Monte Pulciano.

Under orders from Van Buren, the Secretary of the Treasury on June 23 instructed all subordinates to discontinué depositing the government's moneys in banks that had refused to pay in specie. This was the first indication of what Van Buren's recommendations to the special session would be. On Tuesday, September 5, the second day of the sitting, his son Abraham delivered his message to Congress. Rare courage and statesmanship were blended in this historic document. It was more than a message to Congress; it was an appeal to the people to sustain him in his revolutionary design. The bills carrying out his proposal for a Sub-Treasury, or Independent Treasury—as it was first known —and suggestions for immediate relief, were in the hands of Silas Wright. The message not only considered the immediate causes of the financial and commercial crisis, but answered those who looked to the government for material relief by thus reminding them of the designs of the Republic:

It was not intended to confer special favors on individuals, or on any classes of them; to create systems of agriculture, manufactures, or trade; or to engage in them, either separately or in connection with individual citizens or organized associations. . . . If its operations were to be directed for the benefit of any one class, equivalent favors, must in justice, be extended to the rest; and the attempt to bestow favors with an equal hand, or even to select those who most deserve them, would never be successful. All communities are apt to look to Government for far too much. Even in our own country, where its powers and duties are so strictly limited, we are prone to do so, especially at periods of sudden embarrassments and distress. But this ought not to be. The framers of our excellent constitution, and the people who approved it with calm and sagacious deliberation, acted at the time on a sounder principle. They wisely judged that the less Government interferes with private pursuits, the better for general prosperity. It is not its legitimate object to make men rich, or to repair, by direct grants of money or legislation in favor of particular pursuits, losses not incurred in the public service. This would be substantially to use the property of some for the benefit of others. But its real duty—that duty the performance of which makes a good Government the most precious of human blessings—is to enact and enforce a system of general laws commensurate with, but not exceeding, the objects of its establishment, and to leave every citizen and every interest to reap, under its benign protection, the rewards of virtue, industry, and prudence.

Equally sound was his lacerating arraignment of the paper-bottomed financial system of the time. To understand his fear of financial institutions as a menace to the integrity of the Republic, we must go beyond his message. In his *Inquiry into the Origin of Political Parties* Van Buren wrote: "Such aggregations of wealth and influence, connected as they usually are with social distinctions, naturally come to be regarded as the fountains of patronage by those who are in search of it. The press, men of letters, artists, and professional men of every denomination, and those engaged in subordinate pursuits who live upon the luxurious indulgences of the rich, are all brought within the scope of their influence." He apprehended that "these aggregations of wealth and influence," unless checked, would lead to the formation of a party "constructed principally of a network of special interests." There is a hint of this in his message. In recounting to Congress his objections to the reëstablishment of a national bank, he said that it "would impair the rightful supremacy of the popular will; injure the character and diminish the influence of our political system; and bring once more into existence a concentrated money power, hostile to the spirit, and threatening the permanency, of our republican institutions."

He justly attributed the immediate cause of the panic to

"over-action in all departments of business; an over-action deriving, perhaps, its first impulses from antecedent causes, but
stimulated to its destructive consequences by excessive issues of
bank paper and other facilities, for the acquisition and enlarge-
ment of credit." In addition to the domestic inflation and "the
spirit of reckless speculation engendered by it, were a foreign
debt, estimated in March last at thirty million dollars; . . . the
diversion of much of the labor [to needless improvements projected by speculators] that should have been applied to agriculture, thereby contributing to the expenditure of large sums in
the importation of grain from Europe—an expenditure which,
amounting in 1834 to two hundred and fifty thousand dollars,
was, in the first two quarters of the present year, increased to
more than two millions of dollars; and finally, without enumer-
ating other injurious results, the rapid growth, among all classes,
and especially in our great commercial towns, of luxurious habits,
founded too often on merely fancied wealth . . ."

Then he surveyed the panic as it affected other countries:
"It has appeared that evils, similar to those suffered by ourselves,
have been experienced in Great Britain, on the continent, and indeed, throughout the commercial world. . . . Two nations
[Great Britain and the United States], . . . but recently enjoying the highest degree of prosperity, and maintaining with each
other the closest relations, are suddenly, in a time of profound
peace, and without any national disaster, arrested in their career,
and plunged into a state of embarrassment and distress. . . .
The history of these causes and effects in Great Britain and the
United States, is substantially the history of the revulsion in all
other commercial countries."

Speaking of the failure of the banks to honor the government drafts in gold, as required by law, he said: "A system which
can, in a time of profound peace, when there is a large revenue laid
by, thus suddenly prevent the application and the use of the
money of the people, in the manner and for the objects they have
directed, cannot be wise; but who can think, without painful
reflection, that, under it, the same unforeseen events might have
befallen us in the midst of a war . . . To such embarrassments
and to such dangers will this Government be always exposed,
whilst it takes the moneys raised for, and necessary to, the public

service, out of the hands of its own officers, and converts them into a mere right of action against corporations entrusted with them. . . . The money received from the people, instead of being kept till it is needed for their use, is . . . a fund, on which discounts are made for the profit of those who happen to be owners of stock in the banks selected as depositories. . . ."

Van Buren thus voiced his faith in the class from which he sprang, the tillers of the soil: "The proceeds of our great staples will soon furnish the means of liquidating debts at home and abroad, and contribute equally to the revival of commercial activity, and the restoration of commercial credit." He closed his message with a regret that he had to dwell on anything but the history of the country's unalloyed prosperity. "Since it is otherwise, we can only feel more deeply the responsibility of the respective trusts that have been confided to us, and under the pressure of difficulties, unite in invoking the guidance and aid of the Supreme Ruler of nations, and in laboring with zealous resolution to overcome the difficulties by which we are environed."

The opposition met this sound analysis with the balderdash of the hustings. Clay said the panic was due to the fight against the Bank. He attacked hard money with: "It was paper money that carried us through the Revolution, established our liberties, and made us a free and independent people." He characterized Van Buren's proposals as "a cold and heartless insensibility to a bleeding people." After noting the Whig victories in the spring and summer elections he truthfully observed that instead of a majority of Democrats in the Senate, "there would be thirty-two or thirty-four Whigs to eighteen or twenty friends of the administration." This was followed by: "We are told that it is necessary to divorce the Government from the banks. Let us not be deluded by sounds. Senators might as well talk of separating the Government from the States, or from the people, or from the country. We are all—people—States—Union—banks, bound up and interwoven together, united in fortune and destiny, and all entitled to the protecting care of a parental government. . . . A hard money Government and a paper money people! A Government, an official corps—the servants of the people—glittering in gold, and the people themselves, their masters, buried in ruin and surrounded with rags." He twitted Calhoun on what he had said about the official corps when he was fighting Van Buren—"one hundred thousand office holders and their dependents, directed by the will of a single man."

Wright and Benton reiterated all Van Buren's arguments in defense of the Sub-Treasury measure, but witnessed a defection of many Democrats in the House and the Senate. These styled themselves Conservative Democrats. The bill passed in the Senate 26 to 20. One who voted against the bill was taking his first step out of the party. This was Tallmadge of New York, whose speech reads as if it were written by a committee from the "pet" banks. He uttered one grain of truth worth recording here: "The tendency of this scheme [the Sub-Treasury] is to bring this country, virtually, to an exclusive metallic currency."

The Sub-Treasury bill was lost in the House on October 16 by a vote of 120 to 106. Four days earlier Webster and three other Senators presented petitions against the annexation of Texas. Many of these protests contained several thousand names each. Most of the signers were from the Northern and Eastern States. Jackson, just before leaving office, had acknowledged the independence of Texas. The slave-holding states were clamoring for her admission, as it would add to their representation in Congress. Jackson covertly and shamelessly aided the insurrection against Mexican dominion; but Van Buren was against annexation, and had so informed Memucan Hunt, envoy and minister extraordinary of the Republic of Texas, when he presented his country's plea for admission to the Union.

The Panic Session, as the first sitting of the Twenty-fifth Congress became known, adjourned *sine die* October 16 after six weeks of talk. It accomplished nothing of moment beyond the enactment of two of Van Buren's recommendations: empowering the Treasury Department to issue $10,000,000 in interest-bearing notes for the Government's current obligations—a singular situation for a country that had wiped out its national debt; permitting importers to pay custom dues in paper.

The coalition of the Conservative Democrats and the Whigs in the lower house of Congress anticipated the sentiment of the people in the November elections. The Whigs carried the legislatures of most of the Northern and Eastern States. In New York there had never been such a rout of any party since the early days of the nation. Of the one hundred and twenty-eight candidates for the Assembly, the Whigs elected one hundred and one; six of the eight Senators chosen were of the same faith. Throughout most of November the Whigs celebrated: news of the results from some distant community being a sufficient excuse for more torchlight processions.

One of these celebrations was out of the ordinary, and bore the earmarks of careful planning. Some three hundred Whigs roused Washington from its sleep on the night of Tuesday, November 22. About midnight the celebrants, mildly described by Adams as riotous, staged mock demonstrations before the homes of the members of the Cabinet. They were equipped with a heavy brass cannon. They first visited the White House and awakened its occupants with jeering huzzas and the rumble of the gun carriage. What Van Buren and other inmates of the Presidential mansion thought when the cannoneers discharged the piece of artillery, has not been recorded. The merry mob then made the rounds of the houses of the heads of Departments, cheering and firing a salute of mockery before each.

Van Buren continued on his plotted course. When Congress reassembled in December it heard the President's analysis of the elections. In again recommending the enactment of the Sub-Treasury bill he made light of the Whig victories by saying that "questions of far deeper and more immediate local interest than the fiscal plan of the National Treasury were involved in those elections. Above all, we cannot overlook the striking fact, that there were at the time in those States more than one hundred and sixty millions of bank capital, of which large portions were subject to actual—and most of it, if not all, to a greater or less extent, dependent for a continuance of its corporate existence upon the will of the State legislatures to be then chosen." He assailed all financial institutions with: "Indeed, I am more than ever convinced of the dangers to which the free and unbiased exercise of political opinion—the only sure foundation and safeguard of republican Government—would be exposed by any further increase of the already overgrown influences of corporate authorities." In the State elections not only the State banks, but the influences of insurance companies, mercantile houses, and other "large aggregations of wealth" were "spread through all the ramifications of society." All the forces of entrenched wealth were at war with him because of his advocacy of the Sub-Treasury. He was asking no quarter. He called attention to the nation's balance of more than $34,000,000, of which only a little more than $1,000,000 was immediately available: most of the rest was in banks which had suspended specie payments.

The Senate was still with Van Buren; but the House was again controlled by the continued coalition of Whigs and Conservative Democrats. Until there was a change in the political complexion of the House he could not hope to enact the Sub-Treasury bill. The November results had not shattered his faith in the people. They had erred; but he was relying on their inherent righteousness; and consoled himself by calling to mind his favorite phrase, which Matthew Henry, the English divine, had coined in 1710: "the sober second thought of the people." He knew that the return of the mass mind to sane thinking could be hastened by the propagation of easily assimilable truths.

In his message he blazed away at Biddle and the Bank for reissuing some ten million dollars in notes under the charter which had expired on March 4, 1836. It was improper, he told Congress; but the Government was powerless, as this dishonesty had not been anticipated by the lawmakers. He spoke regretfully of the non-realization of his expectations for a settlement of the country's claims against Mexico which Jackson had pressed; there was his familiar conciliatory note in his references to the dispute over the Northeastern Boundary, which remained in the unsettled state the signers of the Treaty of Peace had left it in, in 1783; and he discussed minor topics of domestic concern.

Washington society was disappointed. It had expected frequent and colorful receptions at the White House in keeping with the reputation Van Buren had earned during his long residence in the national capital. But not until New Year's Day were the doors thrown open. In this he had no choice: it was traditional to keep the President's house open from eleven in the morning until eight in the evening. The day was like a bit of June. An endless stream passed in and out of the house. In the afternoon Henry Clay called. He sardonically observed to Van Buren that he must feel happy in being surrounded by so many friends. Van

Buren looked out on the sun-kissed lawn as he parried the thrust with: "The weather is very fine."

Dolly Madison also kept open house this day. She had returned to Washington in October after an absence of twenty years. Age had been kind to her; and suffering had not robbed her eyes of their girlish winsomeness, nor her face of its beauty. She was queenly as ever. When Clay entered the room, she "rose at his approach, extended her hand, and gave him one of those smiles which no doubt helped to make the dominant party adhesive, in the days of her [husband's] presidency."

The fashionables among these New Year's callers discussed "the shabby court of Martin the First": they had dubbed Jackson King Andrew. He was patronizing letters: first it was Washington Irving; now he had named George Bancroft Collector of the Port of Boston; and Bancroft appointed a young author named Nathaniel Hawthorne to a subordinate place. But they preferred Lucullus to Mæcenas. And all hoped that his son Abraham would marry a daughter of The Patroon, as gossip had it. That would make the court of Martin the First endurable, and the White House the heart of the city's social life, as it should be. We can see Dolly Madison nodding acquiescently to these idle chatterers, and smiling to herself. She could have told them that the daughter of The Patroon would not be the lady of the White House; for she herself, within a month after her return to Washington, had presented her cousin, Angelica Singleton, at the White House. This charming daughter of a South Carolina planter, with her corkscrew curls, fresh from Madame Grelaud's seminary at Philadelphia, had won the affection of Van Buren and the love of his son. But Dolly Madison said nothing of this: she was a perfect matchmaker.

Another morsel of gossip concerned the insurrection of Upper Canada. Rensselaer Van Rensselaer, a son of Solomon, had been made Commander-in-chief of the revolting Canadians, and as a consequence, many Americans were joining the Patriot Army, as the insurrectionists styled themselves. This revolt was giving Van Buren concern. There was much sympathy with the followers of William Lyon Mackenzie, Toronto's first Mayor, who had been routed by royal troops early in the month of December.

This was the second insurrection within a month. The first

was led by Louis Joseph Papineau, Speaker of the Legislative Assembly of Lower Canada, and Thomas Storrow Brown; but the military quelled it after three weeks.

Both had their origin in the same causes: corruption and misrule. Reform was impossible while the upper house of each parliament, appointed by the Governor General, who owed his office to London, could negative all acts of the lower house, whose representatives were chosen by the people. Mackenzie, a journalist, had been elected five successive times to the Provincial Parliament, and as often expelled, for having published the truth about the venal ruling clique. Five years before the revolt Mackenzie went to London and induced the Whig ministry to dismiss the Solicitor General and the Attorney General of Upper Canada, and to veto a vicious bank act. On his return conditions grew more intolerable, and the despotic acts of Sir Francis Bond Head, the Lieutenant Governor, culminating in interference in elections, led to the establishment of a provisional republic.

Before the actual outbreak of hostilities, Rensselaer Van Rensselaer, who had been secretary to William H. Harrison when he was Minister to Colombia, had left Albany "for the purpose of picking up news and new subscribers for the *Albany Daily Advertiser.*" When Van Rensselaer reached Buffalo, his name and his training at West Point induced Mackenzie and two of his aides, Dr. John Rolph, and M. S. Bidwell, Speaker of the Legislative Assembly of Upper Canada, to offer him the commission of Commander of the Patriot Army. Van Rensselaer assumed command on December 14, and shortly thereafter seized Navy Island, in the Niagara River, and within speaking distance of the Canadian shore. When Van Rensselaer took the island he had twenty-eight men, and two six-pounders; but within a few days his force was augmented to nearly eight hundred. Mackenzie and other leaders of the uprising were in various parts of the United States enlisting fresh recruits.

On December 27 the royal forces began to shell Navy Island. News traveled slowly then, and the gossips at Washington on New Year's Day knew nothing of this, nor of the indefensible atrocity committed at the American village of Schlosser, opposite the island, at midnight on the 29th. January 1 fell on a Monday. On the following Saturday Van Buren received a letter from H.

W. Rogers, District Attorney for Erie County, dated Buffalo, December 30, reading: "Our whole frontier is in commotion, and I fear it will be difficult to restrain our citizens from revenging, by a resort to arms, this flagrant invasion of our territory. Every thing that can be done will be by the public authorities to prevent so injudicious a movement. The respective sheriffs of Erie and Niagara have taken the responsibility of calling out the militia, to guard the frontier, and prevent any further depredations."

An affidavit, sworn to by Gilman Appleby, captain of the steamboat *Caroline*, and supported by nine other Americans, recited that the boat had made three trips between Schlosser and Navy Island during the day, landing men and freight (recruits and ammunition for Van Rensselaer), and had tied up to the dock at Schlosser for the night. ". . . the crew and officers of the *Caroline* numbered ten; . . . in the course of the evening, twenty-three . . . citizens of the United States, came on board . . . and requested to remain . . . during the night, as they were unable to get lodgings at the tavern nearby; these requests were acceded to, and the persons thus coming on board retired to rest, as did also all of the crew and officers of the *Caroline*, except such as were stationed to watch . . . about midnight, this deponent was informed by one of the watch that several boats filled with men were making toward the *Caroline* . . . this deponent immediately gave the alarm and before he was able to reach the deck the *Caroline* was boarded by seventy or eighty men . . . they immediately commenced a warfare with muskets, swords, and cutlasses upon the defenseless crew and passengers of the *Caroline*,  under the fierce cry of 'G—d damn them, give them no quarter; kill every man; fire; fire!' . . . the *Caroline* was abandoned without resistance, and the only effort made by either crew or passengers seemed to be to escape slaughter. . . ."

Only twenty-one of the passengers and crew escaped. The boat was set adrift in the river and fired by the invaders, who then returned to the Canadian side, where their return was received with loud cheers. The following morning the charred fragments of the slaughtered were seen swirling in the eddies below the Falls.

On January 8 Van Buren transmitted to Congress the documents quoted with a message which made no attempt to palliate the "extraordinary outrage," yet couched in language to obviate hostile discussion. A demand for redress would be made, and while he did not doubt that the Government of Upper Canada would "do its duty in punishing the aggressors and preventing future outrage, the President notwithstanding, had deemed it necessary to order a sufficient force on the frontier to repel any attempt of a like character, and to make it known to you that if it should occur, he cannot be answerable for the effects of the indignation of the neighboring people of the United States." The restrained tone of the message was dictated by Van Buren's dominating idea since he had been Secretary of State, to "lay a lasting foundation for perpetual peace & harmony between the two countries." The phrase is from a letter marked "Private & confidential," written by Jackson to Van Buren on December 17, 1831.

Actual hostilities ended on January 14, when Van Rensselaer and his troops evacuated Navy Island after parleys with General Winfield Scott and Governor Marcy. Van Rensselaer was arrested on a charge of accepting a commission from a foreign government and released on bail; but subsequently imprisoned. A Canadian who boasted that he was in command of the force which slaughtered the crew and passengers of the *Caroline* was arrested in New York, tried, and acquitted. Mackenzie was taken in Rochester, where he was publishing a newspaper, and imprisoned. Mackenzie, described by Van Rensselaer—after they had quarreled—as "a meddling little body but fully devoted to the cause of freedom," had a long memory and an effective pen. We shall meet him eight years hence, a member of the *Tribune* staff, and a successful pamphleteer. While Mackenzie remained a citizen of the United States, the reforms for which the Canadian liberals had fought were largely realized. An act of amnesty was passed; Mackenzie returned to Toronto; served in Parliament; and published a weekly, *Mackenzie's Message*.

It was not until March that the White House drawing room was opened. Van Buren, fond as he was of society, had little heart for it while the financial crisis, and the suffering it entailed, was at its height. But relief was in sight: England was relieving the stringency by shipping gold here, and most of the banks would resume the payment of gold and silver in a month or two at the most. In April Van Buren gave another reception at the White House. These were his contributions to the social side of Washington for the season. He entertained members of Congress at the traditional Saturday night dinners. At one of these a servant whispered: "The house is on fire." Excusing himself, Van Buren went to the kitchen: a few pailfuls of water quenched the blaze. On returning to the table he explained the reason for his absence. Clay, his hand on his heart, protested loudly: "Mr. President, I am doing all I can to get you out of this house; but believe me, I do not want to burn you out."

On April 11, Butler, who had consented to remain with his old preceptor and law partner for a year, resigned as Attorney General. Senator Felix Grundy, of Tennessee, was appointed his successor. Once, when Van Buren inquired what Hugh Lawson White was doing in his retirement, Grundy gave this picture of a defeated aspirant for Presidential honors: "I will tell you: he sits all day long in the chimney corner, spitting tobacco juice by the gallon, cursing everything and everybody, except his Creator, but thinking devilishly hard of him."

Dickerson was anxious to retire from the Navy Department. Van Buren offered the post to Irving. When the author declined, Van Buren tendered the post to another man of letters in his cabinet, James K. Paulding, satirist, humorist, poet, and novelist, related by marriage to Irving, with whom he collaborated on the first numbers of *Salmagundi*. Paulding accepted.

Congress sat until July 9, and one of its last acts was to pass one of Van Buren's recommendations: making the reissuance of old notes of the Bank of the United States a crime. About three weeks before adjournment, Senator William C. Preston, of South Carolina, who did not share Calhoun's support of the administration, withdrew his resolution for the annexation of Texas. The Washington house of the Prestons was also the home of their charming kinswoman, Angelica Singleton, since the preceding fall. And after the adjournment of Congress she returned with them to South Carolina, where, in her father's house, in the month of November, she was married to Captain Abraham Van Buren; and shortly after started north with him to be the mistress of the White House.

Van Buren also left Washington after the adjournment of

Congress. It was his first vacation in two years. From early in July until late in September he rested at White Sulphur Springs. We have this glimpse of him on the way down, sent by the correspondent of the *Richmond Enquirer* on his arrival at Louisa Court-house: "About one o'clock he arrived, travelling in the plainest manner, with two of his sons, drawn by four horses; his servant riding the horse presented to him by the late John Randolph, of Roanoke." His two sons were Abraham and Martin.

On his return to Washington, Van Buren appraised the surveys of the Democratic canvassers in States which went Whig in the preceding fall. The reports showed that the panic was little more than a painful memory; the banks that had survived were paying in specie, and credit was gradually being restored. News came from London of the regal time Van Buren's son John was having in the British capital. John had left for England in the late spring. At the state dinner given by Queen Victoria on July 25 the Queen received him with marked consideration. The *Courier*, the British court journal, on July 26, published the list of guests in this wise: "Prince Nicholas Esterhazy; Prince Windisch Gratz; John Van Buren, son of the President of the United States; the Lord Chancellor and Lady Cottenham; . . ." Then followed dukes and duchesses; marquises and marchionesses; earls; counts, viscounts, lords, baronets, and commoners of distinction.

The Whig journals seized upon this list as a choice morsel. Who were the princes at Queen Victoria's state dinner? Prince Nicholas Esterhazy; Prince Windisch Gratz; Prince John Van Buren. And then they told, with much fanciful elaboration, how Prince John danced with Queen Victoria; and how Prince John was given precedence over the Hero of Waterloo and other lesser and greater dukes. And they dwelt on the dinner given a few days later by the Lord Mayor and Corporation of London to illustrious foreigners, where Prince John was placed on the right hand of the Lord Mayor with the Prince de Nemours, son of Louis Philippe. Now the Whig press talked of Prince de Nemours and Prince John van Buren; for to heighten the effect, some printed the surname with a small *v*. Mockingly they called him "our Prince John."

Prince John—the name thereafter clung to him—returned in time to take active part in the November elections. The slavery question was playing a large part. This was due to the autocratic attitude of the slaveholders in Congress; they forced upon the lower house a rule prohibiting debate on petitions relating to slavery, or even their reference to a committee. This was the undemocratic "gag rule" which Adams mocked daily in the House by presenting petitions from Abolitionists, whose course he disapproved, but whose right of free speech he defended. The Abolitionists asked candidates if they were for or against the gag rule. In New York, Marcy, candidate for reëlection, when asked: "Do you believe in the right of Abolitionists to petition Congress?" replied: "No." Seward, who again opposed him, answered: "Yes." Seward was elected Governor by 10,000 majority. But it was not a complete rout of the Regency: they reduced the Whig majority in the Assembly to 79, and maintained their ascendancy in the upper house.

Van Buren found consolation in the country-wide returns. The Whigs carried only four States besides New York: Rhode Island, Indiana, Kentucky, and North Carolina. The loss of Ohio, Harrison's home State, offset the loss of New York to the Democrats. The Whigs made slight gains in Illinois and Missouri. But for the Canadian insurrections the Democratic gains in New York and elsewhere in the North would have been more pronounced; for Van Buren's laudable neutrality earned for him and his administration the unwarranted charge that they were "the tools of Victoria." Solomon Southwick, now a bitter foe of Van Buren, told Mackenzie during the canvass that Washington was "a sink of iniquity, corruption, and British influence." The Whig vote, generally, was a conservative poll. Outside of the South, the Democratic ranks were augmented by the addition of most of the liberal element. The Equal Rights, or Loco-focos, had returned to the party because of Van Buren's demand for a Sub-Treasury and his radical pronouncements in advocating it. His insistence upon the divorcement of bank and state signally embraced the twin objectives of the Loco-focos: no special privileges, and no class legislation.

On the second day of its sitting Van Buren communicated his annual message to Congress. He spoke cheerfully of the state of the country: the harvest had been abundant; industry was prospering; plague had not visited us; peace reigned among us.

"These blessings, which evince the care and beneficence of Providence, call for our devout and fervent gratitude." He noted that "the present year closes the first half century of our Federal institutions; and our system—differing from all others in the acknowledged, practical, and unlimited operation which it has for so long a period given to the sovereignty of the people—has now been fully tested by experience. . . . It was reserved for the American Union to test the advantage of a Government entirely dependent on the continual exercise of the popular will; and our experience has shown that it is as beneficent in practice as it is in theory."

The major part of his report was a reiteration of his sound economic theories in advocating the Sub-Treasury. He regarded the rapid recovery of the nation without the aid of the Bank (which had done what it could to prevent the State banks from resuming specie payments) as refutation of the arguments of the opposition. "The scenes through which we have passed conclusively prove how little our commerce, agriculture, manufactures, or finances, require such an institution, and what dangers are attendant on its power—a power, I trust, never to be conferred by the American people upon their Government, and still less upon individuals not responsible to it for its unavoidable abuses."

He told of the progress made by the administration, of the settled policy of the nation, dating back to Monroe, to move the Indians "to a country west of the Mississippi, much more extensive, and better adapted to their condition, than that on which they then resided; the guarantee to them, by the United States, of their exclusive possession of that country forever, exempt from all intrusions by white men . . ." He noted a regrettable exception: 2,000 Seminoles in Florida under Osceola were unwilling to leave their old hunting grounds. "The continued treacherous conduct of these people; the savage and unprovoked murders they have lately committed, butchering whole families of the settlers of the Territory, without distinction of age or sex, and making their way into the very center and heart of the country, so that no part of it is free from their ravages; their frequent attacks on the lighthouses along that dangerous coast; and the barbarity with which they have murdered the passengers and crews of such vessels as have been wrecked upon the reefs and keys which border the Gulf, leave the Government no alternative but to continue the military operations against them until they are totally expelled from Florida." The Florida War was an inheritance from the Jackson administration, and it was to out-last Van Buren's by a year.

Van Buren, although expressing a hope that Congress would pass his Sub-Treasury bill at this session, knew that the House was still controlled by a coalition of Conservative Democrats and Whigs.

England's provocative colonial policy was threatening Van Buren's hope of an enduring peace between the two countries. Adams thus described the English colonial attitude: "The policy of the British government has been to maintain and excite divisions of interest among the colonies themselves, as well as to nour-ish and stimulate their animosities against the neighboring States [of the United States]. . . . There are very perceptible mutual rivalries and jealousies between the provinces, and a great indif-ference in both the Canadas. They levy an impost duty of five per cent upon all imported goods from one to the other, and it is very apparently part of the political system at home to keep them as much as possible alienated from each other, that all may be perfectly dependent upon the common parent. Another precaution at home is a rigorous prohibition to recruit any of the regiments in the provinces. . . . The men are enlisted for life, and as they are all taken from the paupers of the three kingdoms, and are fed, clothed, and lodged at the King's expense, and trained ex-clusively to the performance of military service, they are nested in a condition of existence from which they have little temptation to depart, especially at the risk of capture and severe imprison-ment. . . ."

A series of high-handed acts of aggression by the Canadian authorities, having their origin in the disputed Northeastern Boundary, culminated this winter in the seizure of an agent of the State of Maine who had been sent to investigate reports that bands of trespassers from Canada were cutting timber in the Aroostook region. This agent was taken to Fredericton, the capi-tal of New Brunswick, where he was held by Sir John Harvey, Lieutenant Governor of the province. Sir John then dispatched more of his lawless lot to the timber lands within Maine's boundary; but they were driven back into Canada by the State militia.

As soon as credible information of the border trouble reached Washington, Van Buren—after negotiations between the Secretary of State and the British Minister had failed—transmitted the correspondence to Congress with a message sustaining the action of Maine. He hoped that mutual exercise of jurisdiction over the disputed territory by the authorities of Maine and New Brunswick would be continued pending arbitration, which had been agreed upon by the two nations years back. But "if the authorities of New Brunswick should attempt to enforce the claim of exclusive jurisdiction set up by them, by means of a military occupation of the disputed territory, I shall feel myself bound to consider the contingency provided by the Constitution as having occurred on the happening of which a State has the right to call for the aid of the Federal government to repel invasion. . . . As, however, the session of Congress is about to terminate, and the agency of the Executive may become necessary during the recess, it is important that the attention of the Legislature should be drawn to the consideration of such measures as may be calculated to obviate the call for an extra session. . . ."

Congress unanimously empowered the President to call out fifty thousand volunteers to aid Maine if he deemed it necessary. On the day the measure reached the Senate, March 2, it was immediately acted upon and unanimously passed.

No necessity arose for a military demonstration, as a memorandum was signed binding Maine and the Province of New Brunswick to release all prisoners, and to act "in concert, jointly or separately, according to agreements between the Governments of Maine and New Brunswick" to disperse intruders or trespassers in the disputed territory.

Before this amicable solution had been reached, the border States were in a ferment. In New York when it seemed as if the militia of the several States would be ordered to Maine, Solomon Van Rensselaer, now approaching his sixty-eighth year, called on Governor Seward. And lest his gold-headed cane be mistaken as an old man's support, he carried it under his arm when he asked for command of the State troops in the event of war. Seward humored the old veteran, who then called on Judge John Sanders and asked him to be one of his aides. The local newspapers, under such heads as "Fire of the Old Flint" published: "We learn from the highest authority that Maj. Gen. Solomon Van Rensselaer, who was distinguished in the Indian War of the last century, and who led the American troops at the Battle of Queenstown, has promptly tendered his services as the senior major general of New York State infantry to the commander-in-chief in the event of war between England and America. This hero of two wars . . ." A few weeks later, in the same paper, the *Albany Evening Journal*, under date of March 18, there appeared a story which began: "General Solomon Van Rensselaer, our excellent and respected Post Master, has received a letter from Amos Kendall announcing that he has been instructed by the President of the United States to say that in his judgment the public interests will be promoted by a change of Post Master at Albany, and that such change will be made at the close of the present quarter." But the old man, pretending not to mind, raised his head higher, and continued with his preparations for the war with his old enemy. He thought the foe would be England: but it was his still older foe, the fear of want.

Van Rensselaer was the first of the victims to fall in Van Buren's campaign to capture the next Congress as a preliminary to his campaign for reëlection in 1840. Some six months before the blow fell, the old veteran, in writing to Vice President Johnson to thank him for being reappointed, said that many in Albany were seeking his place. Had he written in like strain to Van Buren —but he was a Dutchman, too, and could not—he would have been permitted to end his years overseeing the mails at the ancient seat of the Manor of the Van Rensselaers. We have evidence tending to support this belief in Van Buren's refusal, shortly after his inauguration, to permit the removal of the old soldier on fictive charges of shortage in his accounts. The Regency persisted in its demand for his place; and Van Buren could not continue deaf to it. It was an important office, as the spoilsmen saw it, and one of the faithful must fill it. Yet within a month after the proscription of the most picturesque of the Van Rensselaers, Van Buren showed his other side. William Leggett, a brilliant journalist, whose caustic pen had often made Van Buren wince, was dying of tuberculosis at his home in New Rochelle. Since the *Plaindealer* had failed in 1836, Leggett had been too weak to work. Doctors advised a trip to a warmer climate; but Leggett was penniless and in debt. Van Buren solved the problem by appointing him diplomatic agent to Guatemala. With a lighter heart than he had known in many months, Leggett made ready; but on May 29, a few days before his ship was to sail, he died.

# CHAPTER XXXVIII

In the last week of June Van Buren left for New York. His progress was deliberately slow. In several places in Pennsylvania he addressed partisans. Gradually it dawned upon the nation that Van Buren was campaigning for a Democratic Congress, and for his own reëlection, although it would be a year or so before he would be renominated. The stage was carefully set for his return. He arrived in Newark "in the railroad cars at half past 9 a.m." The *New Era*, which alone of New York journals assigned a reporter to meet him, then continued: "At a quarter before 11 o'clock, the President and a procession of vehicles and equestrians which extended apparently more than a mile in length, departed for Jersey City amidst cheers . . . At the several villages of Bergen County on his way, Mr. Van Buren was honored with repeated salutes of cannon procured for the occasion. . . ."

From Jersey City Van Buren saw New York for the first time since November, 1836. The whole Upper Bay and the mouth of the Hudson were dotted with gayly decorated craft when he stepped aboard the *Utica*. Midway between the New Jersey and New York shores the frigate *North Carolina* lay at anchor. Instead of heading straight for the opposite shore, the *Utica* plied her way "gracefully for some time among the vessels that thronged the bay." As she approached the frigate, whose yards were covered "by rows of sailors in white uniforms," the forty-four pound guns fired a double-broadside salute. This was returned by the forts on Bedloe's Island, Staten Island, and Governor's Island; and the several companies of artillery on the Battery thundered a welcome home; and for more than half an hour "the whole atmosphere was filled with the smoke and rent by the thunder of the continued discharge of cannon."

Not since the visit of La Fayette had New York seen such a spectacle. At least one hundred thousand men and women, in gaudy summer raiment, cheered Van Buren as he stepped ashore at the Battery. He was escorted into Castle Garden, where a

428

citizens' committee, headed by John W. Edmonds, a former State Senator, received him. In his greeting, Edmonds repeatedly referred to the Democratic party of the State. The *Evening Post* —William Cullen Bryant was his most loyal and steadfast editorial supporter in his fight for a Sub-Treasury and other reforms—thus quotes Van Buren's response: "Gentlemen: I am deeply and gratefully affected by this cordial reception on the part of my Democratic fellow citizens of the City and County of New York. . . . Your observations upon an . . . independent treasury show a very mature and just consideration of the subject in all its bearings; tested by the principle which has been opposed to it—that of giving a temporary use of the public money, and a consequent control over it, to private corporations irresponsible to the people—it may well be regarded as a question of involving the nature, and to some extent the existence of republican institutions, as well as a consideration of the main purposes for which our government was established; whether for the safety of the many or the aggrandizement of the few, whether or not to secure the greatest good to the greatest number, in our view, the only legitimate object of the government among men. . . ."

In his reference to the Canadian insurrectionists, he answered his critics who accused him of being a foe to the spread of republican principles: ". . . we may, I am sure, count, with confidence upon a vigilant support, by our citizens, of those great principles of international justice, the maintenance of which is alike indispensable to the preservation of social order and the peace of the world. In doing so it does not follow that we are either to surrender the right of opinion, to suppress a solicitude for the spread of free government, or, to withhold our best wishes for the success of all who are in good faith laboring for their establishment."

"At the conclusion of the ceremonies in the garden," the *Evening Post* chronicled, "the President, mounted on a very graceful and spirited black horse, reviewed the six thousand troops gathered at the battery, when they were formed into ranks and the procession began slowly to move up Broadway, surrounded on all sides by multitudes of persons of both sexes and of all ages. The line of march was from Broadway up Chatham street [now Park Row] and the Bowery, through Broome street into Broadway again from whence it returned to the park. . . ." Here he dismounted and was escorted into the City Hall, where Isaac L. Varian presented him to the members of the Common Council. Both the Council and the Mayor were of his own political faith, the Democrats having regained control of the city in the April election.

Van Buren's ill-chosen phrase in his opening sentence—"my Democratic fellow citizens"—was included by the Whig press in its array of exhibits assembled to support the charge that Van Buren was violating the unwritten law forbidding a President to canvass for office.

The following day Van Buren received local political leaders and a large number of citizens in his suite at the Washington Hotel. The third day of his stay he journeyed to Staten Island in Captain Cornelius Vanderbilt's boat to attend the Fourth of July celebration of the Sunday schools of the metropolitan district. On Friday nine thousand people called to shake his hand. Commenting on this demonstration, the *New Era* said: "And this is the man that the Whigs, a year ago, asserted did not dare to come to our city for fear of assassination." Not even a member of the local police force was detailed to guard him.

From Hone's diary we learn that toward the end of the week he attended a performance at the Bowery Theater, where *The Lion King, or The Bandit's Doom* was showing nightly, followed by some other popular melodrama, such as *Nick of the Woods, or The Jibbenainosay*. It had not become the fashion for newspapers to assign reporters to record the movements of a President. Van Buren went to the playhouse with several Loco-focos, including Alexander Ming. This was the same Ming who had signed the call for the meeting in the Park in February, 1837, when he and other speakers incited their hungry listeners to storm and sack the flour warehouses. Ming was still shouting "Down with monopolists and extortionists!" It distressed Hone to see Van Buren associating with such radicals. On Monday morning Hone paid his respects to the President. Later in the day Van Buren visited the Navy Yard in Brooklyn, whose citizens turned out to honor him.

The next morning he left the city to visit friends in Westchester County. He was accompanied through the sylvan roads of upper Manhattan by Mayor Varian and several Councilmen in barouches. Mounted members of the Young Men's Democratic Club escorted them to the village of Harlem. Farmers, on horseback and in wagons, joined the procession along the route, now massed with skyscraping apartment houses. An *Evening Post* reporter noted: ". . . before reaching Harlem the train extended for more than a mile."

After spending a night with Colonel Hunter on his island estate in the East River, he shared the hospitality of Irving at his home at Sunnyside. Then he journeyed to Sing Sing, where several villages united in an official welcome. Three old farmers were so overjoyed to see one of their own blood elevated to the Presidency, that they kissed his hand. It was a fair stretch from the scene of the ceremonies to the boat landing. Van Buren walked the distance, the center of a cheering crowd that moved with him. From the windows women waved handkerchiefs. Hat in hand, he bowed right and left in acknowledgment. A venerable graybeard decided he must protect the President from the scorching sun, and persisted in keeping an umbrella over his head until the landing was reached. These spontaneous attentions were distorted by the local Whig weekly, the *Hudson River Chronicle*, in this wise: "We are not disposed to withhold from Mr. Van Buren any of the glory he received at Sing Sing, and therefore, though we confess it a disgrace to our place, we state the fact, that three of his faithful followers kissed his hand, with which he seemed greatly gratified. . . . On the way to the boat, a person was appointed to hold over his head an umbrella, after the fashion set by slaves of the Chinese emperor."

At Peekskill some little schoolboys, who had learned their pieces by heart, bade him welcome. This surprise moved Van Buren; for the children mentioned Kinderhook. And as he shook hands with each, he doubled the tiny fist over a five-dollar gold piece. The small boys now knew why he was called the Little Magician.

Van Buren was making his way by easy stages, the guest of the local authorities of every village and town on the east bank of the Hudson, until he reached the city of Hudson. It was here, as we remember, that he first practiced law on a large scale; here his first child was born. Here, at the seat of Columbia County, he had sat as Surrogate; and it was while a resident of Hudson that he was elected to the State Senate. He arrived in Hudson Friday, July 19, ten days after he left New York. He had been prepared for the rebuff, as he had received several days before a copy of the churlish resolutions the Whig Common Council of "the city of his adoption" had adopted the preceding Saturday. These resolves read in part:

It is therefore plain—beyond the power of argument to make it plainer, that Mr. Van Buren's tour is one of a political and partizan character.—Therefore be it

Resolved, by the Mayor and Common Council of the city of Hudson, in Common Council assembled, that we do not feel bound by any consideration of *justice, prudence,* or *hospitality,* to expend the people's money, or descend from the dignity of our official stations, for the purpose of aiding political partizans in their endeavors to carry out their favorite schemes.

These exalted ones had taken their cue from the Jovian Seward, who in declining to attend the celebration in New York City, wrote: "I have regarded his policies and his measures as injurious to the country. . . . It would be an extraordinary demonstration of respect on the part of the Chief Magistrate of this State towards any public functionary, were he to leave his duties at the capital to receive such functionary in your city."

The "discourtesy and illiberality"—as the Albany *Argus* characterized it—of the common Council, reacted to Van Buren's advantage; for many thousands journeyed from Ulster, Albany, and Rensselaer counties to make certain that he was not greeted by a handful. Several detachments of militia, including a company of artillery, participated in the celebration. Impartial witnesses of the reception to Van Buren who had been present at La Fayette's visit to Hudson a decade and a half earlier compared the two favorably. After the cannon had roared a Presidential salute, and the citizens' committee had formally welcomed him back to the "city of his adoption" and the county of his birth, Van Buren spoke. There was no suggestion of politics in his utterances, so the Democratic papers of New York City did not republish the report in the *Argus.* "Let me add," said Van Buren midway in his short response, "that to me it is a source of pleasure to meet so many of the associates of my youth, and of my maturer years." As we read we hear him speak, not in his usual rapid delivery, but slowly, in the manner of one who has been unexpectedly called upon to speak and searches his heart for something to say.

That night he slept in Hudson. In the morning, at nine o'clock, accompanied by his youngest son and sixteen friends, most of them blood relatives, he set out for Kinderhook. They rode in four barouches and two one-horse wagons. There were no outriders. A mile outside his native village the six vehicles halted as they came within earshot of a group of horsemen. They were the reception committee of Kinderhook. At their head was Mordecai Myers, President of the village. His aides were officers in the militia and veterans of the War of 1812 who had not grown too rotund for their faded uniforms. The mounted men flanked themselves on either side of the Presidential party, and presently the little procession moved forward at a brisk trot. It lacked a few minutes of noon, the hour fixed for Van Buren's arrival at Stranahan's Hotel, which was set in the heart of Kinderhook, three miles north. They could barely make it in the time remaining.

A four-page draft, in Van Buren's hand, of the speech he was to make that day, is in the archives of Congress. The only printed record is found under "Kinderhook Correspondence" in the *Argus* of the following Tuesday. The unknown chronicler has placed Van Buren on the balcony of the squat, two-story village hotel. From his vantage Van Buren glimpses the weather-beaten pile of shingles and clapboards—now untenanted—the tavern where he was born. In front of the doorway has been raised a flagpole from whose top the Stars and Stripes floats in the noonday sun. Through the trees to the northwest, a few rods away, bits of marble gleam against the restful green of the grass. He cannot avoid seeing these, and recalling, as he does, the sentiment he uttered the day before at Hudson: "I am happy in finding myself once more in the midst of those with whom my career in life commenced, and among whom I hope to be permitted to close it." The Parian shafts marking the resting places of his wife and parents grow indistinct as the closely packed mass in the square below cheers again. The chairman has finished speaking: it is now his turn.

After Van Buren formally acknowledged the welcome, he

began to talk of his toil-filled childhood; of scenes that had changed or were now no more; of his father and mother, and others whose voices had long been silent, from whom he had learned his first concepts of truth and honor. He was back home among them all. None of them had died; for their spirits lived. And when he laid down the cares of the Presidency he would come back again, this time to stay as long as the hills of Kinderhook endured. The surging mass in the village square became still; eyes moistened, and many sobbed softly. Tears coursed down Van Buren's cheeks, and he had to struggle with his emotions to keep his voice. There is mute supporting evidence of this scene, which local tradition has hallowed, but could not embroider. We find in the *Argus* of July 23: ". . . His reply was one of the most effective and beautiful addresses I have ever heard . . . the feeling allusions to the scenes he had passed through from the time he was a youth to the present, was such that all hearts were melted; and he himself was almost overcome by the bare repetition of them. . . ."

The soul-baring speech is over, and there is "another outburst of feeling in the repeated cheers." And we will let the unknown correspondent of the *Argus* continue: "He now took all by the hand that approached him, and exchanged congratulations with old neighbors and friends. When dinner was announced he sat down with them at the public table [in Stranahan's Hotel]. It was, however, understood beforehand that there were to be no set speeches nor toasts. . . ."

We have not used Van Buren's draft of the speech he intended to deliver on this day; for the things he said from the balcony of the inn are not put down on paper in advance.

Four days he remained in Kinderhook. He lived at the old Van Ness home, to which he had recently acquired title. Part of his stay was spent in devising improvements. But—these were his imperative instructions—under no circumstances was the half-door with its brass knocker to be altered in any manner. He wanted them to remain as souvenirs of that day, thirty-five years ago, when he hurried to the house in answer to the call for help from Billy Van Ness, a fugitive after the Burr-Hamilton duel, and found Billy's father seated under the brass knocker, oblivious to his presence and to his repeated rapping. A sad smile played around Van Buren's mouth as he recalled the scene which ended when Billy came down the long hall and whispered to his father, who never forgave Van Buren for supporting Morgan Lewis against Burr for Governor in the April election of 1804.

Van Buren's youngest son remained a day at Kinderhook, and then went on to Albany, where the father followed him. Here, the Whig municipal authorities followed the example set by their partisans in Hudson, and declined to welcome the President. But the citizens of the State Capital organized a celebration, which ended with speeches on the steps of the City Hall. In his reply to ex-Governor Marcy's address of welcome, Van Buren uttered a thought worth recording: "Deception and delusion may, for a time, depress the worthy and elevate the undeserving, but the final judgment of this people as to the tendency of public measures and the motives of public men, is alike unerring and inflexible."

Van Buren and his son stopped at Congress Hall while in the capital. The Whig authorities of two other cities on his way to Saratoga—Schenectady and Troy—also snubbed him. Said the Trojans: "Resolved, That the occasion of the President's visit calls for no public action on the part of the city authorities." Before leaving Albany Van Buren wrote to Jackson recounting the splendid receptions he had, and voiced the conviction that the State was redeemed politically. The next day his son wrote to his brother Martin in Washington:

My dear Mat,

The old man has just gone to Schenectady—and intends to bring up at the United States Hotel, Saratoga, tomorrow. I shall follow on this afternoon with the luggage. We have had a very pleasant time since I last wrote you. At Kinderhook we spent a day & dined at the Van Ness Place—Kleirood no more! We had a capital dinner of Fricasse [*sic!*] and ham, washed down with champaigne [*sic!*] We tried hard to get up a good name; but it is very tough work. The present favorite is "The Locusts" of which there are a great number about. The only objection is that the same name is used by Cooper in the "Spy" for one of his places. . . .

Believe me

Yrs ever affectionately

S. T. Van Buren

Albany July 31st 1839

Mat's younger brother should have added his brother's title to his name; for he was Acting Secretary to the President of the United States. Abraham and his bride were enjoying a brief holiday in Europe. No American couple received such attentions. He was the Secretary and son of the President, and she the niece of Andrew Stevenson, Minister to Great Britain. They were accorded regal honors. After dinner at St. Cloud, Louis Philippe conducted them through the palace; and all doors opened to them save the entrance to the sleeping apartment of the Comte de Paris, the grandson of the Citizen King. When Mrs. Van Buren told the Queen of their failure to obtain admittance, she explained laughingly: "Ah! that is all the King knows about it! After his mother left with the Duc d'Orléans for Algiers, I caused the child to be removed to a room nearer my own." Victoria was equally gracious in her informal reception of America's first lady of the land and her amiable husband.

While Van Buren was at Saratoga he wrote to Abraham to be home for the opening of Congress; for he depended on his daily reports for his news of the two houses. We have glimpses of Van Buren at Saratoga. Hone and Mrs. Hone are there, and Van Buren sends his bottle of wine to their table. Morgan Lewis, still active despite his eighty-three years, at whose home Van Buren has often been a guest, is seen walking with him. Henry Clay is expected, and the Democratic papers copy this thrust at him in the *Cincinnati Advertiser and Journal:* "The vindictive demagogue may meet the Little Magician there who may conjure him into a nonentity." Secretary Forsyth arrives with "others of the faithful," notes Hone. Another member of the Cabinet, Poinsett, follows. Van Buren "is conducting himself with his usual politeness and making the best of everything, as he is wont to do. . . . I have studied to treat him with all the respect due to his high station and the regard I have for an old friend, and I acknowledge the kindness with which my advances have been received." And all have forgotten old hatreds. But there has been "one exception, on the part of a lady, which, in my judgment, was equally at variance with good taste and proper feeling." This reference was the public snub administered to Van Buren by the widow of De Witt Clinton. Members of the gentle sex do not forgive a wrong done to the man they love.

There are two common tables in the dining room. "The President takes the head of one of the tables," writes Hone, "and the *modest* Mr. Bennett of the *Herald*, the other. The President cannot help this, to be sure, and the juxtaposition is somewhat awkward. Bennett will make a great thing of this with those who are not aware that any person may take this seat who has impudence enough . . ."

Clay arrived on Friday, August 9. Van Buren had been escorted to the hotel by a motley horde. The local Whigs had been divided over the nature of the reception to their leader, a minority protesting against an elaborate welcome because of the presence of Van Buren. Their problem was solved by Van Buren himself, who told them that he would leave before Clay arrived, and would return on Monday. He went to Troy where the citizens made amends for the inhospitality of the Whig municipal governing body. Clay was led to the hotel at the head of a formal procession which moved to the martial music of a brass band. As he was entering the hotel, he was detained on the porch long enough to enable a chaplet of roses and hyacinths to be lowered from the window of Mrs. Clinton's room. Clay suspected nothing until the garland touched his brow, when he pushed it to one side.

Clay had been looking forward to a visit to the battlefield of Saratoga. Van Buren anticipated this, and arranged that Morgan Lewis be his guide. This thoughtfulness, and the honor involved, delighted Clay. And Lewis enjoyed it just as much. There was the spot where his regiment first came in contact with Burgoyne's troops; and there the British broke; and . . . Clay warmed the spry old hero's heart by observing that a colonel of a fighting unit should not have been saddled with the duties of Quartermaster General of the entire Northern Army. And he talked of other battles Lewis fought in the fight for freedom. Clay had been well primed.

General Winfield Scott, another aspirant for the Whig nomination for President, arrived during Van Buren's absence. The three met in the drawing room on Van Buren's return. Clay was unable to get close enough to shake Van Buren's hand because of a group of ladies in the promenade, so he called out to him. Van Buren smiled as he saw Clay's predicament, and returning his greeting, exclaimed: "I hope I don't obstruct your progress."

"Not at all," came the quick response: "I have found the utmost facility in my progress since I entered your dominions." Scott, from a distance spied the meeting, and joined them, and "for an hour the three luminaries continued their promenade."

Van Buren threw no obstacles in Clay's path while he was in his "dominions." When the Kentuckian arrived in New York City, nine days later, Van Buren saw to it that the Loco-foco municipality placed the Governor's Room in the City Hall at Clay's disposal. Here the hosts of Whigs thronged to do Clay homage. This unusual mark of respect accentuated the lack of sportsmanship—to use a most charitable expression—of Van Buren's political adversaries.

The Whig papers afforded Van Buren and his friends a hearty laugh, somewhat at his expense. Black Bess, the horse he had ridden in the New York parade, had been loaned by Thomas S. Hamblin, the Shakespearian actor, and a Whig. The *New York Express* said that had it the power it would confer the privilege of suffrage on Black Bess that she might always vote the Whig ticket. The *Era* retorted: "A horse vote for the Whig ticket! What does that show?" "Shows that he is not a jackass," riposted the *Louisville Courier*.

Van Buren took his leave of the Springs on August 20; and on the following day was the center of a celebration in the village of Whitehall. Other large villages and cities were thereafter visited, including Buffalo and Auburn; and in the third week of September, the political tour ended, he enjoyed a fortnight's rest in Kinderhook. This was followed by a brief stay in New York on his return to Washington.

The November elections justified his expectations, the Democrats electing a bare majority in the House, thus giving him control of both branches for the first time since he began his fight for a Sub-Treasury. Congress convened on December 2. The House of Representatives was thrown into a turmoil by ten rival claimants for five of New Jersey's six seats. Governor William Pennington, a Whig, had given commissions to five of his partisans who had lost to their Democratic opponents on the face of the official returns. The Whigs charged that returns in the contested districts had been falsified. Excluding these seats, the Democrats had 119, and the opposition 118. At noon, the Clerk of the House, Hugh A. Garland, of Virginia, began calling the roll. When he reached New Jersey, he called the name of Joseph F. Randolph, and "then said that there were five other seats from the State of New Jersey which were contested; and not feeling himself authorized to decide the question between the contending parties, he would, if it were the pleasure of the House, pass over the names of those members and proceed with the call till a House shall be formed, who will then decide the question." Adams, who has left us the most replete account of the two weeks' tumult which this announcement started, continued: "This gave rise to a debate, which continued until past four o'clock, when a motion was made to adjourn. The Clerk said he could put no question, not even for adjournment, until the House itself should be formed. . . . There was a general call to adjourn; and, although one voice cried 'No!' and others called out to adjourn to eleven o'clock, the Clerk declared the House adjourned to twelve o'clock. This movement has been evidently prepared to exclude the five members from New Jersey from voting for Speaker; and the Clerk has had his lesson prepared for him. . . . His two decisions form together an insurmountable objection to the transaction of any business and an impossibility of organizing the House."

For three days the House of Representatives was made a mock parliament by the Clerk. The fiery Henry A. Wise, of Virginia, in leaving the chamber on the second evening, observed to those near him: "We are a mob." Not until the evening of the third day did the Clerk condescend to put a question, and then only on a motion to adjourn. On the fourth day, Adams addressed his associates, summed up their predicament, and said: "If we cannot organize in any other way,—if this Clerk will not consent to our discharging the trusts confided to us by our constituents, —then let us imitate the example of the Virginia House of Burgesses when the colonial governor [Dinwiddie] ordered it to disperse, and like men—"

Adams never finished the sentence, although his corrected speech has rounded it out. The House broke into cheers; the galleries, forgetting that visitors must remain silent, joined in the boisterous demonstration to the "old man eloquent." He offered a resolution directing the Clerk to call the names of the five Whigs from New Jersey who had credentials, explaining that any member might offer an amendment to his resolve, and thus bring the question to an immediate issue. To the more exasperated this seemed ineffectual, and they shouted from all parts of the House: "Who will put the question?" and "How shall the question be put?" Adams, still holding the floor, astonished all with his answer, which rang out clear like the peal of cathedral chimes above the roar of an angry mob on the square below: "I intend to put the question myself." This was usurpation; but it was also a solution. Now the Clerk tried to define his position. But his words were drowned in the uproarious shouts of "Organize without him!" Robert Barnwell Rhett, of South Carolina, mounted a desk and moved that Lewis Williams, of North Carolina, dean of the House, take the chair. Williams objected: his choice was Adams. "Adams! Adams!" chorused the House. Rhett, who named Williams solely because he was older than any other man in the House, instantly substituted the name of the ex-President, who was chosen by a thunderous volley of ayes.

A ten-day struggle to elect a Speaker began, the House having decided to suspend the inquiry into the New Jersey elections until a presiding officer was chosen. On the 16th Robert M. T. Hunter, of Virginia, was chosen. It took another week to organize the House, and then the President's annual message was read. The five Democrats from New Jersey were thereafter seated. They had as much color to their claims as their Whig opponents; both sides had been guilty of frauds in the election.

During the first week of the sitting the Whigs met at Harrisburg and again nominated General Harrison for President. John Tyler, of Virginia, a Democrat, and a Strict Constructionist, was named for Vice President. Clay, who never doubted that he would be the choice of the convention, "was sitting in a room at Brown's Hotel, anxiously waiting to hear of his nomination." Wise, who called on him, relates that Clay "made most singular exhibitions of himself in that moment of ardent expectancy. He was open and exceedingly profane in his denunciation of the intriguers against his nomination. We had taken two Whig friends of our district to see him; and after they had sat some time listening to him, in utter surprise at his remarks, full of the most impudent, coarse crimination of others, in words befitting only a bar-room in vulgar broil, of a sudden he stopped, and turning to the two gentlemen, who were dressed in black and both strangers to him, he said, 'But, gentlemen, for aught I know, from your cloth you may be parsons, and shocked at my words. Let us take a glass of wine.' And, rising from his seat, he walked to a well-loaded sideboard, at which, evidently, he had been imbibing deeply before we entered.''

When word was brought that Clay had been defeated, Wise noted: "Such an exhibition we never witnessed before, and pray never again to witness such an ebullition of passion, such a storm of desperation and curses. He rose from his chair, and, walking backwards and forwards rapidly, lifting his feet like a horse string-halted in both legs, stamped his steps upon the floor, exclaiming, 'My friends are not worth the powder and shot it would take to kill them!' He mentioned the names of several, invoking upon them the most horrid imprecations. . . . 'It is a diabolical intrigue, I now know, which has betrayed me. I am the most unfortunate man in the history of parties: always run by my friends when sure to be defeated, and now betrayed for a nomination when I, or any one, would be sure of an election.' ''

Clay had not overstated the nature of the intrigue. The younger Joseph Gales had told Adams "that the nomination of Harrison at Harrisburg was the triumph of Anti-Masonry and was entirely the work of W. H. Seward, the present Governor of New York." Seward effected Clay's defeat through a most ingenious invention. This was the famed Triangular Correspondence. Seward, knowing that New York would control the nomination, induced his aides, pretended friends of Clay, residing in Rochester, Utica, and New York City, to write each other to this effect: "Do all you can for Mr. Clay in your district, for I am sorry to say that he has no strength in this." These letters were then shown to Whig leaders in the three great sections of the State. In this manner Clay's strength was destroyed before the New York delegation went to Harrisburg, and the delegates were committed by Seward to support Scott, the stalking horse for Harrison.

On Christmas Eve Congress heard Van Buren's annual message. He again assailed the paper banking system in his fourth plea for the Sub-Treasury. The collapse of Biddle's Bank of the United States in the second week of October, with the consequent suspension of banks in the West and South, he adverted to in the course of a plea for regulation of the banks. The several State governments, he said, ought to limit the activities of banks to banking, and "take from them . . . the unjust character of monopolies; to check . . . by prudent legislation, those temptations of interest, and those opportunities for their dangerous indulgence which beset them on every side . . ." After dwelling on the immense power of the banks over politics and trade, and the wholesome effect the Sub-Treasury and other imperative reforms would have on them and on the nation, he observed that in most other countries the ends aimed at could be achieved only "through that series of revolutionary movements, which are too often found necessary to effect any great and radical reform; but it is the crowning merit of our institutions that they create and nourish in the vast majority of our people, a disposition and a power peacefully to remedy abuses which have elsewhere caused the effusion of rivers of blood, and the sacrifice of thousands of the human race."

When the message was read, in the Senate, William Allen, of Ohio, moved that it be printed. Allen, ever coining phrases—it was he who invented five years later, during the Oregon boundary dispute, "Fifty-four forty, or fight!"—was at his happiest on this occasion. He was brief, and did not construct a bewildering labyrinth of rhetorical expressions. Thus he summed the evils of paper money and Van Buren's struggle:

> To guarantee forever the rights, the happiness of individual man —to protect the feeble against the rapacity of the strong—the whole against the combinations of the parts, by an equal distribution of burdens and of blessings among all—was the cardinal object of our civil institutions. But, notwithstanding this, these rights have been violated —this happiness perilled—this rapacity allowed—these combinations formed—and this equality destroyed. These things have been done, and that, too, under the authority of law. Corporations innumerable freckle the face of the land. Corporations which, not content with absolute power over the currency—over the property—over the labor of the entire people, now seek to render themselves immortal, and their dominion complete, by political associations. . . .

When, in 1837, after the universal crash of the banking system, the President recommended its severance from the Government, and the Government's restoration to its ancient policy, the people, unprepared alike for the ruin around them, or the remedy proposed, re-mained for a moment, equally confounded by both. State after State reeled from its perpendicular and slid from its support; politician after politician fled for safety or for succor to the arms of his foes; yet he, almost alone, amidst the general consternation, amidst the desertions of the venal and the shrieks of the timid, stood unappalled —confiding, as he ever has, does, and ever will, in that "sober second thought" of his countrymen which is "never wrong, and always efficient."

The opposition realized that Van Buren's stand on the Sub-Treasury would not lend itself to a popular form of attack. But they were not in a dilemma because of this, as Van Buren's supporters had forged the very steel they sought. When Harrison was nominated, the *Baltimore Republican* sneered at his poverty with: "Give him a barrel of hard cider, and settle a pension of two thousand a year on him, and my word for it he will sit the remainder of his days in his log cabin . . ." The Washington correspondent of the *Evening Post* defiled the columns of Van Buren's metropolitan organ with this: "General Harrison's poverty has awakened the sympathy of the ladies of this District, and they are now at work getting up a subscription to supply the 'war-worn hero' with a suit of clothes. If you have any old shoes, old boots, old hats, or old stockings, send them on, and they will be forwarded to the Hero of North Bend."

Shortly after the Senate confirmed a new Cabinet officer. The election of Grundy in November to succeed Senator Ephraim H. Foster had created the vacancy. Van Buren at first invited Buchanan to be Attorney General. When he declined, he named another Pennsylvanian, Henry D. Gilpin, author of several legal tomes, patron of the arts, and philanthropist. Until he joined Van Buren's official family, Gilpin had been Solicitor General of the Treasury. Grundy, an old friend of Calhoun, had been laboring for some months to effect a personal reconciliation between the Great Nullifier and the President. He was aided by Francis W. Pickens, a Representative from South Carolina.

The day following Christmas, Calhoun was a guest at the White House. No one was astonished, as the South Carolinian had been a zealous supporter of Van Buren's policies for some time. Had Grundy alone attended this little dinner, and participated

in reuniting the two, the Whig press would have been furnished
with fresh ammunition for the impending campaign. Pickens had
been one of the most caustic critics of the Van Buren administration. No one had played more on Marcy's "to the victor
belong the spoils."

The bellwether of the opposition journals, the *American*, in
satirizing the reconciliation, recalled the speech Pickens made at
the opening of the regular session of Congress in 1837, when he
said: "The rooks, together with the obscene birds, have perched
themselves in the high places of the land, and we sit here beneath,
surrounded by their filth and corruption."

On January 27 the *American* said that the enactment of the
Sub-Treasury bill would reduce "the wages of free labor in the
United States to the lowest standards of overtaxed and overpopu-
lated Europe." This, of course, Rufus King's son, and those who
reëchoed his editorialisms, knew to be untrue. But canards of this
type were leaving their impress on the masses in the cities, who
were again beginning to feel the pinch of poverty, as they had
felt it in 1837.

Through Hone we have a glimpse of Van Buren on the last
day of the month, at one of his Saturday night dinners. "The
party consisted of about five and twenty gentlemen; a splendid
affair . . . The President does the honours with dignity and
graciousness. There is no fuss in the business, and every guest has
his full share of the attentions of his host. I thought myself
particularly favoured, and so I presume others did. The President
sat on one side of the table, with Mr. Southard on his right, and
Mr. Sturgeon, the new senator from Pennsylvania, on his left.
Immediately opposite to him was Mr. Forsyth, Secretary of State,
with General Scott on his right and me on his left,—an arrangement which the Secretary informed me before the dinner was made
by the President's order. The President's first glass of wine was
drunk with General Scott, and the second with me." This was
typical of Van Buren: distinguished Whigs who visited Washington were invited to these Cabinet dinners and shown marked
attention at his table.

The Whig campaign was actively under way in the month
of February. The slurs on Harrison's poverty were the materials
out of which the opposition beclouded issues and fashioned the

most dramatic appeal ever submitted to the American electorate. The log-cabin home of the Whig nominee symbolized not only the struggles of the frontiersman, but the simple ways of the majority; and to their prejudices the Whig journals made daily appeals. In the month of March, during the height of the New York charter elections, the log cabin was first used as the Whig emblem, and hard cider was distributed free and freely at Whig rallies. On Friday, April 10, four days before election, Hone noted: "Immense meetings take place every night at the general and ward places of rendezvous. Processions parade the streets at night with music, torches, and banners; the prevailing device for the latter is the *log-cabin;* and we had hard cider, which has become the fountain of Whig inspiration. . . . on all their banners and transparencies the temple of Liberty is transformed into a hovel of unhewn logs; the military garb of the general, into the frock and shirt-sleeves of a laboring man. The American eagle has taken his flight, which is supplied by a hard cider barrel, and the long established emblem of the ship has given way to the plough." Biddle and his host of paper bankers had become more democratic than the most radical of the Loco-focos. The Whigs lost the city; but the Democratic majority was greatly lessened.

The following day Van Buren was the victim of a most virulent attack in the House of Representatives by Charles Ogle, of Pennsylvania. This speech is an unexcelled example of partisanship run riot. For almost the entire day the Whigs sat enthralled as their spokesman wove a record with warp of fact and woof of fancy. Ogle fabricated a figure so like Van Buren as to deceive the unknowing. More than twenty years before this speech was made, William Lee, American Consul at Bordeaux, purchased for the Presidential mansion many exquisite pieces of French cabinetry, and other furnishings, including a service of gold spoons. Monroe, the second Adams, and Jackson had used these things. Ogle said that Van Buren had bought these luxuries: and plated spoons and divers other articles of base metal, became, in the orator's crucible, expensive examples of the goldsmith's art. This, and similar ridicule, was heaped on Van Buren:

And now, sir, having seen that this democratic President's house is furnished in a style of magnificence and regal splendor that might well satisfy a monarch, let us examine the manners, habits, conduct, and political principles of the person who dwells in it, and see if they correspond to the grandeur of the mansion. I do this to show the People some facts, from which they may judge whether this is that plain, simple, humble, hard-handed democrat whom they have been taught to believe is at the head of the democratic party. . . . He may call himself a democrat—such, no doubt, he professes to be—but then there is a great difference between names and things. You have heard the story of the farmer's son, who said to his father, "Father, if I should call that calf's tail a leg, how many legs would the calf have?" "Why, five to be sure," said his father. "Why, no it wouldn't," says the boy, "because my calling it a leg wouldn't make it so."

So, in this case, I strongly suspect that, when we look a little closely, we shall find that the democratic leg is nothing but a tail, after all.

Ogle next transformed the White House into a palace, and Van Buren into His Majesty. Even the President's churchgoing came in for Ogle's gibes, who contrasted Henry Clay walking from his lodgings to St. John's Church, with Van Buren riding the short three hundred yards between the White House and the Episcopal church "in His Democratic Majesty's British State-coach." It should be noted that Van Buren had not embraced Episcopalianism: he was but following the example of the Patroon and other New York Dutchmen in worshiping at the historic edifice on La Fayette Square, there being no Dutch Reformed Church in Washington.

Ogle assailed Van Buren through Prince John, who "had been honored with wine-sipping with 'the pretty little Queen,' and 'the Queen was highly delighted' with 'our Prince!'" Here Ogle exclaimed: "Our Prince! mind you. We must get familiar with these things, for we must come to them. We have a President who was so great a favorite with the English nobility that when his son goes there they rank him above their titled noblemen." Ogle was certain that Jackson or Harrison or any other heroes of the War of 1812 would not have received any honors from British hands. "What has John Van Buren done for his country to distinguish him? Nothing. . . . But our Prince, I am informed, is a very clever gentleman, and by the way, possesses a great deal of drollery. I am told that one day he went into the palace, and seeing his father rather melancholy at the prospect of Old Tippecanoe coming in, he patted him on the back, and said: 'Pa, you need not despair, because, if you are beat, I will take you in to practice law with me.' " He told how the Secretary to the President was honored by British royalty. "Is not this all enough to sicken an old-fashioned democrat? And this is Van Buren democracy! This is bringing up the sons of a democratic President in fine style!"

Many wild tales were told of Prince John, most of them sheer inventions. His mad pranks suggested many of them. A few months before Ogle's speech, with other members of New York State's Board of Law Examiners, he was a guest of the budding Solons. John Bigelow, who had just passed the examinations, was one of the youthful hosts. He recounts that immediately after all had risen and drunk solemnly to the toast, "To George Washington, the Father of his country!"—many impromptu toasts had been drunk earlier in the evening—Prince John rose and proposed: "To the health of Martha Washington, the Mother of Her Country!" A few had difficulty swallowing their wine because of the merriment that convulsed them.

Van Buren—we have Ogle's partisan speech for it—never mingled with the people on the street: he always rode in his "gilded coach." "He was out, to be sure, at the ball at Carusi's on the 22d of February. He appeared about 9 o'clock . . . the bank struck up 'Hail to the Chief.' What a glorious chief to be sure! I wonder where he fought his battles." And where was Van Buren in the War of 1812? Opposed to Madison and the war along with the Federalists and the Peace party who supported De Witt Clinton for President. Ogle appealed to the prejudices of the South by recalling that one of the reasons advanced by Clinton's friend for their opposition to Madison in 1812 was that Madison "is devoted to the Southern policy." Continued Ogle: "Was it a crime then to be 'devoted to Southern policy'? And is it a virtue now to be 'a Northern man with Southern principles'? . . ."

Ogle played with the phrase "a Northern man with Southern principles." What would the Southerners think of a Southern man with Northern principles?

After reading "the base assaults on General Harrison's poverty" in the New York *Evening Post*, Ogle said: "I can inform this insolent Loco-foco that General Harrison, though not

rich, has always had money sufficient to pay for hemming his own
dish rags and grinding his own knives, and that he would scorn
to charge the people of the United States with foreign cut wine
coolers, liquor stands, and golden chains to hang golden labels
around the necks of barrel-shape flute decanters with cone stop-
pers. And I can further inform this Loco-foco calumniator that the
hands of the 'Hero of North Bend' have become so hard by the use
of the flail and the plough tail, that a cordial grasp of his dexter
would cause the big tears to flow from the eyes of the taper, lily
fingered aristocrat who made the people pay for his Fanny
Kemble green finger-cups, larding needles, and certain other
articles which dare not be named to ears polite."

We had forgotten to mention that the Countess of Westmorland stayed at Saratoga when Van Buren was there. She
was beautiful, and all who made her acquaintance paid her
homage. But Ogle, to perfect his fictive figure of the aristocratic
Van Buren, imaged Saratoga as a lonely trysting place where Van
Buren spent all his time "in gallanting the Countess of Westmorland."

Ogle had sneers for "the cabbage garden at Kinderhook,"
and Van Buren's fondness for society. He was not an ordinary
aristocrat, but a leader of cotillions in the gay salons of the
opulent, a fop who used pomatum on his hair, powder on face,
and perfume—the most expensive French *Triple Distillée Savon
Daveline Mons Sens*—on his whiskers and lily-fingered hands.

Ogle had made a campaign text book—typical of these quadrennial imprints—for the Whig spouters.

A fortnight later Congress was deserted by Whig and Democratic leaders. All were headed for Baltimore, where the Democrats were holding their National Convention, and the Whigs had
staged a rival gathering to divert attention from the proceedings
of the Democrats. From all parts of the country the Whigs came
to the number of thirty thousand. They had a procession with
floats, including log cabins on wheels and barrels of hard cider.
The Baltimore *Patriot* tells us that "a thousand banners, burnished by the sun, floating in the breeze, ten thousand handkerchiefs waved by the fair daughters of the city, gave seeming life
and motion to the very air."

Hoodlums attacked the procession. Stones and brickbats

injured several; and a local carpenter who was marching in the parade was slain. Webster and his fellows from Massachusetts raised more than $1,000 for the dead Whig's family. Other delegates contributed more than $6,000. No one was permitted to contribute more than a dollar.

The next day, Tuesday, May 5, the convention renominated Van Buren. The presiding officer was William Carroll, sometime Governor of Tennessee, whose duel with Jesse Benton in 1813 led to the street brawl in which dirks, sword canes and pistols were used, Jackson receiving an ugly pistol wound. On motion of Buchanan there was no ballot for President, there being no opposition to Van Buren. There were many objections to renaming Johnson for second place; several States, in local convention by legislative caucuses, had nominated favorite sons for Vice President. In the resolution placing Van Buren before the people, it was also resolved, "That the convention deem it expedient at the present time not to choose between the individuals in nomination, but to leave the decision to their Republican [*sic!*] fellow-citizens in the several states, trusting that before the election shall take place, their opinions shall become so concentrated as to secure the choice of a vice president by the electoral college." In an appeal to the people the Convention denounced the Abolitionists, and accused the Whigs of enlisting them in support of Harrison. The hard cider and log cabin processions were properly described as costly and stately pageants addressed merely to the senses, which would be met with the truth and reason of democracy. The document unjustly reflected on Harrison's military achievements; and with a like disregard of truth, wrote him down a Federalist.

Letters which passed between Van Buren and Jackson indicate that the failure to name a Vice President was an expedient devised by Van Buren. On April 3 Jackson wrote to Van Buren that a Vice President ought to be named: he was against the renomination of Johnson and favored James Knox Polk, long a member of Congress from Tennessee, several times Speaker of the House. Forsyth, supported by his fellow Georgians and friends in other States, was an open aspirant for the place. Tazewell, of Virginia, was a candidate. Van Buren remained loyal to Johnson, holding that the personal habits of a man, provided they did not interfere with his labors as a public servant, were not a bar to office. But he did not dare assert himself openly.

Unlike the Whigs, the Democrats adopted a platform epitomizing the cardinal principles of Van Buren's political faith. He was for a strict construction of the Constitution, and a Sub-Treasury, and economy in government; he was against government aid to private enterprise or internal improvements; he denied that Congress had the power to interfere with slavery in the States, or to create a national bank; he denounced Abolitionists as enemies of the Union, and the few who sought to abridge the privilege of citizenship as kin to the advocates of the Alien and Sedition Laws of the first Adams.

On the day he was renominated Van Buren received a letter that effaced politics and Washington from his mind, and conjured up a picture of his childhood, of Kinderhook blanketed in snow, when young and old sang: *"Sint Nikolaas goed heilig man!"* And what was it they asked Santa Claus to bring from Muscat? Ah, yes, it ran: *"Noten van Muskaat."* Never till now had he thought of anything save nuts coming from Muscat. This was the letter:

To His Excellency Martin Van Buren, President of the United States of North America, Washington:

Sir: Hope the Almighty God will protect you, and keep you in good health. From this part of the world, having no news to communicate them to your Excellency; and, whenever opportunity offers for this place, we shall feel happy to hear from your Excellency. With any thing that we can do for you, little or plenty, shall feel happy.

Written by the order of His Highness,

Seyd Seyd Bin Sultan Bin Ahmed,

Imaum of Muscat.

Seyd Bin, Calfaun.

Dated Muscat, 25th December, 1839.

He could not help noting that the quaint letter was dated Christmas Day—the day associated with the song. And then there was a second note from the merchant house of Barclay and Livingston advising him that on His Highness's ship, *Sultanee*, there arrived in the Metropolis on May 2, these gifts from the Imaum of Muscat: two Arabian horses, one case of attar of roses, five demijohns of rose water, one package of Cashmere shawls, one bale of Persian rugs, one box of pearls, a box containing a sword. The Constitution prohibited the acceptance of presents "from any King, Prince, or Foreign State" without the consent of Congress, which had never yet granted this permission. Van Buren intended to shatter this tradition, as he had so many others. The third day following the receipt of the Imaum's letter, Van Buren, with the aid of an Oriental epistolarian, penned this answer:

To His Highness Seyd Seyd Bin Sultan Bin Ahmed, Imaum of Muscat, from Martin Van Buren, President of the United States of America—Greeting:

Great and Good Friend: By the hands of Ahmed Ben Haman, commanding your Highness's ship Sultanee, I had the satisfaction of receiving your Highness's letter of the 19th of the Moon of Shawal, the 1,255 of the Hegira. It has been a source of lively satisfaction to me, in my desire that frequent and beneficial intercourse should be established between our respective countries, to behold a vessel bearing your Highness's flag enter a port of the United States, to testify, I hope, that such relations will be reciprocal and lasting.

I am informed that Ahmed Ben Haman had it in charge from your Highness to offer for my acceptance, in your name, a munificent present. I look upon this friendly proceeding on your part as a new proof of your Highness's desire to cultivate with us amicable relations; but a fundamental law of the Republic which forbids its servants from accepting presents from foreign States or Princes, precludes me from receiving those your Highness intended for me. I beg your Highness to be assured that, in thus declining your valuable gift, I do but perform a paramount duty to my country, and that my sense of the kindness which prompted the offer is not thereby in any degree abated.

Wishing health and prosperity to your Highness, power and stability to your Government, and to your people tranquillity and happiness, I pray that God may have you, great and good friend, in his holy keeping.

M. Van Buren

By the President:
John Forsyth,
Secretary of State.
Washington, May 8, 1840.

The Emperor of Morocco, not to be outdone, sent a lion and a lioness to Van Buren, who induced the Senate to permit him to accept the gifts and sell them and place the proceeds in the Treasury, and the House ratified. A number of Whigs, persuaded by Adams to respect the ancient tradition, voted in the negative.

Kendall tendered his resignation as Postmaster General on May 16. He was not too robust and wanted to conserve his energies to spit Van Buren's enemies on his pen. Kendall privately recommended that John Milton Niles, Senator from Connecticut, be named in his stead. Van Buren doubted that Niles would accept: he was a philanthropist, a distinguished writer, and founder of the Hartford *Times*. He wrote Niles immediately, marking the communication "Strictly confidential," so that his declination could not be capitalized by the opposition. Niles, to Van Buren's delight, accepted.

It was a long session, after the manner of sittings in Presidential years. The Whigs assailed Van Buren for the expensive campaign against the Seminoles, and for using bloodhounds to track the Indians through the swamps of Florida; he was accused of trying to emulate Napoleon, Cromwell, and Cæsar, because Poinsett recommended a Federal organization of the militia— this was "Van Buren's standing army of 250,000"; he was not a Democrat, but a Kinderhook man, and his followers were the men of Kinderhook, although occasionally they were referred to as the Kinderhook Democrats. The Bank men were making their last stand against the Sub-Treasury. As had been the case since he first recommended the measure, the real battle was in the House: the Senate, following its practice, passed the bill shortly after Congress was convened. On the last day of June the House sent the bill to the President. A few Whigs, realizing that this was the most forward-looking measure that had been submitted to any Congress, voted for it. On July 4 Van Buren signed the Sub-Treasury Act, thus striking the golden chains of the banks from the hands of government.

When Congress adjourned on July 21, the campaign was rapidly approaching the high note of its hilarious crescendo. Adams was far from sanguine of Whig success in June. At this time Van Buren wrote Jackson that the prospects of reëlection were favorable. Adams and others of conservative leanings did not approve the mob appeals of the Whigs, who were erecting log cabins in every important community in the country where barrels of hard cider were the principal furnishings, and where all comers might drink themselves into a drunken stupor. Banners adorned these free saloons depicting Harrison in the buckskins of a frontiersman trapping the Red Fox of Kinderhook, or bearing some kindred device. Raccoon skins adorned the walls, and quite frequently live raccoons ran around the cabins within the orbits of their chains. In commemoration of Harrison's farewell to his soldiers, when he invited them to call at their pleasure, assuring them that his door would be never shut, or the string of the latch pulled in; the doors of these log cabins had conspicuous latchstrings, always out.

The largest of these log cabins was erected a few streets north of New York's City Hall, on Broadway, at the corner of Prince street, and covered a plot of ground fifty by one hundred feet. It was formally dedicated on the night of June 16 with speeches by Whigs from Kentucky, Indiana, and Ohio. One of the local attractions was Joseph Hoxie, a wealthy importer of textiles, a dabbler in politics, and with no pretensions to oratory. He sang. Before the summer was well under way he had organized a glee club and toured the country. Whig glee clubs sprang up everywhere, in imitation of Hoxie's. To the air of "Little Pig's Tail" they sang—and the audiences sang it with them:

What has caused this great commotion, motion,
    Our country through?
    It is the ball a-rolling on,
For Tippecanoe and Tyler too, Tippecanoe and Tyler too.
And with them we'll beat little Van, Van, Van;
    Van is a used-up man.

The ball referred to was taken from Benton's speech on the night the expunging resolution was adopted by the Senate, when he boasted that "solitary and alone" he had "put the ball in motion." Another of the many uses of this figure ran:

As rolls the ball,
Van's reign doth fall,
And he may look
To Kinderhook.

There was more of it, and soon the Whigs everywhere were singing it, for the melody was popular. They mocked Van Buren's ruffled shirt and golden plate in sounding the praises of Harrison's simple garb:

> Ole Tip he wears a homespun suit,
>   He has no ruffled shirt—wirt—wirt;
> But Mat he has the golden plate,
>   And he's a little squirt—wirt—wirt.

When this was sung in the taprooms by those who chewed tobacco, the *wirt—wirt* was simulated by ejecting tobacco juice through the clenched teeth. A parody on "John Anderson, My Jo, John!" found favor in the drawing rooms as well as on the hustings and in the taverns. The first three verses ran:

> O Matty Van, my jo, Mat,
>   I wonder what you mean
> By such a naughty act as that
>   Which lately has been seen.
> What want you with an army, Mat?
>   Ah, why do you do so?
> 'Twill march you back to Kinderhook,
>   O Matty Van, my jo.
>
> O Van Buren, my jo, Van,
>   You've clomb the hill o' State,
> And monie a cunnin' trick, mon,
>   Was fathered in your pate;
> But now you're tottering down, Van;
>   How rapidly you go!
> You'll soon be sprawling at the fit,
>   O Matty Van, my jo.
>
> O Matty Van, my jo, Mat,
>   When we were first acquaint,
> 'Tis true you were not slow, Mat,
>   With sinner or with saint;
> But now you have grown ould, Mat,
>   You never seem to know
> How fast you're goin' "bock agen,"
>   O Matty Van, my jo.

Nor did the Whig versifiers forget those who preferred recitations. The most noted of these pieces told of Tippecanoe coming out of the West, where his fame was best; "for, save his log cabin, he station had none." Of course he boldly entered the President's hall; and Van Buren, overwhelmed by Harrison's goodly form and honest face, surrendered the White House to him. And then:

> One touch to Blair's hand and one word in his ear,
> As Van reached the door, and his carriage was near:
> "We are gone, we are gone, by hook or by crook,
> I must wend my way back to my own Kinderhook;
> My light English coach, though often it flew,
> Couldn't match the hard gray of old Tippecanoe."
>
> There was mounting and tramping of Cabinet clan,
> And the Kitchen concern, some rode and some ran;
> There was racing and chasing o'er Capitol lea,
> But the little Magician no more could they see!
> So dauntless in war, to his country so true,
> Who could clear the Kitchen but Tippecanoe?

Picturesque as were the meetings, they were outdone by the parades. As the campaign progressed, women and children were infected by the enthusiasm; they rode in wagons from which they chorused partisan ditties to the accompaniment of brass bands or fife and drum corps. The fusion of the Conservative Democrats with the Whigs was epitomized in the couplet emblazoned on nearly every third banner:

> National Republicans in Tippecanoe,
> And Democratic Republicans in Tyler too.

Lurid daubs of paint on transparencies depicted Harrison on a charger bidding farewell to his soldiers; a log cabin with the legend, "The latchstring will be always out"; Harrison attired as a hunter standing beside a trapped fox with the face of Van Buren; Harrison building a rude stockade; Harrison leading a charge; Harrison guiding a plow; Harrison fighting Indians; Van Buren riding in a gilded coach—a British state-coach— driven by a redcoat; and plain white banners on which the cabalistic K.K.K.K.K. was inscribed in black. There was not a child in the land who did not know that this stood for Kinderhook

Kandidate Kant Kome it Kwite. No parade was complete without this rude couplet borne aloft:

> With Tip and Tyler
> We'll burst Van's biler.

These artificially stimulated demonstrations of popular protest against Van Buren were, in themselves, insufficient to move the mass behind Harrison. No one expected that the thinking element of the electorate would be swayed by theatrical claptrap. Webster and others who knew better, using the hustings and the press as their vehicles, sought to drive fear into homes not moved by the costly street pageants or swigs of hard cider. Day after day the prostitute press sang the praises of paper banknotes, denounced gold and silver, and cried the need of another national bank to save the nation from financial ruin. The Sub-Treasury was pictured as a menace to our institutions.

Van Buren, citing the record, said that the Bank had been originally devised by friends of privileged orders.

Webster, in one of his most dramatic outbursts, recalling that the first Bank of the United States had been chartered when Washington was President, and the second Biddle institution created under Madison, argued that this statement of Van Buren's was a direct accusation of corruption against Madison and Washington. Still essaying the rôle of a debased demagogue on the hustings, Webster added: "I may forgive this; but I shall not forget it." Biddle could not say that this laborer was not worthy of his hire.

It is an old device of politicians to accuse their opponents of traducing the venerated dead. Old Federalists were reminded that Washington had been their leader. Democrats had Van Buren held up to them as the quondam campaign manager of Rufus King, "Federalist, Missouri restrictionist, and advocate of negro suffrage." And most monstrous crime of all, Van Buren had supported Clinton and opposed Madison and the war. There was no reference to his advocacy and aid of the war after the people had spoken at the polls, nor of his intense democracy in his maturer years.

The officers of the suspended banks, still hoping to see the day return when the Sub-Treasury Act would be repealed, and the vast revenues of the government once more placed in their hands —without interest—were still powers in their respective communities. These civic and social leaders had no difficulty in persuading commission merchants and other middlemen to advertise in this manner: "The subscriber will pay five dollars a hundred for pork if Harrison is elected, and two and a half if Van Buren is." and "The subscriber will pay six dollars a barrel for flour if Harrison is elected, and three dollars if Van Buren is." Employers appealed to Democratic workmen to abandon Van Buren, saying if Harrison were not the next President their wages, then at a low ebb, would be still further reduced—provided any work was to be had. Similar appeals were made editorially, of which this from the *Morning Courier and New York Enquirer*, of October 2, is typical:

"To the Laboring Classes and Workingmen in the City and State of New York—If you wish to be poor and trodden down, and to see your wife starving and your children in ignorance, vote for Martin Van Buren."

The Whig spouters repeated the fiction of the gold spoons and falsely charged Van Buren with extravagance in the administration of government. They truthfully said the payments from the Treasury during his term had exceeded $130,000,000: they neglected to say that $14,000,000 had been spent in removing the Indians west of the Mississippi; that the pension roll had been increased to more than $10,000,000; $3,000,000 for public buildings, and nearly $7,000,000 which had been received from foreign governments for indemnities had been transferred through the Treasury to citizens.

Throughout the campaign Van Buren remained in Washington, answering letters of Whigs and his own partisans, confining his replies to the issues of the campaign. He knew that if the election was to be decided on the issues, he would receive a larger Electoral vote than any President save Washington and Madison. He knew also that if the canvass was to turn solely on the relative values of himself and Harrison, "Old Tippecanoe" would not receive a single vote.

Harrison, following the precedent established by Van Buren, campaigned for the office. In a speech at Dayton he asked himself if he was in favor of paper money, and answered: "I am." He branded the charge that he was an Abolitionist as a slander. He made an appeal to the South by declaring that the Constitution did not sanction the discussion of slavery in slave states by citizens of free states. He dodged the question of what should be done with petitions to Congress to abolish slavery with the announcement that he stood for the right of petition. The "gag rule," while prohibiting the discussion, or even the reference to a committee, of Abolitionist petitions, conceded the right to petition. No one denied this right.

Van Buren dramatized Harrison's evasion when he was interrogated concerning the "gag rule." He replied that as President he had no concern with the "gag rule." He could have stopped here; but he added that Congress was justified in its treatment of the memorials from Garrison and his followers. Not an inquiry addressed to him remained unanswered by Van Buren.

Jackson was restless. His health prevented a country-wide tour, but he canvassed western Tennessee where the Whigs were making heavy inroads. Historians have doubted that in a tavern on this tour Jackson said: "The Whigs sent Daniel Webster over to England to negotiate for a great Bank of America; the dukes, lords, and ladies over there are to be the stockholders, and the Whigs' campaign expenses are being defrayed by British gold sent here for that very purpose." Had they access to Jackson's private correspondence with Van Buren they would not have questioned that the Old Hero believed that "the combined money power of England, and the Federalists"—the phrase is Jackson's—was being used to bribe the electorate. Without Van Buren at his side, the victor of New Orleans was feeding on his old hate. In a public letter Jackson charged the opposition with resorting to "falsehood and slander of the basest kind"; but he was confident that the "virtue of the people" would triumph over the "money power." He pitilessly compared the two candidates. Harrison had only military achievements of small merit to commend him: Van Buren by his firmness and ability had earned a rank not inferior to Jefferson or Madison.

As the election drew near Van Buren's friends centered their efforts on New York, knowing that if he did not hold the State, he would not only lose the election, but suffer a severe blow to his prestige. Here the Whigs were repeating Marcy's "To the victor belong the spoils," and warning the people against corruption at the polls in the Metropolis. Two years earlier the Whigs had out-done the city Democrats in the use of repeaters, and in making false returns. There had been current for many months rumors that in 1838 Whig ballot box stuffers had been paid with money furnished by five distinguished citizens, including Moses H. Grin-nell, one of our merchant princes, as friendly journals alluded to him.

A fortnight before election James B. Glentworth, an ap-pointee of Governor Seward, was imprisoned on sworn charges that at the instance of Grinnell—then a member of Congress—and others he had imported repeaters from Philadelphia. Letters of the accused were impounded and made public. One referred to the repeaters as pipe-layers for the Croton Aqueduct. Grinnell and his associates were in a tight box. Their guilt was beyond question. They could not deny that they had supplied money which went to the repeaters; so they posed as philanthropists, and said that they had drawn upon their private funds, not to corrupt the electorate, but to prevent illegal voting. A friendly grand jury returned their reputations restored.

Nine days after the balloting in New York Jackson wrote Van Buren:

Hermitage
Nov<sup>br</sup>. 12<sup>th</sup> 1840

My dear Sir,
Your letter of the 1<sup>st</sup> instant * has been rec<sup>d</sup>. its contents duly noted, and which will be passed in review by me in a letter to you soon—Corruption, bribery & fraud has been extended over the whole Union—still, altho our friends here are all gloom, and the Federal Whigg [*sic!*] pipe layers are rejoicing, and saying they have carried Pennsylvania and will have New York, I do not believe one word of it, nor will I believe that you are not elected untill [*sic!*] I see *all* the official returns—I trust in a kind providence that he has not so early doomed us to fall by bribery, & corruption. Corruption, bribery & fraud has been resorted to over the whole Union—Tennessee & Ohio has fell victims to it—I am sure good old Pennsylvania will prove proof against the mass of corruption, & bribery that has been lavished upon her,—if New York proves democratic your election is safe—I

---

* Van Buren's letter to Jackson is not extant.

cannot believe otherwise—My Household join me in kind regards & success to you—

Yr friend<br>Andrew Jackson

M. van Buren
    President, U. S.

Not only had Van Buren lost his own State, but he carried only three States in the South: Alabama, Virginia and South Carolina: Calhoun had been faithful. He lost the entire East save New Hampshire; and carried only three western States: Illinois, Missouri, Arkansas. These seven gave him only sixty votes in the Electoral College to the two hundred and thirty-four in the twenty States that went for Harrison and Tyler. One of the Virginia electors voted for Polk for Vice President; and South Carolina's eleven votes were cast for Tazewell. The popular vote was far from being four to one against him; it stood: Harrison, 1,275,017; Van Buren, 1,128,702. James G. Birney, candidate of the Abolitionists, polled 7,059 votes. New York's count for the two major candidates was: Harrison, 225,812; Van Buren, 212,519.

Before the complete returns from the entire State were tabulated, Rufus King's son Charles printed in his *American:* "The Empire State casts out her recreant son; and by a voice of 10,000 at least condemns his measure, and supplants his power." He let no opportunity pass to void his venom on Van Buren. Six days after the election he printed a half-column of doggerel slurring the President. The first verse ran:

> Who killed small Matty?
> We, says Tippecanoe,
> I and Tyler too:
> We killed small Matty.

This attack was not sheer wantonness. King was only one of many. The Whig press, or more precisely, the journals under control of the paper-money bankers were beginning a new campaign of scurrility and vilification against Van Buren. He must be destroyed politically to serve as a warning. He had dealt them a wound which they thought the next administration would heal.

They expected to recover; but all they could hope for was a respite: Van Buren's blow was mortal. Van Buren had asked no quarter, and the banks were giving none. The leading New York morning opposition daily, the *Courier and Enquirer*, commenting on his defeat, said:

> In 1836, the State of New York, anxious to do honor to one of her citizens, gave Martin Van Buren her electoral vote by a majority of twenty-eight thousand, two hundred and seventy-two! After a period of four years, during which he has been at the head of the nation, the people of his native state have again been called upon to give him their confidence and support, and the result is that he has been declared unworthy of his station, and an enemy to the welfare of the Republic by a majority of more than ten thousand of the very people who only four years since, gave him a majority of 28,272! Let the advocates of corrupt and unprincipled politicians and demagogues who dare to trample upon the rights of the people, bear in mind this rebuke of a profligate and unscrupulous public functionary. The history of the United States can furnish no such instance of an unworthy public servant being thus severely rebuked by his fellow citizens. . . .

Van Buren ignored these attacks. Nor did he bear any ill-will toward his journalistic libelers, save King: they had to live. Years later, when King was President of Columbia College, he conversed familiarly with Van Buren at the opening of a new club house. Van Buren mistook him for his brother James, and made him feel perfectly at home. Suddenly he discovered his error: His whole attitude changed. King, sensing the situation, withdrew as gracefully as the circumstances permitted. As King walked away, Van Buren's eldest son joined him and smiling said: "I saw that you did not at first recognize your old friend Charles." This restored Van Buren to his amiable self. Years had elapsed since King had assailed him: he had made an overture for peace:  Van Buren immediately sought him out and resumed the conversation.

Three days after the *Courier and Enquirer* attack, Van Buren wrote to Jackson. We get a suggestion of the tenor of his missing letter of November 1 in the opening sentence: "The apprehensions expressed in my last have been fully realized." He then continued:

"The experience in N York had the effect of assisting, at that place, in Philadelphia & the neighbouring Counties, the frauds of the opposition, but it came too late for general effect. We carried all the counties with only one exception on both sides of the River to Albany, and a majority of 5000 to the margin of the last District in the State composed of but six Counties, and have these overthrown by a majority of three or four thousand. So complete was our success in the old parts of the State that I can go from the City to my Home 150 miles without touching a Whig County. You will recollect the caution expressed in my last about Penn. not to trust to the results in the City and County until we heard whether the business of pipe laying had been extensively carried on in the interior. The result you have seen. ... Time will unravel the means by which these results have been produced, & the people will then do justice to all. Having pursued a course in which my confidence was daily increased and which has left me nothing to regret, it is, I hope, unnecessary to say to you, you know me well, that the result causes me no personal regrets. Of this my enemies shall have abundant evidence. . . ."

After reading Van Buren's letter Jackson was more convinced that the election had been bought by English and Federalist gold. There is a touch of unconscious humor in Jackson's explanation of the reverse in Tennessee. The Old Hero began by noting Van Buren's mistake in writing October in dating his last. Jackson then continued:

The democracy of the United States have been shamefully beaten, *but I trust not conquered.* I still hope there is sufficient virtue in the unbought people of this Union, to stay the perjury, bribery, fraud, and imposition upon the people by the vilest system of slander, that ever before has existed, even in the most corrupt days of Ancient Rome, who will unight [*sic!*], and by their moral force check this hydra of corruption in its bud, or our republican system is gone, and the Federalists doctrine will be verifyed [*sic!*], "that the people are incapable of self government," and that they must be governed by corruption and fraud. I do not yet despair of the Republick, altho the scenes of corruption at our late elections, are now so probable, and so general, that unless soon met by the indignant powers of the virtuous portion of the whole community, and all those who have been engaged in these monstrous scenes of fraud perjury & imposition upon the unsuspecting portion of the people, hurled from their confidence, we will [be] ruled by the combined money power of England and the Federalists of this Union. But I trust, still, in the virtue of the great working class, that they will rally & check at once this combined corrupt coalition & on their native dunghills set them down.

I would be thankful to be informed of the componant [*sic!*] parts of the next Congress that is to say the congress of 1841—will Harrison have a majority in both Houses.

The census law—I mean the foolish questions of how much soop [*sic!*] how many chickens, geese, &c. &c. &c. lost us the State of Tennessee—the Whiggs [*sic!*] used it with great dexterity—they had their whoppers in [*sic!*], in every precinct in the State & alarmed all the old ladies with the idea that all soop [*sic!*] &c &c &c were to be taken to support your standing army of 200,000 men—& I have no doubt now but that scamp Goodlow of Louisiana, had the amendment proposed by him introduced for this purpose. But the scene is now for the present, closed, and it must be the duty *now* of all the democratic papers, to hold forth in flowing [*sic!*] colors before the people these base slanders and frauds, and the people must & will reflect on the baseness of these demagogues who originated & circulated them throughout our whole country—this is the only way by which the people can be brought to know the great injustice done you, and the democracy of the country.

For yourself you have nothing to regret, altho your Secretary of War may—you have done your duty well and I trust the people will do you justice yet, by hailing you with the approbation of "well done [thou] good & faithfull [*sic!*] servant.["]

My whole Household with Major A. J. Donelson joins me in kind regards & best wishes for your future prosperity, fame & happiness and believe me Sincerely your friend,

Andrew Jackson

Martin Van Buren
P. U. States

P. S. Some of our Republican friends—Genl Armstrong & Marshall &c was determined to resign—I have said to them no—this would be playing into the hands of the Harrisonites—Let him remove them—*Tip* has said in his speeches, that he would turn out no man for his political opinion. let us therefore test it.

Van Buren's answer to this letter is also lost. Replying to Jackson's query on party divisions in the Congress which would go into office with Harrison, he would have said that the Whigs would control the Senate by seven, and would have a comfortable working majority of nearly fifty in the House. One of the Democratic seats would be held by his son John. He had expectations that there would be a second family of which it could be said that the father and son had filled the highest office in the land.

# CHAPTER XXXIX

VISITORS to the White House found Van Buren as amiable and cheerful as if he had been given another four years' lease on the President's mansion. On the opening day of Congress, he was in his office engaged in lively conversation with a dozen or more members of both houses. A few had supported Harrison. All had been received with the same cordiality. While the friends were chatting pleasantly, Senator Preston entered. Van Buren received him with marked respect, and invited him to a chair. Preston noticed that the greeting had not been as cordial as usual. When Preston had settled himself in his seat, Van Buren remarked on the unusual severity of the weather. Talking about the weather . . . and in that frigid tone. But Preston understood. He immediately rose, bowed, and withdrew. Senator William H. Roane, of Virginia, on finding Preston gone, exclaimed: "What has become of Preston—what made him leave so soon?" All knew the intimate relations that existed between the Van Burens and the Prestons since Abraham began paying court to his future wife under the roof of the Prestons. No one had noticed anything singular in Van Buren's attitude toward Preston; and he diverted the discussion to other channels. But all Washington was talking of it within a few days as Preston made no secret of his sudden departure. Meeting a common friend almost immediately after leaving the White House, he volunteered:

"Well, I have been to pay my respects to the President. He received me with all the respect that was due to a Senator of the United States. Spoke of the coldness of the weather, and treated me and received me in a way that was a damned deal colder than the weather. But that was not the worst of it; he was perfectly right, and treated me no worse than I had deserved. . . . I was goose enough during the recent canvass to make myself a party in one of my Virginia speeches to the absurd gold spoon story. . . . I was heartily ashamed the moment I had done it, and have been so ever since."

Van Buren would readily forgive and forget unfairness in the heat of a canvass from an ordinary political foe, but not where his adversaries, as in the cases of Preston and Charles King, had risen from his table to malign him. No one had campaigned more zealously against him than Clay; but the Kentuckian had fought fair; and when he called two days after the rebuke to Preston, Van Buren received him privately, and for an hour they were closeted together. They had one thing in common: their dislike of Webster, which with Clay was gradually assuming the dimensions of a hatred. The sagacious and wily New Englander—to borrow one of Van Buren's milder descriptions of Webster— had already succeeded in convincing Harrison that Clay must have no voice in the incoming Administration. Clay was not discreet in his speech when Webster was involved. He loathed venality; Webster was not avaricious, but he had expensive habits: money trickled through his fingers. Back in the session of 1825, when Buchanan was about beginning his career, Clay, in discussing the payment of the Spanish claims then pending in the House, told Buchanan that Webster had a financial interest in the legislation. "That ———— yellow rascal is to have $70,000 of the money," said Clay.

On the day of Clay's visit to Van Buren, the President's fourth and last annual message was read in Congress. He had been working on it for weeks. As in his other public documents, there is a polish of which he was incapable; but the sentiments are his. "Fellow Citizens of the Senate and House of Representatives" was the greeting, followed by: "Our devout gratitude is due to the Supreme Being for having graciously continued to our beloved country, through the vicissitudes of another year, the invaluable blessings of health, plenty and peace. . . . With all the powers of the world our relations are those of honorable peace. . . . If clouds have lowered above the other hemisphere, they have not cast their portentous shadows upon our happy shores. Bound by no entangling alliances, yet linked by a common nature and interest with the other nations of mankind, our aspirations are for the preservation of peace, in whose solid and civilizing triumphs all may participate with a generous emulation. Yet it behooves us to be prepared for any event, and to be always ready to maintain those just and enlightened principles of national intercourse, for which this Government has ever contended. In the shock of contending empires, it is only by assuming a resolute bearing, and clothing themselves with defensive armor, that neutral nations can maintain their independent rights. . . ."

After a review of the suspension of specie payments at the outset of his term, "and the excesses in banking and commerce out of which it arose," and the consequent losses to the government, he said:

Among the reflections arising from the contemplation of these circumstances, one, not the least gratifying, is the consciousness that the Government had the resolution and ability to adhere, in every emergency, to the sacred obligations of law; to execute all its contracts according to the requirements of the constitution, and thus to present, when most needed, a rallying point by which the business of the whole country might be brought back to a safe and unvarying standard—a result vitally important as well to the interests as to the morals of the people. . . .

The policy of the Federal Government in extinguishing, as rapidly as possible the national debt, and consequently, in resisting every temptation to create a new one, deserves to be regarded in the same favorable light. Among the many objections to a national debt, the certain tendency of public securities to concentrate ultimately in the coffers of foreign stockholders, is one which is every day gathering strength. Already have the resources of many of the States, and the future industry of their citizens, been indefinitely mortgaged to the subjects of European Governments, to the amount of twelve millions annually, to pay the constantly accruing interest on borrowed money —a sum exceeding half the ordinary revenues of the whole United States. The pretext which this relation affords to foreigners to scrutinize the management of our domestic affairs, if not actually to intermeddle with them, presents a subject for earnest attention, not to say, of serious alarm. Fortunately, the Federal Government, with the exception of an obligation entered into on behalf of the District of Columbia, which must soon be discharged, is wholly exempt from any such embarrassment. It is also, as is believed, the only Government which, having fully and faithfully paid all its creditors, has also relieved itself entirely from debt. . . . Never should a free people, if it be possible to avoid it, expose themselves to the necessity of having to treat of the peace, the honor, or the safety of the Republic, with the Governments of foreign creditors, who, however well disposed they may be to cultivate with us in general friendly relations, are nevertheless, by the law of their own condition, made hostile to the success and permanency of institutions like ours.

This last note we find dominating the mental processes of Van Buren in all his later years. No man, since Jefferson, had a more profound knowledge of foreign affairs, or a deeper understanding of the varied and subtle influences set in motion by the ruling classes of the Old World to destroy our experiment in democracy. After sounding this warning, he continued:

Another objection, scarcely less formidable, to the commencement of a new debt, is its inevitable tendency to increase in magnitude, and to foster national extravagance. He has been an unprofitable observer of events, who needs at this day to be admonished of the difficulties a Government, habitually dependent on loans to sustain its ordinary expenditures, has to encounter in resisting the influences constantly exerted in favor of additional loans; by capitalists, who enrich themselves by Government securities for amounts much exceeding the money they actually advance—a prolific source of individual aggrandizement in all borrowing countries; by stockholders, who seek their gains in the rise and fall of public stocks, and by the selfish importunities of applicants for appropriations for works avowedly for the accommodation of the public, but the real objects of which are, too frequently, the advancement of private interests.

He answered the false charges of extravagance his foes had made during the canvass with a presentation of the state of the Government's finances. He observed that in the few months the Sub-Treasury had functioned nothing had occurred "in the practical operation of the system to weaken in the slightest degree . . . the confident anticipation of its friends." He assailed the Whig proposal for a new Bank because "it had been so clearly demonstrated that a concentrated money power, wielding so vast a capital, and combining such incalculable means of influence, may, in those peculiar conjunctures to which this Government is unavoidably exposed, prove an overmatch for the political power of the people themselves; when the true capacity of its character to regulate, according to its will and its interests, and the interests of its favorites, the value and production of the labor and property of every man in this extended country, had been so full and fearfully developed . . ."

To avoid a national debt, he advised economy; in lieu of a Bank, he urged the continuance of the Sub-Treasury. And thus he summed up his stand against subsidizing private enterprise: ". . . Not deeming it within the constitutional powers of the General Government to repair private losses sustained by reverses in business having no connection with the public service, either by direct appropriations from the Treasury, or by special legislation designed to secure exclusive privileges and immunities to individuals or classes in preference to, and at the expense of, the great majority necessarily debarred from any participation in them, no attempt to do so has been either made, recommended, or encouraged, by the present Executive."

He had nailed his colors to the mast.

Six days after the message had been read, Clay introduced a resolution to repeal the Sub-Treasury Act. He knew that the repealer had no chance in this Congress; but it was a dutiful gesture, as he explained. Calhoun rebuked him for assuming that the people had decided against the Sub-Treasury in the late election, and reminded the Whigs that at their national convention they had "solemnly resolved that they would make no declaration of their opinions." On motion of William Allen of Ohio, Clay's resolution was amended by striking out all its language after the word, resolved, and inserting an indorsement of the Sub-Treasury. It was a temporary triumph for the people.

New Year was ushered in by a blinding storm of snow, hail, and sleet, which did not abate until nightfall. At the White House Van Buren's daughter-in-law stood in the receiving line with the members of his Cabinet and their wives. Clay was there. Other members of Congress, with their wives and daughters, had braved the weather to pay their respects. Most of the callers were Whigs. Democrats who knew him only politically remained beside their own hearths. They could not get anything more from him; he had nothing more to give. Van Buren had a keen appreciation of dramatic contrasts. As he greeted Clay, he could not but recall his first New Year's Day in the White House; the endless stream of visitors; Clay sardonically complimenting him on being surrounded by so many friends; and his own cynical retort: "The weather is very fine." He had anticipated the loss of his fair-weather friends.

On Tuesday, February 9, Harrison arrived in Washington, and he called the following day at the White House. For half an hour they chatted pleasantly.

On Thursday Van Buren shattered another tradition, when, accompanied by his entire Cabinet, he returned the visit by calling on Harrison at his lodgings in Gadsby's Hotel. The strict etiquette of official Washington is that the President shall not return visits. He next played host to Harrison. The President-elect was the only Whig at this White House dinner. The Democratic leaders of Congress, and the heads of departments, assisted in entertaining Harrison, whose heart was warmed by these unexpected attentions. Turning to Van Buren's spokesman in the upper house, he exclaimed: "Benton, I beg you not to be harpooning me in the Senate; if you dislike anything in my administration, put it into Clay or Webster, but don't harpoon me."

Hone reached the city on the Thursday following the dinner to Harrison. The next morning he called at the White House. Van Buren escorted him into his study. Van Buren was "fat and jolly," and "a stranger would be greatly at a loss to discover anything to indicate that he was a defeated candidate for the high office he is about to vacate." Van Buren assured Hone that his opposition during the campaign had not diminished his friendship for him, and expressed his gratification because Hone had not indulged in personalities. The few Whigs who had not maligned him had earned his gratitude. To be grateful because one is not basely slandered: this is the pathos we would expect to find in a Greek tragedy. Yet Sumner, in his life of Jackson, said: "He [Van Buren] was thick-skinned, elastic, and tough." Yale's professor of political and social sciences had found a well drilled by the hirelings of the corrupt financial system Van Buren destroyed.

The last day of February fell on Sunday. While driving to St. John's, Van Buren saw Hone walking churchward. As Hone ascended the steps he was greeted by Van Buren's son Smith, who extended his father's invitation to share his pew. Hone had "to stand some shots from the Whigs who have not the taste to understand how a man may continue on good terms with a gentleman whose election he has worked hard to defeat." Hone naïvely added: "I . . . did not find my devotions interfered with, nor my political principles contaminated, by the company I had the honor to be placed in."

Van Buren vacated the White House the day before the inauguration, and took his lodgings with his Attorney General. He had offered to break up his household on February 20 so Harrison might have a needed rest: this was impossible at any of the overcrowded hotels. At Gadsby's, where Harrison lodged, the dining room had been converted into a dormitory. A rude shed, seating four hundred, hastily erected in the court, housed the hungry diners. Harrison would not permit Van Buren to make this sacrifice. Harrison's enfeebled frame and sixty-eight years had badly weathered the buffetings of the campaign.

The visiting Whigs made the inauguration the climax of the Presidential campaign. In the taprooms of hotels and taverns they celebrated. Joseph Hoxie was welcomed by every drinking group; and the *Evening Post* correspondent wrote that "he has already made a deep impression on the *profanum vulgus* by his splendid execution of some choice Tippecanoe songs, although hardly in the city forty-eight hours." The small boys, who always run with the herd, paraded Pennsylvania Avenue, singing:

> Couldn't come it over Tip,
> Couldn't come it nohow,
> Couldn't come it over Tip,
> Because they didn't know how.

The custom of a retiring President participating in the inauguration of his successor had not been established. Van Buren remained in Gilpin's home. Van Buren had work to do. The Legislature of Missouri had nominated him for President four years hence, and had also honored him by naming a new county after his native village. In his reply, addressed to Governor Thomas Reynolds, he avoided saying that he would run again. "I did not on that occasion [when first nominated], nor do I now, profess to be indifferent to a station to which every citizen of the United States may aspire. . . . No one can expect, or should desire, to be always in office under a government and institutions like ours; and I have enjoyed that privilege long enough to satisfy my utmost ambitions. . . . The circumstances under which the Democracy of my native county, of my native State, and of the sister

States, have raised me from the first to the last step of advancement, the opportunities they have afforded me to exemplify to the world the principles by which I have been governed, and the indomitable spirit with which they have sustained me in the late struggle to baffle the exertions and appliances of selfish and political interests combined against me, and against the measures which I have uniformly advocated, and in part succeeded in establishing, have imposed upon me an obligation lasting as life, and leaving on my heart a debt of gratitude I can never discharge."

This letter was dispatched on March 6. Two days later he wrote to the Tammany leaders planning a welcome home that he would be in the Metropolis on the 23rd. He informed the committee: "I come to you now with a political ambition more than satisfied by the many and distinguished honors which have been conferred upon me, and with no higher aspirations, if there be higher, than to occupy the station, enjoy the privileges, and discharge the duties of an American citizen."

He returned home by easy stages. He was entertained at Baltimore and Philadelphia. On March 17 he reached the Quaker City, accompanied by Silas Wright, and in the evening visited the Democratic Reading Room at 8th and Chestnut streets. New York impatiently awaited the day of his arrival, and when it came, wished that any other day in the year had been chosen. A gusty wind from the ocean swept sheets of rain through the city streets. At three o'clock Van Buren and Wright arrived in Jersey City. It was still pouring. Half an hour later he landed at Castle Garden, and the waiting thousands at the Battery were wet to the skin.

He laughed at the suggestion that he ride in a closed barouche. There was "a corps of lancers . . . beautifully dressed and equipped" and "a numerous body of armed firemen" to escort him to Tammany Hall. He insisted that he and Wright sit in the barouche with its top down. Several times the parade was halted in its course up Broadway by mobs massed around the ex-President's carriage. Women waved handkerchiefs from windows draped with dripping flags. At Bleecker street the cortège turned east, and thence south on the Bowery to Chatham street [renamed Park Row] to Tammany Hall, where Robert H. Morris formally welcomed Van Buren back to his native State. The response was very short. He expressed the hope "that Providence may enable me to demean myself worthily toward the great cause to which I have been long and devotedly attached, and toward the virtuous and devoted yeomanry by whom I have been intrepidly sustained in the hour of difficulty."

After dinner Van Buren went to the Bowery Theater where he saw the "immense Attraction—Dramatic and Equestrian— . . . The Greek Warrior's Return . . . followed by varied and beautiful selections of Arena Entertainment by the whole Equestrian Company . . . concluded with the Equestrian Drama in 3 acts, of El Hyder, or, Love and Glory." He visited the menagerie of wild animals. We also learn from the advertisement for the evening's bill that there was no advance in prices, which remained: "boxes 50c, pit 25c, gallery 12½c." All evening long the audience took turns in applauding the performers and huzzaing for Van Buren.

That night he slept at the house of his law partner. Butler had a home on Waverly place and Greene street. On the morrow he rested. Thursday found him in the City Hall where he received eight thousand admirers. Friday evening he attended the Park Theater where Mrs. Sutton played the leading part in "The Ladder of Love," followed by "the grand opera of Norma," Mrs. Sutton singing the title rôle; and as soon as the curtain had been rung down on Bellini's work, Mrs. Sutton sang "a grand *scena* from Otello" and "Woodman, Spare That Tree!" The evening was rounded out as it began—with a farce, "Shocking Events," in which the versatile and tireless Mrs. Sutton appeared as the leading lady.

When Van Buren had been in New York a week, Webster visited the city. Webster not only had succeeded in making Clay an unwelcome visitor at the White House, but had so played upon Harrison that the Kentuckian was constrained to write the President:

. . . I was mortified by the suggestion you made to me on Saturday, that I had been represented as dictating to you, or to the new Administration—mortified, because it is unfounded in fact, and because there is danger of the fears, that I intimated to you at Frankfort, of my enemies poisoning your mind toward me.

In what, in truth, can they allege a dictation, or even interference, on my part? In the formation of your Cabinet? You can contradict them. In the administration of the public patronage? The whole Cabinet as well as yourself can say that I have recommended nobody for any office. I have sought none for myself, or my friends. I desire none. A thousand times have my feelings been wounded, by communicating to those who have applied to me, that I am obliged to abstain inflexibly from all interference in official appointments. . . .

If to express freely my opinion, as a citizen and as a Senator, in regard to public matters, be dictation, then I have dictated, and not otherwise. There is but one alternative which I could embrace, to prevent the exercise of this common right of freedom of opinion, and that is retirement to private life. That I am most desirous of, and if I do not promptly indulge the feeling, it is because I entertain the hope—perhaps vain hope—that by remaining a little longer in the Senate, I may possibly render some service to a country to whose interests my life has been dedicated. . . .

The new Administration was heading into a storm. Webster and Clay were each ambitious to succeed Harrison; his age precluded any thought of a renomination. Toward the end of March New York heard that Harrison was gravely ill; and on April 4, "thirty minutes before one in the morning" as the official announcement had it, he died. Van Buren was the principal mourner at the obsequies held in the Metropolis.

Saturday morning, May 8, Van Buren boarded the *Albany* at the foot of Barclay street. He was at last going home. "Early in the afternoon, a numerous and respectable portion of the citizens of Kinderhook, Stuyvesant and the adjoining towns assembled on the steam-boat wharf, to await the arrival of the Ex-President. When the . . . boat . . . came in sight, she was saluted by a heavy piece of artillery which continued firing until the boat reached the wharf. Several popular airs were also played by the Spencertown Brass Band the members of which, without distinction of party, volunteered for the occasion." Butler was with him, and together they entered Van Buren's private carriage and led a procession "composed of a long line of citizens in carriages and on horseback." Their approach to the village "was announced by the firing of cannon and ringing of bells. . . . The procession having arrived in front of Stranahan's hotel, Mr. Van Buren was conducted . . . to the piazza of the spacious building, which was already graced by a goodly company of

ladies. . . ." Again, as two summers ago, Mordecai Myers spoke
the welcome.

The outside world learned of Van Buren's return from the
*Albany Argus* of three days later, which published a paragraph
beginning: "We understand that Mr. Van Buren came up the
river on Saturday last, on the steam-boat. . . ." A full week later,
the *Argus* reprinted the account of the reception from the *Kinderhook Sentinel*. Van Buren had not given up hopes of again
presiding over the destinies of the nation as this excerpt from
Myers's speech indicates: "Here, surrounded by friends and connections, may you, under the protection of Divine Providence,
pass many and happy years under the shade of your own vine
and fig tree, unless again called by the voice of the people into
public life, a mandate which you ever have and doubtless ever will
obey."

All else in the "thrice welcome home" was devoid of politics.
Van Buren ended his response with: ". . . I come to take up my
final residence with you, not, I assure you, in the character of a
repining, but in that of a satisfied and contented man. Of this
even my opponents, if they are not already, will soon, I trust, be
entirely satisfied." He emphasized that he had no regrets, defended
the financial system he had given to the country, and added:
". . . all I desire is, that my future political standing with the
people of the United States shall be graduated by the opinion
which they may ultimately form of the soundness of the principles and measures referred to." There was to be no compromise
with the social and economic forces which defeated him.

Van Buren evidently sent a clipping from the *Sentinel* to
Jackson in the first known letter that he wrote after his return,
from which we quote: "You will see by the enclosed that I have
at last got home. My health has never been better, nor my spirits
either. I found the improvements I had directed on my place in
great forwardness, & hope to get into it by the 1st of June. How
greatly would its value be encreased [*sic!*] if I could promise
myself to see you at it. To come as near that as is practicable, I
have our friend Col. Earle's likeness of you (which is the best he
took) well framed, & mean to surrender to it, and to an excellent
likeness of Mr. Jefferson which I have had the good fortune to
procure, in my dining room."

Extensive alterations were made on the old red brick pile, built by Billy Van Ness's father in 1797. The plain brick mantels in the fireplaces on the first floor gave way to chaste marble, worked in Ionic design. Two additional kitchens were built at the rear of the house: there would be large gatherings at Lindenwald. An observation tower, from which the Hudson could be seen, was raised four stories above the old gables. A new pump was installed outside the original kitchen door, and the well in the cellar—still used in old country houses in the north when the pump freezes—cleaned out. The spacious hall was papered with a colorful hunting scene designed by an Alsatian craftsman toward the end of the eighteenth century. A lodge at either end of the arched driveway lent a manorial tone to the place. New chicken houses, a stable, and a cattle shed had been built in the rear of the house.

For two months Van Buren lived alone. Every morning, before breakfast, he would mount the gift of John Randolph of Roanoke and ride to the village, exchanging salutations with neighbors, and pleased when greeted in Dutch. He would have liked to have one of his children with him; but Prince John was in Washington, serving his first term as a member of Congress in the special session convoked by President Tyler on May 31; and he was marrying sometime in June. His bride was Elizabeth Vanderpoel, a native of Kinderhook. It would be a long session; he would like to be near John; but all accounts concerning him were highly flattering. As July was ending, Abraham came to Lindenwald, bringing his wife and their infant son. Van Buren was a grandfather. The old house was now worth living in. He turned to politics with added zest. He kept up a voluminous correspondence with lieutenants throughout the country, and directed the contest to reclaim New York from the Whig control.

The Whigs in Congress were in a sorry state. In his inaugural message Tyler voiced disapproval of a new Bank of the United States and of Van Buren's Sub-Treasury. He signed a bill repealing the act creating the crowning achievement of Van Buren's administration; and on August 16, vetoed a bill creating another Bank. The Whigs regarded Tyler as a traitor to the banks who had lavished their money to elect him and Harrison. Had he forgotten what had happened to Van Buren? A second bank bill

—the word bank was omitted, and corporation used throughout the measure, in the hope that Tyler would accept this puerile substitution—was rushed through both houses. On September 9 Tyler vetoed it. Within forty-eight hours, the entire Cabinet, save Webster, resigned. Mighty was the power of the men who could bribe legislatures to yield them bank charters, and with this grant in their vaults—and little else beside—turn out paper money as fast as the presses could print it.

The November elections justified Van Buren's expectations. In New York the Democrats captured some sixty Whig seats in the Assembly: it would take another year to win the Senate, where only a third of the membership was chosen annually; and all indications pointed to the election of a Democratic Governor twelve months hence. Democratic gains in other States showed the trend of the next Presidential election.

Congratulations poured in on Kinderhook. Letters from Judge John Law, of Indiana, and John Hastings, one of Ohio's Representatives in Congress, especially pleased him: both described the elections as the return of "the sober second thought of the people." Not since Jefferson had any President out of office wielded such influence with the masses. Lindenwald was becoming another Monticello.

His old enemies talked of Calhoun for President in 1844 with Silas Wright for Vice President. They uncooped a canard that Van Buren declared he would not run again. In denying this he volunteered that he would take no step toward being the party's choice for President.

Shortly after the election John A. Dix visited Kinderhook. Dix, who was distinguished as an educator and a lawyer, had been elected to the Assembly from an Albany district: service in humble places was not then regarded as bemeaning. When he returned to his home, he wrote an editorial for the *Argus*. It appeared December 1 under the heading: "Mr. Van Buren in Retirement." It was a tactless production, and in sum, said that Van Buren must be nominated by the next Democratic National Convention, whether he wished it or not. Bryant, ever loyal to Van Buren, apologized in his *Evening Post* for the dictatorial tone of the editorial. Thurlow Weed, the bellwether of the Whig journalists, disposed of it in his *Albany Journal* with: "Written by

Dix, revised by Butler, approved by Van Buren." To which the *Argus* rejoined that neither Van Buren nor Butler had any hand in preparing it.

On December 14 a grand jury in Philadelphia indicted Biddle and several directors of the defunct Bank of the United States for looting the institution. Biddle was specifically charged with having conspired to rob the stockholders of $400,000. He succeeded in escaping jail on a technicality. This did not destroy his unholy sway over the politics of the land.

In the second week of February Van Buren began a tour of the South. The announced reason was a visit to the Hermitage, but its immediate purpose was to circumvent the moves Calhoun and his friends were making to destroy Van Buren's strength in the South. He was accompanied by his former Navy head, James K. Paulding, who acted as secretary. When Clay learned that Van Buren had started, he invited him to be his guest. Clay's invitation overtook Van Buren at the High Hills of Santee, South Carolina, on March 26, five days before Clay delivered his valedictory to the Senate. His retirement emphasized the Whig party's repudiation of Tyler, who now occupied the unique position of a President without a party. Van Buren replied that, plans permitting, he would be in Kentucky early in May. He was declining numerous invitations from Southern communities anxious to do him honor. Nashville and Jackson greeted him affectionately.

Early in May Van Buren bade farewell to the most devoted friend he ever had. On arriving in Lexington, he and Paulding were met by Clay and invited to his home. The next morning Van Buren and Paulding went to Ashland where they remained two days. No one enjoying Jackson's friendship, save Van Buren, could have gone from the Hermitage to Ashland without forfeiting the Old Hero's esteem; for Jackson cherished the delusion that Clay had corruptly robbed him of the Presidency in 1828. There was drama in this meeting—and mystery. No one knows what passed between these potential rivals for the Presidency in another two years. The general surmise was that they agreed to keep the question of the annexation of Texas out of the campaign. Both saw eye to eye on this problem which the servilocracy hoped to make the issue in 1844. Annexation would stop the reconquest of Texas by Mexico. The slave-owners were ready to plunge the nation into war if necessary to add Texas to the Union, and thus increase their strength in Congress. Jackson, whose encounters with Spaniards made him detest the whole race, sympathized with the Texans; but since Van Buren had taken a position against admitting Texas without Mexico's consent, he had maintained silence.

Van Buren's reception in Lexington so delighted him that he made special mention of it in a letter to Jackson telling of his visit to Clay, and his departure for Frankfort. At St. Louis he was regally received. This was repeated at Cincinnati, Columbus, Indianapolis, and elsewhere on the route. On his return to Kinderhook Van Buren went over his broad acres—there were more than a hundred cleared and nearly as many in timber—and was satisfied with the husbandry. On July 30 he wrote to Jackson: ". . . I find my farm in excellent condition, crops good and promising & hope to sell *enough of it to pay the workmen in the garden, & on the farm* which is my ultimatum. . . ." He marketed his large potato crop in New York.

The New York Whigs made Van Buren an issue in the fall campaign and met defeat. William C. Bouck was elected Governor. Seward, sensing the shift, had declined to run again. The Democratic gains throughout the Union were acclaimed by Van Buren's friends as evidence of his return to popular esteem. He had now several rivals for the nomination; the most formidable, next to Calhoun, were Buchanan and Cass.

Tyler was feeling the long arm of the Bank through its controlled press. These were almost wholly Whig. Van Buren organs in quoting from their rivals invariably distinguished them in this wise: "We copy the following from the Boston *Courier,* a Whig paper independent of Bank influence." Whig journals not of the type of the Joseph Tinker Buckingham paper had maintained a vituperative campaign against Tyler since he vetoed the two measures designed to incorporate another Bank of the United States. When a mild form of influenza was epidemic, the Bank papers called it the "Tyler grippe." He was branded as a tyrant and a traitor, and all to one end: to prepare the people for his impeachment. Their intentions were known when Congress convened, and on January 10 the impeachment resolution was presented to the House. Tyler's spokesman in the House and biographer, the fiery Wise, does not name the author of the resolution, merely indicating him as "the coarse creature" and "the ogre of Whig politics." Nor would Wise name the State which sent him to Congress. The mover of the resolution was John Minor Botts, of Virginia. Appended to the resolution calling for a committee to institute the impeachment proceedings were the charges on which the Bank men sought to remove from office the President of the United States. Wise fairly disposes of the accusations as "foul, false, pointless, and offensive to every sense of good morals and good taste." This first attempt to indict a President has one count which betrayed the motive of Botts:

> I charge him with the high crime and misdemeanor of withholding his assent to laws indispensable to the just operations of government, which involved no constitutional difficulty on his part; of depriving the Government of all legal sources of revenue; and of assuming to himself the whole power of taxation, and of collecting duties of the people without the authority or sanction of law.

This was the rub of it: Tyler had vetoed the Bank's bills. The resolution was defeated 127 to 83. All save ten who voted for impeachment had voted for the Bank bills which Tyler disapproved. Only six New York representatives voted for the proposal, Prince John and twenty-one other Democrats from New York voting no. Millard Fillmore, who was to reach the Presidency after the manner of Tyler, was one of the New York Whigs to support the Botts resolution.

Had Botts the evidence of the secret negotiations then being carried on between agents of Tyler and Texas, he would have had ample reason for moving an impeachment. This intrigue to annex Texas was conducted without even the actual knowledge of Tyler's Secretary of State. Only the arch-leaders of the servilocracy knew, although Joshua R. Giddings, of Ohio, and other Congressmen suspected that they were under way as early as the second week in February. There was no secret, however, of the intentions of the South. Wise in a speech on the floor of the House thus voiced them: "True, if Iowa be added on the one side, Florida will be added on the other. But there the equation must stop. Let one more northern state be admitted, and the equilibrium is gone—

gone for ever. The balance of interests is gone—the safeguard of American property—of the American constitution—of the American union, vanished into thin air. This must be the inevitable result, unless, by a treaty with Mexico, the south can add more weight to her end of the lever! Let the south stop at the Sabine [the eastern boundary of Texas], while the north may spread unchecked beyond the Rocky Mountains, and the southern scale must kick the beam."

There was little likelihood that the plot could be consummated in Tyler's term: it was essential, therefore, that his successor be favorable to the scheme. Accordingly a second conspiracy was contrived against Van Buren because he opposed annexation. This design began with the publication of a letter signed by Thomas W. Gilmer, a member of the House, and former Governor of Virginia, urging that Texas be annexed "soon, or not at all" to prevent Great Britain from imposing a military and political control over Texas. The *quid pro quo* was to be a loan and the guarantee of the independence of Texas. The political control would lead to the abolition of slavery. Many believed all the representations in the Gilmer letter, whose authorship has been traced to Duff Green, the steadfast ally of Calhoun. In the month of February, Aaron Vail Brown, a member from Tennessee, and an avowed friend of Van Buren, was induced by Representative George W. Hopkins, of Virginia, to mail a copy of the Gilmer letter to Jackson with a request for his opinion.

It did not require much to rouse Jackson's suspicions of Great Britain. Moreover, he favored annexation from the beginning, and in 1829 directed Van Buren, then Secretary of State, to instruct Poinsett to negotiate the purchase of Texas from Mexico. In 1835 the offer was renewed and, again, Mexico declined to sell, although this time the offer was increased. The sentiment for annexation in the North was universal, provided it could be accomplished honorably and did not increase the power of the servilocracy. On March 12, three days before Jackson celebrated his seventy-sixth birthday, he wrote to Brown that he favored immediate annexation. Gilmer obtained possession of the letter, and exhibiting it in confidence to a friend of Benton, boasted it would destroy Van Buren. He explained he would have Van Buren and Calhoun interrogated on immediate annexation just before the convention; after Van Buren had declared against it, it was planned to read Jackson's letter to the delegates: this would drive Van Buren's Southern delegates to Calhoun.

About this time it became desirable that the Secretary of State be made a party to the secret negotiations carried on with Texas. Webster was inflexibly opposed to annexation as proposed: he must be supplanted. A few months back he had successfully completed the most important foreign undertaking Van Buren had left unfinished—the settlement of the Northeastern Boundary question. On May 8 he resigned. Neither he nor Tyler gave any reason. Wise, with delightful naïveté, recites that Webster "magnanimously retired to make way for a Southern statesman, when the time came to take up the next most important matter of foreign relations,—Texas." The "Southern Statesman" was Abel Parker Upshur, of Virginia. Webster left office undoubtedly ignorant of the moves that had been already made in that direction; but he could not have been unaware of the rumors which reached Adams and other New Englanders. Six weeks after his resignation he accompanied Tyler to the dedication of the Bunker Hill monument on the anniversary of the battle it commemorated. On this particular June 17 Adams entered in his diary: ". . . Daniel Webster is a heartless traitor to the cause of human freedom; John Tyler is a slave-monger. What have they to do with the Quincy granite pile on the brow of Bunker's Hill? What have these to do with a dinner in Faneuil Hall, but to swill like swine, and grunt about the rights of man? . . ." These sentiments are explained by an entry made nine days earlier: "Webster has undertaken to dragoon the Whigs of this State [Massachusetts] from their allegiance to Henry Clay, whom he proposes to supplant as a supplementary candidate for the Presidency by a double coalition with John Tyler and John C. Calhoun. . . . This is but a step to that flagitious coalition which is to prostrate the freedom of this Union to its slavery." Webster's silence made many suspect him of a secret bargain with the servilocracy; but he was not found wanting when the hour arrived.

While the plot against him was in being, Van Buren continued to answer interrogatories on political subjects. In proclaiming himself a low-tariff advocate, he said that the chief sufferers from a high protective tariff were the mechanics and laborers. All aspirants for the nomination were asked if they would abide the result of the convention. Calhoun in his reply volunteered that he was not a candidate.

Bancroft and other friends advised Van Buren during the summer not to write letters, or at least confine himself to short responses to interrogatories. They did not want him to jeopardize his strength before the convention. But Van Buren, intent as he was on getting the nomination, was not ready to purchase it with silence or evasions. He continued to answer frankly all inquiries. No one disputed his leadership, openly, at least. The Whig journals rounded on the Democrats in the fall campaign as the Van Buren party. The people, surfeited with Whigs and paper money bankers, elected a Democratic Congress. The Whigs had fewer than half as many members in the House as the Democrats, who elected John W. Jones, of Virginia, Speaker, by a vote of 128 to 59.

The national conventions were to have been held in December, but were postponed to May. The Whigs, whose nomination of Clay was a foregone conclusion, agreed to postponement at the suggestion of Democratic leaders. Van Buren's friends, scenting no intrigue in the proposal, joined in the request. This delay was to the success of the plot of the Texas annexationists. Van Buren, unsuspecting, on January 13, wrote Jackson that he expected a harmonious outcome at the convention.

Toward the end of the month the intrigue against Van Buren began to appear in the open. Advices from Indiana and Illinois revealed his enemies at work among the delegates. In the latter State the feeling over annexation was bitter; here a mob, in the first months of Van Buren's administration, had shot to death Elijah P. Lovejoy, a Presbyterian minister, publisher of an Abolitionist newspaper. The pro-slavery men had thrice before destroyed Lovejoy's printing presses. Wright wrote Van Buren on March 1 that Washington teemed with rumors that he intended to withdraw as a candidate. A copy of the *Evening Post* reached him about the same time with comment on Biddle's death. Bryant wrote that Biddle died "at his country seat, where he passed the last of his days in elegant retirement, which, if justice had taken place, would have been spent in the penitentiary."

The next day New York was shocked by news which arrived

by express from Washington. The preceding afternoon a new gun, called the "Peacemaker," exploded on the steam-frigate *Princeton*, killing several officials, including two of Tyler's Cabinet, Upshur and Gilmer. The latter had resigned from Congress only ten days before to become Secretary of the Navy. Wives, sisters and daughters of the distinguished guests had prevailed on the President to remain below decks while the big gun was being fired. Tyler escaped death through the timidity of the women.

A week later Calhoun was named Secretary of State to complete the secret negotiations with Texas. Within two weeks of his taking office, the conspirators passed the word that a treaty of annexation had been signed and would soon be submitted to the Senate. Stocks and bonds tumbled, as a war would hurt commerce. But a bloody conflict was nothing if it prevented the southern scale from kicking the beam—to borrow Wise's image. It was not, however, until April 12, that the treaty was signed by Calhoun. Some speculators profited by the premature report,—the gamblers in Texas scrip and Texas land.

Van Buren's steady growth in popularity made the intriguers alter their plans respecting the use of the Jackson letter. After the signing of the treaty, Brown went to the office of the Washington *Globe*, which had been the official organ of both Jackson and Van Buren during their administrations, and asked as "a friend of Van Buren," that Jackson's letter favoring immediate annexation be published. Blair instantly saw through the scheme, but asked time to think it over. He held the letter long enough to copy it, and on March 18, forwarded a transcript to Van Buren. Blair went as far as he could, without leaving himself open to the charge of dictation, to suggest that Van Buren not oppose the powerful slave-States on the eve of the convention. Four days later Jackson's letter—now a year old—was printed in the Richmond *Enquirer*, another loyal organ of Van Buren. The date had been changed to March 12, 1844, to give it the appearance of having been recently written. On March 26 another member of the conspiracy, William H. Hammett, a Representative from Mississippi, wrote to Van Buren, professed friendship, said he was an uninstructed delegate to the Baltimore Convention, and urged him to say if he was for or against immediate annexation.

Van Buren began work at once on a reply to Hammett, and

dispatched Butler to the Hermitage to apprise Jackson how their enemies had made use of him. The Old Hero wrung his hands futilely as he protested that his letter to Brown should not have been used to serve any partisan purpose. This he would say in seeking to undo the harm; he would also say—as he did—that his confidence in Van Buren's love of country was so strengthened by years of intimacy, and his regard for Van Buren so great, that no difference over Texas would change his opinions. But he would like to see him change his views on annexation; and this he communicated to Van Buren through Butler and by letter; but knowing Van Buren he did not expect to see his wishes realized.

Twenty-five years earlier, or even less, Van Buren would have found a way to please both sides; but he was long past that. His reply to Hammett takes prime rank among public documents stamped with rare courage. He answered categorically, as requested. He was against immediate annexation of Texas. He went beyond this and said that annexation, without Mexico's consent, meant war,—an unjust war. He was for annexation when it could be done honorably and with justice to Mexico. He reviewed his own record of fair dealing on the subject. He reminded the people that the Texas which the Jackson administration had sought to acquire only extended as far west as the Rio del Norte, and did not include the larger domain extending to the Rio Grande, now claimed by the Texans. After a lengthy discussion of the law in the case, and of the belligerent relations between Texas and Mexico, he said:

We must look at this matter as it really stands. We shall act under the eye of an intelligent, observing world; and the affair cannot be made to wear a different aspect from what it deserves if even we had the disposition (which we have not) to throw over it disguises of any kind . . . if, as sensible men, we cannot avoid the conclusion that the immediate annexation of Texas would, in all human probability, draw after it a war with Mexico, can it be expedient to attempt it? Of the consequences of such a war, the character it might be made to assume, the entanglements with other nations which the position of a belligerent almost unavoidably draws after it, and the undoubted injuries which might be inflicted upon each— notwithstanding the great disparity of their respective forces, I will not say a word. God forbid that an American citizen should ever count the cost of any appeal to what is appropriately denominated the last resort of nations, whenever that resort becomes necessary either for the safety or to vindicate the honor of his country. There is, I trust, not one so base as not to regard himself and all he has to be forever and at all times subject to such a requisition. But would a war with Mexico, brought on under such circumstances, be a contest of that character? Could we hope to stand justified in the eyes of mankind for entering into it; more especially if its commencement is to be preceded by the appropriation to our own uses of the territory, the sovereignty of which is in dispute between two nations, one of which we are to join in the struggle? This, sir, is a matter of the gravest import, one in respect to which no American statesman or citizen can possibly be indifferent. . . .

Van Buren knew the passions of many were inflamed in favor of annexation by friends and relatives who had settled in Texas. We must not be misled by these, or by the fact that most of the Texans were once American citizens, because "nothing is either more true or more extensively known, than that Texas was wrested from Mexico, and her independence established, through the instrumentality of citizens of the United States." The present proposal of annexation, he stressed, bore no analogy to the efforts of two other administrations to acquire Texas by purchase and peaceful negotiation—the first was during the administration of John Quincy Adams. Even granted that they were, they did not justify the committing of a wrong to accomplish the object desired. His jealousy of the nation's good name was no less than his apprehensions of the dangers lurking to our experiment in democracy: immediate annexation would place a weapon in the hands of those who looked upon our republican institutions with distrustful eyes, and would do us more injury than the new territory, however valuable, could repair.

Duff Green had fabricated a second letter—it was not then known that he was the author, although he was suspected—bolstering up the charge in his Gilmer letter that the British government had designs on Texas. Van Buren scoffed at these charges, which had been officially denied by England, and said it would be time for the United States to interfere when England sought more than the usual commercial favors.

In writing his answer, which equaled in length the longest

of his messages to Congress, he left no phase of the subject untouched; he anticipated everything that the annexationists might bring forward in rejoinder. The question was no longer a subject of underhand intrigue, for on April 12—and he had not yet completed his reply to Hammett—public announcement was made of the signing of the treaty with Texas. It was now a campaign issue, and not merely a question of annexation, but an extension of slave territory. He could be charged with attempting to ride into the Presidency on his popularity and dictating to a Congress elected on the issue. This he precluded by declaring that if after a full discussion of the subject, the people chose representatives favorable to immediate annexation, he would yield to the popular will. Yet this could be translated into truckling for the nomination if permitted to stand alone; so he ended the answer to Hammett with: "Nor can I in any extremity be induced to cast a shade over the motives of my past life, by changes or concealments of opinions maturely formed upon a great national question, for the unworthy purpose of increasing my chances for political promotion."

There were mingled emotions among Van Buren's friends when the letter appeared in the Washington *Globe* on April 23. Few doubted his nomination; but many believed that the slave-power—as Van Buren now began to designate the Southern Democrats to his intimates—with Calhoun at its head, would nominate Tyler on a third ticket and defeat him. Clay made himself equally objectionable to the servilocracy with his declaration against immediate annexation printed in the *National Intelligencer* simultaneously with Van Buren's. John C. Rives, who shared control of the *Globe* with Blair, on May 20, wrote to Van Buren that four-fifths of the Democratic members of Congress were opposed to him. A more careful survey led him to say three days later that Van Buren would be nominated on the first ballot.

The Van Burenites on reaching Baltimore, where both conventions would meet on the 27th, found the trail of Calhoun everywhere. More than three-fourths of the States had instructed their delegates, explicitly, or indirectly, to vote for Van Buren. Some of the Southern delegates rather than carry out their instructions to vote for Van Buren resigned. Delegates from Calhoun's own State declined to enter their names in their official capacity, but continued to remain in the convention as spectators. This was Calhoun's way of saying that, officially, he would have no voice in the convention while it considered Van Buren. Unofficially he was ably represented on the floor. Before the convention was called to order, it was known that the strategy of the slave-holders would be to adopt the two-thirds rule. After the convention organized, Romulus M. Saunders, of North Carolina, moved the adoption of the rules of the convention of 1832, which nominated Van Buren for Vice President—Jackson had been nominated by the States and the convention merely indorsed their actions. These included the two-thirds rule by which the slave-power aimed to crush Van Buren. Butler, knowing how the Van Buren ranks had been thinned by the Calhoun corps, rose to oppose the motion. He was sure of a majority of the delegates on the first vote; but many of these had told him that they would vote for the adoption of the two-thirds rule. All day long the Van Buren men and the slavery representatives debated the proposal. Butler deliberately prolonged the argument. He was fighting to delay decision until the next day, and succeeded. After adjournment Butler and his aides visited their followers favoring the two-thirds rule to persuade them to vote for a majority rule. That night Butler posted a brief note to Van Buren at Kinderhook saying that if the two-thirds rule was not adopted his nomination was certain.

The following morning the free territory and slave territory advocates resumed the contest. Not a delegate among the 325 who had answered the roll call on the first day was missing from his seat. Some of these had only split votes. Virginia, with fifty-three delegates, had only seventeen votes. The total number of votes in the body was 266. Every one of these was cast when the angry debate ended at noon, and the undemocratic two-thirds rule, originally adopted to lend a greater appearance of strength to Van Buren's nomination for Vice President, was carried 148 to 118. More than fifty of the delegates instructed to vote for Van Buren had gone over to the slave-power on this test vote.

There was no applause from the victors. The occasion was too solemn. Butler held back the welling tears. He had not lost hope. Pencil in hand, he kept tally as the first ballot was being taken, and when the result was announced the Van Burenites cheered. He had a total of 146 votes, thirteen more than all the others combined. Had these voted against the two-thirds rule, Van Buren would have been nominated on this ballot. Cass was second with 83; Johnson, who had publicly announced that if he could not get first place he would take second, was a poor third with 24; Calhoun trailed behind with 6; Buchanan had 4; a lone complimentary vote was given to another Pennsylvanian, and Levi Woodbury, United States Senator from New Hampshire, received 2. All of Van Buren's strength, save twelve votes, came from the North.

On the second ballot, while Van Buren again headed the list, he no longer had a majority. Cass was gaining on him. The clerk announced: Van Buren, 127; Cass, 94; Johnson, 33; Buchanan, 9; scattering, 3. The third ballot saw Van Buren still losing. Now he mustered only 121; Cass still held second place, but with only 92; Johnson with 38, had gained 5; Buchanan made a similar gain, reaching 11; scattering, 4. On the fourth ballot ten more abandoned Van Buren. Now he stood only six ahead of Cass, the result being: Van Buren, 111; Cass, 105; Johnson, 32; Buchanan, 17. Van Buren lost first place on the fifth ballot, which stood: Cass, 107; Van Buren, 103; Johnson, 29; Buchanan, 26. Cass climbed still higher on the sixth ballot with 116 to 101 for Van Buren. Johnson and Buchanan were also sliding; Buchanan had but 25; Johnson, 23. Van Buren also fell behind on the seventh vote, Cass adding seven, making his total 123 to 99 for Van Buren. Buchanan and Johnson continued to fall, being reduced to 22 and 21 respectively.

By this time the day was ending. Nerves were frayed. The Van Burenites were bitter. They murmured and muttered against the slave-power. Van Buren had more than two-thirds of the delegates, and they had robbed him of several before the balloting began. Then they forced the adoption of the two-thirds rule, designed as a piece of theatrical claptrap for Van Buren's benefit while he was in England. As John L. O'Sullivan, then engaged with Wright and Samuel J. Tilden in forming a new daily, the *Morning News*, wrote to Van Buren, the atmosphere was laden with corruption. Some of the Van Burenites found consolation in the knowledge that the unjust rule could work both ways, for they had arrived at their irreducible minimum when the ninety and nine voted for the ex-President on this ballot. But others who followed his fortunes, remembering the arguments advanced by Butler, that a President should have a second term who had faithfully served the people, and that a majority rule was acceptable to Jefferson, let their anger get the better of them. Butler had emphasized this last by reminding the Convention that the true democratic rule called upon the minority to submit to the majority. These angry ones recalled the point Butler made in opposing the adoption of the two-thirds rule, that at the last convention, which Van Buren's followers controlled, and which had renominated him unanimously, the majority rule had been adopted.

Above the angry murmur a voice rose clear and piercing, and in tones reflecting the temper of his associates, moved that Martin Van Buren, having received a majority of the votes on the first ballot, be declared the convention's choice for President. The Calhoun men instantly became a shouting, maddened, gesticulating mob. They had not anticipated this. Delegates were tired and anxious to go home. It would not do to let this motion go to a vote. After order had been restored, the chair ruled that the motion would require a two-thirds vote for adoption. From the Ohio delegation, whence originated the motion, came the cry: "I appeal from the ruling of the chair!" This was reëchoed throughout the hall. Several were on the floor speaking at once. A confused and violent debate followed, and at the request of the Van Buren leaders, the appeal from the decision of the chair was withdrawn, and the convention proceeded with the eighth ballot. When the roll call was completed a new candidate was in the race, Polk, of Tennessee. He received the solid delegations of his own State and Alabama, seven from New Hampshire, a like number from Massachusetts, whose representation was headed by George Bancroft. Polk had a total of 44 votes. But Van Buren had gained five votes, his total being 104. Cass, with 114, had lost eleven votes. Johnson had been eliminated. Buchanan's followers had shrunk to 2; and Calhoun, who had not received a single vote in the seventh ballot, now reappeared with 2.

A motion to adjourn to the morrow was put and carried. That night Baltimore and Washington talked of the new entrant. Congress was in session, and the members who remained at their tasks had been kept informed of every important action by "the new invention of the electro-magnetic telegraph of Professor [Samuel F. B.] Morse . . . in manuscript bulletins suspended in the rotunda [of the Capitol]" as Adams noted. Three days before the convention met, the first public message had been sent over the line, which extended from Washington to Baltimore. Congress, two years earlier, had appropriated $30,000 to aid the penniless inventor.

That night the Van Buren and the slave-power leaders reached an agreement; and when the convention met in the morning, Butler withdrew Van Buren's name. Immediately the South Carolina delegates, who had been sitting as mere spectators, had their names enrolled as the representatives of their State. Then the ninth ballot was started, and 232 of the 264 votes cast —some did not vote—were for Polk. Before the clerk announced the result there was a scramble by the delegates who had voted for losers to change their votes. While the convention was noisily cheering the winner, some of Van Buren's old friends were disconsolate. In a letter to Van Buren Bancroft wrote:

. . . Butler wept like a child; . . . the delegation of Ohio was distinguished for gallantry, though rather precipitate & fiery. It remained in the power of your friends to have dissolved the convention without any nomination; but such an issue I deprecated as wrong in itself, and as injurious to your Fame. . . .

I have many personal causes for regretting the result; but do not include among them the week I gave to the more particular study of your political career. The present ceases to be the fittest moment for the publication of the little sketch I had prepared. . . .

After Polk's nomination, a recess was taken until the afternoon. Wright was named Vice President, Georgia's six delegates alone voting against him. He was in the rotunda of the Capitol, reading the bulletins, and within a few minutes after his nomination the clerk read his telegram declining. The nomination of Wright was a gesture by the servilocracy toward his defeated friend; they knew Wright would decline. A week before the convention opened Van Buren had instructed Butler by confidential letter to fight for Wright for first place if the slave-power would not accept him. Wright was as opposed to the extension of slave territory and the annexation of Texas as his leader. The insincerity of Wright's nomination was demonstrated on the second ballot for Vice President. Governor John Fairfield, of Maine, received the highest number of votes in a field of five, but he lacked the required two-thirds. The convention, anxious to adjourn, was willing to make Fairfield's vote unanimous if his friends could say definitely that he was for immediate annexation—and war, if necessary. In Fairfield's absence no one could give definite word, so the slave-States chose George M. Dallas, of Pennsylvania, for whose warped principles Buchanan could vouch.

The platform adopted was a confession by the servilocracy that they had sacrificed the ablest leader and statesman since Jefferson. Everything that Van Buren had advocated, save his opposition to immediate annexation and the extension of slavery, was incorporated into the appeal on which Polk and Dallas were submitted to the people. The document opened with this denunciation of the log cabin, hard cider, and coonskin campaign of four years ago:

Resolved, That the American Democracy place their trust, not in fictitious symbols, not in displays and appeals insulting to the judgments and subversive of the intellect of the people; but in a clear reliance upon the intelligence, the patriotism, and the discriminating justice of the American masses.

There was an attack on the bigotry of the newly formed Native American Party which had elected a Mayor in New York City in the preceding month in this:

That the liberal principles embodied by Jefferson in the Declaration of Independence, and sanctioned in the constitution, which makes ours the land of liberty, and the asylum of the oppressed of every nation, have ever been cardinal principles in the Democratic faith; and every attempt to abridge the present privilege of becoming citizens and owners of soil among us, ought to be resisted with the same spirit which swept the alien and sedition laws from our statute books.

The platform closed with this tribute to Van Buren:

Resolved, That this convention hold in the highest estimation and regard their illustrious fellow citizen, Martin Van Buren, of New

York; that we cherish the most grateful and abiding sense of the ability, integrity, and firmness with which he discharged the duties of the high office of president of the United States, and especially of the inflexible fidelity with which he maintained the true doctrines of the constitution, and the measures of the Democratic party during his trying and nobly arduous administration; that in the memorable struggle of 1840, he fell a martyr to the great principles of which he was the worthy representative, and that we revere him as such; and that we hereby tender to him in his honorable retirement, the assurance of the deeply seated confidence, affection, and respect of the American Democracy.

Polk's nomination astonished the country. The jargon of the race track was drawn on to describe his unanticipated victory; he was the added starter, the winning black pony, the dark horse. The last became part of the argot of politics. Many believed that Butler had made a premature surrender in withdrawing Van Buren's name. This thought was embodied in a letter to Van Buren from James S. Wadsworth, a New York delegate. The fault did not lie with Van Buren's managers. Bancroft and others who were loyal to him, perceived at the end of the first day that he could not be nominated. The South said: "Let the North name the candidate, provided he is for immediate annexation." Bancroft was the first Van Buren leader to advocate the switch to Polk, the best of the mediocrities available. The failure of the Democracy of Tennessee to instruct its delegates for a candidate for first place, while declaring for Polk for Vice President, raised suspicion that Polk was a party to the Calhoun intrigue. Before many months had passed, Van Buren had evidence of its truth.

Van Buren received the news with philosophic calm. He made good his promise to support the nominees of the convention. But his friends in New York, led by William Cullen Bryant and David Dudley Field, instituted a secret campaign against the election of Democratic candidates for Congress who favored immediate annexation. Within ten days after the convention adjourned, Van Buren had the satisfaction of seeing Congress reject the war-making treaty for the immediate annexation of Texas.

Had Clay not truckled for Southern votes, he would have triumphed over Polk. The movement initiated by Bryant and others against immediate annexation was the sentiment of the

North, and especially so in New York. Wright had been drafted as candidate for Governor by Van Buren. He, too, labored for Polk and Dallas. Twice during the campaign Clay declared he had no personal objections to the immediate annexation of Texas. At once the leading Whigs of the North, who had pledged their reputations for Clay's adherence to the resolves of the Whig Convention, ceased their labors. Clay now rushed to explain. "In my second letter, assuming that the annexation of Texas might be accomplished without war, and with the general consent of the States and upon fair and reasonable terms, I stated that I should be glad to see it," said Clay. "I did not suppose it was possible I could be misunderstood." He carried but one Southern State, and that was Polk's own State. He lost Maine's nine votes and New York's twenty-six in the Electoral College, where he lacked only twenty-three votes to win. Nearly ten thousand voters remained away from the polls in Maine. These were moderate anti-slavery men who could not square their consciences with a vote for either Polk or Clay, or for Birney, the Abolitionist, who again had been nominated for President by the Liberty party. The Maine vote for Clay was 34,378, being 12,234 less than Harrison received. Polk's vote fell 500 below Van Buren's. Birney polled 4,836 in Maine. Here a switch of 5,576 would have given Clay the State.

The result in New York must have made Clay spout brimstone. Here Birney received 15,812, more than twice as many as the Abolitionists polled in the entire nation in 1836. The number of New York votes for Birney, which would have gone to Clay but for his change of front, has been placed at 10,000. The moderate anti-slavery men of New York who remained from the polls because they could not bring themselves to vote with the Abolitionists, also reached high in the thousands. The vote in New York was: Polk, 237,588; Clay, 232,482. Polk's small majority of 5,106, in a total of nearly 276,000 votes, was due solely to Clay's vain bid for Southern votes. A switch of 2,554 ballots would have given Clay the election. The result in the Electoral College stood: Polk, 170; Clay, 105. Had Clay carried New York the count would have been: Clay, 141; Polk, 134.

Not a vote was cast, or counted, in the slave-States, for

Birney. His vote in the thirteen free-States had increased nine-fold in four years, the total counted—there were many that were not—being 62,300. Some regarded the increase as a fungous growth. The excesses of slavery were to metamorphose the mush-room into an oak.

# CHAPTER XL

POLK owed his victory to the faithful performance of Van Buren's pre-convention promise. He offered the post of Secretary of the Treasury to Silas Wright, although Van Buren had written him that Wright would be inaugurated Governor of New York on January 1 and could not abandon his elective office. Moreover, Polk also knew that New York, by virtue of the election returns, was entitled to the first place in the Cabinet, the Secretary of State. Nor was he left in ignorance of Van Buren's sentiments on this. Wright was against immediate annexation and the extension of slave territory. Polk wanted no one in his Cabinet opposed to the aims of the servilocracy. In furtherance of his crafty design, Polk then asked Van Buren to suggest a fit man for the Cabinet. Van Buren named Butler, Cambreleng, and Azariah Cutting Flagg.

But Polk had no intention of naming any Van Burenite to the first place in the Cabinet. He offered Butler the Secretaryship of War, and appealed to Van Buren to induce him to accept, knowing, of course, that Van Buren would disapprove. Van Buren continued the amicable correspondence with Polk until he heard that Marcy had been invited to head the War Department. Marcy and Van Buren had broken on annexation, and his former lieutenant was now the leader of the pro-slavery Democrats of New York. Polk's design was no longer a subject of conjecture: the slave-power sought Van Buren's political annihilation. It was now time to act. He sent his son Smith to Washington to protest against the naming of Marcy. Polk listened politely but stood by his selection. That evening he wrote to Van Buren that any error he had made was unintentional and disavowed any hostile intentions. Van Buren would have been satisfied with matters as they stood; but Polk besought Butler to accept the highly remunerative fee office he had held under Van Buren after he resigned from the Cabinet—the United States Attorneyship for New York. Cambreleng, as loyal to Van Buren as Butler, wrote a spirited defense of Butler's course, saying that it would have been impolitic to appear too independent.

Van Buren would have preferred nothing more than peaceful retirement. But it was again too late to retire—he must kick or be kicked. Often did Burr's cynical advice recur to him. They left him no choice save fight. He had everything he could wish for, but peace. His family was grown up; all save Martin, Jr., were married; Smith had espoused the daughter of William James, a rich merchant of Albany, some months before.

On January 18 his enemies saw indisputable evidence of his control of the State when the Legislature reëlected Dickinson to the United States Senate, and John A. Dix was chosen to succeed Wright. The next month, on February 17, would be the thirtieth anniversary of Van Buren's first big step toward the Presidency, his appointment as Attorney General of the State. A fortnight before that day arrived, his son John was named to the same office. There was too much similarity in this retracing of his father's footsteps for the Whigs to let the opportunity pass. Both started as lawyers; Van Buren's first political office was Surrogate; Prince John, as the Whigs always called him, started as a Law Examiner; Van Buren was then elected to the State Senate; the electors sent his son to Congress; and then the next step in the career of each was appointment to the highest law office in the State. The Whigs lampooned father and son anew. A State's choice for the Presidency is called the favorite son. Prince John was derisively named the favorite grandson, and the Magician's son. A Whig who had not plucked his lyre since the Harrison-Van Buren campaign, sang from the slopes of the political Parnassus:

O, "favorite grandson of the Empire State!"
O, son of magic, wherefore not be great!
What! canst thou pause, and shall it then be told
Thou are not worthy of thy father's fold?
Forbid it, tall John, prove thyself thy sire's,
The world a braggart, and her children liars;
Show that the wand the great Magician sways,
Thee being good, still lengthens out thy days,
Feeds thee with pap, and gives thee every good,
Clothes thy long back, and to thy fire adds wood:

Nor stop thou here, but emulate the man
Who scorns to lie, or touch the flowing can.
These are thy faults: and must I add, that play
Takes up thy time, and leads thee much astray?

There was a lack of sportsmanship in the reference to Prince
John's personal habits. He had been temperate until three months
before his appointment, when he sought forgetfulness of the loss
of his wife in the gaming table and the flowing bowl. But the
example set by his father soon rewon Prince John to a saner way
of living. There was a well-stocked cellar at Lindenwald, but the
modest meal at Kinderhook, or wherever else Van Buren chanced
to be, was washed down with a single small wine-glass of Madeira.
John Bigelow, on his visit to Lindenwald with Samuel J. Tilden,
noted this. It was Bigelow's first meeting with the ex-President,
but he was made to feel so much at home, that he commented
on his host's avoidance of the sweets upon the table. Van Buren
replied that he never took puddings or pastries, preferring a little
fruit. On this occasion he ate an apple. His simple life was reflected in his well-being, for he mounted his horse with the agility
of a youth of twenty, and rode every morning before breakfast.

The first shoots had appeared in Van Buren's farm when
he received a letter from Bancroft, now Polk's Secretary of the
Navy, offering him his old post at the Court of St. James's, which
had just been declined by Calhoun. The South Carolinian regarded himself as in line for the Presidential succession, and did
not wish to be too far removed from his political lieutenants.
Calhoun, too, was annoyed that Polk made Buchanan Secretary
of State. The offer was put on the loftiest grounds; the dispute
over the Oregon boundary had reached a delicate stage; there
were distinguished precedents: "In Europe the prime ministers
are always selected on such occasions. Witness Metternich to
Napoleon; Guizot lately to England; and Talleyrand, Marshal
Soult, and others. On great occasions the highest men are to be
taken; where war is to be averted, none but the highest. I must
quote your own avowed opinion also. Mr. Butler told me, that
you had expressed to him that in your view an Ex-President could
be honorably employed in a foreign mission. . . ."

Van Buren answered that he did not recollect having voiced

this opinion, and added: "I have, however, no hesitation in saying that . . . there would be no incompatibility with his former
position in the councils of the Nation, for an Ex-President to
accept, under suitable circumstances, an important Foreign Mission; and farther, that an emergency in the affairs of the country might arise . . . which would make it his imperative duty
to overlook minor considerations, and devote himself to the public
service in the form proposed, at almost any expense of personal
feeling or preference for retirement." But the Northwestern
Boundary dispute was not a crisis; and moreover, he did not
find "the circumstances by which [the] offer is surrounded,
agreeable." Polk would now see in this unelaborated phrase that
Van Buren viewed the tender as a sentence of exile—such as he
had contemplated for Clinton.

There was a Machiavellian cunning in Polk's offer. If Van
Buren had accepted, it would have given color to the false cry that
England was preparing to war upon us, a stratagem designed to
becloud the Administration's evil intentions toward Mexico. A
messenger dispatched by Tyler on the last day of his term
was now in Texas, offering, on authority Congress assumed
to itself, immediate annexation as a State of the Union. Van
Buren's acceptance would also have placed the stamp of his
personal approval on the Administration's wholesale extension
of slave territory, as the resolutions of annexation provided that
four additional States might be carved out of pro-slavery Texas.
There was a condition in the measure that nothing should be
attempted in violation of the Missouri Compromise. But this was
an empty gesture to make annexation less obnoxious to the opponents of slavery extension.

After answering Bancroft, Van Buren whipped the streams and
ponds of Kinderhook with new rods Tilden had sent him from
New York. On the eve of the anniversary of the Battle of Waterloo he draped a small Stars and Stripes over one corner of the
portrait of Jackson; on the opposite side he placed a bit of crape.
The Old Hero had died ten days before while the sun was sinking
behind the trees of the Hermitage.

In the first week in September, Prince John was sentenced
to serve a day in jail. His father was distressed at the first reports, but when he heard all, he, too, joined in the laughter and

applause. The Dutch counties, where the ancient manorial grants were still in possession of the heirs of the original owners, had been in a turmoil—as they had been on and off for more than a century—during most of the five years following the death of The Patroon in 1839. Armed bands of men, disguised as Indians on the war-path, made incendiary speeches in the manor towns, crying: "Down with rent!" This tenant uprising had been precipitated by the unjust exactions of The Patroon's heir. In Albany County a Sheriff's posse sent to accompany the rent collectors had been driven back by an armed body of farmers who claimed possession in fee simple. In Columbia County the violence ended in December, 1844, when the Anti-renters shot and killed a citizen named W. H. Rifenburg.

Two leaders of the Anti-renters, Dr. Smith A. Boughton, and Mortimer C. Benton, were immediately thereafter captured in the back room of a tavern, and locked in the county jail at Hudson charged with the assassination. Threats to rescue the prisoners brought out a detachment of infantry, a troop of cavalry, and a company of artillery. Four months later Boughton went on trial for his life. Public sentiment being wholly with the prisoner, the jury disagreed. He was again put on trial at the opening of the September term of court. Prince John was in charge of the prosecution. During the selection of the jury, he objected to the manner in which Ambrose L. Jordan, chief counsel for the defense, was examining the talesmen. A dispute ensued; Jordan called Prince John a liar, and was answered with a blow. Presently they were pummeling each other, wholly oblivious of the sitting court. Judge John W. Edmonds ordered the Sheriff to stop the fight and arrest Jordan and Prince John. This done, he committed them to jail for twenty-four hours. The trial was resumed the following day. The story took Van Buren back thirty-four years, when Prince John was only a babe in arms, and he had posted John Sudam as a coward after Sudam had challenged him to a duel and then refused to fight. Fists were an improvement on pistols. This time Boughton was convicted and sentenced to life imprisonment. He was pardoned two years later.

Under the leadership of Marcy, by grace of Van Buren thrice Governor and six years in the United States Senate, opposition candidates for the Legislature were entered against the Van

Buren nominees in many districts. Van Buren had seen the same thing when the Virginia Dynasty ruled the Nation: the Virginia Presidents, from Jefferson to Monroe, had muted New York's voice in the councils of the party by recognizing the minority faction. Yet the Barnburners—the term of opprobrium fastened upon the Van Burenites—won sweeping victories at the polls. The issue was the extension of slave territory. The opposition conceded that the followers of the ex-President might have grounds for their differences, but the inflexibility of the Van Burenites was likened to the farmer who burned his granary to destroy the rats. Van Buren followers retaliated with "Hunkers," an epithet which stuck to the followers of Marcy. Our lexicographers have erred in deriving Hunker from the Dutch *honk*,—a stake marking the terminus of a racetrack; a goal, or home, as used in the children's game of tag. If they would visit, even to-day, any of the old Dutch counties, they would find an occasional scholar who would inform them that Hunker is a corruption of *hunkerer*,—one who desires, a selfish person. *Hunkerer*, in turn, is derived from *hunkeren*, the infinitive of "desire"; *ik hunker* is "I desire." The opponents of Van Buren—they had long been called Conservative Democrats—were led by office holders whose motto, in the language of the Van Burenites, was "to get all they can and keep all they can get." It was to designate this type that "Hunker," with its roots in *hunkeren*, was coined. To the accepted derivations we prefer the humorous suggestion of Bryant in an editorial of October 7, 1847, that "Hunker" was derived from *Henker*, German for "hangman." The poet thought the appellation appropriate, observing that the Hunkers, if given enough rope, would hang themselves.

A week or so after the campaign all relations were broken off between Polk and Van Buren when it was publicly revealed, as Van Buren had long suspected, that the President was responsible for the savage attacks on him in a pamphlet which appeared in September. The booklet bore the title: "The Lives and Opinions of Benj'n Franklin Butler, United States Attorney for the Southern District of New York; and Jesse Hoyt, Counsellor at Law, formerly Collector of Customs for the Port of New York; with anecdotes or biographical sketches of Stephen Allen; . . . John Van Buren; Martin Van Buren; . . . Silas Wright; . . .

and their friends and political associates." The author was William L. Mackenzie, the quondam Canadian leader, now an American citizen. Intimate letters of the Van Burens and their friends which had been written to Jesse Hoyt were sprinkled throughout the 145 pages of text. Mackenzie was employed in the New York Custom House when appointees of Polk forced a locked trunk labeled: "J[esse] and L[orenzo] Hoyt's Law Papers." In May, Mackenzie, having copied many of the letters with the consent of Polk's appointees, sent the transcripts to Polk by a common friend. On May 30, under a government frank, Mackenzie received a note from one of Polk's subordinates from which we cull: "The discovery of these letters seems to be providential, and is duly appreciated in the right quarter. All will go well. . . . on any occasion, in which I can serve you, write me without reserve. You will find me ready to render you any aid in my power." With this equivalent for a royal warrant in his possession, Mackenzie prepared to feed his ancient grudge against Van Buren.

Van Buren could understand Mackenzie's deep hatred for him; for he had, among his papers at Lindenwald, a twelve-page memorial dated: "Rochester Prison, 23rd October, 1839," wherein Mackenzie made a pitiful plea for less rigorous confinement. He wrote of his ill-health and the refusal of the authorities to permit him to exercise in the open air; of his mother of ninety, a wife in delicate health, and six small children. "We are contented with our lot if let alone," he continued, "but that I should be singled out for official proscription, as it seems to me simply because I am an object of dislike to the Canada authorities, and my family left to struggle thro' the world, may be worldly policy, but it is not doing as you would wish to be done by were our places reversed."

Polk, of course, could not afford to place himself before the nation as indorsing the unjust attacks on Van Buren which Mackenzie worked into his pamphlet; so Mackenzie was removed from his Custom House berth. A new volume was issued in the spring. It was more venomous than the first, and bore the misleading title: "The Life and Times of Martin Van Buren." The casual reader, skipping through this book, would close it with the impression that Van Buren was unscrupulous in money matters to the point of corruption. This false atmosphere was created by a most adroit use of references to the corruption of men who had betrayed Van Buren's confidence and robbed the people.

Polk was now offering places right and left to the key men of the Barnburners. Those who were worth while remained steadfast. Tilden, a member of the Assembly, and poor as a churchmouse, spurned the place of Naval Officer with fees of twenty thousand dollars annually. Tilden described the Hunkers as "the venal gathered from all former parties." Dickinson, the senior Senator from New York, had become a Hunker. On July 10, 1846, Polk tried to seduce Dix with the post of Minister to the Court of St. James's. On this same occasion Polk requested Dix to advise Wright that "he had no schemes of conquest in view in respect to Mexico." This was two months less a day after war was declared against Mexico, "not in terms, but by circumlocution," as Adams phrased it. On August 6, the bill carrying out the platform pledge to restore the Sub-Treasury became law. Van Buren's great reform was back on the statute books to stay.

Before this session of Congress adjourned, David Wilmot, of Pennsylvania, a follower of Van Buren in the House, introduced a rider to a bill appropriating $2,000,000 for the purchase of New Mexico, which Texas unjustly claimed as part of her territory. This clause, known as the Wilmot Proviso, provided that "neither slavery nor involuntary servitude shall ever exist in any part of said territory." The House, reacting to the growing sentiment against the slave-power, passed the measure as amended. Every member of the New York delegation voted for the famous proviso. But it was rejected by the Senate. The Whigs, too, were divided on the question. There were Commercial Whigs—also called Cotton Whigs—and Conscience Whigs. The latter were akin to the Barnburners.

The war of conquest was bringing the Barnburners and Conscience Whigs into a common fold. The issues raised by the annexation of Texas had ceased to be abstract questions with those who daily scanned the casualty list. Van Buren's eldest had rejoined the colors. In September, at the battle of Monterey, he was again under fire. During the height of the three days' conflict, while the Mexican cannon balls were falling near where General Zachary Taylor and his staff stood, Colonel Balie Peyton rode up with a message from General William J. Worth. Van

Buren was standing beside Taylor while Peyton was making his communication. Peyton did not recognize him. As Peyton was about to return, he remarked that a letter from Santa Anna had been found in the pocket of a slain cavalry officer. For days the American troops had been asking: "What are Santa Anna's plans?" Taylor, in the hope that the letter revealed the Mexican General's future movements, asked: "Which way is he moving?" Enemy shot and shell were dropping all around the little group. Peyton, as violent a Whig as Taylor—he had served in Congress during Van Buren's Vice Presidency—drew upon the political argot to emphasize his answer. "Upon that point," replied Peyton, "his letter is quite Van Burenish and leaves us altogether in the dark." Taylor forgot that an army was under his command. Bowing to Peyton he said: "Colonel Peyton, allow me to introduce my aide, Major Van Buren." Men were falling on both sides while Peyton in his Louisiana drawl, protested that the discourtesy was unintentional; that while he differed politically with the ex-President, he always entertained toward him the kindest and most respectful feeling. A smile wreathed Van Buren's face as he said Peyton could obtain forgiveness only on condition that he would permit him, on his return to Kinderhook, to give his father a hearty laugh by recounting the incident. And laughter mingled with the thunder of the enemy's guns.

Again the slave-power through Marcy directed an attack against Van Buren. This time their treachery defeated Wright for reëlection. On the following August 27, Wright died at his farm in St. Lawrence County. Toward the close of the short session of Congress of 1846-7, the appropriation for the purchase of New Mexico was increased to $3,000,000. Again the Wilmot Proviso was added to the measure, which was once more passed by the House. The Senate once more rejected the proviso, and passed a measure from which the free soil clause was omitted. The House finally accepted the slave-power's dictation. During the acrimonious debate there were many threats of disunion and civil war. Dix, voicing the sentiments of the Barnburners, answered Calhoun and the slave-power with: "It is virtually declaring that unless we will consent to bring free territory into the Union, and leave it open for the extension of slavery, the Union shall be dissolved. Our Southern friends have heretofore stood upon the ground of defense; of maintaining slavery within their own limits against interference from without. The ground of extension is now taken, and of extending slavery upon free territory. .... I say for the State of New York—I believe I do not misunderstand her resolutions *—that she can never consent to become a party to the extension of slavery to free territory on this continent."

In the month following Wright's death, the New York Democrats met in State convention to nominate State candidates for State office below the rank of Governor. In 1846 the people had decreed that the Secretary of State, State Treasurer, Comptroller, and Attorney General were to be elected by them, instead of being appointed by the Governor with the consent of the Senate.

No local convention ever assembled fraught with greater consequences. The Hunkers controlled the machinery of organizing the convention; but the Barnburners had a bare majority of the delegates. The Hunkers threw out nearly a dozen Barnburners and seated Hunkers in their stead. Among the delegates unseated was John Van Buren. But there were still 63 followers of Van Buren in the Convention. A few of these were elected to empty honors, which they promptly declined. Among them were Cambreleng, Preston King, James S. Wadsworth, and David Dudley Field. These four led the Hunkers a merry dance; and on the fourth day an obscure Van Burenite introduced a resolution indorsing the principles of the Wilmot Proviso, from which we quote: ". . . we declare uncompromising hostility to the extension of slavery by any act of the National Government, in free territory hereafter to be acquired."

It was now Saturday. The convention had been in session since Wednesday. The adoption of this resolution would be binding on the delegates sent to the next national convention. The Barnburners, to the last man, were for the resolves. And there were many Hunkers, who, if the motion were put, would vote for it, as they would not dare vote against a proposition which had received the unanimous approval of the State Legislature. Robert H. Morris, of New York, was in the chair. His strategy was to

* The resolutions adopted unanimously by the New York Legislature directed its representatives in Congress to oppose the extension of slavery. Similar resolves had been voted by the Legislature of Pennsylvania.

prevent a roll call on the motion. Accordingly he entertained a motion to table the resolution. The debate lasted through the day and night, and after midnight, Morris declared the motion carried by a viva voce vote. The Barnburners remained until Morris vacated his chair; they did not secede from the convention as some historians have it.*

After the ruling, Field moved the adoption of another resolution of similar purport. Morris ruled that Field's motion was not in order. The Hunkers cried previous question as the Barnburners appealed from the chair's ruling. "Why this cowardice and recreancy?" exclaimed Wadsworth. "Are the gentlemen too craven to meet this question?"

"Here a scene of indescribable tumult arose," chronicled the *Evening Post*. "Every member of the Convention and the lobby gathering in the center of the room, and gestures, threats, denunciation, and discordant noise, for fifteen minutes, drowned all attempts of discussion of the question."

Many Hunkers, fearful that a roll call might be had on the Barnburners' resolution, and not anxious to commit political suicide by voting against free soil, made a hasty exit, leaving less than a quorum. Morris now refused to heed the angry demands of the Barnburners that he determine if a quorum existed, and declaring that he heard a motion to adjourn, adjourned the convention *sine die*.

A more shameless fraud could not have been perpetrated. The Barnburners, representing the vast majority of the Democratic electors of the State, denounced the fraudulent Syracuse convention, and issued a call for a convention to be held at Herkimer on October 26. In the interim the Hunker press denounced them as traitors; the Whigs held their State convention, nominated a ticket, and adopted the Barnburners' resolution which the Hunker convention tabled. Bryant called this document The White Man's Resolution.

For months local and State conventions were held in the South at which the Southerners formally resolved not to attend a national convention unless opposition to slavery extension was abandoned. The Legislature of Virginia solemnly proclaimed this doctrine as an article of Democratic faith.

* *Vide* Shepard 358 *et seq.*

This new challenge of the slave-power, whose presses re-echoed the local cry of "traitors" hurled at the Van Burenites for calling the Herkimer convention, was answered on Tuesday, October 26, when the delegates assembled. Cambreleng, for many years Van Buren's spokesman on the floor of the House of Representatives, was elected President. Several Democrats from other States attended, including the author of the Wilmot Proviso. The principal speech was made by Prince John. As the ex-President's son took the platform the delegates shouted a noisy welcome. "Fellow Democrats," he began. There was defiance in his tone, and the delegates responded to it with cheers. Quiet restored, he added dramatically: "and fellow traitors." At this assumption of the opprobrious epithet as a badge of honor, the Barnburners, who had heretofore winced at the very sight of the word in the Hunker journals, applauded and laughed by turns. For more than an hour the delegates sat and listened to Prince John, who held their hearts in his hand, and made them beat fast or slow, as the humor seized him. They rose to cheer when he denounced the slave-power's demand that it be permitted "to plant black slavery on foreign free soil." He ended his speech with: "I am aware that a fierce political storm is raging, and that the political sea is rolling mountain high; but I have an undoubting conviction of the correctness of my course, and I think I see the spirit of justice and liberty walking upon the waters, reaching out its arms to my support, saying, 'Be of good cheer, it is I—be not afraid.'" Had this last been declaimed from an ancient pulpit in an Old World cathedral, the effect could not have been more solemn. Silence took possession of all for what seemed an age. But the tall figure of Prince John was presently bowing to the cheers of frenzied delegates whose doubtings were transmuted into an unshakable faith. The resolution proposed at Syracuse was adopted. A second resolve, after reciting that the slave-owners had pledged themselves not to attend a convention which countenanced the principle of free soil, set forth that the Democrats of New York "will be obliged to adopt a counter declaration and proclaim their determination to vote for no man, under any circumstances, who does not subscribe to the preceding resolution." This, too, was adopted unanimously.

The Herkimer Convention did not nominate a State ticket.

As Prince John declared in his speech, the nominees of the Syracuse Convention would have an opportunity to subscribe to the free soil resolution. Only a week remained before New York would go to the polls. The Whig candidates subscribed unanimously to the free soil principle of the Barnburners. The Hunker candidates trusted to luck. They lost, the vote being ten to one against them in several normally Democratic counties. The Whigs carried both branches of the Legislature, outnumbering the Democrats three to one in both houses. The Democratic majority of the New York Congressional delegation was also swept away.

All through the election the *Wilkes-Barre Farmer* had carried Van Buren's name as its choice for President in 1848. Copies of the *Farmer* of October 30, containing a letter from Van Buren, reached the New York newspapers after Election Day. Van Buren said that he was sincerely and heartily desirous to partake of the honors and enjoyments of private life uninterruptedly to the end; his aspirations were of the past; he was conscious of having performed his duty to the people, and had neither heart burnings to allay, nor resentments to gratify by a restoration of power. But being only sixty-five, and with the mind and body of a far younger man, he did not close the door to a unanimous call of his party. This last, Van Buren well knew, was highly improbable.

Van Buren spent New Year's at Lindenwald. All day long he played host to Kinderhook. New Year's calling among New York's Dutch was a ceremony of obligation; its impress has not been wholly effaced. It still flourishes in the cities on the Hudson, and in the interior, where the skyline is still steeple-dotted; and even where the spires of the churches have been overtopped by cloud-piercing creations of steel and stone, the custom is not quite forgotten. Lindenwald this particular January 1 was no different from others that the old pile had seen. On a sideboard in the dining room stood rows of bottles and decanters of brandy and Schiedam and other potent beverages for the grown-ups. On a mahogany console in the great hall was the familiar punchbowl, filled with lemonade, and sparkling red from a generous dash of Burgundy; flanking the bowl were dishes of raisins and figs and the cookies of Van Buren's childhood. While the servants poured for the men and women, the ex-President waited upon the children. Some of the little girls, like their mothers, clung to the ancient custom of wearing two or more warm dresses, one at least being of quilted lamb's fleece. But it was a rare one who gave him the greeting in the tongue they all had spoken not so many years ago.

At nightfall the visits ended. He was now alone save for the servants. Abraham was still at the war. Mat was in Washington making confidential reports to him. Smith was in Albany with his family. Prince John had moved to New York. The house was very lonely; he must go to the city. This wish he gratified before the end of the month. He took lodgings at Julien's, on Washington place, just off the Square. Shortly after his arrival he read the glad news of the signing of the treaty of peace: Abraham would soon be home, wearing a Colonel's epaulettes.

The hostelry of Monsieur Julien was noted for its *"bon diners à la Paris."* But after Van Buren's arrival it became a center of political activity. Prince John and Tilden invariably attended the conferences in Van Buren's chambers. The most important of these occurred after the Hunkers met in Albany on January 26 and appointed thirty-six delegates to the national convention in Baltimore. Every one was looking forward to a gathering of Barnburners on Washington's Birthday; for the two factions at their respective State conventions in the fall had made similar provisions for selecting delegates to Baltimore. Van Buren recalled that the time-honored way was for the Democratic members of the Senate and Assembly to caucus and issue a call for a convention. The Barnburners outnumbered the Hunkers in the Legislature. Accordingly a caucus was held, and a convention called to meet in Utica on February 16.

At noon on the day appointed, the delegates assembled in the Oneida County Court House. The inns and lodging houses of Utica were overflowing with hundreds of enthusiastic Democrats from all parts of the State. Within half an hour after the temporary chairman's gavel fell, the convention was adjourned to the Methodist Church, to accommodate the unexpected throng.

Save for a speech by Prince John, nothing of moment transpired beyond the formal selection of thirty-six delegates, headed by Cambreleng. The purpose of this speech was to stress that the convention had been convoked by a call of a caucus of the Democratic members of the Senate and Assembly. This, said Prince John, was the only legal way in which a State convention could be summoned.

Early in April, during a visit to Julien's, Van Buren handed a mass of manuscript to Tilden, saying: "If you wish to be immortal, take this home with you, complete it, revise it, put it into proper shape, and give it to the public." Tilden, whose law practice kept him toiling day and night, answered that if Prince John would aid him, he would gladly undertake the task. This, of course, was intended, and Prince John and Sammy—as Van Buren affectionately called Tilden—worked over the document. Save for a brief preamble by Prince John, and a still briefer insert by Tilden, the manuscript was, in all essentials, as it had left Van Buren's hands.

This historic document—longer than his reply to Hammett —was the first real assault on slavery. The Abolitionists, with their extremes of phraseology and program, had appealed only to the emotionalists. But here, in the restrained language of statesmanship, was a pitiless indictment of the trade in human flesh, and the arrogant society built upon it. When this arraignment of the servilocracy was published in the second week of April it was received with silence from the high places in Washington; for interwoven with the presentment was an ultimatum to the managers of the Democratic National Convention which would meet within six weeks. The thirty-six delegates chosen at the Convention of Barnburners at Utica must be seated. Equally masterful was the manner of bringing it before the public: Van Buren—whose hand never openly was shown—had it put forth as the traditional address made to the people of the State at the close of each legislative session by the Democratic members.

The Barnburner delegates to the Democratic National Convention "will but illy reflect the spirit of the Convention which nominated them, and the sentiment of their mass constituency, if they do not unyieldingly claim to represent them without corival in that body, and fully assert and firmly maintain, under any and all circumstances the principles, the rights, and the honor of the Democracy of New York." This is outlawing the Hunker delegates. In a review of the decline of the party strength in New York, the Polk administration is assailed because of its recognition of the Hunkers—a "meager list of hirelings" who enjoy "the whole patronage of the Federal Government."

The address then takes up slavery. Here the genius of Van Buren is apparent. He opens the tombs of the hallowed great and calls them forth to bear true witness against the system. Washington is first called upon. His words to Robert Morris are reuttered: "I can only say that there is not a man living who wishes more sincerely than I do to see a plan adopted for the abolition of it." Patrick Henry's stricture on slave-holding is next heard: "I believe a time will come when an opportunity will be offered to abolish this lamentable evil." Jefferson is again thundering against George III for the encouragement he had given the slave trade, in having "waged a cruel war against human nature itself . . . to keep up a market where men could be bought and sold; he has prostituted his negative for suppressing any legislative attempt to restrain this traffic." Then Monroe's testimony is adduced: "We have found that this evil has preyed upon the very vitals of the Union, and has been prejudicial to all the States in which it has existed."

In bringing this dramatic phase of his case to a close Van Buren observes that Madison and other Virginians had displayed an "aversion to slavery of the deepest character." He next assails the slave-owners for denying the constitutional power in Congress to legislative control over slavery in the territories, citing acts of Congress, during every administration from Washington to his own, in which the right was acknowledged. Van Buren does not ascribe this sentiment to the people of the South, but to "the struggles of party leaders at the South for local ascendancy." The cupidity of politicians, and not the avarice of cotton growers, is Van Buren's concept of the root of the evil. This theory, which the student of history cannot reject, Van Buren supports by instancing the hordes of Southern planters who sold their slaves and emigrated to Indiana and to Iowa when they were admitted to statehood as "abodes of free labor."

The vast region ceded by Mexico—all of New Mexico and California—for which we paid $15,000,000 and assumed the claims of American citizens against the Mexican Government, had given added impetus to the cause of the slavery extensionists. To these Van Buren said: ". . . the principle of extending slavery into territories now free from it can never be made acceptable to the freemen of the North."

He closed the address in the key he began it: the thirty-six delegates chosen by the Utica Convention were the sole representatives of the Democratic party of New York. There was talk even now of seating both Barnburners and Hunkers as the easiest way out. This proposed injustice Van Buren rejected in advance with: "If a question is made of their right [to sit as delegates], it must be decided, not compromised. . . ."

Cambreleng, Wadsworth, Prince John and the rest of the delegates went to Baltimore. The convention organized on the morning of the second day. Then ensued two days of wrangling over the rival New York delegations. South Carolina was not represented; yet a lone delegate cast the State's nine votes on all motions. Dickinson of New York asked that the Barnburners be excluded on the sole ground that they had adopted a free soil resolution at Utica. On the evening of the 24th of May the convention seated the Hunkers and Barnburners, giving each delegate half a vote. Immediately the Barnburners withdrew. On the fourth ballot Cass was nominated by the slave-power, with W. O. Butler of Kentucky for Vice President.

On June 6 the Barnburners met in New York City. There was not an unoccupied square foot of the Park when Cambreleng read: "Resolved, That the nominations made at Baltimore by the persons who remained there after the convention was dismembered, and by the aid of nine votes from South Carolina, which were never sent there, are of no validity or force whatever . . . and as invalid as an Act of Congress passed after arbitrary expulsion of the members from any State. . . ."

Throughout Cambreleng's reading the vast crowd interrupted with cries of: "John Van Buren!" A motion to adopt the resolutions was carried unanimously. Prince John was then introduced, and the crowd howled its satisfaction, which he answered with smiles and bows that prolonged the applause.

"The war," he said, "was not fought by us at the North to extend slavery into free territory; it was not for that purpose that the blood and treasure of the North was poured out like water."

When the hand clappings and shouts of approval ceased, he

told of the experiences of himself and his fellow delegates in a manner which made his hearers indignant and amused in turn. He knew the value of a laugh. He reviewed the organization of the convention lasting more than a day. Not a single vote was cast by a New York delegate, Hunker or Barnburner, because the committee on credentials had refused to act. He waxed humorous as he recounted the nine votes cast by one purporting to represent South Carolina.

"I am unwilling," he continued, "that one man should count nine when seventy-two of our people count nothing, considering the vast obligations of the Democratic party to the Democracy of New York. What have they done that they should be made to suffer stripes from such a cat-o'-nine-tails as this from South Carolina?"

He had given them the looked-for hearty laugh. He grew serious again, as he was sounding the call to arms of all the opponents of slavery. And his speech ended, as most of his speeches did, with a bit to stir the soul. "You who hear me may not live to see the end of this contest, but your children will reap its benefits," he said. "You may rely on it that the future historian will look back to the present time to confirm those noble words of the poet—

> "Freedom's battle once begun,
> Bequeathed from bleeding sire to son,
> Though baffled oft, is ever won."

The Barnburners adjourned to meet in convention on June 22 at Utica.

The day after the meeting in the Park, the Whigs met in Philadelphia and nominated General Taylor, of Louisiana, whom we left on the battlefield of Monterey, and Millard Fillmore of New York. This was a hybrid ticket: Taylor owned one hundred slaves; Fillmore was from a State which had abolished slavery in 1827, and whose people, outside of New York City, were anti-slavery. The selection of the colorless Fillmore was dictated solely by the hope of appealing to the disaffected Democrats of his State. The surrender of the traditional party of the North to the slave-power was made complete when the platform was written: there was not a reference to slavery.

Slavery was the only note sounded by the Barnburners in their two-day convention at Utica. Cambreleng, Wadsworth, Field, Tilden, Preston King, and Prince John were there. A letter from Van Buren characterized the demand made by the Baltimore Convention that the Barnburner delegates pledge themselves to support the choice of the convention before their claims to seats had been decided as an indignity of the rankest character. New York had not been given fair representation and the acts of the convention were not binding upon them. He repeated the arguments he had made in the April address of the Barnburner legislators against the abandonment of the right of Congress to impose freedom as a condition of Statehood. As the Baltimore Convention had rejected this doctrine, which had been recognized by Jefferson, Madison, Monroe, and Jackson, all undoubted Democrats—Van Buren, too, had signed a bill imposing freedom on an application for Statehood—he would not vote for its candidates; and if there were no other candidate but Taylor, he would not vote for President. His stand against Northern attacks on slavery in the District of Columbia and in the slave-States was dictated by "convictions that slavery was the only subject that could endanger our blessed Union." He was aware that he had gone further in this than many of his best friends approved; but he would go no further. Anticipating the intentions of the delegates, he protested that it was his "unchangeable determination never again to be a candidate." In spite of this he was nominated for President by the Free Soil Democrats, as his adherents styled themselves. Henry Dodge, United States Senator from Wisconsin, was named for Vice President.

As this was little more than a State convention, a national convention of the new party was summoned to meet in Buffalo on August 9. Free Soil Democrats and Conscience Whigs from most of the States signified their intention to attend. A platform must be adopted and Van Buren and Dodge renominated by the national body. The newspapers supporting Van Buren—he had fifty in New York State alone—carried his and Dodge's names in a box as the paper's choice for President and Vice President. Beneath the names, following the example set by Bryant, the Free Soil press carried this excerpt from Jackson's letter to Butler,

written June 24, 1844, a few days after he learned that the Baltimore Convention of that year had rejected Van Buren:

I cannot hope to be alive to witness the acclamation with which
the people of the United States will call Mr. Van Buren to the Presidency at the end of Mr. Polk's term; but you will, and I know you
will rejoice at it as a consummation of an act of justice, due alike
to him and the honor and fame of the country.

The well-informed knew that Van Buren was a reluctant candidate. It was known also that he would be far from displeased if
the Buffalo Convention should select another nominee for President. On June 29 Dodge declined in a letter beginning: "I have
long been the friend personally and politically of Mr. Van Buren
and under other circumstances would be glad to have my name
associated with his." But Dodge's State had been represented at
Baltimore, had concurred in the nominations, and he felt obligated to support them. Not long after Dodge declined, Salmon
P. Chase, who became Secretary of the Treasury under Lincoln,
and later rose to be Chief Justice of the United States Supreme
Court, discussed the forthcoming gathering of Free Soilers with
another Ohioan, Edwin M. Stanton, who was also to serve in
Lincoln's Cabinet. That night Chase wrote to Prince John:

. . . One of the best and ablest Democrats in the State, I mean
Edwin M. Stanton, said to me to-day that if John Van Buren should
be the nominee of the Buffalo convention he would roll up his sleeves
and go to work till election for the ticket; and I am sure that to all
the young Democrats and all the young Whigs in the State your name
would be more acceptable than your father's. . . . Our contest is
with the slave power, and it will break us down unless we break it
down. . . .

Many shared Stanton's views that Prince John would make
the most popular nominee; no one in the movement had a greater
hold on the hearts of the multitude.

The Buffalo conventions—two were held simultaneously—
were held in the Brick Church, and in a circus tent erected in the
park opposite the court house. The canvas sheltered 5,000, and
was believed adequate to accommodate all. Here was held the
popular, or mass convention, whose opening session was attended

by 30,000, five-sixths of whom sat under the broiling rays of the
midsummer sun. In the church, Charles Francis Adams, son of
John Quincy Adams, presided. Every New England State was
represented. Delegations also attended from New Jersey, Pennsylvania, Ohio, Michigan, Wisconsin, Iowa, Indiana, Delaware,
Maryland, Kentucky, Virginia. Illinois, who numbered Abraham
Lincoln among her representatives in Congress—his only term
was nearing its end—had her proportionate share in the deliberations.

Adams was not a tyro in politics; he had served six years in
the Massachusetts Legislature, and the death of his father made
him the leader of the Conscience Whigs of New England. Moderate Abolitionists such as Chase were there as delegates, as well
as the other extreme, typified by Joshua Leavitt, a member of
Adams's delegation.

A letter from Van Buren informed the delegates that "the
convention of which you will form a part, may, if wisely conducted, be productive of more important consequences than any
which have gone before it, save only, that which framed the
Federal Constitution." He told them also to abandon his nomination if the great end of their proceedings "can be better promoted." On the evening of the second day the convention balloted. Leavitt presented Van Buren's name. John P. Hale, of
New Hampshire, who was proscribed by the Democratic party
of his State because he refused to follow its instructions and vote
in Congress for Texas annexation, received 129 of the 288
ballots cast. This was a complimentary vote to Hale, and a bid
for the support of the Abolitionists whose nomination for the
Presidency Hale had declined. Van Buren was nominated by
acclamation.

There was only one nominee for Vice President—John
Quincy Adams's son. The platform was next adopted; and at ten
o'clock the delegates adjourned to the mass convention in the
park where nearly fifty thousand—their numbers had increased
hourly—roared a welcome as Adams, Chase, Prince John, Tilden,
Dix, Butler, and other leaders ascended the wooden platform.
The nominations were ratified with a thundering aye. Adams was
forced to his feet by the repeated huzzas which greeted the
mention of his name. Scattered among the multitude, dispelling

the darkness, were hundreds of oil torches affixed to saplings and trees, or tied to poles stuck in the ground. The night, the torches, and the trees, added to the religious fervor of the assemblage. The first plank of the platform was a prayer as well as a declaration of political principles: ". . . we, the people here assembled, remembering the example of our fathers in the days of the first Declaration of Independence, putting our trust in God for the triumph of our cause, and invoking His guidance in our endeavors to advance it, do now plant ourselves upon the national platform of freedom, in opposition to the sectional platform of slavery."

There was nothing in the platform to appeal to the Abolitionists of the Garrison school. The next plank read: "Resolved, That slavery in the several States of this Union which recognize its existence, depends upon the State laws alone, which can not be repealed or modified by the Federal government, and for which laws that government is not responsible. We therefore propose no interference by Congress with slavery within the limits of any State."

The platform was replete with ringing phrases leveled at the slave-power, such as: "Congress has no more power to make a slave than to make a king; no more power to institute or establish slavery than to institute or establish a monarch . . . we accept the issue which the slave power has forced upon us; and to their demand for more slave territory, our calm but final answer is, no more slave States and no more slave territory. . . . the only safe means of preventing the extension of slavery into territory now free, is to prohibit its extension in all such territory by an Act of Congress."

The sixteenth and last plank read: "Resolved, That we inscribe on our banner, 'Free Soil, Free Speech, Free Labor, and Free Men,' and under it we will fight on, and fight ever, until a triumphant victory shall reward our exertions."

A little before midnight the mass convention adjourned, after paying a signal tribute to Prince John by unanimously adopting a resolution directing him to make a nation-wide speech-making tour on behalf of his father and Charles Francis Adams.

A holy zeal possessed the Free Soilers, and many of the younger leaders believed that Van Buren and Adams would be swept into office. But Van Buren had no illusions; there was not a Federal office holder among his followers. If he but had the political machine, manned by office holders, Federal and State, which supported Cass! It was he who had introduced this creation of New York politics into the life of the nation. The two-thirds rule, invented to lend an appearance of greater strength to his nomination for Vice President in 1832, had destroyed him in 1844. This, he knew, could not be undone in his lifetime, as to do so would be an acknowledgment by the slave-power that it had robbed him of the nomination in 1844 by this undemocratic device. Nor did he expect an abatement of the evil he had wrought by organizing office holders, high and low, into a well-drilled corps to sway conventions and elections. He had fought against it in his retirement, and the Free Soil platform called for "the election by the people of all civil officers in the service of the government, so far as the same may be practicable." The civil service was as yet an amorphous concept.

In New York, Dix was nominated for Governor on the Free Soil ticket. Elsewhere in the North, men of substance, following the example set by Van Buren and Dix, lent their names to the movement; they ran for the lowliest offices, and gave their time and labor in awakening the country to the menace of slavery.

It did not matter to the slave-States whether Cass or Taylor was elected. The Whig candidate had two qualities that made him preferable to the Democratic South; he was a slave-owner and a Southerner. He had a greater popular appeal because of the glamour of his military achievements. Bigotry was also aiding him. The Native American party at its first national convention, held in Philadelphia, nominated Henry A. S. Dearborn, of Massachusetts, for Vice President, and recommended Taylor for President, although not formally nominating him. This organization was a logical outcome of the Anti-Masonic party, for the sword of intolerance is two-edged. There was a refinement and improvement in methods in the Know-Nothing movement; its members were oath-bound, and held together by a secret ritual. While primarily aimed at all foreign-born, the party was essentially anti-Catholic.

Election Day blasted the hopes of the more sanguine Free Soilers. The returns from the South demonstrated to the country that the slave-owners had used the Democratic party solely for its own perpetuation; that the teachings of Jefferson and all else associated with the party were subordinate to their interests. With the exception of Virginia, Alabama, South Carolina, and Mississippi, Cass lost every Southern State; and these he carried by the slimmest of majorities. But the treachery of the South alone would not have defeated Cass. Taylor's victory would not have been possible without the votes polled by Van Buren and Adams in New York, Pennsylvania, Vermont, Massachusetts, and Connecticut. In each of these five States the combined vote of the Free Soilers and the Democrats exceeded Taylor's pluralities. The thirty-six Electoral votes in these States would have elected Cass by a majority of thirty-nine. The vote in the Electoral College stood: Taylor, 163; Cass, 127. Had Cass carried the other four Northern States where Taylor won by pluralities less than the aggregate polled by the Democrats and the Free Soilers, he would have received 194 Electoral votes to 96 for Taylor.

The popular vote was: Taylor, 1,360,099; Cass, 1,220,544; Van Buren, 291,263. Van Buren polled more votes than Cass in Massachusetts, Vermont, and New York. In his own State the vote was: Van Buren, 120,510; Cass, 114,318. Here Taylor's vote was 218,603, some 16,000 less than the number cast for Van Buren and Cass. The Whig candidate for Governor, Hamilton Fish, also carried New York because of the split. Delaware, Maryland, and Virginia were the only States in the South where any votes were counted for Van Buren. In Virginia he was credited with the ridiculously low poll of nine votes. "Fraud!" exclaimed the Van Burenites, pointing to the nine votes in Virginia. A wag of Virginia conceded the fraud, and solemnly explained that the prosecuting authorities of the entire State were seeking the Van Burenite who had fraudulently cast eight ballots in addition to his own. The country laughed as it marched onward to its Great Tragedy.

# CHAPTER XLI

THE slave-owners' support of a slave-owning Whig demonstrated to the Democrats of the North that they were slave-owners before they were Democrats. Democratic Congressmen from Northern commonwealths reflected the temper of their constituencies in uniting with Northern Whigs against the extension of slavery into the land that had been Mexico's. When the session of 1848-1849 adjourned, Van Buren knew that he had not falsely prophesied to the delegates to the Buffalo Convention when he wrote: "The convention . . . may . . . be productive of more important consequences than any which have gone before it, save only, that which framed the Federal Constitution." Evidence was not lacking that the ideal for which he had fought was a living thing.

Seven months before the Buffalo Convention met, men were opening a trench for a mill race near what is now the city of Sacramento. Their overseer was named James Wilson Marshall. As the ditch diggers turned up the earth Marshall noticed a nugget of gold. Back in 1771, Rudolf Ingulf, in his *Lehrbuch der Geographie von Californien*, had proclaimed to the world that California was a vast gold field. No one paid any heed to the scientific observations of the German sculptor and explorer. But the ring of Marshall's few ounces of gold was heard by adventurous spirits in every corner of the earth. A dauntless courage was all that most of these modern Argonauts possessed; and those who braved the perils of the mountains, the deserts, and the plains, and the treacherous voyage around the Horn, found the land a Colchis of the day. The few who journeyed from the South were typical pioneers, propertyless, and free spirits all.

When Congress was nearing its end in the sitting of 1848-1849, these intrepid ones had increased the population to the proportions of a commonwealth. Accordingly, a convention to frame a Constitution was summoned by Bennett Riley, the military Governor, to meet in Monterey on September 1. On October 13 the delegates finished their labors. One of the sections prohibited slavery. This clause was unanimously adopted by the Forty-niners. On November 13—more than eighty thousand gold seekers had entered the territory since Marshall's find—the people ratified the document adopted at Monterey by a vote of fifteen to one.

About the time the Forty-niners ratified their Constitution, of California, Prince John echoed the sentiments of his father when he voiced the hope that the Democratic party would be "the great anti-slavery party of the Union." Van Buren himself was silent: he had withdrawn from public life; his ambition of more than a generation was realized at last. In politics, as Burr had said, it was a case of kick or be kicked. Prince John must take and give the kicks henceforward. Van Buren would work the farm.

When the Forty-niners were giving added momentum to the Free Soil movement, Kinderhook was thrilled as it had not been since Van Buren, after more than two years in the White House, revisited the village. Henry Clay was fulfilling his promise to call on his old friend. Clay addressed the villagers from the veranda of Stranahan's Hotel, with Van Buren at his side. Clay stayed overnight at Lindenwald. The two compared notes on Calhoun and Webster, and talked pleasantly of their friends. Clay, who came from the West by way of the Great Lakes, then went on to New York, where he remained until it was time to leave for the convening of Congress.

As Van Buren pored over the accounts of the debates in the Capitol during the early part of 1850, he could not have helped wishing at times that he was back in the thick of it and looking forward to his fifty-seventh, instead of his sixty-seventh, birthday. All the great leaders in Congress were now old: Clay, Webster, Benton, and Calhoun. The great nullifier was at the portal of the tomb, and on March 4, when he rose to discuss the dominant issue, he was so weak that another member of the Senate read his speech on Clay's compromise scheme. Clay proposed to admit California as a free State; organize the territories of New Mexico and Utah without reference to slavery; purchase the land Texas claimed in New Mexico; abolish trading of slaves in the District of Columbia, while permitting slavery therein; affirm that Congress had no power over inter-State slave trade; enact a workable fugitive slave law. Calhoun, who had no plan, uttered defiance in his last speech: the Forty-niners had been guilty of a piece of gross impertinence, and the admission of California would be equivalent to notice that the North sought to overwhelm the South. One of the Senators from Mississippi active in the discussion was Jefferson Davis, who had married a daughter of President Taylor. Webster astonished the North on March 7 when he approved Clay's compromise and denounced the Wilmot Proviso as a taunt and a reproach to the South.

Taylor did not live to tarnish his name by signing the oppressive and provocative fugitive slave law: Fillmore, who succeeded to the Presidency on July 9, bears this odium. The act denied a jury trial to a reclaimed slave. Charles Sumner, in Faneuil Hall, said the public conscience would not allow one who had trodden the streets of Boston as a free man to be dragged away as a slave. With only slight variations from its original scope, the Clay Compromise was enacted into law.

During the discussion on the Clay Compromise, Van Buren, through Prince John, told a Free Soil convention in Connecticut that there never was a time when the opponents of slavery extension were called upon to act with more energy or decision to prevent their representatives in Congress from faltering or betraying their trusts.

The nation accepted the Clay Compromise as the lesser of two evils. The Northerners, with few exceptions, believed that the legislation would end all talk of disunion and remove slavery from politics. It did for a while.

On August 27, at the dedication of the monument to Silas Wright, at Weybridge, Vermont, Van Buren made his first public address in years. Here Wright's father farmed while his son studied at Middlebury College. This speech was a simple tribute to his old friend.

While the politicians were scheming for place in the next Presidential campaign, Van Buren was paying court to Margaret Silvester, the spinster daughter of his first preceptor. She had turned forty on January 24, 1851; Van Buren had celebrated his sixty-eighth birthday the month before. She graced the round table at Lindenwald on many festive occasions, and Van Buren's saddle-horse was frequently hitched outside the Silvester home in the village. Her father had died in 1845.

Margaret's mother, who had been Lydia Van Vleck Van Schaack, looked with approval on the ex-President's suit. Her charming daughter was also flattered, but truthfully replied that she would never marry. He had hoped that she would say "Yes," that he might have her companionship on his European trip; but her "No" did not end their friendship. His son Martin was living with him, and while his trip to Europe was still indefinite, Smith, now a widower, also quartered at Lindenwald. Prince John was an irregular visitor; and Abraham and his family lived there only during the summer. One winter day, while Van Buren and his grandchildren, Singleton and Martin III, were walking along the banks of the creek near where he and Billy Van Ness had discussed what should be done in the event of Billy's arrest for his part in the Burr-Hamilton duel, the children slipped and fell headlong into the icy stream. Van Buren plunged in after them. Presently he wrapped the shivering lads in the folds of his blue Spanish cloak, which he had discarded as he leaped into the water, and carried them to the house. This was a feat for a man of Van Buren's size and years; but to the three of them it was only a grand lark.

Most of Van Buren's correspondence now is with his old friend, Francis Preston Blair, who has retired from active journalism and President-making, as he tells Van Buren in one of his letters. Blair has a farm at Silver Spring, Maryland. They talk of fishing and farming. Samuel Houston is dazzling Washington with his leopard skin vest, and there is a movement on foot to nominate him for President and Marcy for Vice President. Van Buren enjoys this intelligence hugely. A gift of seed potatoes from Lindenwald is reciprocated with enough wheat for the fall planting on the old Van Ness place. Blair has "borrowed" the grain from General Harman, who is as proud of his wheat as Van Buren is of his tubers. And Mrs. Blair, knowing that Van Buren always has fruit for dessert, sends some of their peaches which she has preserved in brandy.

The Clay Compromise had not satisfied the extremists in the servilocracy now known as Disunionists. Had the entire problem been left to the people of the South and their moderate leaders, short shrift would have been made of the talk of disunion. Howell Cobb, a slave-holder, of Georgia, who from the floor of the House of Representatives demanded the extension of slavery into California and New Mexico by Act of Congress, was typical of the moderates. When the extremists in his State openly made Disunion an issue in their local campaign of 1851, Cobb ran for Governor on the Union ticket and was overwhelmingly elected. But "the struggles of party leaders at the South for local ascendancy"—to use Van Buren's phrase—kept the slavery issue to the fore.

Fears for the safety of the Union were expressed by many who had followed Van Buren in 1848. Bradford R. Wood, of Albany, wrote to Prince John voicing these apprehensions. He suggested Benton for President and Prince John for Vice President to avoid disunion. Wood, with the Van Burens and most of their followers in New York, had returned to the Democratic fold after the passage of the Clay Compromise.

At their convention in Baltimore, on June 6, 1852, the Democrats nominated Franklin Pierce, of New Hampshire, for President, and William R. King, of Alabama, for second place. The hopelessly divided Whigs convened in the same hall ten days after the Democrats had adjourned. The contest lay between Webster, Fillmore, and Scott. Webster and Fillmore were alike objectionable to their Northern partisans because of their stand on the Clay Compromise. The South stood by Fillmore until the fiftieth ballot, and on the fifty-third, Scott, whose views on the Compromise were concealed from the public, was chosen. William A. Graham, of North Carolina, was named for Vice President. On August 11 the Free Soilers met in Pittsburgh and nominated John P. Hale, of New Hampshire, and George W. Julian, of Indiana.

Six weeks before the Free Soil delegates met, Van Buren indorsed Pierce and King. This pronouncement was embraced in a letter declining an invitation to Tammany's annual celebration of Independence Day. This had been anticipated, as the Tammany broadside for the occasion revealed: it was headed:

Union! Strength!! Victory!!!
Past Grievances to be Buried in Exertions for the Future.

Chase, who had been chosen a member of the United States Senate following the reunion of the Free Soil Democrats and old line Democrats in 1849, was now the heart of the Free Soil movement. In 1850 he had again broken, this time irrevocably, with the Democratic party because it had accepted the Clay Compromise. His vision was neither dimmed by age nor by the conservatism of the East. Three days before Van Buren penned his Tammany letter, Chase wrote to him in the vain hope that his influence would remain with the Free Soil party. But Van Buren had drunk too deeply of the lethal cup Clay had offered the nation.

Various attempts were made to draw Van Buren into the canvass. But beyond a letter to Henry G. Miller and G. H. Pierson, of the Democratic Union Club of Chicago, thanking them for resolutions praising his indorsement of Pierce, he took no active part in the campaign. His views on slavery were voiced by Prince John in his speech at Albany, who said that the Free Soil movement of 1848 had scored two triumphs: the admission of California as a free state, and the abolition of the slave mart in the District of Columbia.

Both parties had declared for the Clay Compromise. The framers of the Whig platform made the error of singling out the fugitive slave act in its indorsement of the Kentuckian's plan. This irritated the Conscience Whigs, who voted for either Hale or Pierce. Scott lost his own State of New Jersey; he carried only Massachusetts, Vermont, Tennessee, and Kentucky. He would have lost Kentucky but for the loyalty of its citizens to the memory of Henry Clay, who died at the beginning of the campaign. Hale polled little more in the country than Van Buren received in New York in 1848. The popular vote was: Pierce, 1,601,274; Scott, 1,386,580; Hale, 155,825. The result for the Electoral College stood: Pierce, 254; Scott, 42.

After the election, Blair, with Van Buren's sanction, sought the post of Secretary of State for Dix. But the appointment of Marcy to the first place in the Cabinet taught the Free Soil Democrats not to expect a voice in the new Administration.

A few weeks after Pierce was inaugurated, Van Buren and his son Martin sailed for Europe. The father was hopeful that the sea voyage and the spas of the Continent would restore young Mat to health. Beyond assembling data for a history of political parties and the *Political Memoirs* which his father contemplated, he had done little for nearly two years. As Van Buren was the first ex-President to leave the United States, court circles were in a quandary as to how to receive him. He solved the problem by requesting that his reception differ in no wise from that accorded other civilians. He visited most of the noted statesmen, calling on Count Camillo Benso di Cavour at his villa in Turin in October.

After his visit to Cavour he heard of his appointment as umpire of the British-American Commission for the adjustment of claims against the two countries for all losses since 1812. On the twenty-second of the month he wrote from Florence to the commissioners, who were sitting in London, declining the honor.

The following month he was received by Pope Pius IX. During his prolonged stay in Rome he was frequently entertained by prelates of the church. A waggish correspondent of a Dublin journal said that hopes were entertained of the ex-President's conversion. In like strain Van Buren wrote to Augustus Wynkoop, a neighbor in Kinderhook. He told of a visit to the monastery of St. Silvester, where he heard the story of the miracle of the turnips; and in the simple tale told by the monks Van Buren saw a great truth: Mother Earth heals all who work in her garden.

. . . If a letter from here which I saw in a Dublin paper, expressing hopes of my conversion, founded on my social intercourse with some of the High Church Dignitaries, should find its way into the American papers, I must beg you to say to my friend, Mrs. Silvester, that there is no danger of any such thing. Thank her and Miss Silvester at the same time for their kind messages which I appreciate very highly. I could not forget them here if I would, for the name is as familiar here as in Kinderhook. About forty miles from Rome stands Soracte. . . . Like the dome of St. Peter's, it is seen from everywhere and stands in that regard as its rival. On the highest point is the convent of St. Silvestro, built by the Uncle of Charlemagne, on the site of a church built by St. Silvester before he became pope. His garden where he planted turnips in the afternoon for his next day dinner is still shown by the monks. Although I can hardly believe the turnip story, I have no doubt he was a good man. . . . By the bye do we not find in the turnip story the secret of the old Lady's healing of us all in gardening? . . .

From Blair he hears that all is not going well with the Pierce Administration; the old struggle between the slavery and the anti-slavery forces is renewed; the Know-Nothings are playing havoc with political lines; and he inquires of young Mat's health.

In the spring of 1854 he settled down, as he thought, at the Villa Falangola, Sorrento, overlooking the bay which has stirred the soul of every Latin poet. On June 21 he began work on his *Political Memoirs.*\* His opening sentence reads: "At the age of seventy-one, and in a foreign land, I commence a sketch of the principal events of my life." That same day he wrote: "What I may write will not . . . proceed, as is so often the case with those whose public career has been abruptly closed, from a wounded spirit, seeking self-vindication, but will, on the contrary, be under the control of a judgment which satisfies me that I ought to be, as my feelings lead me, at peace with all the world." Although he labored long, and produced an interesting tome, he did not complete his task. On page eight of the *Memoirs*, after a fleeting allusion to his defeat for the nomination at Baltimore in 1844, he promised to discuss the intrigue which led to this dramatic event. But save for three other bare references on pages 227, 393, and 513, he is silent on the subject. And he has not written a word on the Free Soil movement. There are many other gaps in the book.

In the month of October he heard of the engagement of Smith to Henrietta Irving, a niece of Washington Irving. On the twenty-eighth of the month he wrote to Martin that his brother was going to make this pleasing alliance. The letter, written from Nice, shows his concealed concern over the state of the health of Martin, who was in London hoping that the English physicians would succeed where the French at Aix-les-Bains had failed.

In December Van Buren received a letter from his old law partner telling of the political confusion resulting from the repeal of the Missouri Compromise during the last sitting of Congress. The mischief-making law, which Pierce signed without scruple, made slavery the outstanding issue before the nation, as the repeal permitted the extension of slavery into the territory north of the line of thirty-six degrees thirty minutes latitude wherein slavery was "for ever forbidden" by the Act of 1820.

\* Van Buren so calls the work which the Government published in 1920.

Van Buren was indignant at the passage of the repeal, and wondered how any but half-baked politicians could have voted for it.

In the first week of January, a measure, popularly known as the Kansas-Nebraska Bill, was introduced by Stephen Arnold Douglas of Illinois. As drafted, it did not contain the provision permitting the States formed out of the vast territory in the Louisiana Purchase not yet admitted to Statehood, to be free or slave soil "as their constitution may prescribe at the time"; nor did it include the declaration that the Act of 1820 prohibiting slavery north of the Missouri Compromise line was inoperative, being contrary to, and superseded by, the Clay Compromise of 1850.

The day following its appearance in its amended form Chase and other objectors described the measure as "a gross violation of a sacred pledge . . . a criminal betrayal of precious rights . . . an atrocious plot to exclude from a vast unoccupied region immigrants from the Old World and free laborers from our own States, and convert it into a dreary region of despotism inhabited by masters and slaves." And this document, known as the "Appeal of the Independent Democrats," characterized the assertion that the Clay Compromise had suspended and rendered the Missouri Compromise inoperative as "a manifest falsification of the truth of history." Sumner said that the bill raised an issue which said to every man in the land: "Are you for freedom or are you for slavery?"

Butler did not overdraw the picture of confusion resulting from the enactment of this bill. Of the forty-two Northern Democrats who voted for the measure, only seven were reëlected. The whole North was at last aroused to the gravity of the issue. Until 1854 Free-Soilism appealed only to analytical and idealistic minds. It had lacked that emotion-evoking ingredient necessary to the popular success of any radical political movement. But the repeal of the Missouri Compromise not only outraged the moral sensibilities of the people, but stirred their souls. The invasion of Kansas in March of this year by bands of pro-slavery Missourians, armed with bowie knives, pistols, rifles, and cannon, who forced the election inspectors to accept their votes for candidates for the Kansas Territorial Legislature, intensified the resentment of the North.

The repeal of the Missouri Compromise originated in the

cunning mind of Seward, then a member of the Senate, and like every other New Yorker of consequence, a vigorous opponent of slavery extension. Only the purblind failed to see that the complete domination of the Democratic party by the servilocracy, and its death grip on the Whig party, would lead to the formation of a third party to give the advocates of Free-Soilism a vehicle of expression. After Douglas introduced his Kansas-Nebraska bill Seward went to Archibald Dixon, Clay's successor in the Senate, and secretly put him up to move the repeal of the Act of 1820. No one suspected Seward at the time; but he later boasted of his unscrupulous act to Montgomery Blair, son of Van Buren's friend and correspondent, and Postmaster General under Lincoln. Blair repeated Seward's boast in a letter to Gideon Welles, Secretary of the Navy when Blair, Seward and he were members of Lincoln's Cabinet. Seward, artful in the ways of machine politics, was aware that this would solidify the anti-slavery elements as naught else. But he did not see beyond the Whig party; nor did he, or any one else, dream that the climax would be an unleashing of passions unparalleled in history's gory annals.

While the Kansas-Nebraska legislation was pending in Congress, a handful of Whigs, Free Soil Democrats, and old line Democrats, met in the Congregational church at Ripon, Wisconsin. This was on the last day of February. Forty-eight hours before the meeting, Alvan E. Bovay, its sponsor, wrote to Horace Greeley: ". . . Advocate calling together in every church and schoolhouse in the free states all the opponents of the Kansas-Nebraska Bill, no matter what their party affiliations. Urge them to forget previous political names and organizations, and to band together under the name I suggested to you at Lovejoy's Hotel in 1852 . . . 'Republican.' . . ." On March 20, seventeen days after the inflammatory measure passed the Senate, a second meeting was held in the little schoolhouse at Ripon; and to quote Bovay: ". . . We went into the little meeting . . . Whigs, Free Soilers, and Democrats. We came out of it Republicans. . . ." The glamour of the name worn by Jefferson and other Virginians, whose faith the Democrats professed and profaned, was not recognized by Greeley until June. On the twenty-fourth of the month he published the second half of Bovay's suggestion in *The Tribune.*

Greeley's tardiness was dictated by caution and a belief, prevalent in the East, that it would be impossible to form a third party. Tilden, and other New Yorkers who followed Van Buren in 1848, held this view. On the August 26 following Greeley's "Republican Party" editorial, Tilden wrote to a friend: ". . . A third party organization, if attempted, would not in my judgment, embody a quarter of the force or numbers our movement did in 1848. I do not know a man who bore any considerable share of the heat and burden of that day, who would enter *actively* into a similar campaign now. . . ."

In September Greeley was a delegate to the Republican State Convention at Syracuse, which indorsed Myron Holley Clark, the Whig nominee, for Governor. Greeley was read out of the Whig party by Thurlow Weed and Seward. The prohibitionists, flushed with their recent success in Maine, indorsed Clark at their convention. Never was the phrase used by Marcy in a letter to Van Buren—"the tangled skein of New York politics"—more applicable than now. Voters of the two old parties were divided into three parts: slavery, Free Soil, and Know-Nothings. The last, under the name of the American party, nominated Daniel Ullmann for Governor. Many Democratic and Whig leaders were, clandestinely, members of this secret, oath-bound solidarity. Among the Democrats were Soft Shell and Hard Shell Hunkers; the Barnburners, or Free Soilers, were dubbed Soft Shells. The Soft Shells, or anti-slavery Democrats, outnumbered the Hard Shells five to one. The combination of temperance voters, anti-slavery Whigs and Republicans, outvoted their rivals. The Know-Nothing candidate for Governor polled only thirty-four thousand less than Clark; but the American party nominee for the state-wide office of Canal Commissioner was elected.

Three months and eighteen days after Clark took office, Van Buren's trip abroad was cut short by the death of Martin. And in the summer, at the head of a newly made barrow, beside the resting place of his wife, Van Buren raised a Parian shaft on which was graven: "Martin Van Buren, Jr." He reserved the place on her right for his own last sleep. Smith acted as his amanuensis when Van Buren resumed his literary labors. He divided his time between his desk and his farm. He still rode to the village every day on his favorite mount. A greeting from a neighbor would cause him to rein up; and in the first few weeks of his return he heard from half the village the story of last December 5 when all Kinderhook celebrated his seventy-second birthday.

On Sundays he was to be seen in his high-backed pew in the little Dutch Reformed church, invariably accompanied by his son Smith and family. Occasionally Prince John accompanied him. Weather permitting, he drove in his famed English coach; and when snow covered the countryside he came in a high-fronted sleigh, horse and vehicle jangling with brass bells that shone like gold, and himself muffled up in a buffalo robe. As he entered the pew on wintry Sundays he would set a small foot stove in a convenient spot, then shake the snow from one of his huge bear-skin gloves, and carefully place it on his head for warmth. His shock of yellow locks was only a memory. When he rose to join in the congregational singing, he would hold his hand on the furry gauntlet to prevent it from falling. And crowded though the church might be, and every voice raised in song, Van Buren's rendering of the hymn could be heard above the rest.

The Presidential campaign of 1856 began on Washington's Birthday when the American party held its national convention at Philadelphia. Fillmore was nominated for President, and Andrew J. Donelson, of Tennessee, for Vice President. The former President was driven into the Know-Nothing movement by Seward and Weed: they never liked him. The Whig party existed only in name. The Republican party had supplanted it. Seward and Weed joined it only when they saw their own party disintegrating. Fillmore's nomination was unsatisfactory to some of the Know-Nothing delegates, who seceded and nominated for President the picturesque soldier, John C. Frémont, of California, surnamed the Pathfinder. William F. Johnston, former Governor of Pennsylvania, was chosen for Vice President by the bolting Know-Nothings.

The Democrats met in Cincinnati in the first week of June. They indorsed the repeal of the Missouri Compromise Act of 1820 and the enactment of the Clay Compromise of 1850. The old doctrine of State rights was reasserted, and an appeal made to Van Buren's followers by pronouncements against a Bank, and against internal improvements by the Federal Government. They denounced the Republicans as a sectional party and the Americans for their proscription of citizens of the Roman Catholic faith or of alien birth. Buchanan, of Pennsylvania, was named for President. Pierce, who—in the language of Blair—"had sold himself to the South," was discarded when Northern delegates threatened to bolt if he was renominated.

The first Republican National Convention was held in Philadelphia on July 17. The choice for President had been pre-arranged; the leaders had cast aside Chase and other abler men to nominate Frémont in return for the Know-Nothing vote. Supporters of John McLean, Justice of the United States Supreme Court, insisted on a ballot, which resulted: Frémont, 359; McLean, 196; Charles Sumner, 2; Seward, 1. William L. Dayton, of New Jersey, was nominated for Vice President. His vote on the first ballot was 259. Lincoln was second, with 110, Johnston, Frémont's running mate on the Know-Nothing ticket, received only two votes.

With the exception of the border States of Maryland, Delaware, and Kentucky, only Northern commonwealths sent delegates to the Republican convention. Many of Van Buren's intimates had joined the new party. His faithful correspondent, Blair, had presided at the preliminary convention held in Pittsburgh during the winter. Robert Emmet, son of Thomas Addis Emmet, was elected temporary chairman of the national convention. His Irish birth was an answer to the charge that the new party in accepting Frémont had accepted Know-Nothingism. The author of the Wilmot Proviso was a delegate. Charles Francis Adams was also prominent in its deliberations.

The platform contained "a clear-cut statement of the Free Soil doctrines as enunciated by the followers of Van Buren in 1848," to borrow a phrase from Professor Myers's *The Republican Party: A History*. The repeal of the Missouri Compromise was condemned; Federal aid for building a railroad to the Pacific Ocean was favored; and the immediate admission of Kansas as a free State was demanded. Responsibility for the invasion of Kansas by armed bands of pro-slavery men, who for months past had burned, pillaged and slaughtered, was properly laid at the door of the Pierce Administration.

The acts of terrorism, instituted by the pro-slavery Missourians, were more than outmatched by an atrocity committed a fortnight before the Democrats convened. On the night of May 24, a party of eight or nine led by a crack-brained Abolitionist named John Brown, invaded the sleeping settlement built up around Dutch Henry's Crossing on the Pottawatomie, and dragged five men from their cabins. These unfortunates were innocent of wrong-doing. All save two of the raiding party were members of Brown's family. Armed with old cutlasses, they slashed and hacked their helpless prisoners to death. After perpetrating this barbarous massacre, Brown and his band of assassins committed the lesser crime of robbery. Brown escaped before he could be apprehended.

The Whigs met in Baltimore on September 17. It was a national convention in name only. They indorsed the candidacies of Fillmore and Donelson. They adopted a platform criticizing the Democratic and Republican parties as sectional, and declared that the success of either "must add fuel to the flame which now threatens to wrap our dearest interests in a common ruin." The outlawry in Kansas was dignified with the name of civil war; and the platform added: "we proclaim that the restoration of Mr. Fillmore to the Presidency will furnish the best if not the only means of restoring peace."

After the Democrats had nominated, the Tammany Society invited Van Buren to its annual Fourth of July celebration. In a long response declining to attend because of his age, he announces his intention to support Buchanan. This letter breathes despondency. There is an indirect plea to the party to return to the ancient traditions of Jefferson. He speaks in praise of the destruction of the Bank and the establishment of the Sub-Treasury. He laments for his party's departure from its historic attitude toward slavery by the repeal of the Missouri Compromise. He relates that no one was more sincerely opposed to the repeal than himself; but the Kansas-Nebraska Act has become less obnoxious to him. This, he frankly adds, may be due to the unanimous acceptance of it by the party in which he had been reared. He knows that Kansas will be admitted as a free State if the people of the territory are not molested by the armed bands of pro-slavery men. This thought is in his mind when he declares that Buchanan's promise to use his power as President to restore harmony among the sister States can be redeemed only by securing to the settlers a "full, free, and practical enjoyment" of the privilege of suffrage. Slavery is now the living issue; he believes that in Buchanan's election there will be "good grounds for hope" that the Union will be saved.

Van Buren said that this would be his first and his last letter during the campaign. He kept this promise, save for a confidential communication to Moses Tilden, the elder brother of Samuel J. Tilden. Moses, who had been wavering between Frémont and Buchanan, wrote Van Buren he had at last decided to support Buchanan. In his sad and prophetic reply, Van Buren spoke freely of Buchanan and the great issue.

I am happy to find that the "sober second thought" has brought you to the right conclusion. . . .

. . . the crisis is, in my judgment, the most imminent and critical of any we have ever experienced. That union should so long have been preserved in a confederacy which contains an element of discord of such magnitude and so disturbing a nature as that of slavery, is a wonder—more surprising than its dissolution would be. This has been owing to . . . the single fact that there have always been neutralizing considerations of sufficient force to maintain party cohesions between men of the free and slave States. Slavery questions . . . have never before had the effect of dissolving old party connections and sympathies, and the balance wheel has thus been preserved. Now, for the first time in our history, one side, and that the one in which we reside, has undertaken to carry an election . . . against the united wishes of the other. It has placed itself in a position which, for the first time cuts itself loose from all hope, if not desire, of assistance to the slave States. It not only admits that this is its position, but avows that it is a desirable one. It wishes to accomplish its mastery by its own unaided arm. Now, it needs no ghost to tell us that one successful effort of this description will be followed by another, for men have too much the quality of wild beasts in them to stop the pursuit when they have once tasted blood, and it would be against reason and experience to expect a Union, in which political mastery is so plainly exhibited and organized, to continue. . . .

Slavery agitation must be eradicated in some way or another, or institutions cannot continue in their present form. . . . if Mr. Pierce had from the beginning taken the stand he now seems to be taking, . . . the country would have been saved from the disgrace to which our institutions have been exposed in the estimation of the world

Kansas would have been a Territory so decidedly free as to put an end to attempts to make it a slave State, the country would have been quiet, the party united, and he renominated. All that is wanted now to secure many of the most important of these results is a rigid and effectual execution of the Kansas Organic Act. Although I am not a particular friend of Mr. Buchanan, I have reasons that satisfy my mind that he will, if elected, secure to the country this great advantage. . . . I do have a favorable opinion of Col. Frémont personally, but cannot for a moment doubt, from his utter want of experience in the affairs of government, and his inexperience in everything that belongs to it, that he would, if elected, inevitably be thrown into the hands of Seward, Greeley, and Weed . . . there is the greatest reason to fear that to commit the power of the government into such hands, at a moment so critical as the present, would be but "the beginning of the end" in regard to the confederacy . . .

Weed and Seward were out of one matrix. Greeley, as he knew from bitter experience, was easily swayed, like a feather in the wind, by every passing emotion; he was clay in the hands of the cunning or unscrupulous. Greeley had been crying freedom and Free Soil early in 1848; but on the eve of the election he cast his influence with the slave-owning Taylor. Seward and Weed had taken him to the top of the mountain.

The Republicans paraphrased Van Buren's slogan of 1848 with: "Free Speech, Free Soil, and Frémont." It took in the North where more than 1,300,000 voted for Frémont, Free Soil, and Free Speech. Fewer than a thousand Republican ballots were cast in the border States of Delaware, Maryland, and Kentucky. Virginia, with 291 Republican votes, recorded the only Southern support. Buchanan was elected by a minority vote. His total of 1,838,169 was 377,629 less than the combined totals of Frémont and Fillmore. In two of the three Northern States which Buchanan carried, New Jersey and Illinois, the Republicans and Know-Nothings heavily outvoted the Democrats. The division of his opponents also gave California to Buchanan. Frémont's total was 1,341,264; Fillmore, 874,534. Fillmore ran a close second in the South. He carried Maryland, whose eight votes were cast for him in the Electoral College, where Buchanan received 174. and Frémont 114.

Van Buren is writing for posterity, he informs his old law partner on December 3. Butler and Smith Thompson Van Buren are to be his literary executors. At Christmas he receives a letter from Blair, who fears that Buchanan will truckle to the South. Blair's son, Montgomery, writes of his argument in behalf of Dred Scott before the United States Court. Within a month Van Buren clipped from a newspaper Buchanan's inaugural address wherein he said that whether slaves could be carried into free territory and maintained there as slaves, would be decided in the Dred Scott decision soon to be pronounced.

This was the one point not covered by the Kansas-Nebraska Act, and the prediction of Buchanan was fulfilled within a few days. Dred Scott was a slave. His master took him from Missouri to Illinois, permitted him to marry in the free State, and in 1838 brought him back to Missouri. After the death of his master, Dred was hired out to various persons in Missouri. Disliking this, he sued for his freedom. A lower court in Missouri found in favor of Dred, but an appellate bench, with two of the three judges concurring, held that the condition of slavery reattached to the negro on his return to Missouri. Before this decision was made, the widow of Dred's master deeded over the negro, his wife, and their child, to a relative in New York. Dred, with the aid of white friends, now brought suit in the United States Circuit Court. Losing here, he took an appeal to the United States Supreme Court.

A majority decision written by Chief Justice Taney held that the Missouri Compromise was unconstitutional; that slave-owners could carry their slaves, as property, into any territory; that negroes born of slave parents in the United States were not only not citizens of any of the States when the Constitution was formed in 1787, but could not be made citizens by the States or by Congress. In a dissenting opinion, concurred in by Justice McLean, Benjamin Robbins Curtis held that Congress had the right to pass the Missouri Compromise, and also refuted Taney's contention that negroes born of slave parents could not be citizens by citing the record to show that many such were citizens, and enjoyed even the privilege of suffrage, at the time of the formation of the Constitution. McLean further held that slavery was contrary to right and had its origin in power; and in this country was maintained only by local laws.

The majority decision, instead of allaying the North, as the legalistic believed, inflamed the people the more. The opinions of McLean and Curtis were printed in pamphlets and extensively distributed by the Free Soilers; and like use was made of Taney's decision by the servilocracy. Seward, without revealing any basis for the charge, accused Taney of having divulged the decision of the court to Buchanan so that he could avoid taking a stand on the issue in his inaugural address. Thousands believed the charge, and Lincoln, in one of his speeches, hinted at it.

The Blairs maintain a regular correspondence with Van Buren. In the fall there is another gift of brandied peaches from Silver Spring. The times are hard. A financial panic has seized the country. The Sub-Treasury and the hard money system that Van Buren fought for no longer require defenders. But the new financial structure is not perfect. A relative, John Dash Van Buren, is working on an improvement. It will call for legislative enactment. He proposes that Van Buren run for member of Assembly next fall and introduce his currency reform. This Newburgh Van Buren is very serious; and the ex-President, in declining to return to the State Legislature in his seventy-seventh year, discusses currency reform as though he were writing to an economist.

Blair, evidently chidden for not writing oftener, pleaded on February 6, 1859, that he did not want to distress Van Buren with a recountal of political conditions in Washington. A month later he receives a pamphlet containing the speech of another talented son of Blair, Francis Preston Blair, Jr., whose journalistic pen was at the service of Van Buren in 1848. Young Blair is now representing his adopted State of Missouri in the House of Representatives, where he advocates colonizing the negro population of the United States in Central America. He and all the Blairs are Republicans. Blair senior, on April 3, talks of the possibility of secession and civil war.

A few days later another of those who had striven wisely to keep the balance between the North and South passes on. Benton was the last of Van Buren's able contemporaries in the Senate. Van Buren settles down with renewed efforts to his literary work: he would like to write *Finis* to these two volumes before his own last page is reached.

Blair grows gossipy in his next: all Washington is again

discussing Peggy Eaton. La Bellona is twenty-seven years older now; but she, after the manner of beautiful women, has forgotten the passage of years. Eaton had died in 1856, leaving her a large estate. Along came a poor Italian, young enough to be her son. He raved over her charms. His words took her back many years. He made her young again; she forgot she was a grandmother. And so they were married. Then he robbed her of a large part of her estate before she awakened from her dream of love. Poor Peggy!

Shortly after Peggy has separated from her third husband, Van Buren receives a printed invitation to a dinner of the Order of the Cincinnati. He uses the reverse side to make notes on Jackson's dissolution of his Cabinet over Peggy. In the spring of 1859 Blair invites Van Buren to Silver Spring. The trip will do him good, and after a little rest he can go on to Washington to do research for his *Memoirs*. And Blair will be happy to aid him in the work of revision. The tempting offer is declined. A New York book publisher, Sheldon Smith, appeals to Van Buren to let his house bring out anything he writes.

It was in October that John Brown and eighteen men seized the United States Arsenal at Harpers Ferry. When a detachment of marines from Washington under Colonel Robert E. Lee arrived at the little Virginia village, only six of Brown's band were left. Brown's two sons were killed by the bullets of the townspeople, and he was thought to be dying. After his capture Brown sent word to the zealots who had supplied him with funds and ammunition for the enterprise not to attempt his rescue. The ill-starred curtain-raiser ended December 2 when this descendant of Peter Brown, passenger on the *Mayflower*, died on the scaffold.

In the winter of 1859-1860 John Brown meetings are held throughout the country. They are attended almost wholly by extremists and the curious. In January Van Buren declines to attend one in Albany. In the second week of the month he writes to Tilden. He is concerned over the future of Prince John. He incidentally mentions his hope to see Prince John and Tilden partners. Tilden has one of the largest and most remunerative practices in the city. The financial returns are not the dominating thought in Van Buren's mind: he wants his brilliant son kept occupied. Prince John is more conservative and circumspect in his gaming, and he has become temperate in his drinking. In the latter he has had no choice, as drink has affected his liver. On February 21 Tilden replies to Van Buren that the partnership would not be either to his own or to Prince John's interest, as the nature of his practice would furnish "few occasions which would give scope to his powers."

There was one matter that he had been putting off for some time. But it must not be delayed. He must not be taken unaware. So he sits down and writes: "I, Martin Van Buren, of the town of Kinderhook, County of Columbia and State of New York, heretofore Governor of the State, and more recently President of the United States, but for the last and happiest years of my life a Farmer in my native town . . ." The will finished, he resumes his literary labors.

Before the Democrats met in national convention at Charleston, South Carolina, on April 23, it was apparent that they were hopelessly divided on sectional lines. The servilocracy, which had forced Buchanan to pattern his political conduct on the Dred Scott decision—a course which evoked criticism from Van Buren —demanded that the principles of Taney's opinion be incorporated in the party's platform. When the Northern delegates refused to agree to this, most of the Southern delegates seceded. They were followed by a few from the North.

Both factions postponed making nominations until June. The bolters assembled at Richmond on June 11, and nominated John C. Breckenridge, of Kentucky, for President, and Joseph Lane, of Oregon, for Vice President. The following week the regular Democrats reconvened at Baltimore and named Douglas, of Illinois, for President. Benjamin Fitzpatrick, of Alabama, was given second place, but declined. Herschel V. Johnson, of Georgia, was substituted. Meanwhile the Republicans had nominated Lincoln at Chicago on the third ballot after Seward had led him on two. Hannibal Hamlin, of Maine, was named for Vice President on the second trial. A fourth ticket was placed in the canvass by the Constitutional Union party which had convened in Baltimore on May 9—a week before the Republican Convention. John Bell, of Tennessee, and Edward Everett, of Massachusetts, were the choice of the new party, which carried Virginia and the border States of Tennessee and Kentucky. The result in the Electoral College was: Lincoln, 180; Breckenridge, 72; Douglas, 12; Bell, 39. Lincoln, who swept every State in the North save New Jersey, had a minority of the popular vote, which stood: Lincoln, 1,866,452; Breckenridge, 847,953; Douglas, 1,375,157; Bell, 590,631.

Bennett, whose snobbishness increased with the years, assailed Lincoln before and after the election. He was a "rough-spun, disputatious village politician . . . without education or refinement . . . an illiterate Western boor . . . a satyr." He had said almost the same of Van Buren. Bennett was wealthy now: he was no longer a blackmailer.

The secession of South Carolina on December 20 was not unexpected. During the canvass William L. Yancey, who represented Georgia in the United States Senate, speaking in several cities in the North, said that the South would regard the election of the Republican ticket as a notice that it could not expect justice from the Government. Van Buren was aghast at the timidity of the machine politician in the White House, who let things drift while he talked of his conscientious scruples against coercing a sovereign State.

The New Year found Van Buren afflicted with a severe attack of asthma, from which he had been suffering for many months. By the time he was convalescent, Mississippi, Florida, Alabama, Georgia, Louisiana, and Texas had followed the example of Calhoun's State. Lincoln's declaration in his inaugural address that "the Union is unbroken" speeded Van Buren's restoration to health. There was a man again in Washington. Lincoln's proclamation calling for seventy-five thousand volunteers to suppress the "combination, and to cause the laws to be duly executed," gave Van Buren a complete renewal of his strength. He again mounted his horse and galloped to the village. And as he rode, his mind could not have helped galloping back to the end of Jackson's first term. At that time South Carolina had authorized the raising of 12,000 troops to support Calhoun's scheme of nullification. And he thought of Jackson's plan, confided to him by letter, to raise a *posse comitatus* in Virginia and Tennessee, while en route to the seat of trouble, and seize Calhoun, Hayne, and the rest of them and deliver them to the judicial power of the United States. Only a Buchanan or a Pierce would have let things drift into the deplorable condition that confronted Lincoln. And then there was that first Jefferson Day Dinner which Calhoun had planned to make his own. But he and Jackson had spoiled this plan with the toasts they had prepared at the White House the day preceding that memorable April 2. Calhoun was Vice President then, and Van Buren was Secretary of State. Jackson's toast that night—"Our Union—it must be preserved" —was Lincoln's policy now. The servilocracy had also been deaf to his own toast that evening: "Mutual forbearance and reciprocal concessions; thro' their agency the Union was established— the patriotic spirit from which they emanated will forever sustain it." And the warning of John Quincy Adams to the nullifiers, although spoken on a later occasion, was complementary to his: "From the instant that your slave-holding States become the theater of war, from that instant the war-powers of the Constitution extend to interference with the institution of slavery in every way." But the generation of inflammable speeches of slave-holding politicians, big and little, had envenomed almost the whole South.

At this time there was a letter on its way to Lindenwald from Concord, New Hampshire, the home of Buchanan's predecessor. It was written on April 16, the day after Lincoln's proclamation for volunteers. Besides Pierce and himself, there were three other ex-Presidents living: Tyler, Fillmore, and Buchanan. Pierce suggested that Van Buren, as the senior of the five, summon the ex-Presidents to meet in Philadelphia. Van Buren knew that the time for parleying was past. It was now the moment to put down the "combination and to cause the laws to be duly executed." Van Buren's reply to Pierce is dated April 20, and reads:

I have received your friendly letter suggesting for my consideration the propriety of summoning a meeting of the Ex Presidents, at Philadelphia, to consult on the present alarming condition of public affairs, & adopt such action in the premises as they may think, might be useful, & have given the subject all the consideration to which it is entitled. . . . I regret however, to be obliged to say, that after the most careful consideration of the subject in all its bearings, I have not been able to repress the serious doubts I entertain in regard to the practicability of making a volunteer movement of that description, on our part, with such action in the matter as we might think allowable.

. . . But it does not follow . . . that views of the subject imbibed by one, who, like myself, have been longest out of public life, & more completely excluded from all connection with public affairs than any of his associates, will also prove to be those of the rest of the Ex Presidents . . . The belief that such is the case [the suggestion that Van Buren assume the duties of a chairman] can only have arisen from the erroneous supposition that I was entitled to precedence in such matters, on account of my being the Senior Ex President—while in truth, that distinction, as far as it goes, is, according to the opinions of those most conversant in such matters, accorded to the individual of the class, who was the latest incumbent of the principal office. But this is a matter which may, I think, had better, be entirely laid out of view, & all the Ex Presidents regarded, in that respect, as standing on the same footing. If then you, who entertain more hopeful expectations upon the point, continue to think the proposed call, free from the embarrassment under which I labor, or either of our associates, who entertain similar views to your own, shall deem such a call expedient, & ask my attendance, I will accept the invitation without hesitation, & comply with the request it contains, if it be in my power to do so. . . .

Pierce is sufficiently schooled in the language of diplomacy to know that the qualification, "if it be in my power to do so," signifies that Van Buren will plead his inability to attend if Buchanan or another issues the call. When a Philadelphia correspondent urges him to reconsider, Van Buren replies that his mind is unchanged, and that there is a growing disposition in New York—the stronghold of pro-slavery sentiment in the North —to support the Administration. Three weeks later Van Buren makes the same response to a friend in the West. The issue is not to be decided by diplomats, but by grim warriors amidst

> ". . . blood
> And darkness and the barrows of the slain."

To circumvent the work of the Hard Shells, Prince John and other War Democrats address meetings nightly throughout the State. To a war meeting at Kinderhook, Van Buren, unable to attend because of a sudden recurrence of his malady, sends a message to support the Administration. In obedience to the counsel of his physicians he avoids all strenuous exercise. He misses the daily canter to the village and around the farm. The war is entering into its ninth month when he celebrates his seventy-ninth birthday. In spite of his illness, he manages to put in a little time occasionally on his manuscript.

In the early part of 1862 he is well enough to go to New York. There, the most noted physician of his day, Dr. Alonzo Clark, treats him from early in March to late in May. Many of his old friends visit him. One is a Clintonian, Azariah Cutting Flagg, who served as Secretary of State under De Witt Clinton. Flagg is led into Van Buren's room. Flagg has been sightless for two years, but this does not prevent his philanthropic work from continuing, nor dim the ardor of his support of the war.

When Van Buren returns to Kinderhook, his plowed fields are green with young life. After resting from the journey he writes to Flagg:

May 28/62

My Dear Sir,

I had hoped to be able to return in person, before I left the City, the visit with which you honored me notwithstanding your unhappy condition; but the state of my health continues to render that gratification impracticable.

Thus driven to the necessity of taking leave in this way, probably for ever, of yourself and your amiable & excellent family and of expressing my earnest wish for the happiness of you all, I must notwithstanding the trespass I fear I will commit on that modest bearing and personal reserve by which your whole political and official career has been so signally characterized, avail myself of the not unfitting occasion to express the opinion with which the latter has impressed one under whose observation so much of it has been exhibited.

With those to any considerable extent acquainted with my own public life, I need not I think fear being thought assuming in making the declaration that there are few still amongst us who have enjoyed a wider and closer intercourse with public functionaries, State & National, during the last half century, or possessed better opportunity to witness their action than myself. With an experience thus enlarged I feel that I can repeat here an opinion which I have often conscientiously expressed elsewhere, that I never met in any branch of the

Public Service a single man who more invariably entered upon the discharge of the duties entrusted to his management with views more exclusively devoted to the promotion of the public interest or who labored with a purer or more disinterested zeal for their advancement than yourself.

As ever your friend

M. Van Buren

A. C. Flagg, Esquire.

All through June he remains in his room on the second floor. This was the sleeping chamber of Billy Van Ness's father. Two windows face the south; and two others catch the rays of the rising sun. On days when he is not too weak he sits in an easy chair covered with chintz. Against the southern wall, between the valanced windows, stands a large wardrobe with a mirror door. The sleigh-bed, of the same warm-toned mahogany from which the rest of the furniture is fashioned, is flanked on either side by a plain chest of drawers. On one of these is an unframed portrait of Silas Wright. It is small; and of the type our early artists called a cabinet. On top of the other is a Bible. In the center of the windowless west wall hangs an illuminated tribute to Jackson. On either side of this memento of his friend is a silhouette of Van Buren. These, too, are simply framed. A shaving stand occupies a corner. Small rugs, woven of vari-colored rags, and three fiddle-back chairs, with seats of gray horse-hair, complete the furnishings.

About the middle of July Smith wrote to Prince John and Abraham to hasten to Lindenwald. When they arrived Van Buren bade his three sons farewell. Shortly after he lost consciousness; and on Thursday morning, July 24, at nine o'clock, he became one of the nation's glorious dead.

For three days his neighbors and friends from various parts of the State entered the big hall where Van Buren lay in a simple rosewood coffin, his feet to the opened half-door. A small silver plate had graven upon it: "Martin Van Buren. Died July 24, 1862, aged 79 years, 7 months, 19 days." On the third day the Reverend J. Romeyn Berry offered prayer beside the bier. Then some of Van Buren's townsmen lifted the coffin on their shoulders and carried it to the village hearse which was drawn up to the porch. In one of the first of the eighty-one carriages rode Edwin

Morgan, Governor of the State; the Tildens were close behind. In some of the others were members of the Common Council of the cities of Troy, Albany, Hudson, and New York, and a deputation from Tammany. Hundreds followed on foot.

In accordance with Van Buren's wishes, there was no ringing of bells, and no music, save the hymn, "O God Our Help in Ages Past." His old friend, Dr. Alonzo Potter, now the Episcopal Bishop of Pennsylvania, and the Reverend Benjamin Van Zandt, the former pastor of the church, occupied the pulpit. The Stars and Stripes was draped on the altar. After Dominie Van Zandt said the closing prayer, the coffin was borne past the only empty pew: this was draped with black crape. From the church the procession to the cemetery was led by the red-shirted members of the Kinderhook Fire Engine Company. Most of the firemen were old: these had taken the places of those who had joined the colors. Bishop Potter read the Burial Office of the Episcopal Church. When the casket was being lowered into the grave, cannon thundered throughout the land. Some of these became silent, in accordance with Lincoln's proclamation, after they had fired a Presidential salute to the memory of Martin Van Buren. Others thundered on until the ideal for which he had unselfishly striven was a reality.

FINIS

# BIBLIOGRAPHY

Adams, Charles Francis (Edited by). *Memoirs of John Quincy Adams, Comprising Portions of His Diary from 1795 to 1848.* 12 volumes. Philadelphia: J. B. Lippincott & Co. 1875.

Barnes, Thurlow Weed. *Memoir of Thurlow Weed.* Boston: Houghton-Mifflin & Co. 1884.

Beardsley, Levi, Late of the New York Senate and President Thereof. *Reminiscences, Personal and Other Incidents, etc.* New York: Charles Vinten. 1852.

[Benton, Thomas Hart.] *Thirty Years' View, etc.* 2 volumes. New York: Appleton and Company, 1856.

Bigelow, John. *Letters and Literary Memorials of Samuel J. Tilden.* 2 volumes. New York and London: Harper & Brothers, 1908.

Bigelow, John. *Retrospections of an Active Life.* 3 volumes. The Baker & Taylor Co., 1909.

Bigelow, John (Edited by). *The Writings and Speeches of Samuel J. Tilden.* 2 volumes. New York: Harper & Brothers, 1885.

Bonney, Mrs. Catharine V[an] R[ensselaer] (Compiled by). *A Legacy of Historical Gleanings.* 2 volumes. Albany: J. Munsell, 1875.

Bowers, Claude G. *The Party Battles of the Jackson Period.* Chautauqua, New York: The Chautauqua Press, 1923.

Bradbury, Mrs. Anna R. *History of the City of Hudson, New York, etc.* Hudson, New York: Record Printing and Publishing Company, 1908.

Bradford, Alden. *History of the Federal Government, etc.* Boston: Samuel G. Simpkins, 1840.

Byrdsall, F. *The History of the Loco Foco or Equal Rights Party, etc.* New York: Clement & Packard, 1842.

Carlyle, Thomas. *Chartism.* Boston: C. C. Little & J. Brown, 1840.

Carter, Nathaniel H., and William L. Stone, Reporters; and Marcus T. C. Gould, Stenographer. *Reports of the Proceedings and Debates of the Convention of 1821, Assembled for the Purpose of Amending the Constitution of the State of New York, etc.* Albany: E. and E. Hosford, 1821.

[Clinton, De Witt.] *Letters on the Natural History and Internal Resources of the State of New York.* By *Hibernicus.* New York: E. Bliss & E. White, 1822.

Colton, Calvin (Edited by). *The Private Correspondence of Henry Clay.* New York: A. S. Barnes & Co., 1855.

*Columbia County at the End of the Century—A Historical Record of Its Foundation, etc.* 2 volumes. Hudson, New York: The Record Printing and Publishing Company, 1900.

*Columbia County, New York, History of, With Illustrations and Biographical Sketches, etc.* Philadelphia: Everts & Ensign, 1878.

Collier, Edward A., D.D. *A History of Old Kinderhook, etc.* New York and London: G. P. Putnam's Sons, 1914.

Curtis, George Ticknor. *Life of Daniel Webster.* 2 volumes. New York: D. Appleton and Company, 1870.

[Cutts, L. B.]*Memoirs and Letters of Dolly Madison, etc.* Edited by Her Grand-Niece. Boston: Houghton-Mifflin & Co., 1886.

Dix, Morgan (Compiled by). *Memoirs of John Adams Dix.* 2 volumes. New York: Harper & Brothers, 1883.

547

Dwight, Theodore (Secretary of the Hartford Convention). *History of the Hartford Convention, etc.* New York: N. & J. White; Boston: Russell, Odiorne & Co., 1883.

Fernow, Berthold (Compiled and Edited by). *Calendar of Wills on File and Records in the Office of the Clerk of the Court of Appeals, of the County Clerk at Albany, and of the Secretary of State: 1626-1836.* New York: Colonial Dames of the State of New York, 1896.

Forney, John W. *Anecdotes of Public Men While He Was Clerk of the House of Representatives, Secretary of the Senate of the United States, etc.* 2 volumes. New York: Harper & Brothers, 1881.

Gallatin, Count (Edited by). *The Diary of James Gallatin, Secretary to Albert Gallatin, a Great Peace Maker: 1813-1827. With an Introduction by Viscount Bryce.* New York: Charles Scribner's Sons, 1916.

Glenn, Thomas Allen, *Some Colonial Mansions and Those Who Lived in Them, With Genealogies, etc.* Philadelphia: Henry Coates & Company, 1898.

Glenn, Thomas Allen. (Same title and publisher as preceding.) Second Series. 1900.

Greeley, Horace. *Recollections of a Busy Life, etc.* New York: J. B. Ford & Co., 1869.

Hall, Benjamin F. *The Republican Party, etc.* New York and Auburn: Miller, Orton and Mulligan, 1856.

Hammond, Jabez D. *The History of Political Parties in the State of New York, etc.* 2 volumes, Albany: C. Van Benthuysen, 1842.

Holloway, Laura C. *The Ladies of the White House, etc.* Philadelphia: Bradley & Company; Boston: R. H. Curran & Company, 1882.

Hopkins, James H. *A History of Political Parties in the United States, etc.* New York and London: G. P. Putnam's Sons, 1900.

Hosack, David. *Memoir of De Witt Clinton: With an Appendix Containing Numerous Documents, etc.* New York: J. Seymour, 1829.

Howe, M. A. De Wolfe. *The Life and Letters of George Bancroft.* 2 volumes. New York: Charles Scribner's Sons, 1908.

Hunt, Charles Havens. *Life of Edward Livingston. With an Introduction by George Bancroft.* New York: D. Appleton and Company, 1864.

Jephson, Henry. *The Platform—Its Rise and Progress.* 2 volumes. New York: Macmillan and Co., 1892.

Kent, Frank R. *The Democratic Party—A History.* New York: The Century Company, 1928.

Kent, William. *Memoirs and Letters of James Kent, LL.D., Late Chancellor, etc.* Boston: Little Brown, and Company, 1898.

King, Charles R. (Edited by). *The Life and Correspondence of Rufus King, etc.* 6 volumes. New York: G. P. Putnam's Sons, 1900.

Lee, Robert E. *Memoirs of the War in the Southern Department of the United States, by Henry Lee, Lt. Col. of the Partisan Legion During the American War, A New Edition with Revisions and a Biography of the Author by Robert E. Lee.* New York: University Publishing Company, 1869.

McGrane, Reginald C. (Edited by). *The Correspondence of Nicholas Biddle, Dealing With National Affairs, 1807-1844.* Boston: Houghton-Mifflin & Co., 1919.

Martineau, Harriett. *Retrospect of Western Travel.* London: Saunders and Otley, New York: Sold by Harper & Brothers, 1838.

Martineau, Harriett. *Society in America.* 3 volumes. London: Saunders and Otley, 1839.

Morley, John. *The Life of Richard Cobden.* 2 volumes. London: Chapman & Hall, 1881.

Munsell, Joel. *The Annals of Albany.* 10 volumes. Albany: Joel Munsell, 1869.

Myers, Gustavus. *The History of Tammany Hall.* New York: Boni and Liveright, 1917.

Myers, William Starr. *The Republican Party—A History.* New York: The Century Co., 1928.

Ogden, Rollo (Edited by). *Life and Letters of Edwin Lawrence Godkin.* 2 volumes. New York: The Macmillan Company, 1907.

Pearson, Jonathan. *Contributions for the Genealogies of the First Settlers of the Ancient County of Albany from 1630 to 1800.* Albany: Joel Munsell, 1872.

Pearson, Jonathan. *Early Records of the City and County of Albany and Colony of Rensselaerswyck, 1656-1675; Translated from the Original Dutch With Notes.* Albany: Joel Munsell, 1869.

Phillips, William. *The Conquest of Kansas by Missouri and Her Allies, etc.* Boston: Phillips, Sampson and Company, 1856.

Quincy, Josiah. *Memoir of the Life of John Quincy Adams.* Boston: Phillips, Samson and Company, 1859.

Robinson, Sara T. L. *Kansas; Its Interior and Exterior Life, etc.* Boston: Crosby, Nichols and Company, 1856.

Sargent, Epes, and Horace Greeley. *The Life and Public Services of Henry Clay, etc.* New York: C. M. Saxton, Barker & Co., 1859.

[Scott, Winfield.] *Memoirs of Lieut.-General Scott, LL.D. Written by Himself.* New York: Sheldon & Company, 1864.

Stanwood, Edward. *A History of Presidential Elections.* Boston and New York: Houghton-Mifflin and Co., 1892.

Tuckerman, Bayard (Edited by). *The Diary of Philip Hone, 1828-1851.* 2 volumes. New York: Dodd Mead and Company, 1889.

Tyler, Samuel. *Memoir of Roger Brooke Taney.* Baltimore: John Murray & Co., 1872.

[Van Buren, Abraham and Smith Thompson, Editors.] *Inquiry Into the Origin and Course of Political Parties in the United States. By the Late ex-President Martin Van Buren. Edited by his sons* (Prince John had died the preceding year). New York: Published by Hurd and Houghton, 1867.

van Laer, A. J. F. (Translated and edited by). *Van Rensselaer Bowier Manuscripts, Being the Letters of Kiliaen Van Rensselaer, 1630-1643, and Other Documents Relating to the Colony of Rensselaerswyck. With an Introductory Essay by Nicolaas de Roever, late Archivist of the City of Amsterdam.* Albany: University of the State of New York, 1908.

Walsh, Robert, Jr. *An Appeal from the Judgments of Great Britain Respecting the United States of America, etc.* Second Edition. Philadelphia: Mitchell, Ames, and White, 1819.

Watson, John F. *Annals of Philadelphia and Pennsylvania in the Olden Time, etc.* 2 volumes. Philadelphia: Whiting and Thomas, 1856-7.

Weed, Harriet A. (Edited by). *Autobiography of Thurlow Weed.* Boston: Houghton-Mifflin and Co., 1883.

Wise, Henry A. *Seven Decades of The Union. The Humanities and Materialism, Illustrated by a Memoir of John Tyler, etc.* Philadelphia: J. B. Lippincott & Co., 1876.

## A Complete List of Books on Van Buren

Bancroft, George. *Van Buren to the End of His Public Career.* New York: Harper & Brothers, 1889. This work, intended as a campaign pamphlet, was written in 1844. It is typical of its kind: it is a distortion and perversion of the record. (*Vide* 221 *et seq.* of *An Epoch and a Man.*) Bancroft's production was not published until 1889, when the author was in his eighty-ninth year. Bancroft's age explains its appearance forty-five years after he had spent a week in compiling it (*vide* his letter to Van Buren of June 14, 1844).

Butler, William Allen. *Martin Van Buren: Lawyer, Statesman and Man.* New York: D. Appleton and Company, 1862. In this memorial booklet of forty-seven pages, appropriately bound in black, the son of the law partner of Van Buren presents a scholarly sketch of his subject.

Crockett, David, *The Life of Martin Van Buren, Heir-Apparent to the "Government," and the Appointed Successor of General Andrew Jackson. Containing Every Authentic Particular by Which His Character Has Been Formed. With Concise History, etc.* Philadelphia: Robert Wright, 1835. A scurrilous campaign "life," largely untrue, designed to aid the pre-convention candidacy of Crockett's friend and fellow Tennesseean, Hugh L. White, one of Van Buren's rivals for the Presidential nomination. The book is not without its amusing side.

Emmons, William (Compiled and Edited by). *Biography of Martin Van Buren, Vice President of the United States. With an appendix containing selections From His Writings, Including his Speeches in the Senate of the United States on the Claims of the Soldiers of the Revolution, and in Favor of Abolishing Imprisonment for Debt—With Other Documents, Among which Will Be Found the Late Letter of Colonel Thos. Hart Benton, to the Convention of the State of Mississippi.* Washington: Jacob Gideon, Jr., 1835. A friendly campaign "life" of Van Buren.

Fitzpatrick, John C. (Edited by). *Annual Report of the American Historical Association for the Year 1918. Vol. II. The Autobiography of Martin Van Buren.* Washington: Government Printing Office, 1920. This memoir of Van Buren's political career was never finished. He recites but one incident of his youth, which was one of hardships. *Vide* 527 of *An Epoch and a Man.* It describes, at times, with a refreshing frankness, some of his political struggles. He began to write these memoirs in his seventy-first year.

Grund, Franz J[osef]. *Martin Van Buren als Staatsmann und Kunstiger Präsident der Vereinigten Staaten von Nord-Amerika.* Boston: (publisher's name omitted), 1835. This untruthful partisan appeal of twenty-nine pages is solemnly described as a biography in *Appleton's Cyclopædia of American Biography.* To win votes of men of German birth or extraction, Grund makes Van Buren "a son of truth-loving people of German descent;" and elsewhere the irresponsible Grund speaks of Van Buren as a man "of German ancestry, with a German heart, and of German thought"—*von deutscher abkunft, mit deutschem herzen und deutschem sinn.*

Holland, William M. *The Life and Political Opinions of Martin Van Buren, Vice President of the United States.* Hartford: Belknap & Hammersley, 1835. This is a voluminous campaign document; and while silent on events which would not add to the political stature of Van Buren, it is truthful in so far as it goes. Typical of the omissions is Holland's silence on the tavern at Kinderhook.

Irelan, John Robert, *The Republic; or a History of the United States of America in the Administrations, from the Monarchic Colonial Days to the Present Times.* 18 volumes. Chicago: Fairbanks and Palmer, 1887. Volume III bears the sub-title: *History of the Life, Administration, and Times of Martin Van Buren, Eighth President of the United States. Seven Years' Seminole War, and Period of Great Financial Convulsions.* Save the first eight pages, which deal with Van Buren's ancestry and youth, and the last chapter, which considers his retirement, the book treats largely of Van Buren's public career in Washington. The author is impartial and sympathetic.

M'Elhiney, Thomas. *Life of Martin Van Buren.* Pittsburgh: J. T. Shryock, 1853. An inane pamphlet. The author vainly attempted to enlist Van Buren's aid in obtaining a place in the Cabinet under Pierce.

Mackenzie, William L[yon]. *The Life and Times of Martin Van Buren: The*

*Correspondence of His Friends, Family and Pupils; Together with Brief Notices, Sketches, and Anecdotes Illustrative of the Public Career of* (here follow the names of fifty-one politicians and statesmen). Boston: Cooke & Co., 1846. A noxious mixture of truths, half-truths, and scurrilous fictions. This is an elaboration of an earlier pamphlet sponsored by the Polk Administration.

Mackienzie [*sic!*], William L. *The Lives and Opinions of Benjamin Franklin Butler, etc.* Boston: Cooke & Co., 1845. For Mackenzie's motives *vide* 501 *et seq.* of *An Epoch and a Man.*

Peckham, H. C. Waite Van B[uren]. *History of Cornelius Maessen Van Buren.* New York: Tobias Wright, 1913. A genealogy brought down to the present generation.

Shepard, Edward M. *Martin Van Buren.* (American Statesmen Series.) Boston and New York: Houghton-Mifflin and Company, 1888. Shepard deliberately suppresses much that would reflect on "the tangled skein of New York politics" in which he himself put a snarl or two. In an attempt to appear impartial in this self-serving volume, Shepard accepts the ridiculous gold spoon story. This, if true, would reflect on Van Buren. But Shepard systematically suppresses all incidents reflecting on the organization which nominated him for Mayor of New York City in 1901. Shepard was a son of Lorenzo B. Shepard, a Grand Sachem of Tammany Hall.

Stoddard, William O. *Andrew Jackson and Martin Van Buren.* (The Lives of the Presidents Series by Stoddard.) New York: Frederick A. Stokes, 1887. The author makes no pretense to present more than a hurried sketch which is embraced in the last nine chapters.

No attempt has been made to enumerate the numerous pamphlets read in the preparation of this work. Nor is there a complete listing of the memoirs and lives consulted: only those which have been used as sources are mentioned. Newspapers, periodicals and pamphlets which have been productive are indicated in the text: the same is true of public documents and other source material.

# INDEX

Adams, Charles Francis, Free Soil nominee for Vice President, 516; Republican Convention, at, 532.

Adams, John, 307, 450.

Adams, John Quincy, first Presidential campaign, 229 *et seq.;* House of Representatives, in, 376 *et seq.;* how a prayer elected him President, 279-281; offers British mission to Clinton, 281; offers Secretaryship of State to Clinton before naming Clay, 281; peace envoy, 139; silent under scurrilous attacks, 312; when the House sought his leadership, 440.

Albany Regency, its leaders hanged and burned in effigy, 266.

Allen, Peter, 146, 147.

Allen, Stephen, 501.

Allen, William, 442, 469.

Ambrister, Robert, 336.

American Party, bolters nominate John C. Frémont for President, 531; splits old parties, 530.

Anti-Clintonians, 142 *et seq.*

Anti-Masonic Party national convention, 347; its genesis, 314, 315; State convention, 320.

Arbuthnot, Alexander, 336.

Aristides (*see* William P. Van Ness.)

Armstrong, John, 52, 56, 110.

Astor, John Jacob, 256, 257.

Astor, William B., valet hired for Van Buren, 329.

Bancroft, George, advice to Van Buren, 483; appoints Nathaniel Hawthorne to office, 416; Baltimore Convention, at, 490; distorts history for politics, 221, 223, 227; Secretary of Navy, 498; tries persuasion on Van Buren, 499.

Bank of America, 126 *et seq.*

Bank of United States, 88; buys Bennett, 370; collapses, 441, 442; corruptly uses money in elections, 359, 360; feeds the multitude, 375; far-reaching powers, 304; Jackson on

Bank of United States (*continued*) its control of the Government, 372; Jefferson on, 262, 263; manufacturing public opinion, 372, 373.

Barker, Jacob, 144, 198.

Barnburners, 501, 505, 506.

Barney, William, Major, 97, 98.

Barry, William T., 325, 331.

Bayard, William, 148.

Beardsley, Levi, 35.

Bellona, La (*see* Mrs. John H. Eaton.)

Bennett, James Gordon, as a blackmailer, 369, 370; assails Lincoln, 540; impudence of, 437.

Benton, Mortimer C., 500.

Benton, Thomas Hart, 254, 294-298, 379.

Berrien, John M., 331.

Berry, Rev. J. Romeyn, 544.

Beverly, Carter, 311.

Biddle, Nicholas, Bryant on, 483; called "Czar Nicholas," 358; indicted for conspiracy to rob, 478; Van Buren's coldness to, 408.

Bidwell, M. S., 417.

Bigelow, John, 447.

Binns, John, rouses fellow Irish, 268.

Birney, James G., nominated for President, 460, 494.

Blair, Francis Preston, Clay to, 277; corresponds with Van Buren, 523 *et seq.;* fears Buchanan will truckle to South, 536; heads Jackson's editorial corps, 357.

Blair, Francis Preston, Jr., 537.

Blair, Mrs. Francis Preston, sends Van Buren brandied peaches, 523.

Bleecker, Harmanus, 238.

Bloemingdael, Maes, 23.

Bogardus, Everardus, Rev., 19.

Boughton, Smith A., 500.

Botts, John Minor, 480.

Bouck, William C., 479.

Bovay, Alvan, 529.

Bradley's Boarding House, 245.

Bradford, Gamaliel, 93.

Branch, John, 331.

553

Breckenridge, John C., nominee for President, 539.
Brooke, Francis, 277.
Brown, Aaron Vail, 481.
Brown, John, Harpers Ferry raid, 538; terrorism of, 533.
Brown, Thomas Storrow, 417.
Bryant, William Cullen, 493, 501; loyalty to Van Buren, 429; "The White Man's Resolution," 506.
Buchanan, James, fails Jackson, 311; nominee for President, 531; President, 535; Van Buren offers Attorney Generalship to, 443; Van Buren's renomination at, 449.
Buckingham, Joseph T., 479.
Bucktail Bards, The, 239.
Bucktails (*see* Tammany.)
Buel, Jesse, 137.
Buren, town in Holland (*see* Van Buren, origin of name), 16.
Burr, Aaron, 29, 39, 43, 48-50, 52, 53, 59; associate counsel of Van Buren, 319; praises Jackson, 133; recounts treason trial to Van Buren, 132, 133.
Burrites, 52, 53.
Butler, Benjamin F., 198, 200 201, 474, 488, 501.
Butler, W. O., nominated for Vice President, 512.
Buurmalsen, village in Holland (*see* Van Buren, origin of name), 16.

Cabot, George, 137.
Calhoun, John C., aids Solomon Van Rensselaer, 230; Jackson's dislike of, 337; retires from Presidential race, 483; Secretary of State, 484; harsh characterization of Van Buren, 401; Van Buren's political machine, on, 412, 413; reconciliation with Van Buren, 443; thinks he has ended Van Buren's career, 352.
Callender, house of, 57, 75.
Cambreleng, C. C., 310, 311, 496, 514.
Canadian Insurrection, 416 *et seq.*
Canal, Erie (*see* De Witt Clinton).
Cantine, Moses I., 133.
Carlyle, Thomas, his prayer, 192.
*Caroline*, massacre on the, 418, 419.
Carroll, Henry, 139.
Carroll, William, 293, 449.
Cass, Lewis, minister to France, 405; nominated for President, 512.
Castlereagh, Lord, 106.
Charles I, Van Buren likened to, 408.
Chartism, 192.

Chase, Salmon P., Free Soil leader, 524; Missouri Compromise, repeal on, 528; on John Van Buren, 524.
Churches—Brick Church, Buffalo, 515; Dutch Reformed at Kinderhook, 531, 545; Old Middle Dutch Church (New York), 42; St. John's Episcopal Church (Washington), 446, 470; St. Mark's In-the-Bouwerie, 143; St. Paul's Church, New York, 42; Trinity Church, New York, 42.
Clay, Henry, 40, 254, 361, 437, 466, 482, 494; "Bargain and Corruption" charge, groundlessness of, 277-279, 281; breaks with Harrison, 473, 474; defeated for President, 494; defense of Bank, 372-374; demagogy, 412; Lindenwald, visits, 521; President in 1844, nominated for, 483; Presidential canvass, first, 229 *et seq.*; Presidency in 1824, how he lost the, 273, 274; profanity, his, 440, 441; undone by the Triangular Correspondence, 441; Clay Compromise, 521 *et seq.*
Clark, Alonzo, Dr., 543.
Clark, Myron Holley, 530.
Clinton, Charles, 49.
Clinton, De Witt, believes Van Buren is for him, 308, 309; Canal opened, 284; candidate for President against Madison, 79, 92; contributing editor of *American Citizen*, 51; death, 317; duel with Swartwout, 50-51; La Fayette, visited by, 269; lampooned, 109, 239; lampooning, 239, 240; Livingstons, warfare on, 68; national figure, 272, 283; political faith, 241; poverty, 151, 318; reappointed Mayor, 75; reëlected Governor, 160; removal enrages people, 261; removed from Canal Board, 260; row with Tammany, 201-203; United States Senator, 48, 52; Van Buren's reëlection to U. S. Senate, supports, 310; Van Buren's style, on, 206; War 1812, supports, 134; withdraws in favor of Jackson, 312.
Clinton, Mrs. De Witt, her look at Van Buren and Marcy, 309.
Clinton, George, casting vote ends first Bank, 372; death of, 89; Governor, 27, 54, 60; New York's choice for President, 77; nominee for Vice President, 61 *et seq.*; Vice President, 69.
Cobb, Howell, 522, 523.

College, Middlebury, 522.
College, Union, 131, 342.
Constapel's Island, 23.
Constitutional Union Party, 539.
Coodies (*see* Anti-Clintonians).
Corn Laws, opposition to, 188, 189.
Corruption (*see* Bank of America, Nicholas Biddle, Jesse Buel, Moses H. Grinnell, Ebenezer Purdy, Ruggles Hubbard, Solomon Southwick, Samuel Swartwout, Daniel B. Tompkins, William W. Van Ness).
Council of Appointment, 54 *et seq.*
Cowper, Lord, 192.
Crabb, Richard S., 94, 98, 99.
Cralo, Fort, 23.
Crary, John, 260, 320.
Crawford, William H., 253, 254; Van Buren manages his Presidential campaign, 229 *et seq.*
Crockett, David, unjust charge against Van Buren, 385, 386.
Crolins, Clarkson, 206.
Croswell, Edwin, 298.
Cunningham, Henry, 260.
Curtis, Benjamin Roberts, 536.
Cuthbert, Alfred, 275.

Dallas, George M., nominated for Vice President, 492; Vice President, 494.
Davis, Jefferson, 522.
Davis, Matthew L., 46.
Davis, Wiley, 379.
Dawes, Thomas, 93.
Dayton, William L., Republican nominee for Vice President, 532.
Delafield, John, entertains La Pedrotti, 361.
Democratic Republican Party, origin, 321.
Democrats, origin of name, 32.
de Nemours, Prince, 421.
Desha, Joseph, on evils of banks of day, 304.
di Cavour, Count Camillo Benso, 525.
Dickerson, Mahlon, 405.
Dickinson, Daniel S., 503.
Dinwiddie, Robert, 439.
Disunionist Party, 523 *et seq.*
Dix, John A., 477, 478, 497, 518.
Dodge, Henry, declines Free Soil nomination for Vice President, 515.
Donelson, A. F., 333.
Donelson, Andrew J., Know-Nothing choice for Vice President, 531.
Douglas, Stephen Arnold, Kansas-Nebraska bill, 528 *et seq.*

Douglas, William, 362.
Duane, William J., 370.
Dudley, Charles E., succeeds Van Buren in U. S. Senate, 322, 323.
Duels, Benton-Carroll, 293; Clay-Randolph, 292-298; Clinton-Swartwout, 50-51; Hamilton-Eacker, 43-45; Hamilton-Burr, 64; Jackson-Benton *et al*, 292-293; Van Buren-Sudam (abortive), 82-84.
Duer, John, 240, 379.
Duer, William A., 146.

Eacker, George I., 44, 45.
Eaton, John H., his "licentious life," 332; marries the Widow Timberlake, 332; Secretary of War, 331.
Eaton, Mrs. John H., as a grandmother marries a youth who robs her, 538; Jackson defends her, 332; Van Buren champions her, 332 *et seq.;* Washington snubs her, 332, 334, 335; why she was snubbed, 332.
d'Eendracht, West India Company's ship, 16.
Edmonds, John W., 429, 500.
Education, lotteries aid learning, 131.
Eldred, Caleb, 206.
Ellmaker, Amos, 347.
Embargo Act, 77.
Emmet, Robert, Irish martyr, 106.
Emmet, Robert, presides at first Republican Convention, 532.
Emmet, Thomas Addis, 106-109 *et seq.*
Equal Rights Party, 397 *et seq.*
Esleek, Welcome, 208.
Esterhazy, Prince Nicholas, 421.
Everett, Edward, nominee for Vice President, 539.
Evertsen, Volckert, 21.
Expunging Resolution, 374, 397.

Fairfield, John, 492.
Federal interference in State elections, 201, 202, 204, 205, 209.
Federalists, 37.
Fellows, Henry, 163.
Ferlin, Jaspaer, 15.
Field, David Dudley, 493.
Fillmore, Millard, Know-Nothings name him for President, 531; President, 522; Tyler impeachment, votes for, 480; nominated for Vice President, 513; Vice President, 519; Whigs indorse, 533.
Fish, Preserved, 374.
Fitzpatrick, Benjamin, 539.

Flagg, Azariah C., 496, 543, 544.
Follett, Oran, 274.
Foot, Ebenezer, 89, 108.
Forrest, Edwin, 363.
Forsyth, John, 405, 436, 449.
Foster, Ephraim H., 443.
Free Masons, 315, 364 *et seq.*
Free Masons (*see* William Morgan).
Free Soil Party, Buffalo Convention,
    514–517; genesis of, 505, 506;
    Herkimer Convention, 507, 508;
    motto of, 517; platform, 517, 518;
    Syracuse Convention, 505, 506;
    Utica Convention, 514; John Van
    Buren's Park speech, 512, 513;
    Martin Van Buren its candidate
    for President, 512 *et seq.*
Frémont, John C., Republican nomi-
    nee for President, 532.
Fugitive Slave Act, 522, 525.
Fulton, Robert, first steamboat, 74.

Gag Rule, 422.
Gaither, Ephraim, 94, 95, 97, 98, 99.
Gaither, Harry, 95, 98, 99.
Gaither, William, 95, 98, 99.
Gales, Joseph, 441.
Gallatin, Albert, 139, 254 *et seq.*
Gallatin, Frances, 256.
Garland, Hugh A., 439.
Garrison, William Lloyd, 375.
Genêt, Edmond Charles, minister
    from France, 30.
George II, 24.
George III, 188, 511.
Gerry, Elbridge, a Signer and Vice
    President, 40.
Gerry, Elbridge, son of Signer, re-
    moved, 328.
Giddings, Joshua R., 480.
Gilbert, William W., 106.
Gilmer, Thomas W., 481, 483.
Gilpin, Henry D., 443, 471.
Glentworth, James B., 459.
Goes, Hannah, love for Van Buren,
    58.
Goes, Mary (*also* Maria), faith of,
    28.
Gold spoon canard, 445.
Graham, John A., Dr., 152.
Graham, William A., nominee for
    Vice President, 524.
Granger, Francis, 320.
Grant, J., Jr., 360.
Green Bag Message (*see* Federal in-
    terference in State elections).
Green, Duff, 481.
Greeley, Horace, 529, 530.

Grinnell, Moses H., 459.
Grosvenor, Thomas P., 82, 85.
Gulian, George W., Free Soil nomi-
    nee for Vice President, 524.
Gwin, Stephen, 375.

Habeas Corpus Act, England sus-
    pends, 188.
Hager, Henry, 123.
Hale, John P., Free Soil nominee for
    President, 524.
Hall, Stokely, 292.
Hall, Thomas, 21.
Halleck, Fitz-Greene, 171.
Hamblin, Thomas S., 438.
Hamilton, Alexander (*see* Duels),
    29, 45, 55; Jefferson, on, 263, 264.
Hamilton, Alexander, Jr., gambling,
    379.
Hamilton, Alexander, Mrs. 45, 49.
Hamilton, James A., aide to Van
    Buren, 313, 314, 330.
Hamilton, John C., 164.
Hamilton, Philip (*see* Duels), 43, 44.
Hamiltonians, *see* Federalists.
Hamlin, Hannibal, nominee for Vice
    President, 539; Vice President, 540.
Hammett, William H., 484.
Hammond, Jabez B., 145, 164.
Hanson, Alexander C., 94, 95, 100,
    102, 103.
Hard Cider Campaign (*see* William
    H. Harrison and Martin Van
    Buren).
"Hard Shells," 530 *et seq.*
Harrison, J., Reverend, 189.
Harrison, William H., campaigning,
    457, 458; court clerk, 381; death in
    White House, 474; humor, 470;
    nominated for President, 440; pov-
    erty, 443; President, 460.
Hart, Eli, 398.
Hartford Convention, 137–139, 278.
Harvey, Sir John, 424.
Hastings, John, 477.
Hawley, Gideon, 208.
Hawthorne, Nathaniel, 416.
Hayne, Robert Y., 310, 338.
Head, Sir Francis Bond, 417.
*Henri Quatre,* 255.
Henry, Patrick, 511.
Hibernicus (*see* De Witt Clinton).
High-Minded Federalists, 197, 198,
    240.
Hildreth, Matthias B., 105.
Hill, Isaac, 336.
Hillhouse, James, 137.
Hoes (*see* Goes).

Hogeboom, John C., 79, 122, 199.
Holmes, Oliver Wendell, 40.
Hone, Philip, 361 *et seq.*
Hone, Mrs. Philip, 436.
Hopkins, George W., 481.
Hosack, David, Dr., 240.
House of Commons, 185-188.
House of Lords, 188.
Houston, Samuel, 523.
Hoyt, Jesse, 181, 200, 201, 203, 323, 502.
Hoyt, Lorenzo, 200.
Hoxie, Joseph, 453, 471.
Hubbard, Ruggles, 116, 143.
Humphreys, Reuben, 113.
Hunkers, 501 *et seq.*
Hunt, Henry, 189.
Hunt, Memucan, 413.
Hunter, Robert M. T., 440.
Huygens, Chevalier A. de Bangeman, Van Buren's friendship with, 331.

Ingham, Samuel D., 331.
Ingulf, Rudolf, 520.
Irish, riot for Jackson, 374.
Irving, Henrietta, marries Smith Thompson Van Buren, 527.
Irving, Peter, Dr., 51.
Irving, Washington, contributor to Burr's organ, 51; tutors children of William P. Van Ness, 347; Van Buren appoints him to diplomatic post, 346.

Jackson, Andrew, anger, 328; Anti-Masons oppose him, 320; assails Jefferson, 133; Bank of United States, fight on, 337; Bargain and corruption charge, revives, 311; Burr, defends, 133; Mrs. Eaton, linking his name with, 257; intentions toward "The Monster," 355; Irish ancestry derided, 357, 374; New Orleans, at, 139; plans resigning Presidency that Van Buren may serve, 340, 341, 348; shot at on Capitol steps, 381; Tammany's present to, 400; U. S. Senator, 252; Van Buren, dependence on, 360, 371; Van Buren's defeat, on, 458-460, 462, 463; Van Buren drapes his portrait, 499; Van Buren as a son, loves, 371; Van Buren, repeats whispers to, 367; Van Buren, used to injure, 481, 482.
Jackson, Mrs. Andrew, name assailed in campaign, 312; Clinton denounces attacks on, 317.

Jacobins, American sympathy for, 30, 31, 32.
Jacobsen, Rutger, 22.
Jacques, Moses, Dr., 397-399.
Jay, John, 29, 37.
Jay, Peter, 213.
Jefferson, Martha (*see* Mrs. Thomas Mann Randolph).
Jefferson, Thomas, cities, on, 221; opposes Jackson for President, 278, political credo, 40, 41; poverty, 318; praise of Washington, 265; punctuality, on, 264; repudiates Genêt, 32; Secretary of State, 30; slavery, on, 511.
Jenkins, Elisha, 86.
Jenkins, Robert, 86, 87.
Jenkins, Seth, 86 87.
Jesup, T. J., General, 291 *et seq.*
Jogues, Isaac, Father, 20.
Johnson, Francis, 277.
Johnson, Henry M., 262.
Johnson, Herschel V., nominee for Vice President, 539.
Johnson, Josiah, 296.
Johnson, Richard M., 346; candidate for Vice President on Van Buren ticket, 382, 383; Vice President, 395.
Jones, John W., 483.
Jordan, Ambrose L., 500.

Kansas-Nebraska Act, 528 *et seq.*
Keese, Mrs. Rosa, Van Buren at her boarding house, 91, 109.
Kemble, Charles, 363.
Kemble, Fanny, 362, 447.
Kendall, Amos, 328.
Kent, James, 125, 203; fears universal suffrage will destroy Republic, 218, 219.
Kinderhook, Martin Van Buren buys tract, 23.
Kilgour, Charles K., 94, 98, 99.
King, Charles, abuse of Van Buren, 460.
King, John A., 206, 216.
King, Rufus, aids spoilsmen, 231-233; conventionality, 235; delegate to New York Constitutional Convention, 213; Emmet assails, 106, 107; fears of a hereditary President, 251, 252; intrigues for Van Buren, 247-249; nominated for U. S. Senator, 115; supports War 1812, 135.
King, William, General, 109.

King William, of England, 330; conversation with Van Buren, 346; Van Buren, on, 354.

King William I of Holland, suggests he is kin to Van Buren, 354.

King, William R., nominated for Vice President, 524; Vice President, 525.

Kitchen Cabinet, its membership, 336.

Knower, Benjamin, 207, 232, 233.

Know-Nothings (*see* American Party, and Native American Party).

Kremer, George, 278, 381.

Krudener, Baron, aids Van Buren's intrigue against Calhoun, 335.

La Fayette, General, exults over popular government, 220; received by Solomon Van Rensselaer, 268.

Lane, Joseph, nominee for Vice President, 539.

Lansing, John, 59, 232, 233.

Law, John, 477.

Lawrence, Abbott, 408.

Lee, "Light Horse Harry," 94-96, 100-105.

Lee, Robert E., 538.

Leggett, William, 426.

LeRoy, Abraham, 374.

Lewis, Morgan, 52, 61, 435, 436, 437; Governor, 68; fights legislative corruption, 72; Chief Justice, 60; recalls his prediction of Van Buren's greatness, 364; supported by Van Buren, 63, 64.

Lewis, William B., 310.

Lincoln, Abraham, member House of Representatives, 515, 516; nominee for President, 539; President, 540; policy, his, 541; proclaims salute to Van Buren's memory, 545.

Lingan, James, General, defends free press, 94, 98-103; slain by mob, 104-105.

Livingston, Brockholst, 52.

Livingston, Edward, author of The *Louisiana Code*, 55; Victor Hugo and Royalty pay him tribute, 56; Mayor of New York, 51, 52; resigns offices and goes to New Orleans, 55; Secretary of State, 344, 345; short in his accounts, 55; U. S. Attorney, 55; United States Senator, 310; Van Buren's preceptor studies law under, 39; writes Jackson's proclamation on nullification, 366.

Livingston, Edward P., defeated for State Senate by Van Buren, 85-88; eats turtle with "Mawne" Bleecker and Van Buren, 238; one of "the immortal seventeen," 266.

Livingston, Gertrude, wife of Morgan Lewis, 52.

Livingston, Maturin, 68, 70.

Livingston, Peter R., an important motion, 227; defends democratic institutions, 220; delegate to New York Constitutional Convention, 213; denounces political judges, 216; State Senator, 163.

Livingston, Robert R. (Chancellor), 48, 49.

Livingstone, Alexander, Sir, 49.

Loco-focos (*see* Equal Rights Party).

Log-Cabin campaign (*see* William H. Harrison and Martin Van Buren).

Louisiana Code (*see* Livingston, Edward).

Louis Philippe, 384, 388, 421, 436.

Lovejoy, Elijah P., 483.

Lowrie, Walter, 257.

Lynch, Domenick, 182.

MacDonough, Thomas, 136.

Mackenzie, William Lyon, Canadian leader, 416; imprisoned, 502; journalist, 419; writes pamphlets against Van Buren, 501-503.

McIntyre, Archibald, 179.

McLane, Louis, 253, 341.

McLean, Joseph, 325.

MacNeven, William J., 143.

Macon, Nathaniel, 259.

Madison, James, 77, 92, 109, 511.

Madison, Mrs. James (Dolly), matchmaker, 416.

Magnum, Willie P., nominated for President, 382.

Manhattan, settlement of, 16.

Manley, Joseph R., Dr., 323.

Marcy, William L., 166, 167, 208, 232; Governor, 361; informs Van Buren of his selection as Vice President, 352; leads pro-Slavery men against Van Buren, 496; Secretary of State, 525; "to the victor belong the spoils" speech, 351.

Marshall, James Wilson, 520.

Martling Men (*see* Tammany).

Maynard, William H., 323.

Meigs, Return, J., 205, 231, 232.

Mercer, Charles F., 281.

Miffin, Thomas, Governor, 31.
Miller, Henry G., 525.
Miller, Sylvanus, 52.
Milton, Lord, 192.
Ming, Alexander, Jr., 397, 429.
Minuit, Peter, purchase of Manhattan, 17.
Missouri Compromise, repealed, 527, 528.
Monarchists assail democracy, 185-193, 384, 385.
Monroe, James, 231-234, 286, 326, 337, 511.
Montresor, James, Colonel, 24.
Mooers, Benjamin, 196.
Morell, George, Van Buren's second in abortive duel, 82.
Morgan, Edwin, 544, 545.
Morgan, William, assassination, 314; Clinton falsely accused of ordering assassination, 315; Clinton offers reward for assassins, 314; Jackson's name falsely linked with assassination, 315; Van Buren counsels truth in references to, 314.
Morocco, Emperor of, 451.
Morris, Robert, 511.
Morris, Robert H., 472, 505, 506.
Mumma, John, 99, 100-104.
Muscat, Imaum of, 450, 451.
Myers, Mordecai, 433, 475.
Myers, William Starr, 532.

National Republican Party, name first used, 321.
Native American Party, assailed in Democratic platform, 492; nominates Henry A. S. Dearborn for Vice President, 518; recommends Taylor for President, 518.
Nativism (see also American Party, and Native American Party), 255, 267.
New Amsterdam, settlement of, 16.
Newspapers—Aboliva, 199; Albany Daily Advertiser, 417; Albany Evening Journal, 426; American, 275, 395, 401, 444; American Citizen, 51, 109, 110, 166; Argus, 137, 298, 314, 432, 434, 475; Baltimore Patriot, 116, 448; Baltimore Republican, 443; Boston Courier, 479; Cincinnati Advertiser and Journal, 436; Columbia Observer, 278; Courier, London, 421; Courier and Enquirer 337, 457, 461; Daily Advertiser, 261; Evening Post, 261, 274, 429,

Newspapers (continued)
443, 447, 477; Federal Republican, 94; Gazette, New York, 139; Hartford Times, 452; Herald, 407, 437; Hudson River Chronicle, 431; Kinderhook Sentinel, 475; Liberator, 376; Louisville Courier, 438; Mackenzie's Message, 419; Monitor, Washington, 93; Morning Chronicle, 51, 60; Morning News, 489; National Intelligencer, 278, 487; New Era, 428; Pennsylvanian, 369; Pittsfield Sun, 112; Plebian, 112; Public Advertiser, 112; Register, Albany, 75; Richmond Enquirer, 71, 420, 484; Telegraph, 309; Times, London, 190, 192, 353; Tribune, 419, 529; United States Telegraph, 337; Washington Globe, 358, 484, 487; Wilkes-Barre Farmer, nominates Van Buren for President in 1848, 508.
Nicholson, James, 256.
Nicolson, John B., 346.
Nicholson, Sir Francis, 256.
Niles, John Milton, 452.
Noah, Mordecai M., chief of Van Buren's editorial corps, 244; efforts to found a new Jerusalem, 244; Grand Sachem of Tammany, 244; rupture with Van Buren, 344; self-styled King of Israel, 244.
North, Lord, 130.
Northeastern Boundary, Van Buren prepares for war, 424.
Nott, Eliphalet, 387.
Nullification, Calhoun's fiery report on, 390; Jackson on, 366; originates in New England, 138, 139; South Carolina's threat, 365.

Oakley, Thomas J., 178, 179, 197, 317.
Ogle, Charles, 445-448.
Oldstyle, Jonathan (see Washington Irving).
O'Neale, Peggy( (see Mrs. John H. Eaton).
Opera, introduced in America, 285.
Orange, Fort, 20.
Oregon Boundary, 498.
Osgood, David, 92.
Otis, Harrison Gray, 93, 137, 367, 377.

Palmerston, Lord, 353.
Panama Mission, 308.
Papineau, Louis Joseph, 417.
Patriot Army (see Canadian Insurrection).

Paulding, James K., 420, 478.
Paulding, William, 307.
Payne, John Howard, 94, 98, 99.
"Peacemaker" Explosion, 483, 484.
Pennington, William, 438.
People's Party, 260 *et seq.*
Peterloo Massacre, 189-192.
Peyton, Balie, 503.
Pickens, Francis W., 443.
Pierce, Franklin, nominated for President, 524; President, 525.
Pierson, G. H., 525.
"Pipe-laying," 459, 460.
Pitcher, Nathaniel, 319.
Platt, Jonas, 242.
Poinsett, Joel R., 405, 481.
Polk, James Knox, aspires to Presidency, 449; duplicity, attempts to conceal, 502; nominated for President, 490, 491; President, 494; treachery to Van Buren, 496-499; Van Buren break with, 501.
Pope Pius IX., 526.
Porter, T. H., 315.
Potter, Alonzo, Bishop, 545.
Prendergast, Jedaiah, 163, 164.
Preston, William C., 420.
"Prince John" (*see* John Van Buren).
Prohibition, 530.
Public Schools, affected by Spoils System, 208, 209; origin of, 208, 209.
Purdy, Ebenezer, 71, 72.

Quackenbosh, Maritje, 23.
Quakers, 209.
Queen Victoria, dances with John Van Buren, 421.
Quids, 72.
Quincy, Josiah, 377.

Randolph, Ellen Wayles, flirtation with Van Buren, 235, 236, 237.
Randolph, John (of Roanoke), descent from Pocahontas, 291; drinking, 289; duel with Clay, 292-298; gambling, 288; genius, 288; origin of hatred of the Adamses, 291; presents horse to Van Buren, 421; "Puritan and blackleg" speech, 289-292; ribaldry, 289, 290.
Randolph, Thomas Mann, 236.
Randolph, Mrs. Thomas Mann, daughter of Jefferson, 236; presides at Van Buren's table, 334.
Reforms—Americans agitate for, 193, 194, 201-203, 228, 270; English fight for, 186, 187, 189-191, 210.

Rensselaer, Kiliaen, the first Patroon, 15, 20, 21.
Rensselaerswyck, settlement of, 16.
*Rensselaerswyck,* the ship, 18.
Republican Party, adopts Free Soil Party's doctrines, 532; how it acquired name, 529, 530; paraphrase Free Soil motto, 535.
Republicans, 37.
Rhett, Robert Barnwell, 440.
Riker, Richard, 50, 71, 105.
Riley, Bennett, 520.
Riots—Abolitionist, 377, 385; Anti-Catholic, 376, 377; Anti-Rent, 500; Baltimore riot of 1812, 94-105; Food, 397-399; Irish and Whigs, 374.
Ritzema, Johannes, Dominie, 26.
Rochester, William B., 308.
Rolph, Dr. John, 417.
Romaine, Samuel B., 206.
Root, Erastus, 113.
Ross, William, 110.
Rowan, John, 304.
Rucker, Edward, 382.
Rutgers, Henry, 154, 155.

St. Peter's Field (*see* Peterloo Massacre).
Sanford, Nathaniel, 206, 213, 317.
Saunders, Romulus M., 382, 488.
Schellinger, Captain, of the *Rensselaerwyck,* 18.
Schuyler, Philip, General, 49.
Schuyler, Pieter, Colonel, 49.
Scott, Dred, 536, 537.
Scott, Winfield, aspirant for Presidency, 437; at Navy Island, 419; nominee for President, 524; on a vile calumny, 314; predicts Presidency for Van Buren, 131.
Secession, 540 *et seq.*
Seditious Meetings Act, 188.
Seward, William H., 422, 432, 441, 479, 529.
Seymour, Henry, 163 *et seq.*
Sidmouth, Lord, 191.
Silvester, Cornelius, interest in Van Buren, 35.
Silvester, Francis, Van Buren's first preceptor, 33, 37, 213.
Silvester, Margaret, Van Buren's affection for, 522, 523, 526.
Silvester, Peter, 33.
Singleton, Angelica, 416, 420.
Slavery (*see* Texas), 34, 185, 194, 421, 422, 504, 506, 524.
"Soft Shells," 530 *et seq.*

Southard, Samuel L., 444.
Southwick, Solomon, bribes legislators, 117; corruption of, 88; indicted, 108; informs on another criminal, 136; thief as well as briber, 230.
Smith, John, U. S. Senator, 115.
Spencer, Ambrose, 73, 109, *et seq.*
Spoils System, a national institution, 325 *et seq.;* origin, 51, 52, 53, 54; its working, 325, 327-329; Whigs make it the issue against Van Buren, 377.
Sprigg, Otho, 94, 98, 99.
Starvation Laws (*see* Corn Laws).
State Convention, origin of, 156.
Stevenson, Andrew, 253, 382.
Stirling, Earl of, 243.
Stricker, John, General, 98.
Strong, George D., 374.
Sturgeon, Daniel, 444.
Sub-Treasury, 413, *et seq.*
Sudam, John, challenges Van Buren, 82, 500.
Sumner, Charles, 522, 532.
Sumner, William Graham, 470.
Sutherland, Jacob, 242, 366.
Swartwout, John, duel with Clinton, 50-51.
Swartwout, Samuel, canvasses for Jackson, 310; defalcation, his, 327; Spoils System, and, 326, 327.
Swift, Zephaniah, 137.

Talcott, Samuel A., 207.
Tallmadge, James, 213.
Tallmadge, Nathaniel P., 366.
Tammany, 70, 79, 115, 162, 166, 170, 171, 201, 213, 230, 233, 284, 319, 397, 472, 545.
Taney, Roger B., 370, 536.
Tappan, Arthur, 376.
Tappan, Lewis, 376.
Tariff, 318, 319.
Tatnall, Edward F., 292 *et seq.*
Tayler, John, 109, 112, 117.
Taylor, John W., cynical opinion of Presidential aspirants, 129.
Taylor, Zachary, death, 522; nobleness, 503; nominated for President, 513; President, 519.
Tazewell, Littleton W., 349, 449.
Temple, John, Sir, 107.
Teunisz, Cornelis, 17, 18, 20.
Texas, 413, 478, 480, 496, 499.
Thomas, David 88, 108, 117.
Thompson, John, 103.

Thompson, Smith, and Spoils System, 231; breaks pact with Van Buren, 161; hoodwinks Van Buren, 247-249; Secretary of Navy, 167.
Thompson, William, 168.
Throop, Enos T., 320.
Timberlake, J. B., 332.
Timberlake, the Widow (*see* Mrs. John H. Eaton).
Tilden, Moses, 534.
Tilden, Samuel J., 489, 509, 510, 514, 530.
Tillotson, Thomas, Dr., 52, 72.
Tompkins, Daniel D., aids ballot frauds, 46; Clinton, falsely accuses, 135; Governor, 73; intemperance, 181; Monroe, denounces, 231; poverty 212; Presidential hopes, 122, 129; presides at New York's Constitutional Convention, 212 *et seq.;* prosecutes bribers, 108; re-elected Governor, 148; shortage in his accounts, 179 *et seq.;* Vice President, 244.
Triangular Correspondence (*see* Henry Clay).
Troup, Robert, 45.
Two-thirds rule, 382, 488, 489.
Tyler, John, corrupt bankers attempt to remove him from Presidency, 479, 480; integrity, 477; nominated for Vice President, 381, 440; succeeds Harrison as President, 474.

Ullman, Daniel, 530.
Ulshoeffer, Michael, 162, 201, 227.
Universal Suffrage (*see* Reforms).
University, Columbia, 131, 461.
Upshur, Abel Parker, 482, 484.

Van Alen, James I., law-partner of Van Buren, 59; Van Buren's half-brother celebrates Federalist victory, 37.
Van Alen, John I., Van Buren's half-brother sends him money, 57.
Van Beuren, Pieter, 26.
Van Buren, origin of name, 23.
Van Buren, Abraham, Captain of Militia, 27; marries, 25; political faith, 32; tavern, his, 24, 27, 28, 29, 67; brother of Martin, 25.
Van Buren, Abraham, Jr., Battle of Monterey, at, 503, 504; birth of son, 476; enters West Point, 251; father inaugurated, sees, 400; horseback rides with father, 409; Lindenwald, at, 523; marries, 420; Mexican War,

Van Buren, Abraham, Jr., (*contin'd*) in, 509; royalty entertains, 436; Secretary to the President, 399; summarizes daily work of Congress for father, 436.

Van Buren, Mrs. Abraham, Jr., White House, mistress of, 469.

Van Buren, Catelijntje Martense, marries Cornelis Maesen, 17; death, 21.

Van Buren, Cornelis Maesen, birth of first child, 18; children of, 21; contract with Van Rensselaer, 17; death, 22; Greenwich Village, buys, 21; first voyage to America, 16; leadership qualities, 20, 23; marriage, 17; second voyage to New Netherlands, 18.

Van Buren, Dirckie, sister of Martin, 25.

Van Buren, Hendrick Maesen, brother of Cornelis Maesen, 17.

Van Buren, Jannetje, sister of Martin, 25.

Van Buren, John, 317, 396, 501, 505, 514, 522; accompanies father to England, 346; addresses pro-war meetings, 542, 543; Attorney General, 497; attack on, 446, 447; emotion-stirring Free Soil speech, 507; extravagance, 285, 286, 319; Lawrence Godkin on, 251, 286; Herkimer speech, 507; jail, spends day in, 499, 500; lampooned in rhyme, 497, 498; lives with Rufus King's family, 251; marries, 476; member of House of Representatives, 464; political aide of father, 377, 378; popularity, 512, 515; President, Edwin M. Stanton proposes him for, 515; "Prince John," how he came by the name, 421; profanity, Hoyt provokes him to, 378; Tyler's impeachment, votes against, 480; Utica Convention speech, 509, 510; Vice President proposed for, 524; Yale, progress at, 316; Yale, trouble at, 319.

Van Buren, John Dash, 537.

Van Buren, J. M., 387.

Van Buren, Lawrence, brother of Martin, 25.

Van Buren, Martin, Adams, John Quincy, attacks, 306, 307; Adams, his debt to, 241; Adams on, 283, 287, 391; Albany, moves to, 141; ancestry, 16-24; anecdotes on, 299; anonymous letters against, 181;

Van Buren, Martin (*continued*) artifice, favorite, 145, 368; Attorney General, 141; Attorney Generalship, seeks, 105, 106; Bank of United States, attack on, 317; on corruption of, 391, 392; bank reform, 322; banks, deals mortal blow to, 460, 461; banks, on, 429; banking system, assails, 441, 442; banking system, begins fight against, 404; banking, first attack on corrupt, 126, 127; banking system, no compromise with, 475; baptized, 26; Benton on, 136; Biddle, assails, 415; birth, 26; boast, his, 23; borrowing, on, 199, 316; boyhood politics, 37; boy-lawyer, as famous, 38; boyhood poverty sneered at, 407; British-American Claims Commission, declines post on, 526; Buchanan's administration, criticizes, 539; Buchanan, why he supported, 534, 535; Burr advises him to stay in politics, 149; Burr, assailed for opposing, 60-62; Burr, befriends, 132, 133; Burr, compared to, 313, 314; Burr, defends opposition to, 62, 63; Burr's second, advises, 66; Calhoun dinner, the toast to him at a, 346; calumny, silent under, 281; campaign literature censors, establishes, 313; campaign scurrilities, on, 322; campaign songs on, 453-456, 460, 471; campaigning, 73, 74, 457, 458, 478; Canal, opposes, 144; characteristics, 370; Chairman U. S. Senate Judiciary Committee, 229; charitableness, 199, 387, 396, 397; children, 127; Church and State, on, 284; Clay, advice to, 276, 277; Clay his ideal orator, 277; Clay, visits, 479; Clinton, breaks with, 116-119; Clinton, eulogy on, 318; Clinton, hatred of, 198; Clinton, on, 173-176; Clinton's peace proposals, rejects, 151-156, 161, 177, 274; Clinton's power of ridicule, on, 308; Clinton, plots against, 163; Clinton, proposes exile for, 171, 172; Clinton's removal, protests against, 143; Clinton removes him as Attorney General, 178; Clinton, supports, 69; Clinton for President, supports, 110; Clinton's return to power, vainly tries to prevent, 157-160; Clinton routs him, 273; Clinton, unjustly suspects, 180; Mrs. De

Van Buren, Martin (*continued*)
Witt Clinton, snubbed by, 436; Clintonians, leader of, 111 *et seq.;* Congress, his last message to, 467-469; Congressional delegate at eighteen, 41; constitutional amendments, on, 226; conscription bill, drafts, 136; counsellor of Supreme Court, 73; Countess of Westmorland, attentions to the, 448; court, last appearance in, 319; Crawford's campaign for Presidency, manages, 253; criticism, silent under, 209; cynicism, 415, 416, 469; death, 544; defeat, on his, 461, 462; defeated for reëlection, 460; defeated for renomination, 491; defensive publications, against, 312, 313; delegate New York Constitutional Convention, 211 *et seq.;* demagogy, 377; democracy, his talisman of, 391; derided, 282, 431; dinners, his Saturday night, 444; diplomacy, 330, 331, 341; diplomacy, Washington Irving on, 389; disposition, 39, 76, 385; downcast, 274; drink, warns son against, 339; duel, abortive, with John Sudam, 82-85; W. A. Duer judge, makes, 241, 242; Dutch accent, 158; "Dutch brother," his, 331 *et seq.;* Dutch rejected him, when the, 211, 212; Eaton Imbroglio, uses to eliminate Calhoun, 332-337, 339-340, 342-344; economy, practises and preaches, 316; education, 28, 33; education, recognized his lack of, 115; emotion-stirring speech, 433, 434; Embargo Act, favors, 77; England, life in, 347 *et seq.;* "English coach of State," his, 372; "entangling alliances," against, 466, 467; Europe, leaves for, 525; faith in the people, 415, 423; false report of his engagement to Jefferson's granddaughter, 236, 237; to a widow, 321; farewell letter, 543, 544; farming, 479 *et seq.;* Van Buren, father, (*see* Abraham Van Buren); favorite phrase, a, 415; favors for none, 409, 410; fearing attack, carries pistols, 381; fearlessness, 172, 301-304; federalist opposition to, 76; financial integrity, 371; Hudson, moves to, 77; finance, knowledge of, 410-412; first appearance before appeals bench, 76; first appearance in rhyme, 239; first case, wins, 36;

Van Buren, Martin (*continued*)
first important address, 118; first mentioned publicly for President, 275, 276; first political battle, 79-81; first Presidential intrigue, 139, 140; first vote challenged, 63, 64; foreign affairs, knowledge of, 468; forgiveness, spirit of, 84, 461, 466; Free Soil articles of faith, 510-512; Free Soil candidate for President, 514; frailties of friends, discounts, 330; patronizing with his fellow farmers, 476; gambling, 309, 321, 361, 379; generosity, 438; goes a-fishing, 499; Hannah Goes, love for, 58; government, aim of, 429; Governor, 320-323; Governorship, resigns, 323; gratitude, 470, 472; Hamilton's political formula, adopts, 120; "happiest years, the," 539; hard money advocate, 408; hard times during administration, 406 *et seq.;* Harrison's chief mourner in New York, 474; helps his runaway slave to remain "free," 276; Holy Alliance, on the, 287, 288; honesty, 165; horse-races, attends, 310, 311; Hoyt's threatening letter, answers, 329, 330; humor, 299, 321, 437, 447; hymn, favorite, 545; hymns, fondness for, 309, 531; ideal, his great, 545; imprisonment for debt, fights, 124-126; inaugural address—conciliation of North and South; defense of democracy; denounces mobs; monarchical intrigue, warns against; prayer; proud boast, his, 400 *et seq.;* inauguration, description of, 400; independence, 394; indifference to falsehoods, 138; internal improvements, against Federal aid for, 300; intrigues, 305; intrigues against Adams, 286, 287; Irving, Washington, on, 347; Jackson, admiration for, 475; Jackson, advice to, 312, 313; Jackson for President, opposes, 257, 258; Jackson on, 458; Jackson plans that he run for Vice President, 343; Jackson suggests British mission for, 343; Jackson, visits, 478; Jackson's campaign for Presidency 1828, manages, 310 *et seq.;* Jackson's faith in, 340; Jackson's opinion of, 337; Jackson's State papers, supervises, 388, 389; Jackson's successor, publicly proposed as, 337; Jefferson Day din-

Van Buren, Martin (*continued*)
ner, first, 338, 339; Jefferson, compared to, 468; Jefferson's stand, champions, 78; judge, 125; judiciary reform, for, 214, 215; Kent, controversy with, 137; "killing a man too dead," on, 271; Kinderhook land titles, defends, 69, 70; Kinderhook, leaves New York for, 57; Kinderhook, returns to, 474; kindness, 427, 471; Rufus King in the dark, leaves, 275; Rufus King, outwits, 245; Rufus King, praises, 182-184, 193; Rufus King secretly aids him, 207; Rufus King, secretly plots to elect, 167 *et seq.*; lampooned, 259; "large aggregations of wealth," warns against stifling of political opinion by, 414; law, begins practice of, 59; law office, description of, and his law students, 200; laws of other lands, familiarity with, 217; letter of acceptance, 383, 384; letters he burned, 347; Lincoln's policy, supports, 540 *et seq.*; literary labors, 527 *et seq.*; literary style, 174-176, 224; Lindenwald improvements, 476; loan, seeks a, 46, 47; lodges at Stewart's, 200; Madison's reëlection, opposes, 110; Madison, rhyming lampoon on, transcribes, 114; Marcy polishes Van Buren's English, 182; marriage, proposes, 73, 522, 523; marries, 73; "martyr to principles," 493; master of surprise, 154; masterly intrigue, 308; methods, 119-122, 137, 154-156, 222, 223, 229, 230, 287; Minister to England, 345; Minister to England, Senate rejects him as, 349-352; miracle of the turnips, on the, 526; mission to England, declines, 498; mocked by mob, 414; monarchical attacks on the Republic, warns against, 384, 385; Monroe opposes, 145; Monroe will not aid the spoilsmen, 230-234; Morgan affair, on political effect of the, 321; mother of, *see* Goes, Mary; national debt, on evils of a, 467-469; nepotism, 208; New Year's Day at Lindenwald, 508, 509; New Year's at the White House, 415, 416, 469; New York, considers moving to, 198; New York, triumphal return to, 428-435; nicknames, 282, 342, 394, 416; nominated for President, 382, 383; non-committalism,

Van Buren, Martin (*continued*)
322; non-committalism charge, its origin, 299; "Northern man with Southern principles," 447; Nullificationists, conciliation for, 367, 368; oath, an, 198; opera, goes to the, 473; opposed to appointive judges, 263; opposition press distorts utterances, 404, 405; out of office, 200; "Panic Session" of Congress, convokes, 409; parents, 127; patron of letters, 416, 420; patronage controlled by theft of Assembly seat, 146, 147; patronage controlled by theft of a Senate seat, 163, 164; peacemaker, 111; personal appearance, 28, 34, 58, 235, 312, 313, 356, 470, 531; personal appearance as Bennett pictured it, 407; personal appearance, as "Davy" Crockett pictured it, 386; Phi Beta Kappa, elected to, 341, 342; Pierce's proposal to call meeting of ex-Presidents, 540, 541; Pierce, supports, 524; Poindexter tries to pick a duel with, 379-381; political conduct, Acts 23 guide, 128; political faith, 321; political philosophy, 245, 435; politics, studies, 53; politics, weary of, 149; popular government, on superiority of, 442; poverty, 38, 41, 46, 48, 57; poverty keeps learned man in office, 323; preparedness, on, 466, 467; President, 395, 396; President, renominated for, 449; Presidency, second campaign for the, 444-460; Preston, snubs, 465, 466; prophecy of John P. Van Ness, 47; public career, begins, 59; public servant, his ideal, 543, 544; public currents, studies, 228; quarrel with Hogeboom, 122; quarrel with Rufus King, 253, 254; quarrel with Swart, 158; radicalism, 430; Radicals, leader of the, 258; Thomas Mann Randolph visits, 236; Regent of the University of the State of New York, 144; reliance on a controlled press, 243; religion, 128, 309, 446, 470, 531; removal of Clinton enrages people who challenge Van Buren's vote, 270, 271; removal of deposits, won over to, 369; Republic, objects of, 410; republican principles, devotion to, 429; rescues grandchildren from icy stream, 523; response to demand that he run again, 508; Sara-

Van Buren, Martin (*continued*) toga, rests at, 436-438; retirement at last, 525; retirement, in, 471 *et seq.;* retires Clinton to private life, 238; royal gifts for, 450-452; Saratoga Springs, rests at, 369; scurrilous attacks on, 357; Secretary of State, 323; Secretary of State, resigns as, 343, 344; Seminole War, on the, 423; Shakespeare, his, 174; Francis Silvester, studies law under, 33, 34; Margaret Silvester's hand, asks, 523; skepticism, 108; slander, Charles King's, 395; slanders concerning, 375; slave runs away, his, 141; slave-owners' plot against, 481-491; slavery, on, 375, 387, 392, 393, 511; slavery extension, votes against, 194; snubbed by municipalities, 432, 435; snuff, a borrowed pinch of, 373, 374; social graces, 363, 385, 436, 444; social graces, Clay on, 401; social lion, 361 *et seq.;* society, fondness for, 236; sorrow, 340; South, tours, 478; Solomon Southwick on, 422; "special interests," fears a party of, 410; Specie Circular, refuses to recall, 408; speech moves to tears, 197; Ambrose Spencer, plots to remove, 203, 204; Spencer's jealousy of, 141; Spoils System, 230-234; Spoils System, directs it, 325, 326; Spoils System, extending, 205; Spoils System, plans to make New York's national, 196; Spoils System, visions it as national institution in 1822, 326; State rights, speaks on, in South Carolina, 310; State Senator, nominated and elected, 85-90; State Senator, reëlected, 148; statesmanship, 409; State Supreme Court, misses appointment to, 169; style, Charles A. King on, 401; Sub-Treasury Act, signs, 452; suffrage, on extension of, 222-226; Supreme Court appointment, declines, 236; Surrogate, 75; Surrogate, removed as, 122; Tammany Hall, at, 364; Tammany pays tribute to, 142; tariff, favors, 262; Texas annexation, against, 481; Texas annexation letter, 485-487; theater, attends, 430, 473; Thompson for Presidency, opposes, 245; Tilden, seeks to place John Van Buren with, 538, 539; toad-eaters, dislikes, 172; Tompkins, defends,

Van Buren, Martin (*continued*) 184; tradition, shatters an old, 470; turtle feast, at a, 238; unmoved by clamor, 113; ultra-conservative pose, 215, 217, 227, 228; United States Senator, 206; United States Senator, reëlected, 310; U. S. Supreme Court, criticism of, 301-304; U. S. Supreme Court bench, seeks place on, 246-250; Universal suffrage, opposes 214, 215, 227; vagueness, 360; William P. Van Ness, obtains pardon for, 76; William P. Van Ness, studies under, 41, 43; Vice President, 361; Virginia Dynasty aids his war on Clinton, 179; vilest calumny hurled at him, the, 313, 314; virulent attack on, 445-448; voice, 400; war speech earns kiss, 123; War of 1812, supports, 119, 122; Webster, hatred of, 131, 466; White House, last days in the, 465-471; White Sulphur Springs, rests at, 421; wholesale removals from office in New York, 207-209; wife dies, 169, 170; Elisha Williams, compared with, 66; wine and oysters supper, gives, 132; wine fondness for, 181, 182, 409; wine, orders, 316; wine robs him of his caution, 246; wine to Jackson, sends, 409; world politics, knowledge of, 121; Wright, eulogizes, 522; writes anonymous pamphlet, 182-184, 193; writes party's appeal, 133; Gov. Yates, differences with, 242, 243.

Van Buren, Martin, Jr., accompanies father to Europe, 525; Acting-Secretary to the President, 435; bachelor, 497; dies in Europe, 530; makes confidential reports to father, 509.

Van Buren, Mary (Maria), death, 165; marries, 25.

Van Buren, Smith Thompson, 404, 433, 509; dinner at Kinderhook, 435; father's emmissary to Washington, 496; marries Miss Ellen James, 497; marries Washington Irving's niece, 527; widower, a, 523.

Vanderbilt, Cornelius, 430.

Vanderpoel, Elizabeth, wife of John Van Buren, 476.

Van der Veere, Marinus Adriaensz, 15, 17.

Van Ness, John P., 41, 46, 47, 63.

Van Ness, Peter, 39.

Van Ness, William P., author of anti-Livingston pamphlet, 51; Burr's affection for, 48; evades election law, 73; intrigues for Senatorship, 85-88; seeks Van Buren's aid, after Burr-Hamilton duel, 64, 65; law student of Edward Livingston, 39.

Van Ness, William W., 126, 194, 213, 219.

Van Rensselaer, Jacob Rutsen, 79-81, 213.

Van Rensselaer, Rensselaer, commander of revolting Canadians, 416 *et seq.;* his arrest, 419.

Van Rensselaer, Solomon, 161, 205, 208, 211, 229-234, 324, 325, 425, 426.

Van Rensselaer, Stephen, 37, 42, 70, 105 *et seq.*, 215, 275, 279-281.

Van Schaack, Peter, challenges Van Buren's vote, 63; home at Kinderhook, 29; retires in favor of Van Buren, 70; Van Buren's last visit to, 358, 359.

Van Twiller, Wouter, Governor of New Netherlands, 16, 21.

Van Zandt, Rev. Benjamin, 545.

Varian, Isaac L., 430.

Vaughan, Sir Charles R., Van Buren's relations with, 330, 331, 334.

Verbeeck, Jan, 22.

Verplanck, Gulian C., 142, 240.

Virginia Dynasty, 70, 172, 253, 255.

Wadsworth, James S., 493, 506, 514.

Waldo, Daniel, 137.

War of 1812, opposition to, 93 *et seq.*

Warfield, Peregrine, 94, 98, 99.

Washington, George, 33, 511.

Webster, Daniel, 40, 129; Adams on, 482; nominated for President, 381;

Webster, Daniel (*continued*) on civil war, 130.

Weed, Thurlow, 124, 477, 530.

Wellington, Duke of, 421.

West India Company, 16.

Westmorland, Countess of, 448.

Whallon, Ruben, 80.

White, Hugh Lawson, nominated for President, 381; what he did when defeated, 420.

White, Joseph L., 325.

Williams, Elisha, 36, 40, 66, 79, 80, 129, 213; defies government, 115; on *vox populi vox dei,* 220, 221.

Williams, John, 237.

Williams, Lewis, 440.

Wilkins, William, 361.

Willet, Marinus, 72.

Willis, W. P., 400.

Wilmot, David, 503, 505.

Wilmot Proviso, 503 *et seq.*

Wilson, Isaac, 163.

Windisch Gratz, Prince, 421.

Wirt, William, 347.

Wise, Henry A., 439-441; on the Tyler impeachment, 480.

Wolseley, Sir Charles, 189.

Wood, Bradford R., 524.

Woodbury, Levi, 405.

Woodworth, John, 242.

Woodworth, Samuel, 134.

Worth, Graham A., 198, 199.

Worth, William J., 503.

Wright, Silas, 266, 307, 361, 366, 477, 489, 501; declines Vice Presidential nomination, 491, 492.

Wynkoop, Augustus, 526.

Yankee, derivation of, 87.

Yates, Henry, Jr., 163.

Yates, Joseph C., 151, 156, 238.

Young, Samuel, 137, 206, 219.